RETHINKING AUTISM
Variation and Complexity

RETHINKING AUTISM
Variation and Complexity

LYNN WATERHOUSE

Professor, Graduate Global Studies,
Center for Global Engagement,
Director Emeritus, Child Behavior Study,
The College of New Jersey,
Ewing, NJ

ELSEVIER

Amsterdam • Boston • Heidelberg • London
New York • Oxford Paris • San Diego • San Francisco
Singapore • Sydney • Tokyo
Academic Press is an imprint of Elsevier

Academic Press is an imprint of Elsevier
32 Jamestown Road, London NW1 7BY, UK
225 Wyman Street, Waltham, MA 02451, USA
525 B Street, Suite 1800, San Diego, CA 92101-4495, USA

First edition 2013

Notice
No responsibility is assumed by the publisher for any injury and/or damage to persons or
property as a matter of products liability, negligence or otherwise, or from any use or
operation of any methods, products, instructions or ideas contained in the material herein.
Because of rapid advances in the medical sciences, in particular, independent verification of
diagnoses and drug dosages should be made

British Library Cataloguing-in-Publication Data
A catalogue record for this book is available from the British Library

Library of Congress Cataloging-in-Publication Data
A catalog record for this book is available from the Library of Congress

ISBN: 978-0-12-415961-7

For information on all Academic Press publications
visit our website at elsevierdirect.com

Typeset by TNQ Books and Journals Pvt Ltd.
www.tnq.co.in

Printed and bound in United States of America

12 13 14 15 16   10 9 8 7 6 5 4 3 2 1

CONTENTS

Autism is a clinical reality. Autism has been around, if not from the beginning of time, at least for thousands of years. It has been on the minds of people not affected by autism for a minimum of two centuries, albeit under different labels. It has been in the medical textbooks for nigh on seventy years (or more than a hundred if you just think of the word that Bleuler once coined for autism as a core symptom of schizophrenia). As a word, it has come from relative obscurity to the forefront of everyone's mind in little more than a decade. It is now the best-funded neurodevelopmental disorder, in terms of research, in many parts of the world. It is said to be at once one of the most common neuropsychiatric disorders and the most devastating. Its prevalence has purportedly increased, although the evidence supporting this claim is equivocal to say the least. Yet it remains an illusive butterfly, escaping clear-cut definition. Operationalized criteria have tried to capture it for years, and such criteria have changed, usually without a strong scientific evidence base to support any shift from one algorithm to another.

Having said this, I realize it may sound as though I do not "believe" in autism. To the contrary, I am acutely aware of the reality of autism; my endless flow of patients is convincing in itself. However, the fact is that we do not know what autism "is." I have been in the field for forty years, and I can honestly say that I do not believe we are any closer now than twenty years ago to a real understanding of what it is about autism that makes experienced clinicians "certain" that it is autism regardless of whether operationalized criteria for the disorder are met or not. The gestalt of autism has yet to be semantically conceptualized.

For more than twenty years we have had sufficient knowledge about "autism" to know that the unitary concept of it (and even that of an (= one) autism "spectrum" disorder) will not take us further in research or clinical practice. Unfortunately, this insight has been overshadowed by populist cries for cures (or even of *one* cure) and uncovering *the* cause of autism. We have been hitting a wall for a long time, and there has been little in terms of well-funded research and service development that would indicate that a scientifically sound change of track might be in the offing.

Lynn Waterhouse, with her long clinical and research experience of autism and other "early symptomatic syndromes eliciting neurodevelopmental clinical examinations" (ESSENCE), has written the definitive text that, if read and pondered, will guide us onto new tracks in the field. She takes apart the whole argument that autism is "one," and a concept that can be studied without attention to subgrouping. She does it in the most didactic and systematic way, arguing her point, step by step, bit by bit. And the best thing about it is, she does it with such humor, verve and intelligence that, far from simply sweeping you away, she leaves you feeling convinced and scientifically supported at a much higher level than before — on safe ground.

This book is a must for researchers and specialist clinicians in neurodevelopment. Not least, it needs to be read by all those influential people at top levels who, through lobbying, scientific advisory boards and committees of funding bodies, now funnel huge amounts of money to the study of — and intervention for — "one autism." Lynn Waterhouse's book will guide the quest for supporting clinical and research work focusing on the autisms (with all their complex connections with all the other ESSENCE) rather than on "pure" autism *per se*.

Christopher Gillberg, MD, PhD
Professor of Child and Adolescent Psychiatry
Gillberg Neuropsychiatry Centre (gnc.gu.se)
Gothenburg University, Sweden
Institute of Child Health, London, UK
Glasgow University, Glasgow, UK

The public, the National Institutes of Health, and the American Psychiatric Association have supported a vision of autism as a single disorder or spectrum of closely related disorders. However, the research evidence does not support this vision. In fact, all the research to date on autism suggests the opposite: that "Autism" is not one disorder or many "Autisms" but is a set of symptoms. The heterogeneity and associated disorders suggest that autism symptoms, like fever, are not themselves a disorder or multiple disorders. Instead, autism symptoms signal a wide range of underlying disorders. This book lays out all the research evidence for readers to draw their own conclusions. If, after reading through this, you come to believe as I do that autism symptoms are exactly that—symptoms, our next step is to shift research to the many underlying brain dysfunctions and their causes in order to more effectively find the neurobiological targets for potential treatments for those who suffer from autism symptoms.

The book begins with a description of what is required for a group of symptoms to be considered a single disorder and then presents the evidence that demonstrates that autism cannot be a single disorder. There is no replicated evidence of a shared pathophysiology that accounts for a majority of cases of autism. There is no drug treatment that directly addresses the symptoms of autism. All autism diagnostic symptoms—social interaction impairment, repetitive and restricted behaviors, and sensory abnormalities—vary in form and severity. Equally important, the expression of autism nearly always occurs with one or more additional non-diagnostic symptoms including but not limited to intellectual disability, attention deficit/hyperactivity disorder symptoms, perceptual problems, motor disorders, epilepsy, and language development problems. In addition, research findings do not support the vision of multiple autisms. No meaningful subgroups of autism have been discovered, and genetic and environmental risk factors tie autism symptoms to many other disorders and outcomes.

The eight chapters of this book offer evidence for extensiveness of heterogeneity in autism. Chapter 1 summarizes variation in autism, and Chapter 2 outlines symptom variation in siblings with autism, siblings at risk for autism, and other family members of individuals with autism. Chapter 3 reports evidence for varied social brain circuit deficits in autism, Chapter 4 reviews the many gene and chromosomal risk factors that

link autism symptoms to other disorders, and Chapter 5 catalogs environmental risk factors that link autism symptoms to other symptoms and disorders. Chapter 6 matches savant and superior mental skills in autism with
the same skills in typical individuals. Chapter 7 considers the variation in
autism prevalence rates and reviews claims that DSM-5 diagnostic criteria
for autism spectrum disorder may limit both heterogeneity and prevalence.
Chapter 8 proposes that researchers and theorists have been unable to construct validated diagnostic criteria or valid unifying theories of autism
because the causes, brain deficits, and behaviors found for autism are so
varied.

Given the accumulated evidence, the book concludes that autism is not,
in fact, a single disorder or a spectrum of related disorders. Why does this
matter? It matters because if you are searching for the cure for fever, you are
trying to cure a symptom, and are not focusing on the real disorder, which
is the pathogen whose effects on the body triggered the immune system to
generate a fever. Researchers should stop the continually failing quest to
find a brain dysfunction that unifies autism. Evidence has demonstrated that
a unifying brain dysfunction does not exist. Ending this quest will free
researchers to concentrate on causes, plural, for the brain dysfunctions,
plural, that generate the full range of symptoms expressed by individuals.
The complex relationship between causes and brain dysfunctions alone is a
difficult problem, but the diagnosis of autism has complicated the task by
errantly defining a set of symptoms as evidence for a single disorder or
spectrum of closely related disorders.

Research should instead focus on the developmental brain disruptions
that cause autism symptoms along with other symptoms, and focus on etiological agents that cause developmental brain disruptions. All individuals
expressing autism symptoms and who have a known genetic or chromosomal
disorder such as fragile X syndrome or Down syndrome should be identified
as having fragile X syndrome with autism symptoms or Down syndrome
with autism symptoms. All individuals expressing autism symptoms who have
suffered known environmental insults such as fetal alcohol syndrome or
extreme prematurity should be identified as having fetal alcohol syndrome
with autism symptoms or extreme prematurity with autism symptoms. As
research isolates more causes for autism symptoms co-occurring with other
symptoms, an expanding set of neurobiological targets would accrue.

The rejection of the vision of autism as a set of subgroups will also yield
benefits in research. If researchers stop searching for autism symptom subgroups—the "Autisms"—and accept that a range of more varied symptoms

results from global brain development disruptions caused by risk factors, they will be freed to focus on the mechanisms of disruption. Understanding the mechanisms of brain disruption is the basis for translational research.

Advances in the understanding of causes for autism symptoms that occur with associated non-autism symptoms will depend on increased knowledge of the genetics, epigenetics, and gene–environment interactions involved in brain development, as well as increased knowledge of environmental risk factors for brain development. Advances will also depend on increased knowledge of individual brain circuits, the whole brain connectome, and the mechanisms of the dynamic processes involved in brain development. The disorders discovered as causes for autism symptoms will not be autism. However, future discoveries should be able to better isolate specific brain circuits that when disrupted result in neurodevelopmental social impairment.

ACKNOWLEDGEMENTS

My deepest debt is to the 340 children and adolescents with autism and their parents who participated in my studies over many years. Thank you all. Because our research was longitudinal, I visited each child and adolescent many times. The individual variation among you was and is remarkable.

Although I told every parent our studies would not yield any treatment for autism, nonetheless, many parents did hope that something would come of our findings. Their belief in the potential of autism research shamed me. As our research and the research of others uncovered more and more variation in behavior, brain deficits, and risk factors for autism, I felt the intense frustration that most autism researchers and most parents have felt. Shame and frustration are powerful motivators. They propelled me to read every piece of research I could, and pressed me to repeatedly question why no shared brain deficit for autism could be found.

The call made in 2010 by Dr. Thomas Insel, Director of the National Institutes of Mental Health, and his colleague Dr. Philip Wang for researchers to rethink mental illness was the match that lit the kindling for this book. This book and its title are a direct response to their call. They doubted the validity of psychiatric diagnostic categories, and their doubt affirmed my own. I would also like to thank Dr. Sanislow and his colleagues, as well as an anonymous reviewer for providing the analogy to fever as a symptom.

Elsevier editors made this book possible. I am most grateful to Nikki Levy for her belief in the book's thesis, for her patience and continued support throughout the writing of the book, and for her key contributions to this Preface. I would like to thank Caroline Johnson for her care and kindness. Last but nonetheless, first, Colin Macnee was the most erudite, funny, polite, and thoughtful of copy editors.

Most importantly, I owe this book to the three loving, supportive, and brilliant critics in my life, each of whom proposed challenges to the thesis of this book. Do you have enough evidence? My husband, Michael, is an archaeologist who believes the best ratio of data to theory is the ratio of stars in the Milky Way to the sun. What are the core mechanisms? My son, Bennett, is an engineer who has imagined and built many things that have never before existed. Happily, unlike the Russian engineers of the past, who were forced to stand with their families under the bridges they had designed while multitudes of soldiers on horses pounded over them, the tests of my son's inventions do not endanger my grandsons: calculations and model simulations have replaced horses and riders. What are the specific differences between brain disruptions? My daughter, Emily, is a molecular neurobiologist and physician. Her work on BDNF in neurogenesis sharpened my attention to the complexity in the brain that neuroscience has yet to delineate. Moreover, seeing her dedication to the treatment and well-being of her patients increased my feelings of obligation to all the children and adolescents with autism I have studied.

Autism Heterogeneity

Contents

Rethinking Autism
http://dx.doi.org/10.1016/B978-0-12-415961-7.00001-0

Belief in autism exists worldwide. Teachers, psychologists, doctors, and social workers are trained to recognize or diagnose autism. Parents whose children were diagnosed with autism learn about the disorder and search for treatments. Celebrity parents of children with autism, such as golfer Ernie Els, quarterback Doug Flutie, and comedian Jenny McCarthy, have made public statements about their children and publicly advocated for autism research and treatment. Numerous groups such as Autism Speaks and the Global Autism Project have advocated for autism. Individuals with autism Donna Williams (1998) and Temple Grandin (1996) have written memoirs. The movie *Rain Man* (Levinson, 1988) and the novel *The Curious Incident of the Dog in the Night-time* (Haddon, 2003) each told dramatic stories of autistic savants—individuals with autism who have remarkable memories or remarkable skills.

In most countries, magazines, newspapers, television broadcasts, and social media have reported news of autism, and many reports have raised alarm about the increased prevalence of autism. In the United States, the National Institutes of Health, as well as other government agencies, and private funding sources provide grant money to study autism, and the Centers for Disease Control and Prevention has monitored the startling increase in the diagnosis of autism.

In 1975 when I began studying autism I believed it was a distinct behavioral syndrome, and believed a unitary brain basis for it would soon be discovered. But by the middle of the 1990s many brain deficits had already been found in association with autism. Evidence suggested that subsets of individuals diagnosed with autism had deficits in one or more brain regions and brain neurochemicals, including the amygdala, the hippocampus, temporal and parietal regions of the cortex, and the neurohormone oxytocin (Waterhouse, Fein, & Modahl, 1996). Our research group did find evidence for abnormal oxytocin in autism (Green et al., 2001; Modahl et al., 1998). However, despite substantial financial support from the National Institutes of Mental Health, National Institutes of Child Health and Development, and support from several private funding agencies, and despite the intellectual effort of all on our research teams, we failed to find meaningful brain-based behavioral subgroups of autism (Stevens et al., 2000; Waterhouse et al., 1996). Our problems reflected the field's problems.

No researcher or research group has found valid, empirically based behavioral subgroups within autism spectrum disorder (ASD) (Rutter, 2011; Witwer & Lecavalier, 2008). More significantly, no one has yet proven any specific brain deficit predicts a specific autism diagnostic behavior

(Rutter, 2011; Waterhouse, 2008, 2011). Boucher (2011) suggested "the concept of autism as a unitary disorder resulting from a single common cause ... may be at the point of being abandoned" (p. 473).

AUTISM HETEROGENEITY IS EXTENSIVE AND UNEXPLAINED

The central challenge to understanding autism has been its heterogeneity. While any psychiatric disorder can be expected to include heterogeneity, the amount of heterogeneity in autism exceeds that found in other psychiatric disorders. Schaaf and Zoghbi (2011) stated, "It is well established that the ASDs represent a heterogeneous group of disorders" (p. 806). Jones and Klin (2009) stated, "Individuals with autism show a vast clinical variability in the expression and severity of their symptoms. This heterogeneity spans the entire range of IQ and language function and a wide array of communicative, social, and behavioral disabilities" (p. 471). Amaral (2011) asserted, "A hallmark of virtually every biological parameter assayed in individuals with autism is the enormous heterogeneity—far greater than in the general population" (p. 6). Happé, Ronald, and Plomin (2006) declared, "Heterogeneity within the autism spectrum is perhaps the biggest single obstacle to research at all levels" (p. 1220). Heterogeneity exists in autism diagnostic behaviors and in a wide range of additional behavioral impairments, medical conditions, brain deficits, as well as in genetic and environmental risk factors.

Autism researcher Robert Schultz said, "If you've seen one child with autism, you've seen one child with autism. Autism's like a snowflake" (Scott, 2011). Lord (2011) noted that anyone who has met more than one person with autism is struck by the differences between diagnosed individuals. For example, researchers Sullivan, Laverick, and Lewis (1995) described a young girl, Vanessa, who experienced repeated seizures as a child, did not talk, had little eye contact, and had such poor muscle tone her body had to be strapped into an orthopedic chair. She was diagnosed with autism and diagnosed with Rett syndrome caused by a gene mutation (Sullivan et al., 1995). Daniel Corney, like Vanessa, experienced repeated seizures as a child, was socially aloof, and he was diagnosed with autism. Unlike Vanessa, Daniel had intact motor skills, could speak, and had a remarkable memory. As a young adult he set the European record for reciting pi to 22,514 decimal places in just over 5 hours. He changed his name to Daniel Tammet, and wrote two books about his experience of being an autistic savant with synesthesia: *Born on a Blue Day* (2007), and *Embracing the Wide Sky, A Tour Across the Horizons of the Mind* (2009).

AUTISM HETEROGENEITY HAS BLOCKED MEDICAL TREATMENT DISCOVERY

The most serious problem caused by the failure to understand autism heterogeneity is the failure to discover any autism-specific effective drug. Unlike other psychiatric disorders, the core diagnostic symptom of autism—impaired social interaction—is not improved by any psychotropic medication (Rutter, 2011). Levy, Mandel, and Schultz (2009) pointed out that "existing pharmacotherapeutic agents are not effective for treatment of core symptoms of autism spectrum disorders" (p. 1633), and they noted that drug treatments are rarely effective for addressing non-diagnostic symptoms in autism. Rogers and Vismara (2008) reported that no one knows which treatments or combinations of types of treatments will be most effective for which symptoms of autism, and no one knows if there are subgroups of individuals with autism who would benefit from a particular medical treatment. McPheeters et al. (2011) concluded, "Although many children with ASDs are currently treated with medical interventions, strikingly little evidence exists to support benefit for most treatments" (p. e1312).

Effective medication for autism cannot be developed until the heterogeneity in autism is understood, and the heterogeneity in autism is extensive. Many different efforts have been made to resolve the heterogeneity. One line of attack has been to refine the diagnosis of autism. Unfortunately, reformulations of diagnostic criteria for autism have not decreased heterogeneity.

DIAGNOSTIC CRITERIA HAVE NOT CONSTRAINED AUTISM HETEROGENEITY

Although diagnostic criteria are designed to narrowly define a disorder, the diagnostic criteria for autism have allowed for wide heterogeneity. The fifth Diagnostic and Statistical Manual of the American Psychiatric Association (www.dsm5.org) recognized the heterogeneity within autism by expanding Autism Disorder to become Autism Spectrum Disorder (ASD). Throughout this book, I have used the term autism rather than the DSM-5 diagnostic label Autism Spectrum Disorder. As used here the term autism is intended to include or represent diagnoses used in research and theory, including the proposed DSM-5 (APA, 2011) and the previous DSM-IV (APA, 1994) and DSM-IV-TR (APA, 2000).

DSM-5 mandated two diagnostic criteria for autism spectrum disorders. The first was social communication and interaction deficits as shown in impaired social approach, impaired social reciprocity, impaired non-verbal communication, and impaired social relationships. The second was restricted repetitive behavior patterns, including interests or activities such as repetitive phrases, resistance to change, over- or under-reactivity to sensory experience, and unusually intense and/or limited interests.

Kuenssberg, McKenzie, and Jones (2011) reviewed research on the DSM-IV and DSM-IV-TR diagnostic criteria for autism: (1) qualitative impairment in social interaction; (2) qualitative impairments in communication; and (3) restricted repetitive and stereotyped patterns of behavior, interests, and activities. They concluded that only the two criteria now mandated for DSM-5 autism spectrum disorder—social interaction and repetitive and restricted interests—best characterized individuals with autism. Conversely, Szatmari (2011) argued against the change from three to two criteria for the DSM-5. He stated, "The two dimensions of social communication and repetitive behaviours may not be the most useful for categorising children with autistic spectrum disorder in terms of the causes, outcomes, and response to treatment because variation in these dimensions seems to be only weakly associated with variation in outcome and response to treatment, which are more closely related to cognitive and language abilities" (2011, p. 6).

Because Kanner first identified autism, his 1943 observations about autism have been identified as "classic" autism. Kanner (1943) proposed that a profound lack of understanding of social interaction and a need for sameness were the core diagnostic characteristics of autism. The increase in autism prevalence and heterogeneity led some researchers to call for a return to Kanner's autism in hopes of limiting prevalence and reducing heterogeneity. For example, autism researcher Folstein (2006) asserted that Kanner's autism was a true unitary disorder because Kanner "did not diagnose autism in every child who had social impairment or repetitive behaviors. The children Kanner diagnosed needed to 'look' intelligent, to be alert and to show interest in things (although not people). He excluded children who had dysmorphic features or very low IQ, below perhaps 35 or 40" (p. 116). Folstein argued that autism heterogeneity resulted from the autism diagnosis being applied to too many non-Kanner's autism cases including "those who have profound mental handicap, dysmorphic features, and specific etiologies" (2006, p. 116).

Rosenberg, Daniels, Law, Law, and Kaufmann (2009) also called for a more restricted diagnosis of autism. They argued, "as knowledge increases about the heterogeneity of the ASD ... changes and expansion in classification are likely contributing to the increase in ASD diagnoses during the past two decades" (p. 1099). Rosenberg et al. (2009) appealed for a return to a more stringent diagnosis of autism.

Instruments for diagnosing autism have also been proposed as a means to reduce heterogeneity. Hus, Pickles, Cook, Risi, and Lord (2007) stated that use of the Autism Diagnostic Interview—Revised (ADI-R) significantly decreased variance within identical twin pairs. However, Boucher (2011) cautioned that diagnostic instruments "run the risk of impeding progress in that they instantiate circularity" (p. 475). In other words, defining autism by symptoms on a particular diagnostic instrument means that autism effectively becomes what the instrument defines autism to be.

Contrary to the hope that redefining the autism diagnostic criteria would reduce heterogeneity, studies found the opposite: changes in autism criteria were linked to an increase in prevalence, thus increasing heterogeneity within autism. Volkmar, Klin, and Cohen (1997) argued that changes in the criteria from DSM-III (APA, 1980) to DSM-III-R (APA, 1987) broadened the concept of autism, increasing prevalence and heterogeneity, and asserted that the changes from the DSM-III-R to the DSM-IV (APA, 1994) criteria were helpful in narrowing the definition of autism. Williams, Higgins, and Brayne (2006), however, found that, in fact, DSM-IV and DSM-IV-TR (APA, 2000) criteria yielded autism prevalence estimates two to three times that obtained using earlier DSM-III-R criteria. Wazana, Bresnahan, and Kline (2007) suggested that changes in autism diagnostic criteria over time may have produced up to a 28-fold increase in autism prevalence, and with the increased prevalence, an increase in autism heterogeneity.

VARIATION IN AUTISM DIAGNOSTIC FEATURES

If diagnostic changes have increased the prevalence and heterogeneity in autism, it has been through the open nature of the criteria. Social impairment is the central diagnostic feature of autism, but, as noted above in the brief description of Vanessa and Daniel Tammet, individuals with autism may range from completely asocial and mute to not more than socially awkward.

Variation in patterns of impaired sociability has been found for all stages of development. Many infants later diagnosed with autism did form attachments to their parents, but some did not. Some attachments are unusual, wherein the infant with autism may appear to be attached to a part of the parent, and attachments to unusual objects may also occur. Many infants later diagnosed with autism responded differentially to those around them but many did not. Some infants later diagnosed with autism paid no attention to social stimuli as babies, smiled infrequently, and vocalized little. However, this was not true for all, because many infants later diagnosed with autism did smile, vocalize, and pay attention to other people as infants. Some toddlers with autism never reached to be picked up, some never spontaneously sought their parents or caretakers, some never engaged in simple social interaction games. Conversely, other toddlers with autism did go to parents, reach to be picked up, and play simple interaction games. Some children with autism did and some did not respond to their own name. Individuals with autism may or may not have limited eye contact with others, and may or may not direct attention to the behavior of others. Some with autism may initiate interaction with others and some may not; some may show empathy for others, but many may not (Volkmar, Chawarska, & Klin, 2005).

There is also great variation in social communication deficits in autism. Children with autism may or may not orient toward speech, may or may not respond to their name by 6–12 months, may or may not acquire words and word combinations more slowly, and may or may not have any speech at all by the age of 2 (Stefanatos & Baron, 2011). Children with autism may or may not have persisting receptive language problems, may or may not have verbal imitation skills, and may or may not use appropriate gestures along with speech (Stefanatos & Baron, 2011). Communications skills may develop as individuals mature and receive training, but some with autism remain impaired in social communication as adults.

Autism-diagnostic rigid interests and repetitive behaviors have also been found to be varied. Four subtypes of these behaviors have been identified: preoccupation with restricted interests; non-functional routines or rituals; repetitive motor mannerisms; and persistent preoccupation with parts of objects. The last two subtypes have been more often found in younger or lower-functioning individuals with autism (Leekam, Prior, & Uljarevic, 2011). However, all individuals diagnosed with autism may or may not express stereotyped language patterns, such as repeating exact phrases again and again (Stefanatos & Baron, 2011), and may or may not have repetitive sensory interests such as staring at a moving ceiling fan, or staring at their own hands waving back and forth in front of their faces. They may or may not express other forms of hand or finger mannerisms, including flicking or twisting their fingers or flapping their hands. All individuals diagnosed with autism may or may not express more complex repeated motor behaviors such as repetitively spinning in circles. Most individuals diagnosed with autism have abnormalities of sensory system functioning, such as over- and under-reaction to sound, pain, food texture, and physical touch.

Higher functioning individuals with autism are more likely to have rituals and preoccupations. However, individuals with autism at any level of functioning may or may not express an inflexible need for the same route, the same foods, the same clothing. Individuals with autism may repetitively line up objects in a row. Individuals with autism may or may not be preoccupied with particular objects, activities, or information. Trains, planes, vacuum cleaners may be objects of interest; the weather and particular television shows may be topics of obsessive interest (Kim & Lord, 2010).

In addition to the wide range of variation found for autism diagnostic features, there is also great heterogeneity in brain deficits, associated medical conditions, and non-diagnostic symptoms in autism.

Variation in Autism Brain Deficits, Medical Conditions, and Non-Diagnostic Symptoms

The heterogeneity in autism brain deficits is considerable. Stigler, McDonald, Anand, Saykin, and McDougle (2011) reported that individuals with autism may or may not have larger heads, or smaller heads, or increases in total brain volume, or deficits in total brain volume, or general gray matter abnormalities, or increased or decreased white matter, or cerebellum abnormalities, or amygdala abnormalities, or hippocampal and or hypothalamus abnormalities. Individuals diagnosed with autism may or may not have insula or fusiform gyrus abnormalities, or caudate or thalamus abnormalities, or left temporal abnormalities, or inferior frontal gyrus abnormalities, or cingulate cortex or corpus callosum abnormalities, or brainstem abnormalities (Stigler et al., 2011). Diagnosed individuals may or may not have major neurotransmitter system deficits in serotonin, dopamine, glutamate, or GABA (Gupta & State, 2007; Lam, Bodfish, & Piven, 2008). Diagnosed individuals may or may not express abnormalities in the neurohormones oxytocin and vasopressin (Andari et al., 2010; Insel, 2010).

There is also considerable heterogeneity in associated medical conditions and non-diagnostic symptoms in autism. As many as 25–33% of individuals with autism develop epilepsy (Levy et al., 2009), and 55–70% have intellectual disability (Chakrabarti & Fombonne, 2005; Charman et al.,

2011). Moreover, individuals with autism may or may not have sleep disorders, eating disorders, intestinal disorders, or motor skill deficits or tics (Levy et al., 2009). Between 24% and 59% of individuals with autism have an anxiety disorder and 28% meet criteria for ADHD (Ronald & Hoekstra, 2011).

In addition to the heterogeneity in brain deficits, associated medical conditions and other disorders found in autism, there is significant heterogeneity in genetic risk factors for autism.

VARIATION IN GENETIC RISK FACTORS FOR AUTISM

More than 100 gene variants have been linked to autism (Betancur, 2011), and Sanders et al. (2011) stated that autism was linked to between 130 and 234 submicroscopic chromosomal deletions and duplications called copy number variants or CNVs. Miles (2011) asserted that the extremely high heritability rates of .85 to .92 found for autism made geneticists "confident that autism will be the first behavioral disorder for which the genetic basis can be well established" (p. 278). Not all findings have suggested such high rates of genetic causality for autism, however. Though Ronald and Hoekstra (2011) found high genetic heritability for autism, Hallmayer et al. (2011) reported that shared environment accounted for more variance than genetic risk factors. The researchers reported that genetic factors accounted for 38% of co-twin variance, but shared environmental components accounted for 58% of co-twin variance.

Independent of the level of gene influence on autism, autism cannot have a unitary genetic source. Whatever portion of autism is accounted for by genetic factors, those genetic factors are likely to include many different gene variants, chromosome deletions or duplications, and combinations of gene and chromosomal variations.

Consequently, it will not be *a* genetic basis that is established for autism, it will be *many* different patterns of varied and combined genetic bases for different individuals with autism. This scientific work is unlikely to be easy or swift.

Autism diagnosed in an individual known to have a specific genetic syndrome such as Rett syndrome or fragile X is called "syndromic autism," whereas autism diagnosed in the absence of a known genetic cause is labeled "idiopathic autism," idiopathic meaning having no known cause.

Sanders et al. (2011) noted that that no single genetic risk variant occurs in more than 1% of individuals with autism, and not all individuals carrying a genetic risk variant will express autism symptoms. The researchers pointed out, "remarkably diverse outcomes have been identified for apparently identical CNVs" (2011, p. 864). In addition, many individuals with autism have new or de novo genetic mutations. Often siblings with autism do not share the same genetic variant or chromosomal deletion or duplication as their diagnosed brother or sister. Moreover, while relatives of individuals with autism express higher rates of autism behaviors, these behaviors vary within families and between families.

Gene variants found for autism vary widely in function. Some gene variants alter genes that contribute to the construction of the brain's neurons and neuron connections, the synapses. Some genes affect basic brain building through cell-adhesion molecules, and some gene variants alter the functions of attachment neurohormones oxytocin and vasopressin (Harony & Wagner, 2010).

In addition to the hundreds of genetic risk factors for autism, there are many environmental risk factors.

VARIATION IN ENVIRONMENTAL RISK FACTORS FOR AUTISM

Research has uncovered many environmental risk factors associated with autism, but the full range of heterogeneity in the environmental risk factors for autism is not yet known. Older mothers and older fathers have been shown to confer a greater risk for autism (Foldi, Eyles, Flatscher-Bader, McGrath, & Burne, 2011; Rutter, 2011). Some environmental effects have been found to occur during the birth process (Gardener, Spiegelman, & Buka, 2011). Additional factors such as spacing of pregnancies appear to confer a risk factor for autism (Cheslack-Postava, Liu, & Bearman, 2011). Extremely premature birth has also been shown to be an environmental risk factor for autism (Limperopoulus, 2009).

Gestational environmental factors such as maternal alcohol use or maternal infection have also been associated with an elevated risk for autism (Kinney, Barch, Chayka, Napoleon, & Munir, 2010). One set of infectious agents is commonly referred by the acronym TORCH: T for Toxoplasmosis; O for Other including syphilis, varicella-zoster, and parvovirus B19; R for Rubella; C for Cytomegalovirus (CMV); and, H for Herpes infections. Stigler, Sweeten, Posey, and McDougle (2009) reported that all TORCH infectious agents have been found in association with autism.

In addition to the thousands of infectious agents that can be harmful to brain development, there are more than 50,000 known neurotoxicants.

A neurotoxicant is a chemical compound that may cause brain damage. One well-known neurotoxicant is lead, which caused intellectual disability in children who ingested flakes of lead-based household paint. Few neurotoxicants have been studied as possible causes of autism. Researchers Shandley and Austin (2011) studied pink disease (also called infantile acrodynia), theorized to be caused by the neurotoxicant mercury used in infant teething powders in the last century. Shandley and Austin (2011) found that the prevalence rate of autism among the grandchildren of pink disease survivors (1 in 22) was significantly higher than the comparable general population prevalence rate of autism (1 in 160).

In 1998, the now infamous Dr. Andrew Wakefield published a paper in the British medical journal *The Lancet* claiming that a vaccination for measles, mumps, and rubella (MMR) was the cause for autism. It was also theorized that mercury in the MMR vaccine binding agent thimerosol could be a cause for autism. The Institutes of Medicine (Stratton, Ford, Rusch, & Clayton, 2011), however, reviewed research and reported that neither vaccines nor their preservatives were linked to autism. Contrary to Wakefield's dire claim, after more than 10 years of research on the effects of vaccines and the mercury and thimerosol in vaccine preservatives, and numerous court rulings, the general finding was that neither MMR vaccine, nor its preservative thimerosol, nor trace amounts of mercury in the thimerosol were the cause of autism (Stratton et al., 2011).

In 2010, *The Lancet* retracted Dr. Wakefield's paper, but vaccination rates had tumbled and outbreaks of measles needlessly claimed the lives of numbers of children (Baker, 2008). Measles, mumps, and rubella had been controlled in the United States by the MMR vaccine, but after Wakefield's claim, there was an increase in these diseases, and England, Wales, Italy, France, Spain, and Germany reported substantial increases in measles outbreaks.

Offit's book *Autism's False Prophets* (2008) exposed Wakefield and the politics intertwined with the misguided public beliefs that arose following the publication of the *Lancet* paper. Most unfortunately, the mistaken belief that vaccinations cause autism has persisted despite all empirical evidence to the contrary.

SUMMARY: VARIATION EXISTS IN ALL AUTISM DOMAINS

As outlined above, heterogeneity in autism occurs in all aspects of affected individuals. Diagnostic symptoms are expressed heterogeneously, and there are many associated non-diagnostic symptoms such as sleeping, eating, and motor problems that vary widely across diagnosed individuals. There are numerous associated disorders, including seizures, intellectual disability, anxiety, and ADHD. There are an unknown number of distinct brain deficits, and nearly 200 distinct genetic and chromosomal risk factors have been identified to date. Environmental risk factors for autism include the age of sperm and ova, the imprinting interaction of maternal gene variants and paternal gene variants, as well as potentially thousands of infectious agents, and more than 50,000 neurotoxicants exist that, in theory, could negatively affect the embryo, fetus, newborn, and toddler.

The main research approach to autism variation has been to seek subgroups and explore unifying theories.

AUTISM SUBGROUPS AND UNIFYING THEORIES FOR AUTISM HAVE ADDRESSED HETEROGENEITY

Research has followed two paths to understand and explain variation in autism. One path has been to search for subgroups within autism. Another path has been to construct theories unifying autism by a brain deficit or causal agent or pattern. As noted in the opening section of this chapter, unfortunately, most subgroups proposed have been abandoned or disconfirmed by research, and, to date, no unifying brain deficit and no unifying cause has been proven and accepted (Rutter, 2011; Szatmari, 2011; Waterhouse, 2009, 2011). While a flood of creative and reasonable theories have been proposed, most often the theories are abandoned by the field, or disconfirmed by further research.

Although theory competition, orphaned hypotheses, and disconfirmed theories are a normal part of the scientific process, it is not normal science that autism research has developed no standard model. It is not normal science that 70 years of refinements to the diagnostic criteria, and seventy years of autism research have done nothing to synthesize competing autism subgroup proposals into a standard set. It is not normal science that the competing theories of autism deficits and causality have not been synthesized into a standard explanatory framework. Critically, as noted above, none of the competing theories has led to any autism-specific drug or other medical treatment.

The following sections provide selected examples of competing proposals for autism subgroups, competing brain deficit theories, and competing genetic cause theories and complex environmental cause theories. All these theories either have languished without further attention or have been disconfirmed by further research.

Competing Proposals for Autism Subgroups

Although Mayes and Calhoun (2011) argued, "autism is a single spectrum disorder and not comprised of separate and discrete subtypes" (p. 756), researcher Mary Coleman proposed that future research would discover hundreds of distinct autism subgroups (Feinstein, 2010, p. 266). Reiss (2009) also suggested, "autism will, ultimately, be found to be comprised of many subgroups" (p. 95). Amaral (2011) similarly concluded, "given the incredible heterogeneity of this disorder, understanding that one size will never fit all is a reasonable perspective to frame all future findings" (p. 8). However, Amaral did hold out hope that some deficit in the neuron synapse would be found to be a unifying basis for autism.

One autism behavioral subgroup, Asperger's syndrome, was identified as a diagnosis in the fourth version of The Diagnostic and Statistical Manual of the American Psychiatric Association, DSM-IV-TR (APA, 2000). Asperger's was eliminated from the fifth version of the manual because many studies failed to find significant differences between individuals diagnosed with Asperger's and individuals diagnosed with autism who were cognitively high functioning (Kamp-Becker et al., 2010). Psychiatrist Allen Frances (2010) worried that folding Asperger's into Autism Spectrum Disorders would increase autism prevalence and also worried that "the spectrum concept will likely further fuel the 'epidemic' of loosely defined autism that has already been triggered by the introduction of Asperger's in DSM4" (2010, p. 4).

Genetic subgroups of autism such as fragile X, Rett syndrome, and tuberous sclerosis, called syndromic autism, include individuals who receive dual diagnoses—genetic and psychiatric. These subgroups have not been incorporated into the research model of autism or the diagnostic categorization of autism and are considered to be a problem in understanding autism (Rutter, 2011). Hall, Lightbody, Hirt, Rezvani, and Reiss (2010) wondered if dual diagnosis for individuals with autism and fragile X would become obsolete. The researchers argued that dual diagnosis was a scientific category mistake because the diagnosis of autism and the diagnosis of fragile X exist at different levels of explanation: autism is explained at the behavioral level, but fragile X is explained at the genetic level.

Rosenberg et al. (2009) argued that, although "the taxonomy of what are now known as the autism spectrum disorders (ASD) remains in flux" (p. 1099), nonetheless, the existence of subgroups could be discovered by refining the diagnosis of autism spectrum disorder. However, changes in the diagnosis of autism over decades have not yielded valid replicated autism subgroups. Rosenberg et al. (2009) offered no explanation why the many prior changes in autism diagnostic criteria failed to yield valid differentiated subgroups, nor did they explain how future refining of diagnostic criteria could succeed where past refining of criteria had failed.

Researchers Liu, Paterson, and Szatmari along with the Autism Genome Project Consortium (2008) created six autism dimensional trait sets. One set was IQ-based, another was based on social interaction skill, another was based on presence of restricted, repetitive, and stereotyped patterns of behavior, still another based on age of first words, another based on age of first phrases, and finally a comparative group was formed wherein individuals were designated with a verbal or non-verbal IQ. These subphenotypes of autism, however, did not show strong association with abnormal chromosomal sites.

Happé, Ronald, and Plomin (2006) reported that the three autism diagnostic criteria—impaired social interaction, impaired communication, and restricted and repetitive behaviors—were separately heritable in a sample of 3000 typical twin pairs. The researchers noted that relatives of individuals with autism might show one of the three diagnostic symptoms of autism and express communication impairment without social impairment or restricted and repetitive behavior. Happé et al. (2006) argued that their findings indicated that the genes that contribute to autism vary in relatives, and "have distinct influences on the different parts of the phenotype" (p. 1219).

Ingram, Takahashi, and Miles (2008) reported that three types of behaviors could be used to subgroup individuals with autism: (1) social interaction and communication; (2) intelligence; and (3) essential autism without any dysmorphic physical features versus complex autism with dysmorphic physical features. The researchers reported, however, that four other behaviors were dimensional and could not be used as a means to subgroup individuals with autism: (1) insistence on sameness; (2) repetitive sensory motor actions; (3) language development; and (4) daily living skills.

Despite these and a myriad of other competing proposals for subgroups within autism, no accepted subgroups have been established. Rutter (2011) cautioned, "All that can be concluded firmly at the moment is that it is highly likely that there are meaningful subcategories of autism spectrum disorders but that these are not well identified" (p. 399). A similar failure has plagued efforts to resolve autism heterogeneity by theories of a unifying brain deficit.

Competing Brain Deficit Theories of Autism

Neurologist Margaret Bauman asserted that researchers "should still be hunting for what is similar, for the unifying characteristic" (Feinstein, 2010,

p. 210). Bauman stated, "Even if Mary Coleman refers to 70 different kinds of autism, she's still calling it autism. There may be different ways of getting there, but I am not ready to give up the hunt for some core, unifying feature of the brains of children with autism" (Feinstein, 2010, p. 210). Many autism researchers have shared Bauman's conviction, and have remained committed to the belief that there must be a unique defining brain deficit for autism.

Autism is Unified by a Shared Brain Disruption in Social Information Processing

Pelphrey, Schultz, and Hudac (2011) claimed that autism heterogeneity did not prevent unity in autism; it was only that researchers "have overemphasized the heterogeneity in ASD, at the expense of recognizing the homogeneity of core disruptions in social information processing" (p. 633). Pelphrey et al. (2011) asserted that although autism is heterogeneous in phenotype and genotype, autism is unified by impaired reciprocal social interaction. The researchers claimed, "Our contention is that despite the etiological heterogeneity and despite such high phenotypic variability … a circumscribed set of neural structures and their interconnections … will be found at the level of brain systems particularly those regions devoted to social information" (Pelphrey et al., 2011, p. 633). Pelphrey et al. (2011) did not interpret the wide variation in autism brain deficits as a possible reason why a shared circumscribed set of brain structures might not be found for all individuals diagnosed with autism.

Autism is Unified by a Failure to Sparsify Information to Prototypes

Unlike Pelphrey et al. (2011), Fabricius (2010) claimed that autism was not a social cognition brain deficit but a general information-processing brain deficit. Fabricius argued that typical individuals take in all the information from their environment but then immediately "sparsify their neural signal to a smaller subset of neurons that capture an approximation of the signal" (p. 257). Fabricius (2010) argued that key information is "sparsified" and becomes a prototype signal used to make multiple associations throughout the brain. Fabricius argued that individuals with autism fail to make prototypes, but retain some segment of the un-sparsified sensory information. He theorized that individuals with savant syndrome, whether diagnosed with autism or not, retained all primary sensory information through to higher level processing without "sparsifying" information. Treffert (2010) found that half of those with savant syndrome were diagnosed with autism, and Howlin, Goode, Hutton, and Rutter (2009) claimed, "unusual talents are found in at least a third of individuals with autism" (p. 1364). The particular challenge for the theory proposed by Fabricius (2010) is that many individuals with autism do make associations and learn prototype category knowledge (Soulières, Mottron, Giguère, & Larochelle, 2011).

Clearly, heterogeneity has not hindered researchers from asserting unifying theories. Similarly, disconfirming evidence has not hindered the influence of many theories. Three creative and powerful competing theories have been disconfirmed by further research but continue to be accepted, cited, and studied:

autism is the result of a failed ability to understand that others have different thoughts—called Theory of Mind theory (Baron-Cohen, Leslie, & Frith, 1985);

autism is the result of failed brain interconnectivity caused by maldevelopment of the white matter of the brain (Just, Cherkassky, Keller, & Minshew, 2004);

autism is the result of the inability to attend to biological motion (Klin, Lin, Gorrindo, Ramsay, & Jones, 2009).

Autism is Unified by the Failure to Have a Theory of Mind

Baron-Cohen et al. (1985) hypothesized that the crucial unifying characteristic of autism was a failure to have a Theory of Mind: that is, a failure to be able to imagine that other people have their own beliefs and thoughts. However, multiple studies have demonstrated that many individuals with autism do have the ability to imagine the minds of other people, and many studies have also demonstrated that skill on tests of the Theory of Mind depends on cognitive and language abilities (van Buijsen, Hendriks, Ketelaars, & Verhoeven, 2011). In addition, other studies have shown that failure to imagine that other people have their own beliefs and thoughts is not unique to autism—this failure occurs in schizophrenia and other psychiatric and neurological disorders (Fett et al., 2011).

Autism is Unified by Brain Underconnectivity

Autism was also claimed to be unified by underconnectivity of the brain, stemming from underdevelopment of the brain's white matter (Just et al., 2004). However, here too, variation was discovered that undermined underconnectivity as the unifying brain deficit of autism. There is evidence that white matter abnormalities do exist in many individuals with autism, but not in so many as to unify autism as a syndrome of underconnectivity.

Schuman et al. (2010) found that longitudinal brain growth patterns in some individuals with autism were not abnormal. The researchers did find that many males with autism had significantly enlarged frontal and temporal lobe gray matter volumes, and many females with autism had significantly enlarged gray and white matter volumes. Boddaert et al. (2009) found mild to moderate isolated regional white matter abnormalities in just 30 of 77 children with autism. Booth, Wallace, and Happé (2011) compared under-connectivity in autism to failure of the development of the corpus callosum, tissue connecting the left and right hemispheres of the cerebral cortex. They noted that many individuals with the absence of the corpus callosum—a most severe lack of interconnectivity in the brain—expressed typical social development. This challenged the idea that failed interconnectivity could explain the core autism deficit of social interaction impairment.

Barnea-Goraly, Lotspeich, and Reiss (2010) reported that both individuals with autism and their unaffected siblings showed significantly reduced white matter. However, the siblings showed no autistic behaviors, therefore the researchers suggested that white matter deficits may be a family marker but are unlikely to be a unifying cause of autism diagnostic behaviors. Moreover, underconnectivity is not unique to autism. It has been found in many disorders, including dyslexia (Richards & Berninger, 2008), schizophrenia (Cole, Anticevic, Repovs, & Barch, 2011), and depression (Cullen et al., 2010).

Autism is Unified by Impaired Attention to Biological Motion

Klin et al. (2009) proposed that autism was unified by impaired attention to biological motion wherein children with autism express diminished attention to the eyes of other people, leading to failed social learning, which, in turn, leads to increasing impairment in social interaction. However, Brady, Fitzgerald, and Troje (2009), Saygin, Cook, and Blakemore (2010), and Rutherford and Troje (2012) found no significant difference between adults with autism and typical adults in the perception of biological motion. Moreover, a review of research on face recognition in autism concluded that the "versatility and abilities of face processing in persons with autism have been underestimated" (Jemel, Mottron, & Dawson, 2006, p. 102). Jemel et al. (2006) concluded that autism was not characterized by any deficit in perceiving faces, or in attending to face features, or recognizing specific faces or facial expressions of emotion. Additionally, Rutherford and Troje (2012) reported that autism group performance on a biological motion perception task was significantly correlated with IQ, indicating that failure to detect biological motion was likely to be a function of intelligence, and not a dysfunction characterizing autism.

South, Schultz, and Ozonoff (2011) asked, "What are the neural organizing principles and shared pathways that lead to a group of behaviors that can be defined by the common term of autism?" (p. 237). To date, among the many competing theories of unifying brain deficit in autism there is no answer to this question.

Competing Genetic Risk Factor Theories of Autism

Brain deficit theories have not been the only competing unifying hypotheses proposed for autism. Competing theories to unify autism by genetic variants have also been proposed. Because so many gene variants and altered chromosome sites have been discovered in association with autism, relatively few unifying genetic theories have been proposed. These competing theories have not been synthesized, and there has been no field-wide effort to construct a standard genetic causal model for autism. Most theories have not been disconfirmed but left isolated, without replication.

Several difficulties have to be overcome by any theories to unify autism through genetic causality. First, nearly all gene variants and chromosomal site alterations associated with autism are also associated with intellectual disability (Betancur, 2011). Second, many gene variants link autism to other psychiatric and neurodevelopmental disorders including schizophrenia, bipolar disorder, and attention deficit disorder (Owen, O'Donovan, Thapar, & Craddock, 2011; Rapoport, Chavez, Greenstein, Addington, & Gogtay, 2009). A third difficulty is the more general question whether autism should be seen as a common disease caused by common genetic variants or as a common disease caused by many different rare single genetic variants or combinations of rare variants. To date, both common genetic variants and rare variants have been found in association with autism (Miles, 2011). Maher (2008) wondered, "Medicine tries hard to lump together a complex collection of symptoms and call it a disease. But if thousands of rare genetic variants contribute to a single disease, and the genetic underpinnings can vary radically for different people, how common is it? Are these, in fact, different diseases?" (p. 7).

Despite the heterogeneity of gene and chromosome variants associated with autism, researchers have developed competing unifying genetic theories of autism. Yrigollen et al. (2008) proposed that multiple affiliation hormone gene variants together produced abnormal sociality in autism. Gregory et al. (2009) proposed that dysfunction of the oxytocin receptor gene alone was sufficient to cause the syndrome of autism. Bill and Geschwind (2009) proposed that a set of faulty genes causing aberrant brain connectivity was the cause of autism. In addition to these genetic causal theories, three other complex evidence-based genetic theories were proposed to unify autism.

Voineagu et al. (2011) measured messenger RNA levels in three regions of postmortem brains from 19 patients with autism and 17 controls. They concluded that autism is characterized by the increased and decreased transcription of 444 genes in the brain's frontal and temporal lobes: 209 genes less-expressed in autistic cortex had growth functions related to the neuron connections or synapses; 235 genes more-expressed in autistic cortex had reactive functions associated with immune and inflammatory responses. Korade and Mirnics (2011) cautioned, however, that these mass genetic expression changes were not found in all 19 autism patient brains. Nonetheless, Korade and Mirnics proposed a molecular genetic-linked-to-behavior classification of autism into three subgroups: gene splicing deficit autism; synaptic deficit autism; and inflammatory impairment autism. Korade and Mirnics (2011) asserted that if specific molecular genetic patterns were found to be linked to specific autism behaviors, "it would revolutionize autism research, and open the door to developing more targeted and individualized therapies" (p. 295).

Ploeger, Raijmakers, van der Maas, and Galis (2010) noted that autism was associated with errors in early embryogenesis, varied brain deficits, and with major and minor physical anomalies. From this, they concluded that autism was likely to be caused by the mutation or environmental disruption of imprinted genes—known to have many varied or pleiotropic effects on development. The researchers proposed that interference with the function of these imprinted genes during organogenesis of the embryo resulted in autism. This model, like the transcription model of Voineagu et al. (2011), of course, cannot account for perinatal or post-birth environmental causes of autism.

Zhao et al. (2007) theorized that autism was genetically transmitted in two familial patterns: (1) families in which 50% of males have autism resulting from the dominant transmission of a single gene with high penetrance; and (2) families for whom male offspring are at a low risk of autism. The researchers further theorized that most dominant transmission was of a new gene mutation, deletion, duplication, rearrangement, or point mutations in the germ line of one parent. They countered the evidence that only 10% of autism was caused by novel mutations by arguing that the 10% figure was "a gross underestimate because of the low resolution of the technique for discovering these copy–number mutations" (Zhao et al., 2007, p. 12835).

At present, the competing genetic theories outlined above remain separate unsynthesized hypotheses. One problem for any potential synthesis is that evidence for gene variants in autism has been shown to be so heterogeneous: no risk variant is present in more than 1% of affected individuals. Moreover, often the diagnosed siblings of individuals with autism do not share the same risk variants as their brother or sister.

Competing Speculative Environmental Cause Theories of Autism

In addition to the many competing brain deficit and genetic cause theories of autism, a plethora of competing environmental causes have been proposed. Many have been based on speculation. Sadly, a number of competing speculative environment theories have been fraudulent, dangerous, or foolish. Worse still, the fraudulent, harmful, and foolishly speculative notions have been widely disseminated, and too often have been believed by parents and the public.

The Wakefield Vaccine Theory Fraud

One of the most widely disseminated fraudulent theories of an environmental cause for autism was the Wakefield vaccine theory. As outlined earlier in this chapter, in 1998, Wakefield claimed autism was caused by the combined measles–mumps–rubella vaccination. His claim was not simply a mistaken hypothesis; Wakefield's paper in *The Lancet* was based on multiple frauds. It took years of investigative journalism by Brian Deer to uncover the fraud behind the now retracted paper (Deer, 2011). The deception included Wakefield's failure to disclose his financial payment for supporting future potential parent lawsuits and his financial interests in his own patents for single vaccine administration. The fraud also included Wakefield's false assertion that all 12 children described in the paper had regressive autism, when only one child actually did experience regression. Moreover, Wakefield's claim that the association between MMR, autism, and bowel disease was discovered via the study of these 12 children was itself a lie, as Wakefield had been able to select these children from the files of hundreds of children collected by an attorney planning a massive lawsuit (Deer, 2011).

Wakefield also falsified the parents' reports of vaccination after-effects in their children. In the article in *The Lancet* (1998), Wakefield stated that the affected children's autism behaviors appeared within 14 days following the

MMR vaccination. However, most parents had actually reported to Wakefield that their children experienced crying, fever, rash, and irritability. These are not autism symptoms but instead are common and benign consequences of vaccination. No competent pediatrician would have characterized these behaviors as signs of regressive autism.

Two Harmful Theories of Environmental Causes for Autism

One of the most harmful speculative theories of environmental cause was proposed by Dr. Leo Kanner, the doctor who in 1943 first identified autism as a syndrome. Dr. Kanner speculated that cold parenting caused autism. Following Dr. Kanner's speculations, Dr. Bruno Bettelheim (1967) argued that autism was caused by the failure of parents to love their child. The notion that autism was caused by cold parenting and particularly cold mothering indicted mothers and parents for more than 30 years. In 1964, a parent, Dr. Bernard Rimland, published *Infantile Autism: The Syndrome and Its Implications for a Neural Theory of Behavior.* Rimland argued that the cause for autism was not parental coldness but brain dysfunction. Kanner had come to believe that autism was not caused by cold parenting, and he wrote an enthusiastic introduction to Rimland's book.

Many other potentially harmful theories have been proposed since the refrigerator mother theory was abandoned. For example in *The Myth of Autism* (2011), Goldberg and Goldberg claimed that autism was caused by a neuroimmune viral disorder that should be treated by the repeated administration of antiviral and antifungal drugs, and the administration of a serotonin reuptake inhibitor antidepressant to "induce speech in the temporal lobes." Goldberg and Goldberg defended against empirical investigation of their theory by declaring that standard tests for impaired immune system function in blood, stool, or urine were "notoriously" inaccurate and thus could not be informative about the state of a patient's immune system.

Four Foolishly Speculative Theories of Environmental Causes for Autism

Most foolish theories of environmental cause for autism are purely speculative; however, some have supporting evidence. Three purely speculative theories and one speculative theory with minimal evidence argued that autism was caused by: lack of lard; watching TV; use of the internet; and an increase in technology specialist intermarriage. Loos (2011) argued that as fewer and fewer people cooked with lard, autism increased in prevalence. Lard, Loos argued, is an important precursor for utilization of vitamin D, and lack of fully utilized vitamin D was the cause of autism. Waldman, Nicholson, and Adilov (2007) claimed that watching cable television was likely to be a core cause for autism. The neuroscientist Baroness Susan Greenfield suggested that increasing use of the internet had led to an increase in autism (Swain, 2011). Researcher Dorothy Bishop (2011) rebuked Greenfield, stating, "You may not realise just how much illogical garbage and ill-formed speculation parents of children with these conditions are exposed to … inoculations, dental amalgams, faulty diets … the list is endless." Bishop claimed that increased prevalence of autism was largely due to changes in diagnostic criteria, that autism prevalence increased "well before internet use became widespread," and that "autism is typically evident by 2 years of age, long before children become avid users of Twitter or Facebook" (Bishop, 2011).

Roelfsema et al. (2012) hypothesized that autism was caused by brain hyper-systematizing, and they reasoned that autism would occur more frequently if more adult male and female systematizers chose to marry one another. The researchers speculated that talented systematizers would be found in areas with concentrations of information technology businesses. They tested for the prevalence of autism in children in the technology-concentrated Eindhoven region of The Netherlands and compared prevalence of autism in two other regions without concentrations of technology businesses: the Haarlem and Utrecht regions. They reported that the prevalence of school-aged children with a diagnosis of autism was significantly higher in the Eindhoven region than in the Haarlem and Utrecht regions. The researchers claimed this finding supported the theory that children born to two systematizing parents where neither parent was diagnosed with autism were subject to a significant risk factor for autism. However, it seems unlikely that a sufficient number of systematizers could have married one another to account for the actual increase in autism prevalence.

Competing Gene–Environment Interaction Theories of Autism

Complex competing gene–environment interaction theories have been proposed to unify autism. Pardo and Eberhart (2007) proposed that autism resulted from "environmental factors (e.g., neurotoxins, child infections, maternal infections) in presence of genetic susceptibility and the immuno-genetic background" (p. 493) of a child. They argued that the interaction of genetic and environmental factors caused the development of abnormalities in cortical organization and neuronal circuitry and neuroinflammatory changes, which together caused autistic symptoms.

Casanova (2007) and Williams and Casanova (2010) proposed that a "triple hit" of faulty vulnerability genes, environmental agents, and a specific time of the insult to the fetus caused autism. They argued that if negative environment effects occur during the early stages of fetal development, and if a fetal brain is specifically vulnerable to those environmental factors, autism will result.

In 2005, Herbert and Ziegler argued that autism was unlikely to be a prenatal gene effect, because the genes of strongest effect in autism, fragile X and Rett syndrome, did not consistently result in autism, and because many brain changes in autism occurred postnatally during the course of development. They proposed a cascading mechanism. First, a pregnant woman's infection would cause her body's cells to increase numbers of inflammatory cytokines, triggering fetal cells to increase their cytokines, including interleukin 1, interleukin 6, tumor necrosis factor, and interferon. The fetal cytokine increase would trigger the production of free radicals, and these free radicals would damage nuclear and mitochondrial DNA in neurons in the fetal brain, and trigger the brain's microglia cells to produce superoxide, nitric oxide, and peroxynitrite, and these microglia products would damage mitochondrial DNA in an ongoing developmental cycle of damage (Herbert and Ziegler, 2005).

In 2008, Herbert and Anderson restated their theory, arguing that neuroinflammation caused autism by a series of insults: first, static encephalopathy; second, an epigenetic reaction to environmental toxins; and finally, by the ensuing chronic encephalopathy.

To date, none of the many alternate gene-in-environment theories has been confirmed by further research.

SUBGROUPS AND UNIFYING THEORIES HAVE NOT EXPLAINED THE VARIATION IN AUTISM

There is now a large pile of competing orphaned, disconfirmed, and unsynthesized theories of autism subgroups, and theories of unifying brain deficits and unifying patterns of genetic and environmental risk factors for autism. Instead of explaining the variation in autism, the mountain of unproven competing theories has only made understanding autism more difficult. The mountain will grow higher. Bishop (2010) reported that autism prevalence and severity are comparable to those of Down syndrome, yet funding for autism is six times the amount allocated to study Down syndrome. Bishop also noted, "the slope showing increase of NIH funding over time is dramatically higher than for any other condition. It seems likely that government initiatives play a large role in explaining the extraordinary rise of publications in autism" (2010, p. e15112).

Rutter (2011) argued that, because of the "huge investment in clinical research that goes back for well over half a century, it might be supposed that all that needed to be known is already well established and free of controversies. However, that is far from the case" (p. 395).

In fact, the orphaned and disconfirmed theories that have failed to explain variation in autism are, in large part, examples of theory underdetermination. Science philosopher Peter Lipton (2005) argued, "Theories go far beyond the data that support them; indeed, the theories would be of little interest if this were not so. However, this means a scientific theory is always 'underdetermined' by the available data concerning the phenomena" (p. 1261). The theory of underdetermination, called the Duhem–Quine principle, is a formal acceptance that theories make claims that data do not fully support. Theory succession, as from Hippocrates' theory of pangenesis to Darwin's gemmules, to DNA and transcriptomes, moves from one underdetermined theory to the next. However, Stanford (2001) pointed out that not all theory underdetermination is acceptable. It can be a Devil's bargain: a serious threat to scientific discovery.

The wide variation in behavior, brain deficit, and risk factors found for autism has meant that all theories to unify autism have been significantly underdetermined by the available data, primarily because the data have been insufficiently homogeneous. This lack of homogeneity is most often revealed in studies attempting to replicate an earlier study's findings in autism. Too few individuals with the unifying feature is not the only problem, however. Most unifying theories are also insufficiently autism-specific because the unifying feature is not unique to autism but also occurs in intellectual disability, schizophrenia, Alzheimer's disorder, or other disorders.

HAS AUTISM BEEN REIFIED?

Not only are findings too heterogeneous to provide support for single cause theories of autism, the existence of autism is itself a theory, and the theory that autism spectrum disorder exists is underdetermined. The existence of autism spectrum disorder has not been supported by evidence for a drug treatment that successfully addresses autism symptoms, or by any evidence for a unifying genetic or environmental cause, or any unifying explanatory brain deficit. The heterogeneity has meant that the theory that autism spectrum disorder exists has remained unproven.

Although autism spectrum disorder has not been proven to exist either as a set of meaningful subgroups, or as the expression of a unifying deficit or causal pattern, nonetheless, autism appears to have been unified as a real entity in public opinion. Autism blogger Rudy (2011) complained that the symptoms of autism were real, but the spectrum of autism disorders was a theory invented by those in power in the American Psychiatric Association. Of course, autism was first hypothesized by Kanner in 1943, and was not invented by the APA. Moreover, Kanner did propose autism as a real and unitary disorder. However, autism was Kanner's theory, and his theory was based on a limited set of observations. Some researchers have argued that, over time, autism has been transformed from a hypothesis to an assumed reality. This transformation is called reification. Reification is the conversion of a theorized entity into something assumed and believed to be real.

Sociologists have argued that reification of autism is reflected in diagnostic substitution. Diagnostic substitution occurs when an autism diagnosis replaces the diagnosis of intellectual disability, severe language disorder, or other developmental disorder. In their book *The Autism Matrix*, sociologists Eyal, Hart, Onculer, Oren, and Rossi (2009) argued that autism has been reified as the most prototypical form of brain development disorder. The researchers claimed that autism was reified through the gradual shift to an autism diagnosis for more and more individuals formerly diagnosed with childhood schizophrenia and for more and more individuals formerly diagnosed with intellectual disability.

Sociologists King and Bearman (2009) studied diagnostic substitution in California. Their analysis revealed that 9% of cases of autism were cases of intellectual disability wherein a diagnosis of autism had been substituted. They reported that an earlier case review also found that 10% of children with a sole diagnosis of intellectual disability qualified for a diagnosis of autism. King and Bearman (2009) noted that California's diagnostic practice was conservative. The researchers argued that the ongoing process of providing an autism diagnosis where a diagnosis of intellectual disability should have been made was likely to be responsible for a significant portion of the increasing prevalence of autism. They further argued it was likely that diagnostic substitution of autism for developmental language disorder and other learning disabilities was also increasing the prevalence of autism.

Although there may be many different causes for diagnostic substitution, diagnostic substitution does reflect the reification of autism. As more professionals and parents believe in the reality of autism, it is likely that diagnostic substitution will increase. In the United States, the Centers for Disease Control reported that for 2008, the estimated prevalence of ASDs was 11.3 per 1000 (1 in 88) children aged 8 years (Autism and Developmental Disabilities Monitoring Network Surveillance Year 2008 Principal Investigators, CDC, 2012). Mandell et al. (2011) found that 10% of patients in a psychiatric hospital met the criteria to be diagnosed with autism. Kim et al. (2011) screened more than 55,000 7–12-year-old children in South Korea with the Autism Spectrum Screening Questionnaire. They found the astoundingly high autism prevalence of 2.64%. One in every 37 children tested met diagnostic criteria for autism; this prevalence rate was the highest ever reported for autism. This exceedingly high prevalence supported Eyal and colleagues' (2009) assertion that autism has been reified as the main prototypical developmental disorder.

Diagnostic substitutions may not be a public process, but the intense public discussion of autism, the long history of autism in the diagnostic manuals of the American Psychiatric Association, and the long history of autism research and theory are in full view, and they all have made autism seem more concrete and less hypothetical. Researchers, parents, doctors, teachers, and the public do believe autism is real. Paradoxically, however, if greater belief in the reality of autism has caused more diagnostic substitution and more diagnosis of autism in general, the resulting increase in heterogeneity and prevalence has led to concerns about the reality of autism.

Reiss (2009) asked readers to imagine it was 2025 and a child with a brain development disorder was being evaluated. He projected that in 2025 the evaluation would determine brain, gene, and environmental factors that contributed to the child's neurodevelopmental problems independent of labels from different disciplines. Reiss argued that present disciplines, including psychiatry, genetics, and neurology needlessly limited the ideal evaluation of children. Reiss (2009) and colleagues (Hall et al., 2010) asserted that psychiatric and genetic categories were in conflict in cases like Rett syndrome and autism, and fragile X and autism. Although Reiss did not claim the diagnoses from different disciplines were reified inventions, he did suggest that "saving the phenomena" (the heterogeneity in behaviors, brain deficits, and in genetic and environmental risk factors) from conflicting diagnostic labels from different disciplines was crucial.

SAVING THE PHENOMENA OF AUTISM VARIATION

Equally problematic, autism brain research findings have not uncovered the underlying complexity of the phenomena. Bogen and Woodward (1988) argued that what can be measured is "rarely the result of a single phenomenon operating alone, but instead typically reflect the interaction of many different phenomena .... Nature is so complicated that ... it is hard to imagine an instrument which could register any phenomenon of interest in isolation" (pp. 351–352).

The heterogeneous phenomena in autism are complex, and our ability to understand the complex brain deficits and complex genetic and environment causes for autism is hobbled by our lack of knowledge. Congdon, Poldrack, and Freimer (2011) baldly stated, "One of the main obstacles to progress in genetic dissection of brain and behavioral disorders is that our basic knowledge of the function of the human nervous system remains so incomplete ... making it difficult to design studies that map the comparative genetic architecture of particular disorders with specific neurocognitive phenotypes" (p. 220).

Our awareness of the complexity of the phenomena in autism has increased as the scientific understanding of genetics and neuroscience has increased. When autism was first claimed as a disorder by Kanner in 1943, almost nothing was known about the many varied brain circuits and neurotransmitters that contribute to typical social behavior, and the helical structure of DNA had yet to be discovered. Only now are we beginning to understand the complex processes of genetic control of brain development and brain function. Research has just begun to shed light on the varied patterns of complex multi-causal regulation of the expression of genetic variants, and we remain largely in the dark on the disruptive effects many environmental factors may have on brain development.

Congdon et al. (2011) pessimistically concluded, "there is little to suggest that our current knowledge of the biological pathways involved in neurocognitive function provides a sufficient basis to make strongly motivated hypotheses regarding which genes are associated with these functions. Such hypothesizing is further complicated by an even greater lack of understanding of the potential effects of regulatory mechanisms, epigenetic influences, and environmental factors on variation in complex phenotypes" (p. 219).

HOW SHOULD WE VIEW THE VARIATION IN AUTISM?

We know that autism is not a single disease. We know that autism includes brain development disorders that appear with varied symptoms early in development. We define autism to include social impairment and rigid interests or repetitive behaviors, but we know that these symptoms are expressed heterogeneously. We know that autism has not been divisible into meaningful subgroups, and we know that the evidence uncovered to date indicates that there will be no discovery of a unifying brain deficit or unifying genetic or environmental risk factor for autism.

Some researchers have accepted the variation as an inevitable aspect of autism. For example, autism researcher Tager-Flusberg (2010) stated, "We may never find the single clue (genetic, neurobiological, or behavioral) that can unequivocally predict who will have ASD—it simply may not exist. Instead, ASD may be more accurately viewed as an emerging syndrome that unfolds over time in a probabilistic way as a result of alterations in the dynamic interaction between the infant and his or her environment" (p. 1076). As outlined earlier, Pelphrey et al. (2011), like Tager-Flusberg, accepted autism phenotype and genotype heterogeneity. However, Pelphrey et al. (2011) claimed that autism was unified by a brain deficit that impaired social cognition.

Conversely, other researchers have seen the problem of heterogeneity as serious enough to require a completely different research strategy. Goos (2008) argued that using a diagnosis to form groups for genetic risk studies "is a very serious mistake, as heterogeneity is rampant within diagnostic categories, and individuals with the same diagnosis may vary significantly in phenotype and etiology, even in the presence of high heritability" (p. 270). Consequently, many autism researchers have worked to identify autism endophenotypes—specific brain deficits or specific behavioral impairments—in the hopes of linking an endophenotype to a single gene mutation or chromosome alteration.

Rommelse, Geurts, Franke, Buitelaar, and Hartman (2011) proposed exploring many different autism endophenotypes. They recommended temperament and personality traits, specific brain domains, brain volume, cortical thickness, brain connectivity, as well as intelligence, language, executive functioning, sensory functioning, and motor coordination. Congdon et al. (2011) also asserted that an important means for "reducing heterogeneity has been to focus investigation on ... endophenotypes" (p. 219). However, autism is so very heterogeneous that autism endophenotypes themselves have been shown to include heterogeneous brain deficits and heterogeneous causes (Waterhouse, 2011).

Researchers Happé et al. (2006) argued that heterogeneity in autism was not "noise or the complex unfolding of development, but is an unavoidable consequence of variation along at least three largely independent (although of course interacting) dimensions of impairment" (p. 1220). The researchers further claimed that the three DSM-IV diagnostic criteria of social impairment, communication difficulties, and rigid and repetitive behaviors resulted from three separate sets of non-overlapping genes.

Holt and Monaco (2011) proposed that the "ASDs should not be considered a set of discrete disorders, but a continuous range of individually rare conditions. The rarity of specific variants, combined with the sample sizes employed to date, mean that caution must be adopted in assigning a pathogenic role to a specific variant based solely on its uniqueness within an ASD sample" (p. 455). Although the researchers argued in favor of the existence of unique variant forms of autism, they cautioned that unique variants might be meaningless. They also proposed that individual forms of autism do exist, but nonetheless claimed that individual forms of autism could not be separated and must be maintained in a "continuous range." It is unclear how individual forms of autism might be maintained in a continuous range.

Szatmari (2011) suggested the field should start over. He theorized that autism could be re-envisioned as a family of dimensional phenotypes including symptom phenotypes, intelligence phenotypes, psychiatric phenotypes, and medical disorder phenotypes. In Szatmari's model, autism phenotypes are created by networks of genes, and each individual "with autistic spectrum disorder represents an overlap of phenotypes, and the degree of overlap represents the clinical profile of any individual child" (p. 2). Of course, Szatmari's model will not account for cases of autism caused by environmental risk factors.

Like Szatmari, Boucher (2011) proposed that autism be redefined as a spectrum of many separate behavior and physical disorders that happen to occur together in autism more than would be expected by chance. Boucher noted that many autism behaviors are not correlated, but are instead dissociable. She hypothesized that the heterogeneity of brain deficits and causal factors, and the many dissociable diagnostic behaviors must "fan in" to converge onto a single brain abnormality.

Although Happé et al. (2006), Holt and Monaco (2011), Szatmari (2011), and Boucher (2011) addressed autism variation directly, their proposals included two unexplained processes. First, their proposals all argued that a specific subset of autism behaviors, brain deficits, and causes must "happen to occur together" in any given individual with autism. However, none of the four proposals theorized any mechanism that could cause the varying features to occur together. Happé et al. (2006) argued that each of the three diagnostic criteria for autism was entirely separate, and stated, "Clearly a question remains of why these three features co-occur at above-chance rates" (p. 1219). Similarly, Boucher (2011) admitted that it would be difficult to explain, "how the multiplicity of susceptibility factors underlying ASDs might in their different combinations" (p. 479) have created a single unified autism brain dysfunction.

Second, three of the four proposals argued that the variation within each diagnosed individual must contribute to a meaningful continuum of autism. Holt and Monaco (2011) argued that a continuous range of individual variation must be created; Szatmari (2011) argued that the autism spectrum depended on overlapping phenotypes; and Boucher (2011) argued autism is a spectrum of overlapping deficits in which some combinations of deficits are more prototypical than others. However, none of the researchers hypothesized any mechanism that would cause the wide range of individual variation in autism to form itself into a meaningful continuum.

SERIOUS CONCERNS FOR MAINTAINING THE AUTISM DIAGNOSIS

Given all that is known about autism and its diagnosis, there are two serious concerns for continuing to maintain the diagnostic category of autism spectrum disorder for research. As noted earlier, the most critical concern is that effective drug treatments require knowledge of explicit causal brain and gene mechanisms. Diagnosed individuals do not all share the same deficits in brain mechanisms and brain neurochemistry, or share gene variants for aberrant brain development, thus effective treatments will be extremely difficult to discover when the autism spectrum disorder criteria are used to form study groups. Another concern is that studying groups of individuals diagnosed with autism spectrum disorder will not permit researchers to achieve an understanding of the significance of the full range of symptoms of the autism phenotype. The diagnosis excludes symptoms that risk factor research suggests are part of the complex autism phenotype.

These two concerns are serious. If we accept autism spectrum disorder diagnostic criteria as creating a valid group, we are accepting a theory of autism that is underdetermined and unproven. In Stanford's (2001) view we are making a "Devil's bargain" because in accepting the diagnosis of autism spectrum disorder we are accepting a definition that is not consonant with the reality of phenotypic heterogeneity. This will limit crucial scientific discovery.

EIGHT CLAIMS CONCERNING AUTISM VARIATION AND THE AUTISM DIAGNOSIS

The book proposes three general arguments organized into eight claims. These three arguments are the operating assumptions for the book's eight claims. The first general argument is that autism variation in etiology, brain deficits, behaviors, and life course is real and extensive and carries important information, therefore this variation should be explained rather than be accepted, minimized, or ignored.

The second argument is that prior DSM diagnostic criteria for autism and the DSM-5 diagnostic criteria for autism spectrum disorder have mistakenly excluded frequently occurring symptoms of the autism phenotype as being outside the autism diagnosis. Intellectual disability, attention deficit/ hyperactivity disorder symptoms, motor disorders, epilepsy, and, in DSM-5, developmental language disorder symptoms, have been excluded from the autism diagnostic phenotype. Excluding these symptoms from a diagnosis of autism has not helped us to understand the varied complex autism phenotypes, and has consequently hampered research discovery.

The third general argument is that there are multiple causes for complex autism phenotypes, and understanding these causes will not be advanced by theories that propose a single unifying cause or feature for autism. Advances in the understanding of causes for complex autism phenotypes will depend on increased knowledge of the genetics, epigenetics, and gene–environmental interactions involved in brain development, and on increased knowledge of social brain circuits and the entire brain connectome. Advances in the understanding of causes for complex autism phenotypes will also depend on the increased knowledge of environmental impacts on brain development, and increased knowledge of the mechanisms of the dynamic processes involved in brain development.

Chapter 1 Claim 1: Autism Heterogeneity is Meaningful

This chapter has argued that the wide variation in behavior, brain deficit, and risk factors found for autism represent meaningful complex phenotypes. The variation in autism has meant all theories to unify autism have been significantly underdetermined by the available data, primarily because the data have been insufficiently homogeneous. Therefore, studying groups of individuals diagnosed with autism spectrum disorder will not permit researchers to achieve an understanding of the significance of the heterogeneous phenomena within the diagnosis and crossing the boundary of the diagnosis.

Finding too few individuals with any presumptive unifying feature is not the only problem, however. Most unifying theories have been insufficiently autism-specific because most presumptive unifying features have been shown to occur in other disorders or in unaffected siblings of individuals with autism. Given the evidence of autism research to date, it is clear that diagnosed individuals do not all share the same deficits in brain mechanisms and brain neurochemistry, thus effective focal medical treatments have been and will remain extremely difficult to discover.

Chapter 2 Claim 2: Autism Symptom Heterogeneity Exists in Family Members

Researchers have conducted many family studies of autism (Mosconi et al., 2010). Identical (monozygotic) and fraternal (dizygotic) twins have been studied (Hallmayer et al., 2011; Ronald & Hoekstra, 2011), siblings have been studied (Orsmond & Selzer, 2007), and baby siblings of individuals with autism have also been studied (Hutman et al., 2011; Ozonoff et al., 2011). Studies of the family members of individuals with autism have found heterogeneity in diagnostic features, comorbid disorders, and even in causal agents for affected siblings, co-twins, and other family members.

Despite the heterogeneity found in various forms of family study in autism, researchers have attempted to find unity in the features of affected and unaffected family members. However, where variation in the behavior, genes, or brain impairments in family members of individuals with autism has been explored, a unitary broader phenotype of autism has seemed less likely.

Ozonoff et al. (2011) reported that one in five siblings of an autistic child will be diagnosed with autism. This powerful inheritance pattern is not unitary but depends on hundreds of genes and chromosomal loci, and surprisingly, may also depend on repeated action of environmental factors.

Hallmayer et al. (2011) reported high heritabilities for identical and fraternal twins, but were surprised to find that the shared environment component was larger than the genetic heritability component. The researchers estimated that genetic factors accounted for 38% of co-twin variance, but shared environmental components accounted for 58% of co-twin variance. Hallmayer et al. (2011) argued, "Because the prenatal environment and early postnatal environment are shared between twin individuals, we hypothesize that at least some of the environmental factors impacting susceptibility to autism exert their effect during this critical period of life" (p. 1101). However, the researchers also argued that parental age, low birth weight, multiple births, and maternal infections during pregnancy might account for the 58% of co-twin variance.

In sum, all forms of family studies show heterogeneity. This heterogeneity is likely to preclude establishing one broader familial phenotypic form of autism.

Chapter 3 Claim 3: The Social Brain is a Complex Super-Network

Because social interaction depends on so many brain systems, and because there are many structural and functional elements in these brain systems, there are many ways in which any one of these brain systems may be disrupted at any point during development. Consequently, the central diagnostic trait of autism, social interaction impairment, is likely to vary widely because this impairment is caused by multiple brain deficits, multiple genetic variants, and multiple environmental risk factors. The heterogeneity of brain deficits and causal agents in autism suggests that there are many different disruptions in brain systems mediating social behavior.

Brain systems that contribute to social interaction include the superior temporal sulcus of the temporal lobe, the fusiform gyrus, the amygdala, the prefrontal cortex (PFC), and areas comprising the mirror neuron system, the neurohormones oxytocin and vasopressin (Insel, 2010), and neurotransmitters of reward, including dopamine (Neuhaus, Beauchaine, & Bernier, 2010). These brain tissues, circuits, and neurotransmitters contribute to our interest in the behavior of others around us, trigger mirror neuron activity in the presence of others, make us especially alert to the human voice, generate rewards for being with other people, and generate our perception of human faces and our ability to responsively coordinate our behaviors with others.

Because there are so many brain systems that shape our ability to be social, there are likely to be myriad forms of brain disruption from widespread brain disruption to specific brain disruptions associated with autism symptoms. In addition, brain systems that contribute to our ability to be social are interconnected with brain systems for other abilities. This increases social brain circuit vulnerability.

Chapter 4 Claim 4: Genetic Risk Factors Link Autism to Many Other Disorders

Most known genetic and chromosomal syndromes associated with autism have been defined independently of autism. Examples include Rett syndrome, fragile X, and tuberous sclerosis. Although autism diagnosed in an individual known to have a specific genetic syndrome is called "syndromic autism," there is no diagnostic difference between syndromic autism and idiopathic autism—autism diagnosed in the absence of a known genetic cause. Nonetheless, a girl diagnosed with both Rett syndrome and autism spectrum disorder would be identified as having autism *comorbid* with Rett syndrome. The term comorbidity means being diagnosable with more than one disorder at the same time. For example, when people suffer colds, they may have both a viral and a bacterial infection at the same time.

Declaring the comorbidity of Rett syndrome and autism claims that the individual has two separate disorders. But unlike the person with a cold, who has both a viral and a bacterial infection, an individual diagnosed with autism and Rett syndrome cannot be demonstrated to have two distinguishable diseases. Although strep bacteria can be reliably differentiated from a respiratory virus by culturing both pathogens, autism cannot be reliably differentiated from Rett syndrome by examination of brain deficits or behavioral patterns. Despite this lack of differentiation, and despite the fact that autism researchers accept the known genetic basis of Rett syndrome, most researchers still view autism as distinct from Rett syndrome: "the overall undivided ASD category should be used for the period when children with Rett syndrome show features similar to autism" (Rutter, 2011, p. 398).

However, it is unlikely that autism and Rett syndrome are distinct disorders that just sometimes happen to co-occur such that "children with Rett syndrome show features similar to autism" (Rutter, 2011, p. 398). What is most likely is that Rett syndrome brain deficits are the cause of autism behaviors (Monteggia & Kavalali, 2009). Specifically, Rett syndrome includes alterations in the levels of the protein MECP2 that in turn alters the ongoing development of neurons, and this brain development deficit is most likely to generate the autism behaviors observed in individuals known to have Rett syndrome.

Comorbidity is a definitional boundary problem for the presence of symptoms from many other disorders that appear with autism. In DSM-5, the Neurodevelopmental Disorders group includes six subgroups: Intellectual Developmental Disorder, Communication Disorders, Autism Spectrum Disorder, Attention Deficit/Hyperactivity Disorder (ADHD), Learning Disorders, and Motor Disorders. The reality is that genetic, environmental, and brain deficit research has demonstrated causal links between Intellectual Disability and autism, Communications Disorders and autism, ADHD behaviors and autism, and Motor Disorders and autism. Consequently, many individuals diagnosed with autism do exhibit behaviors that would permit other DSM-5 neurodevelopmental diagnoses.

Although two-thirds of individuals diagnosed with autism have also been diagnosed with intellectual disability, most researchers have argued that intellectual disability is comorbid with autism. Many autism researchers have excluded individuals with intellectual disability from their research based on the assumption that intellectual disability is a brain impairment that has nothing to do with autism brain impairment.

Despite the common use of comorbidity assignments for autism, in fact, Rett syndrome, intellectual disability, and autism are most likely to be features of a shared brain development disorder. For example, Shinawi and colleagues (2011) reported on four children each with a mutation on chromosome 11 in the 11p13 region with deletions that affect several genes crucial for the maturation and differentiation of neurons and for synaptic transmission between neurons. Two of the four children met the criteria for a diagnosis of autism, and met the criteria for a diagnosis of ADHD, and met the criteria for a diagnosis of intellectual disability. Thus these two children were identified as comorbid for ASD, ADHD, and intellectual disability. However, neither child is likely to have three separate brain disorders. What is most likely is that the chromosomal deletion disrupting crucial brain development genes has given rise to all of their behaviors that fit the criteria for ASD, ADHD, and intellectual disability.

Owen et al. (2011) argued that many psychiatric diagnoses are likely to be linked through multiple gene vulnerabilities. They noted that that schizophrenia and intellectual disability are often found together, that symptoms of autism are also seen in adult schizophrenia, and that autism is often found in conjunction with intellectual disability and ADHD. Owen et al. (2011) argued that genetic evidence makes it "hard to avoid the conclusion that these disorders (autism, ADHD, intellectual disability, schizophrenia) represent a continuum of genetic and environmentally induced neurodevelopmental impairment" (2011, p. 174).

In sum, where autism shares gene variants with other disorders, comorbidity is unlikely and comorbidity should not be assumed.

Chapter 5 Claim 5: Environmental Risk Factors Link Autism to Many Other Outcomes

Most people are not aware of any other environmental risk factors for autism beyond childhood vaccination—the one risk factor that research has disconfirmed. For example, Anne Dachel (2011), a blogger for the anti-vaccine *The Age of Autism* website, commented bitterly, "Suddenly we're hearing that scientists believe there are environmental factors. There are a number of candidates from pesticides, older moms, older dads, too much TV watching, living too close to freeways, having siblings too close together among others. It seems that experts will continue to guess at autism and allow another generation to become its victims."

In fact, research has uncovered many environmental risk factors associated with autism, and, as noted above, Hallmayer and colleagues (2011) found that shared environmental factors accounted for a very surprising 58% of co-twin variance. Environmental risk factors for autism are wide-ranging and include older parents, birth process problems, spacing of pregnancies, and extremely premature birth. Gestational environmental factors such as maternal alcohol use or maternal infection have also been associated with an elevated risk of autism. Many infectious agents confer a risk for autism (Stigler et al., 2009).

All environmental agents link autism to other outcomes. For example, extreme prematurity has a range of outcomes, including typical development, intellectual disability, physical disabilities, and autism. A wide range of outcomes also occurs with exposure to other environmental agents.

Certainly part of the reason why the public and parents are unaware of many environmental risk factors beyond the discredited vaccine theory is that very few scientific theories of autism unified by an environmental agent have been proposed. Many researchers have seen autism as primarily a genetic disorder. However, many varied environmental risk factors contribute to autism heterogeneity.

Chapter 6 Claim 6: Savant Skills, Special Skills, and Intelligence Vary Widely in Autism

Treffert (2010) reported that 50% of individuals with savant syndrome were diagnosed with autism, and Howlin and colleagues (2009) stated that one third of individuals with autism have special information-processing talents. However, the true prevalence of savant skills in autism has not been determined. Savant and special skills found in autism all occur in typical individuals. As noted earlier, Fabricius (2010) theorized that all individuals with autism had a variant of savant sensory information processing. He argued that while typical individuals compress sensory data to prototypes for association across brain systems, savants and individuals with autism who were not savants failed to make prototypes, but retained uncompressed sensory information. He further claimed that individuals with savant syndrome retained *all* primary sensory information to higher-level processing without compressing any sensory details.

Not only are savant skills an unexplained form of heterogeneity in autism, there is heterogeneity within savant and other special skills that has remained unexplained.

Chapter 7 Claim 7: Increasing Prevalence and the Problem of Diagnosis

From Kanner's 1943 claim to the present DSM-5 criteria, the diagnosis of autism increased from 4 in 10,000 children to Kim and research colleagues' (2011) finding of 1 in 37 children, or 2.64%, diagnosed with autism. No other brain development disorder has such a high prevalence. Even the 1 in 110 prevalence rate reported for a set of regions in the United States by the Centers for Disease Control for the year 2006 (Autism and Developmental Disabilities Monitoring Network Surveillance Year 2006 Principal Investigators, CDC, 2009) increased to a rate of 1 in 88 just 2 years later in 2008 (Autism and Developmental Disabilities Monitoring Network Surveillance Year 2008 Principal Investigators, CDC, 2012). These high rates of prevalence and their apparent continuing upward course are a significant epidemiological problem.

Researchers have argued that changes in DSM diagnostic criteria, increased sensitivity to social disorders in young children, and diagnostic substitution have each contributed to increased autism prevalence. As more individuals are diagnosed, more heterogeneity is included in the autism spectrum diagnosis. Rutter (2011) wondered why autism did not become extinct, as the vast majority of individuals with autism do not have offspring. If the prevalence rate of 2.64% were replicated worldwide, autism would reduce world population growth.

It is more likely, however, that the extremely high prevalence rate reported by Kim and colleagues (2011) is evidence that the increased diagnosis of autism spectrum disorder has resulted from many causal factors. These include diagnostic substitution, interpretation of diagnostic criteria, increased sensitivity to social impairment, increasing awareness of autism, and possibly, a real increase in incidence.

Chapter 8 Claim 8: Autism Symptoms Exist but the Disorder Remains Elusive

Heterogeneity in autism has not been explained. Researchers have continued to try to establish a unifying deficit behavior, brain deficit, or causal agent. A persistent problem with theories designed to unify autism is the process of ignoring heterogeneity that would disconfirm a theory. For example, one unifying theory argued that autism is the result of early brain overgrowth (Courchesne, Campbell, & Solso, 2011). However, only 20% of individuals diagnosed with autism have a larger head (macrocephaly) by the age of 2 or 3. In addition, studies have shown regional abnormal growth in some individuals with autism: in the frontal lobe, temporal lobes, the amygdala, the hypothalamus, and the cerebellum.

Brain overgrowth in autism might develop from any one of the 164 conditions associated with increased head size (Williams, Dagli & Battaglia, 2008). The condition most commonly found in autism with macrocephaly is a *PTEN* gene mutation. The *PTEN* gene generates the phosphatase and tensin homologue protein, in which the phosphatase is involved in preventing brain cells from growing and dividing too rapidly. However, Buxbaum and colleagues (2007) found only one boy with PTEN mutations in a sample of 88 individuals with autism who also had macrocephaly.

If only 20% of individuals with autism have increased head size, brain overgrowth cannot be the unifying basis for autism. Equally important, increased head size in those 20% may be caused by any of a sizeable subset of 164 possible sources for head overgrowth in children.

To define autism as a syndrome of brain overgrowth ignores 80% of individuals diagnosed with autism. As stated earlier, this limits research ability to find brain mechanisms that might lead to potential drug treatments.

In fact, the only treatment for autism at present is intense and focused education programs. Helt and colleagues (2008) claimed that between 3% and 25% of children with autism recover to a typical level of functioning. They pointed out that although "Ideally, treatment methodologies are based on an understanding of the underlying brain abnormalities" (p. 360), in fact most treatment is conducted blind to what brain abnormalities may exist for a diagnosed individual. Warren and colleagues (2011) reviewed 10 years (2000 to 2010) of studies of behavioral intervention for autism. They noted that a majority of the studies examined one of two general approaches: one established for older children and the other for very young children with autism. Both treatment systems resulted in improvements in children's cognitive and language skills, and adaptive daily living skills.

Brain deficits definitively linked to a cause are more likely to lead to potential clinical treatments, assessments, and possible prevention. Rett syndrome and fragile X are genetic syndromes associated with a range of brain deficits and associated with autism diagnoses. Each has been successfully studied to the point of assessment, potential prevention, and possible treatments. Therefore, one reasonable approach would be to allow Rett syndrome, fragile X, and other genetic syndromes, when present in individuals diagnosed with autism, to take precedence over a diagnosis of autism.

No one knows how many individual brain developmental disorders exist within and linked to the autism spectrum. However, given the additional hundreds of gene variants found in association with autism, and the varied multiple brain dysfunctions, it is likely that within and linked to autism are many yet-to-be-discovered brain developmental disorders that are caused by genetic variants, epigenetic processes, gene–environment interactions, and environmental risk factors. Whether, as Owen, O'Donovan, Thapar, and Craddock (2011) have argued, there is one meshed assemblage of genetic and environmental causality in which minor shifts lead to different expressions of psychiatric disorders, or there are hundreds of individual gene–environment–brain developmental disorders included in or linked to the autism spectrum, there is one major stumbling block to discovering the underlying causal reality. The impediment is the use of the diagnosis of autism in research.

The only viable scientific path to finding the possible gene–environmental mesh of causality linking seemingly distinct psychiatric disorders, and the only viable scientific path to exploring possible individual genomic–environmental–impaired brain development disorders requires researchers to abandon the use of the diagnosis of autism as a basis for research. Why? Because the process of diagnosis excludes meaningful symptoms, calling them associated or comorbid disorders. These excluded symptoms are part of an individual's complete phenotype. Therefore, in excluding these symptoms, the diagnosis creates a group based on truncated symptoms. Because of this the diagnosis hinders research.

For example, if we study a group of 50 individuals each diagnosed with autism spectrum disorder, it is likely we are including many different etiologies. This group of 50 might include: 2 individuals, each with a different known genetic syndrome such as tuberous sclerosis or DiGeorge syndrome; 5 individuals each with a unique gene–environment interaction brain developmental disorder A1 to A5; 11 individuals with varying chromosomal variant disorders B1 to B11; 18 individuals with seven distinct environmental causes C1 to C7; and 14 individuals, each with a slightly different combination of genetic risk factors, D1 to D14, partly shared across individuals diagnosed with schizophrenia, ADHD, and intellectual disorder.

Each one of these hypothetical groups would express a range of non-diagnostic symptoms that would have been excluded by diagnosis. This hypothetical study group of 50 individuals diagnosed with autism would include not only many varied etiologies, but many different neurodevelopmental brain deficits. Nonetheless, because all individuals would have met diagnostic criteria for autism, there would, by diagnostic definition, be overlapping behavioral patterns across the 50 individuals. Therefore, studying the pooled characteristics of the 50 individuals diagnosed with autism could show some statistically significant findings that would appear to characterize autism as a unique disorder. If, however, we recognize that diagnostic features are not effective or consistent markers of etiology or brain dysfunction, we would be able to see that the findings would be an empty artifact of grouping individuals by diagnostic features. Equally important, mean group scores could not identify possible valid individual disorders within the group of 50.

Of course, it is vastly more difficult to take autism apart to find the likely cross-diagnosis and individual brain development disorders. But researchers should consider the possibility that the autism spectrum diagnosis impedes research.

Summary of the Eight Claims Regarding Autism Variation

Claim 1, argued in this chapter, asserted that the wide variation in behavior, brain deficit, and risk factors found for autism reflects meaningful complex phenotypes. Claim 2 asserts that autism heterogeneity extends throughout the families of individuals diagnosed with autism. Research has shown that all forms of family studies show heterogeneity, and family heterogeneity is likely to preclude establishing one broader familial phenotypic form of autism. Claim 3 asserts that autism social impairment variation reflects the varied brain functions supporting typical human social skills. The brain bases of human social skills are varied, including but not limited to the superior temporal sulcus of the temporal lobe, the fusiform gyrus, the amygdala, the prefrontal cortex (PFC), and areas comprising the mirror neuron system, various neurotransmitters, and the neurohormones oxytocin and vasopressin. Consequently, there are many routes to disrupt the development of these systems.

Claim 4 asserts that where autism shares gene variants with other disorders, comorbidity is unlikely. For example, if an individual is diagnosed as comorbid for ASD, ADHD, and intellectual disability, it is unlikely that the individual's brain development was separately disrupted by three disorders, but rather that some causal factor has given rise to all of the behaviors that fit the criteria for ASD, ADHD, and intellectual disability.

Claim 5 asserts that all environmental agents discovered to date link autism to other outcomes. For example, extreme prematurity may result in autism, typical development, or growth problems, and the same is true for other environmental agents.

Claim 6 asserts that the bases for different forms of savant skills remain unexplained, but savant skills are not unique to autism.

Claim 7 asserts that increasing prevalence and increasing heterogeneity suggest that the diagnosis of autism is problematic. Problems are suggested by the astoundingly high prevalence rate of 2.64% reported by Kim et al. (2011) and from evidence for diagnostic substitution, the open nature of diagnostic criteria, increased public sensitivity to social impairment, as well as ever-increasing public and professional discussion of autism.

Claim 8 asserts that autism research currently operates with two opposing theories of autism. One theory proposes that autism is a single multi-etiology disorder (Pelphrey et al., 2011). The other theory proposes that autism is many disorders (Coleman and Gillberg, 2012). Claim 8 also argues that efforts to narrow the autism diagnosis and efforts to find a unifying feature for autism ignore meaningful heterogeneity, and until the many bases for the daunting real complexity of autism are uncovered, autism diagnosis should be replaced by two autism phenotypes: simple and complex.

This book argues that the vast unexplained heterogeneity in autism must be explored seriously rather than accepted, ignored, or discounted. The past 70 years of research and hypotheses resulted in no meaningful subgroups, no unifying theories, but ever-increasing prevalence with increasing heterogeneity. Based on this history, it would seem a safe bet that autism will not be resolved into meaningful subgroups or unified by a single brain deficit or single causal pattern. Consequently, this book proposes that the diagnosis of autism is unlikely to generate homogeneous groups that are needed to uncover mechanisms that could lead to effective medical treatments and informed prevention, and therefore the DSM-5 diagnosis should be abandoned in research.

REFERENCES

Amaral, D. G. (2011). The promise and the pitfalls of autism research: an introductory note for new autism researchers. *Brain Research, 1380*, 3–9.

Andari, E., Duhamel, J. R., Zalla, T., Herbrecht, E., Leboyer, M., & Sirigu, A. (2010). Promoting social behavior with oxytocin in high-functioning autism spectrum disorders. *Proceedings of the National Academy of Sciences of the United States of America, 107*, 4389–4394.

APA. (1980). *Diagnostic and statistical manual of mental disorders* (3rd ed., rev.). Washington, DC: American Psychiatric Association.

APA. (1987). *Diagnostic and statistical manual of mental disorders* (3rd ed.). Washington, DC: American Psychiatric Association.

APA. (1994). *Diagnostic and statistical manual of mental disorders* (4th ed.). Washington, DC: American Psychiatric Association.

APA. (2000). *Diagnostic and statistical manual of mental disorders–text revised* (4th ed., rev.). Washington, DC: American Psychiatric Association.

APA. (2011). *DSM-5 development: A 09 Autism spectrum disorder.* Available at: http://www.dsm5.org/ProposedRevisions/Pages/proposedrevision.aspx?rid=94.

Autism and Developmental Disabilities Monitoring Network Surveillance Year 2006 Principal Investigators, Centers for Disease Control and Prevention. (2009). Prevalence of autism spectrum disorders—Autism and developmental disabilities monitoring network, United States, 2006. *Morbidity and Mortality Weekly Report Surveillance Summaries, 58*(SS10), 1–20.

Autism and Developmental Disabilities Monitoring Network Surveillance Year 2008 Principal Investigators, Centers for Disease Control and Prevention. (2012). Prevalence of autism spectrum disorders—Autism and developmental disabilities monitoring network, United States, 2008. *Morbidity and Mortality Weekly Report Surveillance Summaries, 61*(SS03), 19.

Baker, J. P. (2008). Mercury, vaccines, and autism: One controversy, three histories. *American Journal of Public Health, 98,* 244–253.

Barnea-Goraly, N., Lotspeich, L. J., & Reiss, A. L. (2010). Similar white matter aberrations in children with autism and their unaffected siblings: A diffusion tensor imaging study using tract-based spatial statistics. *Archives of General Psychiatry, 67,* 1052–1060.

Baron-Cohen, S., Leslie, A. M., & Frith, U. (1985). Does the autistic child have a "theory of mind"? *Cognition, 21,* 37–46.

Betancur, C. (2011). Etiological heterogeneity in autism spectrum disorders: More than 100 genetic and genomic disorders and still counting. *Brain Research, 1380,* 42–77.

Bettleheim, B. (1967). *The empty fortress: Infantile autism and the birth of the self.* New York, NY: The Free Press.

Bill, B. R., & Geschwind, D. H. (2009). Genetic advances in autism: Heterogeneity and convergence on shared pathways. *Current Opinion in Genetic Development, 19,* 271–278.

Bishop, D. V. M. (2010). Which neurodevelopmental disorders get researched and why? *PLoS ONE, 5,* e15112.

Bishop, D. V. M. (2011). *An open letter to Baroness Susan Greenfield. August 4.* Available at: http://deevybee.blogspot.com/2011/08/open-letter-to-baroness-susan.html2011.

Boddaert, N., Zilbovicius, M., Philipe, A., Robel, L., Bourgeois, M., Barthélemy, C., et al. (2009). RI findings in 77 children with non-syndromic autistic disorder. *PLoS ONE, 4,* e4415.

Bogen, J., & Woodward, J. (1988). Saving the phenomena. *Philosophical Review, 97,* 303–352.

Booth, R., Wallace, G. L., & Happé, F. (2011). Connectivity and the corpus callosum in autism spectrum conditions: Insights from comparison of autism and callosal agenesis. *Progress in Brain Research, 189,* 303–317.

Boucher, J. (2011). Redefining the concept of autism as a unitary disorder: Multiple causal deficits of a single kind? In D. Fein (Ed.), *The neuropsychology of autism* (pp. 469–482). New York, NY: Oxford University Press.

Buxbaum, J. D., Cai, G., Chaste, P., Nygren, G., Goldsmith, J., Reichert, J., et al. (2007). Mutation screening of the PTEN gene in patients with autism spectrum disorders and macrocephaly. *American Journal of Medical Genetics Part B Neuropsychiatric Genetics, 144B,* 484–491.

Casanova, M. F. (2007). The neuropathology of autism. *Brain Pathology, 17,* 422–433.

Chakrabarti, S., & Fombonne, E. (2005). Pervasive developmental disorders in preschool children: Confirmation of high prevalence. *American Journal of Psychiatry, 162,* 1133–1141.

Charman, T., Jones, C. R., Pickles, A., Simonoff, E., Baird, G., & Happé, F. (2011). Defining the cognitive phenotype of autism. *Brain Research, 1380,* 10–21.

Cheslack-Postava, K., Liu, K., & Bearman, P. B. (2011). Closely spaced pregnancies are associated with increased odds of autism in California sibling births. *Pediatrics, 137,* 246–253.

Cole, M. W., Anticevic, A., Repovs, G., & Barch, D. (2011). Variable global dysconnectivity and individual differences in schizophrenia. *Biological Psychiatry, 70,* 43–50.

Coleman, M., & Gillberg, C. (2012). *The autisms.* New York, NY: Oxford University Press.

Congdon, E., Poldrack, R. A., & Freimer, N. B. (2010). Neurocognitive phenotypes and genetic dissection of disorders of brain and behavior. *Neuron, 68,* 218–230.

Courchesne, E., Campbell, K., & Solso, S. (2011). Brain growth across the life span in autism: age-specific changes in anatomical pathology. *Brain Research, 1380,* 138–145.

Cullen, K. R., Klimes-Dougan, B., Muetzel, R., Mueller, B. A., Camchong, J., Houri, A., et al. (2010). Altered white matter microstructure in adolescents with major depression: A preliminary study. *Journal of the American Academy of Child and Adolescent Psychiatry, 49,* 173–183.

Dachel, A. (2011). *Age of Autism, August 29, 2011.* Available at: http://annedachel.com/2011/08/29/scientific-american-autism-is-a-mental-illness/.

Deer, B. (2011). How the case against the MMR vaccine was fixed. *British Medical Journal, 342,* c5347.

Eyal, G., Hart, B., Onculer, E., Oren, N., & Rossi, N. (2009). *The autism matrix.* London: Polity Press.

Fabricius, T. (2010). The savant hypothesis: Is autism a signal-processing problem? *Medical Hypotheses, 75,* 257–265.

Feinstein, A. (2010). *A history of autism: Conversations with the pioneers.* New York, NY: Wiley Blackwell.

Fett, A. K., Viechtbauer, W., Dominguez, M. D., Penn, D. L., van Os, J., & Krabbendam, L. (2011). The relationship between neurocognition and social cognition with functional outcomes in schizophrenia: A meta-analysis. *Neuroscience and Biobehavioral Reviews, 35,* 573–588.

Foldi, C. J., Eyles, D. W., Flatscher-Bader, T., McGrath, J. J., & Burne, T. H. (2011). New perspectives on rodent models of advanced paternal age: relevance to autism. *Frontiers in Behavioral Neuroscience, 5,* 32.

Folstein, S. (2006). The clinical spectrum of autism. *Clinical Neuroscience Research, 6,* 113–117.

Frances, A. (2010). Opening Pandora's box: The 19 worst suggestions for DSM5. *Psychiatric Times.* February 11.

Gardener, H., Spiegelman, D., & Buka, S. L. (2011). Perinatal and neonatal risk factors for autism: A comprehensive meta-analysis. *Pediatrics, 128,* 344–355.

Goldberg, M., & Goldberg, E. (2011). *The myth of autism: How a misunderstood epidemic is destroying our children.* New York, NY: Skyhorse Publishing.

Goos, L. M. (2008). Imprinting and psychiatric genetics: Beware the diagnostic phenotype. *Behavioral and Brain Sciences, 31,* 271–272.

Grandin, T. (1996). *Thinking in pictures: and other reports from my life with autism.* New York, NY: Vintage.

Green, L., Fein, D., Modahl, C., Feinstein, C. L., Waterhouse, L., & Morris, M. (2001). Oxytocin and autistic disorder: Alterations in peptide forms. *Biological Psychiatry, 50,* 609–613.

Gregory, S. G., Connelly, J. J., Towers, A. J., Johnson, J., Biscocho, D., Markunas, C. A., & Pericak-Vance, M. A. (2009). Genomic and epigenetic evidence for oxytocin receptor deficiency in autism. *BMC Medicine, 7*(62), 1–13.

Gupta, A. R., & State, M. W. (2007). Recent advances in the genetics of autism. *Biological Psychiatry, 61,* 429–437.

Haddon, M. (2003). *The curious incident of the dog in the night-time.* New York, NY: Doubleday.

Hall, S. S., Lightbody, A. A., Hirt, M., Rezvani, A., & Reiss, A. (2010). Autism in fragile X syndrome: A category mistake? *Journal of the American Academy of Child and Adolescent Psychiatry, 49*, 921–933.

Hallmayer, J., Cleveland, S., Torres, A., Phillips, J., Cohen, B., Torigoe, T., & Risch, N. (2011). Genetic heritability and shared environmental factors among twin pairs with autism. *Archives of General Psychiatry, 68*, 1095–1102.

Happé, F., Ronald, A., & Plomin, R. (2006). Time to give up on a single explanation for autism. *Nature Neuroscience, 9*, 1218–1220.

Harony, H., & Wagner, S. (2010). The contribution of oxytocin and vasopressin to mammalian social behavior: Potential role in autism spectrum disorder. *Neurosignals, 18*, 82–97.

Helt, M., Kelley, B., Kinsbourne, M., Pandey, J., Boorstein, H., Herbert, M., et al. (2008). Can children with autism recover? If so, how? *Neuropsychology Review, 18*, 339–366.

Herbert, M., & Anderson, M. (2008). An expanding spectrum of autism models: From fixed developmental defects to reversible functional impairments. In A. Zimmerman (Ed.), *Autism: Current theories and evidence*, Totowa, NJ: Humana.

Herbert, M. R., & Ziegler, D. A. (2005). Volumetric neuroimaging and low-dose-early-life exposures: Loose coupling of pathogenesis-brain-behavior links. *Neurotoxicology, 26*, 565–572.

Holt, R., & Monaco, A. P. (2011). Links between genetics and pathophysiology in the autism spectrum disorders. *EMBO Molecular Medicine, 3*, 438–450.

Howlin, P., Goode, S., Hutton, J., & Rutter, M. (2009). Savant skills in autism: Psychometric approaches and parental reports. *Philosophical Transactions of the Royal Society of London Series B Biological Sciences, 364*, 1359–1367.

Hus, V., Pickles, A., Cook, E. H., Jr., Risi, S., & Lord, C. (2007). Using the autism diagnostic interview–revised to increase phenotypic homogeneity in genetic studies of autism. *Biological Psychiatry, 61*, 438–448.

Hutman, T., Rozga, A., DeLaurentis, A. D., Barnwell, J. M., Sugar, C. A., & Sigman, M. (2010). Response to distress in infants at risk for autism: A prospective longitudinal study. *Journal of Child Psychology and Psychiatry, 51*, 1010–1020.

Ingram, D. G., Takahashi, T. N., & Miles, J. H. (2008). Defining autism subgroups: A taxonometric solution. *Journal of Autism and Developmental Disorders, 38*, 950–960.

Insel, T. (2010). The challenge of translation in social neuroscience: A review of oxytocin, vasopressin, and affiliative behavior. *Neuron, 65*, 768–779.

Jemel, B., Mottron, L., & Dawson, M. (2006). Impaired face processing in autism: Fact or artifact? *Journal of Autism and Development Disorders, 36*, 91–106.

Jones, W., & Klin, A. (2009). Heterogeneity and homogeneity across the autism spectrum: The role of development. *Journal of the American Academy of Child and Adolescent Psychiatry, 48*, 471–473.

Just, M. A., Cherkassky, V. L., Keller, T. A., & Minshew, N. J. (2004). Cortical activation and synchronization during sentence comprehension in high-functioning autism: Evidence of underconnectivity. *Brain, 127*, 1811–1821.

Kamp-Becker, I., Smidt, J., Ghahreman, M., Heinzel-Gutenbrunner, M., Becker, K., & Remschmidt, M. (2010). Categorical and dimensional structure of autism spectrum disorders: The nosologic validity of Asperger syndrome. *Journal of Autism and Developmental Disorders, (40)*, 921–929.

Kanner, L. (1943). Autistic disturbances of affective contact. *The Nervous Child, 2*, 217–250.

Kim, S. H., & Lord, C. (2010). Restricted and repetitive behaviors in toddlers and preschoolers with autism spectrum disorders based on the Autism Diagnostic Observation Schedule (ADOS). *Autism Research, 3*, 162–173.

Kim, Y. S., Leventhal, B. L., Koh, Y.-J., Fombonne, E., Laska, E., Lim, E.-C., et al. (2011). Prevalence of autism spectrum disorders in a total population sample. *American Journal of Psychiatry, 168*, 904–912.

King, M., & Berman, P. (2009). Diagnostic change and the increased prevalence of autism. *International Journal of Epidemiology, 38*, 1224–1234.

Kinney, D. K., Barch, D. H., Chayka, B., Napoleon, S., & Munir, K. M. (2010). Environmental risk factors for autism: Do they help cause de novo genetic mutations that contribute to the disorder? *Medical Hypotheses, 74*, 102–106.

Klin, A., Lin, D. J., Gorrindo, P., Ramsay, G., & Jones, W. (2009). Two-year-olds with autism orient to nonsocial contingencies rather than biological motion. *Nature, 459*, 257–261.

Korade, J., & Mirnics, K. (2011). The autism disconnect. *Nature, 474*, 294–295.

Kuenssberg, R., McKenzie, K., & Jones, J. (2011). The association between the social and communication elements of autism, and repetitive/restrictive behaviours and activities: A review of the literature. *Research in Developmental Disabilities, 32*, 2183–2192.

Lam, K. S. L., Bodfish, J. W., & Piven, J. (2008). Evidence for three subtypes of repetitive behavior in autism that differ in familiality and association with other symptoms. *Journal of Child Psychology and Psychiatry, 49*, 1193–1200.

Leekam, S. R., Prior, M. R., & Uljarevic, M. (2011). Restricted and repetitive behaviors in autism spectrum disorders: A review of research in the last decade. *Psychological Bulletin, 137*, 562–593.

Levinson, B. (Director). (1988). *Rain man*. Los Angeles: United Artists. [Film].

Levy, S. E., Mandel, D. S., & Schultz, R. T. (2009). Autism. *The Lancet, 374*, 1627–1638.

Limperopoulos, C. (2009). Autism spectrum disorders in survivors of extreme prematurity. *Clinics in Perinatology, 36*, 791–805.

Lipton, P. (2005). The Medawar Lecture 2004: The truth about science. *Philosophical Transactions of the Royal Society of London Series B, 360*, 1259–1269.

Liu, X. Q., Paterson, A. D., Szatmari, P., & The Autism Genome Project Consortium (2008). Genome-wide linkage analyses of quantitative and categorical autism subphenotypes. *Biological Psychiatry, 64*, 561–570.

Loos, T. (2011). Lost somewhere in the forest. *High Plains Midwest Agriculture Journal*. Available at: http://www.hpj.com/archives/2011/aug11/aug22/0816LoosTalessr.cfm.

Lord, C. (2011). How common is autism? *Nature, 474*, 166–168.

Maher, B. (2008). Personal genomes: The case of the missing heritability. *Nature, 456*, 18–21.

Mandell, D. S., Lawer, L. J., Branch, K., Brodkin, E. S., Healey, K., Witalec, R., & Gur, R. E. (2011). Prevalence and correlates of autism in a state psychiatric hospital. *Autism*. [Epub August 16, 2011]. doi: 10.1177/1362361311412058.

Mayes, S. D., & Calhoun, S. L. (2011). Impact of IQ, age, SES, gender, and race on autistic symptoms. *Research in Autism Spectrum Disorders, 5*, 749–757.

McPheeters, M. L., Warren, Z., Sathe, N., Bruzek, J. L., Krishnaswami, S., Jerome, R. N., et al. (2011). A systematic review of medical treatments for children with autism spectrum disorders. *Pediatrics, 127*, e1312.

Miles, J. H. (2011). Autism spectrum disorders: A genetics review. *Genetics in Medicine, 13*, 278–294.

Modahl, C., Green, L., Fein, D., Morris, M., Waterhouse, L., Feinstein, C., et al. (1998). Plasma oxytocin levels in autistic children. *Biological Psychiatry, 43*, 270–277.

Monteggia, L. M., & Kavalali, E. T. (2009). Rett syndrome and the impact of MeCP2 associated transcriptional mechanisms on neurotransmission. *Biological Psychiatry, 65*, 204–210.

Mosconi, M. W., Kay, M., D'Cruz, A.-M., Guter, S., Kapur, K., Macmillan, C., & Sweeney, J. A. (2010). Neurobehavioral abnormalities in first-degree relatives of individuals with autism. *Archives of General Psychiatry, 67*, 830–840.

Murphy, P., Brady, N., Fitzgerald, M., & Troje, N. F. (2009). No evidence for impaired perception of biological motion in adults with autism spectrum disorders. *Neuropsychologia, 4*, 225–235.

Neuhaus, E., Beauchaine, T. P., & Bernier, R. (2010). Neurobiological correlates of social functioning in autism. *Clinical Psychology Review, 30*, 733–748.

Offit, P. A. (2008). *Autism's false prophets: Bad science, risky medicine, and the search for a cure.* New York, NY: Columbia University Press.

Orsmond, G. I., & Selzer, M. (2007). Siblings of individuals with autism spectrum disorders across the life course. *Mental Retardation and Developmental Disabilities Research Reviews, 13,* 313–320.

Owen, M. J., O'Donovan, M. C., Thapar, A., & Craddock, N. (2011). Neurodevelopmental hypothesis of schizophrenia. *British Journal of Psychiatry, 198,* 173–175.

Ozonoff, S., Young, G. S., Carter, A., Messinger, D., Yirmiya, N., Zwaigenbaum, L., et al. (2011). Recurrence risk for autism spectrum disorders: A baby siblings research consortium study. *Pediatrics, 128,* e488–e495. Available at: http://pediatrics.aappublications.org/content/early/2011/08/11/peds.2010-2825.

Pardo, C. A., & Eberhart, C. G. (2007). The neurobiology of autism. *Brain Pathology, 17,* 434–447.

Pelphrey, K. A., Schultz, S., & Hudac, C. M. (2011). Research review: Constraining heterogeneity: the social brain and its development in autism spectrum disorder. *Journal of Child Psychology and Psychiatry, 52,* 631–644.

Ploeger, A., Raijmakers, M. E. J., van der Maas, H. L. J., & Galis, F. (2010). The association between autism and errors in early embryogenesis: What is the causal mechanism? *Biological Psychiatry, 67,* 602–607.

Rapoport, J., Chavez, A., Greenstein, D., Addington, A., & Gogtay, N. (2009). Autism spectrum disorders and childhood-onset schizophrenia: Clinical and biological contributions to a relation revisited. *Journal of the American Academy of Child and Adolescent Psychiatry, 48,* 10–18.

Reiss, A. (2009). Childhood developmental disorders: an academic and clinical convergence point for psychiatry, neurology, psychology and pediatrics. *Journal of Child Psychology and Psychiatry, 50,* 87–98.

Richards, T. L., & Berninger, V. W. (2008). Abnormal fMRI connectivity in children with dyslexia during a phoneme task: Before but not after treatment. *Journal of Neurolinguistics, 21,* 294–304.

Rimland, B. (1964). *Infantile autism; The syndrome and its implications for a neural theory of behavior.* New York, NY: Appleton-Century-Crofts.

Roelfsema, M. T., Hoekstra, R. A., Allison, C., Wheelwright, S., Brayne, C., Matthews, F. E., et al. (2012). Are autism spectrum conditions more prevalent in an information-technology region? A school-based study of three regions in the Netherlands. *Journal of Autism and Developmental Disorders, 42,* 734–739.

Rogers, S. J., & Vismara, L. A. (2008). Evidence-based comprehensive treatments for early autism. *Journal of Clinical Child and Adolescent Psychology, 37,* 8–38.

Rommelse, N. N. J., Geurts, H. M., Franke, B., Buitelaar, J. K., & Hartman, C. A. (2011). A review on cognitive and brain endophenotypes that may be common in autism spectrum disorder and attention-deficit/hyperactivity disorder and facilitate the search for pleiotropic genes. *Neuroscience and Biobehavioral Reviews, 35,* 1363–1396.

Ronald, A., & Hoekstra, R. A. (2011). Autism spectrum disorders and autistic traits: A decade of new twin studies. *American Journal of Medical Genetics Part B, 156,* 255–274.

Rosenberg, R. E., Daniels, A. M., Law, J. K., Law, P. A., & Kaufmann, W. E. (2009). Trends in autism spectrum disorder diagnoses: 1994–2007. *Journal of Autism and Developmental Disorders, 39,* 1099–1111.

Rudy, L. J. (2011). *The autism spectrum as a "social construct".* Available at: http://autism.about.com/b/2011/07/04/the-autism-spectrum-as-a-social-construct.htm.

Rutherford, M. D., & Troje, N. F. (2012). IQ predicts biological motion perception in autism spectrum disorders. *Journal of Autism and Developmental Disorders, 42,* 557–565.

Rutter, M. L. (2011). Progress in understanding autism: 2007–2010. *Journal of Autism and Developmental Disorders, 41,* 395–404.

Sanders, S. J., Ercan-Sencicek, A. G., Hus, V., Luo, R., Murtha, M. T., Moreno-De-Luca, D., & State, M. W. (2011). Multiple recurrent de novo CNVs, including duplications of the

7q11.23 Williams syndrome region, are strongly associated with autism. *Neuron, 70,* 863–885.

Saygin, A. P., Cook, J., & Blakemore, S. J. (2010). Unaffected perceptual thresholds for biological and non-biological form-from-motion perception in autism spectrum conditions. *PLoS ONE, 5,* e13491.

Schaaf, C. P., & Zoghbi, H. Y. (2011). Solving the autism puzzle a few pieces at a time. *Neuron, 70,* 806–808.

Schuman, C. M., Bloss, C. S., Barnes, C. C., Wideman, G. M., Carper, R. A., Akshoomoff, N., et al. (2010). Longitudinal magnetic resonance imaging study of cortical development through early childhood in autism. *Journal of Neuroscience, 30,* 4419–4427.

Scott, R. (2011). "Autism's like a snowflake"—doctors study symptoms, possible causes of autism with hopes of learning more. August 28. Retrieved from *Gloucester County Times.* http://www.nj.com/gloucester-county/index.ssf/2011/08/autisms_like_a_sno wflake_-_doc.html. August 28, 2011.

Shandley, K., & Austin, D. W. (2011). Ancestry of pink disease (infantile acrodynia) identified as a risk factor for autism spectrum disorders. *Journal of Toxicology and Environmental Health A, 74,* 1185–1194.

Shinawi, M., Sahoo, T., Maranda, B., Skinner, S. A., Skinner, C., Chinault, C., et al. (2011). 11p14.1 Microdeletions associated with ADHD, autism, developmental delay, and obesity. *American Journal of Medical Genetics Part A, 15,* 1272–1280.

Soulières, I., Mottron, L., Giguère, G., & Larochelle, S. (2011). Category induction in autism: Slower, perhaps different, but certainly possible. *Quarterly Journal of Experimental Psychology, 64,* 311–327.

South, M., Schultz, R. T., & Ozonoff, S. (2011). Social cognition in autism. In D. Fein (Ed.), *The neuropsychology of autism* (pp. 225–242). New York, NY: Oxford University Press.

Stanford, P. K. (2001). Refusing the devil's bargain: What kind of underdetermination should we take seriously? *Philosophy of Science, 68,* 3. Supplement: Proceedings of the 2000 Biennial Meeting of the Philosophy of Science Association. Part I: Contributed Papers, pp. S1–S12.

Stefanatos, G. A., & Baron, I. S. (2011). The ontogenesis of language impairment in autism: A neuropsychological perspective. *Neuropsychological Review, 21,* 252–270.

Stevens, M. C., Fein, D., Dunn, M., Allen, D., Waterhouse, L., Feinstein, C., et al. (2000). Subgroups of children with autism by cluster analysis: A longitudinal examination. *Journal of the American Academy of Child and Adolescent Psychiatry, 39,* 346–352.

Stigler, K. A., McDonald, B. C., Anand, A., Saykin, A. J., & McDougle, C. J. (2011). Structural and functional magnetic resonance imaging of autism spectrum disorders. *Brain Research, 1380,* 146–161.

Stigler, K. A., Sweeten, T. L., Posey, D. J., & McDougle, C. J. (2009). Autism and immune factors: A comprehensive review. *Research in Autism Spectrum Disorders, 3,* 840–860.

Stratton, K., Ford, A., Rusch, E., & Clayton, E. W. (Eds.), (2011). *Committee to Review Adverse Effects of Vaccines; Institute of Medicine. Adverse effects of vaccines: Evidence and causality.* Washington, DC: The National Academies Press. Available at: http://www.nap.edu/cata log.php?record_id=131642011.

Sullivan, M. W., Laverick, D. H., & Lewis, M. (1995). Brief report: Fostering environmental control in a young child with Rett syndrome: A case study. *Journal of Autism and Developmental Disorders, 25,* 215–221.

Swain, F. (2011). Susan Greenfield: Living online is changing our brains. *New Scientist.* August 3.

Szatmari, P. (2011). New recommendations on autism spectrum disorder: Shifting the focus from subtypes to dimensions carries potential costs and benefits. *British Medical Journal, 342,* d2456.

Tager-Flusberg, H. (2010). The origins of social impairments in autism spectrum disorder: Studies of infants at risk. *Neural Networks, 23,* 1072–1076.

Tammet, D. (2007). *Born on a blue day: Inside the extraordinary mind of an autistic savant.* New York, NY: Free Press.

Tammet, D. (2009). *Embracing the wide sky, a tour across the horizons of the mind*. New York, NY: Free Press.

Treffert, D. A. (2010). *Islands of genius: the bountiful mind of the autistic, acquired, and sudden savant*. Philadelphia, PA: Jessica Kingsley Publishing.

van Buijsen, M., Hendriks, A., Ketelaars, M., & Verhoeven, L. (2011). Assessment of theory of mind in children with communication disorders: Role of presentation mode. *Research in Developmental Disabilities, 32*, 1038–1045.

Voineagu, P., Wang, X., Johnston, P., Lowe, J., Tian, Y., Horvath, S., et al. (2011). Transcriptomic analysis of autistic brain reveals convergent molecular pathology. *Nature, 474*, 380–386.

Volkmar, F., Chawarska, K., & Klin, A. (2005). Autism in infancy and early childhood. *Annual Review of Psychology, 56*, 315–336.

Volkmar, F. R., Klin, A., & Cohen, D. J. (1997). Diagnosis and classification of autism and related conditions: consensus and issues. In D. J. Cohen, & F. R. Volkmar (Eds.), *Handbook of autism and pervasive developmental disorders* (2nd ed., pp. 5–40). New York, NY: John Wiley and Sons.

Wakefield, A. J., Murch, S. H., Anthony, A., Linnell, J., Casson, D. M., Malik, M., et al. (1998). Ileal-lymphoid-nodular hyperplasia, non-specific colitis, and pervasive developmental disorder in children. *The Lancet, 351*, 637–641.

Waldman, M., Nicholson, S., & Adilov, N. (2006, revised May 2007). Does television cause autism? Johnson School Research Paper Series No. 01-07, Cornell University.

Warren, Z., McPheeters, M. L., Sathe, N., Foss-Feig, J. H., Glasser, A., & Veenstra-Vander-Weele, J. (2011). A systematic review of early intensive intervention for autism spectrum disorders. *Pediatrics, 127*, e1303–e1311.

Waterhouse, L. (2008). Autism overflows: Increasing prevalence and proliferating theories. *Neuropsychology Review, 18*, 273–286.

Waterhouse, L. (2009). Autism is a portmanteau syndrome. *Neuropsychology Review, 19*, 275–276.

Waterhouse, L. (2011). Autism endophenotypes are not unified by gene variants or chromosome number variants. In D. Fein (Ed.), *The neuropsychology of autism* (pp. 483–498). New York, NY: Oxford University Press.

Waterhouse, L., Fein, D., & Modahl, C. (1996). Neurofunctional mechanisms in autism. *Psychological Review, 103*, 457–489.

Wazana, A., Bresnahan, M., & Kline, J. (2007). The autism epidemic: Fact or artifact? *Journal of the American Academy of Child and Adolescent Psychiatry, 46*, 721–730.

Williams, C. A., Dagli, A., & Battaglia, A. (2008). Genetic disorders associated with macrocephaly. *American Journal of Medical Genetics Part A, 146A*, 2023–2037.

Wiliams, D. (1998). *Nobody nowhere: The remarkable autobiography of an autistic girl*. Philadelphia, PA: Jessica Kingsley Publishing.

Williams, E. L., & Casanova, M. F. (2010). Autism and dyslexia: A spectrum of cognitive styles defined by minicolumnar morphometry. *Medical Hypotheses, 74*, 59–62.

Williams, J. G., Higgins, J. P. T., & Brayne, C. E. G. (2006). Systematic review of prevalence studies of autism spectrum disorders. *Archives of Disease in Childhood, 91*, 8–15.

Witwer, A. N., & Lecavalier, L. (2008). Examining the validity of autism spectrum disorder subtypes. *Journal of Autism and Development Disorders, 38*, 1611–1624.

Yrigollen, C. M., Han, S. S., Kochetkova, A., Babitz, T., Volkmar, F. R., Leckman, J. F., et al. (2008). Genes controlling affiliative behavior as candidate genes for autism. *Biological Psychiatry, 63*, 911–916.

Zhao, X., Leotta, A., Kustanovich, V., Lajonchere, C., Geschwind, D. H., Law, K., et al. (2007). A unified genetic theory for sporadic and inherited autism. *Proceedings of the National Academy of Sciences of the United States of America, 104*, 12831–12836.

CHAPTER 2

Autism Symptom Heterogeneity Exists in Family Members

Contents

Rethinking Autism
http://dx.doi.org/10.1016/B978-0-12-415961-7.00002-2

49

Most family members of individuals with autism do not have social, intellectual, or motor problems. However, some family members do have atypical social skills, language problems, and other autism-related disorders, and sometimes more than one child in a family is diagnosed with autism. Even within a single family, there can be great variation in autism symptoms. As noted by Bernier, Gerdts, Munson, Dawson, and Estes (2011), in one family where two children are diagnosed with autism, one child "may be nonverbal and have repetitive motor mannerisms" but the second child with autism "may speak fluently and have interests of unusual intensity, but no repetitive motor movements" (p. 1).

FOUR PAIRS OF SIBLINGS WITH VARYING AUTISM SYMPTOMS

When two siblings in one family are diagnosed with autism, those two siblings can express distinctly different patterns of autism and associated non-autism symptoms. Following are discussions of four pairs of siblings. In the first pair, the brother showed symptoms of schizophrenia and autism, but his sister was diagnosed with autism and not schizophrenia. In the second pair, two brothers with the fragile X premutation, the older brother had significant intellectual disability and seizures, but the younger brother did not. In the third pair, one brother showed a significant autism regression beginning at age 2 years, but his half-brother did not. The last pair, identical twin brothers with tuberous sclerosis, showed great difference in the severity of their autism symptoms.

Different Symptoms in a Brother and Sister with Autism

In 1976, Beatrix Verhees described a brother and sister in Switzerland. The brother, Markus, was born after a normal pregnancy and delivery, but as an infant he made no movements in preparation for being picked up out of the crib. He avoided eye contact, and the sound of raindrops made him cry. He insisted on things being the same in his environment, he had stereotyped motor behaviors, and he became attached to odd play objects. He did develop speech, but was not interested in social communication. Through his early twenties, his only interest was reading train schedules. Markus developed delusions of persecution and was diagnosed with schizophrenia for which he was treated with insulin.

His sister Lucia was born when he was 11 years old. Like Markus, and her four other unaffected siblings, Lucia arrived without any complications during her delivery. However, Lucia was an unusually quiet, non-reactive baby. According to Verhees (1976) most of the time Lucia lay motionlessly in the crib and showed no reaction to those attending to her. She never adapted her body to her mother while being carried; she remained stiff and rigid whenever she was held. When she sat up, she sat for hours in the same position. She liked to play with marbles. She never learned to talk, but her parents believed that she understood words. When hungry she either screamed or stood silently in front of the refrigerator. Like her brother, she had an overwhelming need for sameness in the environment. Unlike her brother, she engaged in self-stimulating and self-destructive behaviors, including body rocking, whirling, head rolling, head banging, hand flapping, and scratching and poking of her own eyes and ears. She often expressed severe temper tantrums. She developed seizures, and was unable to live independently.

Verhees (1976) argued that both Markus and Lucia met the diagnostic criteria for autism because both brother and sister showed "extreme autistic aloneness combined with the inability to relate themselves in the ordinary way to people and situations as well as an anxiously obsessive desire for the maintenance of a constant, unchanging environment" (p. 56). She reported that although Lucia never spoke and Markus did speak, Markus had autism language symptoms. He reversed nouns, he expressed tic-like echo behavior called echolalia wherein he repeated the words of others, and he repeated his own words, palilalia.

Verhees (1976) argued, "When more than one child of a family is afflicted with autism, this raises the question whether there might be perhaps a genetic basis" (p. 57). She noted that Markus had delusions that led to his diagnosis of schizophrenia, but she maintained that, nonetheless, his behaviors met the diagnostic criteria for autism. She concluded that the autism of Markus and Lucia suggested "a wider concept of genetically determined types of autistic disturbance which … can manifest itself in several forms" (Verhees, 1976, p. 59).

Different Symptoms in Two Brothers with Autism and the Fragile X Premutation

Autism researchers Conchaiya, Schneider, and Hagerman (2009) studied a family that included two brothers with autism. Brother 1 was born after a normal pregnancy and delivery. He had typical early motor development: he sat alone at 6 months, crawled at 8 months, and walked at 10 months. However, his speech was severely delayed. He did not speak until he had language training at age 4 years. Beginning at age 5 years he had staring spells, and electroencephalography (EEG) revealed he was experiencing abnormal multiple spike brain wave discharges. He was treated with valproic acid. He was also given risperidone for mood instability, irritability, and tantrums. Despite the medications, he expressed a lot of anxiety, perseverative behaviors, and tantrums. He had moderate intellectual disability.

Unlike his older brother, Brother 2 developed along a more typical trajectory following most developmental milestones in all except social skills. However, Brother 2 did develop overanxious disorder and he engaged in obsessive-compulsive rituals. He was not social, did not make eye contact with others, and was diagnosed with autism and attention deficit/hyperactivity disorder (ADHD).

Brothers 1 and 2, and their mother, her two sisters, her grandfather, her great uncle, and her nephew were found to have the fragile X premutation. Fragile X syndrome (FXS) is the most common single-gene cause of inherited intellectual disability and autism. Two to six percent of individuals with autism have been found to have the full mutation, FXS. Fragile X syndrome and fragile X premutation are two forms of a group of related fragile X-associated disorders (FXD). The premutation occurs in approximately 1 in 130 to 250 women, and 1 in 250 to 810 men; the full mutation is less common at 1 per 2500 to 1 per 4000 men and women (Hagerman, Au, & Hagerman, 2011).

Fragile X disorders are caused by DNA errors of too many repetitions of cytosine-guanine-guanine (CGG) triplets in the fragile X mental retardation 1 (FMR1) gene on the X chromosome. Our DNA contains approximately 22,000 genes organized onto 23 pairs of chromosomes. The sex chromosome pair is XX in females and XY in males. DNA is made of four nucleotide bases: A, adenine, which pairs with T, thymine; and C, cytosine, which pairs with G, guanine. Our genetic code is stored in a sequence of three bases called base triplets. The triplets act as a template directing the transcription of messenger RNA triplet codons to make proteins.

Individuals who have more than 200 CGG triplet repeats in the FMR1 gene are considered to have the full mutation; these repeats result in a dysfunctional lack of fragile X mental retardation protein (FMRP) in the brain. Individuals who have 55–200 CGG repeats in the FMR1 gene are considered to have a premutation; this generates toxic amounts of FMR1 messenger RNA in the brain. The premutation can also cause a late onset of tremors called X-associated tremor ataxia syndrome.

The FMRP protein regulates the translation of genes crucial for changes in neuron connectivity needed for learning and memory. Consequently, the absence of FMRP protein or the presence of toxic amounts of *FMR1* messenger RNA is the central cause for intellectual disability and autism symptoms in affected individuals. The majority of males and a third of females with the full fragile X mutation will have a significant intellectual disability, and males are likely to have autism symptoms. However, most individuals with the fragile X premutation have normal intellectual abilities, and do not show autism symptoms.

In the family studied by Conchaiya and colleagues (2009), Brothers 1 and 2 and other affected family members had only about 60 CGG repeats, the very lowest level of the fragile X premutation. Therefore, it is surprising that both brothers were diagnosed with autism, and that Brother 1 was diagnosed with intellectual disability. Because the brothers had the same low number of CGG repeats, Conchaiya et al. (2009) found the brothers' autism symptom differences to be unusual. They also suggested that Brother 1's IQ of 46 was a more significant deficit than expected and was in sharp contrast to his brother's higher level of cognitive function. The researchers argued that Brother 1's seizures must have added to the negative effects of the toxic amounts of *FMR1* messenger RNA. They also hypothesized that Brother 1 might have an additional unknown gene mutation contributing to his severe social impairment and seizures.

Different Symptoms in Two Half-Brothers with Autism

Zwaigenbaum et al. (2000) described two half-brothers, JP and MP, sons of the same mother and different fathers. Both brothers met criteria for a diagnosis of autism; however, MP was diagnosed with childhood disintegrative disorder, while JP was diagnosed with autism, obsessive-compulsive disorder, and Tourette syndrome. Gilles de la Tourette syndrome, called Tourette syndrome or TS, is a neurological disorder theorized to result from genetic mutations that cause errors in neuron migration in the basal ganglia during brain development (Bloch, State, & Pittinger, 2011). The basal ganglia are a group of brain nuclei that regulate motor activity. The basal ganglia are also theorized to regulate learning of rewarded behaviors by collecting motivation, emotion, cognition, and sensorimotor information and sending selective inhibitory signals to the thalamus, brainstem structures, cortex, and hippocampus and amygdala. Tourette syndrome occurs in approximately 1 in 180 individuals. Bloch et al. (2011) noted that mutations in the *CNTNAP2* and *NLGN4X* genes have been found for individuals with Tourette syndrome, autism, and intellectual disability.

JP was born after an uncomplicated full-term pregnancy. As an infant, JP did not smile or make eye contact, and did not cuddle or tolerate being held. When he was a toddler, he showed little interest in social interaction, and his preferred activities in childhood were repetitive spinning and lining up objects. Zwaigenbaum et al. (2000) reported that JP rarely sought comfort when he was distressed, and he never offered comfort to others. He never greeted his parents, and never showed anxiety when separated from them. JP's speech developed slowly, and he used no gesture to communicate his wants or needs. At age 4, JP did not interact with others, and he showed many stereotypic movements and behaviors. When JP did speak, he reversed pronouns and used many repeated phrases. However, JP went to school at age 4, and in his first years in school, his language skills improved and he showed some interest in playing with other children. When he was 11 years old, JP felt compelled to use profanity and had a compulsion to call the police emergency phone number. He recognized his compulsions as wrong, and was upset by them. JP met criteria for Tourette syndrome, defined by multiple motor and vocal tics lasting for more than 1 year. The symptoms of TS vary from person to person and range from very mild to severe. JP had both simple and complex tics. Tics are sudden, painless, involuntary sounds or movements. Simple motor tics use only a few muscles: examples are eye blinking, facial grimacing, head jerks or shoulder shrugs that last less than one second. Simple vocal tics range from throat clearing or coughing to barking-like sounds, or hissing. Complex motor tics last longer and involve more complex movements including biting, banging, whirling or twisting around. Complex vocal tics include syllables, words, phrases, and shouted abrupt statements such as "Shut up!" or obscenities, called coprolalia.

JP's brother, MP, was born 11 years later. He was the product of a healthy pregnancy and uneventful delivery. MP was sociable and affectionate, and greeted people cheerfully. Unfortunately, after MP turned 2 he showed a gradual loss of skills, and loss of interest in being with any family members. MP's eye contact and affectionate behavior stopped. He stopped speaking, stopped pointing, and even stopped responding to his name. Over the course of 4 years of training, MP regained some speech and daily living skills. By the age of 6 years, he was able to use several single words, and he learned a few gestures. He started engaging in ritualistic behaviors such as stripping the beds of all their sheets. He was tested for Landau–Kleffner syndrome and fragile X syndrome, but had neither.

Zwaigenbaum and colleagues (2000) argued that the co-occurrence of autism and childhood disintegrative disorder (CDD) in half-brothers

JP and MP suggested the brothers shared one genetic mechanism for their two very different forms of autism. They further argued that individuals with CDD should be included in genetic studies of autism. Zwaigenbaum and colleagues (2000) concluded, "Until we know better how genetic heterogeneity is expressed phenotypically, we cannot assume that including only those … with autism is the best approach" (p. 125).

Different Symptoms in Identical Twin Brothers with Autism and Tuberous Sclerosis

Even identical twins who share a known genetic deficit have shown different symptoms. Humphrey, Higgins, Yates, and Bolton (2004) reported on identical male twins A and B. The twins were delivered by elective cesarean section at 37 weeks, and each boy weighed 5 pounds. Twin A was diagnosed with tuberous sclerosis complex (TSC) at 3 months when he began to have seizures. Although both Twins A and B were found to have a single-base deletion in exon 29 of the tuberous sclerosis *TS2* gene, neither their mother nor father had this genetic deletion. Tuberous sclerosis complex (TSC) results from a mutation in either the *TS1* or the *TS2* gene. The disorder causes tuber-like tumors to form in the brain, eyes, heart, kidney, skin, and lungs. TSC affects one person in 6000. The word complex was added to distinguish tuberous sclerosis complex (TSC) from Tourette syndrome (TS). Some with TSC have intellectual disability and autism. Others with TSC may be unaffected.

Although both twins had a similar number of tubers, Twin A met the diagnostic criteria for autism, but Twin B only had some symptoms of autism. Surprisingly, however, Twin B had cortical tubers in brain areas disrupted in some individuals with autism: the right temporal lobe, the cerebellum, and the face recognition region—the fusiform gyrus. However, Twin A did have a tuber in the right superior temporal gyrus, which may have affected his detection of the gaze of other people. In addition, Twin A had seizures at an earlier age than Twin B did. Humphrey and colleagues (2004) proposed that because Twin B's seizures had a later onset and were better controlled, Twin B experienced less interference with his social and cognitive development.

Symptom Differences for the Four Sibling Pairs

The brother and sister, Markus and Lucia, and the two half-brothers, JP and MP, all had *idiopathic* autism—autism with no known cause. These two sibling pairs illustrate how great the variation in autism symptoms can be in one family. Markus had typical intelligence, but his sister Lucia had severe intellectual disability. Markus had excellent language skill, but Lucia had no language. Markus was obsessed with reading train schedules, his sister never learned to read. Markus developed paranoid delusions and was diagnosed with schizophrenia, Lucia's lack of language and intellectual disability would not have allowed her to express paranoid ideas if she had them. JP exhibited no loss of skills but his brother, MP, showed a marked disintegration of language and social skills. JP had severe tics, causing a diagnosis of Tourette's, but MP had no tics. JP was withdrawn as an infant, but MP was a happy and social baby and toddler.

Brothers 1 and 2 both had the fragile X premutation, and identical twins A and B both had tuberous sclerosis. Because all four boys had a genetic syndrome, their autism is called *syndromic* autism to distinguish it from idiopathic autism (of no known cause). Despite the sibling pairs' shared genetic mutations, they expressed differences in intelligence, and differences in autism symptoms. Brother 1 had intellectual disability, but Brother 2 did not. Brother 2 was diagnosed with ADHD, Brother 1 was not. Twin A had early seizures; Twin B did not. Twin A met all criteria for autism; Twin B did not. Despite having identical genes, identical Twin A and Twin B illustrated the more general finding that some individuals with tuberous sclerosis have intellectual disability and autism, but others are less affected or not affected at all.

Together the case studies of Markus and Lucia, Brother 1 and Brother 2, JP and MP, and identical Twins A and B clearly demonstrate strikingly different autism and associated non-autism symptoms and life courses. While each of the eight siblings had a brain developmental disorder, none of the four sibling pairs shared a matching set of symptoms.

IMPORTANT RESEARCH QUESTIONS RAISED BY VARIATION IN THE FOUR SIBLING PAIRS

These four sibling pairs illustrate three crucial questions for research. First, when different diagnoses occur in siblings of the same family, such as schizophrenia (Markus) and autism (Lucia), or Tourette syndrome (JP) and childhood disintegrative disorder (MP), should the two diagnoses be investigated together as having a possible genetic link? Despite increasing evidence for genetic links between schizophrenia and autism (Guilmatre et al., 2009; Owen, O'Donovan, Thapar, & Craddock, 2011), no studies to date have included both siblings of individuals with schizophrenia and siblings of individuals with autism.

Second, when siblings have the same neurogenetic disorder, such as tuberous sclerosis in Twin A and Twin B, and fragile X premutation in Brothers 1 and 2, if one (Twin A) meets criteria for autism and the other (Twin B) does not, should the sibling who met criteria for autism be studied in samples of individuals with autism or not? Should the neurogenetic disorder diagnosis of tuberous sclerosis or fragile X premutation be considered the primary diagnosis or be viewed as a disorder comorbid with autism? Researchers Hall, Lightbody, Hirt, Rezvani, and Reiss (2010) reported that individuals with fragile X syndrome showed high levels of social avoidance, repetitive behaviors, and language impairment, but the researchers concluded that these symptoms were not identical to symptoms shown by individuals with autism of no known origin. Although Hall et al. (2010) argued that generalized brain dysfunction might cause both intellectual disability and autism symptoms in individuals with fragile X syndrome, the researchers nonetheless concluded that diagnosing autism in fragile X syndrome was likely to be a mistake.

Third, when two siblings in a family both meet the diagnosis for autism, and one of the siblings (Lucia, Brother 1) has intellectual disability, but the other sibling (Markus, Brother 2) does not, should the presence of intellectual disability be a basis for excluding individuals from study? Surprisingly, although autism occurs with intellectual disability in 55–70% of cases, little research has explored the relationship between intellectual disability and autism.

Researchers Matson and Shoemaker (2009) asserted that the study of autism in individuals with intellectual disability was "a relatively new phenomenon" (p. 1111), and they reported that prevalence of the co-occurrence of intellectual disability and autism varies widely from study to study. The researchers also pointed out that the prevalence of intellectual disability in autism was not considered in the formal diagnosis of autism.

These three research questions are considered at greater length in Chapters 4 and 8. Chapter 4 outlines the many genetic links between autism and other disorders, and Chapter 8 argues that known genetic and neurological disorders, and not autism, should be an individual's primary diagnosis, because medical treatment and prevention can ultimately be established for known causes, but not for the behavioral diagnosis of autism.

INFANT SIBLING, TWIN, AND FAMILY STUDIES OF AUTISM

Case studies like the four pairs of siblings discussed above provide details of individual differences within families, but patterns of heterogeneity within families are also revealed by group comparison in family studies (Mosconi et al., 2010). Many different forms of family studies have been conducted. Studies have explored the development of infant siblings some of whom later met criteria for autism (Hutman, Chela, Gillespie-Lynch, & Sigman, 2012; Ozonoff et al., 2011). Other studies have considered the behaviors of older diagnosed and typically developing siblings (Orsmond & Selzer, 2007; Sumiyoshi, Kawakubob, Sugab, Sumiyoshie, & Kasaib, 2011), and still other studies have tested co-twins who did and did not meet criteria for autism (Hallmayer et al., 2011; Ronald & Hoekstra, 2011). Parents of children with autism and their extended family members have also been studied (Bernier et al., 2011; Dawson et al., 2002; Losh & Piven, 2007; Nydén, Hagberg, Goussé, & Råstam, 2011).

Goals differed for different forms of family studies. Studies of baby siblings of individuals with autism looked for onset age of early behavior and brain predictors of autism and estimated the recurrence risk of autism in siblings (Hutman et al., 2012; Ozonoff et al., 2011; Tager-Flusberg, 2010). Twin studies of autism estimated the heritability of autism and explored the shared and non-shared autism symptoms of fraternal and identical twin pairs (Hallmayer et al., 2011; Ronald & Hoekstra, 2011). Family studies explored possible genetic risk factors within and across families (Gai et al., 2011; Levy et al., 2011; Mosconi et al., 2010; Sanders et al., 2011).

Studies of siblings, parents, and extended family members explored atypical social skills, rigid and repetitive interests, and other autism-related disorders (Bernier et al., 2011; Dawson et al., 2002; Losh & Piven, 2007; Nydén et al., 2011). The field searched for a unified set of autism-like behaviors in family members, calling the set of behaviors the broader autism phenotype (BAP). The BAP hypothesis argued that milder forms of atypical social skills, rigid and repetitive interests, and other autism-related traits together comprised a family autism-like phenotype. As will be discussed in detail later in this chapter, many different versions of the BAP were proposed. For example, Losh, Childress, Lam, & Piven (2008) analyzed family symptom data and argued for four features of the broader autism phenotype: social problems, language problems, rigidity, and anxiety. Bernier et al. (2011) had a different vision of the BAP and argued that it included impaired social motivation, conversation skills, expressiveness, and restricted interests.

Symptom Studies have Explored Group Differences, not Individual Variation

Variation in individual symptoms is the key means by which heterogeneity can be discovered in family studies. Unfortunately, family studies of autism have not reported descriptive data on individual variation. Consequently, outside of sibling case studies such as the four sibling pairs discussed above, it is difficult to determine the extent of heterogeneity within families. However, variation in autism symptoms between families can be explored in a number of ways without individual variation data. First, conflicting findings across studies provide insight into heterogeneity. For example, if two studies use similar measures, and one study finds significant differences between infant siblings and typical infants, but the other study does not, population heterogeneity can be inferred. Second, within a single study, when less than a majority of individuals express a specific developmental problem, this indicates that some individuals do and some do not have a developmental problem.

The following sections consider selected research findings for heterogeneity in family members. The first section examines the varying recurrence risk rates, varying onset times of atypical behaviors, and varying patterns of atypical brain growth and brain activity found for infant siblings of children with autism. Also included in this section is a discussion of the problem of inference from small samples. The second section outlines the varying diagnoses found for co-twins of individuals with autism. The final section reviews the heterogeneity of features in the broader autism phenotype in family members of individuals with autism. The final section also compares the continuum and endophenotype theories of the BAP.

Variation in Risk Rates, Onset, Atypical Behaviors, and Atypical Brain Development in Infant Siblings of Children with Autism

Variation in findings for studies of infant siblings of children with autism has caused problems for the interpretation of results. One problem is that all infant sibling studies exploring how likely a family is to have a second child with autism generate a single risk rate. However, that single rate is really the average of many different individual family risk rates. Another problem is that infant siblings who go on to develop autism have shown many different times of onset of autism symptoms, and have shown variation in the types of onset symptoms. The wide variation in onset times and variation in symptoms found at onset make prediction based on infant sibling data very difficult. Linked to the problem of onset and symptom variation is a more general problem of drawing conclusions from small samples. Still another problem is that atypical brain growth and atypical brain activity found for infant siblings of children with autism have only been examined by means of group comparisons of infant siblings with typical infants. Examination of individual variation would permit inferences with greater predictive power.

Any Single Recurrence Risk Rate for Autism Determined for a Group of Infant Siblings of Children with Autism Represents an Average of Many Family Risk Rates

For families with a child with autism, one of the most troubling questions is whether to have another child. From the existing data, we know that most siblings of children with autism are never diagnosed with autism. Nonetheless, infant siblings of children with autism are at risk for developing autism. When a second child in a family is diagnosed with autism, it is referred to as a recurrence. Studies have reported varying rates of recurrence. Rozga et al. (2011) reported that 11% of infant siblings of children with autism were later diagnosed with autism, and Zwaigenbaum et al. (2005) reported a recurrence risk of 29%. In the largest study to date, members of the Baby Siblings Research Consortium of autism researchers analyzed pooled information on 664 infant siblings and reported a recurrence risk of 18.7%: 132 infant siblings were diagnosed with autism spectrum disorder (Ozonoff et al., 2011). This study also reported that 32% of infants who had at least two older siblings with autism developed autism themselves. Infant sibling boys had a 26% risk rate, but infant sibling girls had a significantly lower risk of only 9%.

True recurrence rates, though, require knowing the cause of each case of autism. Ozonoff and colleagues (2011) excluded any family whose child with autism had a known neurologic or genetic condition such as fragile X syndrome. Thus, they did not know the cause for autism in any of the 664 children whose siblings were studied. It is very likely that the 664 cases were caused by a wide range of different genetic and environmental factors.

As a result, the risk rate for recurrence of autism ascertained in the infant sibling studies is not a single rate that can be applied across all families with autism. Each group risk rate, whether it is 11% (Rozga et al., 2011), or 19% (Ozonoff et al., 2011), or 29% (Zwaigenbaum et al., 2005), is the average of many different individual risk rates. Consequently, no individual family can assume that any group risk rate applies to their possibility of having another child with autism.

As discussed in Chapter 1, autism is highly heritable, but this heritability springs from hundreds of known and likely as many or more yet unknown causes. Autism has been found with more than 100 gene variants (Betancur, 2011) such as tuberous sclerosis, and more than 200 chromosomal deletions and duplications (Sanders et al., 2011), as well as with many other varied gene and chromosome alterations. Autism has also been found with numerous varied environmental risk factors, such as extreme prematurity, maternal infection, and parental age.

In sum, for each family the risk of having another child with autism depends on the cause of autism in that family. One example would be a child with autism whose birth was extremely premature, and the child's autism symptoms arose amidst a variety of problems suffered by the infant in the course of development as a premature newborn. If this child's mother is healthy, and premature delivery could be prevented for her future children, the recurrence risk for that mother's future children might close to zero. Another very different recurrence risk would apply if one of the parents of a child with autism carried the fragile X mutation or fragile X premutation. For future children in this family, autism recurrence risk would be between 20% and 60% for boys, and half to a third of that for girls. It is also likely that there would be an autism recurrence risk for future children of any siblings in the family carrying the mutation or premutation.

Public dissemination of research findings on autism recurrence has been swift and widespread. When Ozonoff and colleagues published their infant siblings recurrence risk findings, Alan Zarembo, a writer for the *Los Angeles Times*, declared, "Researchers say there is a 19% chance that a child will have autism if he or she has an older sibling with autism" (2011). However, because the 19% is an average across hundreds of different family recurrence rates, the real recurrence must range from nearly 0% recurrence to 99%.

Zarembo also reported that, because the infant sibling sample was so large, autism experts said this risk rate of 19% "should be used to counsel families" (2011). On the same day, CBS News online (2011) reported that Dr. Ozonoff said, "We were all a bit surprised and taken aback about how high it is," and also said, "parents of autistic children often ask her, 'How likely am I to have another child' with autism? She said her study provides a more up-to-date answer" (2011).

Given the likelihood that recurrence risks range widely from family to family, should a group risk rate be used to counsel parents of a child with autism? Probably not. In fact, it is surprising that reports of recurrence rates in infant siblings do not discuss the fact that the rate they have ascertained is an average of many different true recurrence risk rates, and thus cannot accurately be used to guide any given family's plan to have another child. As Constantino, Zhang, Frazier, Abbacchi, and Law (2010) noted, in the "diversity of genetic mechanisms that give rise to the autistic syndrome … each is associated with its own pattern of intergenerational transmission" (p. 1350). Equally important, in families where the cause for autism is environmental, such as autism associated with extreme prematurity or autism associated with maternal infection, here, too, recurrence rates will vary from family to family depending on the specific mechanism of the environmental cause.

Onset Times Vary Widely in Infant Siblings of Children with Autism, Making Prediction Difficult

Not only do recurrence risk rates vary from family to family, but so do ages of onset at which autism symptoms first appear in infant siblings later diagnosed with autism. The earliest onset symptoms of any disease or disorder are called a prodrome. A prodrome is one or more early symptoms that signal the beginning of a disease or disorder before the full range of diagnostic symptoms emerge. Researchers Yirmiya and Charman (2010) argued that an infant or toddler prodrome for autism "needs to be as specific and universal as possible for it to be of clinical utility" (p. 433). They asserted that specificity means that the prodrome must be unique to autism, and universality means that the autism prodrome must have sufficient coverage to apply to most people who develop autism. However, they claimed it was impossible for autism to have a specific, universal prodrome because autism "risk factors and prodromes may be as diverse as the many etiologies and developmental trajectories underlying ASDs" (Yirmiya & Charman, 2010, p. 433).

The variation in onset times and heterogeneity of early atypical symptoms in infant siblings of children with autism (Ozonoff et al., 2011; Tager-Flusberg, 2010) supported Yirmiya and Charman's pessimistic view (2010) that finding a universal and specific prodrome for autism would be impossible. Heterogeneity of onset time was reported by Feldman and colleagues (2011) who studied 108 infants at risk for autism because they had older siblings diagnosed with autism. The researchers reported that 9 of the 108 infants were diagnosed with autism by professionals at 36 months. However, parent reports on a questionnaire indicated that some parents noticed autism behaviors in their children when the infants were only 3 months old. Using information from parent reports, Feldman et al. (2011) reported that parents of 2 of the 9 infant siblings who later were diagnosed with autism saw autism symptoms in their child when the child was only 3 months old. Other parents identified 2 more infant siblings with autism by age 6 months, and by 9 months of age 3 more infant siblings were identified by parents as having autism. Two more infant siblings were diagnosed by their parents at 18 months of age.

In contrast to the parents interviewed by Feldman et al. (2011), few parents of infant siblings later diagnosed with autism who were interviewed by researchers Hess and Landa (2011) expressed any concerns before their children were 3 years old. In addition, researchers Moricke, Swinkels, Beuker, and Buitelaar (2010) found that none of the autism symptoms that parents reported for their children at 14–15 months of age were consistent with autism symptoms measured in the same children at ages 4 and 5 years. Hess and Landa (2011) theorized, "Parents may have more difficulty identifying social impairment related to ASD at early ages. Perhaps social difficulties are less apparent to parents of toddlers because exposure to peers is as yet limited, thus limiting opportunities for comparison to typical development" (p. 6). Moricke and colleagues questioned whether early measures of autism symptoms were sufficiently sensitive to capture subclinical variants of symptoms.

Ozonoff et al. (2010) studied 25 infant siblings who later were ultimately diagnosed with autism. The researchers saw three patterns of onset in these infant siblings. In one onset pattern, children with autism had atypical low social communication throughout their development. In a second onset pattern, children who were initially highly social suddenly decreased their social communication. In a third pattern, infant siblings later diagnosed with autism behaved like typical children early on but then failed to make developmental progress in social communication.

However, the researchers reported that the three proposed autism onset patterns did not fully capture individual variation among the infant siblings. They proposed that there should be more and varied onset patterns, including a pattern of onset of autism in which children moved through a series of developmental plateaus, and a pattern of onset in which children expressed a mixture of patterns early and then later regressed.

Ozonoff and colleagues (2010) alternatively suggested that autism symptom emergence might be dimensional along a continuum based on the amount of regression and the age when regression began. The researchers suggested that one end of the continuum would be children who showed such an early loss of social interest that the process of regression was so difficult to see that symptoms would seem to have always existed. At the other end of this hypothetical continuum of onset, autism symptoms of impaired social interest and social communication would appear so late that the regression would seem obvious to parents and professionals.

Similarly, Rogers (2009) reviewed infant sibling studies and concluded that onset patterns "emerging from these studies do not fit either the early onset or the regressive patterns … [but] instead involve slower or faster mounting of symptoms, more or less deceleration of general development, earlier or later onset of social difficulties—differences that seem more continuous than dichotomous" (p. 136).

Tager-Flusberg (2010) reviewed studies of infant siblings and claimed the evidence pointed to just two distinct onset times. She argued, "Taken together, the studies of infants at risk demonstrate that subtle behavioral and neurobiological endophenotypes may be identified in the first year of life before the onset of risk signs at around 12 months that are associated with a later diagnosis of ASD" (2010, p. 1075). Essentially Tager-Flusberg defined the abnormalities found for infant siblings in the first year of life as onset signs of the broader autism phenotype, but defined abnormalities found for infant siblings at 1 year of age or later as onset signs of autism itself. Tager-Flusberg cautioned, however, that "many of these studies have not followed the infants through to outcome so what is reported here as patterns associated with the broader autism phenotype at a group level may in fact be risk signs for ASD" (2010, p. 1075).

Tager-Flusberg's claims (2010) that symptoms appearing before 12 months only predicted the broader autism phenotype, but symptoms appearing after 12 months predicted full-blown autism, were countered by data from other researchers. Feldman and colleagues (2011) reported 7 of 9 infant siblings who were later diagnosed with autism were identified as having autism at or before 9 months of age. Elsabbagh et al. (2012) also reported that some infant siblings of children with autism when tested at 6–10 months showed different brain wave patterns in response to the face gaze direction. The atypical gaze response was associated with the diagnosis of autism at 36 months.

Infant sibling studies have shown that the range of onset of any autism symptoms varied from as early as 3 months to as late as 36 months. While the nearly 3-year period from 3 to 36 months may seem like a narrow time window, in fact this is not narrow in developmental terms. Many different time-limited aspects of typical development occur during this period. Children babble, then speak words and phrases and begin syntax development during this 33-month window. Typical children sit, crawl, stand, walk, and develop many other fine and gross motor skills. Children develop skills of self-control, and learn to play with others, and take turns in conversation.

Researchers were not able to determine whether the variation in onset symptoms and time of onset fit into multiple categories or fell along a single dimension (Ozonoff et al., 2010; Tager-Flusberg, 2010). Ozonoff and colleagues (2010) lamented, "Resolution of opposing viewpoints regarding onset (e.g., multiple categories v. a dimensional view that emphasizes timing) is urgently needed for etiologic studies, which have been hindered already by the tremendous heterogeneity of the autism phenotype" (pp. 264–265).

The unresolved variation has meant that researchers do not know which symptoms of infant siblings of children with autism can predict whether an infant sibling will or will not develop autism or other developmental problems. This is due, in large part, to the wide variation in symptoms that appear during the 33-month window of varying onset for infants at risk for autism. The next section describes the range of early atypical social behaviors, language problems, and atypical motor behaviors.

Heterogeneity of Atypical Behaviors in Infant Siblings of Children with Autism

Researchers who have studied infant siblings of children with autism have commented on the heterogeneity in behavior. Iverson and Wozniak (2007) concluded that "more striking than the group differences ... is the fact that within the Infant Sibling group, on a child-by-child basis, the particular patterns of clinically significant delay are hugely variable" (p. 167). Tager-Flusberg (2010) concluded that infant siblings studies revealed, "no single atypical behavior has been found that is shared by all 12 month olds who later go on to meet criteria for ASD .... In this way studies of infants at risk reflect the complex nature of the disorder" (p. 1074).

The heterogeneity of atypical behaviors in infant siblings is extensive (Iverson & Wozniak, 2007; Rogers, 2009; Tager-Flusberg, 2010). Table 2.1 lists a limited set of findings for infant siblings aged 6 months to 24 months. Table 2.1 demonstrates cross-study evidence for variation: at each age, some studies have found abnormalities in development for infant siblings, and other studies have not. Rogers (2009) noted that variation among infant siblings has been reported for social gaze, facial expression of emotion, response to speech, imitation, fine and gross motor development, repetitive behaviors, sensory abnormalities, visual attention, as well as for other skills. Hutman et al. (2010) reported that infant siblings subsequently

Table 2.1 Symptoms Shown by Infant Siblings of Children with Autism Between 6 Months and 24 Months of Age Identified in Selected Studies

Age	Behaviors Reported for Infant Siblings	Research Group
6 months	*More infant siblings than controls:* expressed more frequent social and communication behaviors	Ozonoff et al., 2010
	More infant siblings than controls: expressed little social smiling	Cassel et al., 2007
8–9 months	*More infant siblings than controls:* expressed no interest in faces; expressed no shift of attention to a person; did not respond to name	Feldman et al., 2011
	No difference between infant siblings and controls in learning selective inhibition of attention	Holmboe et al., 2010
	No difference between infant siblings and controls in initiating joint attention	Cassel et al., 2007
12 months	*More infant siblings than controls:* expressed no interest in faces; expressed no shift of attention to a person; did not respond to name; did not imitate sounds or words	Feldman et al., 2011
	More infant siblings than controls: looked longer and expressed more affect to social targets as an examiner feigned distress	Hutman et al., 2010
	More infant siblings than controls: expressed little or no social smiling; expressed little eye gaze to faces	Ozonoff et al., 2011
	No difference between infant siblings and controls in initiating joint attention	Cassel et al., 2007
15 months	*No difference between infant siblings and controls* in attachment	Haltigan et al., 2011
	No difference between infant siblings and controls in social communication gesture with speech	Yoder, Stone, Walden, & Malesa, 2009
18 months	*More infant siblings than controls:* did not imitate sounds or words; did not coordinate point and gaze	Feldman et al., 2011
	More infant siblings than controls: were delayed in producing their first word	Iverson & Wozniak, 2007

(Continued)

Table 2.1 Symptoms Shown by Infant Siblings of Children with Autism Between 6 Months and 24 Months of Age Identified in Selected Studies—*cont'd*

Age	Behaviors Reported for Infant Siblings	Research Group
	More infant siblings than controls: expressed little or no social smiling; expressed little eye gaze to faces; expressed no directed communication	Ozonoff et al., 2011
	No difference between infant siblings and controls in initiating joint attention	Cassel et al., 2007
	No differences between infant siblings and controls in walking	Iverson & Wozniak, 2007
	No differences between infant siblings and controls in attention or affect while looking at social targets as an examiner feigned distress	Hutman et al., 2010
24 months	*More infant siblings than controls:* did not imitate sounds or words; did not coordinate point and gaze; did not point in response to questions; did not imitate actions; did not speak	Feldman et al., 2011
	No differences between infant siblings and controls on standard tests of mental, motor, and language development	Yirmiya, Gamliel, Shaked, & Sigman, 2007
	No differences between infant siblings and controls in attention or affect while looking at social targets as an examiner feigned distress	Hutman et al., 2010

diagnosed with autism paid less attention and showed less emotion to another person's distress.

Researchers Chow, Haltigan, and Messinger (2010) found only very slight differences between 6-month-old infant siblings of children diagnosed with autism and 6-month-old typical infants in a parent social interaction study. Chow and colleagues (2010) used the "FF-SF-RE" protocol. This protocol starts with parent and child seated face-to-face (FF) during which the parent is actively interacting with the infant. After this period of the protocol, the parent stops interacting with the infant and suddenly presents a neutral still face (SF). A final component of the protocol is a reunion episode (RE) during which the parent resumes interacting with their infant. Typical infants experience distress during the still face portion of the protocol and show positive emotions when their parent begins to interact with them again. Chow et al. (2010) found that infant siblings of children with autism differed from typical infants in only one measure of this protocol: 6-month-old infant siblings of children with autism showed less emotional reactivity during their parents' still face than did typical infants.

Conversely, Ozonoff and colleagues (2010) found that 25 infant siblings who were diagnosed with autism at 36 months showed *more* social expression at 6 months than low-risk infants who experienced typical development.

The apparently contradictory findings of impaired social expression in 6-month-old infant siblings (Chow et al., 2010) versus enhanced social expression in 6-month-old infant siblings (Ozonoff et al., 2010) were not truly contradictory because the studies used different measures. However, the sharp difference in results between the two studies of infant siblings of children with autism points to a general problem in small sample research.

The Problem of Inference from Small Sample Studies

Ioannidis (2005) argued, "The smaller the studies conducted in a scientific field, the less likely the research findings are to be true" (p. 697). He concluded, "for most study designs and settings, it is more likely for a research claim to be false than true. Moreover, for many current scientific fields, claimed research findings may often be simply accurate measures of the prevailing bias" (p. 696). Ioannidis and Panagiotou (2011) discovered "inflated results among … highly cited investigations. Many of these studies were relatively small …. Discoveries made in small studies are prone to overestimate or underestimate the actual association. Interest in publishing major discoveries leads to selective reporting from chasing significance" (p. 2206).

The contradictory findings reported on Table 2.1 are likely to be contradictory because of small sample size effects. Researchers Chow et al. (2010) studied only 20 infant siblings of children with autism, and Ozonoff et al. (2010) studied only 25 infant siblings; moreover, they both reported wide variation in onset times and wide variation in atypical behaviors. The effect sizes of their findings are small, and therefore little can be concluded from the wide variation in their data, other than that there is wide variation in onset and in atypical behaviors in infant siblings.

Tatsioni, Bonitsis, and Ioannidis (2007) noted that when studies have reported conflicting results and wide variation in findings, most researchers have presented counterarguments to fend off the possibility that their own findings are problematic. For example, autism researchers Ozonoff and colleagues (2010) presented two counterarguments in support of their widely varied times of onset data across the 25 infant siblings studied. First, the researchers argued that because one of their study measures showed improving social skills in the infant siblings, the measure was inadequate, and should not be used in future studies of infant siblings. They stated that, because this measure failed to show declining skills in infant siblings as would be expected, "the Mullen and other standardized developmental tests will not be good prospective measures for tracking regression, as they appear to be less sensitive to the kinds of behaviors that decline as autism emerges" (Ozonoff et al., 2010, p. 264).

In the second counterargument, Ozonoff and colleagues (2010) defended the variation in their findings of many varied onset patterns by claiming that researchers "need to expand the number of categories used to describe onset ... perhaps there are four rather than two categories of onset (p. 264). In a continuation of this counterargument, the researchers also proposed, "symptom emergence may better be considered dimensionally, as a continuum" wherein "at one end of the continuum lie children who display loss of social interest so early that the regression is difficult to see and symptoms appear to have always been present" (Ozonoff et al., 2010, p. 264).

Chow and colleagues (2010) presented one counterargument to defend the variation in their findings. They noted that although other studies had reported significant differences in emotional expression for infant siblings of children with autism, they found no significant differences in core measures of emotional expression for infant siblings and typical infants. They discovered several minor variables that did show a group difference, and they stated, "It is perhaps even more encouraging that we were able to extract such subtle differences after information due to mean and variability differences had already been removed" (p. 112).

No defense of hard-to-explain findings would be necessary if the researchers had presented individual variation data for the 20 and 25 infant siblings rather than attempting to find significant group differences. The raw data points were and are true for the individual infant siblings studied, and more exploratory data analysis is needed in autism research. Unpacking the heterogeneity found for infant siblings by examining individual variation is a crucial step for future productive translational research.

Atypical Brain Findings in Infant Siblings of Children with Autism

Research has demonstrated great heterogeneity in atypical brain findings for infant siblings of children with autism. Brain growth and brain activity patterns have been shown to be altered in some but not other infant siblings of children with autism. Despite the repeated findings for heterogeneity, studies have focused on group comparisons, rather than exploring the heterogeneity of individual variation.

Brain Growth Heterogeneity in Infant Siblings of Children with Autism

Autism researchers Elder, Dawson, Toth, Fein, and Munson (2008) studied 77 younger siblings of children with autism. The researchers found that autism symptoms were associated with an increased acceleration of head circumference growth from 6 to 12 months, followed by a deceleration of head circumference growth from 12 to 24 months. Average sibling head circumference at 12 months in infant siblings was significantly higher than Center for Disease Controls norms for head circumference in typical children at that age.

Elder and colleagues (2008) argued that their results supported the hypothesis that atypical head growth patterns might be an index of risk for autism in young children. They found that changes in head circumference in infant siblings were correlated with level of social and communication impairment. Both sharper increases in head circumference, and swifter leveling off for head circumference growth were significantly linked to greater impairment in social skills.

Elder et al. (2008), however, did not report individual variation data for the group. The researchers did report sex differences in the sample of infant siblings at risk for autism. Male infant siblings showed the speed-up slowdown pattern of head circumference growth but few infant sibling girls showed any atypical head circumference growth, even though both boys and girls in this sibling study showed the same level of autism symptoms.

Brain Activity Heterogeneity in Infant Siblings of Children with Autism

Luyster, Wagner, Vogel-Farley, Tager-Flusberg, and Nelson (2011) found no differences for two brain activity components—the N290 and the P300—and found the P400 was reduced only over the left hemisphere when data from 32 infant siblings of children with autism and 24 typical children were compared. The N290, P300, and P400 are event-related potentials (ERPs). An ERP is a shift in electrical potential in a person's brain activity as the person reacts to external events. ERPs are measured with electroencephalography (EEG). Each ERP or measured shift in electrical potential occurs at a different time in milliseconds after a specific event, and each may be a positive or negative shift in potential. Each distinct shift, called a component, reflects brain activation associated with one or more mental operations. ERPs are used to identify processes involved in complex cognitive, motor, or perceptual skills.

The N290 is a negative shift that appears 290 milliseconds after an individual experiences an event. The P300 is a positive shift in potential that appears 300 milliseconds after an individual experiences an event. Both components are sensitive to human faces. The P400 in infants is also a reflection of face responsive activity in the brain's fusiform gyrus, or face area. Thus, it is unexpected that Luyster and colleagues (2011) found no differences for the N290 or the P300, and one slight P400 difference for infant siblings of children with autism compared with typical infants.

By contrast, Elsabbagh and colleagues (2009) found significant differences between infant siblings and typical children in the timing of the P400 component. Holmboe et al. (2010) also found a delayed P400 component in infant siblings with autism. The researchers compared brain evoked potentials for 19 infant siblings of children with autism, and 17 control infants with no family history of autism measured while the infants viewed photographs of women displaying direct or averted gaze. The infant siblings of children with autism showed a delayed onset of the occipital P400 event-related potentials component in response to direct gaze. They also showed a delayed onset of induced gamma activity over the right temporal lobe.

The various contradictory findings from the various evoked potential studies of infant siblings are likely to result from the lack of power in small samples. For example, Luyster et al. (2011) studied 32 infant siblings and Holmboe et al. (2010) studied only 19 infant siblings. Because these studies included such small samples of infant siblings, it is difficult to argue that any group findings for evoked potentials are likely to be consistent from study to study.

Bosl, Tierney, Tager-Flusberg, and Nelson (2011) studied the EEG patterns of infant siblings of children with autism. The sample included two infant siblings aged 6 months, five aged 9 months, four aged 12 months, five aged 18 months, and five aged 24 months. The researchers assessed the complexity of EEG signals using an algorithm of the entropy of multiple brain waves. Costa, Goldberger, and Peng (2005) developed the algorithm based on the view that biological processes, such as brain waves, operate across many different brain sites at many different time points. Costa et al. (2005) argued that diseases and disorders cause an increasing loss (entropy) of information in the transmission of signals in many different biological processes. Bosl et al. (2011) measured multiscale entropy in EEG signals registered at three different spots on the heads of infant siblings at five different ages. This yielded 15 comparisons of infant siblings with typical infants. Of the 15 comparisons, 5 were significant and 10 were not. The multiscale entropy differences were significant for the left frontal region at all ages except 9 months (4 comparisons), and for overall multiscale entropy at 18 months (1 comparison).

Given the tiny sample sizes at each age measured, and given only 5 of 15 comparisons showed a significant difference between infant siblings and typical children, it was surprising that the researchers (Bosl et al., 2011) concluded that infant siblings had meaningfully different EEG complexity patterns from 6 to 24 months of age. It was also surprising that the researchers proposed that this entropy measure could determine autism risk at age 9 months. The researchers claimed using this measure might "enable the high-risk population to be subclassified more accurately ... [and] provide a clinically useful psychiatric biomarker using complexity analysis of EEG data" (Bosl et al., 2011, p. 14).

Psychologists Griffin and Westbury (2011) expressed concern regarding the claims made by Bosl et al. (2011). Griffin and Westbury (2011) argued that using EEG entropy to define an endophenotype of high risk for autism might have little research value. They pointed out that twin studies of autism have shown many non-overlapping genetic causes, including new mutations. They also noted that more autism cases have been shown to reflect environmental risk factors. Consequently, Griffin and Westbury (2011) concluded that an EEG-entropy endophenotype for infants at risk of autism would be likely to include so many different genetic and environmental risk factors that the endophenotype would include too much variation to be interpretable.

Summary

The problems of heterogeneity and the weak inference power of small sample studies are endemic to infant sibling research. It is very difficult to find and recruit pregnant mothers who already have a child with autism. Moreover, the heterogeneity in autism insures that infant siblings will show heterogeneous development and heterogeneous atypical behaviors. Exploratory data analysis of individual variation in these small samples of infant siblings of children with autism would remove the problem of lack of power, because exploratory data analysis includes no quest for statistical significance. More importantly, exploratory data analysis of individual variation would be the first step toward making sense of the existing real heterogeneity in infant sibling development.

AUTISM SYMPTOMS IN IDENTICAL AND FRATERNAL TWINS

Autism researchers Folstein and Rutter (1977) conducted the first twin study of autism. They reported that 36% of identical, i.e., monozygotic (MZ) twin pairs, who have identical genes, shared a diagnosis of autism. However, they found that none of the fraternal, i.e., dizygotic (DZ) twin pairs, who share approximately half their genes, shared a diagnosis of autism with their co-twin. Twenty-one years later, Taniai, Nishiyama, Miyachi, Imaeda, and Sumi (2008) reported finding that 88% of identical (MZ) twin pairs shared a diagnosis of autism, and 31% of fraternal (DZ) twin pairs shared a diagnosis of autism. Similar findings were reported by Rosenberg et al. (2009), whose study included 277 twin pairs.

Lichtenstein, Carlström, Råstam, Gillberg, and Anckarsäter (2010) interviewed parents of a population sample of 9- and 12-year-old Swedish twin pairs born between 1992 and 2000 (N = 10,895) regarding autism spectrum disorders. The researchers reported that 0.9% of the twins met criteria for autism, 1.8% for ADHD, 1.6% for developmental motor disorders, and 3.1% for tic disorder. In 47% of identical (MZ) twin pairs both twins were diagnosed with autism, and in 14% of fraternal (DZ) twin pairs both twins met criteria for an autism diagnosis.

Lichtenstein et al. (2010) found autism linked to ADHD. They reported that, although 80% of the variation in causes for autism was likely due to genetic effects, a surprisingly high percent, 75% of the 80%, or 60% of the possible genetic basis for autism in their twin sample was shared with the genetic cause for ADHD. In addition, the researchers found a 71% genetic correlation of autism and developmental coordination disorder, a 60% correlation with tic disorder, and a 71% genetic correlation of autism with learning disabilities in their twin sample.

These high correlations of autism with ADHD, tic disorders, motor coordination problems, and learning disorders in the twin pairs are more evidence of the extensive heterogeneity in autism. This heterogeneity, combined with the high correlation of genetic variation across the disorders, argues that studies organized by the recruitment of samples of individuals diagnosed with autism are unlikely to yield the focal brain mechanism data required for moving toward treatment and prevention research.

Hallmayer et al. (2011) studied 192 twin pairs diagnosed with autism, 54 identical (MZ) pairs and 138 fraternal (DZ) pairs. The researchers' analysis revealed that 38% of the causal variance in autism in the twin pairs was due to genetic factors, but, unexpectedly, 58% of the causal variance in autism was due to shared environmental variance. The researchers argued that their findings provided evidence that the influence of genetic factors in autism had been overestimated. They proposed that the environment of the womb may be an important non-genetic causal factor in autism, whether from maternal age or maternal infection, or the stress on resources made by multiple fetuses. The researchers concluded, "Because of the reported high heritability of autism, a major focus of research in autism has been on finding the underlying genetic causes, with less emphasis on potential environmental triggers or causes. The finding of significant influence of the shared environment, experiences that are common to both twin individuals, may be important for future research paradigms" (Hallmayer et al., 2011, p. 1101).

The lower genetic heritability and high shared environmental variance found by Hallmayer and colleagues (2011) suggested that research attention should focus on environmental causes. All previous twin studies had found very high heritability for autism. Previous twin study heritability estimates of 93% for Rutter and Folstein (1977) or 80% for Lichtenstein and colleagues (2011) were more than double the heritability estimate of 38% determined by Hallmayer and colleagues (2011). Those previous higher heritabilities had suggested that environmental factors were a negligible cause of autism.

Ronald and Hoekstra (2011) reviewed twin studies of autism and noted that twin studies revealed high levels of heterogeneity in autism symptoms as well as heterogeneity in intellectual functioning. They claimed that twin studies provided: (1) new evidence autism behaviors were dimensional; (2) new evidence autism etiology was heterogeneous; and (3) new explanations for the co-occurrence of autism with intellectual disability, language disorders, and other disorders such as anxiety, ADHD, depression, and schizophrenia. Despite their presentation of evidence for heterogeneity, Ronald and Hoekstra (2011) claimed that more research was needed to explore the links between autism and cognitive abilities in order to integrate psychological and biological explanations of autism.

Contrary to the claim of Ronald and Hoekstra (2011), the heterogeneity found in twin studies of autism does not indicate that the integration of psychological and biological explanations for autism is possible. In fact, the co-occurrence of autism with other disorders reported by Lichtenstein and colleagues (2011) in their twin study, and the low genetic heritability and high shared environmental variance found by Hallmayer and colleagues (2011) in their twin study argue against integration of biological and psychological factors. Twin studies have revealed that biological explanations for autism will include too many varied brain dysfunctions, caused by too many varied genetic and environmental causes, to be neatly integrated with the many varied hypotheses of psychological deficits in autism. Moreover, autism twin study findings and results from other types of autism research have indicated that any attempt to integrate biological and psychological explanations will face two serious problems for inference: *symptom convergence* and *symptom divergence*.

Symptom Convergence and Divergence

Symptom Convergence

Symptom convergence occurs when many different brain deficits conjointly cause one symptom. Symptom convergence also occurs when many different genes conjointly yield one symptom or one trait. When only a few gene variants operate conjointly to contribute to the expression of a symptom it is called oligogenic inheritance. When many genes jointly contribute to a symptom, it is called polygenic inheritance. Autism researcher Voineagu (2011) hypothesized that autism was likely to have a polygenic basis of more than 100 different SNPs for each case of autism. SNP is an acronym for single nucleotide polymorphism. An SNP is a variation (polymorphism) in a single nucleotide of the four nucleotides that make up our DNA: A, adenine; T, thymine; G, guanine; and C, cytosine. SNPs occurring in gene DNA sequences create gene variants. Davies et al. (2011) reported that human intelligence is highly polygenic. They explored the nearly 550,000 SNPs of 3500 unrelated adults for whom the researchers had data on cognitive traits. The researchers estimated that half of all genetic variation in human intelligence is accounted for by variation in common SNPs along with some unknown causal genetic variants.

Given that 55–70% of individuals with autism are diagnosed with intellectual disability, if human intelligence is as highly polygenic as reported by Davies and colleagues (2011), then it is possible that there are hundreds of SNP mutations that might contribute to intellectual disability in autism.

Schaaf et al. (2011) proposed that autism can either result from a mutation in a single gene, such the tuberous sclerosis gene mutation found for both Twin A and B, or result from the oligogenic inheritance of milder mutations in several known or unknown genes. Genetic variants in autism are discussed in detail in Chapter 4.

Symptom Divergence

Symptom divergence occurs when a single brain deficit or a single genetic mutation causes multiple symptoms. When a single gene variant produces a wide range of different symptoms or traits it is called pleiotropy. An example of pleiotropy in autism is tuberous sclerosis. Identical Twins A and B each had a single deletion in one component of the tuberous sclerosis *TS2* gene; the single deletion in a single gene caused the production of non-identical tuberous tumors in their brains and bodies, and led to a wide range of symptoms.

Symptom convergence and divergence magnify the problem of drawing inferences from data enormously. Together, the symptoms resulting from diverging and converging gene expression and the symptoms resulting from divergent and convergent effects of environmental factors contribute to the vast heterogeneity of symptoms found in autism and in the broader autism phenotype.

HETEROGENEITY IN THE BROADER PHENOTYPE OF AUTISM

The broader autism phenotype has been defined as milder autism-like symptoms found in family members of individuals with autism. An individual living organism is described by its *phenotype*, and the DNA of that living thing is its *genotype*. A phenotype represents a person's physical and behavioral characteristics; a genotype includes the DNA from the ovum and the sperm. Autism researchers Folstein and Rutter (1977) examined evidence for a broader phenotype of autism in the 21 twin pairs in their study. Folstein and Rutter (1977) reported that a greater number of co-twins among their identical twin pairs shared milder variants of autism symptoms than shared the complete set of diagnostic symptoms. Losh et al. (2009) noted that many studies in the past 25 years found a wide range of evidence for elements of a broader autism phenotype. The researchers also noted that symptoms of the broader autism phenotype "closely parallel the core symptom domains in autism (i.e., impaired social functioning, language and communication deficits, and restricted/repetitive interests, respectively), yet are subtle in expression and not usually associated with any functional impairment" (Losh et al., 2009, p. 519).

Many different sets of behaviors have been defined as the broader autism phenotype. Dawson et al. (2002) proposed that the broader phenotype consisted of six traits: (1) impairment in face processing; (2) impairment in sensitivity to social reward and social affiliation; (3) impairment in motor imitation; (4) impairment in declarative memory feature binding; (5) impairment in planning and organizing skills; and (6) impairment in language ability. As noted earlier in this chapter, Losh et al. (2008) analyzed family symptom data and argued for four features of the broader autism phenotype: social problems, language problems, rigidity, and anxiety.

Scheeren and Stauder (2008) reviewed symptoms proposed as part of the broader autism phenotype. They asserted that the broader autism phenotype "cannot be defined as a fixed pattern of specific mild autistic traits .... [because] As yet, it is not entirely clear which traits make up the BAP" (Scheeren & Stauder, 2008, p. 276). However, they listed groups of symptoms discovered in research as possible components of the broader autism phenotype. Atypical social behaviors reported for family members of individuals with autism included: a lower quantity and quality of friendships; poorer conversational skills; a preference for non-social activities; lack of tact in interactions; emotional unexpressiveness; a hypersensitivity to criticism; and anxiety. Other autism-like symptoms found in family members included rigidity, restricted, and stereotyped behaviors; and diagnosed obsessive-compulsive disorder. Scheeren and Stauder (2008) outlined four cognitive problems found in family members that might also be part of the broader phenotype: impairment in executive function, weak central coherence (where central coherence is defined as the ability to put information together for general meaning unfettered by details of experience); and impaired spatial memory.

Bernier et al. (2011) also proposed that the broader autism phenotype consisted of four features: impaired social motivation, impaired conversational skills, impaired emotional expressiveness, and the presence of restricted interests. Mosconi et al. (2010) studied unaffected parents and siblings of individuals diagnosed with autism and found eight different atypical features that might contribute to a broader autism phenotype. They reported evidence for atypical brain circuits in family members' cerebellums, cortices, and striatal regions. The researchers also reported finding abnormal eye movements in family members, as well as deficits in learning sequential motor tasks, and cognitive control. Family members were also found to report more communication abnormalities and more obsessive-compulsive behaviors than study participants who served as controls.

TWO ALTERNATE HYPOTHESES ABOUT THE STRUCTURE OF THE BROADER AUTISM PHENOTYPE

There have been two general competing hypotheses about the broader autism phenotype. One hypothesis claims that autism symptoms represent the extreme end of a continuum that shades from typical behaviors into atypical behaviors (Constantino & Todd, 2003). In this view, autism symptoms are at the extreme end of the continuum, and the broader autism phenotype includes milder atypical behaviors shading toward typical behavior on the continuum. The alternate view sees autism symptoms as distinct from typical behaviors, and sees the broader autism phenotype as including milder variants of the distinct autism behaviors or including the expression of one of the symptoms of autism. This second view has been enriched by the concept of endophenotypes. Endophenotypes are measurable variables that narrow the heterogeneity of a complex disorder. Sabb et al. (2009) stated that genetic research in psychiatry had failed to make headway because psychiatric diagnoses such as schizophrenia and bipolar disorder were categories too complex for gene discovery. They stated that genetics in psychiatry would benefit from studying "*endophenotypes*, phenotypes presumably 'intermediate' between the overt expression of the syndromes themselves, and more basic levels of gene expression" (Sabb et al., 2009, p. 88).

The concept of autism endophenotypes clearly stands against the concept of a continuum of autism symptoms. Individual endophenotypes have been promoted for research in autism because they might be linked to an individual genetic variant such as an SNP or a chromosome duplication or deletion, and so could therefore provide a greater likelihood of mapping a behavior or feature to a genetic variant. If autism results from a set of unique gene variant-linked endophenotypes of atypical brain structures and behaviors, the symptoms of autism and of the broader autism phenotype are much less likely to exist in a continuum with typical behavior.

The Continuum Hypothesis for Behaviors of Autism and the Broader Autism Phenotype

There have been two notable versions of the general continuum hypothesis. One version proposed a continuum that embraces all three autism diagnostic symptoms as well as milder variants of the broader autism phenotype (Constantino & Todd, 2003). Another version proposed that three separate continuums exist, one for each of the three DSM-IV autism symptoms, wherein each continuum extends from autism severity through milder symptom variants to typical behaviors (Happé et al., 2006).

One Continuum for all Autism Symptoms

Constantino and Todd (2003) argued that autism diagnostic deficits in reciprocal social behavior, communication, and repetitive or stereotyped behaviors were all expressions of one underlying continuously distributed variable:

reciprocal social behavior. The researchers developed a social responsiveness instrument that tested for evidence of reciprocal social behavior, and they asked one parent of each of 788 typical twins to complete the measure. They found that social responsiveness was continuously distributed in the twin sample. They also found that social responsiveness was moderately to highly heritable and was influenced by the same genetic factors in boys and girls.

Constantino and Todd (2003) argued that the continuum of social responsiveness was a distinct domain of social development because it was impaired in autism, was unrelated to IQ, and was found to be genetically independent of all other domains of psychopathology in their male–male twin sub-study. They proposed that "Only when the specific causal influences (both genetic and environmental) on subthreshold autistic traits ... are better understood and are distinguished from ... shyness, extraversion, sociopathy, personality disorder will it be possible to better understand ... subthreshold autistic traits" (Constantino & Todd, 2003, p. 528).

Constantino (2011) moved away from the argument for a single continuum of all autism diagnostic symptoms, and argued instead that impaired social responsiveness was one of many endophenotypes of autism. He outlined possible endophenotypes for brain deficits, impaired social behavior, delayed language development, and atypical motor behaviors. However, despite his apparent theory shift from one continuum for all autism symptoms to many discrete endophenotypes of autism, Constantino (2011) argued that many separate endophenotypes could fall into one continuum. He claimed that "the continuum as a whole ... may be comprised, in part, of an array of clusters, each engendered by its own cause—independent, partially overlapping, or fully overlapping with the underlying causes of other clusters—and varying in range of severity" (p. 55R). Constantino (2011) effectively proposed a lumpy and layered continuum whose lumps and layers were endophenotypes.

Hoekstra, Bartels, Hudziak, Van Beijsterveldt, and Boomsma (2007) also argued for a single continuum of all autism behaviors. They noted that studies of autism traits in the general population and in samples of typical twins demonstrated that autism was "the upper extreme of a constellation of traits that may be continuously distributed in the population" (Hoekstra et al., 2007, p. 372). The researchers reported that quantified autism traits they measured by the Autism Spectrum Quotient were continuously distributed in their sample of 184 adolescent twin pairs. The researchers also reported that individual differences in autistic traits showed high heritability, and were influenced by the same genetic factors in men and women.

Scores on the Autism Spectrum Quotient ranged from 50 to 200: a score of 50 meant no autism traits were reported; a score of 200 meant all autism traits were reported. The measure tested for all three diagnostic symptom autism traits, and the measure itself assumed an equal interval continuum of overall autism severity from a score of 50 for no expression of autism behaviors to a score of 200 for the most severe expression of autism behaviors. Because there were so many scored items, and because only total test scores were counted, this measure was biased in favor of finding a continuum. As discussed in Chapter 1, Boucher (2011) cautioned that diagnostic instruments "instantiate circularity" (p. 475). Because the ASQ provides 150 symptom items to be scored as a cumulative total for each individual, an autism continuum is much more likely to be found. If the ASQ were constructed with several scales, and if each scale included items that could be analyzed separately, a continuum would be less likely to be determined.

Three Continuums of Autism Symptoms

Researchers Happé and colleagues (2006) agreed with Constantino and Todd (2003) that autism behaviors were on a continuum with typical behaviors such that social, communication, and repetitive behaviors formed "a smooth continuum (at least at the behavioral level) between individuals meeting diagnostic criteria for ASD and individuals in the general population" (p. 1218). Distinct from Constantino and Todd, however, Happé and colleagues noted that findings from large sample studies of typical twins and studies of children with autism had discovered only low correlations between the three diagnostic behavioral impairments: impaired social interaction, impaired communication, and restricted and repetitive interests and activities. They concluded, "in middle childhood at least, the degrees of social difficulty, communicative impairment and rigid/repetitive behavior are only modestly related" (p. 1218).

Happé et al. (2006) hypothesized three independent autism symptom continuums. One was a social behavior continuum ranging from typical to atypical to severely impaired. A second was a communication continuum ranging from typical language to no language, and the third was a continuum of motor behaviors ranging from typical to atypical to extremely rigid/repetitive behaviors. The researchers allowed that the three continuums would interact in development and throughout life, but argued that most genetic effects influenced each of the three continuums separately.

Happé et al. (2006) reported that their twin study of typical children revealed that the three autism behaviors were separately heritable, and they proposed that future research should focus on finding the genetic bases for each of three symptom continuums. The researchers noted that evidence for the broader autism phenotype in family studies of autism supported their claim that the three symptom groups were separate: some siblings and some parents expressed only one of the three autism diagnostic behaviors. Happé et al. (2006) concluded that their own twin study data, and data from other studies indicated, "the genes that contribute to autism segregate among relatives and have distinct influences" on the three different continuums (p. 1219).

Happé et al. (2006) noted that Constantino and Todd's (2003) findings for a single continuum of all autism behaviors on the Social Responsiveness Scale stood against their claim of three separate symptom continuums. They attributed the contradiction between their findings and those of Constantino and Todd (2003) to a difference in measures. Happé and colleagues (2006) stated, "It is unclear at this stage to what extent different findings are due to differences in measures. Unlike diagnostic tools, for which 'gold standard' measures exist that are used across studies, measures of autistic traits are still in development" (p. 1219). Happé et al. (2006) asserted that *no* primary deficit has been proposed that can plausibly account for the full triad of social, communicative, and rigid/repetitive difficulties in autism and the broader autism phenotype.

The Endophenotype Hypothesis for Behaviors of Autism and the Broader Autism Phenotype

In psychiatry, endophenotypes are individual behaviors, physical features, or brain features that have been defined as components of a complex disorder. Because endophenotypes are much more narrowly defined than whole disorders, endophenotypes eliminate large chunks of heterogeneity in a disorder. Some endophenotypes are believed to be linked to a single gene mutation or chromosome alteration, and could therefore provide a greater likelihood of mapping a behavior or feature to a genetic variant. Gottesman and Gould (2003) outlined Gottesman's origination of the use of endophenotypes in psychiatry, and they asserted that endophenotypes had been a helpful concept in research on schizophrenia. They noted that endophenotypes of sensorimotor function, eye motion, working memory, as well as the dysfunction of the brain's glial cells had each served to generate productive findings.

McCleery, Akshoomoff, Dobkins, and Carver (2009) proposed that an endophenotype or set of endophenotypes might operate in various ways to produce both autism and the broader autism phenotype. The researchers stated that one possibility was simply that a given endophenotype might be more severe in individuals with autism, and milder in family members without autism. Alternately, the researchers hypothesized that an endophenotype could be equally severe in diagnosed individuals and their family members, but that the diagnosed individual developed autism because his or her system had been unable to compensate for the effects of the endophenotype. Compensation could occur by means of a crucial biological or psychological protection factor that was present in unaffected family members but not present in the family members diagnosed with autism. McCleery et al. (2009) stated that the protection factor could be a specific hormone, brain protein, or personality trait. The researchers also suggested that autism might result from an individual having crossed a threshold of a critical number of different mild or severe endophenotypes. In this view, family members with the broader autism phenotype would have fewer endophenotypes than the family member diagnosed with autism.

Autism researchers enthusiastically embraced the notion of endophenotypes, both as a means to explore autism and as a means to better understand the broader autism phenotype. This enthusiasm led some researchers to propose possible autism endophenotypes, and led other researchers to search for endophenotypes.

Proposals for Possible Autism Endophenotypes whose Milder Expression would Define the Broader Autism Phenotype

Many different autism endophenotypes have been proposed. However, no one has yet found any distinct pattern of endophenotypes in autism or in the broader autism phenotype. Constantino (2011) catalogued 22 possible endophenotypes for autism, where each of the 22 endophenotypes could appear in a milder form as part of the broader autism phenotype. These included brain endophenotypes of atypical infant head circumference growth pattern, handedness, brain responses to auditory and visual stimuli in social interaction, sensory dysfunction, EEG, and event-related potential abnormality. He identified psychological endophenotypes of impaired theory of mind, self–other representation, social motivation, capacity for shared intentionality, abnormalities in gaze cueing, and problems with joint attention. He also listed possible language endophenotypes including problems in sentence sound pattern control and sentence comprehension abnormalities, and delayed appearance of the child's first word or first phrase. Finally, he noted possible motor endophenotypes including motor coordination problems, involuntary repetitive motor movements, insistence on sameness, perseveration, and inattention. Moreover, Constantino (2011) hypothesized that each of these 22 endophenotypes might be caused by a different brain circuit or network. Consequently, a milder form of each of the 22 endophenotypes could be components of the broader autism phenotype.

Panksepp (2006) claimed, "enthusiasm is mounting for reconceptualizing genetic analyses of psychiatric issues with respect to the most pervasive endophenotypes that characterize syndromes" (p. 775). He proposed that seven core emotion systems should be considered endophenotypes: seeking, care, play, lust, fear, panic, and rage. Seeking others, care for others, and play with others are all atypical or absent in autism. For Panksepp, these three emotional systems, if not all seven, should be studied as impaired endophenotypes in autism, and milder impairments of these emotion systems might contribute to the broader autism phenotype.

Rommelse, Franke, Geurts, Buitelaar, and Hartman (2011) reviewed possible brain-based endophenotypes for autism and ADHD. They proposed that pleiotropic genes were likely to cause both autism and ADHD; therefore, the endophenotypes for both disorders should be studied jointly. They noted that ADHD has been found in family members of individuals with autism and that ADHD might be part of the broader autism phenotype as an alternate expression of partly overlapping causes. They also noted that individuals with ADHD often had autism features: lack of awareness of the feelings of others, reduced knowledge of the effects of their behaviors on others, poor social skills, reduced empathy, language delay, pragmatic language skill impairment, stereotypic motor behaviors, and sensory over-reactivity. Similarly, Rommelse et al. (2011) identified ADHD features found in autism. They identified these as attention problems, hyperactivity, impulsivity, and emotional regulation problems.

Rommelse et al. (2011) reported that in clinical samples, 20–50% of children with ADHD met criteria for autism, and 30–80% of children diagnosed with autism met criteria for ADHD. The researchers outlined many overlaps between the two disorders and proposed that genetic studies should look for mutations in multi-outcome pleiotropic genes for ASD and ADHD combined. They identified 11 brain structure and function endophenotypes for autism and ADHD. These included atypical cortical thickness, brain connectivity, brain volume, EEG, processing time, state regulation, arousal, sensory functioning, motor coordination, sustained attention, and response variability. Rommelse and colleagues (2011) also proposed that aberrant function in five brain regions as likely endophenotypes: the frontostriatal system; left medial temporal lobe; left inferior parietal cortex; cerebellum; and the corpus callosum. In addition, the researchers identified atypical scores on seven neuropsychological measures as potential endophenotypes for autism and ADHD: IQ profiles; cognitive control; error and feedback processing; facial emotion recognition; arousal and reward in response to social stimuli; and skill with language use rules for interaction (called pragmatics).

Rommelse et al. (2011) argued that four endophenotypes should not be investigated for autism and ADHD because they were not linked to both disorders and/or they were not heritable. These included atypical functional connectivity, delay aversion, theory of mind, and central coherence.

Like Rommelse and colleagues (2011), researchers Levy and Ebstein (2009) proposed that endophenotypes should take precedence over diagnoses in research. They argued that groups of affected individuals should be studied in endophenotype groups "defined with respect to theoretically motivated traits rather than syndromes … in homogenous and exhaustive groups … crossing syndrome boundaries" (Levy & Ebstein, 2009, p. 665).

Research to Explore Endophenotypes in Autism and in the Broader Autism Phenotype

In their study of twenty 10-month-old infant siblings of children with autism, McCleery, Akshoomoff, Dobkins, and Carver (2009) found that, compared with typical infants, infant siblings showed atypical cortical processing of faces versus objects. The researchers found faster than normal object responses in infant siblings of children with autism, but not abnormal responses to faces. They hypothesized that enhanced object processing could be an early endophenotype of autism. In their hypothesis, the enhanced early processing of objects could generate core neural circuits of enhanced object processing resulting in greater motivation to attend to objects leading to impaired development of human face processing. Although enhanced object processing has been found in some studies of family members of individuals with autism, Scheeren and Stauder (2008) reported that scores of parents of children with autism on the Block Design Test did not differ from those for parents of typical children. The Block Design Test is a visual intelligence test for which enhanced object processing would provide a significant advantage.

Nydén et al. (2011) reviewed evidence for impaired executive functions as a core endophenotype of the broader autism phenotype. Executive functions regulate complex cognition by controlling the operation of various mental operations in order to achieve a goal in a flexible manner. Tasks that require executive function include solving problems, changing behavior given new information, planning strategies, and sequencing complex actions. Working memory is a component of executive function: working memory keeps needed information active while complex processing uses the active information to make decisions and change behavior or plans.

Executive functions are theorized to operate in multiple flexible circuits in the frontal cortex linked to other brain regions, of which the striatum is the most important. The striatum is a component of the basal ganglia that has two functional operation centers both of which get information from the frontal lobe. The dorsal striatum consists of the caudate and putamen and the fundus that joins them. The ventral striatum includes the nucleus accumbens and the olfactory tubercle. The dorsal striatum is a key element in decision-making, especially for action selection and initiation. The ventral striatum is associated with reward. Dopamine neurons in the striatum have been shown to be the basis for feelings of reward. The dorsal and ventral striatum are theorized to regulate the learning of rewarded behaviors by collecting motivation, emotion, cognition, and sensorimotor information and sending selective inhibitory signals to the thalamus, brainstem structures, cortex, and hippocampus and amygdala.

Nydén and colleagues (2011) posited that impaired executive functions have been associated with the broader phenotype of autism in parents and non-affected siblings of children with autism. The researchers noted that some studies found nothing atypical in the executive function skills of parents of children with autism, while other studies did show atypical executive function skills in parents. Nydén et al. (2011) tested neurocognitive skills in 86 individuals in 18 families in which two siblings were diagnosed with autism. The researchers' goal was to establish a neurocognitive profile for the broader autism phenotype. They reported that all family members studied showed impaired planning, but typical visual scanning and mental set-shifting. They reported that no family members had intellectual disability, and that family members as a group had typical fluid and crystallized intelligence. However, siblings of children with autism were found to have better visuo-perceptual than verbal ability.

The findings of Nydén et al. (2011) did not support either weak central coherence or Theory of Mind as components of the broader autism phenotype. Enhanced skill on the Embedded Figures Test was argued to be evidence of weak central coherence because central coherence is the ability to generalize the "gist" of an experience, leaving behind details, and skill on the Embedded Figures Test requires holding onto visual details. However, the family members they tested expressed no more than typical scores on the Embedded Figures Test. The researchers also reported that family members did not show impairment in Theory of Mind. Theory of Mind is defined as the ability to imagine that other people have their own separate thoughts and knowledge.

Like other studies exploring the elements of the broader autism pheno-type, Nydén and colleagues (2011) did not present individual variation data. Such data would allow examination of different patterns of the broader autism phenotype in different families.

Wilson, Freeman, Brock, Burton, and Palermo (2010) investigated the face recognition skills of parents of 20 children with autism. They reported contradictory findings. On one measure of face recognition skill, the Cambridge Face Memory Test, they found significant deficits for parents of children with autism. On another test of face recognition skill, a simpler sequential face-matching task, they found no significant impairment for parents. Embedded in the argument Wilson et al. (2010) made in defense of their contradictory findings was a very valuable suggestion. The researchers argued "It is widely accepted that symptom profiles in ASD are heterogeneous, therefore it is unreasonable to expect that consistent patterns of impairment would be present across relatives of ASD individuals. Our results suggest that, to effectively identify cognitive and behavioural traits that translate to the relatives of ASD individuals, it is important to take account of the corresponding trait in the ASD probands" (Wilson et al., 2010, p. 6).

A proband is the diagnosed member of a family participating in a genetic study. The valuable suggestion made by Wilson et al. (2010) was the statement that to understand the broader autism phenotype it would be important to examine within-family symptom patterns. Their conclusion is logical: heterogeneity in family symptoms cannot be understood by lumping all parents together for group comparison statistics. It will be necessary to match symptoms expressed by the individual with autism (the proband) to the specific symptoms expressed by that individual's own parents.

Wilson et al. (2010) did not describe a method for matching the symptoms of affected and unaffected family members, but the researchers indicated they had collected face recognition data for the children with autism. They reported "Participants were the parents of 20 ASD children, who had been recruited … to take part in other studies of face recognition in our lab" (Wilson et al., 2010, p. 2). Therefore, it would seem possible that the researchers could have matched the face recognition data they collected for parents to the face recognition data they had collected for each of their children. Wilson et al. (2010) could have used exploratory data analysis methods and non-parametric analyses to look for family patterns.

Bernier and colleagues (2011) compared skills of four groups of parents: parents with two or more children with autism: parents with a single child with autism; parents with a child without autism but with developmental delay; and parents of typical children. The researchers reported that parents with two or more children diagnosed with autism showed a greater number and greater intensity of atypical social and communication traits than did each of the other three groups. They concluded that transmission of autism may be different in families with more than one affected child from genetic transmission in families with only one affected child.

Bernier et al. (2011) proposed that in families with only one child with autism, that child's autism is more likely to have resulted from a de novo genetic event. A de novo genetic event is a new genetic variation in an individual that is discovered because it has caused a disease or disorder. This new mutation may have arisen only in the affected individual; however, it may have occurred in one of the parents of the affected individual. Counter to the proposal of Bernier et al. (2011), if the de novo mutation occurred in the sperm of the father or ovum of the mother, the siblings of the affected family member may also be at increased risk for the disorder. Thus, families with more than one child with autism may include de novo mutations as the cause for autism.

Searching for a brain endophenotype, Jou et al. (2011) found atypical white matter functional connectivity in a sample of 15 boys with autism and 8 controls. They noted wide individual variation, but presented only group comparisons. From their findings, the researchers hypothesized that the brain phenotype in autism was variable diffuse, white matter maldevelopment. They further hypothesized that autism social disability was the result of failed function of two white matter tracts: the inferior fronto-occipital and superior longitudinal fasciculi that connect frontal, temporal, and parietal lobes. They argued that because the frontal, temporal, and parietal lobes contain circuits for social functions, consequently, "With the disability of major pathways connecting the modules of the social brain, there is possible reliance on smaller tracts that may lead to inefficient corticocortical communication" (Jou et al., 2011, p. 6). They proposed that degree of social cognitive impairment in autism was likely to depend on how severely white matter fiber tracts were compromised, and whether other tracts were functioning. They concluded that the "overall pattern of tract deficits may not only dictate the expression of autism but also its severity and heterogeneity" (Jou et al., 2011, p. 6).

Although Jou and colleagues (2011) cautioned that their findings were limited by the heterogeneous nature of the autism group, they did not take the obvious step of presenting individual variation data. Tantalizingly, Jou et al. (2011) noted that the individual variation in their overall findings might contribute to autism's "well-known heterogeneity" (p. 6), and they worried that "the widely different degree to which individual tracts are affected, raises the question of whether a unique disconnectivity fingerprint may be ascribed to ASD" (p. 6). Nowhere do the researchers consider the possibility that the widely different degree to which different tracts are affected in different individuals may signal meaningfully distinct patterns of white matter aberration. Exploratory analysis of this wide individual variation would provide the possibility of tracing distinct patterns.

Summary: Heterogeneity in the Broader Autism Phenotype

Table 2.2 lists all symptoms proposed as endophenotypes or symptoms of autism that might be constituents of the broader autism phenotype. Given that the only cognitive symptom in the autism diagnosis is restricted interests, it is surprising that so many specific cognitive deficits have been proposed as either endophenotypes or elements of the broader autism phenotype. Conversely, given that about two-thirds of individuals with autism have intellectual disability, it is surprising that mild intellectual disability has not been identified as a possible element in the broader autism phenotype.

As can be seen from Table 2.2, even this chapter's limited review of possible symptoms and endophenotypes yielded 59 symptoms. Not all 59 symptoms have been studied in family members of individuals with autism. Moreover, conflicting study against study results of symptoms found versus symptoms not found are common for family research. What is clear from these findings is that researchers have not discovered *any* consistent pattern of traits for the broader autism phenotype, and that the great heterogeneity found for autism symptoms is true for symptoms of the broader autism phenotype.

If individual families have different genetic and environmental causes for autism in their family, no consistent homogeneous pattern will ever be found for the broader autism phenotype. If individual families have different genetic and environmental causes for autism in their family, the broader autism phenotype is a collection of many different broader autism phenotypes. While small sample size may be one reason for so many

Table 2.2 Symptoms Proposed as Possible Constituents of the Broader Autism Phenotype Organized by Domain

Domain	Symptoms Proposed
Social	General social problems
	Impaired joint attention
	Abnormalities in gaze cueing
	Impaired social motivation
	Impaired social responsiveness
	Insensitivity to social reward and social affiliation
	Blunted emotional expression
	Impaired face processing
	Impaired identification of emotional expressions
	Poor conversational skills
	Lack of tact in interactions
	Hypersensitivity to criticism
	Atypical quantity and quality of friendships
	Preference for non-social activities
Language	Delayed speech onset
	General impairment in language ability
	Atypical sentence sound pattern production
	Sentence comprehension abnormalities
	Impaired skill with language use rules (called pragmatics)
Motor	Tics
	Abnormal eye movements
	Atypical motor imitation
	Restricted and stereotyped behaviors
	Deficits in learning sequential motor tasks
	Motor coordination problems
Sensory	General sensory dysfunction
Cognitive	Enhanced object processing
	Better visuo-perceptual than verbal ability
	Impaired declarative memory feature binding
	Impaired spatial memory
	General impaired executive functions
	Impaired planning and organizing skills
	Weak central coherence
	Impaired Theory of Mind
	Rigidity in thinking
	Restricted interests
	Insistence on sameness
	Perseveration
	Impaired attention
	Impaired processing time
	Impaired error and feedback processing

(Continued)

Table 2.2 Symptoms Proposed as Possible Constituents of the Broader Autism Phenotype Organized by Domain—*cont'd*

Domain	Symptoms Proposed
Psychiatric symptoms and diagnoses	Anxiety
	Obsessive compulsive disorder
	ADHD
Atypical brain structures	Larger brain volume
	Atypical cortical thickness
	Atypical head circumference growth pattern
	Deficient/insufficient white matter connectivity
	Atypical cerebellar circuits
	Atypical cortical circuits
	Atypical striatal circuits
	Abnormalities in frontostriatal system
	Abnormalities in the left medial temporal lobe
	Abnormalities in the left inferior parietal cortex
	Abnormalities in the cerebellum
	Abnormalities in the corpus callosum
Atypical brain functions	Atypical EEG
	Atypical evoked potentials
	Atypical brain responses to social auditory and visual stimuli

conflicting findings, conflicting findings may also be the result of the noisy variance generated by the aggregation of so many different broader autism phenotypes.

CONCLUSIONS: RECURRENCE RISK RATES AND FAMILY PHENOTYPES REFLECT AGGREGATES

The four sibling pairs discussed in the beginning of this chapter raised three questions regarding heterogeneity. When different diagnoses occur in siblings from the same family, should the two diagnoses be investigated together as having a possible genetic link? Yes, because it is very likely they share an etiology. When siblings have the same neurogenetic disorder, if one sibling meets criteria for autism and the other sibling does not, should the neurogenetic disorder be considered the primary diagnosis? Yes, because a genetic syndrome is a move closer to findings that might translate into focal treatment and prevention. When two siblings in a family meet the diagnosis for autism, but one has intellectual disability and the other does not, should the presence of intellectual disability be a basis for excluding individuals from study? No. Intellectual disability has been excluded from the symptoms of autism. However, complex phenotypes that result from pleiotropy, wherein differing symptoms result from one genetic variant, indicate that intellectual disability when present, should be considered part of the autism phenotype.

The review of infant sibling research pointed out the heterogeneity of symptoms found for infant siblings, and noted the problems for studies with small sample sizes. Exploratory data analysis of individual variation was proposed as a means to investigate patterns that might untangle some of the heterogeneity. However, heterogeneity is endemic to all samples that are based directly or indirectly on the autism diagnosis. This problem will not be resolved until the diagnosis is eschewed in research. Until that time, exploring individual variation within the diagnosis would be the first step toward making sense of the existing real heterogeneity of traits and symptoms in affected children and their unaffected siblings.

Twin studies by many different research groups have demonstrated that heterogeneity of symptoms is endemic in autism because autism results from many varied brain dysfunctions caused by many varied genetic and environmental risk factors. The co-occurrence of autism with other disorders reported by Lichtenstein et al. (2011) in their twin study, and the low genetic heritability and high shared environmental variance found by Hallmayer et al. (2011) have demonstrated the complex heterogeneity that must be untangled.

Finally, because individual families have different genetic and environmental causes for autism in their family, the broader autism phenotype that has been studied is, in fact, an aggregate of many different family broader autism phenotypes, just as the recurrence risk rate ascertained for infant siblings of children with autism is an average of the aggregate of many different family risk rates. To find true family broader autism phenotypes, and true recurrence risk rates, groups of individual families with shared genetic or environmental risks must be identified. The symptoms found for these identified sets of families then must be examined by exploratory data analysis, and family brain studies. This requires opening the door to many different forms of research—particularly forms of research that do not chase significance in small sample group comparisons.

REFERENCES

Bernier, R., Gerdts, J., Munson, J., Dawson, G., & Estes, A. (2011). Evidence for broader autism phenotype characteristics in parents from multiple-incidence autism families. *Autism Research, 4*, 1–8.

Betancur, C. (2011). Etiological heterogeneity in autism spectrum disorders: More than 100 genetic and genomic disorders and still counting. *Brain Research, 1380*, 42–77.

Bloch, M., State, M., & Pittinger, C. (2011). Recent advances in Tourette syndrome. *Current Opinion in Neurology*, *24*, 119–125.

Bosl, W., Tierney, A., Tager-Flusberg, H., & Nelson, C. (2011). EEG complexity as a biomarker for autism spectrum disorder risk. *BMC Medicine*, *9*(18). Available at http://www.biomedcentral.com/1741-7015/9/18.

Cassel, T. D., Messinger, D. S., Ibanez, L. V., Haltigan, J. D., Acosta, S. I., & Buchman, A. C. (2007). Early social and emotional communication in the infant siblings of children with autism spectrum disorders: An examination of the broad phenotype. *Journal of Autism and Developmental Disorders*, *37*, 122–132.

CBS News online. (2011, August 15). *Siblings' autism risk much higher than thought*. Retrieved from http://www.cbsnews.com/stories/2011/08/15/earlyshow/living/parenting/main20092340.shtml.

Chow, S. M., Haltigan, J. D., & Messinger, D. S. (2010). Dynamic infant–parent affect coupling during the face-to-face/still-face. *Emotion*, *10*, 101–114.

Conchaiya, W., Schneider, A., & Hagerman, R. J. (2009). Fragile X: A family of disorders. *Advances in Pediatrics*, *56*, 165–186.

Constantino, J. N., Zhang, Y., Frazier, T., Abbacchi, A. M., & Law, P. (2010). Sibling recurrence and the genetic epidemiology of autism. *American Journal of Psychiatry*, *167*, 1349–1356.

Constantino, J. N., & Todd, R. D. (2003). Autistic traits in the general population: A twin study. *Archives of General Psychiatry*, *60*, 524–530.

Constantino, J. N. (2011). The quantitative nature of social impairment in autism. *Pediatric Research*, *69*(5 Pt 2), 55R–62R.

Costa, M., Goldberger, A. L., & Peng, C. K. (2005). Multiscale entropy analysis of biological signals. *Physical Reviews E Statistical Nonlinear Soft Matter Physics*, *71*, e021906.

Davies, G., Tenesa, A., Payton, A., Yang, J., Harris, S. E., Liewald, D., et al. (2011). Genome-wide association studies establish that human intelligence is highly heritable and polygenic. *Molecular Psychiatry*, *16*, 996–1005.

Dawson, G., Webb, S., Schellenberg, G. D., Dager, S., Friedman, S., Aylward, E., et al. (2002). Defining the broader phenotype of autism: Genetic, brain, and behavioral perspectives. *Developmental Psychopathology*, *14*, 581–611.

Elder, L. M., Dawson, G., Toth, K., Fein, D., & Munson, J. (2008). Head circumference as an early predictor of autism symptoms in younger siblings of children with autism spectrum disorder. *Journal of Autism and Developmental Disorders*, *38*, 1104–1111.

Elsabbagh, M., Mercure, E., Hudr, K., Chandler, S., Pasco, G., Charman, T., et al. (2012). Infant neural sensitivity to dynamic eye gaze is associated with later emerging autism. *Current Biology*, *22*, 1–5.

Elsabbagh, M., Volein, A., Csibra, G., Holmboe, K., Garwood, H., Tucker, L., et al. (2009). Neural correlates of eye gaze processing in the infant broader autism phenotype. *Biological Psychiatry*, *65*, 31–38.

Feldman, M. A., Ward, R. A., Savona, D., Regehr, K., Parker, K., Hudson, M., et al. (2011). Development and initial validation of a parent report measure of the behavioral development of infants at risk for autism spectrum disorders. *Journal of Autism and Developmental Disorders*, *42*, 13–22.

Folstein, S., & Rutter, M. (1977). Infantile autism: A genetic study of 21 twin pairs. *Journal of Child Psychology and Psychiatry*, *18*, 297–321.

Gai, X., Xie, H. M., Perin, J. C., Takahashi, N., Murphy, K., Wenocur, A. S., et al. (2011). Rare structural variation of synapse and neurotransmission genes in autism. *Molecular Psychiatry*, *17*, 402–411.

Gottesman, I. I., & Gould, T. D. (2003). The endophenotype concept in psychiatry: Etymology and strategic intentions. *American Journal of Psychiatry*, *160*, 636–645.

Griffin, R., & Westbury, C. (2011). Infant EEG activity as a biomarker for autism: A promising approach or a false promise? *BMC Medicine*, *9*, 61.

Guilmatre, A., Dubourg, C., Mosca, A. L., Legallic, S., Goldenberg, A., Drouin-Garraud, V., et al. (2009). Recurrent rearrangements in synaptic and neurodevelopmental genes and shared biologic pathways in schizophrenia, autism, and mental retardation. *Archives of General Psychiatry, 66,* 947–956.

Hagerman, R., Au, J., & Hagerman, P. (2011). FMR1 premutation and full mutation molecular mechanisms related to autism. *Journal of Neurodevelopmental Disorders, 3,* 211–234.

Hall, S. S., Lightbody, A. A., Hirt, M., Rezvani, A., & Reiss, A. L. (2010). Autism in fragile X syndrome: A category mistake? *Journal of the American Academy of Child and Adolescent Psychiatry, 49,* 921–933.

Hallmayer, J., Cleveland, S., Torres, A., Phillips, J., Cohen, B., Torigoe, T., et al. (2011). Genetic heritability and shared environmental factors among twin pairs with autism. *Archives of General Psychiatry, 68,* 1095–1102.

Haltigan, J. D., Ekas, N. V., Seifer, R., & Messinger, D. S. (2011). Attachment security in infants at-risk for autism spectrum disorders. *Journal of Autism and Developmental Disorders, 41,* 962–967.

Happé, F., Ronald, A., & Plomin, R. (2006). Time to give up on a single explanation for autism. *Nature Neuroscience, 9,* 1218–1220.

Hess, C. R., & Landa, R. J. (2012). Predictive and concurrent validity of parent concern about young children at risk for autism. *Journal of Autism and Developmental Disorders, 42,* 575–584.

Hoekstra, R. A., Bartels, M., Hudziak, J. J., Van Beijsterveldt, T. C., & Boomsma, D. I. (2007). Genetic and environmental covariation between autistic traits and behavioral problems. *Twin Research in Human Genetics, 10,* 853–860.

Holmboe, K., Elsabbagh, M., Volein, A., Tucker, L. A., Baron-Cohen, S., Bolton, P., & Johnson, M. H. (2010). Frontal cortex functioning in the infant broader autism phenotype. *Infant Behavior and Development, 33,* 482–491.

Humphrey, A., Higgins, N. P., Yates, J. R. W., & Bolton, P. F. (2004). Monozygotic twins with tuberous sclerosis discordant for the severity of developmental deficits. *Neurology, 62,* 795–798.

Hutman, T., Chela, M. K., Gillespie-Lynch, K., & Sigman, M. (2012). Selective visual attention at twelve months: Signs of autism in early social interactions. *Journal of Autism and Development Disorders, 42,* 487–498.

Hutman, T., Rozga, A., DeLaurentis, A. D., Barnwell, J. M., Sugar, C. A., & Sigman, M. (2010). Response to distress in infants at risk for autism: A prospective longitudinal study. *Journal of Child Psychology and Psychiatry, 51,* 1010–1020.

Ioannidis, J. P. (2005). Why most published research findings are false. *PLoS Medicine, 2,* e124.

Ioannidis, J. P., & Panagiotou, O. A. (2011). Comparison of effect sizes associated with biomarkers reported in highly cited individual articles and in subsequent meta-analyses. *Journal of the American Medical Association, 305,* 2200–2210.

Iverson, J., & Wozniak, R. (2007). Variation in vocal-motor development in infant siblings of children with autism. *Journal of Autism and Developmental Disorders, 37,* 158–170.

Jou, R. J., Mateljevic, N., Kaiser, M. D., Sugrue, D. R., Volkmar, F. R., & Pelphrey, K. A. (2011). Structural neural phenotype of autism: Preliminary evidence from a diffusion tensor imaging study using tract-based spatial statistics. *American Journal of Neuroradiology, 32,* 1607–1613.

Levy, Y., & Ebstein, R. P. (2009). Research Review: Crossing syndrome boundaries in the search for brain endophenotypes. *Journal of Child Psychology and Psychiatry, 50,* 657–668.

Levy, D., Ronemus, M., Yamrom, B., Lee, Y.-H., Leotta, A., Kendall, J., et al. (2011). Rare de novo and transmitted copy-number variations in autistic spectrum disorders. *Neuron, 70,* 886–897.

Lichtenstein, P., Carlström, E., Råstam, M., Gillberg, C., & Anckarsäter, H. (2010). The genetics of autism spectrum disorders and related neurospychiatric disorders in childhood. *American Journal of Psychiatry, 167,* 1357–1363.

Losh, M., Adolphs, R., Poe, M. D., Couture, S., Penn, D., Baranek, G. T., & Piven, J. (2009). The neuropsychological profile of autism and the broad autism phenotype. *Archives of General Psychiatry*, *66*, 518–526.

Losh, M., Childress, D., Lam, K., & Piven, J. (2008). Defining key features of the broad autism phenotype: A comparison across parents of multiple- and single-incidence autism families. *American Journal of Medical Genetics B Neuropsychiatric Genetics*, *147*, 424–433.

Losh, M., & Piven, J. (2007). Social-cognition and the broad autism phenotype: Identifying genetically meaningful phenotypes. *Journal of Child Psychology and Psychiatry*, *48*, 105–112.

Luyster, R. J., Wagner, J. B., Vogel-Farley, V., Tager-Flusberg, H., & Nelson, C. A. (2011). Neural correlates of familiar and unfamiliar face processing in infants at risk for autism spectrum disorders. *Brain Topography*, *24*, 220–228.

Matson, J. L., & Shoemaker, M. (2009). Intellectual disability and its relationship to autism spectrum disorders. *Research in Developmental Disabilities*, *30*, 1107–1114.

McCleery, J. P., Akshoomoff, N., Dobkins, K. R., & Carver, L. J. (2009). Atypical face versus object processing and hemispheric asymmetries in 10-month-old infants at risk for autism. *Biological Psychiatry*, *66*, 950–957.

Moricke, E., Swinkels, S. H. N., Beuker, K. T., & Buitelaar, J. K. (2010). Predictive value of subclinical autistic traits at age 14–15 months for behavioural and cognitive problems at age 3–5 years. *European Child and Adolescent Psychiatry*, *19*, 659–668.

Mosconi, M. W., Kay, M., D'Cruz, A.-M., Guter, S., Kapur, K., Macmillan, C., et al. (2010). Neurobehavioral abnormalities in first-degree relatives of individuals with autism. *Archives of General Psychiatry*, *67*, 830–840.

Nydén, A., Hagberg, B., Goussé, V., & Råstam, M. (2011). A cognitive endophenotype of autism in families with multiple incidence. *Research in Autism Spectrum Disorders*, *5*, 191–200.

Orsmond, G. I., & Selzer, M. M. (2007). Siblings of individuals with autism spectrum disorders across the life course. *Mental Retardation and Developmental Disabilities Researcher Reviews*, *13*, 313–320.

Owen, M. J., O'Donovan, M. C., Thapar, A., & Craddock, N. (2011). Neurodevelopmental hypothesis of schizophrenia. *British Journal of Psychiatry*, *198*, 173–175.

Ozonoff, S., Iosif, A. M., Baguio, F., Cook, I. C., Hill, M. M., Hutman, T., et al. (2010). A prospective study of the emergence of early behavioral signs of autism. *Journal of the American Academy of Child and Adolescent Psychiatry*, *49*, 256–266.

Ozonoff, S., Young, G. S., Carter, A., Messinger, D., Yirmiya, N., Zwaigenbaum, L., et al. (2011). Recurrence risk in younger siblings of children with autism spectrum disorders: A BSRC study. *Pediatrics*, *128*, e1.

Panksepp, J. (2006). Emotional endophenotypes in evolutionary psychiatry. *Progress in Neuro-Psychopharmacology & Biological Psychiatry*, *30*, 774–784.

Rogers, S. (2009). What are infant siblings teaching us about autism in infancy? *Autism Research*, *2*, 125–137.

Rommelse, N. N. J., Franke, B., Geurts, H. M., Buitelaar, J. K., & Hartman, C. A. (2011). A review on cognitive and brain endophenotypes that may be common in autism spectrum disorder and attention-deficit/hyperactivity disorder and facilitate the search for pleiotropic genes. *Neuroscience & Biobehavioral Reviews*, *35*, 1363–1396.

Ronald, A., & Hoekstra, R. A. (2011). Autism spectrum disorders and autistic traits: A decade of new twin studies. *American Journal of Medical Genetics B Neuropsychiatric Genetics*, *156*, 4255–4274.

Rosenberg, R. E., Law, J. K., Yenokyan, G., McGready, J., Kaufmann, W. E., & Law, P. A. (2009). Characteristics and concordance of autism spectrum disorders among 277 twin pairs. *Archives of Pediatric and Adolescent Medicine*, *163*, 907–914.

Rozga, A., Hutman, T., Young, G. S., Rogers, S. J., Ozonoff, S., Dapretto, M., et al. (2011). Behavioral profiles of affected and unaffected siblings of children with autism: Contribution of measures of mother–infant interaction and nonverbal communication. *Journal of Autism and Developmental Disorders*, *41*, 287–301.

Sabb, F. W., Burggren, A. C., Higier, R. G., Fox, J., He, J., Parker, D. S., et al. (2009). Challenges in phenotype definition in the whole-genome era: Multivariate models of memory and intelligence. *Neuroscience, 164*, 88–107.

Sanders, S. J., Ercan-Sencicek, A. G., Hus, V., Luo, R., Murtha, M. T., Moreno-De-Luca, D., et al. (2011). Multiple recurrent de novo CNVs, including duplications of the 7q11.23 Williams syndrome region, are strongly associated with autism. *Neuron, 70*, 863–885.

Schaaf, C. P., Sabo, A., Sakai, Y., Crosby, J., Muzny, D., Hawes, A., et al. (2011). Oligogenic heterozygosity in individuals with high-functioning autism spectrum disorders. *Human Molecular Genetics, 20*, 3366–3375.

Scheeren, A. M., & Stauder, J. E. (2008). Broader autism phenotype in parents of autistic children: Reality or myth? *Journal of Autism and Developmental Disorders, 38*, 276–287.

Sumiyoshi, C., Kawakubob, Y., Sugab, M., Sumiyoshie, T., & Kasaib, K. (2011). Impaired ability to organize information in individuals with autism spectrum disorders and their siblings. *Neuroscience Research, 69*, 252–257.

Tager-Flusberg, H. (2010). The origins of social impairments in autism spectrum disorder: Studies of infants at risk. *Neural Networks, 23*, 1072–1076.

Taniai, H., Nishiyama, T., Miyachi, T., Imaeda, M., & Sumi, S. (2008). Genetic influences on the broad spectrum of autism: Study of probands-ascertained twins. *American Journal of Medical Genetics B Neuropsychiatric Genetics, 147*, 844–849.

Tatsioni, A., Bonitsis, N. G., & Ioannidis, J. P. N. (2007). Persistence of contradicted claims in the literature. *Journal of the American Medical Association, 298*, 2517–2526.

Verhees, B. (1976). A pair of classically early infantile autistic siblings. *Journal of Autism and Childhood Schizophrenia, 6*, 53–59.

Voineagu, I. (2012). Gene expression studies in autism: Moving from the genome to the transcriptome and beyond. *Neurobiology of Disease, 45*, 69–75.

Wilson, C. E., Freeman, P., Brock, J., Burton, M., & Palermo, R. (2010). Facial identity recognition in the broader autism phenotype. *PLoS ONE, 5*, e12876.

Yirmiya, N., & Charman, T. (2010). The prodrome of autism: Early behavioral and biological signs, regression, peri- and post-natal development and genetics. *Journal of Child Psychology and Psychiatry, 51*, 432–458.

Yirmiya, N., Gamliel, I., Shaked, M., & Sigman, M. (2007). Cognitive and verbal abilities of 24- to 36-month-old siblings of children with autism. *Journal of Autism and Developmental Disorders, 37*, 218–229.

Yoder, P., Stone, W. L., Walden, T., & Malesa, E. (2009). Predicting social impairment and ASD diagnosis in younger siblings of children with autism spectrum disorder. *Journal of Autism and Developmental Disorders, 39*, 1381–1391.

Zarembo, A. (2011, August 15). Children with autistic sibling face greater risk, study finds. *Los Angeles Times*. Retrieved from http://articles.latimes.com/2011/aug/15/health/la-he-autism-20110815.

Zwaigenbaum, L., Bryson, S., Rogers, T., Roberts, W., Brian, J., & Szatmari, P. (2005). Behavioral manifestations of autism in the first year of life. *International Journal of Developmental Neuroscience, 23*, 143–152.

Zwaigenbaum, L., Szatmari, P., Mahoney, W., Bryson, S., Bartolucci, G., & MacLean, J. (2000). High functioning autism and Childhood Disintegrative Disorder in half-brothers. *Journal of Autism and Developmental Disorders, 30*, 121–126.

CHAPTER 3

The Social Brain is a Complex Super-Network

Contents

Rethinking Autism
http://dx.doi.org/10.1016/B978-0-12-415961-7.00003-4

The central diagnostic trait of autism, impaired social behavior, varies widely because the heterogeneity of genetic and environmental risk factors contributes to a wide variation in brain deficits, which, in turn, contribute to a wide variation in deficits in autism social behavior. The human "social brain" includes many specialized and shared circuits in many different brain systems, and those brain systems appear to operate as a complex super-network to support social interaction. Consequently, there are hundreds of different social brain network elements that may be disrupted, with varied outcomes in behavior. Some individuals with autism are completely aloof and uninterested in other people, some are attached to family members but indifferent to all others, and some individuals with autism are anxious to interact with others but generate hard-to-interrupt obsessive one-sided monologues. Moreover, some individuals with autism express emotions but are unable to understand the emotions of others. Other individuals with autism have trouble regulating their emotions; they may laugh or become angry without cause.

In order to discover the sources of the variation in autism social impairment, it is necessary to understand the brain basis of typical social behavior. Our brains include billions of neurons, each of which is a separate information processor. Each neuron has one or more axons and many dendrites that send and receive information. The brain's billions of neurons form the cerebellum, brainstem, subcortical regions, and the cerebral cortex. The cerebral cortex has four lobes—the occipital, parietal, temporal, and frontal lobes—and is structured by columns of local circuits of neurons. These local circuits are organized into systems, and into networks of systems of circuits. The multiple brain circuits required for typical social behaviors overlap and interconnect with multiple brain circuits in the brain's functional connectome (van den Heuvel & Sporns, 2011). Brain chemicals called neurotransmitters, and hormones such as estrogen and testosterone, contribute to social behavior. The neuropeptides oxytocin and vasopressin, and a key reward neurotransmitter, dopamine, as well as the neurotransmitter serotonin function in varied ways to regulate social behavior. Many brain pathways of neurons with specialized receptors for various neurotransmitters form brain systems by linking local circuits from one brain region to another.

The complex super-network of social brain systems governs our various social behaviors, from a baby's distress cry or everyday conversations, to a judge's raised eyebrow, or the negotiations for a peace treaty. The field of social neuroscience is relatively new, but the research has generated an initial sketch of what constitutes the social brain. Researchers have found evidence for a region called the fusiform face area that processes and stores images of the faces of people we know. Researchers have discovered the mirror neuron system, a distributed set of processing centers that automatically and non-consciously trigger brain activity that mirrors the behaviors of the people we observe. Researchers have found evidence that a network including a tiny brain region at the juncture of the temporal and parietal lobes may be specialized for the mental construction of the thoughts and intentions of other people. These, and still more brain tissues, circuits, neurotransmitters, and systems regulate our emotions, engender our bonding with others, form our interest in the behavior of others around us, and permit social recognition, trust, and empathy, as well as social imitation and social learning. Brain systems also provide internal rewards for social contact, and establish the framework for our ability to coordinate our behaviors with others.

While theorists may concur that multiple brain systems govern social behavior, they differ in their view of the relative importance of various systems governing social behavior. For example, Insel (2010) proposed that the central decision of the social brain was a more complex form of the primitive animal decision to approach or to avoid, regulated in large part by the nonapeptides, oxytocin and arginine vasopressin. Panksepp (2006) proposed that the evolutionary basis for the social brain was the brain circuits for emotions, where the emotions are primary drivers of social behavior. Gallese and Sinigaglia (2011), however, theorized that the central process of the social brain was our reuse of our non-conscious mimicry of the behaviors of other people. Frith and Frith (2012) proposed that the most important function of the social brain was learning about other people as individuals. Higgins and Pittman (2008) claimed that human motivation came from our ability to imagine the past and the future, and from our three social brain skills: awareness that another person's reaction to our own actions may influence an outcome; awareness that other people's thoughts and feelings influence their behavior; and awareness that we must share our reality with other people.

THE PHRENOLOGY PROBLEM

Regardless of the elements in a social brain theory, each theory must face the question of the "phrenology" of social brain circuits and systems. Franz Joseph Gall was an eighteenth century Viennese physician who collected more than 300 human skulls, many from people who in life had special talents, or were mentally ill. Gall believed that bumps and indentations on the brain demarcated separate brain organs of human faculties of thought and personality, and he speculated that bumps and indentations on the surface of the skull matched those of the brain (Van Whye, 2002). Gall simply assigned mental faculties to each skull bump and indentation, but he claimed his skull-localized mental traits were based on scientific observation. When Gall lectured, he called his theory *Schädellehre*, the doctrine of the skull. However, an English physician called Gall's theory "phrenology" or mind-study, and that name stuck (Van Whye, 2002).

Today the word phrenology has a pejorative meaning. It suggests that a proposed link between a specific mental operation and a unique brain circuit is oversimplified and unlikely to be true. The broadest phrenological problem for behavioral neuroscience may be the oversimplified division of brain functions into emotion, cognition, and social systems. Pessoa (2008) argued against any division of emotion and cognitive processes in the brain, asserting that "brain regions viewed as 'affective' are also involved in cognition; second, brain regions viewed as 'cognitive' are also involved in emotion; and critically, third, cognition and emotion are integrated in the brain" (p. 148). Cromwell and Panksepp (2011) argued that cognition, in fact, evolved from emotion processing, stating "our more recently evolved neural spaces for higher-order cognitive-conceptual abilities of an expansive neocortex remain profoundly anchored to more ancient affective state-control processes of the brain" (p. 2033). Niedenthal and Brauer (2012) reviewed research on emotions and concluded that emotional expressions regulate social interaction, and thus the ability to understand emotions was a crucial social behavior.

The amygdala is a specific brain region that exemplifies the difficulty in dividing brain functions into social, emotion, or cognitive. Researchers Edelson, Sharot, Dolan, and Dudai (2011) investigated social conformity to the memories of others, and reported that long-term memory change induced by the social environment involved greater activity in the amygdala, and increased connection with the hippocampus. They concluded, "the incorporation of external social information into memory may involve the amygdala's intercedence, in accordance with its special position at the crossroads of social cognition and memory" (Edelson et al., 2011, p. 111). Moreover, Pessoa and Adolphs (2010) argued against the hypothesis that two pathways that process our ongoing experiences were definable as an emotion pathway and a cognitive pathway. A standard theory claims that we have a speedy emotion-processing pathway linking the amygdala and thalamus, and a slower cognition pathway linking the thalamus and cortex. Pessoa and Adolphs (2010) found, however, that initial processing of "cognitive" visual information occurs in many simultaneous waves, and when we see something that has "emotional" significance these fast waves trigger the amygdala and other regions for more focused processing. Pessoa and Adolphs (2010) argued that the amygdala was not an emotion processor, but functioned more as a value decision center for all forms of information, selectively processing only "those inputs that are the most relevant to the goals of the animal" (Pessoa and Adolphs, 2010).

In sum, brain regions, circuits, and networks regulating human behaviors cannot be phrenologically divided into a cognition super-network, a social super-network, and an emotion super-network. Brain circuits, systems and networks are not separable into neat categories, and circuits and systems may have multiple overlapping functions. Moreover, brain regions serving social behavior include most subcortical regions and many cortical regions. For example, social processing occurs in the frontal lobes of the cortex including the prefrontal cortex, the frontal pole, the orbitofrontal cortex, and the inferior frontal cortex. Social processing occurs in the temporal lobes including superior temporal sulcus and the temporoparietal junction of the temporal lobe. Social processing also occurs in the inferior parietal cortex, the cingulate cortex, the fusiform gyrus, the hippocampus, the hypothalamus, the amygdala, the striatum, the insula, and the cerebellum.

Consequently, the term "social brain" can only be used as a shorthand label for the many distributed, specialized, and shared cognitive–emotional–social brain systems that operate to perceive, understand, and express social information. Moreover, the phrenology warning must also be applied to claims for individual links between specific social behaviors and specific brain circuits.

For example, van Eijsden, Hyder, Rothman, and Shulman (2009) claimed that although most neuroimaging researchers did not engage in a "*very localized phrenology*," many imaging researchers did make the mistake of being too flexible in defining forms of cognition, and too flexible in shaping local brain circuits that could be linked to those forms of cognition. Frith and Frith (2012) asserted, "social cognitive neuroscience needs to break away from a *restrictive phrenology* that links circumscribed brain regions to under-specified social processes" (p. 289).

However, in contrast to the concerns of Frith and Frith (2012), research-ers Wig, Schlaggar, and Petersen (2011) saw evidence accruing for an increasing number of meaningful brain circuits. They concluded that "Unlike the map of the countries of the earth, which delineates geopolitical boundaries, brain science has yet to create a robust and reliable 'brain map' that allows identification of each of the individual cortical areas, or subcor-tical parcellations. Nonetheless, neuroscientific studies of humans and other animals have provided ample evidence that the brain is composed of dis-crete and dissociable brain areas, and that these brain areas exhibit unique properties that allow them to be differentiated" (Wig et al., 2011, p. 133). Moreover, van Eijsden et al. (2009) argued that "Instead of starting with psychological conceptualizations of Mind in the hope they can be explained by brain activity" (p. 9), researchers should look for connections between observed behaviors and specific brain circuits discovered through neuro-physiological investigation.

Wig et al. (2011) argued that imaging studies have provided significant and substantial evidence for local functional specialization in the brain. Nonetheless, they cautioned that belief that the cerebral cortex was made up "of specialized areas that are dedicated to highly complex cognitive tasks or domains [e.g., thinking about others' thoughts …] [was] a relatively extreme position on localization of function" (Wig et al., 2011, p. 126). The researchers advocated a more moderate, less phrenological model wherein human behaviors arose from "orchestrated interactions between multiple distributed brain areas that each mediated functionally specialized process-ing operations" (Wig et al., 2011, p. 127).

Despite the unresolved phrenology localization problem, it is possible to report empirical evidence for brain circuits linked to specific social behav-iors. Table 3.1 illustrates some of the cortical and subcortical brain systems reported to be involved in regulating social behavior, and provides examples of research findings for social deficits and brain deficits of autism that sug-gest deficits in social brain systems in autism. The next section of this chap-ter outlines evidence for brain systems supporting social behaviors. The final section of the chapter examines the social deficits and brain deficits of autism in light of the research findings for circuits and systems of the social brain.

Table 3.1 A Modern "Phrenology" of Brain Hormones, Neurotransmitters, Circuits, and Regions Proposed as Underpinning Human Social Behaviors and Examples of Research Findings for those Brain Elements and Behaviors in Autism

Social Brain Elements	Diagrams of Brain Circuits for a Social Brain with the Left Hippocampus Darkened as a Reference Point	Examples of Brain and Behavior Deficits in Autism
Gonadal hormones		
Testosterone: Receptor sites in the amygdala, hypothalamus, hippocampus, and other regions	Amygdala, Hypothalamus, Hippocampus	Ruta, Ingudomnukul, Taylor, Chakrabarti, and Baron-Cohen, S. (2011) found that autism diagnosis strongly predicted levels of androstenedione, the immediate precursor of testosterone.
Estrogen: Receptor sites in the amygdala, hypothalamus, hippocampus, and other regions	Amygdala, Hypothalamus, Hippocampus	Sarachana, Xu, Wu, and Hu (2011) found that an autism candidate gene, retinoic acid–related orphan receptor-alpha (RORA), transcriptionally regulated aromatase, an enzyme that converts testosterone to estrogen. They reported that aromatase protein is significantly reduced in the frontal cortex of individuals with autism, and they theorized that estrogen protects females against autism by increasing the level of aromatase.

(Continued)

Table 3.1 A Modern "Phrenology" of Brain Hormones, Neurotransmitters, Circuits, and Regions Proposed as Underpinning Human Social Behaviors and Examples of Research Findings for those Brain Elements and Behaviors in Autism—*cont'd*

Social Brain Elements	Diagrams of Brain Circuits for a Social Brain with the Left Hippocampus Darkened as a Reference Point	Examples of Brain and Behavior Deficits in Autism
Nonapeptides		
Oxytocin: Moves from the hypothalamus to the amygdala, hippocampus, striatum, and brainstem regions and influences cortical neurotransmission in various regions	Hypothalamus / Amygdala / Hippocampus / Striatum / Brainstem regions	Campbell et al. (2011) found an association between two regions of the oxytocin receptor gene OXTR and autism susceptibility. They proposed their data along with evidence for abnormal levels of oxytocin in autism (Green et al. (2001) and Modahl et al. (1998)) suggested that polymorphisms, i.e., different forms of the oxytocin receptor gene, exist in a subgroup of families of individuals with autism.
Arginine vasopressin: Moves from the hypothalamus to the amygdala, hippocampus, striatum, and brainstem regions and influences cortical neurotransmission in various regions	Hypothalamus / Amygdala / Hippocampus / Striatum / Brainstem regions	Yang et al. (2010) found three significant correlations between autism and three single nucleotide polymorphisms (SNPs) in the promoter region (DNA near a gene coding region that controls the gene's expression) of the arginine vasopressin receptor gene AVPR1A in families.

Neurotransmitters

Neurotransmitter	Brain regions (diagram labels)	Findings
Dopamine: Found in the sustantia nigra, ventral tegmental area, striatum, nucleus accumbens, frontal cortex, and likely throughout the cortex	Substantia nigra; Ventral tegmental area; Striatum; Nucleus accumbens; Brainstem regions; Frontal cortex; Perhaps throughout the entire cortex	Gadow, DeVincent, Olvet, Pisarevskaya, and Hatchwell (2010) found autism associated with the 7-repeat allele of the dopamine D4 receptor gene (DRD4) that results in less efficient dopamine activity: 7-repeat DRD4 carriers were reported to have more tics, obsessions and compulsions, and more separation anxiety, as well as more severe oppositional defiant disorder behaviors.
Serotonin: Serotonin receptors are found the raphe nuclei of the brainstem, hippocampus, the anterior cingulate gyrus, and throughout the cortex	Raphe nuclei of the brainstem; Hippocampus; Anterior cingulate gyrus; Brainstem regions; Occipital lobe; Parietal lobe; Temporal lobe; Frontal lobe	Nakamura et al. (2011) found a serotonin regulatory protein syntaxin 1A (STX1A) linked to autism in a family study, and found in a study of postmortem brains that STX1A expression in the anterior cingulate gyrus region in the autism group was lower than in controls.

(*Continued*)

Table 3.1 A Modern "Phrenology" of Brain Hormones, Neurotransmitters, Circuits, and Regions Proposed as Underpinning Human Social Behaviors and Examples of Research Findings for those Brain Elements and Behaviors in Autism—cont'd

Social Brain Elements	Diagrams of Brain Circuits for a Social Brain with the Left Hippocampus Darkened as a Reference Point	Examples of Brain and Behavior Deficits in Autism
Social motivation		
Experience of reward: Throughout cortical gray matter in a variety of regions in all four lobes—occipital, parietal, temporal, and frontal—and every subcortical region.	Hypothalamus, Amygdala, Hippocampus, Striatum, Brainstem regions Occipital lobe, Parietal lobe, Temporal lobe, Frontal lobe	Kohls et al. (2011) found that children with ASD showed the same enhancement of performance from a smiling face social reward as controls, but children with autism showed a reduced P3 response, believed to reflect activity of the neural reward circuitry, which determines the reward value of experience.
Infant attachment: Involves oxytocin, arginine vasopressin, and dopamine-dependent reward pathways, the hypothalamic–pituitary–adrenal (HPA) and the hypothalamic–pituitary–gonadal (HPG) axes	See above for oxytocin, vasopressin, and dopamine pathways Hypothalamus, Pituitary	Naber et al. (2007) found that severity of autism at age 2 years was linked to less secure attachment, and disorganized attachment was more frequent in autism. They noted, however, that children with autism were capable of forming attachment relationships with their caregivers.

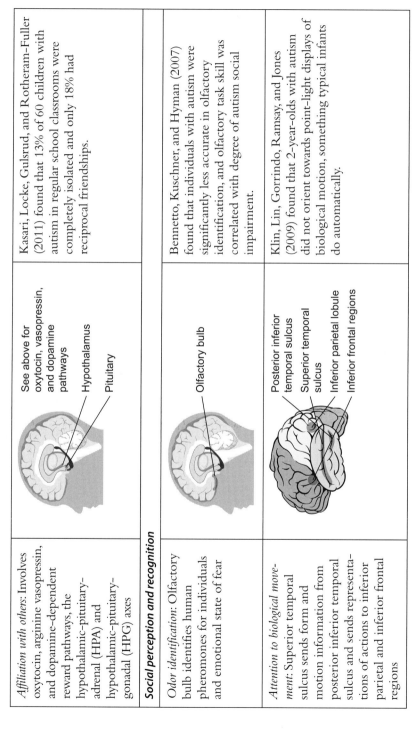

Affiliation with others: Involves oxytocin, arginine vasopressin, and dopamine-dependent reward pathways, the hypothalamic–pituitary–adrenal (HPA) and hypothalamic–pituitary–gonadal (HPG) axes	See above for oxytocin, vasopressin, and dopamine pathways Hypothalamus Pituitary	Kasari, Locke, Gulsrud, and Rotheram-Fuller (2011) found that 13% of 60 children with autism in regular school classrooms were completely isolated and only 18% had reciprocal friendships.
Social perception and recognition		
Odor identification: Olfactory bulb identifies human pheromones for individuals and emotional state of fear	Olfactory bulb	Bennetto, Kuschner, and Hyman (2007) found that individuals with autism were significantly less accurate in olfactory identification, and olfactory task skill was correlated with degree of autism social impairment.
Attention to biological movement: Superior temporal sulcus sends form and motion information from posterior inferior temporal sulcus and sends representations of actions to inferior parietal and inferior frontal regions	Posterior inferior temporal sulcus Superior temporal sulcus Inferior parietal lobule Inferior frontal regions	Klin, Lin, Gorrindo, Ramsay, and Jones (2009) found that 2-year-olds with autism did not orient towards point-light displays of biological motion, something typical infants do automatically.

(Continued)

Table 3.1 A Modern "Phrenology" of Brain Hormones, Neurotransmitters, Circuits, and Regions Proposed as Underpinning Human Social Behaviors and Examples of Research Findings for those Brain Elements and Behaviors in Autism—*cont'd*

Social Brain Elements	Diagrams of Brain Circuits for a Social Brain with the Left Hippocampus Darkened as a Reference Point	Examples of Brain and Behavior Deficits in Autism
Gaze following: Believed to depend on posterior temporal sulcus and the frontal superior gyrus	Posterior temporal sulcus · Frontal superior gyrus	Stauder, Bosch, and Nuij (2011) found that children with autism expressed typical attention shifting, but achieved gaze following with an atypical strategy.
Face recognition of others: Fusiform face area, the amygdala, the occipital face area, a region of the ventro-medial temporal cortex, and the superior temporal sulcus	Occipital face area · Amygdala · Superior temporal sulcus · Fusiform gyrus	Kleinhans et al. (2011) found that adults with autism could recognize faces, but imaging revealed that those with autism failed to engage the subcortical brain regions involved in face detection and automatic emotional face processing, suggesting a core mechanism for impaired socioemotional processing in autism.

		Kita et al. (2011) found that individuals with autism performed as well as controls on self-face recognition tasks, but imaging revealed hypoactivation of the right inferior frontal gyrus, and greater hypoactivation was correlated with more severe social impairment.
Self-recognition: The insula, the fusiform gyrus, precuneus, anterior cingulate cortex, right medial and middle frontal gyri, supramarginal gyrus, the inferior parietal lobule, the inferior temporal gyrus, and the inferior frontal gyrus	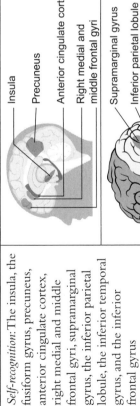 Insula — Precuneus — Anterior cingulate cortex — Right medial and middle frontal gyri — Supramarginal gyrus — Inferior parietal lobule — Inferior temporal gyrus — Inferior frontal gyrus — Fusiform gyrus	

(Continued)

Table 3.1 A Modern "Phrenology" of Brain Hormones, Neurotransmitters, Circuits, and Regions Proposed as Underpinning Human Social Behaviors and Examples of Research Findings for those Brain Elements and Behaviors in Autism—cont'd

Social Brain Elements	Diagrams of Brain Circuits for a Social Brain with the Left Hippocampus Darkened as a Reference Point	Examples of Brain and Behavior Deficits in Autism
Recognizing emotion in face expressions: Amygdala, insula, fusiform face area, occipital lobe, anterior cingulate, middle and superior frontal gyri, bilateral fronto-orbital cortex	Amygdala — Insula — Occipital lobe — Anterior cingulate — Middle and superior frontal gyri — Fronto-orbital cortex — Fusiform gyrus	Farran, Branson, and King (2011) found that individuals with autism were significantly slower but not less accurate than controls in recognizing fear, anger, and sad target expressions.
Recognizing emotion in a voice: Superior temporal sulcus adjacent to the left and right primary auditory cortices	Superior temporal sulcus	Brennand, Schepman, and Rodway (2011) found no deficit for children with autism in identification of four basic emotions—anger, fear, happiness, sadness—in the voice.

Expression of emotions

Face expression of emotions: Amygdala and the associative cortex were both activated for all emotions	 Amygdala Associative cortex	Oberman, Winkielman, and Ramachandran (2009) found that children with autism could recognize and voluntarily imitate happy, sad, fear, anger, disgust, and neutral face expressions; however, their spontaneous, but not voluntary, mimicry activity was delayed by 160 milliseconds.
Voice expression of emotions: Anterior cingulate gyrus to the right inferior frontal gyrus	 Anterior cingulate gyrus Right inferior frontal gyrus	Peppé, Cleland, Gibbon, O'Hare, and Martinez Castilla (2011) found that high-functioning individuals with autism were impaired in their ability to imitate emotional prosody.

(Continued)

Table 3.1 A Modern "Phrenology" of Brain Hormones, Neurotransmitters, Circuits, and Regions Proposed as Underpinning Human Social Behaviors and Examples of Research Findings for those Brain Elements and Behaviors in Autism—cont'd

Social Brain Elements	Diagrams of Brain Circuits for a Social Brain with the Left Hippocampus Darkened as a Reference Point	Examples of Brain and Behavior Deficits in Autism
Language production		
Language production: Vocal circuit involves the lower brainstem and spinal cord, as well as the pons; voluntary language production involves left hemisphere inferior frontal gyrus, commonly called Broca's area, and the laryngeal motor cortex	Lower brainstem / Pons / Spinal cord / Inferior frontal gyrus, a.k.a. Broca's area / Laryngeal motor cortex	Kjellmer, Hedvall, Fernell, Gillberg and Norrelgen (2012) found a general language delay and great variability in the development of receptive and expressive language, and non-verbal communicative skills in 129 preschool children with autism. Cognitive skill and age explained half or more of the variance, while severity of autism symptoms explained only a few percent of the variance.
Language comprehension		
Language comprehension: Involves left hemisphere posterior middle temporal gyrus, anterior superior temporal gyrus, posterior superior temporal sulcus, orbital part of inferior frontal gyrus, and middle frontal gyrus	Posterior middle temporal gyrus / Anterior superior temporal gyrus / Posterior superior temporal sulcus / Orbital part of the inferior frontal gyrus, and the middle frontal gyrus	Kjellmer, Hedvall, Fernell, Gillberg, and Norrelgen (2012) found a general language delay and great variability in the development of receptive and expressive language, and non-verbal communicative skills in 129 preschool children with autism. Cognitive skill and age explained half or more of the variance, while severity of autism symptoms explained only a few percent of the variance.

Social cognitive behaviors

Behavior	Regions	Findings
Empathy: Involves dorso-medial prefrontal cortex, medial prefrontal cortex, and precuneus	Precuneus / Dorsomedial prefrontal cortex / Medial prefrontal cortex	Schulte-Rüther et al. (2011) found a distinctly different pattern of empathy-linked ventro-medial prefrontal cortex activity in individuals with autism compared with controls, and the pattern found for autism was associated with reduced behavioral emotional response.
Non-conscious understanding of the behavior of others: Mirror neuron system links inferior parietal lobule, inferior frontal gyrus, perhaps supplementary motor area and possibly other regions as well	Inferior parietal lobule / Inferior frontal gyrus / Supplementary motor area	Enticott et al. (2011) found when observing a human hand grasping a mug, individuals with autism compared with typical individuals showed reduced motor corticospinal excitability, thought to measure mirror neuron system activity in the premotor cortex, specifically the inferior frontal gyrus.
Theory of Mind: Region of the right temporoparietal junction responds selectively to information describing the mental states of other people	Right temporoparietal junction / Likely additional areas	Lam and Yeung (2011) found a 50% failure rate for children with autism on a Theory of Mind test, compared with a 17% failure rate for controls.
Mentalizing: Region of the right temporoparietal junction responds selectively to information describing the mental states of other people	Right temporoparietal junction / Likely additional areas	Lombardo, Chakrabarti, Bullmore, MRC AIMS Consortium, and Baron-Cohen (2011) found that in adults with autism there was atypical unenhanced activation in the right temporoparietal junction—believed to be the basis for mentalizing, or imagining the thoughts of others. The researchers also reported that activity of the right temporoparietal junction was associated with the degree of reciprocal social impairment in autism.

WHAT BRAIN CIRCUITS SUPPORT SOCIAL BEHAVIORS?

Insel (2010) divided social brain systems into three categories: receiving social information; expressing social information; and the more complex higher-order processing of social information to generate social behaviors. Insel asserted that reception of social information depends on specific neurotransmitters and their receptors and cortical regions dedicated for processing social information, whether that information comes from smelling molecules given off by others, or hearing the voices of others, or seeing others and their expressions of emotion (2010, p. 768).

Employing a metaphor from astrophysics, Insel claimed that between social perception, and social expression, lies social cognition "the great dark matter of social neuroscience" (2010, p. 768). For Insel, the "dark unknown matter" is the brain's neurons, receptors, neurotransmitters, circuits, systems, and networks that link social perception to social action (2010). He asked, "What happens between the stage when a percept is encoded as 'social' to the stage when a 'go' signal is given for initiating social behavior .... What are the neural mechanisms that facilitate or inhibit social interaction?" (Insel, 2010, p. 768).

Although brain circuits for social behavior are not neatly marked as perception, cognition, and expression, Insel's three-part division (2010) offers a means to organize an outline of known brain mechanisms for social behavior. Consequently, the following three subsections discuss brain mechanisms of social recognition, mechanisms of social expression of emotion and language, and the "dark matter" of social cognition.

Brain Circuits for Recognizing Other People, for Self-Recognition, and for Identifying Emotions

A crucial social perception is to perceive others and recognize them as specific individuals. We attend to biological motion, and we attend to the eye gaze of others. We recognize other individuals through their smell, their voices, their faces, and by their general appearance. We recognize ourselves as well. In addition, we recognize emotions expressed in body odor, voices, facial expressions, gestures, and body postures by other people, and we also identify our own emotions.

Attention to Biological Motion

Thompson and Parasuraman (2012) defined biological motion as "The movements of living organisms such as people or animals—both whole-body motion as well as partial movements by hands, head, eye" (p. 4). The researchers outlined the brain basis for attention to biological motion: at some time after 200 milliseconds, the superior temporal sulcus (STS) and anterior inferior parietal sulcus are processing the biological shape and the movement, and slightly later, the inferior frontal gyrus is engaged in processing biological motion. Thompson and Parasuraman (2012) noted that infants only 2 days old prefer to look at abstracted light displays of biological motion rather than any other moving objects, and the same is also true for newborn chicks hatched in complete darkness. They asserted that basic attention to biological motion was innate and automatic, but the function of the dedicated brain circuits for processing biological motion could be influenced by selective attention. They concluded that "Coding the actions of other people is a key function of the STS, as it appears to integrate form and motion signals coming from regions in pITS (posterior inferior temporal sulcus) and then send representations of actions to inferior parietal and inferior frontal regions. It is through the interaction of these regions that the viewer is able to understand and interpret the intentions of others" (Thompson & Parasuraman, 2012, p. 11).

Following the Gaze of Others

Laube, Kamphuis, Dicke, and Their (2011) reported that we pay most attention to other people's eyes, and when we see someone shift their gaze, automatically our eye-gaze shifts to the thing, person, or place that the person is looking at. Laube et al. (2011) posited eye-gaze following is an innate process and is a key component of social cognition. They reported that eye-gaze direction activated the posterior temporal sulcus and the frontal superior gyrus. The researchers also reported that eye-gaze following was associated with a deactivation in the left anterior superior temporal sulcus and the left and right middle superior temporal sulcus. Bayliss, Bartlett, Naughtin, and Kritikos (2011) posited that our ability to see in what direction others are looking depends on the shifting activity of neurons that code information of eyes looking to the left, to the right, and straight ahead. These neurons are thought to be in the anterior superior temporal sulcus and in the inferior parietal lobule.

Specialized Social Odor Recognition

All mammals have many genes for odor recognition. Humans can perceive human body odor molecules. Human body odor includes approximately 120 odor compounds (Blum, 2011). Our ability to use chemical signals to recognize human pheromones is separate from our ability to identify odors coming from food, animals, plants, chemicals, and other sources. The human immune system is linked to specific olfactory receptor genes that allow mothers and their infants to non-consciously recognize each other, allow relatives to recognize one another, and allow us to identify better immune system mates (Hoover, 2010). Women who have had the steroid androstadienone brushed on their upper lip find men more attractive, and androstadienone also increases general attention to the emotional expressions of others (Hummer & McClintock, 2009).

Specialized Social Voice Recognition

Recognizing the unique voice of a specific person depends on activity in two voice-sensitive regions of the temporal lobe along with activity of neurons in the face-sensitive left amygdala (Andics et al., 2010). These regions are separate from the primary auditory cortex that recognizes sounds in general. Interestingly, human voice recognition is different from voice recognition in all other animals. Unlike the brains of other animals, our brains must compute the difference between the sound pattern of another person's voice and the pattern of sounds in a particular language in order to recognize a specific individual voice (Perrachione, Del Tufo, & Gabrieli, 2011). Perrachione et al. (2011) reported that when we do not know the language that a person is speaking, or if we are impaired in our native language, our ability to recognize a specific individual's voice is significantly impaired.

Specialized Face Recognition

Face recognition is one of the most important social perception skills. Brain regions dedicated to human face processing include the amygdala, fusiform face area, the occipital face area, a region of the ventromedial temporal cortex, and the superior temporal sulcus. These brain regions allow us to identify and store patterns for thousands of individual faces. Human face perception depends on identifying specific features, such as the eyes, nose, and mouth, and on perceiving the specific spatial arrangement of those features.

Kanwisher (2010) reported that the face-processing area was one of five areas of the human cortex that appear to be solely dedicated to specific forms of recognition. The fusiform face area on the bottom surface of the cerebral cortex just above the cerebellum responds selectively to specific faces. The extrastriate body area on the lateral surface of the brain next to the visual motion area responds selectively to bodies and body parts of specific individuals. An area of the temporoparietal junction responds selectively to information describing the mental states of other people. A tiny area of the ventral occipitotemporal cortex responds to visually presented words. The parahippocampal place area, a part of the parahippocampal complex, responds selectively to familiar and unfamiliar places and mainly to the spatial layout of a place.

Researchers Zhu, Zhang, Luo, Dilks, and Liu (2011) reported that activity of the occipital face area and fusiform face area determined the overall holistic processing of faces. Activity in these two brain regions was also correlated with skill in recognizing familiar faces and in identifying unfamiliar faces as unfamiliar. Activity in the occipital face area and fusiform face area, however, was not correlated with skill in identifying objects. The researchers argued that their findings indicated that the face recognition circuit was separate from the circuits for recognizing objects, for recognizing global forms and global motions, and separate from global scene processing. Zhu and colleagues (2011) also argued that synchronized spontaneous neural activity between the occipital and fusiform face areas indicated that the entire circuit was crucial for face recognition.

Rutishauser et al. (2011) recorded activity from more than 200 single amygdala neurons in seven neurosurgical patients with implanted depth electrodes. They reported half of these amygdala neurons responded to faces or parts of faces, and 20% of the 200 neurons responded only to the image of a whole face. They noted that these neurons showed sensitivity to the deletion of even small components of the face. Rutishauser et al. (2011) concluded that the face neurons in the amygdala code the identity of a person based on the entire face.

Face and Voice Recognition are Linked

Blank, Anwander, and von Kriegstein (2011) found direct circuits connecting voice-sensitive areas of the superior temporal sulcus, and the fusiform face area. Blank et al. (2011) argued that their findings indicated that recognizing another person could take place at a very early stage of perceptual processing. They also argued that this exchange of information improves recognition of a person's characteristics in noisy or ambiguous contexts.

Self-Recognition

Pannese and Hirsch (2011) asserted that researchers had not been able to come to an agreement on which brain circuits determine the recognition of one's own face. However, they reported finding a self-specific processing region in the posterior parietal lobe. The researchers noted that this region of parietal cortex was a component of the default network. The default network activates when your mind is not actively focused, and you are not disturbed by anyone else or anything in the environment around you. This is the activation state the brain "defaults to" when not engaged in a focused process such as learning to drive, or taking a math test, or participating in a conversation.

Andrews-Hanna, Reidler, Sepulcre, Poulin, and Buckner (2010) argued that the default network has two subcomponents. The researchers proposed that one subcomponent of the default network was in the medial temporal lobe, and its function was to activate episodic memory when individuals made decisions about their future. Episodic memory is the memory of events in your life: episodic memories have specific times or dates, specific people, emotions, places, and actions. Andrews-Hanna et al. (2010) suggested that constructing a scene in an imagined future was a key element in this subcomponent of default state, and they claimed that prediction accuracy was a possible benefit of this default network subcomponent. The researchers identified the second subcomponent of the default network as a region within the dorsal medial prefrontal cortex. They proposed that this subsystem supported the ability to consider our own current mental and emotional state, and supported the ability to infer or imagine the mental states of other people. The researchers argued, "The possible neural overlap among affective, self-referential, and social cognitive processes suggests a broader role for this subsystem in either metacognition, mental state inference, social cognition, or the use of one's own mental states as a model for inferring the mental states of others" (Andrews-Hanna et al., 2010, p. 558). The researchers argued that the posterior parietal cortex contributes to the default network and self-processing concerning one's own sense of personal significance, introspection about one's own mental states, and evoked emotion.

Qin and Northoff (2011) conducted a meta-analytic examination of research on self-awareness and the default mode network. Many researchers have argued that the brain regions involved in self-awareness are not dedicated only to processing information about the self, but process many different sorts of information. Nonetheless, Qin and Northoff (2011) reported that a section of the anterior cingulate cortex was solely involved in self-processing.

Uddin (2011) pointed out that when a person has undergone surgery that splits the two halves of the cerebral cortex, both the left and right cortical hemispheres can each separately recognize the person's own face. Uddin (2011) concluded, "Split-brain patients continue to challenge the notion of a unified self … and suggest instead that different aspects of the multifaceted entity we call the self are subserved by distributed neural systems" (p. 97).

Devue and Brédart (2011) reported that many areas appear to contribute to self-recognition, including the inferior frontal gyrus, the right medial and middle frontal gyri, the inferior parietal lobule, the supramarginal gyrus and the precuneus, the anterior cingulate cortex, the bilateral insula, the fusiform gyrus, and the bilateral inferior temporal gyrus. The researchers posited that these varied regions were unlikely to be dedicated solely for recognition of one's own face, but probably also regulated subjective evaluations, memories, and emotions triggered by the vision of the face. Devue and Brédart (2011) claimed that the brain network for recognizing our own face differed from the network for recognizing others because processing goals are different in each case. They noted, "The aim of processing another person's face is typically to identify that person or to interpret her emotional expressions whereas the goal of processing our own face is normally not identification but an inspection of facial features, for instance when grooming" (Devue & Brédart, 2011, p. 48).

Reward and Self-Recognition

Enzi, de Greck, Prösch, Tempelmann, and Northoff (2009) reported evidence for an overlap in processing information about reward and the self. They found that regions in the anterior cingulate cortex, caudate, putamen, and two regions of the prefrontal cortex were activated during reward and personal relevance processing. Enzi et al. (2009) noted that these areas were part of a valuing circuit that codes the value of an experience for its immediate and long-term relevance for the individual. Vickery, Chun, and Lee (2011) found that reward and punishment signals were widely distributed throughout the cortex and subcortical regions. Enzi et al. (2009) theorized that sense of self might be a highly distributed processing assessment of what is rewarding for the individual. Northoff and Hayes (2011) hypothesized that various aspects of the self were differentially governed across a range of reward levels. They suggested, "self-specific processing could be considered the ground upon which the assignment of value to external stimuli becomes possible" (Northoff & Hayes, 2011, p. 1022). Given the findings of Vickery et al. (2011), this valuing process for the self may include reward and non-reward signals.

Recognition of Emotion in Pheromones

Humans recognize emotions in others through odor, voice tones, and facial expressions. Humans can smell molecules expressed by others when they are afraid (Hoover, 2010), and male hormone odor increases interest in the facial expression of emotion (Hummer & McClintock, 2009).

Recognition of Emotion in the Voice

Ethofer et al. (2012) reported that regions in the left and right temporal lobes in the superior temporal sulcus adjacent to the left and right primary auditory cortices had differentially stronger responses to voices expressing anger, sadness, joy, and relief compared to voices with neutral emotion. The researchers called these parallel regions "emotional voice areas." Ethofer and colleagues (2012) reported increased simultaneous activity in the emotional voice areas with increased activity in the inferior frontal gyrus, and they argued that the inferior frontal gyrus was also crucial for recognizing emotions in voices.

Recognition of Emotions Expressed by the Face

Research suggests that the facial expressions accompanying anger, disgust, fear, happiness, sadness, and surprise are human universals, and the amygdala is central to emotion recognition. Varying patterns of brain activity occur when we see different emotions expressed in others (Jehna et al., 2011; Leppänen & Nelson, 2009; Said, Haxby, & Todorov, 2011). Recognizing anger is linked to activation of the lateral orbitofrontal cortex. Recognizing a look of disgust is tied to differential activity in the insula and globus pallidus. When we see an expression of fear on another's face, there is differential activity in our amygdala and the lateral orbitofrontal cortex. Seeing a neutral expression on another's face triggers activity in the inferior occipital gyrus, the lateral fusiform gyrus, and the superior temporal sulcus. Recognition of sadness is differentiable from recognition of anger, and recognition of smiling, happy faces elicits activity in several areas of the anterior orbitofrontal cortex.

Mechanisms for the Expression of Emotions and Use of Language

The most important communicative social behaviors we generate are our facial expression of emotions, our vocal expression of emotions, our expression of empathy, and our use of language in social interaction. The following sections review the evidence for the brain circuits for feeling and showing emotion in facial expressions, and for language production including expressing emotions in tone of voice.

Brain Mechanisms for the Experience and Expression of Emotion

Panksepp (2006) argued that our core emotions are anger, fear, sexual lust, maternal care, separation distress, social bonding, playfulness, and a seeking emotion. Panksepp (2006) further argued that each of these core emotions was regulated by its own brain circuit of different neuropeptide and non-neuropeptide receptors in different brain tissues. Tettamanti et al. (2012) stated, "each individual emotion recruits a set of interacting subcortical and cortical regions that form specialized, distributed neural pathways. However, it is not completely understood whether the involved neural circuits consistently reflect the salient features of the different kind of emotions" (pp. 1–2).

Tettamanti and colleagues (2012) measured the brain activity of individuals experiencing fear, disgust, sadness, and happiness. They reported that the amygdala and the associative cortex were both activated for all four emotions. However, different patterns of brain activity were also found for each emotion except sadness. Fear uniquely activated the frontoparietal brain system for planning motor behavior. Disgust uniquely activated the somatosensory system responsive in physical disgust. Happiness uniquely activated medial prefrontal and temporoparietal cortices previously found to be involved in understanding joyful interactions.

Lench, Flores, and Bench (2011) conducted a meta-analysis of emotion elicitation studies and also reported support for the discrete neural bases for different emotions. They noted that although the amygdala is a central control for our responses to both positive and negative experiences, there are likely to be differentiated neuropeptide receptors for the expression of different emotions; however, these proposed receptor patterns are as yet unknown.

Experience and Expression of Empathy

Masten, Morelli, and Eisenberger (2011) noted that empathy is a significant element in human social behavior. Through empathy we develop awareness of the feelings of others. Empathy also is an important factor in generating behavior to help others: people who feel empathy are more likely to care for the welfare of others and are more likely to help others. Masten et al. (2011) reported that empathy for the pain of another person's social exclusion activated the dorsomedial prefrontal cortex, medial prefrontal cortex, and precuneus. The researchers found that only the most empathic individuals activated the insula and dorsal anterior cingulate cortex.

Brain Mechanisms for Language Production and Comprehension

We have two pathways for speech production. The evolutionarily older sub-cortical pathway controls innate non-verbal and emotional vocalizations, such as a baby's cry, or spontaneous cries of pain or grief. This innate pathway includes the sensory and motor nuclei of the lower brainstem and spinal cord, as well as the pons.

The "newer" larynx motor cortical pathway controls voluntary voice production and the voluntary production of innate vocalizations as well. Voluntary language production depends on a brainstem region, the peri-aquaductal gray, to trigger a vocal response, and the anterior cingulate gyrus for voice initiation. The left hemisphere inferior frontal gyrus, commonly called Broca's area, and the laryngeal motor cortex together control the form of speech production. Production and processing of language are linked, and processing depends on regions of the temporal lobe. Stevenson, VanDerKlok, Pisoni, and James (2011) found two regions of the superior temporal cortex for language processing, one that aligns auditory and visual input, and another subregion that fuses separate perceptions into one coherent sense of perceived speech. Flinker, Chang, Barbaro, Berger, and Knight (2011) tested four people during open brain surgery, sampling neurons from the superior temporal gyrus, and reported that different sets of neurons responded differently. Some neuron groups responded to whole words only, and other adjacent groups of neurons responded to both speech sounds and whole words. Flinker et al. (2011) argued that either the neurons in the two neighboring populations have different sound response "knowledge" or one population simply has more neurons that respond to sounds that are more complex.

The voluntary language production pathway depends on the anterior cingulate gyrus for emotional prosody. Emotional prosody is the intonation of speech carrying emotional information through rhythm, rate, pitch, and voice quality. The prosody circuit links the anterior cingulate gyrus to the inferior frontal gyrus—with emotional prosody more strongly activating the right hemisphere inferior frontal gyrus, and linguistic prosody, the into-nation pattern of a particular language, more strongly activating the left hemisphere inferior frontal gyrus. Aziz-Zadeh, Sheng, and Gheytanchi (2010) found that the left inferior frontal gyrus and the left dorsal premotor cortex were active for both the expression and perception of emotional and linguistic prosody. This finding suggests that these regions may be "mirror" regions for prosody, wherein these regions imitate the prosody of a speaker we are listening to, even if we do not speak or produce that person's prosody pattern.

Glenberg and Gallese (2012) argued that speech perception and production overlap in Broca's area—the inferior frontal gyrus—and Broca's area contributes to both speech production and hand gestures. The researchers noted that this overlap of functions was evidence for mirror neurons in Broca's area. Hickok, Houde, and Rong (2011) theorized that speech production and speech perception areas overlap in brain language areas "to support speech production, that is, the capacity to learn how to articulate the sounds of one's language, keep motor control processes tuned, and support online error detection and correction" (p. 418).

Pulvermüller and Fadiga (2010) also argued for an extensive overlap of perception and motor processing of language wherein action and perception mechanisms are bound together in distributed cell assemblies that include mirror neurons. They proposed that language comprehension depends on a wide range of brain regions including middle and inferior temporal cortex, where auditory language areas and visual processing join together. They noted that words for odors activate olfactory bulb regions, and action verbs activate motor and premotor areas representing the specific types of action of the verb.

Noordzij et al. (2009) reported that a single cerebral cortex region, the posterior superior temporal sulcus, recognizes communicative intentions and plans communicative actions. This brain region has been shown to process gaze and eye–hand movements. Noordzij et al. (2009) argued that this system not only is separate from the brain bases for language, but evolved before human language evolved. The researchers proposed that this system determines "our ability to communicate without any pre-existing conventions at all, as in the gestures one might use behind the boss' back, or to signal to others out of earshot" (Noordzij et al., 2009, p. 1). Noordzij and colleagues (2009) argued that this brain system predicts the intentions of the other person in an interaction, given the immediately preceding message. The researchers suggested that this prediction of intention in a forthcoming communication was developed based on one's previous experience with the behavior of that person.

Summary: Social Perception and Social Expression

This brief and selective review of the brain circuits found in association with perception and expression of social behaviors reveals three general aspects of the brain bases for social behavior. First, many brain circuits for perception and production overlap. Therefore, perception and expression often function together, and thus, the "input" of social perception, and "output" of social expression of Insel's three-part division (2010) appear to be functionally melded together. Emotion processing and emotion expression areas overlap. Speech production and speech perception areas overlap. There is an overlap in the activity of the left inferior frontal gyrus and the left dorsal premotor cortex for control of the recognition and expression of emotional prosody. There is an overlap in the activity whereby the posterior superior temporal sulcus recognizes communicative intentions and plans communicative actions. The overlapping brain activity for self-recognition is complex: evidence suggests that brain systems for emotion expression and recognition, episodic memories, and cognitive processes all may be activated in self-recognition. The findings for overlapping perception and production suggest that production skill for many social behaviors may rely on specific perception information to help us understand the behavior of others, and help us to pattern the motor expression of our own behaviors.

A second general finding is that many behaviors appear to have dedicated brain circuits. Humans have special receptors to identify odors of specific other individuals, and to identify the smell of fear, and the smell of specific immune system characteristics. We have special brain circuits for the recognition of other people's faces, and for our own face. We have special brain circuits for the recognition and production of emotional voice expression, and we have distinct circuits for experience and expression of individual emotions, including fear, anger, disgust, and happiness. Each emotion has evolved as "an evolutionarily adaptive response that organizes cognitive, experiential, behavioral, and physiological reactions to changes in the environment" (Lench et al., 2011, p. 834). We have special circuits that evolved for the production and perception of language, and may have a special circuit in the temporal lobe that evolved prior to the evolution of language that allows us to recognize communicative intention and to plan communicative actions.

This evidence for so many different specialized brain circuits suggests that social behavior has been so important in human evolution that brain circuits, systems, and networks have evolved to process and produce social behavior. O'Connell and Hofmann (2011) outlined a model for examining cross-species evolution of social behavior. They proposed that social behaviors evolve from an animal's varying forms of approach or avoidance behaviors in response to opportunities, such as for food or mating, and response to challenges, such as for territory. If an animal's social behaviors have survival value, the genes or other genetic factors for the brain basis of the adaptive social behavior will become more prevalent in the population. The genetic adaptation may be in the neurochemicals, or in neural circuits for forms of neural plasticity, or in neural circuit function, or in neural circuit connectivity, or hormonal regulation of behavior, or sensory integration, or motor control, or in gene–environment interactions.

A third general conclusion that emerges from the findings for brain circuits for social behavior is the "over-built" redundant systems for recognition and expression of social information. For example, if you observe another person who is experiencing fear, you can identify the fear in the person's body odor, and you can hear fear in the person's voice. You can also see fear in their facial expressions, and, given that the brain's emotion processing and emotion expression areas overlap, your own brain may begin to activate your emotional expression of fear, which you will recognize and experience. And, of course, the fearful person may speak to you, and tell you they are afraid. No engineer would over-build a recognition system in this way.

MECHANISMS OF THE "DARK MATTER" OF HUMAN SOCIAL COGNITION

In Insel's (2010) heuristic, between social perception and social expression are the mechanisms of social cognition. As noted in the introduction of this chapter, there are many theories of what mechanisms are most crucial for human social cognition. Only five theories are outlined here. These five were selected because each is representative of a distinct vision of the social brain, and each is associated with active lines of research.

Five Theories of Social Cognition
Insel's (2010) Gonadal Steroid and Nonapeptide Model
Insel (2010) argued that higher order social cognition rested on one simple innate social decision: should I "tend and befriend" the other person or should I avoid or attack that person? Insel noted that nearly all social expression was regulated by estrogen and androgens, the gonadal steroids. He stated that research exploring gonadal steroid receptor expression in the brain led to the discovery of brain regions regulating expressive social behaviors. He reported that because research had found that steroid receptors regulate genes, those regulated genes could now be discovered, leading to the beginning of a molecular model of social behavior. Steroid receptors are proteins inside cells that react to steroid hormones and other molecules. Steroid receptor proteins work with other proteins to regulate gene expression, contributing to the development of the individual and to the

operation and stability of the individual's metabolism. Insel listed a variety of expressive social behaviors that are known to be regulated by gonadal steroids: sexual behavior, parental care, affiliation, social play, communication, aggression, and predation.

There is evidence for the role of gonadal steroids in social behavior. For example, van Wingen, Ossewaarde, Bäckström, Hermans, and Fernández (2011) noted that gonadal hormones influence the development of brain regions involved in processing emotions. They reported that men have relatively larger amygdala volumes than women, and that the prefrontal cortex also showed sex differences in organization. Researchers van Wingen et al. (2011) also reported that the hormone progesterone increases amygdala coupling with the medial prefrontal cortex, while testosterone decreases amygdala coupling with the orbitofrontal cortex. They theorized that increased coupling of the amygdala with the medial prefrontal cortex would trigger more elaborated appraisal of emotions, whereas reduced coupling of the amygdala with the orbital frontal cortex would diminish the ability to inhibit behavior, thus promoting impulsivity.

Insel (2010) also argued that neuropeptides and their receptors are a crucial basis for social information processing. Mammals produce and use more than 100 neuropeptides, but the two most important for human social behavior are oxytocin and vasopressin. Both these neuropeptides support the very important and very intense "tending and befriending" affiliation of pair bonding. Oxytocin functions in a woman's labor, delivery, in breastfeeding her child, and her bonding to her infant. Arginine vasopressin functions in male bonding to his sexual partner. Insel noted there are no real differences in location of oxytocin and vasopressin receptors in males' and females' brains, yet pair bonding depends on vasopressin in males and oxytocin in females. Insel theorized that these two neuropeptides link social and sex-related information to the brain's pathways for reward. He also theorized that the two neuropeptides might influence other aspects of social cognition.

There is much empirical support for the role of oxytocin and vasopressin in social behaviors. Goodson and Thompson (2010) noted that nonapeptides, including the mammalian forms of vasopressin and oxytocin, have been present in similar neural pathways for 450 million years from the evolution of fish to humans. In fish, birds, and mammals, receptors for forms of oxytocin have determined sensorimotor processes, social recognition, affiliation, bonding, parental care, appetite, sexual behavior, the regulation of smooth muscle contractions, oviposition in non-mammals, milk ejection in mammals, delivery, appetite, and energy metabolism. Receptors for forms of vasopressin in different regions of the brain have regulated the modulation of sensorimotor processes, social communication, aggression, affiliation, bonding, parental care, pair bonding, social recognition, modulation of social recognition, anxiety, and circadian rhythms. Although the nonapeptides have similar functions across species, the receptor patterns of forms of oxytocin and vasopressin vary widely across species. The differences in receptors may mark the differences in social behaviors across species.

Lee, Macbeth, Pagani, and Young (2009) reviewed the functions of oxytocin. They noted that oxytocin has a role in sexual behavior, birth process, breast feeding, maternal behaviors, attachment, bonding, trust, anxiety, feeding, aggression, pain perception, and social memory. Lee et al. concluded that oxytocin receptors evolved to support species propagation. Meyer-Lindenberg, Domes, Kirsch, and Heinrichs (2011) reviewed the functions of oxytocin and vasopressin. They outlined a model of social behavior control by the two nonapeptides. They posited that both positive and negative social experiences trigger oxytocin release. Positive social interaction and social touch trigger oxytocin release; however, social anxiety also triggers oxytocin release. Initially, social anxiety stimulates the amygdala–cingulate circuit and the hypothalamus–pituitary–adrenal (HPA) axis. Meyer-Lindenberg et al. (2011) stated that arginine vasopressin enhances this function. Social anxiety then promotes social affiliation for the reduction of that anxiety. In sum, oxytocin reduces amygdala and HPA axis reactivity to social stressors. The use of oxytocin as a treatment for psychiatric disorders continues to be studied. For example, Pedersen et al. (2011) reported that 2 weeks of twice-daily intranasal sprays of oxytocin significantly reduced schizophrenia symptoms, and significantly enhanced social cognition in 11 individuals diagnosed with schizophrenia.

Gordon, Martin, Feldman, and Leckman's (2011) Oxytocin and Dopamine Social Motivation Theory

Gordon et al. (2011) proposed that social motivation builds from a base of oxytocin and dopamine in the experience of infant–mother attachment to a more general desire to be with other people. Gordon et al. (2011) argued the dopamine system for reward interacts with oxytocin to generate our motivation to be with other people. They proposed that evidence supports the role of dopamine in linking sensory cues from the individual person to the reward system to create and maintain selective social bonds.

The neurotransmitter dopamine has many distinct receptors and serves many functions in the brain. Northoff and Hayes (2011) outlined dopamine's heterogeneous functions: pleasure, wanting, reward importance or salience, seeking, instrumental learning, conditioning, prediction, and behavioral activation. The researchers argued that dopamine contributes to a reassignment of cognitive resources in relation to the self. Because everything that affects us is highly important to us consciously and non-consciously, dopamine activity may help recruit "more self-related sensory, affective, and cognitive resources compared with nonself-related ones" (Northoff & Hayes, 2011, p. 1023). If dopamine reward is linked to the self, the self may be everywhere in the brain. Vickery et al. (2011) reported finding reward signals from every part of the brain. In fact, the researchers found widespread representations of both reward and punishment that overlapped in many areas of the brain, and concluded that "the distribution of punishment signals might in fact largely be similar to that of reinforcement signals" (p. 174).

Researchers Gordon et al. (2011) noted that the prefrontal cortex and the nucleus accumbens in the ventral striatum receive input from both oxytocin and dopamine neurons and may regulate social attachment behaviors. The ventral striatum is thought to connect emotion signals from the amygdala, with place information from the hippocampus and with planning information from the prefrontal cortex, and link all these signals to dopamine levels that signal level of reward for a particular experience. The model proposed by Gordon and colleagues (2011) posited that oxytocin interacts at multiple levels with the dopaminergic reward pathway and the hormone-producing systems—the hypothalamic–pituitary–adrenal system and the hypothalamic–pituitary–gonadal system—as well as the system for arousal and threat detection. Threat detection is an innate system that includes the ventromedial prefrontal cortex and the periaquaductal gray tissue of the midbrain (Mobbs et al., 2007). Threat detection varies depending on how imminent danger seems to be. When threat is close, the periaquaductal gray may inhibit complex cognitive control to permit a faster, more automatic action to threat (Mobbs et al., 2007).

Gordon and colleagues (2011) noted that oxytocin functions evolved to regulate bonding and parenting behaviors, mate affiliation and mate pair bonding, social recognition, sexual incentive and copulatory behaviors, and aggression. They argued that although the oxytocin system is innate, it is responsive to early environment effects.

In contrast to the model of Gordon et al. (2011), Higgins and Pittman (2008) proposed that human social motivation results from our ability to imagine the past and the future, and from three additional social skills. These three are the awareness that another person's reaction to our own behavior may influence an outcome, the awareness that other people have different thoughts and feelings, and the awareness that we must negotiate a shared reality with others. Higgins and Pittman (2008) argued that "the predominant approach to studying human motivation was as follows: discover the motivational consequences of humans being animals" (p. 363). They argued that the notion that humans have "the mind of a god and the motives of a brute ... is wrong and damaging ... [because] there was development—a fundamental growth that resulted in human motives that are distinct from and advanced compared with other animals" (Higgins & Pittman, 2008, pp. 363–364).

Panksepp's Primacy of Emotions Theory (Panksepp, 2006; Cromwell & Panksepp, 2011)

Panksepp proposed that the evolutionary basis for the social brain is the brain circuits for emotions, which direct social behavior. Panksepp argued that emotions are the core drivers for all social cognition. Panksepp (2006) claimed that there are highly overlapping emotional networks for sexual behavior, separation–distress, maternal care, and physical playfulness. Panksepp (2006) theorized, "basic social feelings emerge from those brain dynamics ... [and] a clear taxonomy of the basic emotions may be essential for making scientific sense of the many higher-level social derived emotions as well as for the complex patterns of emotional turmoil that commonly characterizes psychiatric syndromes" (p. 776).

Bos, Panksepp, Bluth, and van Honk (2012) proposed a model with the same elements outlined by Insel (2010) in which gonadal steroids and neuropeptides regulate brain connectivity. In their model, testosterone acts on vasopressin and on oxytocin in concert with estrogen to regulate brain connectivity of the amygdala, which will shift brain connectivity either to the brainstem or to prefrontal regions, depending on hormone and neuropeptide inputs. Bos et al. (2012) noted that steroid hormone and neuropeptide activity change during social interactions. They theorized that in social interaction, increased testosterone acts on vasopressin, increasing the motivation to engage in rewarding activities, and leading to more fairness, but reduced empathy. Bos et al. (2012) also proposed that increasing oxytocin in social interaction "promotes a greater directed focus on the social environment and perhaps less on the subjective influences of individual self-serving motives, as it increases ... trust, partner bonding, cognitive and affective empathy, and … increased in-group favoritism, as well as jealousy and gloating in an environment in which competition is emphasized" (p. 14). Bos and colleagues (2012) further argued that testosterone and oxytocin have opposite effects on specific social cognitive skills. They posited that oxytocin enhances the identification of emotions, and also enhances the ability to imagine the thoughts of others, while testosterone inhibits these abilities, and leads to an increase in self-serving behaviors. Surprisingly, Bos et al. (2012) offered no model of the specific mechanisms that would link gonadal steroids and neuropeptides to the emotion endophenotypes outlined by Panksepp (2006).

Gallese and Sinigaglia's (2011) Embodied Simulation Theory

Gallese and Sinigaglia (2011) theorized that the core process of social cognition was embodied simulation, in which individuals reuse the actions, emotions, and sensations copied from others through mirror neurons. Glenberg and Gallese (2012) stated that mirror neurons in the premotor regions of the frontal lobe and in the parietal lobe are activated when an animal moves its own hand or the mouth in relation to an object, and are activated when an animal watches the hand and mouth of another. Mirror neurons code the goal and the intention of an observed action of another individual, and can be activated by hearing a sound of an action, such as a candy wrapper being opened, or when an action is described verbally, for example, someone describing how they stuck their hand inside a candy bar dispensing machine. Moreover, some mirror neurons suppress self-movement during action observation.

Because the human mirror neuron system includes the automatic "copying" of actions, speech, face expressions, and emotions of the people we observe, it is likely that mirror neurons are an important component of social behavior. Mirror neurons evolved in primates and, in humans and all other primates, mirror neurons are likely to be a key means for the behaviors of others to influence our own behavior. Embodied simulation theory argues that we reuse what we automatically copy in order to choose actions. Glenberg and Gallese (2012) claimed, "the basic function of cognition is control of action. From an evolutionary perspective, it is hard to imagine any other story. That is, systems evolve because they contribute to the ability to survive and reproduce, and those activities demand action" (p. 14).

There is significant empirical support for the mirror neuron system. From their meta-analysis of 125 studies, Molenberghs, Cunnington, and

Mattingley (2012) concluded that the mirror system included not only the inferior frontal gyrus, dorsal and ventral premotor cortex, and the inferior and superior parietal lobule, but also brain areas regulating somatosensory, auditory, and emotional processing. The researchers also concluded that, depending on the task, these various additional overlapping brain regions are activated when observing or executing certain actions.

In particular, Molenberghs et al. (2012) found that mirror neuron activity in humans not only mirrors the actions of other people, but also mirrors the emotions and the sensations of other people. The researchers reported that when people observed the emotional expressions of others, mirror activity in the observers' own brains occurred in regions that determine emotional expression, including the insula, amygdala, and cingulate gyrus. Molenberghs et al. (2012) also reported that mirror activity occurred in relation to social touch. When an observer saw someone being touched, the observer's primary somatosensory cortex, and the dorsal part of the observer's postcentral gyrus, each involved in higher order somatosensory processing, were both vicariously activated.

Jacob (2009) argued against embodied simulation because of a time lag problem in the mirror neuron system process. He stated that person A engaged in an action and person B observing person A's action could not share a cognition based on mirror neuron activity. He claimed that because each person's brain was engaged in a different task—A, a motor task, and B, a perceptual task—and because A's brain control of the motor task occurred before B's brain perceived A's motor actions, A and B could not share the experience as is suggested by the embodied simulation theory. Jacob (2009) argued that what person A and B shared was a concept: "the mechanism that is active in both the execution of a transitive act (e.g., grasping) and in the perception of the same act performed by a conspecific looks very much like a neural mechanism underlying the concept of the act in question" (p. 242).

Ocampo and Kritikos (2011), however, argued for a more blurred line between mirroring and concepts, asserting that mirror neurons primarily register more abstract properties of the behaviors of other people. They pointed out that human mirror neurons fire in the absence of any visual information. They proposed that mirror neurons were crucial for our ability to construct "a continuous and accurate interpretation of others' behaviors and to coordinate our own responses appropriately" … [through] "a personal understanding not only of what others are doing but also why" (Ocampo & Kritikos, 2011, p. 265).

Frith and Frith's (2012) Understanding the Other

Frith and Frith (2012) claimed that the most important function of the social brain was learning about other people as individuals. Frith and Frith (2012) identified five behaviors they believed important for human social cognition: reward learning; imitation of others; tracking the intentions of others; supervisory control of lower level processes; and metacognition. Frith and Frith (2012) claimed that these five mechanisms were the only mechanisms of social cognition for which there is evidence of underlying brain circuitry. Frith and Frith (2012) outlined specific behaviors serving each of the five general behaviors. Reward learning was defined as gaining food or money, as well as obtaining social rewards, including smiling faces, gain in status or reputation, agreement of others, being imitated, observing mimicry, seeing cooperative people, experiencing fairness and cooperation, seeing similar others being rewarded, and social modulation of more abstract social rewards. Imitation of others was defined as including perception of biological motion, recognizing face identity, following eye gaze, signaling the value of gaze following, mirroring action, and mirroring emotion. Tracking the intentions of others was defined to include implicit mentalizing, and various forms of monitoring—monitoring one's own actions, others' actions, others' trustworthiness, others' generosity, and one's influence on others. The supervisory system of social cognition was defined by Frith and Frith (2012) to include overcoming race prejudice, response to unfairness, overriding trial-and-error learning of reputation by instructed knowledge, and managing conflicting information about emotional states. Metacognition was defined to include explicit mentalizing or theory of mind, intentional stance, mentalizing stance, impression formation, monitoring what others think of us, communicative signaling and pointing, judgment of one's own perception, agency, and strategy of others, and uncertainty about a partner's strategy.

Frith and Frith (2012) proposed that three things were unique to human social cognition. For one, we have language, through which we can make explicit claims about others and ourselves. Second, we have more self-regulation ability than do other primates. Finally, we have the ability to think about our own mental states.

Frith and Frith (2012) outlined a clear and well-justified model of social cognition, and they presented a table citing studies that provided support for each claimed component of their model of social cognition. Two groups of studies, however, not considered by the researchers, suggest limitations of their model of social cognition. One group of studies includes the research supporting the Insel (2010) and Grant et al. (2011) models. There is ample evidence that gonadal steroid hormones and the nonapeptides oxytocin and vasopressin defined by Frith and Frith (2012) to be on the bottom level of social cognition as elements of a "rewarded learning system" actually influence the top level metacognition system defined by Frith and Frith (2012)—our thinking about other people. For example, Pedersen et al. (2011) reported that 2 weeks of twice-daily intranasal sprays of oxytocin not only reduced diagnostic symptoms in 11 individuals diagnosed with schizophrenia, but also significantly improved the patients' accurate identification of second order false belief on a Theory of Mind test. The oxytocin spray also enhanced the patients' accuracy in recognizing deception and their ability to detect untrustworthy faces.

Skuse and Gallagher (2011) reported that a range of studies of oxytocin treatment indicated oxytocin had also been effective in reducing anxiety, increasing trust, generosity, altruism, betrayal aversion, and improving mentalizing skills and social memory. Skuse and Gallagher (2011) noted that the serotonergic system regulates aspects of aggression, social affiliation, and social decision-making. Bilderbeck et al. (2011) reported that lowered serotonin changed the way healthy adults judged or appraised the quality of other people's relationships. Reduced serotonin caused participants to judge couples as less romantic and less intimate.

The findings of Pedersen et al. (2011) and Bilderbeck et al. (2011) along with the review of Skuse and Gallagher (2011) suggest that the two upper level categories of social cognition identified by Frith and Frith (2012) as supervisory and metacognition are influenced by oxytocin and serotonin levels.

The second set of studies insufficiently considered in the Frith and Frith (2012) model of social cognition are studies of the mirror neuron system. Although the researchers did include the mirror neuron system in their model, they identified it only as one of six aspects of imitation, a lower level social cognitive behavior in their model. However, evidence is emerging that has linked the mirror neuron system to the third general behavior Frith and Frith (2012) outlined: tracking the intentions of others. Fogassi (2011) noted that mirror neurons would be excluded from tracking the intentions of others in a model like that of Frith and Frith (2012) in which memory retrieval and inferential processes govern social cognition. Fogassi (2011) argued, nonetheless, that understanding the actions and tracking the mental states of others can occur through the mirror neuron system. Fogassi (2011) proposed that mirror neuron system research indicates that the inferior parietal lobe and ventral premotor cortex constitute an "intentional" circuit, in which the inferior parietal lobule organizes motor acts in intentional chains, and the ventral premotor cortex generates motor act representations for chain building. Fogassi (2011) claimed that the mirror neuron system in monkeys led to the mind-reading skills in humans, and that human mind reading, the metacognitive Theory of Mind, depends on the automatic activation of the parietofrontal mirror neuron circuit, as well as on more elaborated coding of information in the prefrontal and orbitofrontal cortex.

Summary: Five Theories of Social Cognition

Insel (2010) argued that higher order social cognition rested on one simple innate social decision: should I "tend and befriend" the other person or should I avoid or attack that person? Insel noted that nearly all social behavior was regulated by estrogen and androgens, the gonadal steroids, and the nonapeptides oxytocin and vasopressin. Gordon et al. (2011) proposed that social motivation builds from a base of oxytocin and dopamine operating in the prefrontal cortex and the nucleus accumbens for infant–mother attachment to a more general desire to be with other people. They argued that selective social bonds are created when dopamine links sensory cues from individuals to rewards. Panksepp (2006) claimed that there are highly overlapping affective–emotional networks for sexual behavior, separation-distress, maternal care, and physical playfulness, and proposed that emotions are the core drivers for all social cognition. Gallese and Sinigaglia (2011) theorized that the core process of social cognition is embodied simulation, in which mirror neurons in the premotor regions of the frontal lobe and in the parietal lobe are activated when we observe others behaving, and we then non-consciously reuse the actions, emotions, and sensations copied from others to engender our own thoughts and actions.

Frith and Frith (2012) claimed the most important function of the social brain was learning about other people as individuals. Frith and Frith (2012) identified five behaviors they believed to be important for human social cognition: reward learning; imitation of others; tracking the intentions of others; supervisory control of lower level processes; and metacognition.

All five models are supported by empirical evidence, but none of the five represents a standard model of social cognition. Theory testing and theory synthesis, together with new findings, may or may not lead to a standard model.

CURRENT FINDINGS FOR "SOCIAL BRAIN" DEFICITS IN AUTISM

Table 3.1 lists the social brain elements and circuits that were outlined above, along with diagrams of the circuits, and an example of a study of that social brain function in autism. The studies listed in Table 3.1 reveal an extensive catalog of social brain deficits in autism. Table 3.1 studies indicate abnormalities in a male hormone (Ruta et al., 2011), and evidence that aromatase, an enzyme that converts testosterone to estrogen, is significantly reduced in the frontal cortex of individuals with autism (Sarachana et al., 2011). Studies listed also include evidence that oxytocin gene receptor alterations are linked to autism (Campbell et al., 2011), and evidence for correlations between autism and three single nucleotide polymorphisms (SNPs) of the arginine vasopressin receptor gene AVPR1A.

A Table 3.1 study suggests that autism is associated with the 7-repeat allele of the dopamine D4 receptor gene (DRD4) that results in tics, obsessions and compulsions, and separation anxiety (Gadow et al., 2010). Another study found that autism was linked to serotonin regulatory protein syntaxin 1A (STX1A), and also that a neuropathology study found STX1A expression in the anterior cingulate gyrus region in autism was significantly lower than that of controls (Nakamura et al., 2011).

Studies listed in Table 3.1 also indicate possible abnormalities in reward circuits in some with autism (Kohls et al., 2011), and problems in olfactory identifications (Bennetto et al., 2007). Studies listed also suggested atypical attachment and social play for some children with autism (Naber et al., 2007), and difficulties in making friends when in typical classrooms for many but not all high-functioning individuals with autism (Kasari et al., 2011). Studies listed reported that toddlers with autism failed to orient to biological motion (Klin et al., 2009), and some children with autism achieved typical gaze-following by an atypical strategy (Stauder et al., 2011).

Table 3.1 lists studies that report social recognition and expression problems in some with autism. Kleinhans et al. (2011) found that adults with autism could recognize faces but showed hypoactivation of the subcortical face-processing system. Kita et al. (2011) found that individuals with autism could recognize themselves but did so with hypoactivation of the right inferior frontal gyrus. Farran et al. (2011) found that individuals with autism were significantly slower but not less accurate than controls in recognizing face expressions of fear, anger, and sadness. Brennand et al. (2011), however, found no deficit for children with autism in identification of the vocal expression of the basic emotions anger, fear, happiness, and sadness. Oberman et al. (2009) found that children with autism could imitate happy, sad, fear, anger, disgust, and neutral face expressions, but their spontaneous mimicry of emotional expressions was delayed by 160 milliseconds. Peppé et al. (2011) reported that high-functioning individuals with autism were impaired in their ability to imitate emotional prosody. Schulte-Rüther et al. (2011) found a distinctly different pattern of empathy-linked ventromedial prefrontal cortex activity in individuals with autism compared with controls, as well as significant individual variation in autism.

Kjellmer et al. (2011) found a general language delay and great variability in the development of receptive and expressive language, and non-verbal communicative skills in 129 preschool children with autism. The researchers reported that cognitive skill and age explained approximately half of the variance in communication skills, while severity of autism symptoms explained only a few percent of the variance.

Studies listed in Table 3.1 also suggested problems with the mirror neuron system and with mentalizing skills in autism. Enticott et al. (2011) reported that when observing a human hand grasping a mug, individuals with autism compared with typical individuals showed reduced motor corticospinal excitability—a measure of mirror neuron system activity in the inferior frontal gyrus. Lam and Yeung (2011) found a 50% failure rate on a Theory of Mind task for children with autism, compared with a 17% failure rate for controls. Lombardo et al. (2011) found an atypical unenhanced activation in the right temporoparietal junction in autism. This region is theorized to contribute to mentalizing, e.g., imagining the thoughts of others. The researchers also reported significant individual variation in autism: relative activity of the right temporoparietal junction was associated with the degree of reciprocal social impairment in autism.

Given that the studies listed in Table 3.1 are single examples drawn from the wealth of studies of atypical social behaviors and social brain circuit dysfunctions in autism, it is clear that there is evidence for a deficit in every social brain circuit identified in social neuroscience research. However, in many cases, this wealth of evidence has been countered by findings for no deficit in autism. Larson, South, Krauskopf, Clawson, and Crowley (2011) found no deficit in reward processing for individuals with autism, and Rutherford and Troje (2012) found no deficit in the perception of biological motion for individuals with autism. Press, Richardson, and Bird (2010) found no deficit in automatic imitation of emotional facial actions in individuals with autism, and Raymaekers, Wiersman, and Roeyers (2009) found no difference between individuals with autism and controls for EEG mu suppression—evidence for mirror neuron system activity. Chevallier, Noveck, Happé, and Wilson (2010) found no deficit in individuals with autism for ability to understand a Theory of Mind task that depended on being able to process cues in a speaker's voice.

Impaired social behavior is the core diagnostic criteria for autism, but the evidence for variation in every component and circuit of the social brain makes clear that there is no coherence in the core criteria for the autism diagnosis.

THE RANGE AND VARIATION IN AUTISM SOCIAL BRAIN DEFICITS SUGGEST THAT MULTIPLE DISORDERS HAVE BEEN AGGREGATED IN AUTISM

Autism researchers and theorists have long been aware of the variation in deficits in all the components of social behavior. A variety of views have claimed unity of the social deficits in autism. These unifying views of autism social deficit must account for the variation in social deficits in autism. Selected unifying views of the social deficit in autism are examined in relation to the evidence for social deficit variation.

The Social Instinct

Wing, Gould, and Gillberg (2011) asserted, "the fundamental problems underlying all autistic conditions … is absence or impairment of the social instinct …. We hope that research work into the behavioural neurology of the social instinct will be carried out in the near future. Results from recent research in this area suggest that a combination of specific cognitive skills underlies the social instinct" (p. 769).

The first section of this chapter reviewed existing evidence and theories for brain mechanisms governing human social behaviors. This review suggests that there are many elements that contribute to the human social instinct, most notably, oxytocin and vasopressin, gonadal hormones, the brain bases for individual emotions including empathy, and the dopamine reward circuitry throughout the cortex and subcortical regions. In fact, Gordon et al. (2011) specifically theorized that the social instinct is a motivation to be with others, and provided a detailed model of the possible brain basis of social motivation. The researchers posited that highly conserved oxytocin functions integrate with the dopamine reward system in the frontal cortex and nucleus accumbens to generate our need to be social beings.

Gordon et al. (2011) proposed that attachment is the main goal of the social instinct, and we become attached through the process of dopamine linking sensory cues from the individual person to the reward system to create and maintain selective social bonds.

If the model of "social instinct" Gordon et al. (2011) proposed is correct, then it is clear that many individuals who meet the diagnostic criteria for autism *do* have the social instinct, because they are attached to their parents or caregivers. Naber et al. (2007) reported attachment in children with autism, and Haltigan et al. (2011) reported attachment in infant siblings of children with autism. Rutgers, Bakermans-Kranenburg, van IJzendoorn, and Van Berckelaer-Onnes (2004) conducted a meta-analytic review of attachment in autism and reported that most individuals with autism were found to experience attachment with parents or caretakers. Therefore, because attachment is intact in a majority of individuals with autism, the majority do express a crucial form of social instinct.

Some individuals with autism do lack the social instinct. For these individuals, a deficit in oxytocin, vasopressin, and dopamine, or their receptors, or a form of failed integration of the reward system with the neuropeptides might be expected to lead to a failure of infant attachment, and continued social impairment.

Developmental Failure of One or More Brain Systems for Social Information Processing, Particularly the Posterior Superior Temporal Sulcus

Pelphrey et al. (2011) asserted that individuals diagnosed with autism "share the common, pathognomic feature of dysfunctional reciprocal social interaction" and "the reciprocal relationship between brain disruption and atypical social development drives homogeneity in the syndrome's presentation even in the presence of enormous phenotypic and genotypic heterogeneity" (p. 633). Pelphrey et al. (2011) argued for a specific social brain impairment of the posterior temporal sulcus in autism: "the posterior STS in typically developing young adults is highly specialized for detecting biological motion and interpreting the actions and intentions of others. This region is not specialized for these functions in young adults with ASD" (p. 639).

Table 3.1 lists evidence for social impairments in autism, and the first section of this chapter reviewed existing evidence and theories for brain mechanisms governing human social behaviors. Despite the assertion by Pelphrey et al. (2011) that the posterior superior temporal sulcus is dysfunctional in autism, many studies have suggested no evidence of this dysfunction. Stauder,

Bosch, and Nuij (2011) found that children with autism expressed typical attention shifting to the gaze of others, something that requires intact posterior superior temporal sulcus function. Pierce (2011) reported evidence from four sleep-imaging studies that the only consistent early atypical brain activity occurred as reduced activation in the left superior temporal gyrus. Moreover, Rutherford and Troje (2012) found no deficit in the perception of biological motion for individuals with autism, and Press et al. (2010) found no deficit in automatic imitation of emotional facial actions in individuals with autism. These are both skills that require intact posterior superior temporal sulcus function. Chevallier et al. (2010) found no deficit in individuals with autism for ability to understand a Theory of Mind task, and Pelphrey et al. (2011) proposed that Theory of Mind skill and mentalizing would require intact function of the posterior superior temporal sulcus.

Another difficulty for Pelphrey and colleagues' (2011) claim of a unified social deficit is that their claim has two parts, and the parts make conflicting predictions. First, they asserted that autism dysfunction in reciprocal social interaction is *the* common pathognomonic feature, i.e., a feature so specifically characteristic of a disorder that it can be used for diagnosis. Second, they argued that impaired function of the posterior temporal sulcus is the neural signature of autism. However, reciprocal social interaction rests on the function of many more brain circuits than the posterior temporal sulcus. For example, Guionnet et al. (2012) collected imaging results from 23 typical individuals engaged in reciprocal social interaction. The researchers found that reciprocal social interaction involved spontaneous imitation of the social partner. Guionnet et al. (2012) reported that imitation is a common and constant element of social interaction, and that evidence suggests that non-conscious mimicry enhances liking, rapport, affiliation, and prosocial behavior because we are rewarded by and attracted to imitation. The researchers found that imitation involved activity in the dorsolateral prefrontal cortex, dorsal anterior cingulate gyrus, pre-supplementary motor area, as well as the left pars opercularis, the primary sensorimotor cortex, ventral and dorsal premotor frontal lobe areas, supplementary motor areas, inferior frontal gyrus, left inferior parietal lobule, and left insula.

Consequently, if impaired reciprocal social interaction is the diagnostic core of autism, then many different brain areas may be disrupted and result in a disruption of reciprocal social interaction, not just the posterior superior temporal sulcus. If, however, impaired function of the posterior superior temporal sulcus is the neural signature of autism, there are many studies suggesting that in many individuals with autism, this area is not impaired.

Pelphrey et al. (2011) have not addressed the range of findings for autism. Deficits in the neurochemicals oxytocin, dopamine, serotonin, and gonadal hormones in autism suggest there must be social impairment variation based on receptors for, or production of, these social neurochemicals. Deficits in "the cerebellum, frontal lobes, and temporal lobes ... parts of the parietal lobe ... amygdala ... basal ganglia ... hippocampus ... hypothalamus ... thalamus ... the insula ... the fusiform face area ... the brainstem [and] ... the corpus callosum" (Shroeder, Desrocher, Bebko, & Cappadocia, 2010, p. 562) call into question the notion that autism is unified by a dysfunction in the posterior superior temporal sulcus.

There may be a subset of individuals diagnosed with autism who have an isolated developmental abnormality in their posterior superior temporal sulcus. This remains to be determined by future research.

Primary Social Motivation Failure Resulting in Secondary Social Deficits

Dawson (2008) outlined the social motivation theory of autism. She argued that autism social deficits are caused by an initial failure in social motivation. She proposed that the specific social impairments in social orienting, joint attention, responses to emotions, imitation, and face processing are the result of less engagement with the social world (Dawson, 2008, p. 786) rather than being primary deficits themselves. Dawson asserted that "Because experience drives cortical specialization ... reduced attention to people, including their faces, gestures, and speech, also results in a failure of specialization and less efficient function of brain regions that mediate social cognition" (2008, p. 787). Dawson (2008) suggested that the dopamine reward system and the oxytocin affiliation system may be disrupted in autism, causing a lack of social motivation.

Similar to Dawson's hypothesis, Gordon et al. (2011) theorized social motivation to derive from the interaction of oxytocin functions with the dopamine reward system. However, as outlined above, Gordon et al. (2011) proposed that attachment is the primary goal of social motivation, and, as noted above, a majority of individuals with autism have been found to be attached to their parents or caretakers (Naber et al., 2007; Rutgers et al., 2004). In addition, there is significant evidence that many of the impairments in social behavior that Dawson relegates to secondary effects of impaired social motivation are likely to be primary impairments.

Bennetto et al. (2007) reported that individuals with autism were impaired in olfactory identification, and olfactory task skill was inversely correlated with degree of autism social impairment. The olfactory system may be damaged by illness, or maldeveloped due to genetic factors, but would not be disrupted by impaired social motivation. Klin et al. (2009) reported that 2-year-olds with autism did not orient to displays of biological motion. Because orienting to biological motion predates social motivation in animal evolution, it is unlikely that such a primitive and conserved system would be modified by lack of social motivation.

There may be a subset of individuals diagnosed with autism who are born with an impairment in some combination of oxytocin and dopamine, or their receptors, or their integration into a social reward network. For these individuals with autism, the initial failure of social motivation would result in absent social attachment in infancy. This initial lack of social motivation might or might not be a devolving force for social cognition impairment in autism.

Underconnectivity of the Insula

Ebisch et al. (2010) hypothesized that a reduced connection between the insula and the amygdala and between the insula and somatosensory cortex caused the "altered emotional experiences and impaired social abilities" (p. 1025) of autism. Ebisch et al. (2010) found that in a resting state, the brains of individuals with autism showed reduced functional connectivity between the bilateral posterior insular cortex and somatosensory cortex, and reduced functional connectivity between the anterior insula cortex and the amygdala. Because evidence indicates that the anterior insula regulates the degree of awareness of one's own emotions, and because the anterior insula and the amygdala are crucial to understanding the emotional experiences of others, the researchers theorized that these impaired connections could incapacitate sensitivity to self and others in autism. Ebisch et al. (2010) further hypothesized that impaired connections of the insular cortex could damage the automatic basis for empathy, while the impaired emotional awareness of self and others could disrupt the cognitive aspects of empathy, such as imagining the thoughts and feelings of others.

Despite the plausibility of the theory, a range of research findings suggest that insular cortex isolation is unlikely to be the sole cause for the social impairments found in autism. First, Wass (2011) and Stigler, McDonald, Anand, Saykin, and McDougle (2011) noted that not all individuals with autism have disrupted connectivity. Stigler et al. (2011) asserted that the diverse findings were likely due to the heterogeneity in autism as well as sample size and characteristics. In fact, some studies have even reported increased connectivity in autism. For example, Noonan, Haist, and Muller

(2009) reported finding that functional connectivity in autism overall was not significantly different from that of control participants, but where there were differences, networks in autism were more extensive and not less extensive. Even within studies reporting evidence for reduced functional connectivity in autism, evidence for individual variation in connectivity is a constant. Unfortunately, as Wass (2011) noted, "The tendency of many papers to report only group means is regrettable, since it obscures vital information about within-group heterogeneity" (p. 24).

Evidence to date suggests that individual variation is likely to include some with autism whose brains have no impairment in connectivity, others whose brains have atypically enhanced connectivity in various regions, and still others whose brains have a range of different patterns of disrupted connectivity. Given that over 200 gene and chromosome copy number variants have been found in association with autism and many environmental risk factors as well, it is likely that different genetic causes will have different brain development outcomes in autism. As more studies are done of both functional connectivity, i.e., looking at time-linked activity of different brain regions, and structural connectivity, looking at the white matter physical connections of one brain region to another, a better understanding of the relationship between social deficits and aberrant connectivity in autism will emerge.

A second difficulty for the insular cortex theory of social impairment is that studies reporting reduced "functional and anatomical connectivity in autism have established that autism is not a localized neurological disorder, but one that affects many parts of the brain in many types of thinking tasks" (Schipul, Keller, & Just, 2011, p. 9). Given the evidence for widespread disruptions of functional connectivity, it is likely that many systems for social behavior, such as face recognition, voice recognition, language comprehension and production, and imagining the minds of others, may be directly disrupted by impaired connectivity.

Another, more general problem for the insula isolation model of social impairment is the evidence that impaired functional connectivity is a deficit found in many other disorders. Wass (2011) noted that there was evidence for impaired connectivity in schizophrenia, ADHD, and dyslexia. Peters et al. (2011) reported evidence for impaired connectivity in Angelman disorder, as well as social anxiety disorder, bipolar disorder, and schizotypal personality disorder. Wass (2011) also reported that impaired hemisphere connectivity of the corpus callosum was found in dyslexia, developmental language disorder, Tourette syndrome, Down syndrome, Williams-Beuren syndrome, depression, and schizophrenia. The wide expression of problems in functional connectivity across many disorders suggests that underconnectivity may not be a specific marker for autism, or a specific marker for the social impairment in autism.

Northam, Liégeois, Chong, Wyatt, and Baldeweg (2011) reported that deficits in white matter and corpus callosum connectivity in premature infants explained 76% of the variance in intelligence. These data suggest that underconnectivity itself might be a cause for intellectual disability in autism, rather than the source of specific autism social impairments. It is equally likely that underconnectivity occurs as the result of many genetic and environmental risk factors, and that underconnectivity contributes to both intellectual disability and social impairment in some with autism.

Individuals with autism who also have impaired connectivity may be found to exhibit a unique pattern of disrupted connectivity, or impaired connectivity may be a more general sign of impaired brain development and function. In either case, underconnectivity of the insula is an insufficient explanation for the variation of social deficits found in autism. However, it may be that isolation of the insula is a key contributor to social impairment in autism in some individuals.

Mirror Neuron Theory

Rizzolatti and Fabbri-Destro (2010) reviewed the evidence for the mirror neuron theory of social impairment in autism. The researchers reported that all mirror neurons engage the same process, translating "sensory information describing motor acts done by others into a motor format similar to that the observers themselves generate when they perform those acts" (Rizzolatti & Fabbri-Destro, 2010, p. 227). However, location of mirror neurons in the brain dictates what content is mirrored. Mirror neurons in the insula and cingulate cortex mirror emotional states of those we observe and contribute to our empathy for others. Evidence suggests that mirror neurons are likely to determine our ability to learn by imitation of others, and also suggests that the translation of observed behavior to our own internal motor program enables us to understand the other person's behavior without the need for time-consuming cognitive construction of an idea about what the person is doing. Although research has demonstrated that the mirror system allows us to understand the intentions behind the actions of other people, Rizzolatti and Fabbri-Destro (2010) asserted that the tracking of intention of others through the mirror neuron system does not preclude more cognitive ways of "reading the minds" of others.

Imaging and EEG research has generated evidence that mirror neuron system function is disrupted in autism (Rizzolatti & Fabbri-Destro, 2010), and the mirror neuron theory of autism claimed that disrupted mirror system function causes the social impairment of being unable to understand the behaviors and intentions of others, and being unable to have shared feelings with others. However, a number of studies have reported no evidence of mirror system impairment in autism. Rizzolatti and Fabbri-Destro (2010) proposed that studies finding no impairment in the mirror system in autism failed to understand a second important aspect of mirror neuron system function. The researchers noted that the second aspect of the mirror neuron organization is not the result of the activity of individual neurons, but is the result of chains of motor acts.

In mirror neuron activity involving chains of actions, a person recruits that specific chain of acts that fits his or her intention. Many mirror neurons are action-constrained, and will only activate as part of a particular chain. When we observe someone's behavior, our own chain of action matching the action observed is activated. This gives us a motor representation of the action that we could do, but more importantly, activating our own chain of action permits us to track the intended actions of others.

Rizzolatti and Fabbri-Destro (2010) reported that there is evidence that chained motor act organization is impaired in autism. The researchers claimed, "these data strongly suggest that children with autism have a deficit in the chained organization of motor acts and, as a consequence, they are unable to activate it during action observation. Without this internal 'replica' of the actions of others, they cannot grasp directly, without cognitive inferences, the intention of others" (Rizzolatti & Fabbri-Destro, 2010, p. 233). Boria et al. (2009) reported that children with autism were able to interpret the behavior of other people through object function information given by objects the people were shown using, but children with autism could not interpret the behavior of others from the intentional information present in the motor acts of other people. Boria et al. (2009) argued that these data demonstrated a deficit of the chain-based mirror neuron mechanism. Linking their findings to evidence for underconnectivity in autism, Boria et al. theorized that intra-hemispheric alterations may cause a deficit in the development of individual mirror neurons, but would be likely to cause a much more serious deficit in chains of actions.

Boria et al. (2009) recognized the heterogeneity in autism, and stated that even a deficit in the mirror neuron chaining system would not necessarily mean that all individuals with autism would be unable to understand the intentions of others. Boria et al. (2009) noted that the comprehension of the intentions of others could also be mediated by other mechanisms, such as use of objects, seeing objects in context, and drawing inferences. Boria et al. (2009) argued, "However, even with this additional inferential processing the comprehension of others could hardly reach the reliability and, especially, the effortlessness typical of action understanding based on one's own motor competence" (p. 7).

Counter to the findings of Boria et al. (2009), Marsh and Hamilton (2011) reported no difference in the pattern of activation and repetition suppression of the anterior inferior parietal lobule—a key element of the mirror system—between individuals diagnosed with autism and typical study participants. The researchers concluded that "finding that one key part of the mirror system is intact in autism means that theories proposing a global mirror system deficit in autism are not plausible" (Marsh & Hamilton, 2011, pp. 1516–1517). However, Marsh and Hamilton (2011) did find less activation in autism in a region including posterior mid cingulate cortex and supplementary motor area. This area has been reported to contain mirror neurons, and to play a part in action prediction. The researchers also reported finding less activation in the fusiform cortex in autism, which they concluded signaled impaired body perception in autism.

Neither Rizzolatti and Fabbri-Destro (2010) nor Boria et al. (2009), nor their critics, such as Marsh and Hamilton (2011), addressed the findings for abnormalities found in autism for various neurotransmitters. Nor did these researchers address the findings for deficits in brain structures that are not components of the mirror neuron system or mentalizing system. Pelphrey et al. (2011) argued that atypical function of the posterior superior temporal sulcus characterized autism; Pierce (2011) argued that reduced activity in the left superior temporal gyrus so clearly characterized autism it could be a biomarker for autism. Additional regions of deficit have been reported: "the cerebellum, frontal lobes, and temporal lobes ... [non-mirror parts of] the parietal lobe ... amygdale ... basal ganglia ... hippocampus ... hypothalamus ... thalamus ... the insula ... the fusiform face area ... the brainstem [and] ... the corpus callosum" (Shroeder et al., 2010, p. 562). Nor do the researchers consider how the more than 200 gene and chromosomal variants found in association with autism and the many varied environmental risk factors for autism could possibly *all* converge on the creation of a brain deficit for autism in the mirror neuron system alone.

It may be that some individuals with autism have impairments in some mirror neuron system regions, and some have impairments in much of the mirror neuron system. Findings in small samples for and against the mirror system theory are not explanatory. Individual variation analysis in larger samples rather than group differences should be pursued.

CONCLUSION: NO PLAUSIBLE COMPREHENSIVE MODEL OF SOCIAL DEFICITS IN AUTISM

Five models of a unified cause for the social impairment of autism were reviewed: the absent social instinct; impaired social cognition and deficit in posterior superior temporal sulcus; absent social motivation causing the devolution of social orienting, joint attention, responses to emotions, imitation, and face processing; underconnectivity isolating the insula; and an impaired mirror neuron system. Studies identified in Table 3.1 are emblematic of the evidence that exists for the variation in atypical social behaviors and social brain circuit dysfunctions in autism. In fact, there appears to be evidence for an autism-linked deficit in every social brain circuit identified in social neuroscience research to date, and, in many cases, countering evidence finding no deficit in a specific social brain circuit. This amount of variation across studies is staggering.

None of the five models of autism social deficit reviewed here has addressed even a small portion of the existing reported variation in social behavior and social brain deficits in autism. Moreover, only a handful of autism studies have reported data for individual variation in social behavior deficits or social brain deficits.

Most research on the social deficits in autism has been small sample studies that have often followed the tracks of new functions identified in behavioral neuroscience such as the default mode and the mirror neuron system, or new methodologies in behavioral neuroscience such as the ability to image white matter or measure functional connectivity.

Intellectual Disability and Social Impairment

Surprisingly, not one of the five theories of social impairment mentioned that between 55% and 70% of individuals diagnosed with autism have intellectual disability (Chakrabarti & Fombonne, 2005; Charman et al., 2011). In fact, research on the social impairment in autism has not asked one obvious question. Could intellectual disability in some cases of autism be the expression of a brain system impairment that also impairs many functions including the function of processing social information? This question has been addressed, however, in studies of genetic disorders that are found in association with social impairments.

Peters et al. (2011) reported evidence for underconnectivity in multiple white matter pathways in the brains of individuals diagnosed with Angelman syndrome. Angelman syndrome is a neurodevelopmental disorder caused by disruption in the typical expression of the *UBE3A* gene from the maternal chromosome. Angelman syndrome is characterized by intellectual disability, lack of speech, seizures, and deficits in social interaction. Some individuals with Angelman are diagnosed with autism. Peters et al. (2011) found that overall evidence for reduced connectivity was correlated with increased social withdrawal. In particular, the researchers found that impairment on the left hemisphere white matter arcuate fasciculus pathway was linked to impairment in language skill and cognition, and impaired white matter connectivity in the left uncinate fasciculus, a white matter pathway between the amygdala and the orbitofrontal cortex, was correlated with measures of social impairment. The researchers suggested that because reduced arcuate fasciculus connectivity had been found in other developmental brain disorders, it was evidence for a causal connection. Moreover, Peters et al. (2011) also argued that because reduced connectivity in the uncinate fasciculus was found in social anxiety disorder, bipolar disorder, and schizotypal personality disorder, this pattern of underconnectivity might represent "a common endophenotype of affect dysregulation and/or impaired social interactions" (Peters et al., 2011, p. 366).

To summarize, white matter underconnectivity in Angelman disorder is the result of impaired function of the *UBE3A* gene. This brain underconnectivity, in turn, appears to cause both intellectual disability and social withdrawal. More studies of this type will help explore links between intellectual disability and social impairment for the individual disorders in autism.

Northam et al. (2011) reported that total volume of white matter in the brain combined with the cross-sectional size of the corpus callosum predicted 76% of the variance in measured IQ in adolescents who had been premature infants. The researchers hypothesized that intellectual ability was sensitive to differences in white matter volume. Pinto-Martin et al. (2011) reported that 5% of a longitudinal cohort of individuals who had been born weighing less than 2000 grams were diagnosed with autism: many diagnosed with autism also had cognitive developmental delay. Together the findings of Pinto et al. (2011) and Northam et al. (2011) suggest that it is likely that intellectual disability and social impairment co-occur because they share a cause, whether genetic or environmental.

Many Autism Social Deficit Theories are Over-Generalized and Over-Localized

Given the wide variation in social brain deficits reported for autism, it is implausible that the different patterns of social deficits in different individuals with autism can be explained by a single cause, however elaborated. While most researchers accept that autism is a group of disorders—the autism spectrum disorders—researchers and theorists nonetheless continue to attempt to explain all autism social deficits, or even all autism cases, with a single brain deficit. This over-generalization of a single deficit to explain all of autism is not consonant with the wealth of empirical findings for autism variation.

Pelphrey et al. (2011) argued that dysfunction of the posterior superior temporal sulcus was the basis for the social deficits that define autism. Ebisch et al. (2010) proposed that the isolation of the insula was the basis for the social deficits that define autism. Boria et al. (2009) hypothesized that failed chained mirror neurons were the basis for the primary social failure of autism, the failure to understand others. Pierce (2011) argued that dysfunction in the superior temporal gyrus at 14 months could be a biomarker for autism. Lombardo et al. (2011) proposed that atypical activation in the right temporoparietal junction—believed to be the basis for imagining the thoughts of others—was the key deficit defining autism. Lombardo et al. (2011) reported that they found no dysfunction in other regions in the brain thought to contribute to understanding that others have their own thoughts and feelings, such as the ventromedial prefrontal cortex, or the left temporoparietal junction. The researchers concluded that their findings demonstrated "regional specificity within mentalizing circuitry that may be responsible for the component processes that contribute to mindblindness and social-communication deficits in autism" (Lombardo et al., 2011, p. 1837).

It is possible that some individuals with autism do have a dysfunction in one particular brain region theorized to regulate an aspect of social behavior. However, it is not possible that all or even a majority of individuals with autism have a discrete deficit in a particular brain region. Not only does the evidence for variation in social deficit and variation in social brain dysfunction argue against a unitary "social lesion" in autism, but the evidence for more than 200 gene and chromosomal variants, and the evidence for many environmental risk factors argue against a single focal source of social impairment in autism.

With increasing social neuroscience research, more brain regions and circuits are likely to be described as contributors to human social behavior.

Even now, Devue and Brédart (2011) reported that many brain regions contribute to self-recognition, including the inferior frontal gyrus, the right medial and middle frontal gyri, the inferior parietal lobule, the supramarginal gyrus and the precuneus, the anterior cingulate cortex, the bilateral insula, the fusiform gyrus, and the bilateral inferior temporal gyrus. If some individuals with autism have an impaired sense of self, there is likely to be no single locus for that deficit. Vickery et al. (2011) found that reward and punishment processing occurs in every cortical and subcortical area of the brain. If some individuals with autism find social interaction non-rewarding, that deficit is not likely to result from dysfunction of a single brain region. Mar (2011) conducted a meta-analysis of story comprehension and Theory of Mind studies. He concluded that the brain basis for Theory of Mind is larger than the right temporal-parietal juncture, and includes prefrontal cortex, left and right posterior superior temporal sulcus, left and right angular gyri, left and right anterior temporal regions, posterior cingulate cortex, precuneus, and perhaps also the left inferior gyrus. If some with autism are unable to construct a notion of the minds of others, and thus are "mindblind," e.g., have dysfunction in Theory of Mind skills, it is not likely that one brain site will be found to be dysfunctional.

Over-generalization to all with autism, and over-localization in theorizing that one impaired brain circuit impairment causes autism, combined with lack of attention to variation in autism, and a lack of any examination of individual variation in small study samples, along with a nearly complete inattention to the significance of intellectual disability, have combined to drive the field in waves of non-productive research. Studying a known cause linked to known and carefully observed brain deficit in a subgroup of individuals with and without autism by means of exploratory data analysis may help redirect the field to more productive and, hence, translational research.

REFERENCES

Andics, A., McQueen, J. M., Petersson, K. M., Gal, V., Rudas, G., & Vidnyánszky, Z. (2010). Neural mechanisms for voice recognition. *NeuroImage, 52*, 1528–1540.

Andrews-Hanna, J. R., Reidler, J. S., Sepulcre, J., Poulin, R., & Buckner, R. L. (2010). Functional anatomic fractionation of the brain's default network. *Neuron, 65*, 550–562.

Aziz-Zadeh, L., Sheng, T., & Gheytanchi, A. (2010). Common premotor regions for the perception and production of prosody and correlations with empathy and prosodic ability. *PLoS ONE, 5*, e8759.

Bayliss, A. P., Bartlett, J., Naughtin, C. K., & Kritikos, A. (2011). A direct link between gaze perception and social attention. *Journal of Experimental Psychology: Human Perception and Performance, 37*, 634–644.

Bennetto, L., Kuschner, E. S., & Hyman, S. L. (2007). Olfaction and taste processing in autism. *Biological Psychiatry, 62*, 1015–1021.

Bilderbeck, A. C., McCabe, C., Wakeley, J., McGlone, F., Harris, T., Cowen, P. J., et al. (2011). Serotonergic activity influences the cognitive appraisal of close intimate relationships in healthy adults. *Biological Psychiatry, 69*, 720–725.

Blank, H., Anwander, A., & von Kriegstein, K. (2011). Direct structural connections between voice- and face-recognition areas. *Journal of Neuroscience, 31*, 12906–12915.

Blum, D. (2011). The scent of your thoughts. *Scientific American, 305*(4), 54–57.

Boria, S., Fabbri-Destro, M., Cattaneo, L., Sparaci, L., Sinigaglia, C., Santelli, E., et al. (2009). Intention understanding in autism. *PLoS ONE, 4*, e5596.

Bos, P. A., Panksepp, J., Bluth, R. M., & van Honk, J. (2012). Acute effects of steroid hormones and neuropeptides on human social–emotional behavior: A review of single administration studies. *Frontiers in Neuroendocrinology, 33*, 17–35.

Brennand, R., Schepman, A., & Rodway, P. (2011). Vocal emotion perception in pseudo-sentences by secondary-school children with Autism Spectrum Disorder. *Research in Autism Spectrum Disorders, 5*, 1567–1573.

Campbell, D. B., Datta, D., Jones, S. T., Lee, E. B., Sutcliffe, J. S., Hammock, E. A. D., et al. (2011). Association of oxytocin receptor (OXTR) gene variants with multiple phenotype domains of autism spectrum disorder. *Journal of Neurodevelopmental Disorders, 3*, 101–112.

Chakrabarti, S., & Fombonne, E. (2005). Pervasive developmental disorders in preschool children: Confirmation of high prevalence. *American Journal of Psychiatry, 162*, 1133–1141.

Charman, T., Pickles, A., Simonoff, E., Chandler, S. E., Loucas, T., & Baird, G. (2011). IQ in children with autism spectrum disorders: data from the Special Needs and Autism Project (SNAP). *Psychological Medicine, 41*, 619–627.

Chevallier, C., Noveck, I., Happé, F., & Wilson, D. (2010). What's in a voice? Prosody as a test case for the Theory of Mind account of autism. *Neuropsychologia, 49*, 507–517.

Cromwell, H. C., & Panksepp, J. (2011). Rethinking the cognitive revolution from a neural perspective: How overuse/misuse of the term "cognition" and the neglect of affective controls in behavioral neuroscience could be delaying progress in understanding the BrainMind. *Neuroscience and Biobehavioral Reviews, 35*, 2026–2035.

Dawson, G. (2008). Early behavioral intervention, brain plasticity, and the prevention of autism spectrum disorder. *Developmental Psychopathology, 20*, 775–803.

Devue, C., & Brédart, S. (2011). The neural correlates of visual self-recognition. *Consciousness and Cognition, 20*, 40–51.

Ebisch, S. J., Gallese, V., Willem, R. M., Mantini, D., Groen, W. B., Romani, G. L., et al. (2010). Altered intrinsic functional connectivity of anterior and posterior insula regions in high-functioning participants with autism spectrum disorder. *Human Brain Mapping, 32*, 1013–1028.

Edelson, M., Sharot, T., Dolan, R. J., & Dudai, Y. (2011). Following the crowd: Brain substrates of long-term memory conformity. *Science, 333*, 108–111.

Enticott, P. G., Kennedy, H. A., Rinehart, N. J., Tonge, B. J., Bradshaw, J. L., Taffe, J. R., et al. (2011). Mirror neuron activity associated with social impairments but not age in autism spectrum disorder. *Biological Psychiatry, 71*, 427–433.

Enzi, B., de Greck, M., Prösch, U., Tempelmann, C., & Northoff, G. (2009). Is our self nothing but reward? Neuronal overlap and distinction between reward and personal relevance and its relation to human personality. *PLoS ONE, 4*, e8429.

Ethofer, T., Bretscher, J., Gschwind, M., Kreifelts, B., Wildgruber, D., & Vuilleumier, P. (2012). Emotional voice areas: Anatomic location, functional properties, and structural connections revealed by combined fMRI/DTI. *Cerebral Cortex, 22*, 191–200.

Farran, E. K., Branson, A., & King, B. J. (2011). Visual search for basic emotional expressions in autism; impaired processing of anger, fear and sadness, but a typical happy face advantage. *Research in Autism Spectrum Disorders, 5*, 455–462.

Flinker, A., Chang, E. F., Barbaro, N. M., Berger, M. S., & Knight, R. T. (2011). Sub-centimeter language organization in the human temporal lobe. *Brain & Language, 117,* 103–109.

Fogassi, L. (2011). The mirror neuron system: How cognitive functions emerge from motor organization. *Journal of Economic Behavior & Organization, 77,* 66–75.

Frith, C. D., & Frith, U. (2012). Mechanisms of social cognition. *Annual Review of Psychology, 63,* 287–313.

Gadow, K. D., DeVincent, C. J., Olvet, D. M., Pisarevskaya, V., & Hatchwell, E. (2010). Association of DRD4 polymorphism with severity of oppositional defiant disorder, separation anxiety disorder and repetitive behaviors in children with autism spectrum disorder. *European Journal of Neuroscience, 32,* 1058–1065.

Gallese, V., & Sinigaglia, C. (2011). What is so special about embodied simulation? *Trends in Cognitive Neuroscience, 15,* 512–519.

Glenberg, A. M., & Gallese, L. (2012). Action-based language: A theory of language acquisition, comprehension, and production. *Cortex, 48,* 905–922.

Goodson, J. L., & Thompson, R. R. (2010). Nonapeptide mechanisms of social cognition, behavior and species-specific social systems. *Current Opinion in Neurobiology, 20,* 784–794.

Gordon, I., Martin, C., Feldman, R., & Leckman, J. F. (2011). Oxytocin and social motivation. *Developmental Cognitive Neuroscience, 1,* 471–493.

Green, L., Fein, D., Modahl, C., Feinstein, C., Waterhouse, L., Morris, M., et al. (2001). Oxytocin and autistic disorder: Alterations in peptide forms. *Biological Psychiatry, 50,* 609–613.

Guionnet, S., Nadel, J., Bertasi, E., Sperduti, M., Delaveau, P., & Fossati, P. (2012). Reciprocal imitation: Toward a neural basis of social interaction. *Cerebral Cortex, 22,* 971–978.

Hickok, G., Houde, J., & Rong, F. (2011). Sensorimotor integration in speech processing: Computational basis and neural organization. *Neuron, 69,* 407–422.

Higgins, E. T., & Pittman, T. S. (2008). Motives of the human animal: Comprehending, managing, and sharing inner states. *Annual Review of Psychology, 59,* 361–385.

Hoover, K. C. (2010). Smell with inspiration: the evolutionary significance of olfaction. *Yearbook of Physical Anthropology, 53,* 63–74.

Hummer, T. A., & McClintock, M. K. (2009). Putative human pheromone androstadienone attunes the mind specifically to emotional information. *Hormones and Behavior, 55,* 548–559.

Insel, T. R. (2010). The challenge of translation in social neuroscience: A review of oxytocin, vasopressin, and affiliative behavior. *Neuron, 65,* 768–779.

Jacob, P. (2009). The tuning-fork model of human social cognition: A critique. *Consciousness and Cognition, 18,* 229–243.

Jehna, M. C., Neuper, A., Ischebeck, M., Loitfelder, S., Ropele, C., Langkammer, C., et al. (2011). The functional correlates of face perception and recognition of emotional facial expressions as evidenced by fMRI. *Brain Research, 393,* 73–83.

Kanwisher, N. (2010). Functional specificity in the human brain: A window into the functional architecture of the mind. *PNAS, 107,* 11163–11170.

Kasari, C., Locke, J., Gulsrud, A., & Rotheram-Fuller, E. (2011). Social networks and friendships at school: Comparing children with and without ASD. *Journal of Autism and Developmental Disorders, 41,* 533–544.

Kita, Y., Gunji, A., Inoue, Y., Goto, T., Sakihara, K., Kaga, M., et al. (2011). Self-face recognition in children with autism spectrum disorders: A near-infrared spectroscopy study. *Brain & Development, 33,* 494–503.

Kjellmer, L., Hedvall, A., Fernell, E., Gillberg, C., & Norrelgen, F. (2011). Language and communication skills in preschool children with autism spectrum disorders: Contribution of cognition, severity of autism symptoms, and adaptive functioning to the variability. *Research in Developmental Disabilities, 33,* 172–180.

Kleinhans, N. M., Richards, T., Johnson, C., Weaver, K. E., Greenson, J., Dawson, G., et al. (2011). fMRI evidence of neural abnormalities in the subcortical face processing system in ASD. *NeuroImage, 54,* 697–704.

Klin, A., Lin, D. J., Gorrindo, P., Ramsay, G., & Jones, W. (2009). Two-year-olds with autism orient to non-social contingencies rather than biological motion. *Nature Letters*, 1–5.

Kohls, G., Peltzer, J., Schulte-Rüther, M., Kamp-Becker, I., Remschmidt, H., Herpertz-Dahlmann, B., et al. (2011). Atypical brain responses to reward cues in autism as revealed by event-related potentials. *Journal of Autism and Developmental Disorders, 41,* 1523–1533.

Lam, Y. G., & Yeung, S. S. (2012). Cognitive deficits and symbolic play in preschoolers with autism. *Research in Autism Spectrum Disorders, 6,* 560–564.

Larson, M. J., South, M., Krauskopf, E., Clawson, A., & Crowley, M. J. (2011). Feedback and reward processing in high-functioning autism. *Psychiatry Research, 187,* 198–203.

Laube, I., Kamphuis, S., Dicke, P. W., & Their, P. (2011). Cortical processing of head- and eye-gaze cues guiding joint social attention. *NeuroImage, 54,* 1643–1653.

Lee, H.-J., Macbeth, A. H., Pagani, J. H., & Young, W. S., 3rd (2009). Oxytocin: The great facilitator of life. *Progress in Neurobiology, 88,* 127–151.

Lench, H. C., Flores, S. A., & Bench, S. W. (2011). Discrete emotions predict changes in cognition, judgment, experience, behavior, and physiology: a meta-analysis of experimental emotion elicitations. *Psychological Bulletin, 137,* 834–855.

Leppänen, J. M., & Nelson, C. A. (2009). Tuning the developing brain to social signals of emotions. *Nature Reviews Neuroscience, 10,* 37–47.

Lombardo, M. V., Chakrabarti, B., Bullmore, E. T., MRC AIMS Consortium, & Baron-Cohen, S. (2011). Specialization of right temporo-parietal junction for mentalizing and its relation to social impairments in autism. *NeuroImage, 56,* 1832–1838.

Mar, R. A. (2011). The neural bases of social cognition and story comprehension. *Annual Review of Psychology, 62,* 103–134.

Marsh, L. E., & Hamilton, A. F. de C. (2011). Dissociation of mirroring and mentalising systems in autism. *NeuroImage, 56,* 1511–1519.

Masten, C. L., Morelli, S. A., & Eisenberger, N. I. (2011). An fMRI investigation of empathy for "social pain" and subsequent prosocial behavior. *NeuroImage, 55,* 381–388.

Meyer-Lindenberg, A., Domes, G., Kirsch, P., & Heinrichs, M. (2011). Oxytocin and vasopressin in the human brain: Social neuropeptides for translational medicine. *Nature Reviews Neuroscience, 12,* 524–538.

Mobbs, D., Petrovic, P., Marchant, J. L., Hassabis, D., Weiskopf, N., Seymour, B., et al. (2007). When fear is near: Threat imminence elicits prefrontal–periaqueductal gray shifts in humans. *Science, 317,* 1079–1083.

Modahl, C., Green, L., Fein, D., Morris, M., Waterhouse, L., Feinstein, C., et al. (1998). Plasma oxytocin levels in autistic children. *Biological Psychiatry, 43,* 270–277.

Molenberghs, P., Cunnington, R., & Mattingley, J. B. (2012). Brain regions with mirror properties: A meta-analysis of 125 human fMRI studies. *Neuroscience and Biobehavioral Reviews, 59,* 608–615.

Naber, F. B. A., Swinkles, S. H. N., Buitelaar, J. K., Bakermans-Kranenburg, M. J., van IJzendoorn, M. H., Dietz, C., et al. (2007). Attachment in toddlers with autism and other developmental disorders. *Journal of Autism and Developmental Disorders, 37,* 1123–1138.

Nakamura, K., Iwata, Y., Anitha, A., Miyachi, T., Toyota, T., Yamada, S., et al. (2011). Replication study of Japanese cohorts supports the role of STX1A in autism susceptibility. *Progress in Neuropsychopharmacology and Biological Psychiatry, 35,* 454–458.

Niedenthal, P. M., & Brauer, M. (2012). Social functionality of human emotion. *Annual Review of Psychology, 63,* 20.1–20.27.

Noonan, S. K., Haist, F., & Muller, R. A. (2009). Aberrant functional connectivity in autism: Evidence from low-frequency BOLD signal fluctuations. *Brain Research, 1262,* 48–63.

Noordzij, M. L., Newman-Norlund, S. E., de Ruiter, J. P., Hagoort, P., Levinson, S. E., & Toni, I. (2009). Brain mechanisms underlying human communication. *Frontiers in Human Neuroscience, 3,* 1–13.

Northam, G. B., Liégeois, F., Chong, W. K., Wyatt, J. S., & Baldeweg, T. (2011). Total brain white matter is a major determinant of IQ in adolescents born preterm. *Annals of Neurology, 69*, 702–711.

Northoff, G., & Hayes, D. J. (2011). Is our self nothing but reward? *Biological Psychiatry, 69*, 1019–1025.

O'Connell, L. A., & Hofmann, H. A. (2011). Genes, hormones, and circuits: An integrative approach to study the evolution of social behavior. *Frontiers in Neuroendocrinology, 32*, 320–335.

Oberman, L. M., Winkielman, P., & Ramachandran, V. S. (2009). Slow echo: Facial EMG evidence for the delay of spontaneous, but not voluntary, emotional mimicry in children with autism spectrum disorders. *Developmental Science, 12*, 510–520.

Ocampo, B., & Kritikos, A. (2011). Interpreting actions: The goal behind mirror neuron function. *Brain Research Reviews, 67*, 260–267.

Panksepp, J. (2006). Emotional endophenotypes in evolutionary psychiatry. *Progress in Neuro-Psychopharmacology & Biological Psychiatry, 30*, 774–784.

Pannese, A., & Hirsch, J. (2011). Self-face enhances processing of immediately preceding invisible faces. *Neuropsychologia, 49*, 564–573.

Pedersen, C. A., Gibson, C. M., Rau, S. W., Salimi, K., Smedley, K. L., Casey, R. L., et al. (2011). Intranasal oxytocin reduces psychotic symptoms and improves Theory of Mind and social perception in schizophrenia. *Schizophrenia Research, 132*, 50–53.

Peppé, S., Cleland, J., Gibbon, F., O'Hare, A., & Martínez Castilla, P. (2011). Expressive prosody in children with autism spectrum conditions. *Journal of Neurolinguistics, 24*, 41–53.

Perrachione, T. K., Del Tufo, S. N., & Gabrieli, J. D. E. (2011). Human voice recognition depends on language ability. *Science, 333*, 595.

Pessoa, L. (2008). On the relationship between emotion and cognition. *Nature, 9*, 148–158.

Pessoa, L., & Adolphs, R. (2010). Emotion processing and the amygdala: From a "low road" to "many roads" of evaluating biological significance. *Nature Reviews Neuroscience, 11*, 773–783.

Peters, S. U., Kaufmann, W. E., Bacino, C. A., Anderson, A. W., Adapa, P., Chu, Z., et al. (2011). Alterations in white matter pathways in Angelman syndrome. *Developmental Medicine and Child Neurology, 53*, 361–367.

Pierce, K. (2011). Early functional brain development in autism and the promise of sleep fMRI. *Brain Research, 1380*, 162–174.

Pinto-Martin, J. A., Levy, S. E., Feldman, J. F., Lorenz, I. M., Paneth, N., & Whitaker, A. H. (2011). Prevalence of autism spectrum disorder in adolescents born weighing <2000 grams. *Pediatrics, 128*, 883–891.

Press, C., Richardson, D., & Bird, G. (2010). Intact imitation of emotional facial actions in autism spectrum conditions. *Neuropsychologia, 48*, 3291–3297.

Pulvermüller, F., & Fadiga, L. (2010). Active perception: Sensorimotor circuits as a cortical basis for language. *Nature Reviews Neuroscience, 11*, 351–360.

Qin, P., & Northoff, G. (2011). How is our self related to midline regions and the default-mode network? *NeuroImage, 57*, 1221–1233.

Raymaekers, R., Wiersman, J. R., & Roeyers, H. (2009). EEG study of the mirror neuron system in children with high functioning autism. *Brain Research, 1304*, 113–121.

Rizzolatti, G., & Fabbri-Destro, M. (2010). Mirror neurons: From discovery to autism. *Experimental Brain Research, 200*, 223–237.

Ruta, L., Ingudomnukul, E., Taylor, K., Chakrabarti, B., & Baron-Cohen, S. (2011). Increased serum androstenedione in adults with autism spectrum conditions. *Psychoneuroendocrinology, 36*, 1154–1163.

Rutgers, A. H., Bakermans-Kranenburg, M. J., van IJzendoorn, M. H., & Van Berckelaer-Onnes, I. A. (2004). Autism and attachment: A meta-analytic review. *Journal of Child Psychology and Psychiatry, 45*, 1123–1134.

Rutherford, M. D., & Troje, N. F. (2012). IQ predicts biological motion perception in autism spectrum disorders. *Journal of Autism and Developmental Disorders, 42*, 557–565.

Rutishauser, U., Tudusciuc, O., Neumann, D., Mamelak, A. N., Heller, A. C., Ross, I. B., et al. (2011). Single-unit responses selective for whole faces in the human amygdala. *Current Biology, 21*, 1654–1660.

Said, C. P., Haxby, J. V., & Todorov, A. (2011). Brain systems for assessing the affective value of faces. *Philosophical Transactions of the Royal Society of London Series B Biological Sciences, 366*, 1660–1670.

Sarachana, T., Xu, M., Wu, R.-C., & Hu, V. W. (2011). Sex hormones in autism: Androgens and estrogens differentially and reciprocally regulate RORA, a novel candidate gene for autism. *PLoS ONE, 6*, e17116.

Schipul, S. E., Keller, T. A., & Just, M. A. (2011). Inter-regional brain communication and its disturbance in autism. *Frontiers in Systems Neuroscience, 5*, 1–10.

Schroeder, J. H., Desrocher, M., Bebko, J. M., & Cappadocia, M. C. (2010). The neurobiology of autism: Theoretical applications. *Research in Autism Spectrum Disorders, 4*, 555–564.

Schulte-Rüther, M., Greimel, E., Markowitsch, H. J., Kamp-Becker, I., Remschmidt, H., Fink, G. R., et al. (2011). Dysfunctions in brain networks supporting empathy: An fMRI study in adults with autism. *Social Neuroscience, 6*, 1–21.

Skuse, D. H., & Gallagher, L. (2011). Genetic influences on social cognition. *Pediatric Research, 69*(5 Pt 2), 85R–91R.

Stauder, J. E. A., Bosch, C. P. A., & Nuij, H. A. M. (2011). Atypical visual orienting to eye gaze and arrow cues in children with high functioning Autism Spectrum Disorder. *Research in Autism Spectrum Disorders, 5*, 742–748.

Stevenson, R. A., VanDerKlok, R. M., Pisoni, D. M., & James, T. W. (2011). Discrete neural substrates underlie complementary audiovisual speech integration processes. *NeuroImage, 5*, 1339–1345.

Stigler, K. A., McDonald, B. C., Anand, A., Saykin, A. J., & McDougle, C. J. (2011). Structural and functional magnetic resonance imaging of autism spectrum disorders. *Brain Research, 1380*, 146–161.

Tettamanti, M., Rognoni, M., Cafiero, R., Costa, T., Galati, D., & Perani, D. (2012). Distinct pathways of neural coupling for different basic emotions. *NeuroImage, 59*, 1804–1817.

Thompson, J., & Parasuraman, R. (2012). Attention, biological motion, and action recognition. *NeuroImage, 59*, 4–13.

Uddin, L. Q. (2011). Brain connectivity and the self: The case of cerebral disconnection. *Consciousness and Cognition, 20*, 94–98.

van den Heuvel, M. P., & Sporns, O. (2011). Rich-club organization of the human connectome. *Journal of Neuroscience, 31*, 15775–15786.

van Eijsden, P., Hyder, F., Rothman, D. L., & Shulman, R. G. (2009). Neurophysiology of functional imaging. *NeuroImage, 45*, 1047–1054.

Van Whye, J. (2002). The authority of human nature: The Schadellehre of Franz Joseph Gall. *British Journal for the History of Science, 35*, 17–42.

van Wingen, G. A., Ossewaarde, L., Bäckström, T. J., Hermans, E. J., & Fernández, G. (2011). Gonadal hormone regulation of the emotion circuitry in humans. *Neuroscience, 191*, 38–45.

Vickery, T. J., Chun, M. M., & Lee, D. (2011). Ubiquity and specificity of reinforcement signals throughout the human brain. *Neuron, 72*, 166–177.

Wass, S. (2011). Distortions and disconnections: Disrupted brain connectivity in autism. *Brain and Cognition, 75*, 18–28.

Wig, G. S., Schlaggar, B. L., & Petersen, S. E. (2011). Concepts and principles in the analysis of brain networks. *Annals of the New York Academy of Sciences, 1224*, 126–146.

Wing, L., Gould, J., & Gillberg, C. (2011). Autism spectrum disorders in the DSM-V: Better or worse than the DSM-IV? *Research in Developmental Disabilities, 32*, 768–773.

Yang, S. Y., Cho, S. C., Yoo, H. J., Cho, I. H., Park, M., Yoe, J., et al. (2010). Family-based association study of microsatellites in the 5′ flanking region of AVPR1A with autism spectrum disorder in the Korean population. *Psychiatry Research, 178*, 199–201.

Zhu, Q., Zhang, J., Luo, Y. L.L., Dilks, D. D., & Liu, J. (2011). Resting-state neural activity across face-selective cortical regions is behaviorally relevant. *Journal of Neuroscience, 31*(28), 10323–10330.

Genetic Risk Factors Link Autism to Many Other Disorders

Contents

Rethinking Autism
http://dx.doi.org/10.1016/B978-0-12-415961-7.00004-6

Given the very high heritabilities reported for autism, many researchers initially believed that most cases of autism would result from a small set of gene variants unique to autism. Folstein and Rutter (1977) reported that 36% of identical (monozygotic, MZ) but not fraternal (dizygotic, DZ) twin pairs shared a diagnosis of autism. Taniai et al. (2008) reported 88% of MZ and only 31% of DZ twin pairs shared a diagnosis of autism. Ronald and Hoekstra (2011) reviewed twin studies and reported that high identical twin and low fraternal twin concordances indicated a very large genetic contribution to autism. Miles (2011) asserted that the high heritability rates of .85 to .92 found in these twin studies made geneticists "confident that autism will be the first behavioral disorder for which the genetic basis can be well established" (p. 278).

MANY GENE VARIANTS CONTRIBUTE TO AUTISM

Pickles et al. (1995) theorized that between 2 and 10 gene variants would account for the high heritability rate of autism. Pickles et al. (1995) concluded that either each gene variant would contribute to a separate autism symptom, with "independent genes for each component" of diagnosis (p. 725), or all 2–10 gene variants together would cause autism with "the same genes affecting all components" of the diagnosis (p. 725).

A gene variant is a mutation in the gene caused by mistakes in DNA replication, ionizing radiation, chemicals, or viruses. We all carry two copies, called alleles, of every gene. Our 20,000–22,000 genes occur on 23 pairs of chromosomes and comprise just 2% of the chromosomal DNA. Somewhat startling is that 80% of our genes—perhaps 16,000–18,000 genes—are expressed in our brains. Mutations can occur in an allele of any gene, and an allele linked to a disease or disorder is called a risk allele or a risk gene variant. A mutation is defined as "de novo gene variant" if it is thought to have occurred in an individual without having appeared in the genome of either parent. If a mutation occurs in 1–5% of the population, it is called a rare gene variant. By contrast, common gene variants are mutations that are shared by many individuals in a population.

The Pickles et al. (1995) hypothesis of a group of 2–10 gene variants for autism was found to be both an overestimate and a vast underestimate. A number of disorders expressing autism diagnostic symptoms were linked to only one gene variant. The Online Mendelian Inheritance in Man website listed over 4000 known single gene disorders, including 629 single gene neurological disorders (OMIM, 2011). Table 4.1 lists 14 single gene disorders such as fragile X syndrome, and 24 additional gene variants, each of which has been found in association with autism (Aldinger, Plummer, Qiu, & Levitt, 2011).

Table 4.1 names genetic disorders, neurological disorders, and psychiatric diagnoses caused by gene variants that are found with the diagnostic symptoms of autism. These include Angelman syndrome, attention deficit/hyperactivity disorder, Cowden disease, DiGeorge syndrome, Duchenne muscular dystrophy, epilepsy, recessive epilepsy syndrome, fragile X syndrome, intellectual disability, X-linked intellectual disability, Joubert syndrome, lissencephaly, neurofibromatosis, obsessive-compulsive disorder, Phelan McDermid syndrome, Rett syndrome, schizophrenia, Smith-Lemli-Opitz syndrome, specific language impairment, Timothy syndrome, tuberous sclerosis types I and II, and X-linked infantile spasm syndrome.

It is important to note that these genetic disorders are most often found in individuals who have *not* been diagnosed with autism. When any one of these genetic syndromes occurs in an individual diagnosed with autism, the label "syndromic autism" is applied. Syndromic autism has been defined by contrast to idiopathic autism, autism of unknown origin. Schaaf and Zoghbi (2011) estimated that known genetic disorders were likely to account for 30% of autism cases.

Table 4.1 Gene and Chromosome Variants Found for Autism (adapted from Aldinger, Plummer, Qui, and Levitt, 2011)

Chromosome loci[a]	Gene Name	Protein/enzyme name	Protein/enzyme Function	Primary Syndrome Name	Additional Diagnoses Found with Gene Variant
Fourteen Named Syndromes Caused by Single Gene Mutations					
6q23.3	AHI1	Jouberin	Interacts with β-catenin in cilia	Joubert syndrome	Autism
7q35–q36.1	CNTNAP2	Caspr2	Clusters voltage-gated K^+ channels	Recessive epilepsy syndrome	Autism, ADHD, Tourette syndrome, obsessive-compulsive disorder
9q34.13	TSC1	Hamartin	A growth inhibitor for mTOR pathway	Tuberous sclerosis type I	Autism
10q23.31	PTEN	Protein tyrosine phosphatase	Negative regulator mTOR pathway	Cowden disease	Autism
11q13.4	DHCR7		Final enzyme in cholesterol biosynthetic pathway	Smith–Lemli-Opitz syndrome	Autism
12p13.33	CACNA1C		The a–1 subunit of a voltage-dependent Ca^{2+} channel	Timothy syndrome	Autism
15q11.2	UBE3A	Ubiquitination ligase	Targets protein degradation system	Angelman syndrome	Autism

16p13.3	TSC2	Tuberin	Negative regulator mTOR pathway	Tuberous sclerosis type II	Autism
17q11.2	NF1	Neurofibromin	A GTPase activator and a negative regulator of RAS signaling	Neurofibromatosis	Autism
Xp21.2	DMD	Dystrophin	Cytoskeletal protein bridging extracellular matrix	Duchenne muscular dystrophy	Autism
Xp21.3	ARX		Aristaless-related homeobox protein transcription factor	lissencephaly	Autism, epilepsy, X-linked intellectual disability
Xp22.13	CDKl5		Encodes a cyclin-dependent kinase-like 5 protein	X-linked infantile spasm syndrome	Autism
Xq27.3	FMR1	Fragile X mental retardation protein	An RNA-binding protein that traffics mRNA Fragile X	Fragile X syndrome	Autism
Xq28	MECP2		Transcriptional regulation and chromatin organization	Rett syndrome	Autism

(Continued)

Table 4.1 Gene and Chromosome Variants Found for Autism (adapted from Aldinger, Plummer, Qui, and Levitt, 2011)—cont'd

Chromosome loci[a]	Gene Name	Protein/ enzyme name	Protein/enzyme Function	Primary Syndrome Name	Additional Diagnoses Found with Gene Variant
Sixteen Rare Gene Variants Occurring in Less Than 5% of Human Genomes					
1q21.1	Unknown		Unknown		Autism, ADHD, epilepsy, intellectual disability, schizophrenia
2p16.3	NRXN1		Forms intracellular junctions through neuroligin binding		Autism, intellectual disability, language delay, schizophrenia
3p13	FOXP1		Forkhead box transcription factor		Autism, intellectual disability, specific language impairment, schizophrenia
6p16.3	GRIK2		Postsynaptic glutamate receptor subunit		Autism (linked by SNP), intellectual disability
7q11.23	Unknown		Unknown		Autism, intellectual disability, language delay
7q31.1	FOXP2		Forkhead box transcription factor		Autism, specific language impairment
11q13.3–q13.4	SHANK2		Encodes a postsynaptic density scaffold protein		Autism, specific language impairment
16p11.2	Unknown		Unknown		Autism, ADHD, epilepsy, intellectual disability, schizophrenia
16p13.3	A2BP1		Encodes an RNA-binding protein		Autism, ADHD, epilepsy, intellectual disability, schizophrenia

Location	Gene	Function	Syndrome	Disorders
17q11.2	SLC6A4	5-HT transporter		Autism, obsessive-compulsive disorder
17q12	Unknown	Unknown		Autism, epilepsy, schizophrenia
22q11.21	Unknown	Unknown	DiGeorge syndrome	Autism, intellectual disability, schizophrenia
22q13.33	SHANK3	Postsynaptic density scaffold protein	Phelan McDermid syndrome	Autism
Xp22.11	PTCHD1	Encodes a transmembrane protein		Autism, intellectual disability
Xp22.32–p22.31	NLGN4X	Ligand for β-neurexins		Autism, ADHD, intellectual disability, Tourette syndrome
Xq13.1	NLGN3	Ligand for β-neurexins		Autism
Eight Common Gene Alleles Occurring in More Than 5% of Human Genomes				
1q42.2	DISC1	Large transmembrane protein involved in neurite outgrowth and brain development		Autism, schizophrenia, bipolar disorder, intellectual disability
2q31.1	SLC25A12	Mitochondrial Ca^{2+}-binding carrier		Autism
3p25.3	OXTR	G-protein-coupled receptor for oxytocin		Autism
7q31.2	MET	Receptor tyrosine kinase		Autism

(Continued)

Table 4.1 Gene and Chromosome Variants Found for Autism (adapted from Aldinger, Plummer, Qui, and Levitt, 2011)—*cont'd*

Chromosome loci[a]	Gene Name	Protein/ enzyme name	Protein/enzyme Function	Primary Syndrome Name	Additional Diagnoses Found with Gene Variant
Eight Common Gene Alleles Occurring in More Than 5% of Human Genomes—*cont'd*					
7q22.1	RELN		Extracellular matrix protein involved in cell–cell interactions		Autism, schizophrenia
7q36.3	EN2		Homeobox transcription factor critical for hind-brain patterning		Autism
12q14.2	AVPR1A		G-protein-coupled receptor for arginine vasopressin		Autism
17q21.32	ITGB3		Mediates platelet cell adhesion and cell-surface signaling		Autism

[a]The first loci information is the chromosome's number 1 to 22, and X; p indicates the chromosome's short arm, and q the long arm. The numbers following the p or q represent the position on the arm of the chromosome: the first digit is the region; the second is the band; and the third digit, which appears after a period, is the sub-band. Numbers after the dash indicate a loci band range.

The theory that autism was caused by a group of just 2–10 specific genes operating together was also an underestimate of the number of risk gene variants found for autism. Betancur (2011) identified more than 100 different gene variants as possible causes for autism, and Gilman et al. (2011) suggested, "many hundreds of genes could ultimately contribute to the autistic phenotype" (p. 904). Casey et al. (2012) argued that the number of gene variants potentially conferring a risk for autism was more than 300. Sanders et al. (2011) estimated that 234 gene variants contributed to autism. However, Sanders et al. (2012), using the same analytic technique in a different sample of 928 individuals, including 200 sibling pairs, one with autism and one without autism, estimated that 1034 genes might contribute to autism. O'Roak et al. (2012) estimated that 324–821 risk gene variants would be pathogenic for autism.

MANY TYPES OF GENETIC MUTATIONS CONTRIBUTE TO AUTISM

Research has led to ever-increasing evidence for a variety of different types of genetic alterations, from tiny changes in a single gene, to larger changes in a single gene, to alterations in large sections of a chromosome, to whole chromosome alterations associated with autism symptoms.

Autism has been found with many different types of mutations of single genes. When a mutation occurs in a single nucleotide within a gene but is not rare in the population, it is called single nucleotide polymorphism (SNP). For example, Anney et al. (2010) identified an autism-related SNP that regulates *PLD2*, a gene that contributes to neuron axonal growth and metabotropic glutamate receptor signaling. O'Roak et al. (2012) reported finding many different rare or de novo (new in the genome of an individual) single nucleotide gene mutations associated with autism. These are called point mutations and were reported for many genes: *ABCA2, ADCY5, AP3B2, CACNA1D, CACNA1E, CDC42BPB, CDH5, CHD3, CHD7, CNOT4, CTNNB1, CUL3, CUL5, EHD2, FBXO10, GPS1, HDGFRP2, HDLBP, MDM2, MLL3, NLGN1, NOTCH3, NR4A2, NTNG1, OPRL1, PCDHB4, PSEN1, PTEN, PTPRK, RGMA, RPS6KA3, RUVBL1, SESN2, TBL1XR1, TNKS, TSC2, TSPAN17, UBE3C, ZBTB41,* and *ZNF420.* Neale et al. (2012) argued that there was "an important but limited role for de novo point mutations in ASD" (p. 1). Neale et al. (2012) proposed "polygenic models in which spontaneous coding mutations in any of a large number of genes increases risk by 5- to 20-fold" (p. 1) for autism.

Frameshift mutations are also small single gene mutations: they involve a deletion or insertion of a nucleotide. O'Roak et al. (2012) reported finding frameshift mutations in genes *ADNP, ARID1B, BRWD1, CHD8, MBD5, PDCD1, SETBP1, SETD2, TBR1, UBR3*, and *USP15* associated with autism. Still other mutations in single genes include missense mutations wherein one amino acid is substituted for another, nonsense mutations that result in a shortened protein, indel mutations wherein one segment of the gene is deleted and a different segment is added, deletions of gene segments, and duplication of a piece of DNA copied one or more times. Splice site mutations allow introns, gene subsections removed during protein creation, to remain in mature RNA, thus altering protein formation. Missense mutations in the genes *SCN1A*, and *LAMC3* have been found in association with autism. Protein-truncation (nonsense) mutations in the gene *GRIN2B* have been found for autism. Indels in genes *BRSK2* and *GRIN1LA* have been found for autism. Deletions in genes *CNTNAP4, CTNND1*, and *EHMT1* have been reported for autism. Duplications in genes *CHRNA7* and *TBX6* have been discovered in association with autism. Sanders et al. (2012) found 125 de novo single nucleotide variants (SNVs) in a sample including individuals with autism and their siblings, of which five de novo splice site mutations occurred in five individuals with autism. Sanders et al. (2012) concluded, "highly disruptive (nonsense and splice-site) de novo mutations in brain-expressed genes are associated with autism spectrum disorders and carry large effects" (p. 1).

Autism has also been found with errant duplications or deletions of chromosome sections containing one or more genes and non-gene sequences. These chromosome duplications and deletions are called copy number variants or CNVs. A CNV includes 1000 or more DNA base pairs. Benign common CNVs occur in about 12% of a typical human genome. Rare CNVs contain more genes than common CNVs. Approximately 65–80% of healthy individuals carry one moderate sized CNV, 5–10% carry a large CNV, and 1% of healthy individuals carry a very large CNV without clinical effects (Girirajan, Campbell, & Eichler, 2011). A CNV may variably include few or many genes, and many non-gene DNA sequences. Although the 98% non-gene sequences of our DNA "previously known as junk DNA in fact appears a regulatory jungle" (Splinter & de Laat, 2011, p. 4353), many of the regulatory functions of non-gene DNA remain unknown.

Duplications of a gene in a section of a chromosome may have different effects than a deletion of that gene. For example, duplication of the *MECP2* gene results in Lubs X-linked mental retardation syndrome, but deletion of the *MECP2* gene results in Rett syndrome, which has been found in association with the diagnostic symptoms of autism.

Sanders et al. (2011) estimated there were 130–234 ASD-related chromosomal CNVs. The researchers argued specifically for de novo CNVs at 7q11.23, 15q11.2–13.1, and 16p11.2 as causal for autism. The region of a CNV on a chromosome, for example 7q11.23, begins with chromosome number, 7, then upper/short arm p or long/lower arm q, then region number, 1, band number, 1, and sub-band numbers 2 and 3. Neale et al. (2012) pointed out that, although CNVs are important for understanding the genetic base of autism, CNVs "rarely implicate single genes, are rarely fully penetrant, and many confer risk to a broad range of conditions including intellectual disability, epilepsy and schizophrenia" (p. 242).

The deletion or addition of a whole chromosome will cause disorders in which autism symptoms appear. Chromosome 21 has the fewest base pairs, 47 million, and fewest genes, 300–400, of our 23 chromosomes. Down syndrome is caused by an extra 21st chromosome. Autism has been diagnosed in 7–15% of individuals diagnosed with Down syndrome (Ji, Capone, & Kaufmann, 2011). Chromosome X has 155 million base pairs and approximately 1800 genes. Klinefelter syndrome in males is caused by an extra X chromosome. Autism has been diagnosed in 34% of males with Klinefelter syndrome (van Rijn & Swaab, 2011). Turner syndrome occurs in females, caused by a partial or complete absence of the second X chromosome. Autism has been diagnosed in 3% or more of females with Turner syndrome (Knickmeyer & Davenport, 2011).

THREE FUNDAMENTAL QUESTIONS FOR AUTISM GENETICS

Although genetic research in autism is in the early stages, given the many genetic and chromosomal variants already found for autism, crucial questions have already emerged. First, what are the patterns of genetic causality for autism? Second, how do gene variants cause brain deficits in autism? Third, what is the significance of autism gene variants shared with many other disorders?

Table 4.1 lists genetic syndromes known to cause autism symptoms. Table 4.1 also includes a small subset of the possible thousand or more gene variants and CNVs that have been associated with autism. Beyond the known single gene syndromes, no clear or comprehensive pattern of genetic causality has emerged. Research findings suggest that autism is linked to many different patterns of genetic causality including single genes, combinations of several genes, CNVs, and large groups of hundreds of genes. Many possible alternate models have been proposed.

A second fundamental question raised by the burgeoning genetic findings for autism is the mechanisms through which gene variants contribute to autism brain deficits. Hundreds of gene variants have been discovered for autism, and many different patterns of brain deficits have been documented for autism. Given the vast array of both gene variants and brain deficits associated with autism, is it possible to find causal connections between gene variants and brain deficits in autism without ignoring meaningful variation?

Genetics research has discovered that autism shares many gene variants and chromosome duplications and deletions with other disorders, including intellectual disability, schizophrenia, attention deficit/hyperactivity disorder, epilepsy, and specific language impairment. O'Roak et al. (2012) asserted, "It is clear from phenotype and genotype data that there are many 'autisms' represented under the current umbrella of ASD" (p. 3). Therefore, a third fundamental question is how to interpret the gene variants shared across diagnostic groups.

QUESTION ONE: WHAT ARE THE GENETIC CAUSAL PATTERNS FOR AUTISM?

The model proposed by Pickles et al. (1995) underestimated the complexity of genetic causality. Pickles et al. (1995) hypothesized two possible patterns: single genes each contributing to single symptoms, or all of a small group of genes conjointly contributing to all autism symptoms. Since then, many CNVs have been found in association with autism, as have many individual single gene mutations. A wide range of more complex causal patterns has been theorized.

For example, Hyman (2010) asserted, "no single gene variant or genomic locus appears to be necessary or sufficient to produce any of the major, common mental disorders. Evidence that is emerging at an accelerating pace also suggests that in different individuals, autism ... may result either from the interaction of a large number of common genetic variants ... [or] from rare, highly penetrant mutations" (p. 169).

Many other theories of combinations of gene variants and CNVs have been proposed (El-Fishawy & State, 2010; Geschwind, 2011; Levy et al., 2011; Mitchell, 2011; Neale et al, 2012; O'Roak et al., 2012; Sakai et al.,

2011; Sanders et al., 2012; Schaaf & Zoghbi, 2011; State & Levitt, 2011; Visscher, Goddard, Derks, & Wray, 2011;Voineagu et al., 2011). Researchers have attempted to find meaningful patterns in the hundreds of gene variants and CNVs found for autism.

Five types of investigative models have dominated the many varied hypotheses. Each type of model proposed different genetic mechanisms. One model argued that autism resulted from a large group of gene variants (Neale et al. 2012;Visscher et al., 2011;Voineagu, 2011). Another type of model argued either that there were two separate genetic mechanisms for syndromic and idiopathic autism (Grice and Buxbaum, 2006; Schaaf et al., 2011), or two genetic "hits" caused all autism (Girirajan et al., 2010; State & Levitt, 2011). A third model argued that many different single gene variants separately caused autism (Heger, 2011; Mitchell, 2011). A fourth type of model argued that many rare or de novo CNVs caused autism (Joober & Boksa, 2009; Walsh & Bracken, 2011). Finally, some models proposed that epigenetic mechanisms influenced gene variants causing autism (de León-Guerrero, Pedraza-Alva, & Pérez-Martínez, 2011; Grafodatskaya, Chung, Szatmari, & Weksberg, 2010). These five types of investigative models were not necessarily mutually exclusive. Each could contribute an explanatory component to the understanding of the many genetic causes for autism.

The following five sections review selected findings for each of the investigative genetic models.

Model 1: Multiple Gene Variants Operating Together

Formerly, the common disease–rare variant (CDRV) hypothesis proposed that common diseases and disorders, such as cancer or heart disease, were caused by a few rare gene variants, occurring in less than 1–5% of the population, where each gene variant had a high penetrance, i.e., significant power to cause disease. An opposing view, the common disease–common variant (CDCV) hypothesis, argued that diseases like cancer or obesity were caused by a large set of common gene variants widely prevalent in a population, each with a low penetrance, or small power to cause disease. However, research found that *both* the CDRV and CDCV hypotheses held true for some common diseases, such as heart disease and cancer.

The CDCV hypothesis for autism claimed that a very large set of common gene variants operated together to generate autism symptoms (Visscher et al., 2011; Voineagu, 2011). Rucker and McGuffin (2010) reviewed the CDCV threshold model. They noted, "what is inherited is not so much a disorder as a liability to disorder contributed to by multiple genetic and environmental effects. What has emerged in recent studies is an even more complex pattern of polygenic heterogeneity whereby phenotypically different syndromes appear to result from overlapping liabilities" (Rucker & McGuffin, 2010, p. 312). Chen et al. (2011) pointed out that lower penetrance, i.e., less power for a gene variant to cause a disease or disorder, was discovered for a variety of rare gene variants found in association with autism, including *GNB1L*, *SHANK3*, *NRXN1*, and *CNTNAP2*. These findings suggested the possibility of a "common disorder–several rare variants" model for autism. In this model, autism would result from a set of several rare gene variants rather than many common gene variants.

Voineagu (2011), however, argued that "many common variants, likely more than 100, are necessary to cause the disease in each ASD case, while none of the individual sequence variants are either necessary or sufficient to cause the disease" (p. 2). Like Voineagu, Visscher et al. (2011) argued that the hundreds of common gene variants associated with psychiatric disorders like autism and schizophrenia would be found to operate together. Visscher et al. (2011) proposed that psychiatric disorders had a genetic basis similar to that of human height or human intelligence. A person's height is the combined result of nearly 200 different common gene variants, each of which contributes a tiny bit of inheritance to the overall heritability. Visscher et al. (2011) argued that, like the polygene pattern for height, each gene for a complex psychiatric disorder, such as schizophrenia or autism, contributed only a small amount to the genetic variance, and only when the additive effects from a very large set of gene variants crossed a threshold would autism or schizophrenia emerge. Visscher et al. (2011) concluded that research evidence indicates "beyond doubt that most psychiatric disease is not Mendelian in the sense that they are not caused solely by a single mutation …. Mendelian forms … account for very little of the population variance" (p. 481).

Neale et al. (2012) argued that examination of a "range of genetic models reveals that some models are inconsistent with the observed data—for example, 100 rare, fully penetrant Mendelian genes similar to Rett's syndrome—whereas others are not inconsistent, such as spontaneous 'functional' mutation in hundreds of genes that would increase risk by 10- or 20-fold …. Models that fit the data … suggest that de novo SNVs, like most CNVs, often combine with other risk factors rather than fully cause disease" (p. 244).

Model 1, Multiple Gene Variants Operating Together—Challenges to the Model

Many problems face the multiple common gene model. It is difficult to find common variants, few common variants have been discovered, and constructing a meaningful common variants model requires information not yet known. Park et al. (2010) estimated the possible number of gene variants that might contribute to a complex disorder based on existing evidence from genome-wide association studies. The researchers' conclusions were daunting. They proposed that a complex disorder might well depend on "possibly thousands of susceptibility loci with very small effect sizes" (Park et al., 2010, p. 573). In order to discover whether thousands of gene variants of very low effect sizes were the cause of autism, a study of a minimum of 20,000 individuals with autism, and more than 50,000 controls would be required.

Devlin, Melhelm, and Roeder (2011) used the estimation analysis of Park et al. (2010), and calculated that even if researchers could establish a sample of 8000 individuals diagnosed with autism, and 20,000 typical participants as controls, researchers would be able to discover at most only a meager one to five common variants associated with autism.

Devlin et al. (2011) reviewed genome-wide association (GWA) studies in autism and reported, "For ASD, no susceptibility loci have been reliably replicated over GWA studies" (p. 82). They argued, "common variation dredged from simple GWA analyses will not explain a substantial fraction of the heritability of ASD" (p. 83). Similarly, Pinto et al. (2010) concluded, "common variation will account for only a small proportion of the heritability in ASD" (p. 368).

Rodriguez-Murillo, Gogos, and Karayiorgou (2012) reviewed the problem of the genetic architecture of schizophrenia. They noted that, as in autism genetics, the common disease–common variant (CDCV) polygene hypothesis and common disease–rare variant (CDRV) single gene hypothesis were both actively studied. Similar to the conclusion drawn by Devlin et al. (2011) for autism, Rodriguez-Murillo et al. (2012) concluded that schizophrenia researchers should not "invest resources to identify a handful more common loci whose validity would almost inevitably be controversial and whose functional significance would likely remain elusive and, therefore, not conducive to a straightforward path to drug discovery" (p. 13). Rodriguez-Murillo et al. (2012), like Devlin et al. (2011) for autism, reported that there was little evidence for common gene variant candidates for schizophrenia. Moreover, the common variants that had been found carried very small disease risk and had no functional link to schizophrenia. The researchers pointed out that the risk of all the common variants together was much smaller than the effect sizes found for individual rare large de novo chromosome duplications or deletions.

Rodriguez–Murillo et al. (2012) proposed that four key pieces of information were needed to fully define a multiple gene model. One: how many gene variants contribute to the disorder? In autism, although hundreds of gene variants have been identified as candidates, it is not clear which variants would be necessary for an individual case of autism. Two: what is population frequency of each contributing gene variant? Is a gene variant rare, moderately rare, or common? A number of rare gene variants are known to cause autism diagnostic symptoms, but the role of common variants is not clear (Devlin et al., 2011). Three, what is the effect size of each contributing gene variant? While the penetrance, that is, significant power to cause disease, of many known single gene causes for autism is high, the penetrance of other possible variants that may contribute to autism is not yet known.

A final, fourth question Rodriguez–Murillo et al. (2012) proposed was how the gene variants interacted with one another in causing the disease. Does each gene variant contribute in an additive way to the disease? For example, Girirajan et al. (2011) reported an additive effect of two CNVs. Four individuals found to have both a chromosome 16p12.1 microdeletion and an additional chromosomal abnormality or chromosome deletion or duplication had more severe or marked symptoms than did individuals with only the chromosome 16p12.1 microdeletion. This two-hit model is discussed in the following section. However, the additive effect model proposed by Girirajan et al. (2011) is not a true multiple or polygene model: only two genetic causes are proposed, and the two causes both have high penetrance.

Model 2: Two Genetic Mechanisms

A number of researchers theorized that autism resulted from two genetic mechanisms. Some researchers proposed that syndromic autism and idiopathic autism each resulted from separate genetic mechanisms. Other researchers proposed that all autism was the result of the combined influence of two forms of genetic mutation, whether rare gene variants, or de novo or rare chromosome duplications or deletions.

Model 2, Two Mechanisms: One for Syndromic Autism, Another for Idiopathic Autism

As noted above, 30% of cases of autism have been identified as syndromic autism, diagnosed in individuals with known genetic syndromes, such as fragile X syndrome and tuberous sclerosis. Levy, Mandel, and Schultz (2010) claimed that single gene syndromes were not specific to autism, "but rather are specific to a range of phenotypes, including intellectual disability" (p. 5). Levy et al. (2010) hypothesized that the gene mutations affecting neuron function and synapse development that impaired the brain development of individuals with fragile X syndrome, tuberous sclerosis, Angelman, or Rett syndrome would be similar to, but distinct from, the genetic cause of core diagnostic symptoms of autism. Levy et al. (2010) asserted research was needed to discover how a mutation in genes that regulate the maturation of the synapse can impair social functioning in autism, and how brain circuits "mediating social and communicative skills and behavioural flexibility might be vulnerable to a common underlying synaptic defect" (p. 6).

Folstein (2006) claimed that individuals with syndromic autism who have detectable genetic abnormalities or who have a known etiology such as fragile X syndrome or tuberous sclerosis, do not have true autism as Kanner originally defined it. She suggested that Kanner's autism was more heritable than DSM-IV autism disorder. Folstein (2006) argued that DSM-IV autism disorder had effectively become a mix of syndromic autism and Kanner's autism. She asserted that consequently the ASD diagnosis was netting "a much broader range of cases including those who have profound mental handicap, dysmorphic features, and … a known etiology (such as fragile X syndrome, Rett syndrome, tuberous sclerosis, or untreated phenylketonuria); others are children with … detectable cytogenetic abnormalities, such as maternally transmitted duplication of chromosome 15q11–12" (p. 116). The only atypical feature Folstein (2006) proposed as part of Kanner's autism was macrocephaly, an atypically large head. This is because in his original clinical description Kanner commented that 5 of the 11 children he diagnosed with autism had large heads.

Grice and Buxbaum (2006) also asserted that it was "important to distinguish between 'idiopathic' autism and 'secondary' autism, in which a known environmental agent, chromosome abnormality, or single gene disorder can be identified" (p. 161). Grice and Buxbaum proposed further dividing idiopathic autism into "complex autism" and Kanner-like "essential autism." They argued that complex autism was defined by dysmorphic features and/or an atypically small head and occurred in 20–30% of individuals with idiopathic autism. In contrast to Folstein's (2006) claim that pure Kanner autism did include children with atypically large heads, Grice and Buxbaum (2006) argued that those individuals with Kanner-like essential autism were defined by the *absence* of macrocephaly. Grice and Buxbaum (2006), like Folstein, argued that Kanner-like essential autism had a higher heritability than other forms of autism. However, Grice and Buxbaum proposed, "all identifiable genetic conditions were confined to the complex autism group" (p. 166).

Skuse (2007) also theorized that the genetic basis for idiopathic autism was separate from the genetic basis for autism symptoms found with known genetic syndromes. He noted that one-third of individuals with chromosomal or single gene disorders such as Smith-Lemli-Opitz syndrome or Duchenne muscular dystrophy had autism symptoms, and that autism was reported for one-third of idiopathic cases of intellectual disability. Skuse (2007) argued that autism with intellectual disability and autism in genetic syndromes did not reveal neuropathological deficits that would be specific to autism. Skuse (2007) concluded that the single gene variants or chromosome deletions or duplications that caused syndromic autism could not cause essential idiopathic autism. Skuse (2007) argued that "to search for genes that specifically influence susceptibility to the neurocognitive deficits associated with the autistic phenotype, it would make more sense to focus on samples of individuals with normal-range intelligence and good structural language skills" (p. 393).

Schaaf et al. (2011) proposed a different type of dual model for the genetic mechanisms determining syndromic and idiopathic autism. Schaaf et al. (2011) proposed that syndromic autism was the result of many independent severe mutations of rare single gene variants. The researchers theorized that idiopathic autism was caused by the additive effect of a set of milder mutations of the same genes known to cause syndromic autism. Schaaf et al. (2011) further proposed that idiopathic autism would also be caused by mutations in novel genes unrelated to syndromic autism.

Model 2, Separate Mechanisms for Syndromic and Idiopathic Autism—Challenges to the Model

Research challenges for the theory that syndromic autism and Kanner idiopathic autism are caused by separate genetic mechanisms arise from the lack of evidence for a unique genetic cause for Kanner idiopathic autism, from the existing evidence for pleiotropic effects of syndromic genetic causes, and from the history of accumulation of more and more syndromic autism. Folstein (2006), Grice and Buxbaum (2006), Skuse (2007), and Levy et al. (2010) theorized that essential Kanner idiopathic autism, without intellectual disability, without language disorders, without any other comorbid conditions, would be highly heritable and have a unique genetic cause. However, to date, no research has revealed a gene or chromosomal variant that causes only idiopathic essential Kanner autism, without non-diagnostic associated symptoms (Abrahams & Geschwind, 2010; Liu et al., 2011). Equally problematic is the fact that family studies of individuals with idiopathic autism have found evidence in family members for intellectual disability, language impairment, ADHD, and other disorders in what has been described as the broader autism phenotype.

Another problem for the division of syndromic and idiopathic Kanner autism is the history of conversion of idiopathic to syndromic autism. Many individuals with syndromic autism today would have been diagnosed with idiopathic autism 10 years ago. For example, O'Roak et al. (2011) reported four new single gene variants likely to be the cause of autism in four individuals. These and other similar findings are likely to convert cases of idiopathic autism to cases of syndromic autism. Even today, if a boy with fragile X syndrome premutation had unmarked physical features except for a large head, and only mild intellectual disability but severe social withdrawal and communication impairment, this boy would be likely to be clinically diagnosed with idiopathic autism. In the future, it is possible that that idiopathic autism may narrow greatly or perhaps even disappear as more and more genetic and environmental causes are found to be linked to autism along with other associated symptoms.

Another argument against the division of syndromic and idiopathic autism is that the genetic risk factors for syndromic and non-syndromic autism are not different in nature. Sakai et al. (2011) constructed a large-scale interactome of proteins altered in autism and reported functional connections between syndromic autism proteins, and proteins associated with idiopathic autism. The syndromic proteins included CACNA1C (Timothy syndrome), CNTNAP2 (cortical dysplasia–focal epilepsy syndrome), FMR1 (fragile X syndrome), MECP2 (Rett syndrome), NLGN3 and NLGN4X (syndromic autism), PTEN (PTEN hamartoma tumor syndrome), SHANK3 (Phelan-McDermid syndrome), TSC1 and TSC2 (tuberous sclerosis), and UBE3A (Angelman syndrome). Sakai et al. (2011) reported functional connections between all 11 syndromic proteins and 8 proteins defined as associated with non-syndromic autism: AGTR2, ARX, ATRX, CDKL5, FOXP2, HOXA1, NF1, and SLC6A8. The researchers concluded that the interactome connections between syndromic autism proteins "and other ASD proteins lend support to the idea that common pathways lead to the broader ASD phenotypes" (Sakai et al., 2011, p. 7). Schaaf and Zoghbi (2011) asserted that the evidence demonstrated "a significant overlap in the genetics of syndromic and nonsyndromic autism" (p. 808). Thus, the division of research samples might be counterproductive.

Schaaf et al. (2011) also reported evidence linking syndromic to non-syndromic autism. The researchers found that 7% of individuals with idiopathic autism had novel variants of two or more of 21 genes (*ARX, ATRX, CACNA1C, CDKL5, EML1, FMR1, FOXP2, GRID2, HOXA1, KCTD13, MAPK3, MECP2, NLGN3, NLGN4X, PTEN, RS1, SHANK3, SLC25A12, TSC1, TSC2,* and *UBE3A*) already known as causes of syndromic autism. Schaaf et al. (2011) proposed that idiopathic autism was caused by a polygene cluster of hypomorphic variants—i.e., variants causing reduced expression of a gene—of those genes known to cause syndromic autism. Schaaf et al. (2011) theorized that individuals with non-syndromic autism had less severe mutations in several of the 21 genes that each alone could cause syndromic autism when more severely mutated.

Model 2, Two-Hit Genetic Mechanisms

Girirajan et al. (2010) proposed a two-cause model for autism and developmental delay based on data from their genome-wide meta-analysis comparing the frequency of large deletion and duplication events in individuals with neurocognitive psychiatric disabilities. They argued that their findings pointed to "a two-hit model in which the 16p12.1 microdeletion both predisposes to neuropsychiatric phenotypes as a single event and exacerbates neurodevelopmental phenotypes in association with other large deletions or duplications" (Girirajan et al., 2010, p. 204). The researchers further claimed, "Analysis of other microdeletions with variable expressivity suggests that this two-hit model may be more generally applicable to neuropsychiatric disease" (Girirajan et al., 2010, p. 204). The researchers found that 6 of 20 individuals in a large group of individuals diagnosed with intellectual disability, autism, and schizophrenia, had the 16p12.1 microdeletion, and 4 of 22 individuals with the 16p12.1 microdeletion from their replication set had additional chromosomal abnormalities or large chromosome deletions or duplications. Of note is the fact that the researchers found that two-hit 16p12.1 carriers expressed more severe or marked symptoms than did other affected individuals whose genomes showed no evidence of a double hit.

State and Levitt (2011) also outlined a two-cause model for autism in which rare single gene variants and chromosome duplications and deletions would each separately confer the main risk for autism. However, in their model, varying disorders diagnosed along with an individual case of autism, such as intellectual disability, epilepsy, or anxiety, would result from other factors "including environmental factors, epigenetic mechanisms, stochastic events and additional genetic variations, either in the form of multiple rare alleles or additional modulatory common variants" (p. 1504).

Geschwind (2011) proposed a two-hit model of genetic cause that resulted in one unified brain deficit for autism—underconnectivity. In Geschwind's model, the first "hit" was a chromosomal deletion or duplication such as a duplication at 15q11–13, deletion at 22q, or deletion at 16p. The second hit was mutations in genes such as *TSC1* (tuberous sclerosis gene), *FMR1* (fragile X gene), and *CACNA1C* (Timothy syndrome) that each individually resulted in a variety of brain-wide dysfunctional processes. Geschwind (2011) proposed that these two "hits" caused abnormal neuronal migration, abnormalities in connectivity, problems in axon path finding, aberrant synaptogenesis, aberrant synaptic function, dendritic abnormalities, and dysfunctional neural transmission. In Geschwind's model, similar to the two-hit models proposed by Girirajan et al. (2011) and State and Levitt (2011), dysfunctional processes caused by CNVs were hit again by additional gene variants, such as *CNTNAP2* (cortical dysplasia-focal epilepsy syndrome) or other developmentally disruptive gene variants.

Model 2, Two-Hit Genetic Models—Challenges to the Model

No compelling rationale has been provided for the model of two hits other than evidence that some individuals with more severe autism symptoms have been found to carry two risk gene variants (Girirajan et al., 2010). Schaaf et al. (2011) proposed that many milder mutations may cause autism, and argued that the full number of milder mutations "contributing to the etiology of autism will only become evident once large scale, whole exome or whole genome data sets of sequences from autistic individuals are analyzed to evaluate for such combinatorial events" (p. 3372). Schaaf et al. (2011) noted that individuals with autism whose parents both expressed mild autistic traits tended to show more severe diagnostic social impairment. These findings, the researchers argued, supported the hypothesis that several concurrent partial brain deficits "may accumulate either in a specific signaling pathway, or a subcellular compartment (such as the synapse) to exceed a threshold" resulting in autism (Schaaf et al., 2011, p. 3372).

Single rare gene variants and dual rare variants have been found for autism. It is possible that milder forms of rare risk variants will also be found as causal for autism. Dual-hit models thus have the empirical problems of demonstrating that the second hit is crucial to generating the phenotype, and of demonstrating that there are no additional gene variants that also contribute to the autism symptom phenotype.

Model 3: Multiple Single Gene Mechanisms for Multiple Autism Subsyndromes

Mitchell (2011) reported that although "research into epilepsy and mental retardation has mainly proceeded on the model of genetic heterogeneity and has been very successful in defining rare genetic syndromes, research into psychiatric disorders ... largely turned to a common disease/common variant (CD/CV) model" (p. 197). Mitchell (2011) argued that the common disease/common variant model was wrong for psychiatric disorders. He asserted that different genetic causes yielded "hundreds to thousands of such Mendelian syndromes, each very rare" determining neurocognitive and psychiatric disorders (Mitchell, 2011, p. 197).

El-Fishawy and State (2010) proposed that, although many researchers saw autism as resulting from a single underlying neurobiological deficit, it was possible that autism "might well reflect a collection of rare disorders resulting from hundreds of different genetic defects but leading to a shared phenotype, similar to the case of mental retardation" (p. 88). Heger (2011) reported that researchers Spiro and Scherer both argued that the hundreds of gene variants associated with autism would constitute hundreds of separate Mendelian individual single gene disorders. Heger (2011) reported that Spiro asserted that autism was not a biological disorder but was only a behavioral description, and that Spiro claimed autism was really a constellation of rare genetic disorders. Heger (2011) quoted Scherer as saying autism was a "bunch of different genetic disorders that have a common clinical outcome" (p. 398).

Scherer and Dawson (2011) listed 38 genes and 17 chromosome loci known to be linked to autism, and identified another 211 potential candidate genes and 17 candidate chromosome loci. A chromosome locus is a specific region of DNA sequence on the chromosome. State and Levitt (2011) reviewed data for single gene mutations in autism. They reported that rare single gene variants had been found for both idiopathic and syndromic autism. They identified mutations in the gene *CNTN4*, and rare homozygous mutations in *CNTNAP2*, as the source of autism social impairment.

They reported that heterozygous rare mutations in *CNTNAP2* were found in autism and schizophrenia, while common variants in *CNTNAP2* were found in idiopathic autism, as well as in individuals with language delay, selective mutism, and anxiety. Moreover, neuropathological examination found abnormal neuron structure and migration in brain samples from members of consanguineous families expressing autism and epilepsy whose genomes revealed mutations in *CNTNAP2* (State & Levitt, 2011).

O'Roak et al. (2011) examined the exomes, or protein-coding sections of the genomes, of 20 individuals with idiopathic autism and their parents. The researchers found 11 new mutations in the individuals with autism, each in a different gene, and discovered four mutations that were likely to be single gene causes for the autism symptoms in each of the four affected individuals. One mutation was a single base substitution in the *GRIN2B* gene. De novo or new mutations in *GRIN2B* had previously been found in individuals with mild to moderate intellectual disability. In another individual, a mutation was found for the *SCN1A* gene, a gene found previously in association with epilepsy and previously suggested as an autism candidate gene. O'Roak et al. (2011) noted, "Hundreds of disease associated mutations have been described in epilepsy, and typically individuals with de novo events show more severe phenotypes" (p. 587). The third mutation they discovered was in the *LAMC3* gene. O'Roak et al. (2011) noted that *LAMC3* was not known to influence neuron development but the gene was expressed in many areas of the brain. The fourth de novo mutation they discovered was a single base insertion in the *FOXP1* gene. The researchers reported that large de novo deletions and a nonsense variant disrupting *FOXP1* had been reported in individuals with intellectual disability, language deficits, and with or without autism. O'Roak et al. (2011) concluded that the "finding of de novo events in genes that have also been disrupted in children with intellectual disability without ASD, intellectual disability with ASD features or epilepsy provides further evidence that these genetic pathways may lead to a spectrum of neurodevelopmental outcomes depending on the genetic and environmental context" (p. 588).

Myers et al. (2011) argued for the RAME, the rare allele–major effects, model of single gene causes for both autism and schizophrenia. They reported finding two such rare alleles, *GRIN2B* and *MAP1A*, in both autism and schizophrenia, and an excess of rare missense *CACNAF1* variants in autism. Myers et al. (2011) stated that the involvement of *GRIN2B* and *MAP1A* in both autism and schizophrenia suggested a pleiotropic effect for both genes.

Model 3, Multiple Single Gene Variants—Challenges to the Model

A research challenge for many single gene variants each converging on autism symptoms, or single gene variants each causing a separate subgroup of all the "autisms" is that nearly all single gene variants contribute risk to both autism and other disorders. This has stalled the discovery of gene-to-phenotype causes unique to autism. As can be seen in Table 4.1, a Mendelian single gene disorder is likely to be expressed as several different diagnoses. These different diagnoses may reflect pleiotropic effects of the single gene variant. However, several diagnoses that appear to stem from a single gene variant, in fact may be the result of more than a single gene variant effect. The multiple diagnoses associated with a single gene variant may reflect the effect of a second "hit" from another single gene variant, or multiple weaker effects from still other gene variants, or the effects from varying epigenetic modifications, or the effects of the environment. Therefore, different combinations of single variants and second hit gene variants and other modifying effects may cause multiple different expressions in structure, behaviors, and symptoms. In sum, pleiotropy alone or complex causal gene variant combinations may cause one specific gene variant to be expressed as autism, or intellectual disability without autism, or autism with intellectual disability, or specific language impairment without autism, or autism with language disability, or schizophrenia. As Insel and Wang (2010) observed, psychiatric "diagnostic categories, based on clinical characteristics, do not seem to align well with findings from genetics and neuroscience" (pp. 1970–1971).

In addition, if there are hundreds of different single gene sources of autism, finding and understanding the individual and combinatorial mechanisms for those gene variants will be necessary for the development of specific treatments and prevention plans. Neale et al. (2012) noted that existing "data underscore the challenge of establishing individual genes as conclusive risk factors for ASD, a challenge that will require larger sample sizes and deeper analytical integration with inherited variation" (p. 245). Studying large groups of individuals diagnosed with autism may yield candidate gene variants, but will not help to align a specific set of variants unique to a specific set of individuals with autism.

Model 4: CNVs Cause Autism

A number of researchers theorized that autism was largely caused by the effects of chromosomal copy number variants (CNVs) (Casey et al., 2012; Levy et al., 2011; Pinto et al., 2010). Joober and Boksa (2009) argued that

CNVs were likely to explain a significant subpopulation of autism because autism appears early in development and usually has a severe clinical expression. Casey et al. (2012) stated, "the high heritability of ASD (90%) remains poorly explained by common genetic risk variants. However, recent studies suggest that rare genomic variation, in particular copy number variation, may account for a significant proportion of the genetic basis of ASD" (p. 576).

Liu et al. (2011) proposed that "any chromosomal region that has two or more cases with rare copy number variants (CNVs) that are found in association with ASD in at least a portion of cases, and not in controls, harbors a gene or genes that, when function is compromised, lead to autistic behaviors" (p. 1265). Walsh and Bracken (2011) claimed, "A substantial proportion of idiopathic autism may be attributable to CNVs" (p. 380). They noted that studies had detected de novo CNVs in 7–10% of individuals with autism in simplex families, that is, families with only one individual diagnosed with autism, and CNVs in 2–3% of cases from multiplex families, wherein two or more individuals had been diagnosed with autism. Walsh and Bracken (2011) also noted that some chromosome deletions or duplications caused syndromic autism as well, including the Prader-Willi and Angelman syndromes associated with chromosome alterations at 15q11–13, and the DiGeorge velocardiofacial syndrome caused by chromosome alteration at 22q11.21.

Sanders et al. (2011) reported a meaningful pair of contrasting outcomes of a chromosome duplication and chromosome deletion at 7q11.23. Duplication at 7q11.23 was found to be linked to the social withdrawal of autism, while the reciprocal deletion at 7q11.23 was found to be linked to Williams-Beuren syndrome, wherein affected individuals are overly social, empathic, and engaging.

State and Levitt (2011) reviewed findings for CNVs in autism. They noted that large genome-wide studies found CNVs at 16p11.2, 15q11–13, 22q11.2, 7q11.23, and deletions at the Neurexin 1 locus significantly linked to autism, and two additional CNVs at 17q12 and 1q21 more prevalent in autism than in controls. State and Levitt (2011) further argued that evidence suggested autism risk was most pronounced for large de novo CNVs that included multiple genes.

Model 4: CNVs Cause Autism—Challenges to the Model

One research challenge for models based on CNVs is that there are diverse diagnostic outcomes and there is uncertainty about the exact causal source for an individual diagnosis within the range of the duplication or deletion.

As with single gene variant effects, the deletions and duplications of chromosome sections are found with more than one diagnosis. Sanders et al. (2011) pointed out, "remarkably diverse outcomes have been identified for apparently identical CNVs" (p. 864). For example, Moreno-de-Luca et al. (2010) reported, "the 17q12 deletion has been shown to be associated with intellectual disability … ADHD … high risk for ASD and schizophrenia … unexplained neurodevelopmental impairments … [and] for additional psychiatric conditions such as bipolar disorder" (p. 624). The diverse diagnoses pose a difficult inferential problem for research. Is each different disorder caused by the disruption of a separate single gene variant within the scope of the duplication or deletion? Or, do all the different disorders share a cause within the chromosomal duplication or deletion?

Sanders et al. (2011) also reported that the number of genes affected by a chromosome deletion or duplication was a factor in disease risk: the more gene content that was duplicated or deleted, the greater the risk. However, Sanders et al. (2011) cautioned that this association could not help determine whether disrupting more genes just made it more likely that a single gene of great effect was disrupted by the duplication or deletion, or whether it was a dosage effect. A dosage effect would mean that as the number of genes disrupted by a deletion or duplication increased, the more severe the effect on a phenotype would be. To this point, Sanders et al. (2011) argued that four genes—CLIP2, LIMK1, GTF2i, and STX1A—were "leading candidates among the 22 genes within the region for … a range of intriguing studies of the role gene dosage in this region plays in the genesis and maintenance of social behavior" (p. 880).

Model 5: Epigenetic and Genetic Causes

A fifth type of model of autism genetics has focused on possible epigenetic mechanisms such as imprinting, where the allele of one parent is silenced, i.e., turned off (de León-Guerrero et al., 2011; Grafodatskaya et al., 2010; Hogart, Nagarajan, Patzel, Yasui, & LaSalle, 2007). Schanen (2006) claimed that autism was linked to imprinting regions at 15q11–13, 7q21–31.31, 7q32.3–36.3, 4q21–31, 11p11.2–13 and 13q12.3, and Crespi and Badcock (2008) theorized that aberrant imprinting might cause both psychosis and autism, leaving social cognition underdeveloped in autism, but dysfunctionally overdeveloped in psychosis. Jones et al. (2008) theorized that autism might be caused by errors in the epigenetic control of a variety of genes on the X chromosome that caused overexpression or partial silencing of one or more genes.

Grafodatskaya et al. (2010) reviewed genetic causes for syndromic and idiopathic autism that involved epigenetic processes. The researchers pointed out that autism in Rett syndrome is caused by mutation disrupting a key gene expression control protein, MECP2, and that autism in fragile X syndrome involves CGG repeats in *FMR1* alleles that result in knocking out the expression of the FMR1 protein. Grafodatskaya et al. (2010) also observed that autism in Angelman syndrome and autism in Prader-Willi syndrome both involve the epigenetic process of imprinting. Both syndromes result from errors in the chromosome 15qll–13 genomic region. Prader-Willi syndrome involves the functional loss of paternally expressed genes, and Angelman syndrome results from the loss of the expression of *UBE3A*, a gene expressed exclusively from the maternal chromosome in the brain. Grafodatskaya et al. (2010) also reported that idiopathic autism is linked to genes involving epigenetic processes. The Reelin gene, necessary for neuronal migration and synaptogenesis, is epigenetically regulated. The RELN protein has been found to be significantly reduced in the frontal lobes and cerebellum of autistic individuals, and abnormal RELN levels were found in the brains of individuals with schizophrenia.

Swanberg, Nagarajan, Peddada, Yasui, and LaSalle (2009) studied the function of the protein disrupted in Rett syndrome, MECP2. Swanberg et al. (2009) found an interactive relationship between MECP2 and the activity-dependent early growth response gene 2 (*EGR2*), required for both brain development and mature neuron function. Most importantly, they reported that both Rett syndrome and autism postmortem cortex samples showed a significant reduction in EGR2 protein, suggesting that EGR2 affected neuron development in both syndromes, even though MECP2 function in autism without Rett syndrome does not produce typical Rett syndrome phenotypic features.

Similarly, De León-Guerrero et al. (2011) noted that epigenetic processes regulated the suppression of tissue-specific genes, and imprinted genes, as well as regulating X chromosome inactivation. The researchers reported that in Rett syndrome the lack of MECP2 results in abnormal dendritic and axon development in neurons, and causes defects in glial cells in the brain. Derecki et al. (2012) examined a mouse model of Rett lacking Mecp2, and found that the microglia in mouse brain without Mecp2 were not able to do the job of cleaning away debris from the normal process of neuron cell death. Derecki et al. (2012) concluded that this microglia failure to clean debris would lead to malfunction in neurons already challenged by the loss of Mecp2 function.

De León-Guerrero et al. (2011) argued that there are additional mechanisms by which absence of MECP2 may affect development of neurons and glial cells at earlier stages of development. The researchers also proposed that more research on the interactions between epigenetic processes would help to elucidate Rett syndrome, autism, and other neurodevelopmental disorders. De León-Guerrero et al. (2011) further hypothesized that it was possible that SNPs and CNVs affecting genes that code for epigenetic agents, such as DNA methyl transferases, histone-modifying enzymes, or chromatin-remodeling complexes, might be contributors to neurodevelopmental or psychiatric disorders.

Summary: Five Types of Genetic Mechanism Models for Autism

The complexity and variation in the genetic mechanisms for autism are just beginning to be understood. The initial hypothesis of Pickles et al. (1995) that autism would have its own small set of unique causal genes has been replaced by an explosion of findings for hundreds of likely genetic causes for autism symptoms. Moreover, nearly all gene variants and chromosome duplications and deletions found for autism carry risk for other psychiatric and neurological disorders. Many de novo or rare gene variants and de novo CNVs are associated with autism. Gai et al. (2012) stated that their search for CNVs in autism led them to believe that "inherited autism risk is genetically highly heterogeneous" (p. 408). The researchers reported that they found many separate CNVs and many single causes. Gai et al. (2012) noted that the single gene variants they identified were separate from genes included in the scope of any of the chromosome duplications or deletions.

Research findings have not found support for the possibility that autism could be caused by a large set of common gene variants operating together. Moreover, the links found between gene variants for syndromic and idiopathic autism suggested that the distinction may not be valuable for research. Both idiopathic and syndromic autism may result from single gene variants, and both idiopathic and syndromic autism may result from rare or de novo chromosomal deletions or duplications.

Evidence suggests that risk for autism symptoms can come from many distinct single gene variants, combinations of single gene variants, and CNVs, chromosomal alterations, and epigenetic causes. The effect of single gene variants and chromosomal deletions or duplications may be exacerbated by the action of another gene variant, or another CNV, or modulatory common variants, or epigenetic effects. Individual gene variants may have pleiotropic effects such that many different disorders can result from the same causal gene variant. Chromosome duplications or deletions may cause autism by disrupting a single gene, or by disrupting many genes.

Finally, the caution of Manolio et al. (2009) that heritability estimates might be erroneously large is an important consideration. Despite the evidence suggesting approximately 30% of genetic causes are known, there remains substantial "missing heritability" or unexplained genetic variance for many diseases and disorders (Manolio, 2010; Manolio et al., 2009). Manolio (2010) suggested that missing heritability might ultimately be found in rare gene variants or mutations of common genes. Manolio (2010) also proposed that missing heritability might be found in interactions between genes, or between genes and environmental factors. Van IJzendoorn et al. (2011) noted that genome-wide association studies "have documented disappointingly small genetic associations with common human diseases, cognitive abilities and behavioural traits" (p. 1), and like Manolio (2010) they proposed that missing heritability might be accounted for by gene–environment interaction.

Manolio et al. (2009) further suggested that if heritability estimates were erroneously inflated, less heritability was missing. Importantly, Hallmayer et al. (2011) reported that a large-scale autism twin study found only 37–38% genetic heritability for autism. This is in sharp contrast to the typical findings of 85–92% (Miles, 2011; Ronald & Hoekstra, 2011). If only 37–38% of the variance in autism were due to genetic factors, this would be less than half the commonly reported heritability, and there would be significantly less missing heritability for autism. Thus, if the genetic heritability of autism were confirmed to be approximately 37–38%, given that 30% of autism cases are caused by known gene variants and CNVs the "missing heritability" of autism might be significantly less than previously thought.

QUESTION TWO: HOW DO GENE VARIANTS CAUSE AUTISM BRAIN DEFICITS?

A second fundamental question raised by the wealth of genetic findings in autism is the role of gene variants and chromosome duplications and deletions in the development of brain deficits found for autism. Geschwind (2011) pointed out, "Diseases of cognition and behavior have their basis in brain circuit dysfunction. Therefore, we need to understand how specific genetic risk variants lead to changes in neural circuitry and function in those with and without a specific diagnosis" (p. 414). The difficulty of this research task stems both from the wide range of genetic causes and from the variation in the brain deficits found for autism. Autism brain deficits have been reported for "the cerebellum, frontal lobes, and temporal lobes ... parts of the parietal lobe ... amygdala ... basal ganglia ... hippocampus ... hypothalamus ... thalamus ... the insula ... the fusiform face area ... the brainstem [and] ... the corpus callosum" (Shroeder, Desrocher, Bebko, & Cappadocia, 2010, p. 562). There is also evidence of abnormal brain growth patterns and "increased head circumference ... consistent abnormalities in cortical gray and white matter volume ... an increase in intrahemispheric white matter volume along with a decrease in interhemispheric (i.e., corpus callosum) white matter ... abnormalities in cortical activation and specialization.... [and] underconnectivity in distributed cortical networks" (Stigler, McDonald, Anand, Saykin, & McDougle, 2011, p. 155).

Researchers have used three types of strategies to uncover the possible genetic causes for autism brain deficits. Researchers have explored brain deficits in animal models of autism (Ey, Leblond, & Bourgeron, 2011; Horev et al., 2011; Peñagarikano et al., 2011; Sala et al., 2011). Researchers have also explored the brain effects of gene causes found for autism (Bertone Hanck, Kogan, Chaudhuri, & Cornish, 2010; Chen et al., 2011; Gauthier et al., 2011; Hagerman, Au, & Hagerman, 2011; Persico & Bourgeron, 2006; Rubenstein, 2011; Tan, Doke, Ashburner, Wood, & Frackowiak, 2010). Third, for single brain deficit models of autism (Courchesne, Campbell, & Solso, 2011a; Schipul, Keller, & Just, 2011), explanatory genetic causes have been proposed.

Animal Models of Gene Effects on Brain Function

The links between specific gene variants and autism brain deficits have been explored using animal models. Ey et al. (2011) reviewed mouse models and reported that gene knockout (KO), knockin (KI), and other types of animal models of autism had produced evidence of autism-like symptoms in mice. Ey et al. (2011) noted that six mouse models (Nlgn3-KO, Nlgn4-KO, Nlgn3-R451-cKI, Shank1-KO, and two 15q11–13 models) expressed abnormal social and vocal behaviors. Two mouse models (Mecp2Flox and Fmr1/Fxr2-KO) revealed impaired fear and stress reactions. Six mouse models (Nlgn1-KO, Tsc1-HZ, Mecp2-KI, Mecp2-cKO, Nrxn1a-KO, and Pten-cKO) expressed disrupted nesting and abnormal social behavior. Seizures, motor stereotypy, abnormal movement, and deficits in learning appeared in eight different mouse models (maternal and paternal deletion of Ube3a-Gabrb3, Fmr1-KO, Tsc1-cKO, maternal deletion of Ube3a, and Mecp2Tg1, Nlgn2 overexpression, Fmr1-KI, and Mecp2-KO).

Following are descriptions of three additional mouse models: Cntnap2-KO (Peñagarikano et al., 2011); Oxtr-KO (Sala et al., 2011); and deletion and duplication of CNV 16p11.2 (Horev et al., 2011).

The Cntnap2 *Gene Mouse Model Brain Deficits*

Tan et al. (2010) reported significant reductions in gray matter and white matter volume in typical individuals homozygous for a specific *CNTNAP2* risk allele. The gene encodes a neurexin protein that regulates interactions between neurons and the neuron support cells, glia cells, during brain development and contributes to the development of neuron axon structures. The *CNTNAP2* gene covers 1.5% of chromosome 7; it is one of the largest genes in the human genome. It is regulated by forkhead box protein P2 (FOXP2), a transcription factor related to speech and language development. The *CNTNAP2* gene is a risk factor for multiple disorders, including Tourette syndrome, schizophrenia, epilepsy, autism, attention deficit/hyperactivity disorder, and intellectual disability. A homozygous mutation of the *CNTNAP2* gene was found to cause cortical dysplasia–focal epilepsy syndrome (CDFE) in a group of closely related Old Order Amish children from Pennsylvania. All affected children had relatively normal development until the onset of seizures in early childhood. From that point in development, they expressed features of autism, including language regression and social withdrawal.

Gregor et al. (2011) studied cases and reviewed prior findings and identified that *CNTNAP2* structural alterations, gene truncations, and other mutations were associated with autism, Tourette syndrome, epilepsy, severe language delay, severely impaired motor development, and severe intellectual disability.

Peñagarikano et al. (2011) created a mouse without the *CNTNAP2* gene. They reported that homozygous *CNTNAP2* deficiency caused the mice to have features resembling the features of idiopathic autism. Although the mice exhibited normal anxiety responses, visual spatial memory, and sensorimotor integration, they expressed abnormal vocal communication, repetitive and restrictive behaviors, and abnormal social interactions. The mice also experienced seizures, and expressed hyperactivity. Animals with only one *CNTNAP2* allele knocked out did not show any of the deficits that the homozygous *CNTNAP2* knockout mice did. The researchers pointed out that CNTNAP2 is a single pass transmembrane protein that contributes to the regulation of clustering K^+ channels at nodes in myelinated axons, and contributes to the formation of neuron–glia cell adhesion complexes necessary for the proper localization of K^+ channels. Peñagarikano et al. (2011) reported that there was evidence of abnormal neuronal migration, and a reduced number of GABAergic interneurons in the striatum and hippocampus of the knockout mice. The researchers also reported asynchronous neuron firing in the knockout mice, which they concluded was due to a network dysfunction.

The OXTR Gene Animal Model Brain Deficits

Yrigollen et al. (2008) reported evidence for polymorphisms of *PRL, PRLR,* and *OXTR* genes in 177 individuals diagnosed with ASD. Oxytocin (OT) is a peptide involved in affiliative behavior. Autistic children have been shown to have abnormal levels of plasma OT (Green et al., 2001; Modahl et al., 1998). Prolactin (PRL) is a pituitary hormonal peptide also found to be important for affiliative behaviors.

Campbell et al. (2011) conducted a large family study of the association of common oxytocin receptor (*OXTR*) gene variants with risk for autism. They reported a link for autism and two regions of the *OXTR* gene: intron 3 (an intron is a nucleotide sequence removed in the creation of protein) and the 3′ UTR (three prime untranslated region of mRNA that may modify protein production), where markers in intron 3 implicated the *OXTR* gene specifically in autism. The researchers noted that their findings were consonant with earlier reports linking *OXTR* with autism, including a CNV involving the deletion of a chromosome region including the *OXTR* gene, evidence for altered methylation in the *OXTR* gene promoter in autism, and the decreased expression of *OXTR* in postmortem brains of individuals with autism.

Sala et al. (2011) created a mouse line in which oxytocin neurotransmission was eliminated by knocking out *OXTR*. The researchers reported that the oxytocin receptor knockout mice pups expressed reduced vocalization at separation from the mother, and stayed with a strange mouse as long as with the familiar mouse, indicating a failure in social memory. Knockout mice showed impaired cognitive flexibility in a maze-switching task. Knockout mice also had neuronal hyperexcitability and a reduced threshold for seizures. Investigation of hippocampal brain cells showed the oxytocin receptor knockout mice had a lower ratio of inhibitory synapses to excitatory synapses, and the researchers concluded that the hippocampal functioning of the *OXTR* knockout mice was set to an abnormally high level of excitation. Sala et al. (2011) reported that administration of oxytocin or arginine vasopressin to 3-month-old knockout mice normalized the animals' social behavior.

CNV 16p11.2 Animal Model Brain Deficits

Girirajan et al. (2010) noted that there were three microdeletion/microduplication syndromes on the short arm of chromosome 16: a microdeletion/microduplication of 16p11.2 found with autism and intellectual disability; a large microdeletion across 16p11.2 to 16p12.2 found with many different syndromes; and various 16p13.11 rearrangements found with autism, intellectual disability, and other forms of developmental delay.

Horev et al. (2011) created mice with a deletion and mice with a duplication of the chromosomal region corresponding to 16p11.2. Horev et al. (2011) found the deletion had more severe effects than the duplication. The researchers reported that half of the mice with the 16p11.2 deletion died. The mice with duplications and deletions that survived to adulthood were healthy and fertile. The mice with the 16p11.2 deletion exhibited stereotyped motor behaviors and showed abnormal increases in the size of eight regions of the brain, including the hypothalamus and basal forebrain.

Summary of Three Animal Model Findings

All three forms of knockout mice expressed behavior abnormalities that were consonant with autism behavior deficits, and all three forms of knockout mice had specific brain abnormalities. Horev et al. (2011) reported that the 16p11.2 deletion caused abnormal brain volume increases in mice. Peñagarikano et al. (2011) reported abnormal neuronal migration, reduced numbers of interneurons, and asynchronous neuron firing, and seizures in their *CNTNAP2* knockout mice. Sala et al. (2011) reported hippocampal hyperexcitability and a reduced threshold for seizures in the oxytocin receptor gene knockout mice.

Inferential Limitations for Animal Models

As noted by Sala et al. (2011), no animal model can be expected to replicate the full complexity of the human autism symptoms, because a mouse is not a human, and thus an animal may selectively exhibit only a few features of the syndrome, or express quite different behavioral effects than those found in humans. Ey et al. (2011) also noted that there were varying descriptions of similar animal models. They stated that many fragile X syndrome animal models have created *FMR1* mutant mice, but these mice have shown different group phenotypes from study to study. This may be the result of differences in the genetic background of the mice used, or may reflect different environmental conditions, or different measures used to describe the phenotype.

Linking Genetic Causes to Autism Brain Deficits

Gilman et al. (2011) concluded that autism resulted from the disruption of the genes for synaptic and neuronal connectivity. The researchers reported that "autism-associated rare de novo CNVs, observed in an unbiased genome-wide study, form a large and statistically significant functional network responsible for synaptogenesis, axon guidance, and related molecular processes" (Gilman et al., 2011, p. 904). By contrast, Geschwind (2011) reviewed genetic research and concluded, "studies place ASD genes within a multiplicity of pathways, several of which are broad and do not necessarily demonstrate convergence on final common molecular processes in individuals" (p. 414). Geschwind (2011) also argued that the hundreds of gene variants already found in association with autism have been too varied to permit any satisfactory unifying interpretation. State and Levitt (2011), like Geschwind (2011), asserted, "the field has not yet arrived at a new coherent understanding of the relationship of genotype and phenotype in ASDs" (p. 6). Unlike Geschwind, however, State and Levitt (2011) argued that there was no clear genotype for autism because of the "profound genetic heterogeneity", by contrast the researchers claimed that homogeneity of the autism phenotype was clearly established by "the coherence of ASDs observed at the phenomenological and clinical level, as exemplified in replicable neuroimaging, eye-tracking and other neuropsychological findings" (p. 6).

Unfortunately, most clinical researchers would not subscribe to State and Levitt's (2011) claim of clear coherence of autism behaviors and deficits at the phenomenological and clinical level. For example, Jones and Klin (2009) noted that autism "heterogeneity spans the entire range of IQ and language function and a wide array of communicative, social, and behavioral disabilities" (p. 471). Amaral (2011) asserted, "A hallmark of virtually every biological parameter assayed in individuals with autism is the enormous heterogeneity—far greater than in the general population" (p. 6). Consequently, the challenge to develop "a new coherent understanding of the relationship of genotype and phenotype" (State & Levitt, 2011, p. 1504) in autism is made all the more difficult because not only is there enormous heterogeneity in genotype, there is also enormous heterogeneity in phenotype. This heterogeneity extends to the wide range of brain deficits found for autism.

Two Comprehensive Gene Models for Autism

Nonetheless, two comprehensive gene-grouping models for autism brain deficits were proposed (Persico & Bourgeron, 2006; Rubenstein, 2011). Persico and Bourgeron (2006) theorized that three functional groups of genes would produce the particular brain deficits of autism. These were: genes that if disrupted would result in reduced neuron migration; genes that if disrupted would produce an excitatory–inhibitory imbalance in neuron connectivity; and genes that if disrupted would result in abnormal development of synaptic connections between neurons. Persico and Bourgeron (2006) argued that there was evidence for *RELN* gene disruption in autism, which could alter neuronal migration. They also argued that there was evidence for disruption of the genes *MECP2* and *NLGN*, which would result in unbalanced excitatory–inhibitory neural networks. Persico and Bourgeron (2006) argued that evidence for autism appearing in fragile X syndrome suggested the *FMR1* gene disruption would cause abnormal synapse formation and atypically increased numbers of abnormally long and thin dendritic spines. Persico and Bourgeron (2006) concluded that abnormal neuron dendrite structure found with mutations of *MECP2* in Rett syndrome, with mutations of *TSC1* or *TSC2* in tuberous sclerosis, and with mutations of *NLGN* in autism supported their theory that successful development of synaptic contacts between axons and dendrites was crucial for processing of socially relevant information.

Rubenstein (2011) proposed four alternate models of genetic disruption leading to autism brain deficits. Rubenstein's first model (2011) proposed that "molecular brain lesions" impaired the balance of excitatory, inhibitory, and neuromodulatory neuron synapses, thus impairing brain systems that permit the detection of salient sensory signals above ambient noise and thus impairing both social behavior and non-social cognition. Rubenstein suggested that disruptions in the *NLGN3*, *FMR1*, or *MECP2* genes each alone could cause this imbalance. Rubenstein's second model (2011) proposed that the early atypically increased growth of the cerebral cortex in autism and alterations in cortical and cerebellar size might stem from overactivity of the fibroblast growth factor pathway crucial for brain tissue development. Rubenstein (2011) hypothesized that overactivity of fibroblast growth factor signaling could be caused by mutations in *PTEN* and *TSC1/TSC2* genes. Rubenstein's third model proposed that developmental lesions in cortical–basal ganglia circuitry might cause autism by disrupting dopamine signaling that contributes to various forms of learning. Rubenstein's fourth hypothesis concerned the ratio of four or five males for every female diagnosed with autism. Rubenstein (2011) stated, "While there are several ASD-susceptibility genes on the X chromosome (e.g., Arx, Fmr1, MeCP2, Neuroligin3 and 4), numerically this is not thought to account for the increased male prevalence of ASD" (p. 349). Rubenstein proposed that the male prevalence in autism might be due to sex steroid hormone abnormalities that could disrupt brain development through impairing neuron survival, synapse numbers, numbers of dendritic spines, neuronal connectivity, neuron function, as well as excitatory–inhibitory balance.

While plausible, Persico and Bourgeron's model (2006) and Rubenstein's four models (2011) are brief sketches of mechanisms. The sketches need to be developed into full model mechanisms, and then tested in relation to the actual brain deficits found in autism.

Effects of Individual Gene Variants on Brain Deficits

Another approach is the consideration of brain deficits that result from separate genetic mechanisms. The brain deficits of two disorders—fragile X syndrome and Rett syndrome—the most common forms of syndromic autism, are probable causes for autism brain deficits. Many other single gene variants linked to autism are known to be crucial in brain development. Four of these are *NRXN2*, *DRD3*, *FAK*, and *GNB1L*.

Fragile X Syndrome Brain Deficits

Bertone et al. (2010) noted that between 33% and 67% of children with fragile X syndrome meet the diagnostic criteria for autism. In fragile X syndrome lack of the FMRP protein causes an imbalance of inhibitory and excitatory activity, disrupting synaptic plasticity and neuron connectivity. Santoro, Bray, and Warren (2012) outlined the metabotropic glutamate receptor (mGluR) theory of fragile X syndrome. Aberrant gene repeats result in lack of the FMRP protein; this absence disrupts normal metabotropic glutamate receptor function, and causes excessive and persistent protein synthesis in postsynaptic dendrites and dysregulated synaptic function. An excessive amount of α-amino-3-hydroxyl-4-isoxazole propionic acid receptor (AMPAR) builds up in the neuron, with the consequence of exaggerated long-term depression of the neuron's ability to signal. Hagerman et al. (2011) stated that there were two ways the fragile X *FMR1* mutation could result in autism. The full mutation causes severe FMRP deficiency that disrupts the brain's two key neurotransmitter systems, GABA and glutamate, creating an imbalance of inhibitory and excitatory activity, disrupting synaptic plasticity and neuron connectivity. Moreover, FMRP regulates many genes which themselves alone can cause autism. The fragile X lesser mutation, called the premutation, can also result in autism through RNA toxicity ultimately causing early cell death, and mitochondrial abnormalities.

Rett Syndrome Brain Deficits

Wulffaert, Van Berckelaer-Onnes, and Scholte (2009) reported that 42–58% of girls and women with Rett syndrome met the diagnostic criteria for autism. Swanberg et al. (2009) reported that disruption of the chromatin-associated protein MECP2 has many negative effects on brain development and function. The disruption may affect the function of brain-derived neurotropic factor (BDNF), which contributes to synapse function, and may affect a range of gene transcription factors. Disruption of *MECP2* may disregulate *EGR2*, a gene that encodes a transcription factor that contributes to gene expression in the cell body and dendrites of neurons, and is a factor in peripheral myelination, maintenance of synaptic plasticity, and long-term potentiation.

NRXN2 Brain Deficits

Gauthier et al. (2011) described an individual with schizophrenia found to have a de novo truncating mutation in the *NRXN1* gene, and an individual diagnosed with autism found to have a truncating mutation in *NRXN2*. Both genes are in the neurexin family of genes that mediates the differentiation of excitatory and inhibitory synapses. All neurexins have downstream effects on neuroligin genes, and three neuroligin genes, *NLGN1*, *NLGN3*, and *NLGN4*, have been previously reported as disrupted in autism and in intellectual disability.

DRD3 Brain Deficits

Staal, de Krom, and de Jonge (2012) reported finding an association between the autism trait insistence on sameness and a variant of the *DRD3* gene. Paradoxically the variant decreased risk for the insistence on sameness. The researchers pointed out that DRD3 is highly expressed in frontal striatal circuits, and that variants of DRD3 have been found with attention deficit/hyperactivity disorder. Langen, Kas, Staal, van Engeland, and Durston (2011) reported that "different types of repetitive behavior are often correlated and seem to be mediated—at least partly— by similar circuitries" (p. 353), including GABA and glutamate activity in the basal ganglia, and dopamine and serotonin activity in corticostriatal circuits. Hines, Davies, Moss, and Maguire (2011) reported that many disorders, including autism, Angelman syndrome, Rett syndrome, and fragile X syndromes all express GABAergic hypofunction.

FAK Brain Deficits

Wei et al. (2011) studied the lymphoblasts from eight individuals. They reported that protein levels of integrin $\beta 1$ and focal adhesion kinase (FAK) were significantly decreased in autistic lymphoblasts. FAK contributes to the regulation of neural migration in the developing brain, as well as contributing to the development of the structure of neuron dendrites, neuron axon branching, and synapse formation. The integrins are receptors that conduct information from outside the cell to inside the cell, and reveal information about the status of the cell to the extracellular matrix as well. Wei et al. (2011) also found that the lymphoblasts from individuals with autism showed significantly decreased migration, and increased adhesion properties. The researchers reported that overexpressing FAK in autistic lymphoblasts countered the adhesion and migration defects.

GNB1L Brain Deficits

Deletion of 22q11.2 is a fairly common genomic disorder, with a frequency of 1 in 4000 to 1 in 7000 births. The disorder is called DiGeorge syndrome or velocardiofacial syndrome. The chromosomal deletion leads to many abnormalities, including facial dysmorphism, cleft palate, heart and immune system abnormalities, intellectual disability, and language impairment. Autism has been diagnosed in as many as 50% of individuals with DiGeorge syndrome, and schizophrenia or some form of psychosis has been diagnosed in one-third of individuals with DiGeorge syndrome. The *GNB1L* gene is within the span of the chromosomal 22q11.2 deletion. Chen et al. (2011) studied 513 individuals with autism and found three rare missense *GNB1L* variants. A missense variant is a single nucleotide mutation in the gene. (A nucleotide is the structural element in DNA and RNA.) In mice Gnb1l is widely expressed in the brain, and complete absence of Gnb1l results in mouse embryo death. The *GNB1L* gene is part of a family of genes involved in basic cellular processes, including cell cycle progression, apoptosis (programmed cell death), and gene regulation. Chen et al. (2011) found that four of the five males carrying the missense *GNB1L* variant were diagnosed with autism, but only one of three females carrying the variant showed social abnormality.

The Core Inferential Challenge for any Model Attempting to Link Genetic Causes to Autism Brain Deficits

The core inferential challenge for any model attempting to link genetic causes to autism brain deficits is that gene variants and chromosomal deletions and duplications appear to affect the whole brain, but brain deficits reported for autism are not whole-brain deficits. Wei et al. (2011) proposed that three major brain development processes were disrupted in autism: reduced neuron migration; an imbalance of excitatory and inhibitory synapses; and abnormal synaptogenesis. These are not regional brain disruptions, they are global disruptions. The core problem is that this evidence for brain-wide systemic developmental disruptions does not clearly map onto the varied brain deficits reported for autism. For example, it is hard to hypothesize any plausible developmental process through which brain-wide disruption effects could impair *only* the ability to attend to biological motion, or impair *only* the mirror neuron system, or even impair *only* specific axonal connections in the brain. Moreover, it is hard to hypothesize any gene variant or chromosomal duplication or deletion that would yield autism symptoms without some additional associated disorders.

It is even more difficult to provide an empirical rationale for a corollary assumption that each of the many different gene variants, CNVs, and possible compound genetic causes generating different forms of brain-wide disruption in autism would *all* manage to converge on any single brain deficit hypothesized to account for autism.

Working Back from Autism Brain Deficits to Possible Genetic Causes

Many different brain regions and systems have been identified as the key deficit of autism. These have included the brainstem, the cerebellum, the amygdala, left hemisphere functions, right hemisphere functions, the mirror neuron system, orienting to biological motion, the social instinct, executive function system, social cognition, a mentalizing region, axonal underconnectivity, the brain default mode network, as well as many other regions and systems (Shroeder et al., 2010; Stigler et al., 2011).

Because these theories have argued that there is a single key brain deficit in autism, the many varied genetic risk factors for autism causes must be shoehorned into a causal pathway that yields the single core brain deficit. Two active theories that propose the most global core brain deficits for autism are the underconnectivity theory (Schipul et al., 2011) and the early brain overgrowth theory (Courchesne et al., 2011a). These brain deficit models and possible genetic causes for each are outlined here.

Disrupted Cortical Connectivity as a Single Brain Deficit Hypothesis of Autism and its Many Possible Genetic Causes

Schipul et al. (2011) reviewed evidence that underconnectivity of the cortex was the unifying core brain deficit of autism. Schipul et al. (2011)

reported, "The most consistent finding of functional connectivity differences in autism is a pattern of lower frontal–posterior functional connectivity relative to neurotypical individuals" (p. 1). However, Schipul et al. (2011) noted that there were also findings of typical frontal–posterior connectivity, and even contrary findings of *increased* frontal–posterior functional connectivity in autism. Schipul et al. (2011) argued, however, "It should be noted that all findings of overconnectivity in ASD come from studies using non-standard methods" (p. 5).

Model of Genetic Contributions to Underconnectivity

Geschwind (2011) outlined a model in which multiple genetic causes yielded one unified brain deficit for autism: underconnectivity. In Geschwind's model, any one of a number of gene variants and chromosomal deletions and duplications was theorized to cause brain-wide impairments including abnormal neuronal migration, abnormalities in connectivity, disrupted axon path finding, aberrant synaptogenesis, aberrant synaptic function, dendritic abnormalities, and dysfunctional neural transmission. All these dysfunctional brain development processes were theorized to then be modulated by additional gene variants, such as *CNTNAP2* or other autism risk gene variants.

Geschwind's model proposed that aberrant brain development processes caused the specific disconnection of frontal lobe axonal pathways with the temporal lobe, the parietal lobe, and the striatum. Geschwind (2011) stated, "It is tempting to speculate that the abnormalities in cortical patterning and interneuron function provide a molecular basis" (p. 414) for the specific disconnection of frontal lobe axonal pathways with the temporal lobe, the parietal lobe, and the striatum.

Challenges for a Multigene Model of Underconnectivity in Autism

Wass (2011) reviewed the evidence for disrupted connectivity in autism, and noted that "an obstinate factor to be taken into account is that not all subjects with ASD appear to have disrupted connectivity" (p. 24). Wass argued that only a subgroup of individuals with autism have been shown to have disrupted connectivity, and noted "the tendency of many papers to report only group means is regrettable, since it obscures vital information about within-group heterogeneity" (p. 24). In addition, Wass (2011) reported that "patterns of local over-connectivity and long-distance under-connectivity have also been reported in other disorders" (p. 24). Wass stated that underconnectivity had been reported for opioid-dependent patients, extremely low birth weight adults, and individuals diagnosed with ADHD, schizo-phrenia, depression, and dyslexia. Wass (2011) suggested that it was possible that underconnectivity was not specifically characteristic of autism, but was rather the result of impairment to brain development processes.

Barnea-Goraly, Lotspeich, and Reiss (2010) found no significant differ-ences in white matter structure between children with autism and their unaffected siblings, but did find that white matter structure in the children with autism and their unaffected siblings differed significantly from that of typical children studied. The brains of children with autism and their unaf-fected siblings were both found to have reduced prefrontal white matter, and reduced white matter in the corpus callosum, cingulate gyrus, thalamus, left and right superior temporal gyrus approaching the hippocampus and the amygdala, and left and right temporoparietal junctions. Barnea-Goraly et al. (2010) noted that individuals with schizophrenia and their unaffected siblings shared aberrant basal ganglia shape, reduced cortical gray matter and reduced hippocampal volume, and that individuals with attention deficit/ hyperactivity disorder and their unaffected siblings shared abnormalities in prefrontal cortex and cerebellum. Barnea-Goraly et al. (2010) concluded that reduced white matter in the brains of children with autism and their unaffected siblings, while thought to be a clear marker for underconnectiv-ity, may only be a sign of potential vulnerability to autism. The researchers argued that white matter deficits that suggested underconnectivity could simply "be traits that cosegregate with the disorder in families but are not directly related to the actual psychopathology" of autism (Barnea-Goraly et al., 2010, p. 1058).

The Early Brain Overgrowth Autism Brain Deficit and the Possible Genetic Causes

One notable feature in some individuals with autism is atypical increased head size or macrocephaly. Kanner originally observed that 5 of the 11 chil-dren with autism had large heads. Macrocephaly has been found in between 0% and about 21% of individuals with autism (Davidovitch, Golan, Vardi, Lev, & Lerman-Sagie, 2011). Fombonne, Rogé, Claverie, Courty, and Fré-molle (1999) reported that 17% of a sample of 126 individuals with autism had macrocephaly and 15% had microcephaly. Fombonne et al. (1999) asserted that microcephaly was associated with medical disorders in autism but macrocephaly was not. Many genetic disorders have been found that cause microcephaly in autism, including Angelman syndrome, Jourbert syn-drome, Rett syndrome, and Timothy syndrome. These syndromes result in additional medical symptoms as well as autism diagnostic symptoms. However, many genetic disorders have been found that cause macrocephaly in autism, including fragile X syndrome (*FMR1*), neurofibromatosis (*NF1*), tuberous sclerosis (*TSC1* and *TSC2*), Cowden syndrome (*PTEN*), as well as duplications at chromosome 1q21.1. And, contrary to Fombonne et al. (1999), these genetic causes for autism symptoms along with larger heads also result in additional medical symptoms.

Brain size has been measured by head circumference, postmortem brain weight, and brain volume derived from imaging. There are contradictory findings for cortical volume in adults with autism: increased cortical volume has also been reported in adults with autism in some studies (Raznahan et al., 2010), but not in other studies (Wallace, Dankner, Kenworthy, Giedd, & Martin, 2010).

Hazlett et al. (2011) reported larger brains for children with autism at age 2 and at 4–5 years of age. However, the researchers found no evidence for different brain growth rates, comparing children with autism and typical children of the same age. Hazlett et al. (2011) concluded that increased brain volume at age 2 resulted from brain growth that took place earlier in postnatal development. The researchers also noted that children with autism had significantly larger white matter volumes but not significantly larger gray matter volumes compared with typical children. Nordahl et al. (2011) reported finding that 22% of boys with regressive autism, in which a loss of skills is noted in toddler development, had megalencephaly (abnormally increased brain size), whereas only 5% of boys without regression had megalencephaly. Nordahl et al. (2011) reported that head circumference data for the boys in the study suggested that head size began atypical enlargement at about 4–6 months.

Courchesne et al. (2011a, 2011b) asserted that the core deficit of autism was early brain overgrowth followed by a slowing trajectory of brain growth. The researchers called their model "the theory of age-specific anatomic abnormalities in autism," and argued that "Because early abnormal overgrowth occurs at the time of the first detectable behavioral and clinical signs of autism … neural defects that cause overgrowth may be the neural bases of autism" (p. 138). Courchesne et al. (2011b) conducted an analysis of postmortem prefrontal brain tissue from seven autistic and six typical male children and found 79% more neurons in the dorsolateral prefrontal cortex and 29% more neurons in the medial prefrontal cortex in the autistic cases compared with control cases. The autistic group also had larger than average brain weight. Courchesne et al. (2011b) hypothesized that a failure of apoptosis, programmed cell death, in the third trimester of fetal life might be the cause of the frontal lobe overgrowth.

Possible Genetic Sources of the Theory of Age-Specific Anatomic Abnormalities in Autism

Courchesne et al. (2011a) claimed that other than their own findings for excess prefrontal neurons (Courchesne et al., 2011b), "there are no other prenatal biological defects that are known to occur in the majority of young autistic cases" (p. 142), thus implying that no known genetic causes for early brain overgrowth in autism existed. Moreover, the researchers also claimed that brain–gene mapping studies, presumably transcriptome or protein interactome studies, would fail to identify gene variants because such studies "will necessarily run headlong into the problem of age-specific brain effects. Therefore, brain-SNP, brain-CNV (copy number variation), or brain-'deep phenotype' studies of older children, adolescents, and adults with autism will be prone to reflect outcome associations and not original causal ones" (p. 142).

However, Courchesne et al. (2011a) concluded that their "theory of age-specific anatomic abnormalities in autism has significant broad implications for … genotype/CNV-anatomic phenotype studies" (p. 143), suggesting that new gene variants or chromosomal duplications or deletions might be found to explain their data.

Contrary to the claims made by Courchesne et al. (2011a), existing data from studies of syndromic autism offer possible genetic causes for early brain overgrowth in autism. Bray et al. (2011) reported significantly greater brain frontal lobe volume in boys with fragile X syndrome aged 9–12. Meguid et al. (2011) reported increased cortical gray matter, including significantly larger frontal lobe volumes, in boys with fragile X syndrome, half of whom met all criteria for autism. Meguid et al. (2011) attributed the brain overgrowth to failed programmed cell death caused by the absence of the protein FMRP that characterizes the fragile X syndrome. About 25% of individuals with fragile X syndrome are diagnosed with autism. However, up to 90% of children with fragile X syndrome have autism traits such as social anxiety, gaze avoidance, sensory hypersensitivity, tactile defensiveness, stereotypic movements, poor motor coordination, delayed speech development, and echolalia (De Rubeis & Bagni, 2011). Therefore, one or more of the seven cases of brain overgrowth reported by Courchesne et al. (2011b) could have been cases of fragile X syndrome.

In addition to fragile X syndrome, brain overgrowth or macrocephaly is associated with 164 single gene variants and chromosomal duplications and deletions (Williams, Dagli, & Battaglia, 2008), many of which occur with autism, such as neurofibromatosis (*NF1*) and tuberous sclerosis (*TSC1* and

TSC2). Brunetti-Pierri et al. (2008) and Mefford et al. (2008) also reported that duplications at 1q21.1 were associated with macrocephaly and autism.

A variant of the gene *PTEN* is also associated with early brain overgrowth. Mester, Tilot, Rybicki, Frazier, and Eng (2011) reported that 94% of individuals with *PTEN* hamartoma tumour syndrome (PHTS) had macrocephaly. The *PTEN* gene generates a protein involved in preventing cells from growing and dividing too rapidly. Orrico et al. (2008) found *PTEN* gene variants in 3 of 40 patients with macrocephaly. Butler et al. (2005) found *PTEN* gene variants in 3 of 18 children with autism and macrocephaly. However, Buxbaum et al. (2007) found a *PTEN* gene variant in only 1 of 88 individuals with autism and macrocephaly.

In addition to fragile X syndrome, the *PTEN* gene variant, *NF1*, *TSC1* and *TSC2*, and a chromosomal duplication at 1q21.1, there are numerous other genetic links between autism and macrocephaly. Sarasua et al. (2011) reported macrocephaly and autism in Phelan-McDermid syndrome caused by a chromosomal deletion at 22q13. Vozdova et al. (2011) reported autism and macrocephaly in a boy with a translocation of a section of the Y chromosome to the top of the short arms of chromosome 4. López-Hernández et al. (2011) reported autism and macrocephaly in a group of individuals with megalencephalic leukoencephalopathy caused by the recessive *MLC1* gene, and autism and macrocephaly caused by a variant of the GlialCAM/hepaCAM cell adhesion protein encoded by the *HEPACAM* gene. Tsuchiya et al. (2007) reported finding autism infant macrocephaly associated with abnormally low levels of the platelet-endothelial adhesion molecule (PECAM-1).

In sum, there are many possible genetic causes for early macrocephaly in autism. Given the many known genetic causes of macrocephaly in young children with autism, and given that only 0–21% of children with autism are found to have macrocephaly, it is probable that the increased frontal lobes and larger brain size Courchesne et al. (2011b) found in the seven cases resulted from several of these known genetic risk factors.

Challenges to the Brain Overgrowth Model of Autism
Barnard-Brak, Sulak, and Ivey Hatz (2011) reported no evidence for macrocephaly in 100 individuals with autism compared with 8900 nonautistic children studied in the Early Childhood Longitudinal Study Birth Cohort. This study was a nationally representative, community-based sample of approximately 9000 children across the United States who were studied at three time points: 9 months, 2 years, and 3 years old. Similarly,

Davidovitch et al. (2011) also reported finding no macrocephaly in a sample of 317 children with autism in Israel compared with a sample of 534 typical children.

Ioannidis (2011) analyzed 461 data sets in 41 meta-analyses of brain volumes in a range of disorders, including autism, and reported, "the number of positive results is way too large to be true" (p. 5). Ioannidis (2011) found that the number of positive results was nearly twice what it should have been based on the power analyses reported for the study samples. Ioannidis (2011) argued that "If the true effect sizes are only half of those observed in the meta-analyses, then the number of positive results is about 4 times the expected number" (p. 777). Ioannidis (2011) concluded that it is likely that research published on brain volume differences is subject to a significant amount of bias, and that the average level of bias is likely to be large. Ioannidis (2011) recommended that brain volume comparisons should be conducted in large multicenter studies, wherein all investigators use the same consistent definitions of cases, the same protocols for data acquisition, and the same data analyses. Ioannidis (2011) also argued that journal editors should not use significance tests as a criterion for publication, and should require the availability of raw data.

Summary: No Single Brain Deficit Model Accounts for the Brain-Wide Disruption Caused by Single Gene Variants or Chromosomal Deletions or Duplications Found for Autism

Brain dysfunctions found in animal models of autism, and brain dysfunctions found for most genetic causes linked to autism result in globally impaired brain development. This global impairment includes the molecular processes of abnormal neuronal migration, abnormalities in connectivity, disrupted axon path finding, aberrant synaptogenesis, aberrant synaptic function, dendritic abnormalities, and dysfunctional neural transmission. These molecular processes may or may not alter the time trajectory of brain growth, may or may not alter the growth of gray matter and white matter, may or may not confer functional disconnectivity throughout the brain, and may or may not lead to brain undergrowth (microcephaly) or brain overgrowth (macrocephaly).

The two brain development theories of autism reviewed here stimulated much research. One theory asserted that early overgrowth, particularly in the frontal lobes of the brain, was the unique cause for autism (Courchesne et al., 2011b). The other theory asserted that underconnectivity of the brain was the unique cause for autism (Schipul et al., 2011).

While both theories described global brain dysfunctions of development, neither model applied to all cases of autism. Macrocephaly was reported in only 0–21% of children with autism (Barnard-Brak et al., 2011; Davidovitch et al. 2011), and underconnectivity in 0–65% of individuals with autism (Wass, 2011). Moreover, neither macrocephaly nor underconnectivity, when present, was expressed in a consistent pattern across individuals studied (Davidovitch et al., 2011; Schipul et al., 2011; Wass, 2011). There were also conflicting reports of developmental changes in brain overgrowth and underconnectivity. For example, Hardan et al. (2009) reported a decrease in only the gray matter volume and cortical thickness at 30-month intervals in autism, but Hua et al. (2011) reported "a highly significant and widespread reduction of cortical white matter growth in autism" (p. 8).

While it may be that 20% of individuals with autism do experience developmental macrocephaly, and that a significant subset of individuals with autism have some form of brain underconnectivity, both macrocephaly and underconnectivity have been demonstrated in many other disorders and neither condition was present in a majority of individuals with autism. In addition, because unaffected siblings of individuals with autism showed the same pattern of white matter abnormality as that of their siblings diagnosed with autism (Barnea-Goraly et al., 2010) it was not clear that underconnectivity could be a cause of autism symptoms. Finally, as macrocephaly and underconnectivity varied in individual cases, no specific link to the two diagnostic symptoms of autism can be easily determined.

Social Brain Systems Involve Many Diverse Distributed Circuits and Most of these Circuits have been Demonstrated to be Dysfunctional in Autism

Pina-Camacho et al. (2012) reviewed 208 functional imaging studies of individuals with autism and reported that brains of individuals with autism generally demonstrated an abnormal connectivity of cortical and subcortical regions and networks involved in processing social information. These aberrant connections included prefrontal cortex, inferior frontal gyrus, temporal and cingulate cortex, and the amygdala–fusiform system. Pina-Camacho et al. (2012) also reported that functional imaging of individuals with autism showed impaired activity in the default mode network activated when the mind is not focused on any task. The impaired default mode network regions included medial prefrontal cortex, retrosplenial cortex/posterior cingulate cortex, and other regions as well. In addition, the researchers observed that imaging studies showed lower activation and connectivity in frontostriatal structures, and in the posterior parietal lobe, posterior cingulate, posterior corpus callosum, and cerebellum. Pina-Camacho et al. (2012) identified the impaired brain activity and connectivity in these regions as a cause for the autism symptom of restricted, repetitive patterns of behavior, interests, or activities.

As reviewed in Chapter 3, social neuroscience research has been reporting an increasing number of brain regions and circuits underlying human social behavior. Studies have identified autism impairment in self-awareness, social reward, and imagining the contents of the minds of others. According to Devue and Brédart (2011) the inferior frontal gyrus, the right medial and middle frontal gyri, the inferior parietal lobule, the supramarginal gyrus and the precuneus, the anterior cingulate cortex, the bilateral insula, the fusiform gyrus, and the bilateral inferior temporal gyrus *all* contribute to human self-recognition. Vickery et al. (2011) reported that all forms of reward and punishment processing, including social reward, occur in every cortical and subcortical area of the brain. Mar (2011) reviewed Theory of Mind research and concluded that imagining that others have minds with different content requires the right temporal-parietal juncture, prefrontal cortex, left and right posterior superior temporal sulcus, left and right angular gyri, left and right anterior temporal regions, posterior cingulate cortex, precuneus, and perhaps also the left inferior gyrus.

Genetic Causes for Autism Result in Brain-Wide Disruption

Evidence from genetic research suggests broad effects throughout the brain for gene variants and CNVs linked to autism: abnormal neuronal migration, abnormalities in connectivity, disrupted axon path finding, aberrant synaptogenesis, aberrant synaptic function, dendritic abnormalities, and dysfunctional neural transmission. Because so many brain regions and circuits are required for typical social cognition, social expression and social comprehension, and because brain dysfunction caused by genetic disorders has been found to cause brain-wide developmental disruption, it is likely that genetic disorders that are risk factors for the two diagnostic symptoms of autism will cause a range of other symptoms as well.

Can Autism Social Brain System Dysfunctions Map onto Brain-Wide Dysfunctions Caused by Genetic and Chromosomal Variants?

Abrahams and Geschwind (2010) asserted that, for autism, discovering "how broadly expressed genes give rise to regionalized deficits in brain anatomy and connectivity represents a major challenge for the field" (p. 398). The researchers proposed that aberrant gene products might interact with each other in the brain to produce localized disruptions specific to autism, or alternately that brain-wide disruption of brain circuits might preferentially affect circuits for social cognition because social cognition involved higher-order association cortex that required exact timing of inputs from other regions of the brain.

Another possibility, explored in detail in the section following, is that because gene variants and CNVs associated with autism result in brain-wide failures of information transmission and processing, autism symptoms will not be found as the only phenotypic expression of any of the genetic disorders. It is implausible that widespread system disruption in the brain could yield only autism symptoms. Autism symptoms expressed by an individual with a genetic disorder are therefore likely to be two symptoms among many symptoms—such as intellectual disability, hypotonia, epilepsy, attention problems, or language impairment—caused by the brain development dysfunction resulting from a genetic disorder.

QUESTION THREE: WHAT DOES IT MEAN THAT AUTISM SHARES GENES WITH OTHER DISORDERS?

Counter to the initial belief that a small set of genetic variants would be found that caused only autism symptoms, many gene variants and many CNVs have been found to be risk factors for autism, and risk factors for symptoms of other disorders as well. Ramocki and Zoghbi (2008) theorized that there were likely to be thousands of gene variants that caused autism, intellectual disability, or autism and intellectual disability. For example, the mutation of one gene, *DISC1*, whose name is an acronym for disrupted-in-schizophrenia, is linked to schizophrenia and bipolar disorder and autism and intellectual disability (Porteous, Millar, Brandon, & Sawa, 2011).

Van Bokhoven (2011) reported that 450 gene variants resulted in intellectual disability, and, in many cases, autism. Van Bokhoven stated, "a total of 1,500–2,000 genes might be a reasonable estimate" (p. 85) for variants causing intellectual disability, autism, and other neurocognitive disorders. Neale et al. (2012) noted that, although de novo, i.e., newly occurring, CNVs and large CNVs were found in association with autism, these CNVs most often were linked to "a broad range of conditions including intellectual disability, epilepsy and schizophrenia" (p. 242). O'Roak et al. (2012) argued that it was likely the diagnosis of autism did not have causally specific genetic variants. They concluded that, because many genetic variants were linked to autism and intellectual disability and developmental delay, research should compare "mutation patterns in children with developmental delay (without features of autism) to those in children with ASD" (O'Roak et al., 2012, p. 249).

O'Roak et al. (2011) concluded that "finding of de novo events in genes that have also been disrupted in children with intellectual disability without ASD, intellectual disability with ASD features or epilepsy provides further evidence that these genetic pathways may lead to a spectrum of neurodevelopmental outcomes depending on the genetic and environmental context" (p. 588). State and Levitt (2011) argued, "the observation that identical mutations may lead not only to ID and ASD, but to schizophrenia and possibly other neuropsychiatric disorders …would seem to argue for a model based on the pleiotropy of genes underlying fundamental neuronal processes" (p. 257).

Current genetic findings do suggest that many single gene variants and individual chromosomal duplications and deletions contribute to multiple diagnostic phenotypes, including autism, schizophrenia, attention deficit/hyperactivity disorder, intellectual disability without autism, and other disorders. This has two major implications for understanding autism. First, these findings suggest that many disorders considered as separate comorbid disorders in an individual with autism, including intellectual disability, epilepsy, ADHD, and others, are not separate comorbid disorders but instead are concurrent symptoms, of the genetic disorder of that individual. Moreover, when autism is diagnosed in an individual with a known genetic disorder, autism symptoms do not constitute syndromic autism but are symptoms of social impairment and insistence on sameness or motor stereotypies or sensory abnormalities of that genetic syndrome, be it fragile X syndrome or Angelman syndrome. Second, evidence of apparent comorbidities and multiple diagnoses arising from a shared genetic cause suggest that the two symptoms of autism may be a truncated set of all expressed symptoms for an individual with a genetic disorder. To identify autism arising from a known genetic disorder as a separate disorder means including only social impairment and rigid interests and repetitive behaviors and/or sensory abnormalities, while excluding all other co-occurring symptoms. Conversely, if all the symptoms of a known genetic cause are accepted as part of the phenotype of the disorder, the phenotype will include many non-autism symptoms.

Comorbid Disorders are Concurrent Symptoms not Comorbidities

The four disorders most frequently found in individuals with autism are intellectual disability, epilepsy, attention deficit/hyperactivity disorder, and impaired language development. Intellectual disability has been diagnosed in 55–70% of individuals with autism (Chakrabarti & Fombonne, 2005; Charman et al., 2011). Epilepsy has been diagnosed in 25–33% of individuals with autism (Levy et al., 2009). ADHD has been diagnosed in 30–80% of individuals with autism (Rommelse et al., 2011). Because language impairment was a diagnostic criterion until DSM-5, language delay was diagnosed in nearly all individuals diagnosed with autism (Kjellmer, Hedvall, Fernell, Gillberg, & Norrelgen, 2012; Stefanatos & Baron, 2011), and the absence of any language at all was found for 25–50% of individuals with autism (Eigsti, de Marchena, Schuh, & Kelley, 2011).

Epilepsy, intellectual disability, and ADHD have long been considered comorbid with autism, that is, these disorders were thought to be entirely separate disorders that happened to occur alongside autism in the same individual. As outlined above, genetic research findings indicate that symptoms are not evidence of comorbid associated disorders but are concurrent symptoms.

Intellectual Disability and Autism Symptoms

Approximately two-thirds of individuals diagnosed with autism are also diagnosed with some form of intellectual disability (ID). Van Bokhoven (2011) reported "there is growing evidence to support the notion that ID, autism, and probably a range of CDs (cognitive disorders) share a common molecular etiology at the single-gene level" (p. 86). Van Bokhoven (2011) noted that single gene variants for *IL1RAPL1*, *SHANK2*, *SHANK3*, *NLGN3*, *NLGN4*, *GRIN2B*, *TCF4*, *AUTS2*, *CNTN4*, *CNTNAP2*, and *NRXN1* have been expressed in individuals as intellectual disability without autism, autism without intellectual disability, and autism with intellectual disability. Moreover, autism has been diagnosed in a subgroup of individuals with Klinefelter syndrome, Turner syndrome, Down syndrome, Rett syndrome, and fragile X syndrome, and a majority of the individuals diagnosed with each of these genetic disorders expresses some form of intellectual disability. Wall et al. (2009) identified 66 candidate gene variants in the families of individuals with autism: all 66 gene variants were associated with intellectual disability. A majority of the possible CNV regions associated with autism (1p, 1q, 2q37, 3q, 4q21–31, 5p, 6q, 7q21–31.31, 7q32.3–36.3, 8q, 11p11.2–13, 13q12.3, 15q11–13, 15q24, 16p11.2, 17q11, 19p, 22q11.2) have been found with intellectual disability.

Nishiyama et al. (2009) studied a sample of twins with autism and reported that the additive genetic factors contributing to autism diagnostic symptoms are "substantially common to those that influence IQ" (p. 59). Nishiyama et al. (2009) predicted that more single genes and chromosome duplications and deletions would be found that cause autism and intellectual disability together and separately.

The cumulative evidence linking autism to intellectual disability for genetic syndromes and CNVs suggests that autism symptoms and intellectual disability are not comorbid, but are most likely to be concurrent symptoms of a genetic disorder.

Epilepsy and Autism

Fombonne, Du Mazaubrun, Cans, and Grandjean (1997) reported that 25% of children with autism they studied had epilepsy. Fombonne et al. (1997) reported that the rate of epilepsy in autism was significantly higher than in a control group, "consistent with the increased vulnerability of autistic children to epilepsy" (p. 1564). Maski, Jeste, and Spence (2011) identified epilepsy as comorbid with autism, but asserted that epilepsy and autism were likely to have a shared pathophysiology stemming from causal genetic mechanisms such as specific signaling pathways in single gene disorders, chromosomal copy number duplications and deletions, as well as polygenic causes. Thus, Maski et al. (2011) saw epilepsy and autism not as comorbid disorders, but as dysfunctions arising from the same shared genetic disorder.

Brooks-Kayal (2011) observed that epilepsy and autism could together result from abnormal synaptic plasticity producing an imbalance of excitation and inhibition. Brooks-Kayal (2011) noted that abnormal synaptic plasticity occurs in fragile X syndrome, Rett syndrome, mutations of the gene *CDKL5*, tuberous sclerosis, mutations of the neuroligin genes *NLGN3* and *NLGN4*, as well as mutations in the *ARX* and neuropilin 2 (*NRP2*) genes. Brooks-Kayal (2011) proposed that aberrant synaptic plasticity can result from altered receptors, disrupted signaling molecules, or neurotropins linked to both autism symptoms and epilepsy.

As with autism and intellectual disability, a genetic cause linking autism and epilepsy does not indicate the presence of two disorders, but suggests autism symptoms and epilepsy are concurrent symptoms of a genetic cause producing neural dysfunctions that give rise to both autism symptoms and epilepsy.

Attention Deficit/Hyperactivity Disorder and Autism

Rommelse, Geurts, Franke, Buitelaar, and Hartman (2011) argued that autism and attention deficit/hyperactivity disorder were related because the two disorders shared a significant set of pleiotropic gene variants, and shared symptoms. Rommelse et al. (2011) claimed that the inferior frontal cortex, the anterior cingulate cortex, and the precuneus of the brain are disrupted in both autism and ADHD. They noted that some individuals expressed behaviors that changed from autism to ADHD symptoms. They proposed that impairments of the frontostriatal circuits caused the attention problems, hyperactivity, and impulsivity of ADHD, caused these ADHD symptoms of autism, and caused the rigid and stereotyped patterns of behavior of autism. Rommelse et al. (2011) proposed that dysfunction of orbitofrontal cortex and the anterior cingulate cortex caused the cognitive control problems of ADHD and the social cognition problems of autism. Lionel et al. (2011) reported genetic links between autism and ADHD in shared risk gene variants (*ASTN2, GABRG1, CNTN5, CHCHD3, MACROD2*) and chromosome alterations at 16p11.2, and they concluded that their findings supported "the existence of common underlying susceptibility genes for ADHD, ASD, and other neuropsychiatric disorders" (p. 1). Lionel et al. (2011) observed that DSM-IV did not allow a diagnosis of ADHD for a child diagnosed with autism, even though "data suggest upward of 50% of children with ASD would otherwise meet criteria for ADHD" (p. 7).

Again, as with autism and intellectual disability, and autism and epilepsy, the symptoms of autism and ADHD are produced together by gene variants, chromosome alterations, and resulting shared brain deficits. Thus, when these two disorders are diagnosed in the same individual, they are concurrent symptoms, not separate comorbid disorders.

Language Impairment and Autism

Lord (2011) cautioned, "Language difficulties in autism, in which delays in comprehension and onset are common, are not the same as those found in specific language deficit, in which grammatical aspects of expressive language are most affected" (p. 25). Lord (2011) argued that evidence for a *CNTNAP2* variant causing autism and specific language impairment is "not necessarily evidence of direct links between particular behavioral deficits and specific genetic loci" (p. 25).

Conversely, Verhoeven et al. (2011) claimed that the boundary between autism language deficit and specific language impairment (SLI) was not always clear. The researchers noted that language deficits in autism included problems in social language use, intonation, production and comprehension of gestures, as well as speech sound problems, syntax problems, and comprehension problems. However, Verhoeven et al. (2011) noted a differentiation "between pure ASD, SLI, and the apparent 'comorbid cases' who have classic autism with language impairment and are referred to as ASD-LI" (p. 1).Verhoeven et al. (2011) reported that the superior longitudinal fasci-cle, the major white matter tract connecting parietal and frontal lobe, was impaired in individuals with specific language impairment, but, surprisingly, not impaired in individuals with autism who demonstrated serious language impairment. The findings of Verhoeven et al. (2011) contradicted those of Jou et al. (2011), who reported atypical white matter functional connectiv-ity in the inferior fronto-occipital fascicle and superior longitudinal fascicle in autism. In fact, as noted in Chapter 2, Jou et al. (2011) argued that the deficits in these two white matter tracts "may not only dictate the expres-sion of autism but also its severity and heterogeneity" (p. 1612). The contra-dictory findings of Verhoeven et al. (2011) and Jou et al. (2011) for autism deficits in the superior longitudinal fascicle are likely to be the result of both autism heterogeneity and the non-representativeness of small samples. Verhoeven et al. (2011) studied only 19 individuals with autism and lan-guage impairment, and Jou et al. (2011) studied only 15 individuals with autism. Moreover, neither group reported individual variation data that might have uncovered a possible partial overlap in findings.

The relationship between language impairment and autism is similar to that for autism and intellectual disability, epilepsy, and ADHD. If language disorder and autism symptoms are expressed by an individual with a known genetic disorder, such as a risk variant of the *CNTNAP2*, *FOXP1*, or *FOXP2* genes, it is most likely that language impairment and autism symp-toms are concurrent symptoms of the genetic disorder, and not separate comorbid disorders. However, where individuals with autism do not share genetic risk factors or brain deficits with individuals with specific language impairment, separate risk factors for language impairment in autism and SLI may be operating.

Schizophrenia and Autism

Addington et al. (2011) reported a case study of a family in which a protein truncating mutation in the *UPF3B* gene was found to cause the childhood onset of schizophrenia, autism, and ADHD in the same family. The research-ers reported that the *UPF3B* gene encodes a protein theorized to regulate expression of various mRNAs at the synapse. The researchers concluded their finding "adds to the growing evidence of both clinical and genetic overlap that is indicative of a broad neurodevelopmental phenotype, which includes autism, intellectual disability, and schizophrenia" (Addington et al., 2011, p. 239).

King and Lord (2011) reviewed findings for links between autism and schizophrenia and noted that one study found 50% of childhood onset schizophrenia was preceded by autism symptoms, while another study found schizophrenia was diagnosed in 10% of adults who had been diagnosed with autism in childhood. King and Lord (2011) argued that autism and schizophrenia were related, stating, "whether schizophrenia lives on the autism spectrum, or vice versa, or whether there is a sub-population at their intersection, reconnecting these phenotypes may provide new insights" (King & Lord, 2011, p. 39). These and other examples of gene variants shared across diagnostic boundaries indicate that the disruption of some genes may have multiple different effects, i.e., pleiotropy. Also possible is that, in some cases, neuropsychiatric disorders result from separate and overlapping sets of gene variants.

Mandell et al. (2011) reported that 10% of adult patients at a state psychiatric hospital previously diagnosed with other disorders including schizophrenia met criteria for autism. The researchers noted that all had intellectual disability, and concluded that undiagnosed autism may occur with frequency in psychiatric hospitals. Raja and Azzoni (2010) identified 26 individuals with autism in a sample of 126 individuals diagnosed as schizophrenic.

Solomon et al. (2011) reported finding that 20% of individuals aged 11–20 with a first episode of psychosis showed significant autism symptoms, as did 20% of individuals 11–20 ascertained to be at risk for psychosis. Solomon et al. (2011) concluded that because autism and schizophrenia share genetic causes that disrupt neurotransmission and synapse formation and function, research should explore links between genes and neural circuits in both syndromes.

Syndromic Autism is a Symptom Set and not a Syndrome

A brief review of the genetic disorders in which autism symptoms may be expressed suggests that, for these disorders, autism is a symptom set and not syndromic autism. Autism has been diagnosed: in 34% of males with Klinefelter syndrome (van Rijn & Swaab, 2011); in 7–15% of individuals with Down syndrome (Ji, Capone, & Kaufmann, 2011); in 42–58% of girls and women with Rett syndrome (Wulffaert et al., 2009); and in 33% and 67% of children with fragile X syndrome (Bertone et al., 2010). As noted earlier, autism symptoms are also expressed in Angelman syndrome, Cowden disease, DiGeorge syndrome, Duchenne muscular dystrophy, Joubert syndrome, lissencephaly, neurofibromatosis, Phelan-McDermid syndrome,

Smith-Lemli-Opitz syndrome, Timothy syndrome, tuberous sclerosis types I and II, Turner syndrome, and X-linked infantile spasm syndrome. In addition, association with autism has been reported for many chromosome regions including 1p34.2, 1q21.1, 1q42.2 (*DISC1*), 2p16.3 (*NRXN1*), 2q21–33, 3p13 (*FOXP1*), 3p25, 3q25–27, 4q32, 6p16.3 (*GRIK2*), 6q14–21,6q, 7q22, 7q31–36 (*FOXP2, CNTNAP2*), 11q13.3–q13.4 (*SHANK2*), Xp21.3 (*ARX*), Xp22.32–p22.31 (*NLGN4X*), and Xq13.1 (*NLGN3*).

Lord (2011) argued that there was "strong evidence that different genes are associated with ASD, but in almost all instances, these findings as yet have no clinical implications" (p. 25), and she suggested that lack of clinical implications of genes for autism resulted from low standards for research linking genotype to phenotype. However, State and Levitt (2011) observed that because thousands of genes determine phenotypes, and phenotypic behavior is "mediated by hierarchically organized circuitries that include sensory and motor, autonomic regulatory, social-emotional, and cognitive domains … it is not surprising that identifying the path from genotype to autism spectrum phenotype has not been an easy one" (p. 1499).

Nonetheless, despite the doubts and concerns of Lord (2011) and State and Levitt (2011), there is a simple, conservative first assumption regarding links between genotype and autism phenotype. This assumption is that gene variants, CNVs, and epigenetic risk factors cause abnormal protein functions and abnormal transcription factors and other effects causing widespread developmental disruption of the brain. The second assumption is that the resulting brain disruption causes many symptoms including but not limited to autism symptoms. The third assumption is that brain deficits mediating autism symptoms will be a subset of the wider brain development disruption resulting from gene variants, CNVs, and epigenetic risk factors. Consequently, autism symptoms expressed by an individual with a genetic risk factor or factors are likely to be two symptoms among a set of varied symptoms that result from the widespread brain development dysfunction caused by the genetic risk factor or factors.

Therefore, just as it is unlikely that autism and intellectual disability, epilepsy, attention deficit/hyperactivity disorder, and language impairment found together in a single individual represent five separately caused comorbid disorders, it is unlikely that autism symptoms expressed in a genetic disorder represent syndromic autism. The most parsimonious interpretation is that the two diagnostic criteria for autism are not a disorder called "syndromic autism" but instead represent two concurrent symptoms of a larger symptom set that is the outcome of effects of the genetic disorder.

Genetic Disorder-Mediated Brain Disruptions Cause Many Symptoms, Including Autism Symptoms

Hall, Lightbody, Hirt, Rezvani, and Reiss (2010) argued, "the practice of diagnosing children with FXS [fragile X syndrome] as autistic may become increasingly obsolete in the future" (p. 932). Hall et al. (2010) noted that the inclusion of category members that were not at the same level of explanation was a scientific category error. They suggested that "the grouping together of FXS (a biological disease) with autism (a phenomenologically defined behavioral disorder) may be another such type of category mistake" (p. 932). As Hall et al. (2010) pointed out, an individual with fragile X syndrome and autism symptoms does not have two biological disorders, autism and fragile X syndrome. The individual has a genetic disorder, fragile X syndrome, with many phenotypic symptoms including social impairment and rigidities or motor stereotypies and/or sensory abnormalities.

However, it is unlikely that autism symptoms expressed with genetic disorders will *always* be found to be caused straightforwardly by the brain dysfunctions resulting from the genetic syndrome. For many individuals with autism, symptoms will result from the brain dysfunctions caused by the identified genetic disorder. For other cases of autism, given the complex variation in aberrant genetic mechanisms being discovered and hypothesized (Geschwind, 2011; Girirajan et al., 2010; Lionel et al., 2011; State & Levitt, 2011), it is likely that, in some cases, multiple gene variant effects or gene–environment interactions will also be found to conjointly cause autism symptoms. For example, Lionel et al. (2011) argued that the gene variants and chromosomal duplications and deletions could produce functionally overlapping proteins. The researchers argued that resulting diverse symptoms would arise from "different functional domains of a single protein, the interaction between different proteins (such as a ligand and receptor), the interaction of proteins in a multiprotein complex, or different steps in a cellular pathway" (2011, p. 8). However, for these more complex genetic mechanisms, it is equally unlikely that any specific downstream protein interaction or multiprotein complex will be found to be dedicated only to causing an autism symptom. Therefore, here too, autism symptoms will be symptoms of the complex genetic disorder, and not evidence for a separate syndromic or idiopathic autism disorder.

Idiopathic Kanner Autism

Since 1943, autism symptoms have been seen as a unique disorder. As research uncovered impairments such as epilepsy and intellectual disability occurring along with autism symptoms, efforts were made to isolate some form of autism as a unique disorder. Autism with a known cause was called syndromic autism. It was assumed that syndromic autism was caused by an unknown autism-specific cause, along with the known syndromic cause. Idiopathic autism, a term for autism with no known cause, was thought to be caused solely by uniquely autism-specific causes. For example, Skuse (2007) argued that the search for genes specific to autism should study only individuals with autism who had no intellectual disability or language impairment, i.e., "normal-range intelligence and good structural language skills" (p. 393).

Pure autism was called classical autism, Kanner autism, or essential autism. Researchers assumed pure idiopathic autism existed without intellectual disability, epilepsy, hypotonia (low muscle tone), attention deficit/hyperactivity disorder, abnormal EEG, in short, without any additional non-diagnostic symptoms. As noted earlier, the only allowed non-diagnostic symptom for pure Kanner autism was macrocephaly because Kanner had noted that 5 of the 11 children he identified with autism had larger heads.

However, neuroscience research has discovered that the two symptoms of pure Kanner autism are not caused by narrow brain deficits, but are caused by diverse disrupted brain systems. As outlined in Chapter 3, autism social impairment has been shown to result from dysfunction in many diverse brain systems such as the fusiform face region for recognizing faces, and oxytocin receptor function for bonding and affiliative behavior. Autism behavioral rigidity and motor stereotypy also result from dysfunction in diverse brain systems, such as frontostriatal circuits and dopamine receptors.

The search for the brain basis for autism symptoms, and the search for causal genes for autism both uncovered wide patterns of brain disruption. Although Geschwind (2011) asserted that gene variants linked to autism were too diverse to provide a unified narrative, Gilman et al. (2011) proposed a model of brain effects of rare de novo CNVs linked to idiopathic autism. The researchers hypothesized that the CNVs disrupted a brain-wide "network responsible for synaptogenesis, axon guidance, and related molecular processes … [including] the whole arc of molecular processes essential for proper synapse formation and function" (Gilman et al., 2011, p. 904). Wei et al. (2011) proposed a model similar to that of Gilman et al. (2011): autism caused by reduced neuron migration, abnormal synaptogenesis, and a disruption of the relationship between excitatory and inhibitory synapses.

The brain development disruptions proposed by Wei et al. (2011) and Gilman et al. (2011) were brain-wide. The genetic findings for brain-wide disruption have forced a reconsideration of the meaning of the symptoms associated with autism. In fact, it now appears that autism, intellectual disability, epilepsy, hypotonia, language impairment, attention deficit/hyperactivity disorder, and other disorders are most often meaningful concurrent symptoms caused by the brain-wide developmental dysfunction resulting from different genetic syndromes and from a range of environmental insults as well.

The evidence for widespread brain disruption resulting from many autism genetic risk factors makes clear why there has been a continuing failure to find a brain deficit that causes *only* the two autism diagnostic symptoms of persistent deficits in social communication and interaction across contexts, and restricted, repetitive patterns of behavior, interests, or sensory abnormalities. If, as seems likely, brain deficits mediating autism symptoms are embedded in a larger network of brain disruption, it will be very difficult to unpick the links between causal brain deficits and autism symptoms. Shifting to the working assumption that autism represents two symptoms within a larger symptom set, paradoxically may improve research power to distinguish links between brain deficits and symptoms. The shift makes the phenotype findings for gene and chromosomal risk variants more meaningful because *all* the symptoms—that is the autism and non-autism impairments—can be accepted as the manifold phenotypic effects of brain-wide disruption.

The findings that gene and chromosomal variants cause widespread brain disruption also make clear why psychiatry has "little reason to expect phenotypic specificity from a particular genetic variant" (Addington & Rapoport, 2012, p. 2). Addington and Rapoport (2012) noted that the *DISC1* gene and the 22q11 deletion both produced three disorders: autism, schizophrenia, and intellectual disability. A more conservative interpretation is that the *DISC1* gene and the 22q11 deletion each produce variable sets of symptoms.

Smith, Spence, and Flodman (2009) concluded that "success in the study of these complex disorders best referred to as autisms, rather than autism, will require that we abandon our dependence on limited set diagnostic criteria and turn to systematic studies of the wide range of phenotypic presentations" (p. 128). The associated symptoms and autism symptoms together do produce a wide range of phenotypic presentations. Given all the available evidence, however, the least speculative scientific position would not be the creation of autism subgroups or a creation of "the autisms." The least speculative and most phenomena-conserving position would be to view autism as two symptoms expressed in association with a wide range of genetic disorders, and a wide range of environmental causes.

REFERENCES

Abrahams, B. S., & Geschwind, D. H. (2010). Connecting genes to brain in the autism spectrum disorders. *Archives of Neurology*, *67*, 395–399.

Addington, A. M., Gauthier, J., Piton, A., Hamdan, F. F., Raymond, A., Gogtay, N., et al. (2011). A novel frameshift mutation in UPF3B identified in brothers affected with childhood onset schizophrenia and autism spectrum disorders. *Molecular Psychiatry*, *16*, 238–239.

Addington, A. M., & Rapoport, J. L. (2012). Annual Research Review: Impact of advances in genetics in understanding developmental psychopathology. *Journal of Child Psychology and Psychiatry*, *53*, 510–518.

Aldinger, K. A., Plummer, J. T., Qiu, S., & Levitt, P. (2011). SnapShot: Genetics of autism. *Neuron*, *72*, 418–418e1.

Amaral, D. G. (2011). The promise and the pitfalls of autism research: An introductory note for new autism researchers. *Brain Research*, *1380*, 3–9.

Anney, R., Klei, L., Pinto, D., Regan, R., Conroy, J., Magalhaes, T. R., et al. (2010). A genome-wide scan for common alleles affecting risk for autism. *Human Molecular Genetics*, *19*, 4072–4082.

Barnard-Brak, L., Sulak, T., & Ivey Hatz, J. K. (2011). Macrocephaly in children with autism spectrum disorders. *Pediatric Neurology*, *44*, 97–100.

Barnea-Goraly, N., Lotspeich, L. J., & Reiss, A. L. (2010). Similar white matter aberrations in children with autism and their unaffected siblings: A diffusion tensor imaging study using tract-based spatial statistics. *Archives of General Psychiatry*, *67*, 1052–1060.

Bertone, A., Hanck, J., Kogan, C., Chaudhuri, A., & Cornish, K. (2010). Using perceptual signatures to define and dissociate condition-specific neural etiology: Autism and fragile x syndrome as model conditions. *Journal of Autism and Developmental Disorders*, *12*, 1531–1540.

Betancur, C. (2011). Etiological heterogeneity in autism spectrum disorders: More than 100 genetic and genomic disorders and still counting. *Brain Research*, *1380*, 42–77.

Bray, S., Hirt, M., Jo, B., Hall, S. S., Lightbody, A. A., Walter, E., et al. (2011). Aberrant frontal lobe maturation in adolescents with fragile X syndrome is related to delayed cognitive maturation. *Biological Psychiatry*, *70*, 852–858.

Brooks-Kayal, A. (2011). Molecular mechanisms of cognitive and behavioral comorbidities of epilepsy in children. *Epilepsia*, *52*, 13–20.

Brunetti-Pierri, N., Berg, J. S., Scaglia, F., Belmont, J., Bacino, C. A., Sahoo, T., et al. (2008). Recurrent reciprocal 1q21.1 deletions and duplications associated with microcephaly or macrocephaly and developmental and behavioral abnormalities. *Nature Genetics*, *40*, 1466–1471.

Butler, M. G., Dasouki, M. J., Zhou, X. P., Talebizadeh, Z., Brown, T., Takahashi, T. N., et al. (2005). Subset of individuals with autism spectrum disorders and extreme macrocephaly associated with germline PTEN tumour suppressor gene mutations. *Journal of Medical Genetics*, *42*, 318–321.

Buxbaum, J. D., Cai, G., Chaste, P., Nygren, G., Goldsmith, J., Reichert, J., et al. (2007). Mutation screening of the PTEN gene in patients with autism spectrum disorders and macrocephaly. *American Journal of Medical Genetics Part B Neuropsychiatric Genetics*, *144B*, 484–491.

Campbell, D. B., Datta, D., Jones, S. T., Lee, E. B., Sutcliffe, J. S., Hammock, E. A. D., et al. (2011). Association of oxytocin receptor (OXTR) gene variants with multiple phenotype domains of autism spectrum disorder. *Journal of Neurodevelopmental Disorders*, *3*, 101–112.

Casey, J. P., Magalhaes, T., Conroy, J. M., Regan, R., Shah, N., Anney, R., et al. (2012). A novel approach of homozygous haplotype sharing identifies candidate genes in autism spectrum disorder. *Human Genetics*, *131*, 565–579.

Chakrabarti, S., & Fombonne, E. (2005). Pervasive developmental disorders in preschool children: Confirmation of high prevalence. *American Journal of Psychiatry, 162*, 1133–1141.

Charman, T., Pickles, A., Simonoff, E., Chandler, S. E., Loucas, T., & Baird, G. (2011). IQ in children with autism spectrum disorders: data from the Special Needs and Autism Project (SNAP). *Psychological Medicine, 41*, 619–627.

Chen, Y. Z., Matsushita, M., Girirajan, S., Lisowski, M., Sun, E., Sul, Y., et al. (2012). Evidence for involvement of GNB1L in autism. *American Journal of Medical Genetics B Neuropsychiatric Genetics, 159B*, 61–71.

Courchesne, E., Campbell, K., & Solso, S. (2011a). Brain growth across the life span in autism: Age-specific changes in anatomical pathology. *Brain Research, 1380*, 138–145.

Courchesne, E., Mouton, P. R., Calhoun, M. E., Semendeferi, K., Ahrens-Barbeau, C., Hallet, M. J., et al. (2011b). Neuron number and size in prefrontal cortex of children with autism. *Journal of the American Medical Association, 306*, 2001–2010.

Crespi, B., & Badcock, C. (2008). Psychosis and autism as diametrical disorders of the social brain. *Behavioral and Brain Sciences, 31*, 241–320.

Davidovitch, M., Golan, D., Vardi, O., Lev, D., & Lerman-Sagie, T. (2011). Israeli children with autism spectrum disorder are not macrocephalic. *Journal of Child Neurology, 26*, 580–585.

de León-Guerrero, S. D., Pedraza-Alva, G., & Pérez-Martínez, L. (2011). In sickness and in health: The role of methyl-CpG binding protein 2 in the central nervous system. *European Journal of Neuroscience, 33*, 1563–1574.

Derecki, N. C., Cronk, J. C., Lu, Z., Xu, E., Abbott, S. B., Guyenet, P. G., & Kipnis, J. (2012). Wild-type microglia arrest pathology in a mouse model of Rett syndrome. *Nature, 484*, 105–109.

De Rubeis, S., & Bagni, C. (2011). Regulation of molecular pathways in the Fragile X Syndrome insights into Autism Spectrum Disorders. *Journal of Neurodevelopmental Disorders, 3*, 257–269.

Devlin, B., Melhem, N., & Roeder, K. (2011). Do common variants play a role in risk for autism? Evidence and theoretical musings. *Brain Research, 1380*, 78–84.

Devue, C., & Brédart, S. (2011). The neural correlates of visual self-recognition. *Consciousness and Cognition, 20*, 40–51.

Eigsti, I. B., de Marchena, A., Schuh, J. M., & Kelley, E. (2011). Language acquisition in autism spectrum disorders: A developmental review. *Research in Autism Spectrum Disorders, 5*, 681–691.

El-Fishawy, P., & State, M. W. (2010). The genetics of autism: Key issues, recent findings and clinical implications. *Psychiatric Clinics of North America, 33*, 83–105.

Ey, E., Leblond, C. S., & Bourgeron, T. (2011). Behavioral profiles of mouse models for autism spectrum disorders. *Autism Research, 4*, 5–16.

Folstein, S. (2006). The clinical spectrum of autism. *Clinical Neuroscience Research, 6*, 113–117.

Folstein, S., & Rutter, M. (1977). Infantile autism: A genetic study of 21 twin pairs. *Journal of Child Psychology and Psychiatry, 18*, 297–321.

Fombonne, E., Du Mazaubrun, C., Cans, C., & Grandjean, H. (1997). Autism and associated medical disorders in a French epidemiological survey. *Journal of the American Academy of Child & Adolescent Psychiatry, 36*, 1561–1569.

Fombonne, E., Rogé, B., Claverie, J., Courty, S., & Frémolle, J. (1999). Microcephaly and macrocephaly in autism. *Journal of Autism and Developmental Disorders, 29*, 113–119.

Gai, X., Xie, H. M., Perin, J. C., Takahashi, N., Murphy, K., Wenocur, A. S., et al. (2012). Rare structural variation of synapse and neurotransmission genes in autism. *Molecular Psychiatry*, 402–411.

Gauthier, J., Siddiqui, T. J., Huashan, P., Yokomaku, D., Hamdan, F. F., Champagne, N., et al. (2011). Truncating mutations in NRXN2 and NRXN1 in autism spectrum disorders and schizophrenia. *Human Genetics, 130*, 563–573.

Geschwind, D. H. (2011). Genetics of autism spectrum disorders. *Trends in Cognitive Sciences*, *15*, 409–416.

Gilman, S. R., Iossifov, I., Levy, D., Ronemus, M., Wigler, M., & Vitkup, D. (2011). Rare de novo variants associated with autism implicate a large functional network of genes. *Neuron*, *70*, 898–907.

Girirajan, S., Campbell, C. D., & Eichler, E. E. (2011). Human copy number variation and complex genetic disease. *Annual Review of Genetics*, *45*, 203–226.

Girirajan, S., Rosenfeld, J. A., Cooper, G. M., Antonacci, F., Siswara, P., Itsara, A., et al. (2010). A recurrent 16p12.1 microdeletion supports a two-hit model for severe developmental delay. *Nature Genetics*, *42*, 203–209.

Grafodatskaya, D., Chung, B., Szatmari, P., & Weksberg, R. (2010). Autism spectrum disorders and epigenetics. *Journal of the American Academy of Child and Adolescent Psychiatry*, *49*, 794–809.

Green, L., Fein, D., Modahl, C., Feinstein, C., Waterhouse, L., & Morris, M. (2001). Oxytocin and autistic disorder: Alterations in peptide forms. *Biological Psychiatry*, *50*, 609–613.

Gregor, A., Albrecht, B., Bader, I., Bijlsma, E. K., Ekici, A. B., Engels, H., et al. (2011). Expanding the clinical spectrum associated with defects in CNTNAP2 and NRXN1. *BMC Medical Genetics*, *12*, 106.

Grice, D. E., & Buxbaum, J. D. (2006). The genetic architecture of autism and related disorders. *Clinical Neuroscience Research*, *6*, 161–168.

Hagerman, R., Au, J., & Hagerman, P. (2011). FMR1 premutation and full mutation molecular mechanisms related to autism. *Journal of Neurodevelopmental Disorders*, *3*, 211–224.

Hall, S. S., Lightbody, A. A., Hirt, M., Rezvani, A., & Reiss, A. L. (2010). Autism in fragile X syndrome: A category mistake? *Journal of the American Academy of Child and Adolescent Psychiatry*, *49*, 921–933.

Hallmayer, J., Cleveland, S., Torres, A., Phillips, J., Cohen, B., Torigoe, T., & Risch, N. (2011). Genetic heritability and shared environmental factors among twin pairs with autism. *Archives of General Psychiatry*, *68*, 1095–1102.

Hardan, A. Y., Libove, R. A., Keshavan, M. S., Melhem, N. M., & Minshew, N. J. A. (2009). Preliminary longitudinal magnetic resonance imaging study of brain volume and cortical thickness in autism. *Biological Psychiatry*, *66*, 320–326.

Hazlett, H. C., Poe, M. D., Gerig, G., Styner, M., Chappell, C., Smith, R. G., et al. (2011). Early brain overgrowth in autism associated with an increase in cortical surface area before age 2 years. *Archives of General Psychiatry*, *68*, 467–476.

Heger, M. (2011). Genetic insights beginning to divide autism diagnosis. *Nature Medicine*, *17*, 398.

Hines, R. M., Davies, P. A., Moss, S. J., & Maguire, J. (2011). Functional regulation of GABA(A) receptors in nervous system pathologies. *Current Opinion in Neurobiology*, [Epub October 28, 2011], 1–7. doi: 10.1016/j.conb.2011.10.007.

Hogart, A., Nagarajan, R. P., Patzel, K. A., Yasui, D. H., & LaSalle, J. M. (2007). 5q11-13 GABAA receptor genes are normally biallelically expressed in brain yet are subject to epigenetic dysregulation in autism-spectrum disorders. *Human Molecular Genetics*, *16*, 691–703.

Horev, G., Ellegood, J., Lerch, J. P., Son, Y. E., Muthuswamy, L., Vogel, H., et al. (2011). Dosage-dependent phenotypes in models of 16p11.2 lesions found in autism. *Proceedings of the National Academy of Sciences of the United States of America*, *108*, 17076–17081.

Hua, X., Thompson, P. M., Leow, A. D., Madsen, S. K., Caplan, R., Alger, J. R., et al. (2011). Brain growth rate abnormalities visualized in adolescents with autism. *Human Brain Mapping*. [Epub October 10, 2011]. doi: 10.1002/hbm.21441.

Hyman, S. E. (2010). The diagnosis of mental disorders: The problem of reification. *Annual Review of Clinical Psychology*, *6*, 155–179. doi: 10.1146/annurev.clinpsy.3.022806.091532.

Insel, T. R., & Wang, P. S. (2010). Rethinking mental illness. *Journal of the American Medical Association*, *303*, 1970–1971.

Ioannidis, J. P. A. (2011). Excess significance bias in the literature on brain volume abnormalities. *Archives of General Psychiatry, 68,* 773–780.

Ji, N. Y., Capone, G. T., & Kaufmann, W. E. (2011). Autism spectrum disorder in Down syndrome: Cluster analysis of Aberrant Behaviour Checklist data supports diagnosis. *Journal of Intellectual Disability Research, 55,* 1064–1077.

Jones, J. R., Skinner, C., Friez, M. J., Schwartz, C. E., & Stevenson, R. E. (2008). Hypothesis: Dysregulation of methylation of brain-expressed genes on the X chromosome and autism spectrum disorders. *American Journal of Medical Genetics Part A, 146A,* 2213–2220.

Jones, W., & Klin, A. (2009). Heterogeneity and homogeneity across the autism spectrum: The role of development. *Journal of the American Academy of Child and Adolescent Psychiatry, 48,* 471–473.

Joober, R., & Boksa, P. (2009). A new wave in the genetics of psychiatric disorders: The copy number variant tsunami. *Journal of Psychiatry and Neuroscience, 34,* 55–59.

Jou, R. J., Mateljevic, N., Kaiser, M. D., Sugrue, D. R., Volkmar, F. R., & Pelphrey, K. A. (2011). Structural neural phenotype of autism: preliminary evidence from a diffusion tensor imaging study using tract-based spatial statistics. *American Journal of Neuroradiology, 32,* 1607–1613.

Kapranov, P., Willingham, A. T., & Gingeras, T. R. (2007). Genome-wide transcription and the implications for genomic organization. *Nature Review Genetics, 8,* 413–423.

King, B. H., & Lord, C. (2011). Is schizophrenia on the autism spectrum? *Brain Research, 1380,* 34–41.

Kjellmer, L., Hedvall, A., Fernell, E., Gillberg, C., & Norrelgen, F. (2011). Language and communication skills in preschool children with autism spectrum disorders: Contribution of cognition, severity of autism symptoms, and adaptive functioning to the variability. *Research in Developmental Disabilities, 33,* 172–180.

Knickmeyer, R. C., & Davenport, M. (2011). Turner syndrome and sexual differentiation of the brain: Implications for understanding male-biased neurodevelopmental disorders. *Journal of Neurodevelopmental Disorders, 3,* 293–306.

Langen, M., Kas, M. J. H., Staal, W. G., van Engeland, H., & Durston, S. (2011). The neurobiology of repetitive behavior: Of mice …. *Neuroscience & Biobehavioral Reviews, 35,* 345–355.

Levy, D., Ronemus, M., Yamrom, B., Lee, Y. H., Leotta, A., Kendall, J., et al. (2011). Rare de novo and transmitted copy-number variation in autistic spectrum disorders. *Neuron, 7(0),* 886–897.

Levy, S. E., Mandel, D. S., & Schultz, R. T. (2009). Autism. *The Lancet, 374,* 1627–1638.

Lionel, A. C., Crosbie, J., Barbosa, N., Goodale, T., Thiruvahindrapuram, B., Rickaby, J., et al. (2011). Rare copy number variation discovery and cross-disorder comparisons identify risk genes for ADHD. *Science Translational Medicine, 3,* 95ra75.

Liu, X., Malenfant, P., Reesor, C., Lee, A., Hudson, M. L., Harvard, C., et al. (2011). 2p15–p16.1 microdeletion syndrome: Molecular characterization and association of the OTX1 and XPO1 genes with autism spectrum disorders. *European Journal of Human Genetics, 19,* 1264–1270.

López-Hernández, T., Ridder, M. C., Montolio, M., Capdevila-Nortes, X., Polder, E., Sirisi, S., et al. (2011). Mutant GlialCAM causes megalencephalic leukoencephalopathy with subcortical cysts, benign familial macrocephaly, and macrocephaly with retardation and autism. *American Journal of Human Genetics, 188,* 422–432.

Lord, C. (2011). Unweaving the autism spectrum. *Cell, 147,* 24–25.

Mandell, D. S., Lawer, L. J., Branch, K., Brodkin, E. S., Healey, K., Witalec, R., et al. (2011). Prevalence and correlates of autism in a state psychiatric hospital. *Autism.* [Epub August 16, 2011]. doi: 10.1177/1362361311412058.

Manolio, T. A. (2010). Genomewide association studies and assessment of the risk of disease. *New England Journal of Medicine, 363,* 166–176.

Manolio, T. A., Collins, F. S., Cox, N. J., Goldstein, D. B., Hindorff, L. A., Hunter, D. J., et al. (2009). Finding the missing heritability of complex diseases. *Nature, 461,* 747–753.

Mar, R. A. (2011). The neural bases of social cognition and story comprehension. *Annual Review of Psychology, 62*, 103–134.

Maski, K. P., Jeste, S. S., & Spence, S. J. (2010). Common neurological co-morbidities in autism spectrum disorders. *Current Opinion in Pediatrics, 23*, 609–615.

Mefford, H., Sharp, A., Baker, C., Itsara, A., Jiang, Z., Buysse, K., & Eichler, E. (2008). Recurrent rearrangements of chromosome 1q21.1 and variable pediatric phenotypes. *New England Journal of Medicine, 359*, 1685–1699.

Meguid, N. A., Fahim, C., Sami, R., Nashaat, N. H., Yoon, U., Anwar, M., et al. (2011). Cognition and lobar morphology in full mutation boys with fragile X syndrome. *Brain and Cognition, 78*, 74–84.

Mester, J. L., Tilot, A. K., Rybicki., L. A., Frazier, T. W., 2nd, & Eng, C. (2011). Analysis of prevalence and degree of macrocephaly in patients with germline PTEN mutations and of brain weight in Pten knock-in murine model. *European Journal of Human Genetics, 19*, 736–738.

Miles, J. H. (2011). Autism spectrum disorders—A genetics review. (2011). *Genetics in Medicine, 13*, 278–294.

Mitchell, K. J. (2011). The genetics of neurodevelopmental disease. *Current Opinion in Neurobiology, 21*, 197–203.

Modahl, C., Green, L., Fein, D., Morris, M., Waterhouse, L., Feinstein, C., & Levin, H. (1998). Plasma oxytocin levels in autistic children. *Biological Psychiatry, 43*, 270–277.

Moreno-De-Luca, D., Consortium, S. G. E. N. E., Mulle, J. G., Simons Simplex Collection Genetics Consortium, Kaminsky, E. B., Sanders, S. J., & Ledbetter, D. H. (2010). Deletion 17q12 is a recurrent copy number variant that confers high risk of autism and schizophrenia. *American Journal of Human Genetics, 87*, 618–630.

Myers, R. A., Casals, F., Gauthier, J., Hamdan, F. F., Keebler, J., Boyko, A. R., et al. (2011). A population genetic approach to mapping neurological disorder genes using deep resequencing. *PloS Genetics, 7*, e1001318.

Neale, B. M., Kou, Y., Liu, L., Ma'ayan, A., Samocha, K. E., Sabo, A., & Daly, M. (2012). Patterns and rates of exonic de novo mutations in autism spectrum disorders. *Nature, 485*, 242–245.

Nishiyama, T., Taniai, H., Miyachi, T., Ozaki, K., Tomita, M., & Sumi, S. (2009). Genetic correlation between autistic traits and IQ in a population-based sample of twins with autism spectrum disorders (ASDs). *Journal of Human Genetics, 54*, 56–61.

Online Mendelian Inheritance in Man, OMIM®. McKusick-Nathans Institute of Genetic Medicine, Johns Hopkins University (Baltimore, MD), (November 14, 2011). World Wide Web URL: http://omim.org/

O'Roak, B. J., Deriziotis, P., Lee, C., Vives, L., Schwartz, J. J., Girirajan, S., et al. (2011). Exome sequencing in sporadic autism spectrum disorders identifies severe de novo mutations. *Nature Genetics, 43*, 585–589.

O'Roak, B. J., Vives, L., Girirajan, S., Karakoc, E., Krumm, N., Coe, B. P., et al. (2012). Sporadic autism exomes reveal a highly interconnected protein network of *de novo* mutations. *Nature, 485*, 246–250.

Orrico, A., Galli, L., Buoni, S., Orsi, A., Vonella, G., & Sorrentino, V. (2008). Novel PTEN mutations in neurodevelopmental disorders and macrocephaly. *Clinical Genetics, 75*, 195–198.

Park, J. H., Wacholder, S., Gail, M. H., Peters, U., Jacobs, K. B., Chanock, S. J., et al. (2010). Estimation of effect size distribution from genome-wide association studies and implications for future discoveries. *Nature Genetics, 42*, 570–575.

Peñagarikano, O., Abrahams, B. S., Herman, E. I., Winden, K. D., Gdalyahu, A., Dong, H., et al. (2011). Absence of CNTNAP2 leads to epilepsy, neuronal migration abnormalities, and core autism-related deficits. *Cell, 147*, 235–246.

Persico, A. M., & Bourgeron, T. (2008). Searching for ways out of the autism maze: Genetic, epigenetic and environmental clues. *Trends in Neurosciences, 29*, 349–358.

Pickles, A., Bolton, P., Macdonald, H., Bailey, A., Le Couteur, A., Sim, C. H., et al. (1995). Latent-class analysis of recurrence risks for complex phenotypes with selection and measurement error: A twin and family history study of autism. *American Journal of Human Genetics*, *57*, 717–726.

Pina-Camacho, L., Villero, S., Fraguas, D., Boada, L., Janssen, J., Navas-Sánchez, F. J., et al. (2012). Autism spectrum disorder: Does neuroimaging support the DSM-5 proposal for a symptom dyad? A systematic review of functional magnetic resonance imaging and diffusion tensor imaging studies. *Journal of Autism and Developmental Disorders*, *42*, 1326–1341.

Pinto, D., Pagnamenta, A. T., Klei, L., Anney, R., Merico, D., Regan, R., et al. (2010). Functional impact of global rare copy number variation in autism spectrum disorder. *Nature*, *466*, 368–372.

Porteous, D. J., Millar, J. K., Brandon, N. J., & Sawa, A. (2011). DISC1 at 10: Connecting psychiatric genetics and neuroscience. *Trends in Molecular Medicine*, *17*, 699–706.

Raja, M., & Azzoni, A. (2010). Autistic spectrum disorders and schizophrenia in the adult psychiatric setting: Diagnosis and comorbidity. *Psychiatria Danubina*, *2*, 514–521.

Ramocki, M. B., & Zoghbi, H. Y. (2008). Failure of neuronal homeostasis results in common neuropsychiatric phenotypes. *Nature*, *455*, 912–918.

Raznahan, A., Toro, R., Daly, E., Robertson, D., Murphy, C., Deeley, Q., et al. (2010). Cortical anatomy in autism spectrum disorder: An in vivo MRI study on the effect of age. *Cerebral Cortex*, *20*, 1332–1340.

Rodriguez-Murillo, L., Gogos, J. A., & Karayiorgou, M. (2012). The genetic architecture of schizophrenia: New mutations and emerging paradigms. *Annual Review of Medicine*, *63*, 19.1–19.18.

Rommelse, N., Geurts, H. M., Franke, B., Buitelaar, J. K., & Hartman, C. A. (2011). A review on cognitive and brain endophenotypes that may be common in autism spectrum disorder and attention-deficit/hyperactivity disorder and facilitate the search for pleiotropic genes. *Neuroscience and Biobehavioral Reviews*, *35*, 1363–1396.

Ronald, A., & Hoekstra, R. A. (2011). Autism spectrum disorders and autistic traits: A decade of new twin studies. *American Journal of Medical Genetics B Neuropsychiatric Genetics*, *156*, 4255–4274.

Rubenstein, J. L. R. (2011). Annual research review: development of the cerebral cortex: Implications for neurodevelopmental disorders. *Journal of Child Psychology and Psychiatry*, *52*, 339–355.

Rucker, J. J. H., & McGuffin, P. (2010). Polygenic heterogeneity: A complex model of genetic inheritance in psychiatric disorders. *Biological Psychiatry*, *68*, 312–313.

Sakai, Y., Shaw, C. A., Dawson, B. C., Dugas, D. V., Al-Mohtaseb, Z., Hill, D. E., et al. (2011). Protein interactome reveals converging molecular pathways among autism disorders. *Science Translational Medicine*, *3*, 86ra49.

Sala, M., Braida, D., Lentini, D., Busnelli, M., Bulgheroni, E., Capurro, V., et al. (2011). Pharmacologic rescue of impaired cognitive flexibility, social deficits, increased aggression, and seizure susceptibility in oxytocin receptor null mice: A neurobehavioral model of autism. *Biological Psychiatry*, *69*, 875–882.

Sanders, S. J., Ercan-Sencicek, A. G., Hus, V., Luo, R., Murtha, M. T., Moreno-De-Luca, D., et al. (2011). Multiple recurrent de novo CNVs, including duplications of the 7q11.23 Williams syndrome region, are strongly associated with autism. *Neuron*, *70*, 863–885.

Sanders, S. J., Murtha, M. T., Gupta, A. R., Murdoch, J. D., Raubeson, M. J., Willsey, A. J., et al. (2012). De novo mutations revealed by whole-exome sequencing are strongly associated with autism. *Nature*, *485*, 237–241.

Santoro, M. R., Bray, S. M., & Warren, S. T. (2012). Molecular mechanisms of fragile X syndrome: A twenty-year perspective. *Annual Review of Pathology: Mechanisms of Disease*, *7*, 219–245.

Sarasua, S. M., Dwivedi, A., Boccuto, L., Rollins, J. D., Chen, C. F., Rogers, R. C., et al. (2011). Association between deletion size and important phenotypes expands the genomic region of interest in Phelan-Mcdermid syndrome (22q13 deletion syndrome). *Journal of Medical Genetics*, *48*, 761–766.

Schaaf, C. P., Sabo, A., Sakai, Y., Crosby, J., Muzny, D., Hawes, A., et al. (2011). Oligogenic heterozygosity in individuals with high-functioning autism spectrum disorders. *Human Molecular Genetics*, *20*, 3366–3375.

Schaaf, C. P., & Zoghbi, H.Y. (2011). Solving the autism puzzle a few pieces at a time. *Neuron*, *70*, 806–808.

Schanen, N. C. (2006). Epigenetics of autism spectrum disorders. *Human Molecular Genetics*, *15*, R138–R150.

Scherer, S.W., & Dawson, G. (2011). Risk factors for autism: Translating genomic discoveries into diagnostics. *Human Genetics*, *130*, 123–148.

Schipul, S. E., Keller, T. A., & Just, M. A. (2011). Inter-regional brain communication and its disturbance in autism. *Frontiers in Systems Neuroscience*, *5*, 1–18.

Schroeder, J. H., Desrocher, M., Bebko, J. M., & Cappadocia, M. C. (2010). The neurobiology of autism: Theoretical applications. *Research in Autism Spectrum Disorders*, *4*, 555–564.

Skuse, D. H. (2007). Rethinking the nature of genetic vulnerability to autistic spectrum disorders. *Trends in Genetics*, *23*, 387–395.

Smith, M., Spence, M. A., & Flodman, P. (2009). Nuclear and mitochondrial genome defects in autisms. *The Year in Human and Medical Genetics, Annals of the New York Academy of Sciences*, *1151*, 102–132.

Solomon, M., Olsen, E., Niendam, T., Ragland, J. D., Yoon, J., Minzenberg, M., et al. (2011). From lumping to splitting and back again: Atypical social and language development in individuals with clinical-high-risk for psychosis, first episode schizophrenia, and autism spectrum disorders. *Schizophrenia Research*, *131*, 146–151.

Splinter, E., & de Laat, W. (2011). The complex transcription regulatory landscape of our genome: Control in three dimensions. *European Molecular Biology Organization Journal*, *30*, 4345–4355.

Staal, W. G., de Krom, M., & de Jonge, M.V. (2012). Brief report: The dopamine-3-receptor gene (*DRD3*) is associated with specific repetitive behavior in autism spectrum disorder (ASD). *Journal of Autism and Developmental Disorders*, *42*, 885–888.

State, M., & Levitt, P. (2011). The conundrums of understanding genetic risks for autism spectrum disorders. *Nature Neuroscience*, *14*, 1499–1506.

Stefanatos, G. A., & Baron, I. S. (2011). The ontogenesis of language impairment in autism: A neuropsychological perspective. *Neuropsychology Review*, *21*, 252–270.

Stigler, K. A., McDonald, B. C., Anand, A., Saykin, A. J., & McDougle, C. J. (2011). Structural and functional magnetic resonance imaging of autism spectrum disorders. *Brain Research*, *1380*, 146–161.

Swanberg, S. E., Nagarajan, R. P., Peddada, S., Yasui, D. H., & LaSalle, J. M. (2009). Reciprocal co-regulation of EGR2 and MECP2 is disrupted in Rett syndrome and autism. *Human Molecular Genetics*, *18*, 525–534.

Tan, G. C., Doke, T. F., Ashburner, J., Wood, N. W., & Frackowiak, R. S. (2010). Normal variation in fronto-occipital circuitry and cerebellar structure with an autism-associated polymorphism of CNTNAP2. *NeuroImage*, *53*, 1030–1042.

Taniai, H., Nishiyama, T., Miyachi, T., Imaeda, M., & Sumi, S. (2008). Genetic influences on the broad spectrum of autism: Study of probands-ascertained twins. *American Journal of Medical Genetics B Neuropsychiatric Genetics*, *147*, 844–849.

Tsuchiya, K. J., Hashimoto, K., Iwata, Y., Tsujii, M., Sekine, Y., Sugihara, G., et al. (2007). Decreased serum levels of platelet-endothelial adhesion molecule (PECAM-1) in subjects with high-functioning autism: A negative correlation with head circumference at birth. *Biological Psychiatry*, *62*, 1056–1058.

van Bokhoven, H. (2011). Genetic and epigenetic networks in intellectual disabilities. *Annual Review of Genetics, 45*, 81–104.

van Ijzendoorn, M. H., Bakermans-Kranenburg, M. J., Belsky, J., Beach, S., Brody, G., Dodge, K. A., et al. (2011). Gene-by-environment experiments: A new approach to finding the missing heritability. *Nature Reviews Genetics, 12*, 881.

van Rijn, S., & Swaab, H. (2011). Vulnerability for psychopathology in Klinefelter syndrome: Age-specific and cognitive-specific risk profiles. *Acta Paediatrica, 100*, 908–916.

Verhoeven, J. S., Rommel, N., Prodi, E., Leemans, A., Zink, I., Vandewalle, E., et al. (2011). Is there a common neuroanatomical substrate of language deficit between autism spectrum disorder and specific language impairment? *Cerebral Cortex*. [Epub June 23, 2011], 1–9. doi: 10.1093/cercor/bhr292.

Vickery, T. J., Chun, M. M., & Lee, D. (2011). Ubiquity and specificity of reinforcement signals throughout the human brain. *Neuron, 72*, 166–177.

Visscher, P. M., Goddard, M. E., Derks, E. M., & Wray, N. R. (2011). Evidence-based psychiatric genetics, AKA the false dichotomy between common and rare variant hypotheses. *Molecular Psychiatry, 17*, 474–485.

Voineagu, I. (2012). Gene expression studies in autism: Moving from the genome to the transcriptomes and beyond. *Neurobiology of Disease, 45*, 69–75.

Voineagu, I., Wang, X., Johnston, P., Lowe, J. K., Tian, Y., Horvath, S., et al. (2011). Transcriptomic analysis of autistic brain reveals convergent molecular pathology. *Nature, 474*, 380–384.

Vozdova, M., Horinova, V., Wernerova, V., Skalikova, R., Rybar, R., Prinosilova, P., et al. (2011). der(4)t(Y;4): Three-generation transmission and sperm meiotic segregation analysis. *American Journal of Medical Genetics A, 155A*, 1157–1161.

Wall, D. P., Esteban, F. J., Deluca, T. F., Huyck, M., Monaghan, T., Velez de Mendizabal, N., et al. (2009). Comparative analysis of neurological disorders focuses genome-wide search for autism genes. *Genomics, 93*, 120–129.

Wallace, G. L., Dankner, N., Kenworthy, L., Giedd, J., & Martin, A. (2010). Age-related temporal and parietal cortical thinning in autism spectrum disorders. *Brain, 133*, 3745–3754.

Walsh, K. M., & Bracken, M. B. (2011). Copy number variation in the dosage-sensitive 16p11.2 interval accounts for only a small proportion of autism incidence: A systematic review and meta-analysis. *Genetics in Medicine, 13*, 377–384.

Wass, S. (2011). Distortions and disconnections: Disrupted brain connectivity in autism. *Brain and Cognition, 75*, 18–28.

Wei, H., Malik, M., Sheikh, A. M., Merz, G., Brown, W. T., & Li, X. (2011). Abnormal cell properties and down-regulated FAK-Src complex signaling in B lymphoblasts of autistic subjects. *American Journal of Pathology, 179*, 1–9.

Williams, C. A., Dagli, A., & Battaglia, A. (2008). Genetic disorders associated with macrocephaly. *American Journal of Medical Genetics Part A, 146A*, 2023–2037.

Wulffaert, J., Van Berckelaer-Onnes, I. A., & Scholte, E. M. (2009). Autistic disorder symptoms in Rett syndrome. *Autism, 13*, 567–581.

Yrigollen, C. M., Han, S. S., Kochetkova, A., Babitz, T., Chang, J. T., Volkmar, F. R., et al. (2008). Genes controlling affiliative behavior as candidate genes for autism. *Biological Psychiatry, 63*, 911–916.

CHAPTER 5

Environmental Risk Factors Link Autism to Many Other Outcomes

Contents

Rethinking Autism
http://dx.doi.org/10.1016/B978-0-12-415961-7.00005-8

Many genetic risk factors for autism have been identified. Therefore, no environmental risk factor could be the sole cause of autism. However, two earlier disgraceful theories of environmental factors each claimed to be the sole cause of autism. A misapplication of psychoanalytic theory claimed that cold and unloving mothers caused otherwise typical children to withdraw into autism (Bettelheim, 1967). A calculated research fraud motivated by greed asserted that the measles-mumps-rubella vaccine resulted in regressive autism (Wakefield et al., 1998). Although researchers found no evidence to support these two environmental theories, unfortunately, some treatment practices continued to follow the discredited unloving mother theory, and many parents continued to harbor concerns about the safety of having their child vaccinated.

Sound scientific research uncovered many varied environmental risk factors for autism, and ongoing research will likely uncover more environmental risk factors. However, the unloving mother theory cast a long shadow, dimming interest in conducting research on possible environmental causes for autism. Most importantly, though, autism researchers believed that the majority of autism cases resulted from genetic factors. As discussed in Chapter 4, following the publication of an autism twin study by Folstein and Rutter in 1977, researchers identified autism as the psychiatric disorder with the highest heritability. A series of studies suggested that genetic factors accounted for approximately 90% of the risk for autism. However, in 2011, Hallmayer et al. reported findings from the largest population-based twin study of autism ever conducted. The researchers found that genetic factors accounted for only 38% of the variance in autism. They also reported that environmental factors common to the co-twins accounted for approximately 58% of the variance. Hallmayer et al. (2011) observed that environmental effects begin before birth. Identical twins share any new problematic alterations in the genome of their father's sperm or their mother's ovum that contributed to their conception, and identical and fraternal twins share the gestational environment of their mother's womb. Twins also share the perinatal environment of delivery, and the early postnatal environment of infancy in their family life.

Commenting on the Hallmayer et al. (2011) twin study findings published in the *Archives of General Psychiatry*, the journal's editor Dr. Coyle said, "For the first time, we have credible evidence that environmental factors may be as important as genetic factors" (Harvard Mental Health Letter, 2011, p. 1). Dr. Lajonchere, one of the authors of the twin study, predicted, "much more emphasis is going to be put on looking at prenatal and perinatal factors with respect to autism susceptibility" (Tarkan, 2011).

However, a wide range of evidence for prenatal and perinatal environmental factors has already been reported. Older mothers and older fathers were found to have a greater risk of having a child with autism symptoms (Ben Itzchak, Lahat, & Zachor, 2011; King, Fountain, Dakhlallah, & Bearman, 2009; Parner et al., 2012). Closely spaced pregnancies were found to be a risk factor for autism (Cheslack-Postava et al., 2011). Environment risk factors were also found to include a mother's infections (Stigler et al., 2009), a mother's use of antidepressants (Croen, Grether, Yoshida, Odouli, & Hendrick, 2011), a mother's lack of folic acid early in pregnancy (Schmidt et al., 2011), a mother's weight and metabolic health (Krakowiak et al., 2012), or even possibly a mother's lack of a healthy diet (Shamberger, 2011). Events during delivery were found to carry a risk of autism (Gardener, Spiegelman, & Buka, 2011), as were extremely premature birth and low birth weight (Limperopoulos, 2009; Losh, Esserman, Anckarsäter, Sullivan, & Lichtenstein, 2011; Pinto-Martin et al., 2011).

Just as autism symptoms occur as one of many outcomes, such as intellectual disability, epilepsy, motor delay, and language impairment, of each proposed causal gene and chromosomal risk variant, similarly autism symptoms occur as one of many outcomes of each proposed causal environmental risk factor. For example, the outcomes of premature delivery vary from minor developmental problems to severe impairments, including autism symptoms. Pinto-Martin et al. (2011) noted that low birth weight and prematurity conferred a risk for cognitive and motor disability wherein "neurodevelopmental impairment increases with diminishing birth weight and gestational age" (p. 884). McCormick, Litt, Smith, and Zupancic (2011) reviewed outcomes of prematurity. They reported that premature infants may experience bleeding in the brain, may suffer damage to the brain's white matter, may develop a smaller head, or may suffer persistent hydrocephalus. Some preterm infants suffer impaired retinal function that can lead to blindness. Rates of cerebral palsy range from 6% to 28%, and preterm children may experience persistent fine motor skill difficulties (McCormick et al., 2011). Compared with children born at full term, preterm children were more likely to be diagnosed with attention deficit/hyperactivity disorder, and more likely to score higher on measures of autism symptoms. However, only a small percentage of preterm children meet full criteria for the autism diagnosis.

Pinto-Martin et al. (2011) reported that 31 of 623, or 5%, of adolescents and young adults whose birth weight was less than 2000 grams, met criteria to be diagnosed with autism. The researchers noted the estimated prevalence of autism in their sample was "5 times the prevalence reported by the

Centers for Disease Control and Prevention for 8-year-olds in the general US population in 2006" (Pinto-Martin et al., 2011, p. 889).

Evidence also suggested a risk for autism from adverse epigenetic events, including the possible dysregulation of imprinting at the time of conception (Kopsida, Mikaelsson, & Davies, 2011), and other adverse epigenetic factors affecting gene expression crucial to brain development (de Leon-Guerrero, Pedraza-Alva, & Pérez-Martínez, 2011). There was also a wide range of evidence for possible atypical immune system function related to neuroinflammation in autism that might begin in fetal brain development, and might be the result of prenatal gene–environment interactions (Ashwood et al., 2011a; Stigler et al., 2009). Vargas, Nascimbene, Krishnan, Zimmerman, and Pardo (2005) found the neuroinflammation markers of microglia and astroglia activation in the gray and white matter of the brain tissue from patients with autism. Vargas et al. (2005) proposed that innate immune responses in the brains of individuals with autism were in an abnormal state of chronic activation and reactivity similar to that found for Parkinson's and Alzheimer's diseases. Abdallah et al. (2012) found evidence for abnormal immune system activity in the maternal blood samples and amniotic fluid samples for individuals with autism. The researchers proposed that the immune system of mothers reacted to the fetus, causing abnormal levels of immune system activity (Abdallah et al., 2012).

Four sections of this chapter discuss four groups of environmental risk factors for autism. The first section examines the lingering effects of two false but widely disseminated theories of environmental causes for autism: cold mothers and the measles-mumps-rubella vaccine. The second section reviews existing evidence for specific prenatal and perinatal risk factors linked to autism. This evidence suggests that autism symptoms are one of a range of atypical developmental outcomes for each environmental risk factor. The third section reviews evidence for epigenetic neural development disruption in autism. The fourth section considers evidence for possible gene–environment immune system dysfunction in autism.

The fifth and final section of this chapter addresses the meaning of the lack of causal specificity for both environmental and genetic risk factors for autism.

THE LINGERING EFFECTS OF TWO FALSE BUT INFLUENTIAL THEORIES OF ENVIRONMENTAL CAUSE

Although research has found no support for either the unloving mother theory or the vaccine theory of autism, unfortunately effects of these theories lingered. The unloving mother theory lingered in France in a sanctioned basis for treatment of children with autism. The vaccine theory lingered in the minds of many parents who worried that the dangers of vaccination outweighed the benefits.

The Unloving Mother Theory of Autism

Bettelheim (1967) theorized that an unloving mother was the source of autism. He argued that children with autism were similar to victims of the German concentration camps, as Bettelheim himself was, because children with autism passively withdrew from a frighteningly hostile environment. Bettelheim argued, "the precipitating factor in infantile autism is the parent's wish that his child should not exist" (1967, p. 272). Pollack (1997) wrote a scathing biography of Bettelheim in which he asserted that Bettelheim not only lied about having university degrees, but Bettelheim also lied when he said he had conducted therapy with 46 children with autism, because fewer than 20 children diagnosed with autism were ever admitted to Bettelheim's Chicago Orthogenic School. Nonetheless, Bettelheim's thesis of the negative power of an unloving mother was not far removed from psychoanalytic attachment theories of the 1950s and 1960s. Current analytic attachment theories have made more limited claims, such as "a history of insecure–anxious infant–caregiver attachment, characterized by an excessive intensification of distress signals to elicit caregiver responsiveness and maintain proximity, is a risk factor for developing anxiety disorders" (Nolte, Guiney, Fonagy, Mayes, & Luyten, 2011, p. 2).

A 2011 French documentary titled *Le Mur: La psychanalyse à l'épreuve de l'autisme,* or *The Wall: Psychoanalysis put to the test for autism,* interviewed French psychoanalysts regarding their psychoanalytic therapy for children with autism. The film's producer, Sophie Robert, filmed interviews of French psychoanalysts who believed autism resulted from unloving mothers or abnormally over-attached mothers. In the documentary *Le Mur* one of the psychoanalysts argued that Bettelheim's ideas were under-appreciated and wrongly criticized. Sicile-Kira (2011) reported that three psychoanalysts of the School of the Freudian Cause in Lille, France, appealed to the court to ban the release of the documentary because they felt the producer had been deceptive when recruiting their participation in the film. On January 26, 2012, the French court ordered the film's producer to pay the offended French psychiatrists 19,000 euros and their legal fees, and to remove *Le Mur* from its posting on the internet (Autism Rights Watch—Project France, 2012).

Sicile-Kira (2011) noted that a 2004 French government study determined that psychoanalysis was significantly less effective than cognitive behavior therapy. In 2007 the French Comité Consultatif National d'Ethique, a bioethics advisory board, reported that parents of children with autism had trouble obtaining specialized educational programs and had little if any choice in their child's treatment or education. Sicile-Kira (2011) reported that despite the 2004 and 2007 reports, psychoanalysis continued to be the treatment offered to children in France with autism. Speaking in defense of psychoanalysis for children with autism, French child psychiatrist Lauriane Brunessaux argued that autism activists have distorted the psychiatric process in order to discredit psychoanalysis and discredit the concept of the unconscious (Schofield, 2012).

One stark condition that robs a child of a mother's love is being orphaned, or abandoned and put into institutional care. In an institution a child does not receive the caring social attention that occurs in typical healthy family life. Rutter et al. (2007) followed up on a sample of 12-year-old Romanian children adopted into UK families from Romanian institutional care before the age of 4 years. The researchers found that of 144 children, 16 expressed autism symptoms that Rutter et al. (2007) termed a quasi-autistic pattern. However, they found no autism symptoms in a sample of Romanian children who had not been adopted from institutional care, and found no autism symptoms in 51 children adopted within the UK. Rutter et al. (2007) reported that the 16 children with autism symptoms had difficulty understanding that other people had minds with different contents from their own, and had difficulty in reading emotional facial expressions. These children also exhibited restricted non-social interests, a DSM-IV autism criterion. Rutter et al. (2007) stated that over the course of development these children showed some reduction in their autism symptoms, but noted "it is all too obvious that this is not an evanescent set of features that will disappear with time without help" (p. 1206).

Sheridan, Drury, McLaughlin, and Almas (2010) reviewed outcomes from a series of studies of institutionalized children in Bucharest, Romania. Many of the children avoided eye contact, had difficulty forming friendships, had significant deficits in empathy, and were indiscriminately friendly, a sign of abnormal attachment. The most commonly diagnosed psychiatric disorder was attention deficit/hyperactivity disorder. A less stark condition than institutionalization is foster care. Dregan, Brown, and Armstrong (2011) investigated outcomes for 738 children born in the UK in 1970 who had been placed into foster care for a minimum of 4 weeks. Even after controlling for differences in early life conditions, adult adverse outcomes for these children included a risk rate for depression of 1.74, and a doubled risk rate for low sense of self-efficacy as well as for criminal convictions.

Although institutional care or foster care are not exact proxies for lack of maternal love, findings from studies of children placed in institutions or foster care suggest that there may be lasting negative effects on these individuals, and that, though rare, autism-like symptoms have been identified in children who had been institutionalized.

The Fraudulent Study that Claimed MMR Vaccine Caused Regressive Autism

In 1998, Dr. Andrew Wakefield, a British gastroenterologist, and a number of co-authors published a paper in the British medical journal *The Lancet*. Wakefield et al. (1998) reported cases of 12 children whom they claimed had regressive autism and bowel inflammation caused by their measles-mumps-rubella (MMR) vaccinations. Wakefield et al. (1998) claimed that measles virus from the MMR vaccination persisted in the children's intestines, triggering an inflammation that caused leaks of opioid peptides into the bloodstream, and opioid peptides in the brain caused autism.

Wakefield later held a press conference in which he publicized his concerns about the safety of the MMR vaccine. In addition, a second vaccine theory emerged claiming the mercury in the chemical thimerosal used to stabilize the MMR vaccine caused autism. However, between 1999 and 2004, 11 studies conducted in the USA, the UK, Denmark, Japan, and Finland found no evidence that the MMR vaccine triggered autism (Flaherty, 2011). The United States Institutes of Medicine reviewed more than 20 studies and concluded that neither MMR vaccine, nor its preservative thimerosal, nor trace amounts of mercury in the thimerosal caused autism (Stratton et al., 2011).

Brian Deer, an investigative journalist, uncovered many elements of fraud and greed involved in the Wakefield et al. (1998) study. Deer (2011a) discovered that the Wakefield et al. (1998) study never received human subjects approval. Deer (2011a) also discovered that although the study claimed 9 of the 12 study children had regressive autism, in fact, 3 of the 9 had never been diagnosed with any form of autism, 5 had been diagnosed with non-regressive autism, and only 1 child had been diagnosed with regressive autism. In addition, although Wakefield et al. (1998) asserted that none of the 12 children had any developmental problems prior to their MMR vaccine injections, in fact, reports for 5 of the 12 children had documented developmental problems existing before the children's MMR injections. Deer (2011b) obtained the original histology scoring sheets for 62 intestine specimens taken from 11 of the 12 children. Although Wakefield et al. (1998) had asserted that these 11 patients had chronic non-specific colitis, the actual histology reports showed no colitis and no other diseases in the intestinal samples.

Parents of 10 of 12 children in the 1998 study were represented by Richard Barr, a British lawyer planning a lawsuit against MMR manufacturers (Deer, 2008). Wakefield accepted more than $780,000 from Barr, who obtained this money from the United Kingdom's legal aid fund, and Wakefield started his own company, called Immunospecifics Ltd, planning to make millions selling "diagnostic kits" to worried parents in order to test their children for regressive autism (Deer, 2008). Wakefield also had filed a patent application for a single vaccine against measles that would make money only if the standard MMR vaccine were dropped from use. In addition, Wakefield had filed a patent for a bizarre cure for autism and inflammatory bowel disease based on the bone marrow of one person, Hugh Fundenburg (Deer, 2008).

In 2010, *The Lancet* retracted Dr. Wakefield's paper, and he was struck off the UK medical register for misconduct charges, including four counts of research fraud.

The 1998 paper and all ensuing publicity concerning the MMR vaccine theory of autism caused many parents in England to refuse MMR vaccination for their children. In England, vaccination rates dropped from 91% in 1998 to below 80% in 2003, while measles cases increased from 56 in 1998 to 1370 in 2008 (Flaherty, 2011). Vaccination rates dropped around the world, and in the period from 1998 to 2008, Wales, Italy, France, Spain, and Germany reported substantial increases in measles outbreaks. Public worry that vaccines were unsafe continued despite all scientific evidence to the contrary.

On the Age of Autism website, Arranga (2011) claimed that Deer's articles in the *British Medical Journal* exposing the fraud in the Wakefield et al. (1998) paper were "a manufactured piece of gibberish with no basis in fact" because the Wakefield et al. (1998) study was "valid and scientifically sound." Arranga (2011) also claimed, "The *British Medical Journal*'s campaign to discredit Dr. Wakefield may be the greatest suppression of science episode ever attempted." Kirby (2011) argued that the belief that vaccine causes autism is unlikely to disappear soon because children are vaccinated during the time when autism is usually diagnosed. He stated that by the time a typical

American child was 6 months old, he or she would have received 18 inoculations containing 24 vaccines against 9 diseases, and by the time a child was 3 years old he or she would have received another 9 inoculations containing 14 vaccines against 12 diseases. Kirby (2011) proposed that this early childhood series of vaccinations with many possible side effects, including fever, diarrhea, lethargy, or even seizures, could convince parents of children with autism that their child's autism was caused by a vaccination.

Berger, Navar-Boggan, and Omer (2011) pointed out a painful irony in the belief that the MMR vaccine caused autism. From 1963 to 1965, the United States had a rubella epidemic affecting 12 million people, prenatal rubella infection caused thousands of fetal and infant deaths, and more than 20,000 children were born with congenital rubella. The children with congenital rubella suffered a range of impairments including deafness, cataracts, encephalitis, heart abnormalities, intellectual disability, and autism (Chess, 1971, 1977). Berger et al. (2011) calculated that the R (rubella) part of the MMR vaccine in fact *prevented* several thousand cases of autism in the United States during the period 2001 through 2010.

In 2010, the United States Court of Federal Claims ruled on the final case from the National Vaccine Injury Compensation Program (NVICP) for the US Omnibus Autism Proceedings (Keelan & Wilson, 2011). In the beginning of the process, more than 5000 families brought claims to the court, and special hearings assessed three claims of vaccine damage: (1) measles-mumps-rubella vaccine and its preservative thimerosal caused autism; (2) thimerosal alone caused autism; and (3) the measles-mumps-rubella vaccine alone caused autism (Keelan & Wilson, 2011). In 2007, three families, the Cedillos, the Hazlehursts, and the Snyders, sought compensation from the United States NVICP. However, the special masters in these three cases judged that there was no valid scientific evidence that the MMR vaccine caused autism (Cedillo v Secretary of Health and Human Services, No. 98-916V (USCFC Spec Mstr 2009); Hazlehurst v Secretary of Health and Human Services, No. 03-654V (USCFC Sp Mstr 2009); Snyder v Secretary of Health and Human Services, No. 01-162V (USCFC Spec Mstr 2009)). In the case of Michelle Cedillo, Special Master George L. Hastings Jr. personally noted in his ruling, "I feel deep sympathy and admiration for the Cedillo family …. However, I must decide this case not on sentiment, but by analyzing the evidence" (CNN Health News, 2009).

During the hearings of these ultimately rejected vaccine damage claims, the Court did approve a settlement in the case of Hannah Poling, a child with a rare mitochondrial disorder who regressed and experienced seizures after her MMR vaccination (Poling v Secretary of Health and Human Services, No. 02-1466 (USCFC Spec Mstr 2008)). Mitochondria are the energy-producing element within each cell. Dysfunctional mitochondria produce less energy, causing systems throughout the body to begin to fail. Children with mitochondrial disorders may be more vulnerable to metabolic stress, which, in Hannah Poling's case, the vaccine may have caused. Keelan and Wilson (2011) stated, "advocates of the link between autism and vaccines hailed it [the Poling settlement] as a vindication of their viewpoint. Many public health officials and medical experts, however, countered that no such conclusion could be drawn" (p. 2019).

Although Wakefield et al. (1998) conducted a fraudulent study, and although more than 20 studies found no link between vaccines and autism, it remained possible that some aspect of some vaccines might contribute to autism in some vulnerable children. Kuehn (2009) announced the start of a multisite prospective study funded by the National Institutes of Health to explore genetic and environmental factors that contribute to autism spectrum disorders. The Early Autism Risk Longitudinal Investigation (EARLI) studied 1200 pregnant mothers of children with autism during pregnancy and followed the newborn siblings for 3 years thereafter in an effort to look at all possible causes of autism. Results from the multisite study may shed light on both genetic and environmental causes.

Schwartz and Caplan (2011) noted, "Theories about vaccine safety deficiencies circulate widely on the Internet, where networks of parents share resources, theories, and reports that appear to validate their concerns" (p. 718). On March 22, 2009, an internet search for "autism and vaccines" yielded 1,360,000 web pages, while a search for "autism and prematurity" yielded only 142,000 web pages. Just 20 months later, on November 22, 2011, an internet search for "autism and vaccines" yielded 6,070,000 web pages, while a search for "autism and prematurity" yielded only 306,000 web pages. Thus, in the 20 months prior to, during, and after the US Vaccine Court decisions, the number of web pages for autism and prematurity, a true environmental risk for autism, doubled, while the number of pages for autism and vaccines, a non-risk for autism, more than quadrupled. This suggested public interest and concern had not diminished in this period.

Schwartz and Caplan (2011) concluded that "Despite a large and growing body of scientific evidence rejecting the link between vaccines and autism, the debate persists, in part due to a vocal cohort of activists led by celebrities and a small number of health care providers who reject the consensus of the global medical and scientific communities" (p. 718). Poland

(2011) asserted, "There is no law against being foolish; nor any vaccine against ignorance" (p. 871). He proposed that just as we have seatbelt laws to protect drivers, passengers, and the public, we should have laws requiring vaccination to prevent "outbreaks of highly transmissible diseases that threaten the public health" (Poland, 2011, p. 871). Moreover, as Berger et al. (2011) noted, MMR vaccine protects against more than just the immediate effects of transmissible viruses. MMR vaccination prevents thousands of cases of autism that would result from congenital rubella.

ENVIRONMENTAL CAUSES LINK AUTISM SYMPTOMS TO SYMPTOMS OF MANY OTHER OUTCOMES

Some siblings of children with autism develop symptoms of autism. Prospective studies of those siblings who did develop autism found a wide range of the onset times of their autism symptoms, from as early as 3 months to as late as 36 months (Elsabbagh et al., 2012; Feldman et al., 2011; Hess & Landa, 2011; Ozonoff et al., 2010). Even though many early reported symptoms are not specifically diagnostic of autism, and may include motor problems, abnormal sensory reactions, or lack of attention (Guinchat et al., 2012a), the onset of autism or autism-related symptoms in infancy and early toddlerhood suggested that environmental risk factors for autism symptoms must occur prenatally or at the time of delivery. Dietert, Dietert, and DeWitt (2011) argued that the primary environmental risk for autism was the prenatal period, but evidence for perinatal risk factors has also been reported (Gardener et al., 2011).

The term environment is a broad concept. The prenatal environment includes the time prior to conception in which a specific environmental factor or the general effect of increasing age of the parents may alter genes in the sperm and ova. If genes in the sperm and ovum creating the zygote are altered, this may result in an untoward de novo genetic effect for the development of the fetus. The pre-conception environment also contains many other potential sources of negative developmental effects, such as autoimmune diseases of the parents, season of conception or birth, sociodemographic status of the parents, spacing of pregnancies, birth order, and fertility treatments to assist conception.

After conception, the majority of disruptive gestational environmental risks reach the fetus via the placenta. The prenatal gestational environment of the womb is vulnerable to the presence of one or more additional fetuses, as well as a mother's infections, exposure to medications, consumption of alcohol, maternal metabolic problems, and even, possibly a mother's diet.

A third aspect to the environment includes the events immediately before, during, and immediately after delivery; this is the perinatal environment. Perinatal risk factors include premature birth and a low birth weight that may result from environmental factors, but may also reflect gene–environment interactions. Other perinatal risk factors include birth presentation, problems during a delivery, and low Apgar score in the newborn.

Gene–environment risk factors for autism include epigenetic risk factors. Epigenetic processes are mechanisms that permit environmental exposure to have lifelong or inheritable effects on gene expression. For example, at the time of conception, genetic imprinting occurs for some genes, causing only the gene of mother or father to be expressed. Evidence for atypical epigenetic processes in autism has been reported (Fradin et al., 2010; Grafodatskaya et al., 2010; Kopsida et al., 2011). Chapter 4 reviewed altered genes of epigenetic effect and section three of this chapter extends that review.

Another set of gene–environment risk factors have been identified in the evidence for aberrant immune system function in autism (Stigler et al., 2009). This evidence and selected associated theories are outlined in the fourth section of this chapter.

Risk Factors for Autism Symptoms in the Pre-Conception Environment

The pre-conception environment risk factors found for autism include age of the parents, parent autoimmune disorders, season of conception and birth, sociodemographic status of the parents, spacing of pregnancies, birth order, and fertility treatments.

Advanced Parental Age as a Risk for Autism

In a study of 465 children with autism and 1794 typical children in Western Australia, Glasson et al. (2004) found younger mothers had the lowest risk and older mothers had the highest risk for having children diagnosed with autism. However, Glasson et al. (2004) reported that increasing age of the father in their sample was not associated with an increased risk of autism.

Age of Father Effects

A variety of studies, though, reported that risk for autism was related to age of the father (Hultman, Sandin, Levine, Lichtenstein, & Reichenberg, 2011; Lauritsen, Pedersen, & Mortensen, 2005; Reichenberg et al., 2006). In a cohort of more than one million children born during a 10-year period in Sweden, Hultman et al. (2011) found that autism "risk started to increase at the paternal age of 30, showed a plateau after age 40 and further increased from the age of 50 years" (Hultman et al., 2011, p. 1207). The researchers discovered that fathers over 55 years old had a 4.4 times increased risk of having a child with autism. Reichenberg et al. (2006) collected medical assessments for 318,506 17-year-olds from six consecutive years of the Israeli draft board medical registry records. Reichenberg et al. (2006) found no correlation between age of mothers and autism risk, but found fathers over 40 years old were 5.75 times more likely to have children with autism than fathers who were 30 years old or younger. Lauritsen, Pedersen, and Mortensen (2005) studied records for 818 children diagnosed with autism in a cohort of 943,664 Danish children followed from 1994 to 2001. The researchers found no effect of age of mothers on autism risk but found fathers 35 years or older had 1.4 times the risk of having children with autism than fathers who were 25–29 years old at the time of their child's birth.

Age of Mother and Father Effects

A number of studies reported that the age of both the mother and the father were risk factors for autism (Ben Itzchak et al., 2011; Croen, Najjar, Fireman, & Grether, 2007; Durkin et al., 2008; King et al., 2009; Larsson et al., 2005; Parner et al., 2012; Shelton, Tancredi, & Hertz-Picciotto, 2010). Larsson et al. (2005) examined the records of 698 children diagnosed with autism within a cohort of all children born in Denmark after 1972. The researchers reported a significantly higher risk for autism if mothers were over 30 years old, and if fathers were over 35 years old. Parner et al. (2012) studied all children born in Denmark from 1980 to 2003: 1,311,736 children. Increasing age of mother and father each was found to increase the risk of autism for children in this population. Surprisingly, the researchers found no additive increased risk when both parents were older. Parner et al. (2012) theorized that if genetic alterations in the DNA of sperm and ova were causing the increased risk for autism, two older parents should have additive risk. The researchers suggested a variety of other influences that would increase risk with age of both parents. They suggested that age might be a marker for longer environmental and occupational exposures or for increased use of medications for chronic health problems, or for use of fertility treatments. Parner et al. (2012) also suggested that older mothers might have been exposed to more infections and have a more activated immune system.

Ben Itzchak et al. (2011) analyzed data from 529 Israeli children diagnosed with autism. The researchers found significantly more mothers aged 35–44 years and significantly fewer mothers aged 20–29 years whose children were diagnosed with autism compared with mothers of a cohort of Israeli newborns. Similarly, significantly more fathers aged 30–40 years, and significantly fewer fathers aged 20–29 years had children diagnosed with autism.

Durkin et al. (2008) examined data from a 1994 birth cohort of 253,347 births from 10 US study sites participating in the Centers for Disease Control and Prevention's Autism and Developmental Disabilities Monitoring Network. The researchers found that, compared with autism risk rates for parents who were 25–29 years, autism risk was significantly reduced for parents under the age of 20 years, and autism risk was significantly increased for mothers over 35 and fathers over 40 years old. Shelton et al. (2010) analyzed records from a 10-year California birth cohort (1990–1999) and reported that mothers' age increased risk for autism independent of the age of the father, but fathers' age increased the risk of autism when mothers were less than 30 years old. King et al. (2009) linked birth records and autism diagnostic records from the California Department of Developmental Services for children born in California between 1992 and 2000. King et al. (2009) reported that maternal age over 40 years increased autism risk to between 1.3 and 1.8 times that of younger mothers, and paternal age over 40 years increased autism risk to between 1.3 and 1.7 times that of younger fathers. Croen et al. (2007) analyzed records of 593 children diagnosed with autism born at a single hospital in California. The researchers reported that risk rate increased significantly to 1.3 times that of younger mothers with each 10-year increase in maternal age and 1.3 times that of younger fathers for each 10-year increase in paternal age.

Mechanisms for Age of Father and Mother Effects

Paternal age effects may result from genetic mutations in a father's sperm. Reichenberg et al. (2006) theorized that de novo spontaneous mutations could arise, propagate, and accumulate in successive generations of sperm-producing cells, or DNA methylation involved in paternal imprinting may become impaired as fathers grow older. Hehir-Kwa et al. (2011) noted that ova cease being produced in female fetuses after approximately 30 cell generations, thus women produce ova that are not newly generated, whereas cell divisions for men's sperm production are a lifelong process. Therefore, as men age, sperm production suffers reduced fidelity of DNA replication and increasingly inefficient DNA repair mechanisms.

Advanced maternal age, however, may create a risk for autism via maternal immune system dysfunction, or less competent placenta formation with increased age. Increased maternal age may also index the accumulation of maternal exposures to a variety of environmental toxins.

Advanced Parent Age is Associated with a Variety of Adverse Outcomes

Shelton et al. (2010) reviewed the outcomes associated with increased parental age. They noted that increased age of mothers is a risk factor for infertility, early fetal loss, fetal chromosomal aberrations, increased chromosomal copy number variations, low birth weight, and congenital malformations. They also noted that increased age of fathers is a risk factor for schizophrenia, neurocognitive deficits, childhood cancer, low birth weight, and generalized DNA damage in the child. Thus, autism symptoms are one of many outcomes of the environmental risk factor of increased parental age.

Parent Autoimmune Disease as a Risk for Autism

Keil et al. (2010) explored 19 autoimmune disorders as possible risk factors for autism in cases from three Swedish registries. The researchers discovered a 50% higher odds for autism in children whose parents had any autoimmune disease, and found that several maternal autoimmune diseases were correlated with diagnosis of autism in the child. These included type 1 diabetes, idiopathic thrombocytopenic purpura, myasthenia gravis, and rheumatic fever. Rheumatic fever in the father also was correlated with an autism diagnosis. Atladóttir et al. (2009) examined records for a cohort of all children born in Denmark from 1993 through 2004. Of this cohort, 3325 children were diagnosed with autism. Atladóttir et al. (2009) found an increased risk of autism for children whose mothers had a history of rheumatoid arthritis or celiac disease, and an increased risk of autism for children whose mother or father had type 1 diabetes. The researchers suggested that autism and these parental disorders might share some genetic variant cause. Mouridsen, Rich, Isager, and Nedergaard (2007) examined the history of 35 autoimmune diseases in the parents of 111 individuals with autism and in parents of 330 typical children screened through the Danish National Hospital Register. The researchers found two autoimmune conditions linked to autism, ulcerative colitis in mothers, and type 1 diabetes in fathers.

Parent Autoimmune Disease is Associated with a Variety of Adverse Outcomes

Autoimmune diseases of the parents carry risks for their children, and autism is only one of many risk outcomes. Borchers, Naguwa, Keen, and Gershwin (2010) reviewed the effects of autoimmune disorders on infants. The researchers noted, "Women with autoimmune diseases were long advised not to become pregnant or to have therapeutic abortions if they did because of earlier case reports and series indicating poor outcomes for both the mother and the baby" (Borchers et al., 2010, p. J296). One factor that can lead to adverse outcomes is pre-eclampsia. Pre-eclampsia is atypical high blood pressure and excess protein in the urine after 20 weeks of pregnancy. Pre-eclampsia occurs more frequently in pregnant women with autoimmune disorders, including anti-phospholipid syndrome (APS), systemic lupus erythematosus (SLE), multiple sclerosis (MS), rheumatoid arthritis (RA), and type 1 diabetes (T1D). Pre-eclampsia has been associated with fetal loss, slowed fetal developmental, fetal brain damage, and premature delivery (Borchers et al., 2010). Slowed fetal development and fetal brain damage in turn may result in developmental delay, intellectual disability, motor disorders, cerebral palsy, and delayed or impaired language development.

Season of Birth as a Risk for Autism

Season of birth risk studies reported varied findings. Lee et al. (2008) investigated birth date distribution in a sample of 907 singletons diagnosed with autism and 161 multiple births concordant for an autism diagnosis. Data analyses suggested that April, June, and October were peaks for births of singletons diagnosed with autism, and 2–4 weeks earlier for multiple birth children. Zerbo, Iosif, Delwiche, Walker, and Hertz-Picciotto (2011) reviewed research on season of birth as a risk factor for autism. They noted that several Scandinavian studies and one Israeli study reported that more children with autism were born in March. Zerbo et al. (2011) observed that studies in Canada, Japan, the United States, and the UK also found spring birth as a risk factor for autism, but other studies reported higher autism birth rates in summer or fall. Zerbo et al. (2011) investigated birth season risk in 19,238 cases of autism in California from 1990 to 2002. The researchers found that children conceived in December had an increased risk rate of 1.09, January an increased risk of 1.08, February, 1.12, and March an increased risk rate for autism of 1.16. Zerbo et al. (2011) reported that winter conception was associated with a 6% increased risk for autism when compared with conception in summer. Zerbo et al. (2011) stated that, although prior studies found an increased risk in March or August birth, they "found, in a study considerably larger than these earlier investigations, that November births (corresponding to February conception) had the highest risk after controlling for year of birth, maternal education, and child ethnicity" (p. 474).

Lee et al. (2008) concluded that "even if there are true associations between season of birth and autism risk, season of birth is only a proxy for some other true risk factor or factors" (p. 177). Similarly, Zerbo et al. (2011) stated that the month of conception might be a surrogate for seasonal causal factors such as viruses or pesticide application. However, the researchers noted that if season of conception or season of birth is acting as a proxy, birth season data might overgeneralize exposure, leading to an underestimate of the effect of the actual causal agent.

Season of Birth is Associated with a Variety of Adverse Outcomes
Studies have suggested that winter births are associated with a 10% increase in risk for developing schizophrenia (Zerbo et al., 2011). Unusual concentrations of specific seasons of conception and birth have been found in association with a range of other disorders, including epilepsy, language disorders, attention deficit/hyperactivity disorder, and neurodevelopmental disabilities, as well as autism (Lee et al., 2008).

Sociodemographic Status of Parents as a Risk for Autism
Van Meter et al. (2010) investigated the possibility of non-random geographic clusters of higher prevalence of autism in the state of California. The researchers found 10 consensus clusters and 2 potential clusters of elevated autism risk in California. Consensus clusters are a reconciled statistical consensus of different clusterings derived from a dataset. Van Meter et al. (2010) noted that the majority of these 12 autism clusters "were strongly associated with higher education of the parents, a demographic factor previously documented to be associated with increased autism diagnoses" (p. 26). The researchers reported that although these clusters might signal possible local community environmental risks, they concluded that their clusters were best explained by demographic risk factors.

Leonard et al. (2011) investigated the relationships between autism, intellectual disability, and sociodemographic risk factors in a population of singletons born from 1984 to 1999 in Western Australia. They found that increasing socioeconomic advantage was a risk factor for autism without intellectual disability. Conversely, for intellectual disability the researchers found increasing social disadvantage to be a significant environmental risk factor with an increased risk rate of 2.56 for mild to moderate intellectual disability.

Pinborough-Zimmerman et al. (2011) investigated sociodemographic risk factors for children with autism from a population of 26,108 8-year-old children born in 1994 and living in Utah in 2002. The researchers reported that White non-Hispanic mothers were five times more likely than mothers of a minority ethnicity to have a child with autism without intellectual disability, and families with high-adjusted gross incomes were 1.5 times more likely to have children with autism without intellectual disability than other income groups.

Sociodemographic Status of Parents is Associated with a Variety of Adverse Outcomes

Pinborough-Zimmerman et al. (2011) reported greater frequency of autism diagnoses in families with higher socioeconomic status. Opposite to those findings, Kessler et al. (2012) reported a higher prevalence of many different DSM-IV disorders, including anxiety, mood, and behavioral disorders, among offspring of parents with less than college education versus college graduates, with increased risk rates for various disorders ranging from 1.6 to 2.6. However, Kessler et al. (2012) reported that the risk rate of DSM-IV disorders for individuals living in rural areas was one-third to two-thirds the risk rate for individuals living in urban areas. Emerson and Parish (2010) noted, "Decades of research have carefully documented the association between intellectual disability and poverty" (p. 221). Zheng et al. (2012) reported an increasing risk of severe intellectual disability with increasing socioeconomic disadvantage in a national sample of 106,774 young children. The researchers reported that in China the lowest income sector of their sample was associated with a four-fold increased risk for severe intellectual disability. Zheng et al. (2012) stated that the risk of mild to severe intellectual disability "was monotonically increased among children born to women with low levels of education and to families with low per capita incomes" (p. 218).

Spacing of Pregnancies as a Risk for Autism

Cheslack-Postava et al. (2011) looked at time intervals between births of first- and second-born singleton full siblings in 5861 sibling pairs where each pair included one sibling with autism. The researchers found an inverse relationship between the number of months between pregnancies and risk for autism. Cheslack-Postava et al. (2011) reported that an inter-pregnancy interval of 12 months increased the risk rate to 3.39, an interval of 12–23 months increased the risk rate for autism to 1.86, and an interval of 24–35 months was associated with an increased risk rate of only 1.26. The researchers reported that neither low birth weight nor parental age accounted for these increased autism risk rates.

Brief Spacing Between Pregnancies is Associated with a Variety
of Adverse Outcomes

Cheslack-Postava et al. (2011) observed that short intervals between pregnancies have been significantly associated with increased risk for schizophrenia, prematurity, low birth weight, and being small for gestational age.

Birth Order as a Risk for Autism

Turner, Pihur, and Chakravarti (2011) analyzed three large autism datasets
looking for birth order effects in families with more than one child with
autism (multiplex) and families with one child with autism (simplex). The
researchers found a significant increasing linear birth order effect in the simplex families: risk for autism increased with later born children. The researchers found an inverse V-pattern birth order effect in the multiplex families:
middle children were more likely to be diagnosed with autism. Turner et al.
(2011) found the greatest risk was for a second child, and the risk decreased
until the fifth child, after which no birth order effect was observed. The
researchers concluded that their results were likely to represent "a heterogeneous collection of families with differing birth order effects" (p. 10).

Birth Order is Associated with Adverse Effects on Tested Intelligence

Bjerkedal, Kristensen, Skjere, and Brevik (2007) established birth order and
general intelligence scores recorded from 1984 to 2004 for conscripts in the
Norwegian Army. On a test with a total score range of 1 to 9, among 63,951
adjacent sibling pairs, Bjerkedal et al. (2007) reported that the older brother
average score was 5.18, and the younger brother 4.93, and noted that "intelligence has been found to be negatively associated with birth order in
numerous studies over more than a century"(p. 503).

Fertility Treatments as a Risk for Autism

Hvidtjørn et al. (2009) conducted a meta-analysis of studies evaluating children conceived by in vitro fertilization (IVF). Nine studies reported an
increased risk for cerebral palsy in children conceived by IVF, and one study
reported an increased risk for autism with IVF conception. Hvidtjørn et al.
(2011) conducted a study of autism risk associated with assisted reproduction, and found no increased risk for autism overall. However, the researchers reported that a subgroup of children of mothers who had received
follicle-stimulating hormone did have a 1.44-increased risk for autism.
Zachor and Ben Itzchak (2011) noted that assisted reproduction by IVF and
intracytoplasmic sperm injection (ICSI) had increased in the past 20 years.

Zachor and Ben Itzchak (2011) found that a significantly higher percentage, 10.7%, of individuals with autism had been conceived by IVF and ICSI, than the 3.06% rate of IVF and ICSI conceptions among a large Israeli cohort of newborns.

Fertility Treatments are Associated with a Variety of Adverse Outcomes

D'Angelo, Whitehead, Helms, Barfield, and Ahluwalia (2011) reviewed child outcomes for assisted reproduction. D'Angelo et al. (2011) reported that in a sample of 16,748 infants in six states, 10.9% of mothers had used fertility treatments. The researchers found the singleton infants of mothers who used assisted reproduction were more than twice as likely to have a low birth weight, were nearly twice as likely to be born prematurely, and be small for gestational age. Other outcomes of assisted reproduction technology are cerebral palsy, intellectual disability, and delayed development.

Risk Factors for Autism Symptoms During Gestation

The environmental risk factors of pregnancy include multiple fetuses, bleeding during pregnancy, a mother's infections, diet, medications, exposure to alcohol or drugs, and lack of vitamin use.

Multiple Births as a Risk for Autism

Betancur, Leboyer, and Gillberg (2002) found an excess of twins in a group of sibling pairs recruited by the Paris Autism Research International Sibpair (PARIS) study of families with two or more children with autism from Austria, Belgium, France, Israel, Italy, Norway, Sweden, and the United States. Betancur et al. (2002) reported that twins comprised 14% of their sample, six times the 2.5% rate of twins in the general population. Van Naarden Braun et al. (2008) examined rates of multiple births for 8-year-olds born in the United States in 1994 in data from the Autism and Developmental Disabilities Monitoring (ADDM) Network. The researchers, however, found no elevated rates of autism in the multiple birth sample, but did find elevated rates of cerebral palsy and intellectual disability in the multiple births.

Multiple Births are Associated with a Variety of Adverse Outcomes

D'Angelo et al. (2011) reported that in the United States in 2006 assisted reproduction resulted in multiple gestation births 49% of the time, compared with a 3% multiple gestation birth rate for all US births. D'Angelo et al. (2011) noted that infants born as multiples have an increased risk of preterm delivery, low birth weight, infant mortality, and long-term disability.

Van Naarden Braun et al. (2008) found multiple births significantly associated with higher rates of intellectual disability and cerebral palsy.

Bleeding During Pregnancy as a Risk for Autism

Gardener, Spiegelman, and Buka (2009) reported a significant 81% elevated risk for autism in cases where a mother had reported bleeding during pregnancy. Hultman, Sparén, and Cnattingius (2002) also reported increased risk for autism in pregnancies complicated by bleeding during the pregnancy. They theorized that the cause of autism might be intrauterine growth restriction and adverse prenatal lack of sufficient oxygen.

Bleeding During Pregnancy is Associated with a Variety of Adverse Outcomes

Rosenberg, Pariente, Sergienko, Wiznitzer, and Sheiner (2011) reported that bleeding during pregnancy related to placenta previa was associated with infant congenital malformations and early gestational age at delivery, and increased risk of infant perinatal mortality. Rosenberg et al. (2011) noted that placenta previa was associated with infertility treatments, previous cesarean section, and advanced maternal age.

Maternal Infections as a Risk for Autism

Chess (1971, 1977) reported autism as one outcome of an epidemic of rubella (German measles). In the United States, a rubella epidemic from 1963 to 1965 caused 12.5 million cases of the disease, and 20,000 children were born with congenital rubella suffering a range of impairments including deafness, cataracts, encephalitis, heart abnormalities, intellectual disability, and autism. Stigler et al. (2009) reviewed research and case studies of maternal infection in autism and reported that there was some evidence of congenital rubella, congenital cytomegalovirus, and congenital syphilis in autism, linking maternal infections to autism symptoms.

Atladóttir et al. (2010) analyzed data for all children born in Denmark from 1980 through 2005. They reported that maternal prenatal viral infection that required a mother to be hospitalized in the first trimester, and maternal bacterial infection in the second trimester were associated with an elevated risk for autism. For a maternal viral infection in the first trimester the risk increased three-fold, and for maternal bacterial infection in the second trimester the risk increased by 140%.

Libbey, Sweeten, McMahon, and Fujinami (2005) reviewed findings for congenital virus infection as a cause for autism. They reported that evidence linked congenital herpes simplex and congenital cytomegalovirus to autism.

Sweeten, Posey, and McDougle (2004) reported three cases of autism associated with very early cytomegalovirus infection. Two of the children were deaf, an impairment commonly found with congenital cytomegalovirus infection. All three were microcephalic and all three met the diagnostic criteria for autism. Sweeten et al. (2004) hypothesized that congenital infections could trigger an immune response in the fetus that could disrupt brain development. The researchers noted that congenital herpes simplex encephalitis had been associated with autism and temporal lobe damage. Sweeten et al. (2004) suggested, "congenital infections may trigger an autoimmune attack against the developing brain that could lead to the syndrome of autism" (p. 585).

Maternal Infections are Associated with a Variety of Adverse Outcomes

Sweeten et al. (2004) stated that congenital cytomegalovirus was associated with microcephaly, intellectual disability, motor disability, jaundice, cerebral calcifications, hearing loss, seizures, and death. Berger et al. (2011) reported that children with congenital rubella suffered many varied impairments, including deafness, cataracts, encephalitis, heart abnormalities, and intellectual disability. Atladóttir et al. (2010) stated that maternal infections were associated with an elevated risk for prematurity, low birth weight, congenital malformations, and schizophrenia.

Maternal Weight and Metabolic Disorders as a Risk for Autism

Krakowiak et al. (2012) reported that diabetes, hypertension, and obesity were more prevalent in mothers of children with autism and mothers of children with developmental delay. The researchers found that diabetes was significantly associated with great impairment in expressive language in children diagnosed with autism. Krakowiak et al. (2012) noted that extended fetal exposure to elevated glucose levels could induce chronic tissue hypoxia in the fetus. Iron deficiency in the fetus can damage neuron development in the hippocampus. Krakowiak et al. (2012) pointed out that "The prevalence of obesity and diabetes among US women of childbearing age is 34% and 8.7%, respectively … these maternal conditions may be associated with neurodevelopmental problems in children and therefore could have serious public health implications" (p. 7).

Maternal Weight and Metabolic Disorders are Associated with a Variety of Adverse Outcomes

Krakowiak et al. (2012) reported that mothers with diabetes were 2.3 times more likely to have a child with developmental delay. Hawdon (2011) stated, "Congenital anomalies in the offspring of women with diabetes occur with a frequency up to 10 times that observed in the general population .... UK data demonstrate that 4–6% of fetuses of diabetic mothers had one or more major congenital anomalies" (p. 93). Parental diabetes is also a risk factor for child heart problems and developmental delays. Helderman et al. (2012) studied 921 infants born before 28 weeks of gestation during 2002 to 2004. The researchers found that maternal obesity contributed to lower scores on a measure of mental development. They noted that maternal obesity is also associated with many varied pregnancy complications, and their findings revealed a significant association between maternal obesity and fetal growth restriction. Krakowiak et al. (2012) commented that interleukin and other proinflammatory cytokines are produced in the presence of maternal diabetes and maternal obesity. When cytokines can cross the placenta they can disrupt fetal brain development.

Maternal Diet as a Risk for Autism

Shamberger (2011) examined autism prevalence in relation to state participation in the United States Women, Infants, and Children (WIC) program. The WIC program provides supplemental nutritious foods, nutrition education, and health services for low-income pregnant women and postpartum women. Shamberger (2011) found that the states with the highest WIC participation had significantly lower autism rates (p < .02). Shamberger (2011) also reported the same association within 21 New Jersey counties (p < .02) and within 30 Oregon counties (p < .05). Shamberger (2011) suggested that prenatal nutrition might be a causal factor in autism.

Maternal Diet is Associated with a Variety of Adverse Outcomes

Black et al. (2008) provided a comprehensive report on the effects of undernutrition and poor nutrition. The researchers reported that outcomes of prenatal undernutrition are prematurity, restricted fetal growth, increased infant susceptibility to infection, and delayed or impaired cognitive ability.

Maternal Drugs and Alcohol as a Risk for Autism

Dufour-Rainfray et al. (2011) reviewed four drugs—alcohol, valproic acid, thalidomide, and misoprostol—reported to increase risk for autism. Valproic acid is a treatment for epilepsy, thalidomide was intended as a sedative, misoprostol is a treatment for gastric ulcers that also causes uterine contractions, and women have attempted abortions using misoprostol. All four drugs affect development between the 18th and 42nd day of gestation: they disrupt brain development by impairing neuron growth, neuron migration, neuron differentiation, neuron apoptosis or cell death, and synaptogenesis.

Croen et al. (2011a) compared 291 children with autism and 284 children without autism for maternal exposure to terbutaline and other β2 adrenergic receptor (B2AR) agonists used for treatment of asthma. Two B2AR agonists, ritodrine and terbutaline, have also been used to inhibit preterm uterine contractions. The researchers reported no increased autism risk for maternal exposure to B2AR agonists other than terbutaline. However, Croen et al. (2011a) found that maternal exposure to terbutaline for more than 2 days during the third trimester of pregnancy was associated with more than a fourfold increased risk for autism.

Croen et al. (2011b) investigated the risk of autism in children of mothers who took antidepressants in a population of all infants born at a one hospital in California between January 1995 and June 1999. Croen et al. (2011b) found selective serotonin reuptake inhibitor (SSRI) antidepressant treatment doubled the risk of autism. Moreover, the researchers reported that SSRI treatment during the first trimester of pregnancy tripled the risk for autism.

Drug Exposure is Associated with a Variety of Adverse Outcomes

Alcohol, valproic acid, thalidomide, and misoprostol have been shown to cause physical malformations, fetal alcohol syndrome, intellectual disability, and language delay (Dufour-Rainfray et al., 2011). Antidepressant treatment with SSRIs has been associated with motor delay and delay in reaching developmental milestones (Croen et al., 2011b). Rocklin (2011) reported no negative child outcomes where mothers had been given asthma treatment drugs during pregnancy. However, Pitzer, Schmidt, Esser, and Laucht (2001) reported that 123 German children whose mothers had been given beta-sympathomimetic drugs to inhibit preterm labor had developmental impairment. The children had lower scores on tests of cognitive development, and had a significantly higher rate of psychiatric disorders than the children of mothers who had not been given beta-sympathomimetic drugs to inhibit preterm labor.

Maternal Lack of Prenatal Vitamins Including Vitamin B9 as a Risk for Autism

Schmidt et al. (2011) compared 429 children with autism and 278 children with typical development for maternal reported vitamin intake before and during pregnancy. The researchers found mothers of children with autism were less likely than mothers of typically developing children to have taken prenatal vitamins in the 3 months before pregnancy or in the first month of pregnancy. Schmidt et al. (2011) also examined interaction effects with gene variants related to vitamin B9 function, and found significant interaction effects for the presence of two gene variants and autism risk when mothers reported they did not take prenatal vitamins around the time the child was conceived. Normal fetal brain development is dependent on vitamin B9, also called folic acid or folate, because folate is a one-carbon donor to DNA synthesis, and is necessary for DNA methylation, a regulator of gene expression. Researchers theorized that folate deficiency causes errors in DNA synthesis, and causes hypomethylation of genomic DNA, thus disrupting gene expression crucial to neural tube formation and brain development.

Maternal Lack of Folate is Associated with a Variety of Adverse Outcomes

Two outcomes of maternal lack of folic acid, vitamin B9, are higher rates of premature birth, and neural tube defects, one form of which is spina bifida (Black, 2008; Pérez-Dueñas et al., 2011).

Risk Factors for Autism Symptoms at the Time of Delivery

Premature birth and low birth weight, infant lack of oxygen during delivery, infant breech presentation, cesarean delivery, low Apgar scores at birth, and mother's weight at delivery have all been found to be perinatal environmental risk factors for autism.

Premature Birth and Low Birth Weight as a Risk for Autism

As noted in the introduction to this chapter, Pinto-Martin et al. (2011) reported that in a sample of 623 adolescents and young adults who were born prematurely, and who had weighed less than 2000 grams at birth, 31 were diagnosed with autism. This is a very high prevalence: the researchers observed that the rate of autism they reported was five times the United States population prevalence (Pinto-Martin et al., 2011). Losh et al. (2011) examined birth weights in autism-discordant twin pairs, i.e., where one twin was diagnosed with autism and the other was not. The study twins were drawn from a population sample of 3715 same-sex twin pairs participating in the Child and Adolescent Twin Study of Sweden. Losh et al. (2011) found that twins lower in birth weight in autism-discordant twin pairs were over three times more likely to be diagnosed with autism than heavier twins. Losh et al. (2011) analyzed birth weight as a continuous risk factor, and found a 13% reduction in risk for autism with every 100 gram increase in birth weight. Losh et al. (2011) also found that for every 100 gram increase in birth weight, there was a 2% decrease in severity of autism symptoms, with stronger effects for social and language symptoms than ritualistic or repetitive behaviors. Losh et al. (2011) proposed that in identical twins who share gestational age, "differences in birth weight can provide an index of differences in fetal growth that may be relevant to clinical outcome in twin pairs discordant" for autism (p. 8).

Limperopoulos et al. (2008) studied 91 children who had weighed 1500 grams or less at birth. The researchers found that 26% of the 91 children at 18–26 months had autism features as measured by the Modified Checklist for Autism in Toddlers (M-CHAT). The researchers reported that many factors correlated with the M-CHAT score, including lower birth weight, gestational age, male gender, delivery hemorrhage, and abnormal MRI studies. Limperopoulos et al. (2008) reported that toddlers whose neonatal MRIs showed evidence of cerebellar hemorrhagic injury were significantly more likely to have autism features on the M-CHAT screening measure.

Kuban et al. (2009) used the M-CHAT to screen 988 children born before 28 weeks of gestation from a multisite study of extremely low gestational age newborns (ELGANs). More than 21% (212/988) of all children screened positive for autism. The researchers reported that the odds for screening positive on the M-CHAT were increased 23-fold for children unable to sit or stand independently, and increased 13-fold in children with quadriparesis. Kuban et al. (2009) noted that children with major vision or hearing impairments were 8 times more likely to screen positive than children without those impairments. The researchers concluded that serious motor, cognitive, vision, and auditory impairments accounted for more than 50% of the positive M-CHAT screens in their sample of extremely low gestational age newborns. However, Kuban et al. (2009) found that even after eliminating children with those impairments, 10% of their sample screened positive on the M-CHAT.

Mann, McDermott, Bao, Hardin, and Gregg (2010) found that newborn birth weight was significantly inversely associated with the odds of autism in a sample of 87,677 births in South Carolina from 1996 to 2002. Mann et al. (2011) reported that maternal pre-eclampsia/eclampsia was significantly associated with greater odds of autism, even when controlling for birth weight. Pre-eclampsia is high blood pressure and excess protein in the urine after 20 weeks of pregnancy in a woman who previously had normal blood pressure. Eclampsia is seizures experienced by a pregnant woman who was pre-eclampsic. Mann et al. (2010) found that increasing birth weight reduced the risk of autism in their sample, but not when children with intellectual disability were excluded from the sample.

Premature Birth and Low Birth Weight are Associated with a Variety of Adverse Outcomes

The most adverse outcome for premature birth or extremely low birth weight is the death of the fetus or newborn. Other adverse outcomes include cerebral palsy, hypoxic/ischemic encephalopathy, intellectual disability, and developmental delay.

Perinatal Factors as a Risk for Autism

Perinatal risk factors for autism include infant hypoxia during delivery, cesarean section delivery, lower birth weight at full term delivery, and low Apgar scores at birth (Hultman et al., 2002; Larsson et al., 2005). Kolevzon, Gross, and Reichenberg (2007) reviewed epidemiological studies of autism, and reported that the obstetric conditions significantly associated with autism were duration of gestation, birth weight, and newborn hypoxia. Kolevzon et al. (2007) stated that five factors signaled hypoxia: low Apgar score, fetal distress, cesarean delivery, maternal hypertension, and bleeding during pregnancy. The Apgar score rates a newborn as 0, 1, or 2 for heart rate, breathing, muscle tone, skin color, and responsiveness. Burstyn, Sithole, and Zwaigenbaum (2010) studied records for 218,890 singleton children born in Alberta, Canada between 1998 and 2004. The researchers reported that breech or shoulder presentation during labor increased the risk rate for autism to 1.31 and planned cesarean section increased the risk rate to 1.2. Burstyn, Wang, Yasui, Sithole, and Zwaigenbaum (2011) also reported that birth weight less than 2.5 kilograms was associated with an increased autism risk of 1.33, and a 1-minute Apgar score of less than 7 was associated with an increased risk rate for autism of 1.34.

Gardener et al. (2011) conducted a meta-analysis of studies of perinatal and neonatal risk factors for autism. The researchers reported increased risk rates for autism for a variety of events: abnormal presentation had a risk rate of 1.44; breech presentation, a risk rate of 1.81; umbilical-cord complications, 1.50; fetal distress, 1.52; and, birth injury or trauma, 4.90. Gardener et al. (2011) also reported increased risk rates for autism for: maternal hemorrhage, 2.39; very low birth weight, 3.00; congenital malformations, 1.80; low 5-minute Apgar score, 1.67; meconium aspiration, 7.34; ABO or Rh incompatibility, 3.70; and neonatal anemia had a risk rate of 7.87.

Guinchat et al. (2012b) conducted a meta-analysis of 85 studies of prenatal, perinatal, and neonatal risk factors for autism. For perinatal risk, the researchers found seven factors that conferred additional risk for autism: preterm birth, breech presentation, planned cesarean section, low Apgar scores, birth defect, birth weight small for gestational age, and hyperbilirubinemia. Hyperbilirubinemia is abnormally high blood levels of bilirubin, a natural byproduct of the breakdown of red blood cells. Too high a level of bilirubin may result from liver disease, or the excessive destruction of red blood cells, which occurs in hemolytic anemia. Guinchat et al. (2012b) argued that the association between autism and hyperbilirubinemia should be investigated because the condition can be toxic for two brain regions found to be impaired in many cases of autism: the basal ganglia and the cerebellum.

Dodds et al. (2011) studied records for 924 children diagnosed with autism in Nova Scotia, Canada from 1990 to 2002. The researchers reported increased risk for autism for a variety of prenatal, perinatal, and neonatal conditions. Maternal weight at delivery of more than 120 kilograms, and maternal substance abuse during pregnancy each individually increased the risk rate of autism two-fold. The researchers also reported that maternal use of any prescription drug during pregnancy increased the risk rate to 2.7. Dodd et al. (2011) also reported that placenta previa increased the risk rate two-fold, a 5-minute Apgar score below 7 increased the child's risk of autism by a factor of 1.7, and any major central nervous system anomaly in the child was associated with an increased risk rate for autism of 5.4.

Perinatal Risk Factors are Associated with a Variety of Adverse Outcomes

The most adverse outcome in delivery is newborn death. Other outcomes include cerebral palsy, cerebellar and basal ganglia damage, hypoxic/ischemic encephalopathy, intellectual disability, and developmental delay.

Summary: How Much Variance do Prenatal and Perinatal Environmental Risk Factors Account for?

Events and conditions in the pre-conception period, in the 40 weeks of the gestational period, and in the hours of the perinatal period encompass a catalog of many environmental risk factors. These include advanced parent age, autoimmune diseases of the parents, season of conception and birth, spacing of pregnancies, birth order, fertility treatments, one or more additional fetuses in the uterus, a mother's infections, her medications, her alcohol use, her blood pressure, and her diet. Potentially adverse events of labor and delivery include a mother's weight and her infant's premature birth, low birth weight, birth presentation, and low Apgar score after delivery. Each of these factors was shown to increase the risk for autism.

Schieve et al. (2011) noted a 57% increase in reported cases of autism in the United States for 8-year-old children born in 1998 versus 1994.

The researchers created a mathematical model based on three statistics: the baseline risk factor prevalence in the population in 1994, the change in risk factor prevalence from 1994 to 1998, and rate of the environmental risk factors for autism relative to population risk. Schieve et al. (2011) applied their model to population-based surveillance datasets. The researchers hypothesized that results of their model would help explain the 57% increase in autism, instead they found that each prenatal and perinatal factor "most likely accounted for less than 1% of the ASD increase" (Schieve et al., 2011, p. 936). Schieve et al. (2011) concluded that all the prenatal and perinatal risk factors together made only a minor contribution to the 57% increase in autism diagnoses in the USA from 2002 to 2006. They reported that only if environmental risk factor effects increased by 100% between 1994 and 1998, and only if the total relative risk rate for autism were 5 times that of the population, would their model account for a 57% increase in autism. Despite the conclusion drawn by Schieve et al. (2011), it is possible that a more exhaustive list of pre-conception, gestational, and perinatal risk factors would account for more of the increase in autism diagnoses than that proposed by Schieve et al. (2011).

The Hallmayer et al. (2011) twin study suggested that environmental factors might account for more than half the causal variance in autism. Although Hallmayer et al. (2011) asserted that the prenatal environment was likely to be the causal source of autism, researchers have not yet found evidence that prenatal and perinatal risk rates account for a substantial portion of the variance in autism. However, it is possible that additional environmental risk factors for autism may be found in epigenetic risk factors, the prenatal interaction of maternal and child genes and the gestational environment, and the effects of fetal immune system genes in the environment of the developing fetal brain.

EPIGENETIC RISK FACTORS FOR AUTISM SYMPTOMS

Guinchat et al. (2012b) cautioned that it was not clear whether prenatal, perinatal, and neonatal environmental risks were "causal or play a secondary role in shaping clinical expression in individuals with genetic vulnerability" (p. 288). Any signal that influences the expression or action of a gene is a gene–environment interaction. Epigenetic processes are specific mechanisms that regulate environmental exposure and through which environment factors may exert lifelong or even cross-generation effects on gene expression. Evidence for dysregulation of epigenetic processes in autism has been accumulating (Fradin et al., 2010; Grafodatskaya et al., 2010; Kopsida et al., 2011; Nguyen, Rauch, Pfeifer, & Hu, 2010).

Epigenetics is the modification of chromatin, which is genomic DNA with associated proteins, largely histones. Chromatin shapes the DNA to fit in the cell's nucleus, and structures the DNA for replication and for control of gene expression. Environmental effects and within-cell effects modify chromatin, leaving epigenetic modifications, called epigenetic marks. Modification takes place through three core processes: the action of histone proteins, DNA methylation, and chromatin remodeling. Histones provide structural spools that DNA winds around, and histones influence methylation. Methylation is the addition of a methyl (CH_3) group to a cytosine molecule in a gene, causing that gene's suppression, also called silencing. Chromatin remodeling is moving nucleosomes on the DNA, thereby allowing protein transcription factors to transcribe DNA regions previously blocked.

An individual's epigenome may account for considerable phenotypic variation. Epigenetic mechanisms include: imprinting, in which one parent's allele controls gene expression; X-inactivation of one of the two copies of the X chromosome; gene silencing, wherein histone modification switches off a gene; and many other mechanisms as well. Turner (2011) summarized that "histone modifications lie at the heart of mechanisms by which a variety of functionally significant proteins and protein complexes are targeted to, or excluded from, specific regions of the genome. These include transcription factors, chromatin modifying enzymes, the complexes that methylate DNA or the chromatin remodelers that reposition nucleosomes along the DNA strand" (p. 2033). In addition, Jessen and Auger (2011) hypothesized that sex differences in "epigenetic factors not only contribute to sexual differentiation of the brain and social behavior, but that they may confer sexually dimorphic risk and resilience for developing neurological and mental health disorders later in life" (p. 857).

Grafodatskaya et al. (2010) reviewed epigenetic factors in autism, and organized them into four groups. The first group included epigenetic syndromes with an increased risk for autism. These included three syndromes that cause macrocephaly, PTEN, Sotos syndrome, and Beckwith-Wiedemann syndrome, as well as Rett syndrome, fragile X syndrome, Angelman syndrome, Prader-Willi syndrome, Turner syndrome, and CHARGE syndrome caused by a mutation in the *CHD7* gene thought to have an epigenetic role in chromatin remodeling.

The epigenetic syndromes grouped by Grafodatskaya et al. (2010) represented different types of epigenetic processes. For example, Rett syndrome results from a mutation in the *MECP2* gene. The gene produces Methyl–CpG binding protein 2, a protein that regulates epigenetic control, and is required for neuronal maturation and synaptogenesis. Lack of the MECP2 protein results in abnormally structured neurons and, because it causes an over-release of the neurotransmitter glutamate, has a neurotoxic effect on microglia, the immune system's protective cells in the brain (de Leon-Guerrero et al., 2011). Fragile X syndrome involves a different epigenetic process: an alteration in the *FMR1* gene confers increased susceptibility to methylation and consequent silencing of the *FMR1* gene. Angelman syndrome and Prader–Willi syndrome involve yet another epigenetic process: imprinting.

We inherit our 20,000–22,000 genes in pairs. Each pair contains our mother's variant of the gene, called the maternal allele, and our father's variant, the paternal allele. For some genes, only the maternal allele or the paternal allele is expressed and the other allele is silenced by imprinting. At present, nearly 100 human genes have been identified as showing imprinted expression (Barlow, 2011). Most imprinted genes occur in clusters in a chromosomal domain regulated by an imprinting center that controls activation of maternal versus paternal chromosome regions. Most important is that many proteins produced by imprinted genes regulate brain development.

Angelman syndrome accounts for some cases of autism. It results from loss of function of the maternally imprinted *UBE3A* gene, a gene in which the paternal allele is normally silenced. This loss may occur as the result of point mutations in the gene, or of the deletion of the maternally inherited chromosome 15q11–q13 region, or of mutations within a specialized imprinting center in the gene cluster within the 15q11–q13 region. Prader–Willi syndrome, another epigenetic syndrome that can produce autism symptoms, results from the loss of expression of one or more paternally expressed genes at the same chromosomal region, 15q11–q13.

The second group Grafodatskaya et al. (2010) defined was syndromic autism linked to genes or genomic regions regulated by epigenetic marks. This group included genes in the chromosomal duplication of region 15q11–13, such as *UBE3A*, *SNRPN*, and *NDN*. Unlike the deletion of region 15q11–13 and loss of the function of the *UBE3A* gene in Angelman syndrome, the duplication of region 15q11–13 does not produce Angelman syndrome or Prader–Willi syndrome. However, 85% of individuals with this chromosomal duplication have been diagnosed with autism. Grafodatskaya et al. (2010) reviewed the extensive variability in the phenotype of 15q11–13 duplications. In addition to autism symptoms, the variability in this phenotype included a range of cognitive impairments, anxiety, tantrums, hyperactivity, motor delays, seizures, and dysmorphic facial features, as well as social and language deficits.

Grafodatskaya et al. (2010) defined the third group as idiopathic autism linked to epigenetically regulated genes or genomic regions or genes that served epigenetic regulation. This group included the folate metabolism genes, *MTHFR*, *DHFR*, *TCN2*, *COMT*, and *RFC,* and the epigenetically regulated genes *RELN, BDNF,* and *OXTR.* This third group also included an imprinted gene *DLX6.1* on the long arm of chromosome 7 and a uniparental maternal disomy on chromosome 1. Uniparental disomy occurs when both copies of a chromosomal pair are from one parent, and can cause disordered development by disrupting imprinting, or by allowing recessive gene mutations to be expressed.

Two examples of this third group are the *OXTR* and *RELN* genes. Increased methylation of the promoter of the oxytocin receptor gene was linked to autism. The *RELN* gene has an associated region, and the gene together with the associated region is called the long allele variant of the *RELN* gene. The long allele is able to epigenetically suppress gene expression and has been found in association with autism. The RELN protein is critical for neuron migration and synapse formation in much of the brain.

The fourth group Grafodatskaya et al. (2010) defined as epigenetic risk factors for autism comprised treatments that changed epigenetic marks. These included the ova induction process involved in assisted reproduction, and valproate, a drug administered to treat seizures, migraine headaches, and manic or mixed episodes associated with bipolar disorder. The process of inducing ovulation in assisted reproduction has been linked to an increased risk for two imprinting disorders—Beckwith-Wiedemann syndrome and Angelman syndrome—as well as an increase in the risk for autism symptoms. Valproate has been demonstrated to alter folate metabolism, and to interfere with histone functions. Epigenetic alterations caused by valproate taken by a mother during pregnancy cause adverse outcomes such as spina bifida, heart defects, craniofacial abnormalities, skeletal and limb defects, dysmorphic features, decreased intrauterine growth, intellectual disability, and autism symptoms.

In addition to the epigenetic factors reviewed by Grafodatskaya et al. (2010), there are other findings for and theories of epigenetic factors in autism. Evidence for possible epigenetic factors was reported by Fradin et al. (2010). The researchers conducted a genome-wide linkage scan looking for parent-of-origin effects using 16,311 SNPs in two family samples:

the Autism Genetic Resource Exchange and the National Institute of Mental Health autism repository. The researchers found significant parent of origin linkage for chromosomes 4, 15, and 20. Fradin et al. (2010) noted the strongest candidate gene on chromosome 4 was *CLOCK*, a gene that codes a protein regulating circadian rhythm. The strongest candidate genes for chromosome 15 were *RASGRF1*, a gene linked to memory, and *NRG4*, neuregulin 4, and *CHRNA3/B4*, cholinergic receptor, as well as *MTHFS*, a gene involved in regulation of DNA methylation, and thus important for epigenetic mechanisms. The strongest candidate gene for chromosome 20 was *SNPH*, syntaphiliyn gene that produces a protein that contributes to the development of synaptic processing of neurotransmitters. Fradin et al. (2010) also found evidence suggesting additional parent-specific linkage regions on chromosomes 1, 5, 6, 7, 8, 9, 10, 13, 14, 17, and 21. Fradin et al. (2010) concluded that because of "the potential role for imprinting and other epigenetic mechanisms in neuropsychiatric disorders such as autism the regions identified are good candidates for assessment of functional variants and their relationship to epigenetic marks such as methylation status on paternal and maternal DNA" (p. 6).

Additional evidence for epigenetic factors came from the research of Nguyen et al. (2010), who proposed that epigenetic regulatory mechanisms were important in the pathophysiology of autism. Nguyen et al. (2010) conducted neuropathological analyses from the postmortem tissue arrays from the Autism Tissue Program in San Diego, California. The researchers found decreased expression of two proteins, RORA and BCL-2, in cerebellum and frontal cortex tissue, and noted that the expression of both proteins could have been downregulated by aberrant methylation. BCL-2 is important for cell survival, and prior studies had reported a 30% reduction of BCL-2 protein in the parietal lobes and superior frontal cortex of males with autism. The RORA protein has many functions, including regulation of the survival and differentiation of Purkinje cells, and the regulation of the development of the cerebellum.

Several theories of an epigenetic cause for autism have been proposed. Nguyen et al. (2010) concluded that epigenetic mechanisms in autism should be investigated because epigenetic "modifications can be influenced by exposure to biological modulators and environmental factors [mediating] … between genotype and intrinsic [biological] or extrinsic [environmental] factors contributing to ASDs" (p. 3049). Rogaev (2012) hypothesized that genetic–epigenomic interactions (GEI) were likely causes for schizophrenia and autism. Rogaev (2012) argued that alterations in programmed epigenomic transformations during development, or environmentally induced changes in epigenomic processes would alter genomic regions that were the targets of the epigenomic processes, resulting in altered genetic transcription. Kopsida et al. (2011) observed that "environmentally induced changes in epigenomic processes" might be caused by a maternal diet lacking folic acid, vitamin B12, and choline. The lack of these dietary elements can disrupt the epigenetic processes of DNA methylation and histone modification, thus impairing gene function, leading to altered fetal brain growth and development. As outlined above in the discussion of prenatal factors, Schmidt et al. (2011) reported that mothers of children with autism were less likely to have taken prenatal vitamins before and during pregnancy than were mothers of typically developing children. Schmidt et al. (2011) found significant interactions for two gene variants and autism risk in the absence of prenatal vitamins.

Kopsida et al. (2011) proposed a negative cascade of events in which a mother's diet, infections, substance abuse, stress, and trauma could result in dysregulated placental expression of a variety of imprinted genes. The dysregulated imprinted genes of the placenta, in turn, would disrupt the normal flow of oxygen, nutrients, and hormones to the fetus, which then would cause dysregulated fetal expression of imprinted genes, and would thus disrupt the insulin-like growth factors. Disrupted growth factors would result in fetal growth restriction, which, in turn, would result in autism.

In a different theory of epigenetic causality for autism, Ploeger, Raijmakers, van der Maas, and Galis (2010) theorized that autism was the result of a single mutation or environmental disturbance "during early organogenesis, the embryonic stage from Day 20 to Day 40 after fertilization" (p. 605). They argued that, during this embryonic period, the interactivity among body parts makes the embryo very vulnerable to developmental disruptions. Ploeger et al. (2011) argued that evidence linking autism to varied brain deficits, major structural anomalies, minor physical anomalies, and many medical conditions all supported the plausibility of the embryonic 20-day window for an insult that would result in autism symptoms.

Ploeger et al. (2011) theorized that disruption of the epigenetic process of imprinting was likely to be the cause of the insult during the 20-day period of vulnerability. They reasoned that imprinted genes are important in neurodevelopment, are expressed during early embryogenesis, are associated with autism and schizophrenia, are highly pleiotropic, may account for sex ratios in autism, and thus may be the core source of disruption in this embryonic period.

Summary: More Data are Needed to Understand Epigenetic Risk Factors

Some of the gene variants identified as conferring a risk for autism symptoms have been identified as having epigenetic functions. These included *PTEN, FMR1, MECP2, OXTR, RELN, UBE3A, CHD7*, and a number of other genes. In Chapter 4, a number of genes that have not been found to have epigenetic function but have been identified as causal for autism symptoms were outlined. These included *CNTNAP2, TSC1, TSC2, DHCR7, CACNA1C, NF1, DMD, ARX, CDKl5, FOXP1, GRIK2, FOXP2, SHANK2, A2BP1, SLC6A4, SHANK3, PTCHD1, SLC25A12, MET, AVPR1A*, and *ITGB3*. The considerable evidence for genes causal for autism symptoms that have no epigenetic function suggests that the epigenetic imprinting theories of autism proposed by Kopsida et al. (2011), Ploeger et al. (2011), and others will not be able to account for the majority of cases of autism.

The significance of epigenetic risk factors in autism may be clearest for the folate metabolism genes, *MTHFR, DHFR, TCN2, COMT, RFC*, and *CBS*. Folate, a B vitamin, is crucial for fetal development, and must be provided by the mother. Schmidt et al. (2011) reported a link between autism risk, maternal failure to take vitamins before and during pregnancy, and three variants of folate metabolism genes. Among those mothers who had not taken vitamins, there was an increased 4.5 risk rate of autism in the children of mothers with an *MTHFR* variant, an increased 2.6 risk rate of autism in the children of mothers with a *CBS* variant, and an increased 7.2 risk rate for autism in children with a *COMT* variant. This evidence demonstrated significant causal links between the environment—the presence or absence of folate—and variants of genes *MTHFR, COMT*, and *CBS* with epigenetic functions. This evidence also suggested there might be other such epigenetic risk gene–environment interactions that may be causal for autism symptoms.

The complexities of the epigenetic functions of the MECP2 gene protein reveal the need for more knowledge of epigenetic gene effects in the brain. Guy, Cheval, Selfridge, and Bird (2011) noted that the effect of MeCP2 deficiency on the brain "is poorly understood in many respects and is the subject of intense research" (p. 633). Guy et al. (2011) reported that findings suggest that MeCP2 has global effects on all chromatin, and they identified many protein partners for MeCP2: HP1, mSin3a, cSki, YY1, Atrx, YB1, NcoR, Dnmt1, CoREST, CREB, Brahma, H3K9, and MTase. The researchers stated that MeCP2 engages its protein partners in many crucial epigenetic actions including altering histone function, and silencing genes. They also offered evidence suggesting that, despite the absence of MeCP2 protein, the brain develops normally. Adverse effects of the absence of MeCP2 protein occur later, when the absence disrupts synaptogenesis and neuron functions (Guy et al., 2011).

Given that the complexity of MeCP2 disruption is just beginning to be understood, it is clear there is insufficient evidence concerning the effects of the disruption of epigenetic processes in fetal brain development at present to develop a meaningful narrative of the epigenetic causality for autism.

IMMUNE SYSTEM REACTIVITY, DYSFUNCTION, AND NEUROINFLAMMATION IN AUTISM

Stigler et al. (2009) reviewed immune system research in autism. They noted that sparse evidence linked autism to maternal infections in congenital rubella, congenital cytomegalovirus, and congenital syphilis, as well as to evidence for infection in herpes simplex virus encephalitis, Toxoplasma gondii infection, varicella encephalitis, and viral meningitis. Stigler et al. (2009) observed that serological studies suggested children with autism might be at an increased risk for developing infections, which might indicate immune system problems in autism. Stigler et al. (2009) reviewed research that found subgroups of individuals with autism expressed an abnormal ratio of $CD4^+$ to $CD8^+$ T cells, and increased production of inflammatory or antiviral cytokines, as well as other evidence of abnormal immune system activity. The researchers concluded that these data, along with evidence from postmortem studies and immunogenetic and autoimmune family history, pointed to a causal role for neuroimmune mechanisms in autism.

Onore, Careaga, and Ashwood (2011) reviewed evidence for neuroinflammation in autism. They reported that studies had found ongoing neuroinflammation in postmortem brain tissue of individuals with autism across a wide age span, from 4 to 45 years old. Onore et al. (2012) also reported increased microglia activation and increased inflammatory cytokine production in autism, and commented that microglia are abnormally activated in multiple sclerosis, Alzheimer's and Parkinson's diseases. Onore et al. (2012) pointed out that a transcriptome analysis for autism conducted by Voineagu et al. (2011) suggested that immune dysregulation might be the cause of brain deficit in autism. Onore et al. (2012) cautioned that the causes of immune system abnormalities found for autism were unknown, and might "extend from genetic to maternal immune activation, or any number of unknown causes" (p. 8).

Humans have two immune systems: the innate immune system common to animals, plants, fungi, insects, and primitive multicellular organisms, and the adaptive immune system that evolved in jawed vertebrates. The evolutionarily older innate immune system works through a complement protein cascade that identifies bacteria, activates cells, and triggers removal of dead cells. The innate immune system activates the adaptive immune system. The adaptive immune system recognizes and remembers individual pathogens to more effectively counter a pathogen when it reappears in the body.

The innate immune system employs leukocytes, white blood cells that identify and remove foreign substances throughout the body. Leukocytes include eosinophils, basophils, macrophages, neutrophils, monocytes, and three types of lymphocytes: B cells, T cells, and natural killer cells. There are subgroups within these groups. For example, TH1 and TH2 are T helper lymphocytes that direct and activate other immune cells. Fixed position leukocytes include mast cells, dendritic cells, and microglia. Microglia are the primary protective housekeeper cells of the central nervous system; they search for and engulf damaged neurons, plaques, and infectious agents. Microglia also conduct synaptic pruning in normal neurodevelopment. Microglia produce cytokines, a large group of proteins, peptides, or glycoproteins that mediate and regulate immunity and inflammation. The human genome contains about 180 genes thought to encode for cytokine proteins.

As the reviews of Stigler et al. (2009) and Onore et al. (2012) made clear, a wide range of different types of studies have found evidence for abnormal immune system activity in autism, and, in particular, atypical immune activity in the brains of individuals with autism (Abdallah et al., 2012; Ashwood et al., 2011b; Vargas et al., 2005).

Ashwood et al. (2011b) analyzed levels of 12 cytokines in blood samples from 66 children diagnosed with autism and typical controls. Using a standard stimulation protocol, the researchers found increased production of three cytokines, granulocyte–macrophage colony-stimulating factor (GM-CSF), interleukin-13 (IL-13), and tumor necrosis factor alpha (TNFα), and reduced production of the cytokine interleukin-12 (IL-12p40) for autism. They also found alterations in the frequencies of T cell subpopulations expressing CD25, CD134, and CD137 in autism compared with controls. CD abbreviates cluster of differentiation, and each number such as CD25 identifies a specific monoclonal antibody that recognizes an element of an antigen called the epitope—a cell surface molecule—on a white blood cell. Ashwood et al. (2011b) reported that increased inflammatory cytokines occurred mainly in children within their sample who had been diagnosed with regressive autism, and that "proinflammatory/TH1 cytokines were associated with more behavioral impairment, whereas GM-CSF and TH2 cytokine production was associated with better developmental and adaptive function" (Ashwood et al., 2011b, p. 847). Ashwood et al. (2011b) concluded that children with autism had an acquired immune response that promoted cellular activation, and that malfunctioning cellular immune responses in autism might directly cause autism symptoms. The researchers proposed, "separation of ASD into subgroups based on immunological parameters may have important implications for both diagnosis and therapeutic manipulation" (Ashwood et al., 2011b, p. 847).

Vargas et al. (2005) found the neuroinflammation markers of microglia and astroglia activation in the gray and white matter of postmortem brain tissue from patients with autism obtained through the Autism Tissue Program of the Harvard, University of Miami, and University of Maryland Brain Banks. Vargas et al. (2005) reported, "the primary immunocompetent cells of the nervous system were consistently activated in all brain regions of autistic patients, but particularly in the cerebellum" (p. 77). Vargas et al. (2005) proposed that brains of individuals with autism appeared similar to brain tissues in Parkinson's and Alzheimer's diseases because they showed evidence of chronic activation and reactivity of the innate immune system.

Vargas et al. (2005) reported increased expression of inflammatory cytokines, including macrophage chemoattractant protein 1 (MCP1), and transforming growth factor $\beta1$, in the tissue samples from the brains of patients with autism. MCP1, also known as CCL2, is a protein encoded by the CCL2 gene that recruits monocytes, memory T cells, and dendritic cells to sites of tissue injury, infection, and inflammation. The researchers determined that astroglia and microglia were the core sources of the cytokine production. Vargas et al. (2005) also measured the levels of cytokines in the cerebrospinal fluid in a sample of six living individuals with autism. They discovered a significant increase in the levels of MCP1 and other cytokines, such as interleukin-6 and interferon-γ, in the cerebrospinal fluid of these individuals, but found that the expression of transforming growth factor $\beta1$ was not different from that of typical controls.

Like Vargas et al. (2005), Abdallah et al. (2012) found evidence for significantly elevated levels of inflammatory cytokine MCP1 activity in autism.

The researchers analyzed maternal blood samples and amniotic fluid samples for 331 individuals with autism, and found the elevated MCP1 activity only for 145 individuals with autism who were born after 1993. The researchers proposed that these abnormal levels were likely to have been caused by "maternal viral or bacterial infection or, in broader terms, a maternal immune activation" (Abdallah et al., 2012, p. 174). Abdallah et al. (2012) suggested that an insult to the fetus during gestation might result in an overexpression of MCP-1 in the fetal brain.

Momeni et al. (2012) compared complement I activity in blood samples of 30 children with autism and 30 controls. The researchers found significantly higher activity of a component of the innate immune complement system, glycoprotein factor I, in children with autism compared with controls.

Ziats and Rennert (2011) conducted a network analysis of genes they identified as highly expressed in the developing brain, and all genes associated with autism, schizophrenia, and epilepsy. An interactome analysis revealed six highly expressed candidate autism genes as central hubs of all autism gene networks: *NFKB, JNK, MAPK, TNF, TGF-B*, and *MYC*. Ziats and Rennert (2011) concluded that the genes "may converge onto classical cytokine signaling pathways" (p. 8) common to the heterogeneous interactome of the implicated genes.

Ziats and Rennert (2011) commented that two views of autism immune system dysfunction existed. One view argued that environmental factors stimulated neuroinflammation causing autism (Abdullah et al., 2012). The other view argued that no environmental factors were involved because the autoimmune system itself was impaired in autism (Vargas et al., 2005). Ziats and Rennert (2011) proposed a new third view, that cytokine signaling was the cause of autism. They theorized that either genetic variants affect the cytokine system, causing "aberrant signaling regulation of immune cells during neurodevelopment ... [or] genomic aberrations ultimately funnel through core signaling pathways of glial cells to disrupt formation of neural networks independent of an inflammatory mechanism" (p. 9).

Emanuele et al. (2010) found significantly higher serum levels of endotoxin in 22 adults with autism compared to controls. Endotoxin is the outer cell wall membrane of Gram-negative bacteria. Bacteria get into blood circulation from the gut, and the researchers noted that the individuals with autism in their study might have had gastrointestinal inflammation, secondary to diet or other causes, which could have resulted in increased circulating serum endotoxin levels. However, Emanuele et al. (2010) reported that levels of endotoxin were significantly inversely correlated with two measures of social skill and impairment.

Summary: More Data are Needed to Understand Immune System Dysfunction in Autism

Present evidence is insufficient to determine how many different types of immune system abnormalities may contribute to autism symptoms. Present evidence is also insufficient to determine whether inflammation in the brain is caused by an adverse mutation in fetal immune system genes, or by an adverse reaction of the fetal immune system to maternal gene products, or by an over-reaction of the immune system to some other environmental insult in the womb. Moreover, it is not known whether autism symptoms result from the fetal brain inflammation, or result from an environmental insult to the fetal brain. Saijo and Glass (2011) stated that activated microglia produce many proinflammatory mediators, such as cytokines, chemokines, reactive oxygen species, and nitric oxide to address pathogens in the brain, but excessive microglial cell activation may result in pathological inflammation that directly causes brain deficits. Another difficulty for determining the parameters of immune system dysfunction in the brain in autism is that scientific knowledge of neuroinflammation is still developing. For example, the lifespan and replication capacity of microglia are still unknown.

However, as reviewed by Rees, Harding, and Walker (2011), it is clear that an adverse intrauterine environment including fetal neuroinflammation from any cause may confer fetal brain injury and abnormal brain development. This damage may include the death of gray matter in the cerebellum, hippocampus, and cortex and may also include cerebral white matter damage causing long-term deficits in neural connectivity.

CONCLUSION: PRENATAL, PERINATAL, EPIGENETIC, AND IMMUNE SYSTEM RISK FACTORS LINK AUTISM TO OTHER OUTCOMES AND LACK CAUSAL SPECIFICITY FOR AUTISM

The many varied prenatal, perinatal, environmental, epigenetic, and immune system risk factors found in association with autism are risk factors for other adverse developmental outcomes. These adverse outcomes include early fetal loss, death of the newborn, congenital malformations, dysmorphic facial features, microcephaly, cerebral palsy, heart problems, blindness, impaired hearing, childhood cancer, and increased susceptibility to infections. Adverse outcomes also include the death of gray matter in the cerebellum, hippo-campus, and cortex, pervasive white matter damage, epilepsy, basal ganglia damage, a range of cognitive deficits, general developmental delay, intellec-tual disability, motor delay and motor deficits, language delay and language deficits, anxiety, schizophrenia, attention deficit/hyperactivity disorder, and increased susceptibility to other psychiatric disorders. The evidence for so many varied outcomes for prenatal, perinatal, epigenetic, and immune sys-tem risk factors for autism raises the question of causal specificity.

The Problem of Causal Specificity for Autism

In a strict interpretation of causal specificity, an environmental or genetic or gene–environment cause for a disorder must meet five conditions (Kendler, 2005). One, there must be a high strength of association between the cause and the disorder. Two, there must be clear specificity of a cause for a disor-der, such that the cause results in only the specific disorder and no other disorders. Three, there must be no contingent components of the causal claim, such as gene variant "ABCD" causes autism contingent on whether a mother did or did not take prenatal vitamins. Four, there must be close causal proximity between cause and disorder without many intervening additionally causal steps. Five, the causal claim must be at an appropriate level of explanation. Kendler (2005) asserted that none of these five condi-tions is met by evidence for genetic causes for psychiatric disorders. He pointed out that gene–disorder associations are often weak and non-specific, many gene effects are contingent on environmental effects, causal steps from gene to disorder are "embedded in causal pathways of stunning complexity" (p. 1250), and causal explanations for disorders most often do not match a genetic cause with a specific brain deficit.

A less stringent interpretation of causal specificity requires only that the first two conditions be met: there should be a significant association between cause and disorder; the cause should result exclusively in the specific disor-der. This chapter and Chapter 4 have outlined a wide range of evidence meeting the first condition. Many significant findings for increased risk for autism have been reported for prenatal, perinatal, epigenetic, immune sys-tem, gene variant, and chromosomal variant risk factors. However, no risk factors for autism have been clearly determined to meet the second condi-tion, causal exclusivity, where a cause results in autism symptoms, and only autism symptoms.

The problem of failing to meet this second condition of causal specific-ity for autism is exemplified in an immune disorder theory of autism proposed by Buehler (2011) and in the brain deficits reported by Lubsen et al. (2011) for premature infants. Buehler (2011) hypothesized that maternal infection, injury, and autoimmune disease triggered an overproduction of cytokines in the fetus that created a "cytokine-storm" that caused autism. However, Monji et al. (2012) and Meyer (2011) outlined parallel theories for increased cytokines causing schizophrenia. Monji et al. (2012) argued that evidence that perinatal infection can cause microglia to remain permanently activated into adulthood, together with evidence for elevated cytokines in schizophrenia, suggested that schizophrenia was caused by the prenatal or perinatal overproduction of proinflammatory cytokines released by permanently activated microglia. Meyer (2011) similarly argued, "developmental neuroinflammation induced by prenatal immune challenge ... may contribute to disease progression associated with the gradual development of full-blown schizophrenic disease" (p. 10). Girard, Sébire, and Kadhim (2010) reported that white matter damage in the brains of preterm infants was linked to elevated cytokines and linked to phenotypic outcomes of cerebral palsy and intellectual disability. Moreover, Monji et al. (2012) observed, "most, if not all, neuropathologies are to a various extent associated with activation of microglia and astrocytes" (p. 4).

Because early overproduction of cytokines has been found in association with disorders other than autism, such as schizophrenia, cerebral palsy, and intellectual disability, the theory that autism is a disorder defined by overproduction of cytokines (Buehler, 2011) lacks causal exclusivity for autism.

Lubsen et al. (2011) reported that oxygen deprivation was the major cause of impaired brain development in preterm infants, and that preterm infants were found to have globally and regionally smaller volumes of cortical gray and white matter than infants born at full term. Lubsen et al. (2011) noted that hemorrhage within the brain's ventricles and periventricular leukomalacia, the death of white matter patches around the brain's fluid-filled ventricles, were previously thought to cause the cognitive problems of preterm infants. Lubsen et al. (2011), however, proposed that because evidence has demonstrated that there is decreased white matter tract integrity throughout the brains of premature children, the neurocognitive deficits of prematurity are the result of disrupted white matter tracts throughout the brain.

If the model for premature brain deficit proposed by Lubsen et al. (2011) is correct, then prematurity confers diffuse and variable brain-wide white matter deficits, which result in a range of neonatal outcomes including cerebral palsy, motor deficit, attention deficit/hyperactivity disorder, developmental delay, intellectual disability, and autism. Thus, brain deficits resulting from the insult of prematurity are not deficits that specifically target the brain bases for autism symptoms, and yet, in some cases, autism symptoms do result from brain deficits caused by prematurity. However, even if Lubsen et al. (2011) were wrong, and brain ventricle hemorrhage and associated death of white matter patches around the ventricles were found to be the core cause of brain dysfunction of prematurity, neither do these ventricle brain deficits have specific causal exclusivity for autism symptoms.

Accepting the Absence of Causal Exclusivity for Autism as a Valid Finding

All available evidence indicates that known prenatal, perinatal, epigenetic, immune system, gene and chromosomal variant risk factors for autism cause many different patterns of brain deficits, and none of these brain deficit patterns specifically or exclusively causes autism. Losh et al. (2011) worried that it was "unclear how fetal growth restriction might influence brain development in ways specific to autism" (p. 8), and Mann et al. (2010) worried why "low birth weight can cause an insult that brings about both ASD and mental retardation or mental retardation alone, but not ASD alone" (p. 552). Leonard et al. (2011) wondered whether models of gene and environmental causes for autism "might just as likely produce any neurological phenotype" (p. 7), and Boucher (2011) wondered, "how the multiplicity of susceptibility factors underlying ASDs might in their different combinations" (p. 479) cause a unique autism brain deficit. Geschwind (2011) called on researchers to discover "how specific genetic risk variants lead to changes in neural circuitry and function" (p. 414) unique to autism. Losh et al. (2011), Mann et al. (2010), Leonard et al. (2011), Boucher (2011), and Geschwind (2011) each voiced the same implicit concern: What is the brain deficit exclusive to autism?

However, Amaral (2011) stated, "it is unlikely that a single diagnostic biomarker will be discovered that identifies individuals at risk for autism" (p. 6). This is because autism is two yoked symptoms, each of which can occur as the result of many different brain deficits.

The first diagnostic symptom of autism, social interaction impairment, is likely to occur when any of the many brain systems that govern human social behavior are disrupted. These systems include the detection of biological motion, face recognition, emotion recognition, emotion experience and expression, a drive to bond with others, pleasure in human physical contact, ability to communicate, and other component social skills. Chapter 3 outlined evidence demonstrating that social perception, cognition, and emotional expression depend on brain circuits in the prefrontal cortex, the frontal pole, the orbitofrontal cortex, the inferior frontal cortex, superior temporal sulcus, temporoparietal junction of the temporal lobe, inferior parietal cortex, cingulate cortex, fusiform gyrus, hippocampus, hypothalamus, amygdala, striatum, insula, and cerebellum. Chapter 3 also delineated evidence for a range of different dysfunctions in these brain regions and circuits in autism.

The second autism symptom of restricted and repetitive behaviors and/or sensory abnormalities is likely to result from disruption of a variety of brain systems regulating motor planning, motor systems, sensory systems, executive functions, reward circuits, motor repetition, motor inhibition, and other symptom-component skills (Barry, Baird, Lascelles, Bunton, & Hedderly, 2011; Leekam, Prior, & Uljarevic, 2011). Barry et al. (2011) stated, "the basal ganglia have been implicated through case reports describing the emergence of stereotyped behaviour following lesions of the putamen, orbitofrontal cortex, and thalamus" (p. 982). However, Barry et al. (2011) also reported that restricted and repetitive behavior might result from damage to frontal subcortical circuits or damage to dopamine circuits in the brain. Although Langen et al. (2012) found no overall difference in any striatal structure between adults with autism and typical controls, they found smaller total brain white matter volume in autism than controls, and suggested that reduced white matter volume might cause restricted and repetitive behavior in autism. Leekam, Nieto, Libby, Wing, and Gould (2007) reported that most individuals with autism have sensory system impairment in several sensory domains. Sensory abnormalities include deficits in acuity and hyper- and hyposensitivity to sensory stimuli.

Causal specificity would require that *only* brain circuits mediating specific social and specific motor and/or specific sensory behaviors would be disrupted, generating *only* autism diagnostic symptoms. However, as outlined in this chapter, and in Chapters 1, 2, 3, and 4, existing evidence for heterogeneity in brain deficits suggests there are likely to be many different combinations of brain disruptions that could result in autism diagnostic symptoms. Equally important, most risk factors found for autism cause even more widespread brain disruption than the many varied brain circuit deficits known and hypothesized for autism. Consequently, as claimed by Amaral (2011), it is improbable that one brain deficit will be found that consolidates or accounts for the many varied brain deficits in autism, while leaving all other brain functions intact. In addition, even if such a comprehensive brain deficit were discovered, that comprehensive brain deficit would have to have causal specificity for autism diagnostic symptoms, and no other symptoms.

Another neurobiological impediment to finding a cause exclusive to autism symptoms is the interconnectedness of the many different brain systems that when disrupted result in the two autism diagnostic symptoms. As van den Heuvel and Sporns (2011) asserted, "brain function is not solely attributable to individual regions and connections, but rather emerges from the topology of the network as a whole" (p. 15775). Therefore, when a risk factor causes a network of deficits in the brain, including those brain deficits that mediate autism symptoms, it is likely that the complete disrupted brain network will also cause symptoms beyond those defined for autism.

Theorists have proposed many interconnected networks in the brain. Bassett, Brown, Deshpande, Carlson, and Grafton (2011) proposed that information processing organized hundreds of regions and thousands of interconnected white matter networks into a "hierarchically modular structure of anatomical connectivity" (p. 1275). Rubinov and Sporns (2010) described the difference between anatomical neuron-to-neuron brain interconnections, and functional co-activation brain interconnections in which there was co-activation of brain regions and circuits for which there was no anatomical connection. Rubinov and Sporns (2010) proposed that functional networks maintain "numerous connections between anatomically unconnected regions" (p. 1065) and that as anatomical connections become sparse, functional connectivity remains dense.

van den Heuvel and Sporns (2011) proposed that information processing was organized around two densely connected mega-hubs: bilateral frontoparietal regions, including the precuneus and superior frontal and parietal cortex, and subcortical regions including the hippocampus, thalamus, and putamen. However, van den Heuvel and Sporns (2011) stated that the "communication hubs of the brain do not operate as individual entities, but instead act as a strongly interlinked collective" (p. 15784).

Researchers have identified large-scale networks in the brain. Disruption of these networks has been found in autism. Power et al. (2011) identified four large information-processing networks in the brain: the default mode network, somatosensory network, the visual network, and the frontoparietal control network. Bressler and Menon (2010) identified three large networks. One was the central-executive network, situated in the dorsolateral prefrontal and posterior parietal cortices, proposed to regulate higher-order attention and control. The second was the default-mode network, situated in the ventromedial prefrontal cortex, proposed to regulate autobiographical, self-monitoring, and social cognitive functions. The third was the salience network, situated in the anterior insular and dorsal anterior cingulate cortices but densely interconnected with brain circuits for reward and motivation, proposed to regulate attention switching between the default-mode network focused inside the self, and the central-executive network focused on the world outside the self.

All three of the large networks outlined by Bressler and Menon (2010)—central-executive network, default-mode network, and salience network—have been found to be impaired in autism (Gomot & Wicker, 2012; Taylor, Donner, & Pang, 2012; Uddin et al., 2011).

Many defined networks operate within these broader networks. Dysfunction in empathy has been reported for autism (Schulte-Rüther et al., 2011), and Cox et al. (2012) outlined four subordinate networks contributing to empathy. They reported that the brains of typical adults with strong affective empathy demonstrated stronger functional connectivity in four subordinate social–emotional networks: one, a ventral anterior insula–orbital frontal cortex–subcallosal cortex–amygdala network; two, an amygdala–orbital frontal cortex–temporal pole–ventral anterior insula network; three, an amygdala–anterior cingulate gyrus network; and four, an orbital frontal–paracingulate gyrus network.

The action observation network has been found to be impaired in autism (Enticott et al., 2011; Rizzolatti & Fabbri-Destro, 2010) and Ramsey, Cross, and de C. Hamilton (2012) found two separate circuits within the action observation network. They reported that when typical adults observed another person staring at an object, the left anterior inferior parietal lobule and parietal operculum of the typical adults showed heightened response, but when typical adults observed another person grasping an object, premotor, posterior parietal, fusiform, and middle occipital brain regions showed heightened response. Ramsey et al. (2012) concluded that different parts of the action observation network are active when we see someone staring at an object than when we see someone picking up an object.

The evidence for disruptions in larger brain networks in autism reinforces the conclusion drawn from the evidence for many widely distributed brain circuit disruptions in autism. Autism symptoms are found with a range of non-diagnostic symptoms because of the effects of widespread dysfunctions in the brain.

The Meaning of the Absence of Causal Exclusivity in Autism

As argued above, the many networks of the brain and the existence of multiple brain circuits that serve typical social and motor behavior make it unlikely that any risk factor will be found that demonstrates causal specificity for autism. Kendler (2005) concluded that no gene or genes associated with *any* psychiatric disorder would be found to have causal specificity and exclusivity, and he predicted risk genes would be cross-associated with different psychiatric disorders in a many-to-many relationship, wherein each gene caused several phenotypes and each phenotype was caused by several genes. Kendler's (2005) model fits both the genetic and environmental findings for autism. None of the known risk factors for autism is causally exclusive to autism, and many different combinations of brain deficits result in the diagnostic symptoms of autism. Therefore, the failure to find a brain deficit that is causally exclusive for autism is meaningful.

The Conundrum: Is Autism a Meaningful Diagnosis?

Leventhal (2012) affirmed the two DSM-5 symptoms as valid components of autism, stating, "the parsimonious model that lumped all known ASD signs and symptoms into two factors was statistically significant, with a more than satisfactory level of specificity" (p. 6). But other findings have found no correlation between the two symptoms. Robinson et al. (2012) reported that data from 5944 typical twin pairs revealed, "While genetic effects were substantial within each [autism symptom] domain, there was limited genetic overlap between domains" (p. 7). Identical and fraternal twins had non-significant cross-twin correlations ranging from .02 to .19 between the two DSM-5 autism symptoms of social impairment and restricted and repetitive behaviors and interests. Yet another problem for the two proposed DSM-5 diagnostic symptoms was noted by Szatmari (2011). He pointed out, "social communication and repetitive behaviours may not be the most useful for categorising children with autistic spectrum disorder ... because variation in these dimensions seems to be only weakly associated with variation in outcome and response to treatment, which are more closely related to cognitive and language abilities" (p. 2). Moreover, Coleman and Gillberg (2012) noted that "the more autism is studied the greater the trend toward heterogeneity, both phenotypic as well as genetic" (p. 341).

Given the increasing heterogeneity in autism causes, autism brain deficits, and autism phenotypic presentations, along with an exploding prevalence, it is not clear what the next step should be. Kendler (2005) stated that the function of causal genes could not be understood in relation to psychiatric diagnoses, but could only be understood at the more basic level of "biological processes (e.g., neuronal cell migrations during development) and/or mental functions (e.g., processing of threat stimuli)" (p. 1250). Sweeney (2011) argued that psychiatry "may come to accept that major mental illnesses comprise a continuum of pathology with only modestly distinct clinical syndromes that have highly overlapping and heterogeneous clinical features and etiology" (p. 19). Keshavan, Nasrallah, and Tandon (2011) argued that defining "complex psychiatric disorders based on overt externally observable phenotypes (such as behaviors) is not optimal for determining etiology of these entities" (p. 8). Keshavan et al. (2011) proposed that schizophrenia was a poorly defined disorder, and that "the current world of schizophrenia likely includes multiple phenotypically overlapping syndromes and diseases, and that the unitary concept of schizophrenia may have outlived its usefulness" (p. 11).

Has the unitary concept of autism outlived its usefulness? Coleman and Gillberg (2012) claimed that unifying features of autism were not required, because "the autisms represent a group of conditions with multiple etiologies" (p. 6). Amaral (2011) argued that because there were not "even a few genetic smoking guns for autism confirms … that autism spectrum disorders are, in fact, a large number of syndromes that manifest in behavioral alterations consistent with the diagnosis of autism" (p. 5). For these reasons, and because it is unlikely that any causally exclusive brain deficit will be found to cause only autism diagnostic symptoms, it seems clear that the unitary concept of autism has outlived its usefulness.

The next step in disbanding the concept of autism as a unitary disorder should be the acceptance of the totality of an individual's symptoms as part of the disorder of that individual. Each risk factor for autism would be accepted as the causal source of all the symptoms an individual might express. For example, if a child who was extremely premature and had a very low birth weight expressed diagnostic social impairment and restricted and repetitive behaviors, but also expressed intellectual disability, motor delay, and attention deficits, the child should be identified as having all symptoms. The child should not be considered to have autism with comorbid intellectual disability, motor delay, and attention deficits. Accepting the full range of an individual's symptoms, resulting from a risk factor, without segregating autism diagnostic symptoms, has the scientific value of "saving the phenomena" of all the deficits and impairments associated with a risk factor.

However, accepting the full range of an individual's symptoms resulting from a specific risk factor does not logically lead to the idea of "the autisms" or the concept of many autism spectrum syndromes. It argues instead for accepting the risk factor as the defining principle for identifying a disorder. Individuals with autism symptoms and Rett syndrome or tuberous sclerosis or Down syndrome or Angelman syndrome, or who had been born prematurely would be classified by causal etiology. Only where autism symptoms appeared without *any* other identified psychiatric, neurocognitive, or medical symptoms and without any known etiology would autism be a primary diagnosis. This shift would open the door for research focused on children with autism and non-autism symptoms who share etiologies, and research on those children who express *only* autism symptoms and share a brain deficit.

Moreover, somewhat surprisingly, in light of the evidence for all known causal risk factors for autism, the assumption that most risk factors are likely to cause a complex phenotype of autism and non-autism symptoms is a conservative scientific assumption. Conversely, the current research assumption that an environmental or genetic risk factor could generate a unified comprehensive brain deficit that would cause *only* autism symptoms is highly speculative because this assumption stands against the accumulated evidence for complex phenotypes.

This is not a neat or satisfying solution to the problem of autism. It does not argue that all the various possible epigenetic, genetic, chromosomal, prenatal, or perinatal risk factors converge on a single brain deficit unifying autism as a disorder. Nor does this view argue that specific distinct brain regions are disrupted in specific behavioral subgroups of autism. Nor does this view argue that there is a spectrum of autism disorders, or that many thousands of autism syndromes exist. Instead it argues that the path to translational research requires understanding that social impairment and restricted and repetitive behavior and/or sensory abnormalities are symptoms and not a disorder. The best hope for translational research is knowledge of the etiology and the full range of symptoms and brain deficits associated with that etiology.

Because there is no unique unifying deficit, and because there is no evidence for causal specificity for autism, there is a clear detriment to maintaining the diagnostic category of autism spectrum disorder. The diagnosis misguides researchers, parents, professionals, and the public into the illusory belief that research will find a unifying deficit that would lead to a "cure" for the autism spectrum. Equally important, this illusion has driven the expenditure of an enormous amount of research effort in a continuing series of failed quests to unify autism.

272   Rethinking Autism

REFERENCES

Abdallah, M. W., Larsen, N., Grove, J., Nørgaard-Pedersen, B., Thorsen, P., Mortensen, E. L., et al. (2012). Amniotic fluid chemokines and autism spectrum disorders: An exploratory study utilizing a Danish Historic Birth Cohort. *Brain and Behavior Immunology*, *26*, 1970–1976.

Amaral, D. G. (2011). The promise and the pitfalls of autism research: An introductory note for new autism researchers. *Brain Research*, *1380*, 3–9.

Arranga, E. (2011). *BMJ speaks gibberish*. Retrieved December 13, 2011 from the Age of Autism website, http://www.ageofautism.com/2011/12/the-war-on-science-the-british-medical-journal-dr-wakefield.html.

Ashwood, P., Corbett, B. A., Kantor, A., Schulman, H., Van de Water, J., & Amaral, D. G. (2011a). In search of cellular immunophenotypes in the blood of children with autism. *PLoS ONE*, *6*, e19299.

Ashwood, P., Krakowiak, P., Hertz-Picciotto, I., Hansen, R., Pessah, I. N., & Van de Water, J. (2011b). Altered T cell responses in children with autism. *Brain Behavior and Immunology*, *25*, 840–849.

Atladóttir, H. O., Pedersen, M. G., Thorsen, P., Mortensen, P. B., Deleuran, B., Eaton, W. W., et al. (2009). Association of family history of autoimmune diseases and autism spectrum disorders. *Pediatrics*, *124*, 687–694.

Atladóttir, H. O., Thorsen, P., Østergaard, L., Schendel, D. E., Lemcke, S., Abdallah, M., et al. (2010). Maternal infection requiring hospitalization during pregnancy and autism spectrum disorders. *Journal of Autism and Developmental Disorders*, *40*, 1423–1430.

Autism Rights Watch—Project France. (2012, February). *Exclusive: Translation of the court decision of Jan. 26, 2012 "The Wall" (Sophie Robert) vs. Psychoanalysts*. Retrieved April 2, 2012 from, http://www.supportthewall.org/2012/02/exclusive-translation-of-the-court-decision-of-jan-26-2012-the-wall-sophie-robert-vs-psychoanalysts.

Barlow, D. P. (2011). Genomic imprinting: A mammalian epigenetic discovery model. *Annual Review of Genetics*, *45*, 379–403.

Barry, S., Baird, G., Lascelles, K., Bunton, P., & Hedderly, T. (2011). Neurodevelopmental movement disorders—An update on childhood motor stereotypies. *Developmental Medicine and Child Neurology*, *53*, 979–985.

Bassett, D. S., Brown, J. A., Deshpande, V., Carlson, J. M., & Grafton, S. T. (2011). Conserved and variable architecture of human white matter connectivity. *Neuroimage*, *54*, 1262–1279.

Ben Itzchak, E., Lahat, E., & Zachor, D. A. (2011). Advanced parental ages and low birth weight in autism spectrum disorders—Rates and effect on functioning. *Research in Developmental Disabilities*, *32*, 1776–1781.

Berger, B. E., Navar-Boggan, A. M., & Omer, S. B. (2011). Congenital rubella syndrome and autism spectrum disorder prevented by rubella vaccination—United States, 2001–2010. *BMC Public Health*, *19*, 340.

Betancur, C., Leboyer, M., & Gillberg, C. (2002). Increased rate of twins among affected sibling pairs with autism. *American Journal of Human Genetics*, *70*, 1381–1383.

Bettleheim, B. (1967). *The empty fortress: Infantile autism and the birth of the self*. New York, NY: The Free Press.

Bjerkedal, T., Kristensen, P., Skjere, G. A., & Brevik, J. I. (2007). Intelligence test scores and birth order among young Norwegian men (conscripts) analyzed within and between families. *Intelligence*, *35*, 503–514.

Black, M. M. (2008). Effects of vitamin B12 and folate deficiency on brain development in children. *Food Nutrition Bulletin*, *29*, S126–S131.

Black, R. E., Allen, L. H., Bhutta, Z. A., Caulfield, L. E., de Onis, M., Ezzati, M., et al. (2008). Maternal and child undernutrition: Global and regional exposures and health consequences. *Lancet*, *371*, 243–260.

Borchers, A. T., Naguwa, S. M., Keen, C. L., & Gershwin, M. E. (2010). The implications of autoimmunity and pregnancy. *Journal of Autoimmunity, 34*, J287–J299.

Boucher, J. (2011). Redefining the concept of autism as a unitary disorder: Multiple causal deficits of a single kind? In D. Fein (Ed.), *The neuropsychology of autism* (pp. 469–482). New York, NY: Oxford University Press.

Bressler, S. L., & Menon, V. (2010). Large-scale brain networks in cognition: Emerging methods and principles. *Trends in Cognitive Science, 14*, 277–290.

Buehler, M. R. (2011). A proposed mechanism for autism: An aberrant neuroimmune response manifested as a psychiatric disorder. *Medical Hypotheses, 76*, 863–870.

Burstyn, I., Sithole, F., & Zwaigenbaum, L. (2010). Autism spectrum disorders, maternal characteristics and obstetric complications among singletons born in Alberta, Canada. *Chronic Diseases of Canada, 30*, 125–134.

Burstyn, I., Wang, X., Yasui, Y., Sithole, F., & Zwaigenbaum, L. (2011). Autism spectrum disorders and fetal hypoxia in a population-based cohort: Accounting for missing exposures via Estimation-Maximization algorithm. *BMC Medical Research Methodology, 5*, 1–9.

Cedillo v Secretary of Health and Human Services, No. 98–916V (USCFC Spec Mstr 2009).

Cheslack-Postava, K., Liu, K., & Bearman, P. B. (2011). Closely spaced pregnancies are associated with increased odds of autism in California sibling births. *Pediatrics, 137*, 246–253.

Chess, S. (1971). Autism in children with congenital rubella. *Journal of Autism and Childhood Schizophrenia, 1*, 33–47.

Chess, S. (1977). Follow-up report on autism in congenital rubella. *Journal of Autism and Childhood Schizophrenia, 7*, 69–81.

CNN Health News. (2009). *Vaccines didn't cause autism, court rules.* February 12, 2009. Retrieved from, http://articles.cnn.com/2009-02-12/health/autism.vaccines_1_childhood-vaccines-autism-autistic-children?_s=PM2009 HEALTH on December 11, 2011.

Coleman, M., & Gillberg, C. (2012). *The autisms* (4th ed.). New York: Oxford University Press.

Cox, C. L., Uddin, L. Q., Di Martino, A., Castellanos, F. X., Milham, M. P., & Kelly, C. (2012). The balance between feeling and knowing: affective and cognitive empathy are reflected in the brain's intrinsic functional dynamics. *Social Cognitive and Affective Neuroscience.* [Epub September 11, 2011]. doi: 10.1093/scan/nsr051.

Croen, L. A., Connors, S. L., Matevia, M., Qian, Y., Newschaffer, C., & Zimmerman, A. W. (2011a). Prenatal exposure to β2-adrenergic receptor agonists and risk of autism spectrum disorders. *Journal of Neurodevelopmental Disorders, 3*, 307–315.

Croen, L. A., Grether, J. K., Yoshida, C. K., Odouli, R., & Hendrick, V. (2011b). Antidepressant use during pregnancy and childhood autism spectrum disorders. *Archives of General Psychiatry, 68*, 1104–1112.

Croen, L. A., Najjar, D. V., Fireman, B., & Grether, J. K. (2007). Maternal and paternal age and risk of autism spectrum disorders. *Archives of Pediatrics and Adolescence Medicine, 161*, 334–340.

D'Angelo, D. V., Whitehead, N., Helms, K., Barfield, W., & Ahluwalia, I. B. (2011). Birth outcomes of intended pregnancies among women who used assisted reproductive technology, ovulation stimulation, or no treatment. *Fertility and Sterility, 96*, 314–320.e2.

de Leon-Guerrero, S. D., Pedraza-Alva, G., & Pérez-Martínez, L. (2011). In sickness and in health: The role of methyl-CpG binding protein 2 in the central nervous system. *European Journal of Neuroscience, 33*, 1563–1574.

Deer, B. (2008). The MMR–autism crisis—Our story so far. *The Sunday Times.* February 22, 2004; updated August 10, 2008. Retrieved August 20, 2008 from http://briandeer.com/mmr/lancet-summary.html.

Deer, B. (2011a). How the case against the MMR vaccine was fixed. *British Medical Journal, 342*, c5347.

Deer, B. (2011b). Pathology reports solve "new bowel disease" riddle. *British Medical Journal, 343*, d6823.

Dietert, R. R., Dietert, J. M., & DeWitt, J. C. (2011). Environmental risk factors for autism. *Emerging Health Threats Journal, 4*, 7111.

Dodds, L., Fell, D. B., Shea, S., Armson, B. A., Allen, A. C., & Bryson, S. (2011). The role of prenatal, obstetric and neonatal factors in the development of autism. *Journal of Autism and Developmental Disorders, 41*, 891–902.

Dregan, A., Brown, J., & Armstrong, D. (2011). Do adult emotional and behavioural outcomes vary as a function of diverse childhood experiences of the public care system? *Psychological Medicine, 41*, 2213–2220.

Dufour-Rainfray, D., Vourc'h, P., Tourlet, S., Guilloteau, D., Chalon, S., & Andres, C. R. (2011). Fetal exposure to teratogens: Evidence of genes involved in autism. *Neuroscience and Biobehavioral Reviews, 35*, 1264–1265.

Durkin, M. S., Maenner, M. J., Newschaffer, C. J., Lee, L. C., Cunniff, C. M., Daniels, J. L., et al. (2008). Advanced parental age and the risk of autism spectrum disorder. *American Journal of Epidemiology, 168*, 1268–1276.

Elsabbagh, M., Mercure, E., Hudr, K., Chandler, S., Pasco, G., Charman, T., et al. (2012). Infant neural sensitivity to dynamic eye gaze is associated with later emerging autism. *Current Biology, 22*, 1–5.

Emanuele, E., Orsi, P., Boso, M., Broglia, D., Brondino, N., Barale, F., et al. (2010). Low-grade endotoxemia in patients with severe autism. *Neuroscience Letters, 471*, 162–165.

Emerson, E., & Parish, S. (2010). Intellectual disability and poverty: Introduction to the special section. *Journal of Intellectual & Developmental Disability, 35*, 221–223.

Enticott, P. G., Kennedy, H. A., Rinehart, N. J., Tonge, B. J., Bradshaw, J. L., Taffe, J. R., et al. (2011). Mirror neuron activity associated with social impairments but not age in autism spectrum disorder. *Biological Psychiatry, 71*, 427–433.

Feldman, M. A., Ward, R. A., Savona, D., Regehr, K., Parker, K., Hudson, M., et al. (2011). Development and initial validation of a parent report measure of the behavioral development of infants at risk for autism spectrum disorders. *Journal of Autism and Developmental Disorders, 42*, 13–22.

Flaherty, D. K. (2011). The vaccine–autism connection: A public health crisis caused by unethical medical practices and fraudulent science. *Annals of Pharmacotherapy, 45*, 1302–1304.

Fradin, D., Cheslack-Postava, K., Ladd-Acosta, C., Newschaffer, C., Chakravarti, A., Arking, D. E., et al. (2010). Parent-of-origin effects in autism identified through genome-wide linkage analysis of 16,000 SNPs. *PLoS ONE, 5*, e12513.

Gardener, H., Spiegelman, D., & Buka, S. L. (2009). Prenatal risk factors for autism: Comprehensive meta-analysis. *British Journal of Psychiatry, 195*, 7–14.

Gardener, H., Spiegelman, D., & Buka, S. L. (2011). Perinatal and neonatal risk factors for autism: A comprehensive meta-analysis. *Pediatrics, 128*, 344–355.

Girard, S., Sébire, G., & Kadhim, H. (2010). Proinflammatory orientation of the interleukin 1 system and downstream induction of matrix metalloproteinase 9 in the pathophysiology of human perinatal white matter damage. *Journal of Neuropathology and Experimental Neurology, 69*, 1116–1129.

Glasson, E. J., Bower, C., Petterson, B., deKlerk, N., Chaney, G., & Hallmayer, J. F. (2004). Perinatal factors and the development of autism: A population study. *Archives of General Psychiatry, 61*, 618–627.

Gomot, M., & Wicker, B. (2012). A challenging, unpredictable world for people with Autism Spectrum Disorder. *International Journal of Psychophysiology, 83*, 240–247.

Grafodatskaya, D., Chung, B., Szatmari, P., & Weksberg, R. (2010). Autism spectrum disorders and epigenetics. *Journal of the American Academy of Child and Adolescent Psychiatry, 49*, 794–809.

Grisaru-Granovsky, S., Reichman, B., Lerner-Geva, L., Boyko, V., Hammerman, C., Samueloff, A., et al. (2012). Mortality and morbidity in preterm small-for-gestational-age infants: A population-based study. *American Journal of Obstetrics and Gynecology, 206*(150), e1–e7.

Guinchat,V., Chamak, B., Bonniau, B., Bodeau, N., Perisse, D., Cohen, D., et al. (2012a).Very early signs of autism reported by parents include many concerns not specific to autism criteria. *Research in Autism Spectrum Disorders, 6,* 589–601.

Guinchat,V.,Thorsen, P., Laurent, C., Cans, C., Bodeau, N., & Cohen, D. (2012b). Pre-, peri-, and neonatal risk factors for autism. *Acta Obstetrica Gynecologica Scandanavia, 91,* 287–300.

Guy, J., Cheval, H., Selfridge, J., & Bird, A. (2011).The role of MeCP2 in the brain. *Annual Review of Cell and Developmental Biology, 27,* 631–652.

Hallmayer, J., Cleveland, S.,Torres, A., Phillips, J., Cohen, B.,Torigoe,T., et al. (2011). Genetic heritability and shared environmental factors among twin pairs with autism. *Archives of General Psychiatry, 68,* 1095–1102. doi: 10.1001/archgenpsychiatry.2011.76.

Harvard Mental Health Letter. (2011). Autism spectrum disorders revisited. Several recent studies raise new questions about cause and prevention. *October, 28*(4), 1–3.

Hawdon, J. M. (2011). Babies born after diabetes in pregnancy:What are the short- and long-term risks and how can we minimise them? *Best Practices Research in Clinical Obstetrics and Gynaecology, 25,* 91–104.

Hazlehurst v Secretary of Health and Human Services, No. 03–654V (USCFC Sp Mstr 2009).

Hehir-Kwa, J.Y., Rodríguez-Santiago, B.,Vissers, L. E., de Leeuw, N., Pfundt, R., Buitelaar, J. K., et al. (2011). De novo copy number variants associated with intellectual disability have a paternal origin and age bias. *Journal of Medical Genetics, 48,* 776–778.

Helderman, J. B., O'Shea,T. M., Kuban, K. C.,Allred, E. N., Hecht, J. L., Dammann, O., et al. (2012). Antenatal antecedents of cognitive impairment at 24 months in extremely low gestational age newborns. *Pediatrics, 129,* 494–502.

Hess, C. R., & Landa, R. J. (2012). Predictive and concurrent validity of parent concern about young children at risk for autism. *Journal of Autism and Developmental Disorders, 42,* 575–584.

Hultman, C. M., Sandin, S., Levine, S. Z., Lichtenstein, P., & Reichenberg, A. (2011).Advancing paternal age and risk of autism: New evidence from a population-based study and a meta-analysis of epidemiological studies. *Molecular Psychiatry, 16,* 1203–1212.

Hultman, C. M., Sparén, P., & Cnattingius, S. (2002). Perinatal risk factors for infantile autism. *Epidemiology, 13,* 417–423.

Hvidtjørn, D., Grove, J., Schendel, D., Schieve, L. A., Sværke, C., Ernst, E., et al. (2011). Risk of autism spectrum disorders in children born after assisted conception: A population-based follow-up study. *Journal of Epidemiology and Community Health, 65.* 497–502.

Hvidtjørn, D., Schieve, L., Schendel, D., Jacobsson, B., Svaerke, C., & Thorsen, P. (2009). Cerebral palsy, autism spectrum disorders, and developmental delay in children born after assisted conception: A systematic review and meta-analysis. *Archives of Pediatric and Adolescent Medicine, 163,* 72–83.

Jessen, H. M., & Auger, A. P. (2011). Sex differences in epigenetic mechanisms may underlie risk and resilience for mental health disorders. *Epigenetics, 6,* 857–861.

Keelan, J., & Wilson, K. (2011). Balancing vaccine science and national policy objectives: Lessons from the National Vaccine Injury Compensation Program Omnibus Autism Proceedings. *American Journal of Public Health, 101,* 2016–2021.

Keil, A., Daniels, J. L., Forssen, U., Hultman, C., Cnattingius, S., Söderberg, K. C., et al. (2010). Parental autoimmune diseases associated with autism spectrum disorders in offspring. *Epidemiology, 21,* 805–808.

Kendler, K. S. (2005). "A gene for": The nature of gene action in psychiatric disorders. *American Journal of Psychiatry, 162,* 1243–1252.

Keshavan, M. S., Nasrallah, H. A., & Tandon, R. (2011). Schizophrenia, "Just the Facts" 6. Moving ahead with the schizophrenia concept: From the elephant to the mouse. *Schizophrenia Research, 127,* 3–13.

Kessler, R. C., Avenevoli, S., Costello, E. J., Georgiades, K., Green, J. G., Gruber, M. J., et al. (2012). Prevalence, persistence, and sociodemographic correlates of DSM-IV disorders in the National Comorbidity Survey Replication Adolescent Supplement. *Archives of General Psychiatry, 69*, 381–389.

King, M. D., Fountain, C., Dakhlallah, D., & Bearman, P. S. (2009). Estimated autism risk and older reproductive age. *American Journal of Public Health, 99*, 1673–1679.

Kirby, D. (2011). *The autism-vaccine debate: Why it won't go away.* Huffingtonpost.com. Retrieved February 20, 2011 from http://www.huffingtonpost.com/david-kirby/autism-vaccine-_b_817879.html.

Kolevzon, A., Gross, R., & Reichenberg, A. (2007). Prenatal and perinatal risk factors for autism—A review and integration of findings. *Archives of Pediatrics and Adolescence Medicine, 161*, 326–333.

Kopsida, E., Mikaelsson, M. A., & Davies, W. (2011). The role of imprinted genes in mediating susceptibility to neuropsychiatric disorders. *Hormones and Behavior, 59*, 375–382.

Krakowiak, P., Walker, C. K., Bremer, A. A., Baker, A. S., Ozonoff, S., Hansen, R. L., et al. (2012). Maternal metabolic conditions and risk for autism and other neurodevelopmental disorders. *Pediatrics.* [Epub April 9, 2012].

Kuban, K. C., O'Shea, T. M., Allred, E. N., Tager-Flusberg, H., Goldstein, D. J., & Leviton, A. (2009). Positive screening on the Modified Checklist for Autism in Toddlers (M-CHAT) in extremely low gestational age newborns. *Journal of Pediatrics, 154*, 535–540.

Kuehn, B. M. (2009). Autism study. *Journal of the American Medical Association, 302*, 375.

Langen, M., Leemans, A., Johnston, P., Ecker, C., Daly, E., Murphy, C. M., et al. (2012). Fronto-striatal circuitry and inhibitory control in autism: Findings from diffusion tensor imaging tractography. *Cortex, 48*, 183–193.

Larsson, H. J., Eaton, W. W., Madsen, K. M., Vestergaard, M., Olesen, A. V., Agerbo, E., et al. (2005). Risk factors for autism: Perinatal factors, parental psychiatric history, and socioeconomic status. *American Journal of Epidemiology, 161*, 916–925.

Lauritsen, M. B., Pedersen, C. B., & Mortensen, P. B. (2005). Effects of familial risk factors and place of birth on the risk of autism: A nationwide register-based study. *Journal of Child Psychology and Psychiatry, 46*, 963–971.

Lee, L. C., Newschaffer, C. J., Lessler, J. T., Lee, B. K., Shah, R., & Zimmerman, A. W. (2008). Variation in season of birth in singleton and multiple births concordant for autism spectrum disorders. *Pediatric Perinatology and Epidemiology, 22*, 172–179.

Leekam, S. R., Nieto, C., Libby, S. J., Wing, L., & Gould, J. (2007). Describing the sensory abnormalities of children and adults with autism. *Journal of Autism and Developmental Disorders, 37*, 894–910.

Leekam, S. R., Prior, M. R., & Uljarevic, M. (2011). Restricted and repetitive behaviors in autism spectrum disorders: A review of research in the last decade. *Psychological Bulletin, 137*, 562–593.

Leonard, H., Glasson, E., Nassar, N., Whitehouse, A., Bebbington, A., Bourke, J., et al. (2011). Autism and intellectual disability are differentially related to sociodemographic background at birth. *PLoS ONE, 6*, e17875.

Leventhal, B. L. (2012). Lumpers and splitters: Who knows? Who cares? *Journal of the American Academy of Child and Adolescent Psychiatry, 51*, 6–7.

Libbey, J. E., Sweeten, T. L., McMahon, W. M., & Fujinami, R. S. (2005). Autistic disorder and viral infections. *Journal of Neurovirology, 11*, 1–10.

Limperopoulos, C. (2009). Autism spectrum disorders in survivors of extreme prematurity. *Clinics in Perinatology, 36*, 791–805.

Limperopoulos, C., Bassan, H., Sullivan, N. R., Soul, J. S., Robertson, R. L., Jr., Moore, M., et al. (2008). Positive screening for autism in ex-preterm infants: Prevalence and risk factors. *Pediatrics, 121*, 758–765.

Losh, M., Esserman, D., Anckarsäter, H., Sullivan, P. F., & Lichtenstein, P. (2011). Lower birth weight indicates higher risk of autistic traits in discordant twin pairs. *Psychological Medicine, 2*, 1–12.

Lubsen, J., Vohr, B., Myers, E., Hampson, M., Lacadie, C., Schneider, K. C., et al. (2011). Microstructural and functional connectivity in the developing preterm brain. *Seminars in Perinatology*, *35*, 34–43.

Mann, J. R., McDermott, S., Bao, H., Hardin, J., & Gregg, A. (2010). Pre-eclampsia, birth weight, and autism spectrum disorders. *Journal of Autism and Developmental Disorder*, *40*, 548–554.

McCormick, M. C., Litt, J. S., Smith, V. C., & Zupancic, J. A. (2011). Prematurity: An overview and public health implications. *Annual Review of Public Health*, *21*, 367–379.

Meyer, U. (2011). Developmental neuroinflammation and schizophrenia. *Progress in NeuroPsychopharmacology and Biological Psychiatry*. [Epub November 16, 2011]. doi: 10.1016/j.pnpbp.2011.11.003.

Momeni, N., Brudin, L., Behnia, F., Nordstrom, B., Yosefi-Oudarji, A., Sivberg, B., et al. (2012). High complement factor I activity in the plasma of children with autism spectrum disorders. *Autism Research and Treatment*, Article ID 868576, 6. doi:10.1155/2012/868576.

Monji, A., Kato, T. A., Mizoguchi, Y., Horikawa, H., Seki, Y., Kasai, M., et al. (2012). Neuroinflammation in schizophrenia especially focused on the role of microglia. *Progress in Neuropsychopharmacology and Biological Psychiatry*. [Epub December 13, 2011]. doi:10.1016/j.pnpbp.2011.12.002.

Mouridsen, S. E., Rich, B., Isager, T., & Nedergaard, N. J. (2007). Autoimmune diseases in parents of children with infantile autism: A case-control study. *Developmental Medicine and Child Neurology*, *49*, 429–432.

Nguyen, A., Rauch, T. A., Pfeifer, G. P., & Hu, V. W. (2010). Global methylation profiling of lymphoblastoid cell lines reveals epigenetic contributions to autism spectrum disorders and a novel autism candidate gene, RORA, whose protein product is reduced in autistic brain. *FASEB Journal*, *24*, 3036–3051.

Nolte, T., Guiney, J., Fonagy, P., Mayes, L. C., & Luyten, P. (2011). Interpersonal stress regulation and the development of anxiety disorders: An attachment-based developmental framework. *Frontiers in Behavioral Neuroscience*, *5*, 55. [Epub]. doi: 10.3389/fnbeh.2011.00055.

Onore, C., Careaga, M., & Ashwood, P. (2012). The role of immune dysfunction in the pathophysiology of autism. *Brain Behavior and Immunity*, *26*, 383–392.

Ozonoff, S., Iosif, A. M., Baguio, F., Cook, I. C., Hill, M. M., Hutman, T., et al. (2010). A prospective study of the emergence of early behavioral signs of autism. *Journal of the American Academy of Child and Adolescent Psychiatry*, *49*, 256–266.

Parner, E. T., Baron-Cohen, S., Lauritsen, M. B., Jørgensen, M., Schieve, L. A., Yeargin-Allsopp, M., et al. (2012). Parental age and autism spectrum disorders. *Annals of Epidemiology*, *22*, 143–150.

Pérez-Dueñas, B., Ormazbal, A., Toma, C., Torrico, B., Cormand, B., Serrano, M., et al. (2011). Cerebral folate deficiency syndromes in childhood: Clinical, analytical, and etiologic aspects. *Archives of Neurology*, *68*, 615–621.

Pinborough-Zimmerman, J., Bilder, D., Bakian, A., Satterfield, R., Carbone, P. S., Nangle, B. E., et al. (2011). Sociodemographic risk factors associated with autism spectrum disorders and intellectual disability. *Autism Research*, *4*, 438–448.

Pinto-Martin, J. A., Levy, S. E., Feldman, J. F., Lorenz, J. M., Paneth, N., & Whitaker, A. H. (2011). Prevalence of autism spectrum disorder in adolescents born weighing <2000 grams. *Pediatrics*, *1*(28), 883–891.

Pitzer, M., Schmidt, M. H., Esser, G., & Laucht, M. (2001). Child development after maternal tocolysis with beta-sympathomimetic drugs. *Child Psychiatry and Human Development*, *31*, 165–182.

Ploeger, A., Raijmakers, M. E., van der Maas, H. L., & Galis, F. (2010). The association between autism and errors in early embryogenesis: What is the causal mechanism? *Biological Psychiatry*, *67*, 602–607.

Poland, G. A. (2011). MMR vaccine and autism: Vaccine nihilism and postmodern science. *Mayo Clinic Proceedings*, *86*, 869–871.

Poling v Secretary of Health and Human Services, No. 02–1466 (USCFC Spec Mstr 2008).

Pollack, R. (1997). *The creation of Dr. B: A biography of Bruno Bettelheim.* New York: Simon and Shuster.

Power, J. D., Cohen, A. L., Nelson, S. M., Wig, G. S., Barnes, K. A., Church, J. A., et al. (2011). Functional network organization of the human brain. *Neuron, 72,* 665–678.

Ramsey, R., Cross, E. S., & de C. Hamilton, A. F. (2012). Predicting others' actions via grasp and gaze: Evidence for distinct brain networks. *Psychological Research.* [Epub November 27, 2011]. doi: 10.1007/s00426-011-0393-9.

Rees, S., Harding, R., & Walker, D. (2011). The biological basis of injury and neuroprotection in the fetal and neonatal brain. *International Journal of Developmental Neuroscience, 29,* 551–563.

Reichenberg, A., Gross, R., Weiser, M., Bresnahan, M., Silverman, J., Harlap, S., et al. (2006). Advancing paternal age and autism. *Archives of General Psychiatry, 63,* 1026–1032.

Rizzolatti, G., & Fabbri-Destro, M. (2010). Mirror neurons: From discovery to autism. *Experimental Brain Research, 200,* 223–237.

Robinson, E. B., Koenen, K. C., McCormick, M. C., Munir, K., Hallett, V., Happé, F., et al. (2012). A multivariate twin study of autistic traits in 12-year-olds: Testing the fractionable autism triad hypothesis. *Behavior Genetics, 42,* 245–255.

Rocklin, R. E. (2011). Asthma, asthma medications and their effects on maternal/fetal outcomes during pregnancy. *Reproductive Toxicology, 32,* 189–197.

Rogaev, E. I. (2012). Genomics of behavioral diseases. *Frontiers in Genetics, 3,* 45. [Epub]. doi:10.3389/fgene.2012.00045.

Rosenberg, T., Pariente, G., Sergienko, R., Wiznitzer, A., & Sheiner, E. (2011). Critical analysis of risk factors and outcome of placenta previa. *Archives of Gynecology and Obstetrics, 284,* 47–51.

Rubinov, M., & Sporns, O. (2010). Complex network measures of brain connectivity: Uses and interpretations. *Neuroimage, 52,* 1059–1069.

Rutter, M., Kreppner, J., Croft, C., Murin, M., Colvert, E., Beckett, C., et al. (2007). Early adolescent outcomes of institutionally deprived and non-deprived adoptees. III. Quasi-autism. *Journal of Child Psychology and Psychology, 48,* 1200–1207.

Saijo, K., & Glass, C. K. (2011). Microglial cell origin and phenotypes in health and disease. *Nature Reviews Immunology, 11,* 775–787.

Schieve, L. A., Rice, C., Devine, O., Maenner, M. J., Lee, L. C., Fitzgerald, R., et al. (2011). Have secular changes in perinatal risk factors contributed to the recent autism prevalence increase? Development and application of a mathematical assessment model. *Annals of Epidemiology, 21,* 930–945.

Schmidt, R. J., Hansen, R. L., Hartiala, J., Allayee, H., Schmidt, L. C., Tancredi, D. J., et al. (2011). Prenatal vitamins, one-carbon metabolism gene variants, and risk for autism. *Epidemiology, 22,* 476–485.

Schofield, H. (2012, April 2). France's autism treatment "shame". *BBC News.* Retrieved April 7, 2012 from http://www.bbc.co.uk/news/magazine-17583123.

Schulte-Rüther, M., Greimel, E., Markowitsch, H. J., Kamp-Becker, I., Remschmidt, H., Fink, G. R., et al. (2011). Dysfunctions in brain networks supporting empathy: An fMRI study in adults with autism. *Social Neuroscience, 6,* 1–21.

Schwartz, J. L., & Caplan, A. L. (2011). Vaccination refusal: Ethics, individual rights, and the common good. *Primary Care Clinical Office Practice, 38,* 717–728.

Shamberger, R. J. (2011). Autism rates associated with nutrition and the WIC program. *Journal of the American College of Nutrition, 30,* 348–353.

Shelton, J. F., Tancredi, D. J., & Hertz-Picciotto, I. (2010). Independent and dependent contributions of advanced maternal and paternal ages to autism risk. *Autism Research, 3,* 30–39.

Sheridan, M., Drury, S., McLaughlin, K., & Almas, A. (2010). Early institutionalization: Neurobiological consequences and genetic modifiers. *Neuropsychological Review, 20,* 414–429.

Sicile-Kira, C. (2011). *French psychoanalysts take legal action to ban film "The Wall" about autism.* Posted: 12/5/11 06:57 PM ET. http://www.huffingtonpost.com/chantal-sicile-kira/the-wall-film-autism_b_1127680.html.

Snyder v Secretary of Health and Human Services, No. 01–162V (USCFC Spec Mstr 2009).

Stigler, K. A., Sweeten, T. L., Posey, D. J., & McDougle, C. J. (2009). Autism and immune factors: A comprehensive review. *Research in Autism Spectrum Disorders, 3*, 840–860.

Stratton, K., Ford, A., Rusch, E., & Clayton, E. W. (Eds.) (2011). *Committee to Review Adverse Effects of Vaccines; Institute of Medicine: Adverse effects of vaccines: evidence and causality*. The National Academies Press at http://www.nap.edu/catalog.php?record_id=13164.

Sweeney, J. A. (2011). Viewing the elephant from 200 feet: Reconstructing the schizophrenia syndrome. *Schizophrenia Research, 127*, 18–19.

Sweeten, T. L., Posey, D. J., & McDougle, C. J. (2004). Brief report: Autistic disorder in three children with cytomegalovirus infection. *Journal of Autism and Developmental Disorders, 34*, 583–586.

Szatmari, P. (2011). Is autism, at least in part, a disorder of fetal programming? *Archives of General Psychiatry, 68*, 1091–1092.

Tarkan, L. (2011). New study implicates environmental factors in autism. *New York Times*. July 4, 2011 http://www.nytimes.com/2011/07/05/health/research/05autism.html. Retrieved on July 4, 2011.

Taylor, M. J., Donner, E. J., & Pang, E. W. (2012). fMRI and MEG in the study of typical and atypical cognitive development. *Neuropsychology Clinics, 42*, 19–25.

Turner, B. M. (2011). Environmental sensing by chromatin: An epigenetic contribution to evolutionary change. *Federation of European Biochemical Societies Letters, 585*, 2032–2040.

Turner, T., Pihur, V., & Chakravarti, A. (2011). Quantifying and modeling birth order effects in autism. *PLoS ONE, 6*, e26418.

Uddin, L. Q., Menon, V., Young, C. B., Ryali, S., Chen, T., Khouzam, A., et al. (2011). Multivariate searchlight classification of structural magnetic resonance imaging in children and adolescents with autism. *Biological Psychiatry, 70*, 833–841.

van den Heuvel, M. P., & Sporns, O. (2011). Rich-club organization of the human connectome. *Journal of Neuroscience, 31*, 15775–15786.

Van Meter, K. C., Christiansen, L. E., Delwiche, L. D., Azari, R., Carpenter, T. E., & Hertz-Picciotto, I. (2010). Geographic distribution of autism in California: A retrospective birth cohort analysis. *Autism Research, 3*, 19–29.

Van Naarden Braun, K., Schieve, L., Daniels, J., Durkin, M., Giarelli, E., Kirby, R. S., et al. (2008). Relationships between multiple births and autism spectrum disorders, cerebral palsy, and intellectual disabilities: Autism and Developmental Disabilities Monitoring (ADDM) network—2002 surveillance year. *Autism Research, 1*, 266–274.

Vargas, D. L., Nascimbene, C., Krishnan, C., Zimmerman, A. W., & Pardo, C. A. (2005). Neuroglial activation and neuroinflammation in the brain of patients with autism. *Annals of Neurology, 57*, 67–81.

Voineagu, I., Wang, X., Johnston, P., Lowe, J. K., Tian, Y., Horvath, S., et al. (2011). Transcriptomic analysis of autistic brain reveals convergent molecular pathology. *Nature, 474*, 380–384.

Wakefield, A. J., Murch, S. H., Anthony, A., Linnell, J., Casson, D. M., Malik, M., et al. (1998). Ileal-lymphoid-nodular hyperplasia, non-specific colitis, and pervasive developmental disorder in children. *Lancet, 351*, 637–641.

Zachor, D. A., & Ben Itzchak, E. (2011). Assisted reproductive technology and risk for autism spectrum disorder. *Research in Developmental Disabilities, 32*, 2950–2956.

Zerbo, O., Iosif, A. M., Delwiche, L., Walker, C., & Hertz-Picciotto, I. (2011). Month of conception and risk of autism. *Epidemiology, 22*, 469–475.

Zheng, X., Chen, R., Li, N., Du, W., Pei, L., Zhang, J., & Yang, R. (2012). Socioeconomic status and children with intellectual disability in China. *Journal of Intellectual Disability Research, 56*, 212–220.

Ziats, M. N., & Rennert, O. M. (2011). Expression profiling of autism candidate genes during human brain development implicates central immune signaling pathways. *PLoS ONE, 6*, e24691.

CHAPTER 6

Savant Skills, Special Skills, and Intelligence Vary Widely in Autism

Contents

Rethinking Autism
http://dx.doi.org/10.1016/B978-0-12-415961-7.00006-X

"Jake Barnett is one in 10 million. He has been acing college math and science courses since he was 8 years old. Now 13, he attends college, where he tutors fellow students in math. Fascinated with astronomy, Barnett could probably calculate how much fuel it would take to get to his favorite planet, Saturn .... Barnett's unique talent is enabled by his ability to remember anything he wants. The boy can name 200 of the infinite numbers of pi all because he memorized them in a few hours .... His mind is overflowing with new physics problems and theories he often writes down on walls and windows. Does his head ever get cluttered? 'Not at all. I remember math and numbers. I don't remember other things'" (IUPUI News Center, 2012). Jacob Barnett was diagnosed with Asperger's syndrome at age 3, and at age 12, he enrolled at Indiana University attending Indiana University–Purdue University Indianapolis to take advanced astrophysics classes (McFeeley, 2011).

Savant skills, superior perceptual recognition and discrimination skills, unusual conditions of sensory perception, and general intelligence all vary widely in autism, and parallel prodigious skills, superior perceptual recognition and discrimination skills, unusual conditions of perception, and general intelligence all also vary widely in typical individuals. Treffert (1989) used the term savant syndrome to identify markedly exceptional performance in an individual diagnosed with autism spectrum disorder, as exemplified by Jacob Barnett, or with an intellectual disability. Miller (1998) defined savant skill as superior performance that is markedly higher than typical population performance, and markedly higher than all other skills of the individual. Although Ruthsatz and Detterman (2003) defined a prodigy as a child, "under 10 years of age who [can] perform culturally relevant tasks at a level that is rare even among highly trained professionals" (p. 509), most people would label such extraordinarily talented children as child prodigies. In this chapter, the word prodigy describes an individual of any age without autism or intellectual disability who has exhibited extraordinary skill in art, music, memory, or mental calculation. The word savant as used here describes an individual diagnosed with autism who has exhibited extraordinary or superior skill in art, music, memory, or mental calculation performance that is higher than typical population performance, and higher than all other skills of the individual.

Six Savant and Prodigious Skills

Table 6.1 illustrates that for every savant skill reported for autism the same skill has been reported for typical individuals. Table 6.1 lists six skills. They include extraordinary memory for numbers and facts (Hu, Ericsson, Yang, & Lu, 2009; Treffert, 2010), rapid mental mathematical calculation (Anderson, O'Connor, & Hermelin, 1999; Fehr, Weber, Willmes, & Herrmann, 2010), mental calendar calculation (Dubischar-Krivec et al., 2009; Fehr, Wallace, Erhard, & Herrmann, 2011; Heaton & Wallace, 2004), and extraordinary autobiographical memory (Kennedy & Squire, 2007; Sanders, 2011). Savant/prodigious skills also include accurate music replication after hearing a musical piece a single time (McPherson, 2007; Ockelford & Pring, 2005), and drawing an image or scene with detailed fidelity after viewing it for a single time (Crane, Pring, Ryder, & Hermelin, 2011; Drake & Winner, 2009; Golomb, 1999).

The following six sections present information about prodigies and savants with these extraordinary skills.

Extraordinary Memory for Numbers and Facts in Prodigies and Savants

Typical individuals who have demonstrated prodigious memory have come to public awareness through record setting. In 2004, Ken Jennings came to public attention in the United States as the record-holding winner of the most games on the US television show *Jeopardy!* This game show tested

Table 6.1 Comparison of Evidence for the Existence and Brain Basis of Prodigious/Savant Skills, Superior Auditory and Visual Discrimination and Recognition, Expertise in Pattern Perception and Discrimination, and Unusual Conditions of Perception in Typical Individuals and Individuals Diagnosed with Autism

Skill Type	Possible Memory Basis for Skill	Evidence for Skill in Typical Individuals	Exemplar Evidence for Skill Behavior, Brain Basis, and Skill Practice in Typical Individuals	Evidence for Skill in Individuals with Autism	Exemplar Evidence for Skill Behavior, Brain Basis, Skill Practice, and Impairment in Skill in Individuals with Autism
Six Extraordinary Skills Reported for Typical Individuals and Individuals with Autism					
Highly superior autobio- graphical memory (HSAM)	Event memory	YES (Parker et al., 2006)	11 individuals with HSAM (Stix, 2011) BEHAVIOR: All 11 recalled day's events when given specific dates BRAIN: Larger size of left temporoparietal junction, left posterior insula, and lentiform nucleus PRACTICE: Skill occurred without practice	YES (Kennedy & Squire, 2007)	1 savant with possible HSAM (Kennedy & Squire, 2007) BEHAVIOR: DG recalled day's events when given specific dates BRAIN: Not studied PRACTICE: Not known IMPAIRED SKILL IN AUTISM: Significantly impaired autobiographical memory (Maister & Plaisted-Grant, 2011; Zmigrod et al., 2012)

Exceptional memory for facts and numbers	Visual memory	YES (Hu et al., 2009)	1 memory prodigy (Hu et al., 2009) BEHAVIOR: Recited 67,890 decimal places of pi without error BRAIN: Average digit span, conscious strategy relies on visual memory and narrative memory as well PRACTICE: More than a year of intense practice encoding digits to words, those words to images, those images to a story of events at a specific location	YES (Neumann et al., 2010; Treffert, 2010)	1 memory savant (Tammet, 2007) BEHAVIOR: Recited 22,514 decimal places of pi without error in under 6 hours BRAIN: Early activation in right occipital areas might reflect use of visual memory PRACTICE: A year of intense practice
Extremely rapid mental math calculations	Computation skill	YES (Fehr et al., 2010)	1 math prodigy (Fehr et al., 2010) BEHAVIOR: Superior speed in complex mental calculations compared with all controls BRAIN: Greater activation in left precuneus, lingual and fusiform gyrus, and right cerebellum (Fehr et al., 2010) PRACTICE: 15 years of intensive mental calculating practice	YES (Anderson et al., 1999)	1 prime number savant: (Anderson et al., 1999) BEHAVIOR: Superior speed in recognition of prime numbers compared with trained calculators BRAIN: Theory of enhanced function of brain module for calculation PRACTICE: Not reported but likely

(Continued)

Table 6.1 Comparison of Evidence for the Existence and Brain Basis of Prodigious/Savant Skills, Superior Auditory and Visual Discrimination and Recognition, Expertise in Pattern Perception and Discrimination, and Unusual Conditions of Perception in Typical Individuals and Individuals Diagnosed with Autism—cont'd

Skill Type	Possible Memory Basis for Skill	Evidence for Skill in Typical Individuals	Exemplar Evidence for Skill Behavior, Brain Basis, and Skill Practice in Typical Individuals	Evidence for Skill in Individuals with Autism	Exemplar Evidence for Skill Behavior, Brain Basis, Skill Practice, and Impairment in Skill in Individuals with Autism
Mental calendar calculation	Computation skill	YES (Dubischar-Krivec et al., 2009)	1 calendar calculator prodigy (Fehr et al., 2011) BEHAVIOR: Could identify day names rapidly for many dates BRAIN: Mental arithmetic regions, parietal cortex, premotor cortex, left inferior temporal lobe, and the supplementary motor area PRACTICE: Extensive combined with consciously used strategies	YES (Heaton & Wallace, 2004)	2 calendar calculator savants (Cowan & Frith, 2009) BEHAVIOR: Could identify day names for many dates BRAIN: Mental arithmetic regions, parietal cortex, premotor cortex, left inferior temporal lobe, and the supplementary motor area PRACTICE: Extensive
Image replication with extreme fidelity after brief exposure	Visual memory	YES (Golomb, 1999)	3 child art prodigies (Golomb, 1999) BEHAVIOR: Drew and painted intricate accurate images of people, scenes, and objects with correct perspective and relational complexity BRAIN: Theory of enhanced visual memory and enhanced visual analysis PRACTICE: Skill appeared before practice, but practice enhanced skill	YES (Crane et al., 2011)	1 art savant (Corrigan, Richards, Treffert, & Dager, 2012) BEHAVIOR: Drew intricate accurate collections of birds, flowers, trains, and shoes BRAIN: Larger right amygdala and caudate, reduced GABA and glutamate neurotransmitters in the parietal lobe PRACTICE: Skill appeared before practice, some evidence practice enhanced skill

Music replication with extreme fidelity after brief exposure	Auditory memory	YES (McPherson, 2007)	1 child music prodigy (Ruthsatz & Detterman, 2003) BEHAVIOR: Played piano exceptionally at age 6 BRAIN: Highly superior short-term auditory memory PRACTICE: Skill appeared before practice, and practice was variable	YES (Young & Nettelbeck, 1995)	1 music savant (Young & Nettelbeck, 1995) BEHAVIOR: Played piano exceptionally at age 4 BRAIN: Not studied PRACTICE: Skill appeared before practice, and practice was variable

Three Superior Perceptual Recognition and Discrimination Skills Reported Only for Typical Individuals

Superior skill in face recognition and discrimination	Face memory	YES (Russell et al., 2009)	6 super face-recognizing prodigies (Russell et al., 2012) BEHAVIOR: Markedly superior face recognition BRAIN: Size and synchrony of the occipital face area and fusiform face area linked to face recognition skill PRACTICE: Skill appeared without practice	NO	IMPAIRED SKILL IN AUTISM: Review of studies reported impaired memory for and recognition of faces in autism (Weigelt et al., 2012)
Superior skill in taste recognition and discrimination	Taste memory	YES (Urdapilleta, Parr, Dacremont, & Green, 2011)	28 individuals (Okamoto et al., 2011) BEHAVIOR: Taste discrimination BRAIN: More activation in left and right lateral prefrontal areas for taste memories PRACTICE: Skill appeared and then was enhanced by practice	NO	IMPAIRED SKILL IN AUTISM: Individuals with autism were significantly less accurate than matched controls in identifying basic tastes and odors (Bennetto, Kuschner, & Hyman, 2007)

(Continued)

Table 6.1 Comparison of Evidence for the Existence and Brain Basis of Prodigious/Savant Skills, Superior Auditory and Visual Discrimination and Recognition, Expertise in Pattern Perception and Discrimination, and Unusual Conditions of Perception in Typical Individuals and Individuals Diagnosed with Autism—cont'd

Skill Type	Possible Memory Basis for Skill	Evidence for Skill in Typical Individuals	Exemplar Evidence for Skill Behavior, Brain Basis, and Skill Practice in Typical Individuals	Evidence for Skill in Individuals with Autism	Exemplar Evidence for Skill Behavior, Brain Basis, Skill Practice, and Impairment in Skill in Individuals with Autism
Superior skill in odor recognition and discrimination	Odor memory	YES (Plailly, Delon-Martin, & Royet, 2012)	14 expert perfumers (Plailly et al., 2012) BEHAVIOR: Odor identification and discrimination BRAIN: Activation beyond primary olfactory cortex in posterior olfactory cortex, orbitofrontal cortex, and hippocampus PRACTICE: Skill appeared and then was enhanced by practice	NO	IMPAIRED SKILL IN AUTISM: Individuals with autism were significantly less accurate than matched controls in identifying basic tastes and odors (Bennetto et al., 2007)

Four Superior Perceptual Recognition and Discrimination Skills Reported for Typical Individuals and Individuals with Autism

Skill Type	Possible Memory Basis for Skill	Evidence for Skill in Typical Individuals	Exemplar Evidence for Skill Behavior, Brain Basis, and Skill Practice in Typical Individuals	Evidence for Skill in Individuals with Autism	Exemplar Evidence for Skill Behavior, Brain Basis, Skill Practice, and Impairment in Skill in Individuals with Autism
Accurate word reading ahead of comprehension	Visual and verbal memory	YES (Martinez Perez et al., 2012)	50 child readers (Martinez Perez et al., 2012) BEHAVIOR: Word reading in advance of comprehension BRAIN: Verbal short-term memory predicted word recognition skill PRACTICE: Not reported	YES (Newman et al., 2007)	1 hyperlexic child (Turkeltaub et al., 2004) BEHAVIOR: Word reading in advance of comprehension BRAIN: Greater activity in left inferior frontal gyrus, precentral sulcus, and superior temporal cortex PRACTICE: Skill appeared followed by compulsive practice

Superior skill in route and map learning	YES (Woollett & Maguire, 2011)	39 London taxi drivers (Woollett & Maguire, 2011) BEHAVIOR: Superior knowledge of London's streets and patterns of streets BRAIN: Posterior hippocampal gray matter increased with practice PRACTICE: Extensive	YES (Caron et al., 2004)	16 high functioning individuals with autism (Caron et al., 2004) BEHAVIOR: Superior accuracy in transferring a micro to macro map, in cued recall of a path, and in faster map learning BRAIN: Not studied PRACTICE: None reported
Superior chess skill	YES (Chassy & Gobet, 2011)	8 chess experts (Bilalić, Langner, Ulrich, & Grodd, 2011) BEHAVIOR: Superior chess skill BRAIN: Collateral sulcus region and fusiform face area mediate chess expertise PRACTICE: Skill demonstrated before practice but extensive practice enhanced skill	YES (Hilton, 2008; Margan, 2008)	No studies found
Superior pitch discrimination	YES (Schulze, Gaab, & Schlaug, 2009)	12 perfect pitch prodigies (Loui, Li, Hohmann, & Schlaug, 2011) BEHAVIOR: 97% accuracy on musical pitch identification BRAIN: Larger white matter volumes in posterior superior and middle temporal gyri in left and right hemispheres PRACTICE: Skill appeared without practice, then was practiced	YES (Heaton et al., 2008)	1 perfect pitch savant (Heaton et al., 2008) BEHAVIOR: 100% accuracy on tones and pitches in music and in speech BRAIN: Atypical greater right hemisphere activation to all auditory stimuli PRACTICE: Skill appeared without practice, then was practiced

(Continued)

Table 6.1 Comparison of Evidence for the Existence and Brain Basis of Prodigious/Savant Skills, Superior Auditory and Visual Discrimination and Recognition, Expertise in Pattern Perception and Discrimination, and Unusual Conditions of Perception in Typical Individuals and Individuals Diagnosed with Autism—cont'd

Skill Type	Possible Memory Basis for Skill	Evidence for Skill in Typical Individuals	Exemplar Evidence for Skill Behavior, Brain Basis, and Skill Practice in Typical Individuals	Evidence for Skill in Individuals with Autism	Exemplar Evidence for Skill Behavior, Brain Basis, Skill Practice, and Impairment in Skill in Individuals with Autism
Three Unusual Conditions of Perception Reported for Typical Individuals and Individuals with Autism					
Synesthesia		YES (Terhune et al., 2011)	6 synesthetes (Terhune et al., 2011) BEHAVIOR: Saw each alphabetic letter with an associated color BRAIN: Hyperexcitability in primary visual cortex for grapheme–color synesthesia PRACTICE: Occurred without practice	YES (Bor, Billington, & Baron-Cohen, 2007)	1 synesthete savant (Bor et al., 2007) BEHAVIOR: Multiple sensory experiences associated with individual numbers BRAIN: Increased lateral prefrontal activity but not occipital cortex region PRACTICE: Occurred without practice
Heightened auditory sensitivity		YES (Ben-Sasson, Carter, & Briggs-Gowan, 2010)	20 children with sensory over-responsivity (Brett-Green, Miller, Schoen, & Nielsen, 2010) BEHAVIOR: Auditory hypersensitivity BRAIN: Evidence of absent auditory-somatosensory integration at 50 milliseconds; suggests early stage abnormal sensory–perceptual integration	YES (O'Connor, 2012)	Review of sensory responsivity in autism (Marco et al., 2011) BEHAVIOR: Auditory hypo- and hypersensitivity BRAIN: Evidence for abnormal primary auditory cortex processing and auditory hypo- and hypersensitivity

| Heightened tactile sensitivity | YES (Van Hulle, Schmidt, & Goldsmith, 2012) | 20 children with sensory over-responsivity (Brett-Green et al., 2010) BEHAVIOR: Severe symptoms of tactile over-responsivity BRAIN: No auditory-somatosensory integration at 50 milliseconds; suggests early stage abnormal sensory-perceptual integration | YES (Cascio et al., 2008) | 8 individuals with autism and hyper-reactivity (Cascio et al., 2008) BEHAVIOR: Tactile hyposensitivity and hypersensitivity BRAIN: Theory of hyper-reactivity of polymodal C fibers of afferent peripheral nerves to temperature and vibration |

contestant memory for facts from history, geography, science, literature, music, and popular culture. Jennings reported on his blog that he watched *Jeopardy!* every weekday in his childhood, and that winning on *Jeopardy!* had been his desire from childhood onward. To that end, Jennings had successfully captained his university academic information quiz team, and then wrote questions for a company that managed college quiz competitions (Jennings, 2012). In 2011, Jennings returned to fame for being bested at fact memory on *Jeopardy!* by the computer program Watson.

Hu et al. (2009) reported the skills of Chao Lu, who came to public attention by setting a Guinness World Record by memorizing 67,890 decimals of pi. While many prodigious memorizers were found to have above-average digit span memory, Lu had only an average digit span memory of 8.83, slightly below a control group mean of 9.27. Hu et al. (2009) noted that Lu was 23 on November 20, 2005 when he accurately recited the decimals of pi at a rate of 1.28 digits per second over the course of 24 hours and 4 minutes. Chao Lu began practicing reciting pi in 1998, and in 2004 decided to try to break the Guinness record. Consequently, Lu spent 5–13 hours a day for a year in pi decimal place recitation practice (Hu et al., 2009).

Daniel Tammet is an internationally known high-functioning individual with autism. At age 25, on March 14, 2004 he recited 22,514 decimal places of pi from memory in under 6 hours, setting a new European record (Treffert, 2010).

Treffert (2010) described the unusual memory shared by adult savant twins with autism. The core interest for Flo and Kay Lyman was an American television show host, Dick Clark. Starting in 1973, when they were 17 years old, they watched every episode of the television show, *The $100,000 Pyramid*, and they remembered every outfit Clark wore on the show. They also remembered different elements of each individual show from 1973 to 1996. The Lyman sisters also memorized the name, date, and recording artist from an extraordinary number of songs written in the 1960s, 70s, or 80s.

Rapid Mental Mathematical Calculation in Prodigies and Savants

From available reports, the least public of prodigies have been typical individuals who are calendar calculators or rapid mental calculators. However, Fehr et al. (2010) did describe a prodigious mental calculator, CP, who practiced mathematical calculation skill several hours a day for 15 years, and turned his prodigious skill into his livelihood by publicly demonstrating his abilities in calculation, writing a book, and advising others in strategic thinking. By contrast, neither the calendar calculator studied by Fehr et al.

(2011), nor the three typical individuals with calendar calculating skill studied by Dubischar-Krivec et al. (2009) were reported to have made their skills public.

Anderson et al. (1999) studied a prime number calculator, Michael, a 21-year-old man who had been diagnosed with autism at age 3 years. They reported that his ability to identify prime numbers was exceptional. Prime numbers are natural numbers greater than 1, each of which can be divided without remainder only by itself and by 1. Anderson et al. (1999) discovered that Michael, without being aware of it, was mentally using the Sieve of Eratosthenes. Eratosthenes, a Greek mathematician living in the 3rd century BC, created a method to find prime numbers. List all the natural numbers from 2 to infinity and "sieve out" every second number after two. Then move to the next number, 3, and "sieve out" every multiple of 3. Repeating this process yields a list of prime numbers.

Michael was able to determine a majority of the primes in a large set of numbers greater than 10,000 in 38 seconds (Anderson et al., 1999, p. 385). Michael had no speech, and no verbal comprehension, so the researchers' request for prime numbers was made by a printed illustration. Michael responded by printing the correct prime numbers.

Calendar Calculation in Prodigies and Savants

Calendar calculation is the ability to provide the day of the week for a given date. When asked what day of the week December 3, 2011 was, a calendar calculator can instantly say Saturday. Calendar calculation skill varies in speed of response and numbers of years for which the calendar calculator can provide the correct day of the week. Dubischar-Krivec et al. (2009) tested and interviewed three healthy individuals who were able to do calendar calculation. Each of the three healthy calendar calculators knew and used the regularities of the Gregorian calendar to calculate the day of the week. These regularities derive from the fact that the calendar repeats every 28 years. There are just 14 calendar patterns: leap year or not and 7 days for January 1st. In 28 years, 7 leap year calendars occur once but 7 non-leap year calendars occur three times, and two years 28 years apart in a century have identical calendars. Calendar calculation skill has been more frequently studied in individuals with autism or intellectual disability than in typical individuals. Thioux, Stark, Klaiman, and Schultz (2006) tested a savant calendar calculator, Donny, diagnosed with autism. They concluded that Donny had memorized an enormous number of date–weekday associations, he knew arithmetic, and he knew some but not all Gregorian regularities.

Music Replication with Superior Fidelity in Prodigies and Savants

Violinist Maxim Vengerov when a very young child practiced for 7 or 8 hours a day, and at times would finish practicing at 4am, when he would then go out and ride his tricycle in the snow (Nelson, 2009). Mozart famously composed his first piece of music at age 5, toured as a composing pianist at the age of 6, and by age 8 had written his first symphony (Pesic, 2001–2002). Nelson (2009) pointed out that most child prodigies in music exhibited an intense passion for practice, combined with an extraordinary memory for music. Wates (2010) recounted the story of Mozart visiting Rome in 1770 as a young teen, and hearing Allegri's Miserere sung at the Sistine Chapel. Church authorities had forbidden anyone to copy this piece of music. Having heard the piece once, however, Mozart was able to return to his hotel and write out the entire score. Kenneson (2003) provided the details of early childhood triumphs of many child music prodigies. He reported that at the age of 5, many musicians were already giving public performances, including the cellist Yo Yo Ma, the pianist Martha Agerich, and the violinist Akim Camara (Kenneson, 2003).

Young and Nettelbeck (1995) reported on TR, a music savant. He was diagnosed with autism at age 2, and his musical skills were already apparent at age 4. His technique was then judged to be extraordinary. TR regularly entered music competitions. Testing revealed that he could reproduce music he heard, and that his performances improved with practice.

Image Replication with Superior Fidelity in Prodigies and Savants

Golumb (1999) reported that the Chinese child prodigy artist, Yani Wang, "started painting at the age of two years and by the time she was six years old she had completed approximately 4000 paintings, and held her first exhibit" (p. 42). David Hockney began drawing as a toddler, and he would draw on anything available in house; he even drew cartoons of family members on a chores list in the kitchen (Sykes, 2012). The public came to know of Yani Wang and David Hockney through attention to their artwork.

Stephen Wiltshire, a British art savant, produced two detailed and correct drawings of a section of London and a section of Rome after short airplane rides over each city (Treffert, 2010). In a period of several hours after the flight over Rome he drew an accurate image of every street and building, and similarly, after a flight over London, Wiltshire's drawing of a 4 mile section of the city of London included 200 buildings and 12 landmarks all accurately depicted and placed (Treffert, 2010).

Drake and Winner (2011–2012) compared the drawings of a young art savant, JG, with drawings of 43 typically developing children. Not one of their 43 drawings showed the highly skilled realism that characterized the drawings of JG. Although Drake and Winner (2011–2012) tested art savant JG at the age of 10 years, JG had already memorized a number of biology textbooks, and a complete guide to the birds of North America. Drake and Winner (2011–2012) reported that when "Prompted by the name of any bird in this guide, he can describe the bird in great detail as if he were looking right at it" (p. 13). JG preferred drawing birds from the bird guide, but drew from memory. JG described his inner visual memory to the researchers. Drake and Winner stated, "He reports that he can project any image that he has memorized onto a visual field. He not only sees the image in his mind but can project it anywhere, at any time, for any duration of time so that he has the experience of actually looking at the image" (p. 13).

Highly Superior Autobiographical Memory in Prodigies and Savants

One of the six extraordinary skills, highly superior autobiographical memory for events from every day of one's life (Parker, Cahill, & McGaugh, 2006; Sanders, 2011), has been adequately documented only for typical individuals. Prodigious highly superior autobiographical memory came to public awareness in the United States through a 2010 broadcast of the television program *60 Minutes*, during which reporter Lesley Stahl interviewed a group of adults with this form of prodigious memory. The memory form was discovered when Jill Price, identified as AJ in a study of her memory (Parker et al., 2006), wrote to neuroscientist James L. McGaugh seeking an explanation for her own unusual memory. In her email Ms. Price stated, "Whenever I see a date flash on the television (or anywhere else for that matter) I automatically go back to that day and remember where I was, what I was doing, what day it fell on and on and on and on and on" (Parker et al., 2006, p. 35).

In the *60 Minutes* broadcast, Stahl also interviewed five other individuals with highly superior autobiographical memory, including among them Marilu Henner, an actor and long-time friend of Lesley Stahl (CBS News, 2010). Like Ms. Price, each of the five adults had been tested and found to have perfect autobiographical memory for the events of every day of their lives, including what they ate at meals, the weather, conversations, activities, and even details of what they saw on television that day. However, unlike prodigies in music, art, calculation, and number and fact memory, neither

Ms. Price nor any of the five individuals interviewed by Stahl ever practiced storing autobiographical details of each day. They reported that the extraordinarily detailed autobiographical memories simply automatically formed unbidden day after day. Ms. Price complained that the autobiographical memories were "non-stop, uncontrollable and totally exhausting" (Parker et al., 2006, p. 35). Ms. Price's despair contrasted with Ms. Henner's enthusiasm for her flood of memories: Ms. Henner wrote a book (2012) to instruct people without highly superior autobiographical memory how to increase their ability to remember life experiences.

Through the appeal of the television broadcast, and a public invitation for anyone to be tested for this form of prodigious memory, the researchers have recruited and tested more than twenty individuals (Sanders, 2011).

Although several individuals with autism have written autobiographies (Grandin, 1996; Tammet, 2007), evidence for highly superior autobiographical memory in autism is minimal. There is one proposal that autobiographical memory might be superior in some with autism (Lyons & Fitzgerald, 2005). In addition there is an anecdotal report of Flo and Kay Lyman, twins diagnosed with autism who have autobiographical memories linked to memories of an American television show and its host Dick Clark (Treffert, 2010). Just as described for Jill Price (Parker et al., 2006), if a date between 1973 and 1996 was given to Flo and Kay they could report elements of the broadcast on that date. These elements included the time and number of game-related buzzers sounded during each broadcast. In addition, the twins could report the weather on any date named. However, these memories largely center on Mr. Clark and the details of specific broadcasts, with only a few memories containing autobiographical information about Flo and Kay themselves.

There is, however, a single very brief report suggesting that one individual diagnosed with autism might have highly superior autobiographical memory (Kennedy & Squire, 2007). Kennedy and Squire (2007) reported on the skills of two calendar calculators with autism. The father of one of the savants reported that his son, DG, could remember the events of any particular day, and had been able to do so since he was 8 years old. DG's father provided the researchers with 25 receipts that documented specific events that took place from 1995 to 2002. Kennedy and Squire (2007) gave DG a date and asked him to recall the events of that date, which DG was able to do. In contrast to the skill of DG, most studies have reported impairment in autobiographical and episodic memory in individuals diagnosed with autism (Crane, Goddard, & Pring, 2010; Maister &

Plaisted-Grant, 2011; Zmigrod, de Sonneville, Colzato, Swaab, & Hommel, 2012).

Three Superior Perceptual Pattern Discrimination Skills Reported only for Typical Individuals

Table 6.1 identifies three superior perceptual discrimination skills reported only for typical individuals: superior face recognition, superior odor recognition, and superior taste recognition. The superior recognition of faces has been reported only for a few typical individuals (Russell, Duchaine, & Nakayama, 2009). No superior face recognition has been reported for autism. By contrast, face identification and recognition have most often been reported to be impaired in autism (Weigelt, Koldewyn, & Kanwisher, 2012). Moreover, individuals with autism have often been reported to have abnormal taste and odor recognition and abnormal responsivity to taste and odor (Leekam et al., 2007).

Superior Face Recognition

The serendipitous way in which researchers found an individual with highly superior autobiographical memory (Parker et al., 2006) raised the possibility that other unknown prodigious skills existed. Such skills may be extremely rare and may not yield products or performances such as art, music, chess, or remembering pi, and therefore may have not yet come to public attention. Superior face recognition, defined here as a superior perceptual discrimination skill rather than as a prodigious skill, has only recently been reported. Russell et al. (2009) commented that their research team first learned of highly superior face recognizers after the team's research on developmental prosopagnosia was publicized. Prosopagnosia is exceptionally poor face recognition skill despite normal vision and no evidence of brain damage. Russell et al. (2009) reported that a number of people contacted them claiming to have the "opposite condition" from developmental prosopagnosia. Russell et al. (2009) tested four individuals: CS, a 26-year-old female PhD student; CL, a 40-year-old female homemaker; JJ, a 36-year-old female municipal employee; and MR, a 31-year-old male computer programmer. All four had extraordinary skill at face recognition. Russell et al. (2009) concluded that there was likely to be a continuous range of face recognition skill: "On one end of this range lie developmental prosopagnosics, some of whom even have difficulty recognizing members of their nuclear family. On the other end of this range lie super-recognizers, who frequently recognize complete strangers out of context after many years" (p. 256).

Superior Taste and Odor Recognition

Typical individuals have also demonstrated exceptional taste recognition and discrimination (Urdapilleta, Parr, Dacremont, & Green, 2011), and have shown exceptional odor identification and discrimination (Plailly, Delon-Martin, & Royet, 2012). Conversely, taste and odor discrimination have been found to be impaired in many individuals with autism. Bennetto, Kuschner, and Hyman (2007) reported that individuals with autism were significantly less accurate in recognizing basic tastes and odors than typical controls. Leekam et al. (2007) reported that significantly more children with autism had abnormal smell and taste sensitivities than did children with developmental disability and developmental language disorders.

Four Superior Perceptual Pattern Recognition and Discrimination Skills Reported for Typical Individuals and Individuals with Autism

Route and Map Skill

Superior skill in detailed spatial route knowledge has been studied in London taxi drivers (Woollett & Maguire, 2011). Caron, Mottron, Rainville, and Chouinard (2004) reported that although high-functioning individuals with autism displayed no superiority in route learning, or in reversing a route, they were superior to IQ-matched controls in transferring knowledge between micro- and macro-scale maps, in cued recall of a path, and were significantly faster in map-learning. One difference between map skills in the taxi drivers and map-learning skills reported for high-functioning individuals with autism is that the taxi drivers become skilled through immense effort in memorizing. The superior skill in the individuals with autism was not practiced.

Chess Skill

Although Feldman and Morelock (2011) claimed, "there are no savants in chess" (p. 210), public speculation suggested some chess masters exhibited symptoms of high-functioning autism, and expert chessboard pattern recognition was reported for a number of individual skilled chess players diagnosed with autism (Hilton, 2008; Margan, 2008; This is Plymouth, 2008). Moreover, Young and Nettelbeck (1995) reported that the music savant they tested was an expert in chess, and was the British National Chess Junior Champion at an early age. However, the majority of chess expertise has been demonstrated by ranked and unranked chess players with no diagnosis of autism or intellectual disability (Chassy & Gobet, 2011).

Early Word Decoding

Accurate single word decoding in advance of comprehension has been reported for some early readers in the earliest stages of learning to read (Martinez Perez, Majerus, & Poncelet, 2012) as well as for some individuals with autism (Grigorenko, Klin, & Volkmar, 2003; Newman et al., 2007). Newman et al. (2007) posited that parents of other hyperlexic children in their study reported that their children would compulsively read every number and letter on license plates in parking lots, and read every bit of print they saw, including signs, notices, and manuals. Newman et al. (2007) argued that hyperlexic children were engaged in the same reading processes as typically developing children but that hyperlexic children were obsessed with decoding alone.

Absolute Pitch Identification

Absolute pitch is the ability to identify any pitch of the Western musical scale without any tonal context or reference tone for comparison. Absolute pitch discrimination is a skill that has been reported for individuals with autism and typical individuals (Heaton, Davis, & Happé, 2008; Loui, Li, Hohmann, & Schlaug, 2011; Schulze, Gaab, & Schlaug, 2009).

Why are Savant, Prodigious, and Superior Skills Noteworthy?

There is, of course, a much wider range of superior perceptual recognition and discrimination skills than the seven listed in Table 6.1. They include expertise in reading radiological films (Harley et al., 2009), abacus skill (Hu et al., 2011), and expertise in car identification (McGugin, McKeeff, Tong, & Gauthier, 2011) as well as many others.

Some extraordinary and special skills have received more attention. Art and music entertain. Calculation solves problems. Extraordinary memory evokes awe. Few people have perfect pitch, few can be professional tasters, perfumers, or chess masters, and not everyone can pass the London route knowledge test. However, the selection of extraordinary or superior skills for study is not comprehensive or systematic.

Some Skills are Less Noteworthy

There have been problematic claims for superior visual acuity in autism (Falkmer et al., 2011; Tavassoli, Latham, Bach, Dakin, & Baron-Cohen, 2011), but superior visual acuity has been demonstrated in baseball players and other talented athletes (Boden, Rosengren, Martin, & Boden, 2009). Moreover, approximately 12% of men have some form of X-linked color blindness (Jordan, Deeb, Bosten, & Mollon, 2010) and male color blindness frequently confers superior visual pattern recognition (Jägle, de Luca, Serey, Bach, & Sharpe, 2006). Should the extremely rapid registration of visual images in athletes and superior pattern detection in colorblind men be seen as noteworthy superior skills?

The ontogeny of females results in random X chromosome inactivation; therefore, all the daughters of colorblind men have retinas that contain four classes of cone rather than the normal three. Jordan et al. (2010) found that 1 of 24 women with colorblind fathers had tetrachromatic vision, possessing the unusual ability to actually see color from 4 rather than the typical 3 wavelengths. Should being able to see an additional wavelength be identified as a prodigious or superior skill?

In sum, selection of extraordinary and superior skills for study reflects cultural values and scientific curiosity.

Unusual Conditions of Perception

In addition to the six savant and prodigy skills and seven superior perceptual recognition and discrimination skills, Table 6.1 identifies three unusual conditions of perception found for both individuals with autism and typical individuals. These are synesthesia, atypical sensitivity to touch, and atypical auditory sensitivity.

Synesthesia

Simner (2012) defined synesthesia as pairing of one triggering stimulus with a particular resultant experience that incorporates one or more other senses, where the synesthetic experience arises spontaneously and without effort. In synesthesia, one form of sensory experience, such as seeing the letter A printed in black on white paper, simultaneously and consistently activates the visual image of a particular color, say blue, which is not present on the piece of paper. There are more than 60 different forms of synesthesia (Rogowska, 2011). Of the more than 60 forms, the most common is the color–grapheme synesthesia just described, in which individual letters of the alphabet printed in black are seen by the synesthete as having different inherent colors, such as B is green, F is blue, and Z is brown. Some individuals report gustatory–lexical synesthesia, wherein they taste specific tastes when they read or hear certain words, and music–color synesthetes see specific colors when they hear certain pieces of music. Simner (2012) reported ordinal linguistic personification synaesthesia in which letters, numbers, days of the week, trigger an automatic, powerful impression of a personality type or gender. An example would be a synesthete's impression that the letter 'h' was a tall nervous man, and the number 8 was a happy grandmother. Eagleman (2012) argued that the variation of 60 types of synesthesia was important and argued, "we must treat the heterogeneity of the condition as an interesting clue rather than an inconvenience to be swept under the rug" (p. 18).

While synesthesia has been viewed as extremely rare, in fact, synesthesia occurs in approximately 4% of the general population (Simner et al., 2006; Simner, 2012; Terhune et al., 2011). Moreover, not only are there more than 60 categories of synesthesia, the particulars of synesthetic experience vary from person to person. Rogowska (2011) reported, "Synaesthesia is intra-individually variable and idiosyncratic—each synaesthete has a unique configuration of sensations. There are no two persons with identical sensual associations for the same set of stimulus …. Even identical twins" (p. 213).

Because failed sensory integration has been reported as a problem for autism (Marco, Hinkley, Hill, & Nagarajan, 2011), and synesthesia is an error of over-integration of sensory information, it might be expected that synesthesia has only been adequately reported for one savant, Daniel Tammet (Bor, Billington, & Baron-Cohen, 2007; Treffert, 2010). In his autobiography, Tammet (2007) correctly stated, "It is not known how many savants have synesthetic experiences to help them excel in the areas they excel in" (p. 6).

Daniel Tammet (2007), a memory savant calculator with high-functioning autism, stated that seeing a favorite number in a street sign, shop sign, or license plate stirred "a shiver of excitement and pleasure" (p. 6), but seeing a number that did not match his internal sense of that number was "uncomfortable and irritating" (p. 6). Emotional synesthesia has been demonstrated to confer emotional value on numbers, letters, sounds, or images (Ramachandran, Miller, Livingstone, & Brang, 2012; Rogowska, 2011; Ward, 2004).

Tammet (2007) stated that he saw numbers as having colors, sounds, shapes, sizes, textures, motions, and personalities. This last component is ordinal linguistic personification synaesthesia as described by Simner (2012) in which letters, numbers, days of the week, trigger an automatic, powerful impression of a personality type or gender. Tammet identified 289 as ugly, 4 as shy and quiet, 5 as loud as a clap of thunder, 117 as tall and lanky, 37 as lumpy as porridge, and 89 he found similar to falling snow (Tammet, 2007, p. 2).

Tactile and Auditory Sensitivity

Two other unusual conditions of perception shared by individuals with autism and typical individuals are atypical tactile and auditory sensitivity. Researchers have labeled heightened sensory reactions in typical children as "sensory over-responsivity" or SOR (Ben-Sasson, Carter, & Briggs-Gowan, 2010). Auditory hypersensitivity is a feature of Williams-Beuren syndrome (Elsabbagh, Cohen, Cohen, Rosen, & Karmiloff-Smith, 2011) and tactile hypersensitivity has been reported for attention deficit/hyperactivity disorder (Ghanizadeh, 2008). In typical children and adults, tactile and auditory over-responsivity are the two most prevalent forms of sensory sensitivity (Koziol, Budding, & Chidekel, 2011; Van Hulle, Schmidt, & Goldsmith, 2012). In typical children, the prevalence, 5–13%, is very high (May-Benson, Koomar, & Teasdale, 2009). Enhanced processing of pitch and heightened sensitivity to loudness has been reported in autism (O'Connor, 2012), and tactile hypersensitivity have been reported in autism (Blakemore et al., 2006; Cascio et al., 2008).

Additional Sensory Abnormalities in Autism
In addition to atypical tactile and auditory responsivity, many varied forms of atypical sensory processing have been noted in autism, including hypo-responsivity to stimuli as well as aberrant sensation seeking, such as wanting to watch the movement of a ceiling fan for hours (Foss-Feig, Heacock, & Cascio, 2012). Marco et al. (2011) found that more than 96% of children with autism expressed hypersensitivities and hyposensitivities in multiple sensory domains. Leekam et al. (2007) found that 185 of 200 children and adults with autism had sensory-processing problems. The researchers noted sensory abnormalities in multiple domains, including auditory, visual, touch, smell/taste, food type and texture, body sensations, and pain (Leekam et al., 2007).

The high population prevalence of sensory abnormalities in autism is not unique to autism and has been reported for a range of neurodevelopmental disorders including Williams-Beuren syndrome (Elsabbagh et al., 2011), attention deficit/hyperactivity disorder, cerebral palsy, and fragile X syndrome (Cascio, 2010). However, despite the great heterogeneity of sensory abnormalities in autism, and despite the lack of specificity of sensory abnormalities for autism, the accumulating evidence for sensory abnormalities in autism (Ben-Sasson et al., 2010; Foss-Feig et al., 2012; Leekam et al., 2007; Marco et al., 2011) led to their inclusion in DSM-5 (APA, www.dsm5.org). Unusual sensory behaviors were added to the DSM-5 diagnostic criteria for autism spectrum disorders in the category of repetitive behaviors (APA, www.dsm5.org). The complete criterion is "Hyper- or hypo-reactivity to sensory input or unusual interest in sensory aspects of environment; (such as apparent indifference to pain/heat/cold, adverse response to specific sounds or textures, excessive smelling or touching of objects, fascination with lights or spinning objects)" (APA, www.dsm5.org).

Because of the high prevalence and disruptive effects of sensory abnormalities in autism, Marco et al. (2011) theorized, "differences in sensory processing may actually cause core features of autism" (p. 53R). The researchers argued that auditory processing problems caused language delay, and visual processing problems caused failed emotion comprehension. However, although sensory abnormalities have been found in nearly all individuals diagnosed with autism, no validated model of the brain bases of sensory abnormalities in autism has been established (Leekam et al., 2007; Marco et al., 2011).

UNANSWERED QUESTIONS REGARDING SAVANT, PRODIGIOUS, AND SPECIAL SKILLS

Much about savant skills, superior perceptual recognition and discrimination skill, sensory abnormalities, and intelligence in autism remains to be discovered (Happé & Vital, 2009). Neither the population prevalence of savant skills in autism nor the prevalence of savant skills in intellectual disability has been established (Hermelin, 2001; Howlin et al., 2009; Rimland, 1978; Treffert, 2010). Without knowledge of the true prevalence rates in these two populations, the claim that autism is the disorder with the highest rates of savant skills cannot be verified.

Another unanswered question is the full range of variation in causes for extraordinary skills. Researchers have not determined what various combinations of practice and unique brain organization contribute to savant, prodigious, and special skills. Most studies of savant and prodigious skills have been case studies (Anderson et al., 1999; Bor et al., 2007; Corrigan et al., 2012; Cowan & Frith, 2009; Fehr et al., 2010; Heaton et al., 2008; Hu et al., 2009; Neumann et al., 2010; O'Connor & Hermelin, 1992; Sanders, 2011; Treffert, 2010). Consequently, too little evidence has been collected to provide satisfactory explanations for the brain bases of savant skills in autism and prodigious skills in typical individuals.

A third unanswered question is the relationship between measured intelligence and savant, prodigious, and special skills. The existing evidence is minimal and contradictory.

The three following sections of this chapter address these three questions. The first section reviews evidence for the prevalence of savant skills and prodigious skills, and concludes that the prevalence rates of savant and prodigious skills remain to be determined. The second section reviews the evidence for contributions of intense practice to extraordinary skills, evidence for practiced-induced brain alterations, and evidence for atypical brain organization. The third section reports sparse and contradictory findings for relationships between intelligence, savant skills, special skills, and sensory abnormalities in autism. The chapter concludes with a brief evaluation of several theories of savant skill.

WHAT ARE THE PREVALENCE RATES OF SAVANT AND PRODIGIOUS SKILLS?

Feldman and Morelock (2011) noted, "Although both prodigies and savants are very rare, there are no solid estimates of the frequencies of their occurrence in the general population" (p. 212). There are only two population prevalence studies of savant skills in autism, and both have the disadvantage of reliance on parental report for the identification of savant skills. Rimland (1978) reported that 531 of 5400 parents of children with autism who returned mail interview forms identified their children as having savant skills in calculation, music, memory, and art. Howlin et al. (2009) reported that for a sample of 137 individuals previously diagnosed with autism, 24 of 90 parents contacted identified their adult children as having one or more savant skills in calendar calculation, other calculation, memory, music, and art. Howlin et al. (2009) also created a category of exceptional cognitive skill defined as a standard IQ subtest score one standard deviation above population mean, and two standard deviations above the average score on all subtests taken by the individual. For example, if the population mean on a digit span subtest was 9 digits with a standard deviation of 1, and an adult in the Howlin et al. (2009) sample had a subtest average of 80% across all subtests, if that individual scored a 10 on the digit span subtest, the score of 10 was identified as exceptional cognitive skill. Eight of the 24 savants whose parents had identified them as savants demonstrated exceptional cognitive skill, and an additional 15 adults not identified as savants by their parents were found to have an exceptional cognitive skill by this metric.

From these data, Howlin et al. (2009) concluded that 39 of the original sample of 137 adults previously diagnosed with autism had savant skills. Moreover, Howlin et al. (2009) asserted, "at least a quarter, but probably over a third, of individuals with autism show unusual skills or talents that are both above population norms and above their own overall level of cognitive functioning" (p. 1364).

Institutional surveys of individuals with intellectual disability, who may or may not have had diagnoses of autism, generated markedly lower rates of savant syndrome. Hill (1977) obtained reports from 107 hospitals and care facilities that ultimately identified 54 institutionalized individuals with savant skill. This yielded a rate of 1 in every 2000 care facility residents. Saloviita, Ruusila, and Ruusila (2000) reported that 45 individuals with savant skill were identified in a survey of 583 care institutions in Finland. Saloviita et al. (2000) calculated that the rate of savant skill was 1.4 per 1000 individuals with intellectual disability.

Unfortunately, because none of the four savant prevalence estimates included testing the identified individuals for their savant skills, the estimates reported by Hill (1977), Howlin et al. (2009), Rimland (1978), and Saloviita et al. (2000) were not validated. The need for validation of the existence of savant skills is reflected in the findings of a study conducted by Neumann et al. (2010). The researchers tested memory skill in seven male memory savants whose parents all stated that their children had savant memory. The researchers found that although the seven memory savants showed superior map-learning skills, none of the seven memory savants performed better than typical controls on any of the core memory tests the researchers administered. Neumann et al. (2010) found that the memory savants performed significantly less well than controls in recognizing pseudowords and less well on all tests of visual-spatial working memory. The researchers conceded, "Since mnemonist savants did not show excellent mnemonic skills in this study, the experiment did not allow testing our primary hypotheses concerning the mechanisms by which savants exhibit extraordinary memory" (Neumann et al., 2010, p. 119).

Hermelin (2001) estimated from her own research experience that the rate of savant skills was 1 or 2 in 200. While conducting a series of studies of the development of children with autism, I tested, observed, and interviewed 340 children and adolescents diagnosed with autism. Among these 340 children, I identified only two boys with savant skills. One boy had memorized an extraordinary numbers of pairs of names and phone numbers from telephone books (Waterhouse, 1988). The other boy had memorized extended segments of banter for several years of a daily half-hour television show. However, using the Rimland (1978) rate of 10%, I should have found 34 savants, and using the Howlin et al. (2009) proposed prevalence rate I should have discovered over 110 children with savant skills. However, no evidence in testing, or from caretakers, parents, or teachers I spoke with indicated that there were any other savants among the 340 children and adolescents beyond the two boys I had identified with savant skills.

From my experience then, the rate of savant skill in autism would be 2/340, or 1/170, a prevalence rate roughly similar to the estimate of 1 or 2 in 200 suggested by Hermelin (2001). This is much fewer than the 33% of individuals with autism proposed by Howlin et al. (2009), and significantly more than the 1 in 2000 estimated by Hill (1977). However, this is personal experience and not the application of the scientific method.

Treffert (2010) stated that his own experience led him to believe that the prevalence rate of 10% reported by Rimland was "really quite accurate" (p. 19), and Howlin et al. (2009) asserted, "It may be concluded that unusual talents are found in at least a third of individuals with autism" (p. 1364). Despite all estimates, beliefs, personal experience, and assertions, there has been no substantiated population prevalence estimate for savant skills in autism. Although Howlin et al. (2009) claimed that detailed experimental studies were feasible "only for individual case studies or small case series" (p. 1365), screening for savant skills in a large population of individuals with autism followed by testing for savant skills in those ascertained would be feasible, but has never been reported.

Projecting Population Prevalence Estimates of Savants with Autism

Treffert (2010) claimed, "50 percent of persons with savant syndrome have autistic disorder as their underlying disability and the other 50 percent have other disabilities" (p. 19). The recent world prevalence estimate for autism was approximately 1%. Therefore, among 7 billion people, 70 million people worldwide would have autism. Given the evidence that savant skills may occur in individuals at any level of cognitive functioning, but would be unlikely to be expressed in very young children, hypothetically at least 55 million individuals with autism might be tested for savant skills. Applying the Rimland (1978) ascertainment rate of 10% savants in autism, thus, hypothetically there were 5.5 million savants with autism worldwide in 2012. Applying the Howlin et al. (2009) proposal that savant skills occur in one-third of individuals with autism, therefore in 2012, hypothetically there could have been as many as 18 million savants with autism worldwide.

Given the worldwide attention paid to autism since the vaccine scare generated by the Wakefield et al. (1998) paper, and the estimates of increasing prevalence worldwide (Kim et al., 2011; RTEnews, 2012), it is surprising that more of the projected possible 5–18 million individuals with autism and savant skills have not come to attention worldwide. A search on January 18, 2012 of the website PubMed for all 2011 papers using the search term "autism" yielded 2210 papers. On the same date a search for all 2011 papers using the search term "autism savant" yielded only 4 papers: Corrigan et al. (2012); Crane et al. (2011); Fehr et al. (2011); and Pring, Ryder, Crane, and Hermelin (2012).

The US population in 2012 was approximately 314 million; given an autism prevalence rate of 1%, and a savant prevalence in autism rate of 10%, there would be approximately 3.1 million individuals with autism, 310,000 of whom could be expected to exhibit savant skills. Given the heightened autism awareness in the USA, it is therefore very surprising that no teacher, school psychologist, or researcher has yet reported finding significant numbers of savants with autism in US schools.

The question of the missing but expected savants in the autism population becomes even more perplexing if the Korean prevalence rate for autism is considered. Kim et al. (2011) reported a population prevalence rate for autism of 2.64% in a Korean sample. The total population of Korea in 2012 was 50 million people. Thus, the 2.64% prevalence rate reported by Kim et al. (2009) would suggest a population of 1,320,000 individuals with autism in Korea in 2012. Applying the Rimland (1978) and Howlin et al. (2009) proposed rates of savant skill in autism would yield hypothetical populations of 132,500 or 440,000 savants with autism in Korea in 2012. Moreover, Kim et al. (2011) asserted, "Two-thirds of ASD cases in the overall sample were in the mainstream school population, undiagnosed and untreated" (p. 1). Therefore, after adjusting for children too young to be in the Korean school population or adults too old to be in the Korean school population, two-thirds of 61,250 and two-thirds of 220,000, or 40,425 and 145,200 savants with autism could be expected to be found in Korean schools. It is reasonable to assume that parents at home and teachers at school would have noticed children with savant skills and autism. Therefore, just as in the USA, it is surprising that no Korean teacher, parent, school psychologist, or researcher has yet reported finding significant numbers of savants with autism.

As noted earlier, determining the prevalence of savant skill in autism would require that a large population of individuals diagnosed with autism be screened for possible savant skills, and then be systematically tested for those savant skills. Such a study has not been reported.

No Reported Prevalence Rates for Prodigious Skills

Even if a valid prevalence rate for savant skills in autism were established, the significance of that prevalence rate could not be compared with any other prodigious or special skill prevalence rate. There is no valid established prevalence rate for savant skill in intellectual disability (Hill, 1977; Suloviita et al., 2000), and there is no population prevalence rate for prodigious skills in typical individuals (Feldman & Morelock, 2011). Moreover, there is no evidence that prevalence rates have ever been determined for types of prodigious skills. Most prodigies have become known to the public one by one, through public attention given to extraordinary individual achievements or performances either in childhood or later.

Summary: No Evidence to Support the Claim of Very High Prevalence of Savant or Superior Skills in Autism

Treffert argued, "savant and prodigious skills are present in only a fraction of the disabled population, just as genius occurs in only a fraction of the general population" (Denison, 2007, p. 30). Unfortunately we cannot put numbers to those fractions. No validated prevalence rate for savant skills in autism has been determined (Hermelin, 2001; Howlin et al., 2009; Rimland, 1978; Treffert, 2010). No valid prevalence rate for savant skill in intellectual disability has been determined (Hill, 1977; Suloviita et al., 2000). No population prevalence rate for prodigious skills in typical individuals (Feldman & Morelock, 2011) has been determined. Moreover, there is no evidence that prevalence rates have ever been determined for types of prodigious skills.

Howlin et al. (2009) and Rimland (1978) provided the most careful estimates of savant skills, but these require validation of the identified savant skills. However, without knowing the validated prevalence of savant skills in intellectual disability, as well as the validated prevalence of prodigious skills in a population of typical children and adults, the claim that the highest prevalence of savant skills occurs in autism cannot be assessed.

PRACTICE, PRACTICE-INDUCED BRAIN CHANGES, AND ATYPICAL BRAIN FUNCTION CONTRIBUTIONS TO SAVANT, PRODIGIOUS, AND SPECIAL SKILLS

Evidence has suggested that intense practice, practice-induced brain changes, and atypical brain structure contribute to savant and prodigious skills, and superior perceptual discrimination and pattern recognition skills. Evidence also indicates that there is individual variation in practice, in brain activity patterns, brain organization, and memory processes. The relative importance of these causal factors has been debated. Researchers Ericsson, Nandagopal, and Roring (2009), Howe, Davidson, and Sloboda (1998), and Maguire, Wilding, Valentine, and Kapur (2003) argued that all extraordinary skill resulted from exceptional practice alone. Conversely, many theorists proposed that aberrant or enhanced brain function generated savant or prodigious skills (Fabricius, 2010; Mottron et al., 2009; Murray, 2010; Snyder, 2009; Simner et al., 2009).

The first subsection to follow considers the question of practice as the source of savant, prodigious, and superior skills. The second subsection reviews evidence for brain changes associated with practice for savant, prodigious, and superior skills. The third subsection reviews evidence for atypical brain organization as the basis for savant, prodigious, and superior skills.

Evidence for Practice of Savant, Prodigious, and Special Skills

Howe et al. (1998) discounted the idea that special innate brain organization determined any superior skills, and claimed a great deal of practice was needed for the expression of all extraordinary skills. The researchers argued that studies indicated that individual differences in skill reflected how much practice an individual had engaged in. Howe et al. (1998) argued that identifying children as innately talented was unfair, because it prevented children not identified as talented "from pursuing a goal because of the unjustified conviction of teachers or parents that certain children would not benefit from the superior opportunities" (p. 407).

Ericsson et al. (2009) and Maguire et al. (2003) also argued that all extraordinary skill resulted from exceptional practice alone. Ericsson et al. (2009) noted that studies demonstrated that, after hundreds of hours of practice for lists of numbers, some typical college students were able to increase their digit span memory from seven digits to an extraordinary 80 digits. Ericsson et al. (2009) argued that reviews of research on memory skills had not reported evidence of "limiting factors that would impede healthy, motivated individuals from acquiring exceptional performance in specific memory tasks with appropriate instruction and training" (p. 200). Ericsson et al. (2009) concluded that special genes for unique talent were not necessary for developing an extraordinary memory, and stated, "With specific practice, the speed of performance in many performance domains considerably increases" (p. 201).

Evidence that Practice Contributes to Prodigious Skills

The available biographies of prodigious artists, musicians, calculators, and fact and number memorizers have reported evidence of extended periods of unusually intense and consistent skill practice. The devotion to practice reported for typical individuals who have developed extraordinary or superior skills is often unusual and extreme. CP wanted to become a prodigious mental calculator, and spent 15 years practicing (Fehr et al., 2010). Chao Lu wanted to set a world record (Hu et al., 2009) and spent a year practicing. Ken Jennings wanted to win a game show, and spent much of his childhood and early adulthood collecting and memorizing information to that end.

Maguire et al. (2003) studied typical individuals at the world memory championships. Maguire et al. (2003) compared 10 superior memorizers with 10 matched control subjects who had no special memory skills. Maguire et al. (2003) reported that the superior memorizers showed increased activity in the same brain regions as the typical controls when engaged in memory tasks: medial parietal cortex, retrosplenial cortex, and right posterior hippocampus. Maguire et al. (2003) argued, "those with superior memory use a spatial learning strategy and engage brain regions that are critical for spatial memory … [which] may point to a natural human proclivity to use spatial context—and its instantiation in the right hippocampus—as one of the most effective means to learn and recall information" (p. 94). The researchers pointed out that 9 of the 10 world superior memorizers used the memory strategy of visualizing items on a route. This strategy was "attributed to the Greek poet Simonides of Ceos in 477 BC, who describes using routes and visualizing to-be-remembered items at salient points along the routes, and then mentally retracing those routes during recall" (Maguire et al., 2003, p. 93).

Evidence that Practice Contributes to Savant and Special Skills in Autism
Practice by Savant Calendar Calculators

Thioux et al. (2006) saw the intense practice of calendar calculators with autism as the result of an aberrant reward and motivation system. Thioux et al. (2006) proposed that the basis for calendar calculation skill in autism was a narrowed intense interest in numbers and calculation combined with repeated behaviors, leading to exceptional practice, stemming from "a disruption of the reward and motivation system of the orbito-frontal cortex and extended amygdala that controls goal-directed behaviors and reward-motivated learning" (p. 1167). Thioux et al. (2006) argued that savant calendar calculators memorized dates over a number of years, and developed a very large memory base of date–weekday associations that they then used for calculation with learned arithmetic operations.

However, there is some evidence for a shared practice-induced brain basis for processing for calendar calculation, as reported by Cowan and Frith

(2009) and Fehr et al. (2011). Cowan and Frith (2009) imaged two savant calendar calculators and reported that the brain regions active were similar to the activation patterns in healthy individuals for mental arithmetic, including parietal cortex, premotor cortex, left inferior temporal lobe, and the supplementary motor area. Fehr et al. (2011) imaged a healthy calendar calculator and reported generally the same regions of activation: parietal cortex, premotor cortex, left inferior temporal lobe, and the supplementary motor area. Nonetheless, surprisingly, Fehr et al. (2011) had also imaged a savant calendar calculator and found that his brain activation pattern was completely dissimilar to the patterns reported by Cowan and Frith (2009): widely distributed networks in bilateral inferior posterior and left frontotemporal cortical regions, as well as several subcortical regions and the cerebellum.

Evidence that Practice Contributes to Savant Musicians and Artists

Music savants (Treffert 2010) and art savants (Crane et al., 2011; Drake & Winner, 2011–2012) have demonstrated intense practice of their skills. Although savant musicians and artists may not produce the significant style changes in their artwork or musical production that have been found in the developing work of music and art prodigies, most savants continue the intense practice of their skill (Golumb, 1999; Nelson, 2009; Sykes, 2012; Treffert, 2010). Crane et al. (2011) stated that savant art is accurate and detailed, but there is "reduced thematic variation in their artwork ... which might be associated with a lack of flexibility" (p. 791).

Practice by a Savant Mnemonist

Daniel Tammet is an internationally known high-functioning individual with autism. At age 25, on March 14, 2004 he recited 22,514 decimal places of pi from memory in under 6 hours, setting a new European record (Treffert, 2010). Tammet's father had reminded him in 2003 that he had been seizure free for 20 years, so he decided to practice for one year to recite pi in order to raise money for the National Society for Epilepsy in the United Kingdom. Tammet's year of practice was paralleled by the year memory prodigy Chao Lu spent practicing in order to set a Guinness World Record by memorizing 67,890 decimals of pi (Hu et al., 2009).

Practice as the Basis of Hyperlexia

Newman et al. (2007) claimed that hyperlexia was an isolated skill in individuals, "developed by them at a young age, perhaps as a result of deliberate (and often obsessive) practice" (p. 773). Newman et al. (2007) reported that parents told them one child in their study would not go anywhere without his favorite book, and that he read the book continuously throughout each day. Many parents have reported a compulsion to read (without comprehension) words everywhere in the environment. Newman et al. (2007) reported the parents of the boy with the favorite book bought many copies of this book in case one was ruined or lost, because the boy would become extremely distressed if he did not have the book with him.

Practice Contributes to Perfect Pitch Detection in Autism

Heaton et al. (2008) proposed that an able adult with autism, AC, who demonstrated absolute pitch detection, had developed his skills through atypical practice. Heaton et al. (2008) argued that because AC had "an early preoccupation with naming pitches and his language acquisition was delayed and atypical" (p. 2097), he over-attended to music and pitch, thus developing his exceptional auditory discriminative skill through practice.

Limits to the Effects of Practice for Savant Skills

Although many savant and prodigious artists, musicians, mental calculators, and calendar calculators have been shown to practice their skill (Heaton & Wallace, 2004), there may be a limit on the effects of their practice. For example, O'Connor and Hermelin (1992) tested two calendar-calculating savants with autism at two time intervals, 18 months apart. They found no improvement in calendar-calculating skill over this period for either of the two savants. The lack of improvement past some unknown point suggests a ceiling on the effect of practice for savant skills. The possibility of a ceiling effect, in turn, raises the question of limits on the influence of practice for a particular skill.

Practice-Induced Brain Changes in Savant, Prodigious, and Superior Skills

Intense practice of any skill typically results in enhanced memory. Many researchers and theorists have argued that savant, prodigious, and all other notably superior perception, recognition, and discrimination skills depend on enhanced memory for representations of information. However, neuroscience research has made clear that human memory is not a monolith. There are different types of memory, and there are multiple mechanisms and brain regions involved in forming, retaining, and recalling memories (Baddeley, 2012; Lisman, Grace, & Duzel, 2011; McKenzie & Eichenbaum, 2011; Poppenk & Moscovitch, 2011; Roozendaal & McGaugh, 2011; Squire & Wixted, 2011; Solari & Stoner, 2011).

Enhancement of memory may take place at the time of the encoding of representations, or may depend on greater storage of representations in memory, or on the enhanced consolidation of representations, or the enhanced retrieval and reconsolidation of representations that are to be recognized and discriminated. While it is clear that the consolidation of long-term representations is required for all extraordinary and superior skills considered here, the extent of variation in practice-induced brain changes in brain structures, neurochemicals, and neurophysiological processes involved in superior memory formation is not known. Evidence has suggested that practice serves to consolidate a vast number of representations, and practice serves to make discriminations and calculations automatic. Practice is also assumed to generate changes in the brain that support most savant, prodigious, and superior skills. Some brain changes effected by practice might even parallel the innate brain structure and function differences theorized to confer automatic memory formation. These brain changes might include increased size, activity, or connectedness of brain regions such as the hippocampus or surrounding regions, the lentiform nucleus, the amygdala, the caudate, the fusiform face area, or other cortical regions. They might also include enhanced internal reward neurochemistry, enhanced synaptic formation, greater plasticity of the hippocampus, or increased neurogenesis.

Practice-Induced Heightened Activity in Typical Calculation Brain Regions in Savant Calendar Calculators

In an imaging case study of two calendar calculator savants, Cowan and Frith (2009) found heightened brain activation in regions activated by typical individuals during the learned skill of mental arithmetic. These regions included the parietal cortex, premotor cortex, left inferior temporal lobe, and the supplementary motor area. Cowan and Frith (2009) found no brain abnormalities in the scans of either of the two savants, and concluded that their findings countered proposals that all savants are brain damaged. Just et al. (2004) had theorized that autism symptoms resulted from failed integrative brain circuitry and that savant skills in autism would result from the consequent aberrantly increased connectivity in cortically isolated low-level perceptual systems. Cowan and Frith (2009) argued that their findings for increased activation of the typical mental arithmetic brain activity pattern for two savant calendar calculators countered the notion that savant skills result from redirected use of cortically isolated low-level perceptual systems as theorized by Just et al. (2004).

Fehr et al. (2011) conducted an imaging case study of one typical adult (AB) male with prodigious calendar calculating skill, and one adult male with autism (CD) who was a calendar calculator savant and an art savant. Both CD and AB activated the superior part of left inferior frontal cortex during the calendar tasks, and Fehr et al (2011) theorized that this activity reflected either inner verbalization or use of the left inferior frontal cortex for complex mental processing. Other than this commonality, Fehr et al. (2011) reported, "there was generally little overlap between the activation patterns produced by CD and AB" (p. 9). Interestingly, Fehr et al. (2011) reported that the typical adult prodigy, AB, exhibited the same brain activation pattern as Cowan and Frith (2009) reported for the two savant calendar calculators, namely parietal cortex, premotor cortex, left inferior temporal lobe, and the supplementary motor area.

Practice-Induced Parietal Thickness in Savant Calendar Calculation and Savant Drawing

Wallace, Happé, and Giedd (2009) reported a case study of the brain structure of a multiply talented savant. The savant, GW, was expert in calendar calculation and artistic skills. The researchers found that the superior parietal region of GW's cortex was thicker than typical values, but his superior and medial prefrontal, middle temporal, and motor cortices were thinner than found for a neurotypical control group. Wallace et al. (2009) suggested, "GW's increased superior parietal thickness may have been acquired through practice of calendar and drawing skills" (p. 1431). However, Karama et al. (2011) examined cortical thickness in 433 typical children and found a significant positive correlation between cortical thickness and measured IQ. No regional thickness measures were found to be associated with particular subskills, however, and the researchers proposed that cortical thickness reflected the density and arrangement of neurons, neuroglia, and nerve fibers in the cortex, unlikely to be dramatically altered by practice.

Practice-Induced Enhanced Auditory Memory, Visuospatial Processing, and Hippocampal Changes in Talented Musicians

Groussard et al. (2010) found that imaging revealed that musicians compared with non-musicians had brain activity in a network regulating musical familiarity involving subjective recollection tied to visuospatial imagery, and musicians had significantly higher gray matter density in the head of the left hippocampus than did non-musicians. Groussard et al. (2010) reported that two studies had demonstrated associations between gray matter density of the head of the hippocampus and verbal memory skill. The researchers concluded that this structural difference indicated that musical practice induces gray matter plasticity in the hippocampus.

Cohen, Evans, Horowitz, and Wolfe (2011) and Jakobson, Lewycky, Kilgour, and Stoesz (2008) reported superior memory for musicians. Cohen et al. (2011) demonstrated that musicians had superior auditory memory relative to non-musicians for music and sounds, and concluded that music training enhanced memory skill. Similarly, Jakobson et al. (2008) found memory for verbal material enhanced in musicians and concluded that "formal music training is associated with superior performance in multiple domains of memory functioning" (p. 50).

Practice involves the repetition of information in non-conscious working memory. Baddeley (2012) argued that working memory "provides the temporary storage and manipulation of information that is necessary for performing a wide range of cognitive activities ... [including] an executive component and at least two temporary storage systems, one concerning speech and sound while the other is visuo-spatial" (p. 7). He argued that color and shape perceptions as well as touch and spatial perceptions moved first to a visuo-spatial sketchpad and then on to an episodic buffer and from there to a central executive. He asserted that speech and music perceptions moved to a phonological loop equivalent to the visuo-spatial sketchpad, then to the episodic buffer for evaluation and then to the central executive for decision-making. Baddeley (2012) argued that perceptions in the episodic buffer were available to our conscious minds, and could be altered by refreshed attention, but were time-limited. Squire and Wixted (2011) asserted that declarative memory consisted of representations that allowed the brain to create a model of the external world (p. 267). They argued that short-term declarative memory required activity over a period of weeks to years in both the parahippocampal gyrus and hippocampal formation to become long-term declarative memory that is then stored in the cortex.

Although the practice-induced brain changes in music prodigies have not been reported, the evidence for talented musicians suggests that it is possible that prodigious musicians also experience hippocampal size increase, visuo-spatial processing rededication, and enhanced auditory working memory.

Practice-Induced Hippocampal Enlargement in Superior Route Knowledge

Woollett and Maguire (2011) demonstrated that the process of learning enough to qualify for driving a taxi in London caused a measurable increase in posterior hippocampal size. Woollett and Maguire (2011) offered multiple possible bases for the increase in hippocampal size in the successful London taxi drivers, including enhanced neurogenesis in the hippocampus for new neurons to support spatial memory, better communication between neurons through increased number of new synapses, increased numbers of dendrites on neurons, or even an increased number of glial cells. The most crucial component of taxi-driving skill is the actual driving through the street patterns. This is behavioral memory. Squire and Wixted (2011) defined behavioral memory as non-declarative memory that "is expressed through performance rather than recollection" (p. 267). Squire and Wixted (2011) also included "dispositions, habits, and preferences that are inaccessible to conscious recollection" (p. 267) in non-declarative or behavioral memory.

Because fewer than half of those who try to qualify as taxi drivers succeed, Woollett and Maguire (2011) argued that innate hippocampal plasticity was a likely enhancer of memory storage for practice in route learning in London taxi drivers, and they identified a number of known gene variants that might regulate the size of the hippocampus and, thus, memory performance. Woollett and Maguire (2011) suggested that the hippocampal plasticity shown in the successful taxi drivers might be part of innate "individual differences in spatial memory and navigation ability" (p. 2113).

This claim was supported by the findings of Poppenk and Moscovitch (2011), who found that recollection memory skill in typical healthy young adults was correlated with the size the posterior portion of the hippocampus. Poppenk and Moscovitch (2011) reported a significant positive correlation between recollection memory skill and size of the posterior region of the hippocampus in healthy young adults. The researchers stated that the hippocampus was important for encoding and long-term storage of memories, as well as the retrieval of recollection memory, a form of memory involving the detailed re-experience of specific episodes marked by an item and its context. Place memory is also mediated by the hippocampus, and place learning is the key process in London taxi drivers' knowledge.

McKenzie and Eichenbaum (2011) noted that most memory researchers accepted the hypothesis that the hippocampus immediately stored linked cortical representations for place, multiple sensory representations, and episodes, and that, through practice over time, memory was consolidated as cortical connections strengthened, ultimately freeing the long-term memory from the need for any hippocampal activation. McKenzie and Eichenbaum (2011) also proposed that memory consolidation depends on the hippocampus creating links between the representations of places and routes as well as episodes composed of sequences of events. They proposed that memories interacted through generalized representations of features common to multiple experiences called semantic representations. Moreover, McKenzie and Eichenbaum (2011) claimed that all theories of memory consolidation accepted the premise that generalized semantic representations are themselves interconnected to form generalized schemas that provide us with the "big picture" of our knowledge, history, and structure of our environment, behavior, relationships, and selves.

Practice-Induced Reduced Regional Cortical Activity and Brain Reorganization in Expert Perfumers

Plailly et al. (2012) measured brain activity in 14 novice and 14 expert perfumers while they smelled odors or just imagined smelling odors. The researchers reported that novice and expert perfumers activated the primary piriform cortex, formerly called the olfactory bulb, while they smelled and while they just imagined odors, and for both groups the anterior piriform cortex was more strongly activated during mental imagining of odors. However, when imagining an odor, the experienced perfumers exhibited lower levels of activity in key regions involved in olfactory memory, including the primary olfactory cortex, left and right hippocampus, and the left olfactory orbitofrontal cortex. Plailly et al. (2012) concluded that expert perfumers' superior skill was associated with a functional reorganization of key olfactory and memory brain regions for greater efficiency, and therefore, professional perfumers exhibited a reduction in activation in these areas compared with novices. The degree of activation reduction was inversely correlated with amount of experience as a perfumer. Plailly et al. (2012) noted that pianists and professional golfers had been shown to have less activation in motor cortex and that greater reduction in brain activity was correlated with greater skill. Plailly et al. (2012) reported that professional perfumers were able to instantaneously imagine most odors and novices were not, and the researchers concluded that ease of reactivation of the memory representations of pure or complex odors allowed professional perfumers to compare and combine many scents to create new mosaics of fragrance.

Practice-Induced Changes in Collateral Sulcus and Fusiform Face Gyrus Activity in Chess Experts

Bilalić et al. (2011) reported that the collateral sulcus and, to a lesser extent, the fusiform face gyrus, exhibited greater activity in the brains of chess experts than in the brains of individuals who have no expertise in chess. The collateral sulcus is in the ventromedial surface of the temporal lobe, and it defines where the outer reaches of the hippocampal complex are located. This region includes entorhinal, perirhinal, and parahippocampal cortical areas. Bilalić et al. (2011) reported that chess expertise exists in greater memory for relational patterns of positions of chess pieces on the board, and that experts, unlike non-experts, engage in holistic processing of these patterns mediated by increased fusiform face area activity.

Consequently the possibilities suggested by Woollett and Maguire (2011) for structural alterations in the brains of London taxi drivers may apply to the brains of chess experts. The greater activity in the expert chess players' fusiform face areas, and collateral sulcus regions around the hippocampus, may have developed increased communication between neurons through increased numbers of new synapses, increased numbers of dendrites on neurons, or even an increased number of glial cells. Moreover, it is possible that some expert chess players have inherently greater plasticity in these brain regions.

Practice Effects do not Explain all Savant, Prodigious, or Superior Skills

Despite the claims of Ericsson et al. (2009), Howe et al. (1998), and Maguire et al. (2003) that practice alone is the source of exceptional skills, six skills identified in Table 6.1 have been demonstrated to occur without any practice. Three savant/prodigious skills—highly superior autobiographical memory, accurate image replication, and accurate music replication after brief exposures—and three superior perceptual discrimination skills—superior face recognition, perfect pitch, and word decoding—have been demonstrated to occur prior to extensive practice. In addition, even skills that do require practice may be in part determined by some aspect of initial brain organization. For example, Woollett and Maguire (2011) noted that hippocampal volume and memory skill have been linked to gene variants, and they proposed that London taxi trainees who succeeded "may have had genetic predisposition toward [hippocampal] plasticity that the nonqualified individuals lacked" (p. 2113). Gobet and Campitelli (2007) found a significantly higher number of chess experts were either left-handed or ambidextrous than controls. Gobet and Campitelli (2007) theorized that chess skill, like superior mathematical talent, might reflect enhanced visuospatial ability that "is underpinned more by enhanced interhemispheric interaction" (p. 168).

Moreover, there is evidence of extraordinary skill so early in childhood that a child would not yet have been able to have long practice sessions. The violinist Mischa Elman played the violin with beauty and control at the age of 4, and Keng-Yuen Tseng, a department chair at the Peabody Conservatory in the USA, had memorized all 42 Kreutzer studies by the time he turned 7 years old (Nelson, 2009). Ockelford and Pring (2005) tested Derek Paravacini, a British music savant not diagnosed with autism, and found he had exceptional memory for music, beyond even that of a comparable music prodigy. Young and Nettelbeck (1995) tested a music savant with autism. They found TR's ability to recall notes and passages of music exceptional even though his digit span memory was average. Mozart's ability to write down the entire score to Miserere after hearing it once parallels the extraordinary musical memory reported for music savants (Hermelin, 2001; Treffert, 2010).

Parker et al. (2006) reported the case study of the highly superior autobiographical memory of Jill Price. The researchers stated that when they simply gave her a date, "she would, within seconds, produce the day of the week, or what she did on that day, or what event took place on that day. If allowed to talk uninterrupted, AJ would go on at length telling stories about what she did on that day …. A date, a public event, the name of a television program, the name of a public figure can cue her personal recollections, seemingly effortlessly and automatically" (p. 39).

From these cases and evidence of exceptional skill without practice, it appears that some savant, prodigious, and superior skills have brain bases that confer a predisposition for exceptional skills.

Evidence for Brain Bases of Savant, Prodigious, and Special Skills

Evidence for Brain Bases for Savant Skills

Autism Cognitive Processing as a Possible Brain Basis for Savant Skills

Happé and Vital (2009) proposed that savant skill in autism stemmed from innately enhanced memory representation of specific elements of the visual or auditory environment through "exemplar-based memory encoding, [and] veridical [not context-distorted] representation" (p. 1373). Heavey, Hermelin, Crane, and Pring (2012) supported this theory of autism itself as the basis of savant skill. Heavey et al. (2012) explained, "Given the localized processing style associated with ASD, it may appear somewhat paradoxical that savants are able to use calendrical rules and regularities at all. However, rather than being detrimental, autistic cognition is proposed to facilitate the acquisition of calendrical calculation skills" (p. 6).

Heavey et al. (2012) proposed that savant calendar calculators do not learn rules per se. The researchers argued that savant skill results from a form of autism learning in which exposure to repeated instances of lower-level information, which, for calendar calculator skill is specific day–date pairs, automatically and non-consciously build to a larger structure. The savants may not be aware of the structure that has been built in their memory. Heavey et al. (2012) stated, "A detail-focused processing style is argued to 'draw' individuals with ASD towards these individual elements, with knowledge evolving to represent relations between pairings through subsequent experience and practice" (p. 6).

Commenting on the Heavey et al. (2012) study, Howlin (2012) posited, "Many questions, however, still remain. The most obvious is why such skills are evident in only a minority of individuals with autism or intellectual ability. The possible influence of genetic or environmental factors in the development of these abilities is also unexplored. A further issue of practical significance is why such extraordinary abilities seem to confer so little advantage in other aspects of individuals' lives" (p. 1).

Possible Brain Basis for Savant Art Skill

Corrigan et al. (2012) reported findings of magnetic resonance imaging, spectroscopy, and diffusion tensor imaging for a 63-year-old male savant artist diagnosed with autism. The researchers reported that his cerebral volume was larger than the values for typical adult males, his right amygdala was 24% larger than the left, and his right caudate nucleus was 10% larger than the left. However, the putamen was 8.3% larger on the left side. As the putamen is a component of the lentiform nucleus, the finding for increased putamen size may be consonant with the enlarged lentiform nucleus reported for individuals with highly superior autobiographical memory. Corrigan et al. (2012) also reported finding white matter volumes larger on the right side for the amygdala, hippocampus, frontal lobe, and occipital lobe. The researchers proposed that larger right caudate and amygdala supported enhanced implicit and explicit memory formation. Corrigan et al. (2012) also proposed that the dominance of right hemisphere processing might define savant skill in general.

From a meta-analysis of 74 imaging studies of memory processes, Kim (2011) identified the left inferior frontal cortex as a key encoder of verbal information, and the bilateral fusiform cortex as a key encoder of visual images. Kim (2011) observed that left and right hemisphere premotor cortex, and left and right posterior parietal cortical regions showed greater activity during individual item encoding than during associative encoding. Kim (2011) also concluded that bilateral hippocampal regions were more active for visual encoding than for verbal encoding, and that associative links between images were likely to be generated by greater left hippocampal activity.

Evidence for Brain Bases for Prodigious Skills
Possible Brain Basis for Prodigious Highly Superior Autobiographical Memory
Researchers explored the brain basis of highly superior autobiographical memory in 11 individuals and reported finding larger brain volume in the left temporoparietal junction and the left posterior insula, and a larger than typical lentiform nucleus (Sanders, 2011). The insula and temporal lobe regions are associated with self-related memory, but the lentiform nucleus is linked to obsessive-compulsive behavior. Zarei et al. (2011) demonstrated enlargement of a portion of the putamen, a component of the lentiform nucleus, and associated higher-volume white matter tracts in the brains of children with obsessive-compulsive disorder. Therefore, highly superior autobiographical memory might form automatically through enhanced brain activation that confers greater neurobiological importance on every daily life experience. This might then be immediately stored in the atypically larger self-memory brain regions of the cortex.

Brain Damage or Induced Dysfunction as a Possible Cause of Prodigious Skill
Viskontas et al. (2011) measured visual search performance in frontotemporal lobe dementia, and reported that a subgroup of individuals with semantic dementia were as accurate as controls on all measures of visual search, and on one test performed at the test ceiling with numerically superior performance to controls. Seeley et al. (2008) reported the case of Anne Adams, who experienced primary progressive aphasia, a degenerative disease of the human language network. Ms. Adams, a scientist, felt a strong motivation to produce visual art and, as her disease progressed, her artwork became increasingly realistic. She became interested in Maurice Ravel, the French composer who, like Ms. Adams, had suffered from a progressive aphasia, and she painted Ravel's "Bolero" in a work of art. Seeley et al. (2008) theorized that the subjective relatedness of music and art in her paintings reflected some neurological fusing of perceptual and conceptual images.

Neuroimaging revealed that her brain had severe degeneration of left hemisphere inferior frontal-insular, temporal, and striatal regions, but also showed increased gray matter volume in right posterior cortex in sensory integration areas. Seeley et al. (2008) proposed that loss of function in the left anterior temporal lobe region allowed the development of increased cortical connectivity in right hemisphere dorsal parietal regions that motivated Ms. Adams to generate aphasia-savant artwork.

Temporary induced brain dysfunction has also been shown to confer temporary prodigious skill. On the theory that the left hemisphere actively inhibits superior spatial skills of the right hemisphere, Snyder, Bahramali, Hawker, and Mitchell (2006) administered inhibiting transcranial magnetic pulses to the left anterior temporal lobe of 12 typical individuals. Ten of the 12 improved significantly and several generated a near prodigious visual-spatial skill in rapidly determining the approximate number of imaged objects.

Evidence for Brain Bases for Superior Pattern Recognition and Discrimination Skills

Possible Brain Basis for Perfect Pitch Recognition

Loui et al. (2011) reported that the ability to discriminate musical tones in non-savant absolute pitch musicians, who can name the appropriate pitch class of any given tone without a reference, was predicted by greater white matter connectivity in left and right temporal lobe regions responsible for the perception and association of pitch. The researchers found that individuals with absolute pitch had hyperconnected posterior superior and middle temporal gyri in both left and right hemispheres, and had significantly greater white matter volume than individuals without absolute pitch discrimination skill. Loui et al. (2011) concluded that temporal lobe hyperconnectivity resulting from the larger-than-normal number of white matter tract fibers mediated absolute pitch.

Possible Brain Basis for Superior Face Discrimination

Russell, Chatterjee, and Nakayama (2012) theorized that the fusiform face area automatically operates more effectively in superior face recognizers, conferring better discrimination of stored representations of facial appearance by enhanced pooling of lower level patterns of face shape and face reflectance in combined representations.

Possible Brain Bases for Automatic Word Reading in Advance of Comprehension

Borowsky, Esopenko, Cummine, and Sarty (2007) proposed that early word decoding in typical children involved activity in the brain's temporal lobe object identification and visual word recognition area. Samson, Mottron, Soulières, and Zeffiro (2012) and Scherf, Luna, Minshew, and Behrmann (2010) provided evidence to suggest that hyperlexia—early word decoding without comprehension—in autism might be the result of atypically displaced face and object processing. Scherf et al. (2010) found that individuals with autism activated object recognition regions of the brain when engaged in a face-processing task. The researchers argued that this displaced processing could result from impairment of the fusiform gyrus or impairment in the connectivity of the fusiform gyrus. Samson et al. (2012) proposed that higher activity for words in the fusiform gyrus and medial parietal cortex in autism combined with lower brain activity in many reading regions, along with a pattern of occipital and temporal word processing in the brain, created an unusual autonomy of word processing. The researchers argued that this atypical autonomy was the basis for hyperlexia in autism.

Evidence for Brain Bases for all Three Types of Exceptional Skills: Savant, Prodigious, and Superior Pattern Recognition and Discrimination Skills

Altered Reward System or Compulsion Brain Bases of Savant, Prodigious, and Superior Skills

Howe et al. (1998) argued that the "emergence of unusual skills typically followed rather than preceded a period during which unusual opportunities were provided, often combined with a strong expectation that the child would do well" (p. 401). The controlling effect of parental expectation, famous in Wolfgang's father, Leopold Mozart, may be a force in the practice of some prodigies. However, there is evidence that a compulsion to practice occurs without parental control. Why did Maxim Vengerov practice for 7 or 8 hours a day as a very young child? Why did the hyperlexic child carry around a book to continually read and re-read?

One of the brain structure differences reported for 11 individuals with highly superior autobiographical memory was a larger than typical lentiform nucleus (Sanders, 2011). Although highly superior autobiographical memory is not practiced, altered activation of the lentiform nucleus has been shown to be one of the brain bases of obsessive-compulsive behavior (Zarei et al., 2011). Therefore, it might be hypothesized that atypical alteration of the lentiform nucleus contributes to automatic non-conscious rehearsal of episodic information.

Alternatively, a compulsive motivation to practice may reflect alterations in the dopamine reward system. Söderqvist et al. (2012) reviewed evidence for the role of dopamine in reward and in working memory, and Baskerville and Douglas (2010) argued that dopamine abnormalities might be an important element in the symptoms of autism. Thioux et al. (2006) hypothesized that circumscribed interests in autism reflected a disruption of the reward and motivation system.

Dichter, Richey, Rittenberg, Sabatino, and Bodfish (2012) proposed that altered reward system function was a key feature of autism. Dichter et al. (2012) found that while individuals with autism were anticipating a money reward, their brains exhibited hypoactivation in the right nucleus accumbens of the hypothalamus, and hyperactivation in the right hippocampus. The researchers were surprised to find that individuals with autism did not differ from controls in activation of the nucleus accumbens or ventromedial pre-frontal cortex during face anticipation or face presentation, indicating that they found faces as rewarding as did the controls. However, while individuals with autism were anticipating seeing a face, a social reward, bilateral hyper-activation of the amygdala was observed. Dichter et al. (2012) reported that the degree of hyperactivation of the amygdala predicted social symptom severity in autism. The researchers commented, however, that their findings allowed for competing interpretations. Hyperactivation of the amygdala neurons may reflect coding for a rewarding experience, coding for a punish-ing experience, or may reflect increased problem solving by the amygdala in an effort to try to code value for an ambiguous stimulus. Dichter et al. (2012) also reported the findings for amygdala activation in autism were conflicting: some studies documented increased amygdala activation to faces and some studies did not. The possible application of the Dichter et al. (2012) findings for enhanced memory in autism is that hyperactivation of the amygdala and hyperactivation of the hippocampus would enhance memory formation.

Synesthete Daniel Tammet reported experiencing atypical heightened emotion and affiliative or aversive responses to numbers. His narrative suggests an aberrant strong reward and aversion linked to individual numbers. If num-bers trigger amygdala arousal engaging the neuromodulators norepinephrine and acetylcholine that are associated with emotionally charged experiences, the emotions would trigger a conversion of numbers as ordinary information to numbers as information of very great importance and might thus result in ordinary numbers being rapidly converted to long-term memory.

In an fMRI study of Daniel Tammet, Bor et al. (2007) found hyperactiv-ity in lateral prefrontal cortex when Tammet was encoding digits, compared with controls. The researchers also found elevated lateral prefrontal brain activity and a performance advantage for structured versus unstructured digit sequences for controls. For the same two digit tasks, however, Tammet showed no brain activity change or performance difference. Bor et al. (2007) concluded that, for Tammet, digits are organized by his synesthesia. The researchers did not find the usual synesthesia pattern of activation in Tam-met's brain and proposed that he has his own unique form of emotional synesthesia which might enhance digit recall and calculation with digits.

In typical functioning, the amygdala interacts with the hippocampus and other medial temporal lobe areas to consolidate memories of emotionally arousing stimuli (McIntyre, McGaugh, & Williams, 2011). McIntyre et al.

(2011) stated, "emotional arousal–induced norepinephrine actions promote amygdala modulation of synapses in target areas that ... respond to sensory and cognitive input while they are simultaneously infused with the neuro-modulators norepinephrine and acetylcholine" (p. 9). If the amygdala over-functioned aberrantly, conferring emotional value to information that is not important for survival or for maintaining relationships, this "falsely" over-valued information might be automatically processed for long-term memory formation.

Lisman et al. (2011) argued that long-term potentiation (LTP), the physiological process necessary for the formation of long-term memory, could be divided into LTP formed within a short time, and LTP that takes a longer time to form. Lisman et al. (2011) argued that initial or short-term LTP for a representation was relatively insensitive to dopamine, whereas extended-time LTP was sensitive to dopamine. Abe et al. (2011) stated that dopamine was likely to enhance memory through dopamine-dependent long-term potentiation, and noted that human experience of reward, whether social praise or material such as food or money, was tied to increased dopamine in the midbrain and striatum. Abe et al. (2011) reported that only those individuals who were rewarded during training retained the trained skill 30 days later. Individuals who had been punished or who had not been rewarded during training exhibited substantial skill loss 30 days after training.

Roozendaal and McGaugh (2011) reviewed evidence that epinephrine and glucocorticoids enhanced memory consolidation. They also noted that glucose and fructose each enhanced memory formation, and they outlined the many neurohormones that influenced memory consolidation, including vasopressin, oxytocin, substance P, histamine, and endocannabinoids. They observed that the continuous updating process of working memory required medial prefrontal cortex activity and the action of epinephrine and dopamine.

Clearly, there are many contributors to motivation to practice and many contributors to memory consolidation that might, if altered, enhance savant or prodigious skill memory consolidation.

Excess Neurogenesis as a Possible Brain Basis for Savant, Prodigious, and Superior Memory

Sahay, Wilson, and Hen (2011) proposed that autism was caused by excess new neuron generation in the hippocampus, leading to excessive detail in memory. They noted that complex environments stimulated context and space learning based on neurogenesis in the dentate gyrus of the hippocampus. The researchers claimed that, with increased neurogenesis, there was greater pattern separation in the dentate gyrus of the hippocampus and less pattern completion activity in the CA3 regions of the hippocampus. They asserted that decreased neurogenesis impaired pattern separation, resulting in greater generalization of information processed. Sahay et al. (2011) argued that in an enriched or relatively more complex environment, forming detailed discriminable memories would be adaptive because they would support exploration and learning. Conversely, in a dangerous environment, generalization without detail would be an advantage because it supported avoidance of new situations. Sahay et al. (2011) argued that excessive pattern separation through excessive neurogenesis could result in the pathological attention to detail of autism or obsessive-compulsive personality disorder.

Extending the Sahay et al. (2011) hypothesis to the enhanced memory in savant skills in autism would argue that extraordinary or superior memory for detail could be caused by excessive neurogenesis in the hippocampus in savants.

Synesthesia as a Possible Brain Basis for Savant, Prodigious, or Superior Skills

Although synesthesia might seem an unlikely contributor to savant, prodigious, or superior memory, Rogowska (2011) claimed that synesthesia provides "an additional memory clue very often turning the synesthetes into memory masters" (p. 218). The brain basis for synesthesia is under study. Terhune et al. (2011) conducted a transcranial magnetic stimulation study of six grapheme–color synesthetes and concluded that excitation of primary visual cortex did not function to generate synesthesia, but instead functioned as noise in visual cortex, competing with the visual V4 region of the occipital lobe that supported synesthesia.

Synesthesia may contribute to enhanced memory formation (Bor et al., 2007; Murray, 2010; Rothen & Meier, 2010; Simner, 2012; Terhune et al., 2011; Treffert, 2010). Yaro and Ward (2007) tested 16 synesthetes and found they had a significant memory advantage for material that induced synesthesia, and for color memory. Simner et al. (2009) reported that time–space synesthetes demonstrated superior performance in visual/spatial tasks. Radvansky, Gibson, and McNerney (2011) tested 10 grapheme–color synesthetes. The synesthetes demonstrated significantly greater verbal memory than typical controls. Rothen and Meier (2010) tested 40 grapheme–color synesthetes who exhibited consistently significantly better performance on all measures of verbal memory and measures of visual memory. However, the researchers found no advantage for synesthetes in digit span tests, and they argued that the memory advantage for synesthetes was not extraordinary, because their findings of memory advantage only were within one standard deviation above the mean of a comparison sample of typical individuals.

Neufeld et al. (2012) conducted an imaging study of 14 auditory–visual synesthetes while the synesthetes were listening to music chords and pure tones. The researchers reported that synesthetes showed increased activation in the left inferior parietal cortex. This is a brain area known to be involved with feature binding. However, counter to the claim by Terhune et al. (2011) that brain activation in area V4 was involved in synesthesia, Neufeld et al. (2012) found no difference in brain activation in region V4 for synesthetes compared with typical controls.

Neufeld et al. (2011) concluded that the inferior parietal cortex acts as a sensory integration hub, noting that evidence suggests this region has many roles, including mediating audiovisual integration, multimodality processing of objects, object processing, mental imagery, and non-synesthetic feature binding. Neufeld et al. (2011) also noted that a number of researchers have speculated that inferior parietal cortex in synesthesia induces an atypical hyperbinding of information from different sensory modalities. Enhancement of the function of a hyperbinding hub would be likely to enhance memory formation.

Murray (2010) proposed that savant skills were the result of atypical information processing wherein abstract information was converted to concrete images. Murray (2010) argued, "savants may simply inspect their concrete representation of the concept of interest – be it a calendar, number line or other" (p. 1098). Tammet (2007) described seeing calculations as unusual shapes that he could inspect. Bor et al. (2007) tested Tammet and reported that he had little difference in brain functioning during calculation other than apparently greater efficiency in left temporal lobe processes for calculation. The findings that Tammet's calculation occurs in the same regions as typical controls indicate that the synesthetic visual inspection of the results of calculations as certain shapes may be a post hoc phenomenon. Tammet is likely calculating in the same manner as typical controls, but Tammet sees the calculation results in a pattern he can visually inspect (Tammet, 2007). Second, Wallace et al. (2009) reported the case of an art savant, GW, who exhibited poor memory for a standard test image, and his art production from memory "was characterized by a fragmented approach" (p. 1431). Wallace et al. (2009) observed that other savant artists also had a fragmented approach to production. The evidence for fragmented visual image memory suggested that these art savants are not seeing a complete concrete image in their minds for inspection. The most likely case that Murray's theory would describe is the artist, JG, studied by Drake and Winner (2011). Drake and Winner (2011) stated that JG claims, "He not only sees the image in his mind but can project it anywhere, at any time, for any duration of time so that he has the experience of actually looking at the image" (p. 13).

Summary: More Data Needed on Brain Bases of Savant, Prodigious, and Superior Skills

The savant, prodigious, and superior skills considered here all depend on enhanced memory. Beyond that commonality, it is not clear what generalizations might be made across the skills reviewed here. Some extraordinary skills, such as highly superior autobiographical memory and superior face recognition, have only recently been discovered, and these skills appear to require no practice whatsoever. Conversely, prodigious memory for declarable information has been noted since the advent of writing, and has been demonstrated to depend in large part on intense practice.

Practice is important for many savant, prodigious, and superior skills; however, there may be different patterns of typical and atypical motivation governing practice. External rewards such as parental approval, fame, and money may motivate prodigies, and may motivate some savants. In other savants and prodigies, motivation to practice may arise from aberrant reward system function (Dichter et al., 2012; Thioux et al., 2006). Motivation to practice might also result from an alteration in the neurobiological assignment of biological importance of ordinary information, such as may be generated by emotional synesthesia (Tammet, 2007), or by brain bases for repetitive obsessive-compulsive behaviors (Sanders, 2011).

The brain mechanisms for savant, prodigious, and superior skills may be acquired, as in progressive aphasia or forms of dementia, or may be practice-induced, or may be innate. Brain mechanisms vary across skills, and, within skill type, may vary between savants and prodigies. Individual variation may be common in savant, prodigious, and superior skills. More than 80% of the approximately 22,000 human genes are expressed in the brain. Forming memories is one of the main activities of the human brain, and memory is formed through many brain processes and regions. Therefore, there may be significant individual variation in brain regions, neurochemistry, and brain plasticity.

Fehr et al. (2011) offered important advice for the study of savant and prodigious memory. The researchers stated, "behavioural and neuroimaging-based investigations should more intensely consider individual differences in the neural organization of complex mental processing to provide a valid and sufficient basis for discussions about both the functional principles and local-ization of these processes in the human brain" (Fehr et al., 2011, p. 369).

INTELLIGENCE, SAVANT AND SUPERIOR SKILLS, AND SENSORY ABNORMALITIES IN AUTISM

Intelligence

General intelligence varies widely in autism, but the distribution of IQ scores in autism is different from the distribution in the population as a whole. For example, Charman et al. (2011) reported that, in a group of 156 children with autism, 55% had IQs below 70, and 42% had IQs between 70 and 115. By contrast, just 2–3% of the general population has IQs below 70 (van Bokhoven, 2011), and 95% have IQs between 70 and 130. Research has proposed two types of general intelligence. Crystallized-type intelligence is acquired knowledge, such as vocabulary or mathematics. Fluid-type intelligence is the ability to solve unfamiliar visual and verbal reasoning problems. Standardized tests of fluid verbal and visual-spatial intelligence generate an intelligence quotient, or IQ, score.

Intellectual disability, formerly called mental retardation, is defined as an IQ below 70, impaired behaviors in daily living, and presence before age 18 (van Bokhoven, 2011). Intellectual disability was formerly divided into sub-groups. Intellectual disability was labeled profound if an individual had an IQ lower than 20, severe if an individual had an IQ of 20–34, moderate if an individual had an IQ of 35–49, and mild defined the IQ range from 50 to 69.

Definitions of gifted or high IQ have been more variable. Shaw et al. (2006) defined the IQ range of 121–149 as superior, the IQ range of 109–120 as high, and the IQ range of 83–108 as average, but Charman et al. (2010) defined average IQ as 85–115 and posited that an IQ above 115 was high. Michael Kearney was reported to have the highest valid IQ in the world, somewhere over 200, although his parents claimed it was closer to 300. He earned an Associate Degree in geology at age 8 and a BA in anthro-pology at age 10 (Coon & Mitterer, 2006, p. 372). Despite concern that intelligence tests are culturally biased and may be uninformative about the full range of the skill and talent of an individual, IQ tests have been shown to be "strongly associated with many important life outcomes, including educational and occupational attainments, income, health and lifespan" (Davies et al., 2011, p. 996).

Evidence has linked IQ test scores to a range of brain measurements. Karama et al. (2011) reported that general intelligence was significantly linked to a brain network including the parietal lobe, anterior cingulate cortex, and parts of the temporal and occipital lobes, and was significantly positively correlated with brain gray matter, and negatively correlated with lesions in white matter. Karama et al. (2011) found general intelligence positively correlated with cortical thickness in a sample of 433 typical children 4–18 years old. Cortical thickness includes the density and arrangement of neurons and the neuron support cells called neuroglia, as well as the bundled neuron axons or nerve fibers. Takeuchi et al. (2011) reported that resting cerebral blood flow measures in 63 healthy adults revealed significant positive correlations with gray and white matter and individual general intelligence. Martínez et al. (2011) reported that in 185 healthy adolescents, short-term memory, working memory capacity, and executive updating were so strongly correlated with general intelligence that "they were hardly distinguishable from fluid intelligence" (p. 476). Martínez et al. (2011) concluded that the common mechanisms underlying both fluid intelligence and memory span are basic information processing for encoding information, maintaining information, and retrieving information.

Matson and Shoemaker (2009) noted that intellectual disability is "the most common co-occurring disorder with ASD, and a strong predictor of poor prognosis. This combination of factors suggests the need for even greater efforts at better understanding these two phenomena and their relationship to each other" (p. 1111). Although intellectual disability has most often been defined as a comorbid disorder in autism, evidence accumulating for both genetic and environmental risk factors for autism indicates that autism and intellectual disability co-occur as expressions of a single risk factor. As outlined in Chapter 5, intellectual disability and autism symptoms are conjoint outcomes of many environmental risk factors such as prematurity and maternal malnutrition. Similarly, autism symptoms and intellectual disability are conjoint outcomes of many genetic risk factors for autism (van Bokhoven, 2011). For example, as reviewed in Chapter 4, risk gene variants, including *IL1RAPL1, SHANK2, SHANK3, NLGN3, NLGN4, GRIN2B, TCF4, AUTS2, CNTN4, CNTNAP2*, and *NRXN*, have been expressed as autism without intellectual disability, intellectual disability without autism, and autism with intellectual disability (van Bokhoven, 2011). In addition, Wall et al. (2009) identified 66 candidate gene variants for autism, each of which was expressed as intellectual disability.

Intelligence level, therefore, should be part of the complete symptom set describing an individual with autism.

Sparse Evidence for Correlations of Intelligence with Savant Skills, Superior Skills, and Atypical Sensory Processes in Autism

Understanding the link between intelligence and other skills and sensory abnormalities has been unresolved in autism. Coleman and Gillberg (2012) affirmed, "The relationship between each aspect of the autism personality and each level of intellectual disability is yet to be clarified (p. 231).

Intelligence and Sensory Abnormalities in Autism

Engel-Yeger, Hardal-Nasser, and Gal (2011) reported that intellectual disability was associated with number and degree of sensory abnormalities, wherein children with severe–profound intellectual disability showed more extreme sensory processing abnormalities than did children with mild intellectual disability. Hilton et al. (2010) found no significant correlations between IQ and two measures of sensory responsivity in a sample of 36 high-functioning children with autism. In a sample of individuals with autism, Leekam et al. (2007) found that younger individuals and individuals with lower IQ scores had more symptoms of sensory abnormalities.

Intelligence and Superior Skills in Autism

Newman et al. (2007) reported that children with autism who were hyperlexic had higher verbal intelligence than children with autism who were not hyperlexic, but they had a lower verbal intelligence than typical children who were not hyperlexic. Heaton et al. (2008) reported that an individual with autism and perfect pitch scored within the normal range on both verbal and non-verbal intelligence tests.

Intelligence and Savant Skills in Autism

Howlin et al. (2009) reported finding significant differences in IQ between parent-identified savants with autism, and individuals with autism whose parents had not identified them as having savant skills. For verbal IQ, performance IQ, and full scale IQ, the sample of individuals identified as savants by their parents had significantly higher scores than did those not so identified by their parents. Howlin et al. (2009) also noted that many more individuals in the non-savant group had IQ scores of less than 60.

Neumann et al. (2010) reported IQ scores in the average range for the seven memory savants with autism tested. The savant calendar calculator reported by Thioux, Stark, Klaiman, and Schultz (2006) had an IQ of 74. Wallace et al. (2009) reported that, with the exception of superior calculation skill, a savant calendar calculator and savant artist had an average IQ.

Pring, Ryder, Crane, and Hermelin (2010) reported that nine art savants with autism had high scores on the Block Design test, but these scores did not correlate with IQ. Similarly, Crane et al. (2011) reported no significant association between design fluency and score on the Wisconsin Card Sort and IQ in the group of nine art savants with autism.

Summary: The Relationships Between IQ and Savant Skills, Special Skills, and Sensory Abnormalities in Autism Need Clarifying Data

Individuals with autism and savant skills may have higher IQs (Howlin et al., 2009) or lower IQs (Thioux et al., 2006), or average IQs (Neumann et al., 2010; Wallace et al., 2009). Individuals with autism and superior skills may have lower IQs (Newman et al., 2007) or average IQs (Heaton et al., 2008). Individuals with autism who have sensory abnormalities may have lower IQs (Leekam et al., 2007) or higher IQs (Hilton et al., 2010).

The extremely high prevalence of sensory abnormalities in autism would suggest that sensory abnormalities occur at all levels of intelligence. The unknown prevalence of savant and superior skills in autism offers no guidance, but the existing data suggest that savant and special skills may also occur at all levels of intelligence.

CONCLUSIONS: THEORIES OF SAVANT SKILLS DO NOT EXPLAIN VARIATION, AND PUBLIC ATTENTION TO SAVANT SKILLS SUPPORTS AN UNHELPFUL STEREOTYPE OF AUTISM

Theories of Savant Skills do not Explain Individual Variation

This chapter concluded that the prevalence rate of savant skills in autism remains to be determined, and the chapter outlined evidence for six parallel savant and prodigious skills. This evidence suggested that automatic and practice-induced formation of accurate elaborate memories occurs for savant artists, art prodigies, savant musicians, music prodigies, and for individuals with highly superior autobiographical memory with autism and without autism. This chapter also reviewed evidence that savant and prodigy mnemonists, mental calendar calculators, and rapid mental mathematical calculators have engaged in skill practice. In addition, this chapter reviewed evidence and theory suggesting that many different atypical brain structures and processes were associated with savant, prodigious, and special skills.

Published research exploring savant, prodigious, and superior skills has been case studies or small sample studies (Anderson et al., 1999; Bor et al.,

2007; Corrigan et al., 2012; Cowan & Frith, 2009; Fehr et al., 2010; Heaton et al., 2008; Hu et al., 2009; Neumann et al., 2010; O'Connor & Hermelin, 1992; Sanders, 2011; Treffert, 2010). Although researchers have been aware of the parallels between savant and prodigious skill, research reviewed here indicated that savant skill in autism and parallel prodigious skill in typical individuals has rarely been studied conjointly (Dubischar-Krivec et al., 2009; Fehr et al., 2011).

Despite the minimal data reported for the possible brain bases of savant skills, many theories of savant skill have been proposed (Bor et al., 2007; Fabricius, 2010; Hughes, 2010; Mottron, Dawson, & Soulières, 2009; Murray, 2010; Neumann et al., 2010; Simner et al., 2009; Snyder, 2009). However, these theories have not accounted for individual variation in savant or superior skills. Some theories have suggested that unique splinters of intelligence provide the basis of savant skills (Hermelin, 2001). Other theories have argued that impairment in one brain region releases savant skills in another brain region (Snyder, 2009). In fact, measured intelligence varies widely in autism, and the possible causal web of associations between intelligence, savant skills, superior perceptual recognition and discrimination, and sensory abnormalities has not been determined.

These theories proposed unitary explanations for savant skills. However, the individual variation in atypical brain structure and activation reported for savant, prodigious, and superior skills demonstrated that single cause theories would not explain existing variation. For savant, prodigious, and superior skills, atypical brain structure and/or connectivity was reported for the lentiform nucleus, putamen, caudate, hippocampus, parahippocampal regions, amygdala, fusiform face area, specific regions within the occipital lobe, temporal lobe, parietal lobe, frontal lobe, and connections between brain regions. These findings argue against the possibility that a single atypical brain structure or function could explain the six savant skills considered here.

Examples of problems for three selected theories of savant skill are outlined.

We are all Suppressed Savants Theory of Savant Skill

Some theories of savant brain organization have proposed that all humans have savant skills (Snyder, 2009; Treffert, 2010). However, these theories have not based their claims on the evidence for brain function supporting prodigious skills in typical individuals. Instead, they have theorized hidden prodigious skill in all of us. For example, Snyder (2009) argued that savant skills "reside within everyone, but …. Owing to some atypical brain function, savants have privileged access to raw, less processed information—information in some interim state before it is packaged into holistic labels" (p. 1399). Two studies provided evidence for this theory. Snyder et al. (2006) inhibited function of the left anterior temporal lobe of 12 typical individuals with repetitive transcranial magnetic stimulation (rTMS), and reported that 10 of the 12 improved their ability to correctly guess a display of 50–150 discrete items displayed on a computer screen. Seeley et al. (2008) reported that deterioration of the left anterior temporal lobe of a patient with progressive aphasia had conferred increased gray matter in dorsal parietal regions that appeared to govern a development of savant art skill.

Despite this supporting evidence, the evidence outlined in this chapter argues against the Snyder (2009) theory. First, as noted above, no single brain deficit or alteration will explain the brain bases for all savant skills. Second, Cowan and Frith (2009) found no abnormality in the left hemisphere of two savant calendar calculators. Conversely, they reported that left hemisphere anterior temporal lobe activity occurred during the savant's calculations. This left anterior temporal lobe activity was the same as the activity reported for most typical individuals while engaged in calculations. Moreover, the same left anterior temporal lobe activity was found for a healthy adult calendar calculator (Fehr et al., 2011).

Sensory Acuity Theory of Savant Skill

Baron-Cohen et al. (2011) theorized that heightened sensory acuity resulted in sensory hypersensitivity, excessive attention to detail, and the over-systematizing behavior defining autism. Baron-Cohen et al. (2011) argued that savant skill in autism was linked to registration of perceptual details. A core assumption of this theory is the ubiquity of heightened sensory acuity in autism. However, the evidence for sensory abnormalities in autism counters the possibility that ubiquitous sensory acuity characterizes autism. Leekam et al. (2007) stated that their findings showed, "individuals with autism tend to have sensory abnormalities, not only in one sensory domain but in two or three" (p. 907). The sensory abnormalities found in 90% or 96% of autism are deficits in acuity, as well as hyper- and hyposensitivity to sensory stimuli, not sensory acuity (Leekam et al., 2007; Marco et al., 2011). In addition, as noted above, no single brain deficit or alteration will explain the brain bases for all savant skills. Also, Cowan and Frith (2009) found no focus on sensory detail in two savant calendar calculators whose pattern of brain activation during calculation was the same as the activity reported for most typical individuals while engaged in calculations, and the same left anterior temporal lobe activity was found for a healthy adult calendar calculator (Fehr et al., 2011).

Neural Signal Compression Theory of Savant Skill

Fabricius (2010) argued against the belief that intense practice (Thioux et al., 2006) caused savant skills, arguing it "fails to explain why cognitively 'normal' children cannot achieve such feats" (p. 259). Fabricius (2010) hypothesized, instead, that signal compression at the neural level "can explain every artistic savant who can recreate fine details in their artistic medium of choice" (p. 259). First, as noted above, no single brain deficit or alteration will explain the brain bases for all savant skills. Second, there is clear evidence for the six prodigious skills in "cognitively normal" healthy children and adults that parallel the six savant skills in autism. This evidence stands against Fabricius' (2010) claim that extraordinary skills do not appear in typical healthy children. Third, Fabricius (2010) proposed that compressing the signal representation of sensory stimuli depended on the inhibition of the neurons encoding sensory details of an image or a sound. Corrigan et al. (2012) reported findings for brain imaging for a 63-year-old male savant artist diagnosed with autism. The researchers reported that his cerebral volume was larger than that of typical adult males, his right amygdala and right caudate nucleus were larger than the left, and his left putamen was larger than the right. Corrigan et al. (2012) also found white matter volumes larger on the right side for the amygdala. These brain alterations are likely to have contributed to savant art skill, without any signal compression. Fourth, Diamond (2009) pointed out that neural information processing moves from wide but detailed activation blocks to narrower more focal processing, and that perception and cognition and action operate together. Because the brain process of encoding the properties of any stimulus operates in a large blocked fashion, if the neurons of individuals with savant skills compressed information by inhibition, as theorized by Fabricius (2010), it is more likely that the individual's information processing would be completely dysfunctional, rather than yield savant skills.

While the available data reviewed here suggests that all single cause theories of savant skills are insufficient to explain all cases of savant skill, it may be that some single cause theories of savant skill could be reconfigured to explain specific individual cases or specific savant skills.

Public Attention to Savant Skills Supports an Unhelpful Stereotype of Autism

There is public confusion about autism and savant skills. Draaisma (2009) observed, "The past 20 years or so have seen a considerable proliferation of autism stereotypes—so much so that .... There are now autistic persons as characters in novels and movies, as the subject of biographies or autobiographies, as vignettes in introductory courses" (p. 1476). Most prevalent is the stereotype of the savant with autism. According to Draaisma (2009), in film, "there are hardly any autistic characters not having savant skills" (p. 1478). Draaisma (2009) outlined a film, *Mozart and the Whale* (2005), in which the main character, Donald, is a cab driver with autism. He explains to his passengers that he can see the entire fleet of cabs and their relative distances from his cab in his mind's eye, and he knows to the second how long he has been employed.

In fact, the prevalence of savant skills is likely to be significantly less than either popularly cited estimate of 10% or 33%. Moreover, the prevalence of prodigious skills in healthy individuals is likely to be higher than imagined in many comparisons.

Researchers have been too accepting of estimated prevalence rates for savant skills in autism. There have been too few studies comparing brain function in savant and prodigious skills. Causal variation in savant and prodigious skills argue against single cause theories. In addition, Draaisma (2009) observed that researchers and theorists often unwittingly contribute to the myth of the savant with autism whose extraordinary powers are beyond understanding, or whose innate lack of guile permits them to teach others wise lessons. More data, with greater attention to individual variation in the practice-acquired and innate brain bases for savant and prodigious skills, and fewer speculative theories would help to establish a better understanding of savant and prodigious skills.

REFERENCES

Abe, M., Schambra, H., Wassermann, E. M., Luckenbaugh, D., Schweighofer, N., & Cohen, L. G. (2011). Reward improves long-term retention of a motor memory through induction of offline memory gains. *Current Biology, 21*, 557–562.

Anderson, M., O'Connor, N., & Hermelin, B. (1999). A specific calculating ability. *Intelligence, 26*, 383–403.

APA (American Psychiatric Association). (2011). *DSM-V development: A 09 Autism Spectrum Disorder.* January 26, 2011. Available at http://www.dsm5.org/ProposedRevision/Pages/proposedrevision.aspx?rid=942011.

Baddeley, A. (2012). Working memory: Theories, models, and controversies. *Annual Review of Psychology, 63*, 1–29.

Baron-Cohen, S., Ashwin, E., Ashwin, C., Tavassoli, T., & Chakrabarti, B. (2011). The paradox of autism: Why does disability sometimes give rise to talent? In N. Kapur (Ed.), *The paradoxical brain* (pp. 274–288). New York, NY: Cambridge University Press.

Baskerville, T. A., & Douglas, A. J. (2010). Dopamine and oxytocin interactions underlying behaviors: Potential contributions to behavioral disorders. *CNS Neuroscience and Therapeutics, 16*, e92–123.

Bennetto, L., Kuschner, E. S., & Hyman, S. L. (2007). Olfaction and taste processing in autism. *Biological Psychiatry, 62*, 1015–1021.

Ben-Sasson, A., Carter, A. S., & Briggs-Gowan, M. J. (2010). The development of sensory over-responsivity from infancy to elementary school. *Journal of Abnormal Child Psychology, 38*, 1193–1202.

Bilalić, M., Langner, R., Ulrich, R., & Grodd, W. (2011). Many faces of expertise: Fusiform face area in chess experts and novices. *Journal of Neuroscience, 31*, 10206–10214.

Blakemore, S. J., Tavassoli, T., Calò, S., Thomas, R. M., Catmur, C., & Haggard, P. (2006). Tactile sensitivity in Asperger syndrome. *Brain and Cognition, 61*, 5–13.

Boden, L. M., Rosengren, K. , J., Martin, D. F., & Boden, S. D. (2009). A comparison of static near stereo acuity in youth baseball/softball players and non-ball players. *Optometry—Journal of the American Optometric Association, 80*, 121–125.

Bor, D., Billington, J., & Baron-Cohen, S. (2007). Savant memory for digits in a case of synaesthesia and Asperger syndrome is related to hyperactivity in the lateral prefrontal cortex. *Neurocase, 13*, 311–319.

Borowsky, R., Esopenko, C., Cummine, J., & Sarty, G. E. (2007). Neural representations of visual words and objects: A functional MRI study on the modularity of reading and object processing. *Brain Topography, 20*, 89–96.

Brett-Green, B. A., Miller, L. J., Schoen, S. A., & Nielsen, D. M. (2010). An exploratory event-related potential study of multisensory integration in sensory over-responsive children. *Brain Research, 1321*, 67–77.

Caron, M. J., Mottron, L., Rainville, C., & Chouinard, S. (2004). Do high functioning persons with autism present superior spatial abilities? *Neuropsychologia, 42*, 467–481.

Cascio, C. J. (2010). Somatosensory processing in neurodevelopmental disorders. *Journal of Neurodevelopmental Disorders, 2*, 62–69.

Cascio, C. J., McGlone, F., Folger, S., Tannan, V., Baranek, G., Pelphrey, K. A., et al. (2008). Tactile perception in adults with autism: A multidimensional psychophysical study. *Journal of Autism and Developmental Disorders, 38*, 127–137.

CBS News. (2010). *The gift of endless memory.* Retrieved January 12, 2012 from http://www.cbsnews.com/2100-18560_162-7156877.html?pageNum=8&tag=contentMain;content Body2010.

Charman, T., Pickles, A., Simonoff, E., Chandler, S. E., Loucas, T., & Baird, G. (2011). IQ in children with autism spectrum disorders: Data from the Special Needs and Autism Project (SNAP). *Psychological Medicine, 41*, 619–627.

Chassy, P., & Gobet, F. (2011). Measuring chess experts' single-use sequence knowledge: An archival study of departure from "theoretical" openings. *PLoS One, 6*, e26692.

Cohen, M. A., Evans, K. K., Horowitz, T. S., & Wolfe, J. M. (2011). Auditory and visual memory in musicians and nonmusicians. *Psychonomic Bulletin & Review, 18*, 586–591.

Coleman, N., & Gillberg, C. (2012). *The autisms.* New York, NY: Oxford University Press.

Coon, D., & Mitterer, J. O. (Eds.) (2006). *Introduction to psychology: Gateways to mind and behavior.* Belmont, CA: Wadsworth Publishing.

Corrigan, N. M., Richards, T. L., Treffert, D. A., & Dager, S. R. (2012). Toward a better understanding of the savant brain. *Comprehensive Psychiatry.* [Epub December 27, 2011]. doi: 10.1016/j.comppsych.2011.11.006.

Cowan, R., & Frith, C. (2009). Do calendrical savants use calculation to answer date questions? A functional magnetic resonance imaging study. Philosophical Transactions of the Royal Society of London Series B Biological Sciences, *364*, 1417–1424.

Crane, L., Goddard, L., & Pring, L. (2010). Autobiographical memory in adults with autism spectrum disorder: The role of depressed mood, rumination, working memory and theory of mind. *Journal of Autism and Developmental Disorder, 4*, 383–391.

Crane, L., Pring, L., Ryder, N., & Hermelin, B. (2011). Executive functions in savant artists with autism. *Research in Autism Spectrum Disorders, 5*, 790–797.

Davies, G., Tenesa, A., Payton, A., Yang, J., Harris, S. E., Liewald, D., et al. (2011). Genome-wide association studies establish that human intelligence is highly heritable and polygenic. *Molecular Psychiatry, 16*, 996–1005.

Denison, N. (2007). The rain man in all of us. *On Wisconsin, Summer, 2007*, 28–33.

Diamond, A. (2009). All or none hypothesis: A global-default mode that characterizes the brain and mind. *Developmental Psychology, 45*, 130–138.

Dichter, G. S., Richey, J. A., Rittenberg, A. M., Sabatino, A., & Bodfish, J. W. (2012). Reward circuitry function in autism during face anticipation and outcomes. *Journal of Autism and Developmental Disorders, 42*, 147–160.

Draaisma, D. (2009). Stereotypes of autism. *Philosophical Transactions of the Royal Society of London Series B Biological Sciences, 364*, 1475–1480.

Drake, J. E., & Winner, E. (2009). Precocious realists: Perceptual and cognitive characteristics associated with drawing talent in non-autistic children. *Philosophical Transactions of the Royal Society of London Series B Biological Sciences, 364*, 1449–1458.

Drake, J. E., & Winner, E. (2011–2012). Superior visual analysis and imagery in an autistic child with drawing talent. *Imagination, Cognition and Personality, 31*, 9–29.

Dubischar-Krivec, A. M., Neumann, N., Poustka, F., Braun, C., Birbaumer, N., & Boite, S. (2009). Calendar calculating in savants with autism and healthy calendar calculators. *Psychological Medicine, 39*, 1355–1363.

Eagleman, D. M. (2012). Synaesthesia in its protean guises. *British Journal of Psychology, 103*, 16–19.

Elsabbagh, M., Cohen, H., Cohen, M., Rosen, S., & Karmiloff-Smith, A. (2011). Severity of hyperacusis predicts individual differences in speech perception in Williams Syndrome. *Journal of Intellectual Disability Research, 55*, 563–571.

Engel-Yeger, B., Hardal-Nasser, R., & Gal, E. (2011). Sensory processing dysfunctions as expressed among children with different severities of intellectual developmental disabilities. *Research in Developmental Disabilities, 32*, 1770–1775.

Ericsson, K. A., Nandagopal, K., & Roring, R. W. (2009). Toward a science of exceptional achievement: Attaining superior performance through deliberate practice. *Annals of the New York Academy of Science, 1172*, 199–217.

Fabricius, T. (2010). The Savant Hypothesis: Is autism a signal-processing problem? *Medical Hypotheses, 75*, 257–265.

Falkmer, M., Stuart, G. W., Danielsson, H., Bram, S., Lönebrink, M., & Falkmer, T. (2011). Visual acuity in adults with Asperger's syndrome: No evidence for "eagle-eyed" vision. *Biological Psychiatry, 70*, 812–816.

Fehr, T., Wallace, G. L., Erhard, P., & Herrmann, M. (2011). The neural architecture of expert calendar calculation: A matter of strategy? *Neurocase, 17*, 360–371.

Fehr, T., Weber, J., Willmes, K., & Herrmann, M. (2010). Neural correlates in exceptional mental arithmetic—About the neural architecture of prodigious skills. *Neuropsychologia, 48*, 1407–1416.

Feldman, D. H., & Morelock, M. H. (2011). Prodigies and savants. In R. J. Sternberg & S. B. Kaufman (Eds.), *The Cambridge handbook of intelligence* (pp. 212–234). New York, NY: Cambridge University Press.

Foss-Feig, J. H., Heacock, J. L., & Cascio, C. J. (2012). Tactile responsiveness patterns and their association with core features in autism spectrum disorders. *Research in Autism Spectrum Disorders, 6*, 337–344.

Ghanizadeh, A. (2008). Tactile sensory dysfunction in children with ADHD. *Behavioral Neurology, 20*, 107–112.

Golomb, C. (1999). Art and the young: The many faces of representation. *Visual Arts Research*, *25*, 27–50.

Grandin, T. (1996). *Thinking in pictures: and other reports from my life with autism*. New York, NY: Vintage.

Grigorenko, E. L., Klin, A., & Volkmar, F. (2003). Annotation: Hyperlexia: Disability or superability? *Journal of Child Psychology and Psychiatry*, *44*, 1079–1091.

Groussard, M., La Joie, R., Rauchs, G., Landeau, B., Chételat, G., Viader, F., et al. (2010). When music and long-term memory interact: Effects of musical expertise on functional and structural plasticity in the hippocampus. *PLoS ONE*, *5*, e13225.

Happé, F., & Vital, P. (2009). What aspects of autism predispose to talent? *Philosophical Transactions of the Royal Society of London Series B Biological Sciences*, *364*, 1369–1375.

Harley, E. M., Pope, W. B., Villablanca, J. P., Mumford, J., Suh, R., Mazziotta, J. C., et al. (2009). Engagement of fusiform cortex and disengagement of lateral occipital cortex in the acquisition of radiological expertise. *Cerebral Cortex*, *19*, 2746–2754.

Heaton, O., Davis, R. E., & Happé, G. E. (2008). Research note: Exceptional absolute pitch perception for spoken words in an able adult with autism. *Neuropsychologia*, *46*, 2095–2098.

Heaton, P., & Wallace, G. L. (2004). Annotation: The savant syndrome. *Journal of Child Psychology and Psychiatry*, *45*, 899–911.

Heavey, L., Hermelin, B., Crane, L., & Pring, L. (2012). The structure of savant calendrical knowledge. *Developmental Medicine and Child Neurology*, *54*, 507–513.

Henner, M. (2012). *Total memory makeover: Uncover your past, take charge of your future*. New York, NY: Gallery Books.

Hermelin, B. (2001). *Bright splinters of the mind*. London: Jessica Kingsley Publishers.

Hill, A. L. (1977). Idiot savants: Rate of incidence. *Perceptual and Motor Skills*, *44*, 161–162.

Hilton, C. L., Harper, J. D., Kueker, R. H., Lang, A. R., Abbacchi, A. M., Todorov, A., et al. (2010). Sensory responsiveness as a predictor of social severity in children with high functioning autism spectrum disorders. *Journal of Autism ad Developmental Disorders*, *40*, 937–945.

Hilton, J. (2008, September 12). Autistic chess expert wins Horatio Alger scholarship. *Yahoo! Contributor Network*. Retrieved January 9, 2012 from http://voices.yahoo.com/autistic-chess-expert-wins-horatio-alger-scholarship-1873364.html?cat=72.

Howard, R. (2009). Individual differences in expertise development over decades in a complex intellectual domain. *Memory & Cognition*, *37*, 194–209.

Howe, M. J., Davidson, J. W., & Sloboda, J. A. (1998). Innate talents: Reality or myth? *Behavioral and Brain Sciences*, *21*, 399–407.

Howlin, P. (2012). Understanding savant skills in autism. *Developmental Medicine and Child Neurology*, *54*, 484.

Howlin, P., Goode, S., Hutton, J., & Rutter, M. (2009). Savant skills in autism: Psychometric approaches and parental reports. *Philosophical Transactions of the Royal Society of London Series B Biological Sciences*, *364*, 1359–1367.

Hu, Y., Ericsson, K. A., Yang, D., & Lu, C. (2009). Superior self-paced memorization of digits in spite of a normal digit span: The structure of a memorist's skill. *Journal of Experimental Psychology Learning Memory and Cognition*, *35*, 1426–1442.

Hu, Y., Geng, F., Tao, L., Hu, N., Du, F., Fu, K., & Chen, F. (2011). Enhanced white matter tracts integrity in children with abacus training. *Human Brain Mapping*, *32*, 10–21.

Hughes, J. R. (2010). A review of Savant Syndrome and its possible relationship to epilepsy. *Epilepsy and Behavior*, *17*, 147–152.

IUPUI News Center. (2012, February 17). IUPUI math and science prodigy, 13, loves planets, astronomy, but prefers to keep his feet on the ground: "60 Minutes." *newscenter.iupui.edu*. Retrieved March 1, 2012 from IUPUI-Math-and-Science-Prodigy-13-Loves-Planets-Astronomy-But-Prefers-to-Keep-his-Feet-on-the-Ground-60-Minutes.

Jägle, H., de Luca, E., Serey, L., Bach, M., & Sharpe, L. T. (2006). Visual acuity and X-linked color blindness. *Graefe's Archive for Clinical and Experimental Ophthalmology*, *244*, 447–453.

Jakobson, L. S., Lewycky, S. T., Kilgour, A. R., & Stoesz, B. M. (2008). Memory for verbal and visual material in highly trained musicians. *Music Perception: An Interdisciplinary Journal, 26,* 41–55.

Jennings, K. (2012). *Ken Jennings Confessions of a trivial mind.* Blog post retrieved January 12, 2012 from http://www.ken-jennings.com/aboutken.html.

Jordan, G., Deeb, S. S., Bosten, J. M., & Mollon, J. D. (2010). The dimensionality of color vision in carriers of anomalous trichromacy. *Journal of Vision, 10,* 12.

Just, M. A., Cherkassky, V. L., Keller, T. A., & Minshew, N. J. (2004). Cortical activation and synchronization during sentence comprehension in high-functioning autism: Evidence of underconnectivity. *Brain, 127,* 1811–1821.

Karama, S., Colom, R., Johnson, W., Deary, I. J., Haier, R., Waber, D. P., et al. (2011). Cortical thickness correlates of specific cognitive performance accounted for by the general factor of intelligence in healthy children aged 6 to 18. *Neuroimage, 55,* 1443–1453.

Kennedy, D. P., & Squire, L. R. (2007). An analysis of calendar performance in two autistic calendar savants. *Learning and Memory, 14,* 533–538.

Kenneson, D. (2003). *Musical prodigies perilous journeys, remarkable lives.* Milwaukee, WI: Amadeus Press.

Kim, D. (2011). Neural activity that predicts subsequent memory and forgetting: A meta-analysis of 74 fMRI studies. *NeuroImage, 54,* 2446–2461.

Kim, Y. S., Leventhal, B. L., Koh, Y.-J., Fombonne, E., Laska, E., Lim, E.-C., et al. (2011). Prevalence of autism spectrum disorders in a total population sample. *American Journal of Psychiatry, 168,* 904–912.

Koziol, L. F., Budding, D. E., & Chidekel, D. (2011). Sensory integration, sensory processing, and sensory modulation disorders: Putative functional neuroanatomic underpinnings. *Cerebellum, 10,* 770–792.

Leekam, S. R., Nieto, C., Libby, S. J., Wing, L., & Gould, J. (2007). Describing the sensory abnormalities of children and adults with autism. *Journal of Autism and Developmental Disorders, 37,* 894–910.

Lisman, J., Grace, A. A., & Duzel, E. (2011). A neoHebbian framework for episodic memory; role of dopamine-dependent late LTP. *Trends in Neuroscience, 34,* 536–547.

Loui, P., Li, H. C., Hohmann, A., & Schlaug, G. (2011). Enhanced cortical connectivity in absolute pitch musicians: A model for local hyperconnectivity. *Journal of Cognitive Neuroscience, 23,* 1015–1026.

Lyons, V., & Fitzgerald, M. (2005). Early memory and autism. *Journal of Autism and Developmental Disorders, 35,* 683.

Maguire, E. A., Valentine, E. R., Wilding, J. M., & Kapur, N. (2003). Routes to remembering: The brains behind superior memory. *Nature Neuroscience, 6,* 90–95.

Maister, L., & Plaisted-Grant, K. C. (2011). Time perception and its relationship to memory in autism spectrum conditions. *Developmental Science, 14,* 1311–1322.

Marco, E. J., Hinkley, L. B. N., Hill, S. S., & Nagarajan, S. S. (2011). Sensory processing in autism: A review of neurophysiologic findings. *Pediatric Research, 69,* 48R–54R.

Margan, D. (2008). *Autistic chess champion takes on the world.* The 7:30 Report, Australian Broadcasting Corporation, broadcast: January 16, 2008. Retrieved January 9, 2012 from http://www.abc.net.au/7.30/content/2007/s2139990.htm.

Martínez, K., Burgaleta, M., Román, F. J., Escorial, S., Chun Shih, P., Ángeles Quiroga, M., et al. (2011). Can fluid intelligence be reduced to "simple" short-term storage? *Intelligence, 39,* 473–480.

Martinez Perez, T., Majerus, S., & Poncelet, M. (2012). The contribution of short-term memory for serial order to early reading acquisition: Evidence from a longitudinal study. *Journal of Experimental Child Psychology, 111,* 708–723.

Matson, J. L., & Shoemaker, M. (2009). Intellectual disability and its relationship to autism spectrum disorders. *Research in Developmental Disabilities, 30,* 1107–1114.

May-Benson, T. A., Koomar, J. A., & Teasdale, A. (2009). Incidence of pre-, peri-, and post-natal birth and developmental problems of children with sensory processing disorder and children with autism spectrum disorder. *Frontiers in Integrative Neuroscience, 3*(31). [Epub]. doi: 10.3389/neuro.07.031.2009.

McFeeley, D. (2011, March 20). *Genius at work: 12-year-old is studying at IUPUI.* Indystar.com. Retrieved April 8, 2012 from http://www.indystar.com/article/20110320/LOCAL01/103200369/Genius-work-12-year-old-studying-IUPUI.

McGugin, R. W., McKeeff, T. J., Tong, F., & Gauthier, I. (2011). Irrelevant objects of expertise compete with faces during visual search. *Attention Perception and Psychophysics, 73,* 309–317.

McIntyre, C. K., McGaugh, J. L., & Williams, C. L. (2011). Interacting brain systems modulate memory consolidation. *Neuroscience & Biobehavioral Reviews.* [Epub November 7, 2011]. doi:10.1016/j.neubiorev.2011.11.001.

McKenzie, S., & Eichenbaum, H. (2011). Consolidation and reconsolidation: Two lives of memories? *Neuron, 71,* 224–233.

McPherson, G. E. (2007). Diary of a child musical prodigy. *International Symposium on Performance Science,* 213–218.

Miller, L. (1998). Defining the savant syndrome. *Journal of Developmental and Physical Disability, 10,* 73–85.

Mottron, L., Dawson, M., & Soulières, I. (2009). Enhanced perception in savant syndrome: Patterns, structure and creativity. *Philosophical Transaction of the Royal Society of London Series B Biological Sciences, 364,* 1385–1391.

Murray, A. L. (2010). Can the existence of highly accessible concrete representations explain savant skills? Some insights from synaesthesia. *Medical Hypotheses, 74,* 1006–1012.

Nelson, C. (2009). Monster talents. *The Strad,* 32–36. (2009, April).

Neufeld, J., Sinke, C., Dillo, W., Emrich, H. M., Szycik, G. R., Dima, D., et al. (2012). The neural correlates of coloured music: A functional MRI investigation of auditory-visual synaesthesia. *Neuropsychologia, 50,* 85–89.

Neumann, N., Dubischar-Krivec, A. M., Braun, C., Löw, A., Poustka, F., Bölte, S., et al. (2010). The mind of the mnemonists: An MEG and neuropsychological study of autistic memory savants. *Behavior and Brain Research, 215,* 114–121.

Newman, T. M., Macomber, D., Naples, A. J., Babitz, T., Volkmar, F., & Grigorenko, E. L. (2007). Hyperlexia in children with autism spectrum disorders. *Journal of Autism and Developmental Disorders, 37,* 760–774.

Ockelford, A. (2007). *In the key of genius: The extraordinary life of Derek Paravicini.* London: Random House.

Ockelford, A., & Pring, L. (2005). Learning and creativity in a prodigious musical savant. *International Congress Series, 1282,* 903–907.

O'Connor, K. (2012). Auditory processing in autism spectrum disorder: A review. *Neuroscience and Biobehavioral Reviews, 36,* 836–854.

O'Connor, N., & Hermelin, B. (1992). Do young calendrical calculators improve with age? *Journal of Child Psychology and Psychiatry, 33,* 907–912.

Okamoto, M., Wada, Y., Yamaguchi, Y., Kyutoku, Y., Clowney, L., Singh, A. K., et al. (2011). Process-specific prefrontal contributions to episodic encoding and retrieval of tastes: A functional NIRS study. *Neuroimage, 54,* 1578–1588.

Parker, E. S., Cahill, L., & McGaugh, J. L. (2006). A case of unusual autobiographical remembering. *Neurocase, 12,* 35–49.

Pavlowsky, A., Chelly, J., & Billuart, P. (2011). Emerging major synaptic signaling pathways involved in intellectual disability. *Molecular Psychiatry.* [Epub October 25, 2011]. doi: 10.1038/mp.2011.139.

Pesic, P. (2001–2002). The child and the daemon: Mozart and deep play. *19th-Century Music, 25,* 91–107.

Plailly, J., Delon-Martin, C., & Royet, J. P. (2012). Experience induces functional reorganization in brain regions involved in odor imagery in perfumers. *Human Brain Mapping, 33,* 224–234.

Poppenk, J., & Moscovitch, M. (2011). A hippocampal marker of recollection memory ability among healthy young adults: Contributions of posterior and anterior segments. *Neuron*, 72, 931–937.

Pring, L., Ryder, N., Crane, L., & Hermelin, B. (2010). Local and global processing in savant artists with autism. *Perception*, 39, 1094–1103.

Pring, L., Ryder, N., Crane, L., & Hermelin, B. (2012). Creativity in savant artists with autism. *Autism*, 16, 45–57.

Radvansky, G. A., Gibson, B. S., & McNerney, M. W. (2011). Synesthesia and memory: Color congruency, Von Restorff, and false memory effects. *Journal of Experimental Psychology, Learning, Memory and Cognition*, 37, 219–229.

Ramachandran, V. S., Miller, L., Livingstone, M. S., & Brang, D. (2012). Colored halos around faces and emotion-evoked colors: A new form of synesthesia. *Neurocase*. [Epub November 25, 2011]. doi: 10.1080/13554794.2011.608366.

Rimland, B. (1978). Savant capabilities of autistic children and their cognitive implications. In G. Serban (Ed.), *Cognitive defects in the development of mental illness* (pp. 43–65). New York, NY: Bruner Mazel.

Rogowska, A. (2011). Categorization of synaesthesia. *Review of General Psychology*, 15, 213–227.

Roozendaal, B., & McGaugh, J. L. (2011). Memory modulation. *Behavioral Neuroscience*, 125, 797–824.

Rothen, N., & Meier, B. (2010). Grapheme-color synaesthesia yields an ordinary rather than extraordinary memory advantage: Evidence from a group study. *Memory*, 18, 258–264.

RTEnews. (2012). *Autism on the increase according to conference*. Retrieved January 16, 2012 from http://www.rte.ie/news/2012/0113/autism.html January 13, 2012.

Russell, R., Chatterjee, G., & Nakayama, K. (2012). Developmental prosopagnosia and super-recognition: No special role for surface reflectance processing. *Neuropsychologia*, 50, 334–340.

Russell, R., Duchaine, B., & Nakayama, K. (2009). Super-recognizers: People with extraordinary face recognition ability. *Psychonomic Bulletin & Review*, 16, 252–257.

Ruthsatz, J., & Detterman, D. K. (2003). An extraordinary memory: The case study of a musical prodigy. *Intelligence*, 31, 509–518.

Sahay, A., Wilson, D. A., & Hen, R. (2011). Pattern separation: A common function for new neurons in hippocampus and olfactory bulb. *Neuron*, 70, 582–588.

Saloviita, T., Ruusila, L., & Ruusila, U. (2000). Incidence of savant syndrome in Finland. *Perceptual and Motor Skills*, 91, 120–122.

Samson, F., Mottron, L., Soulières, I., & Zeffiro, T. A. (2012). Enhanced visual functioning in autism: An ALE meta-analysis. *Human Brain Mapping*, 33, 1553–1581.

Sanders, L. (2011). Brain parts differ in gifted memory. *Science News, December*, 3, 9.

Scherf, K. S., Luna, B., Minshew, N., & Behrmann, M. (2010). Location, location, location: Alterations in the functional topography of face- but not object- or place-related cortex in adolescents with autism. *Frontiers in Human Neuroscience*, 22, 26. [Epub]. doi: 10.3389/fnhum.2010.00026.

Schulze, K., Gaab, N., & Schlaug, G. (2009). Perceiving pitch absolutely: Comparing absolute and relative pitch possessors in a pitch memory task. *BMC Neuroscience*, 10, 106.

Seeley, W. W., Matthews, B. R., Crawford, R. K., Gorno-Tempini, M. L., Foti, D., Mackenzie, I. R., et al. (2008). Unravelling Bolero: Progressive aphasia, transmodal creativity and the right posterior neocortex. *Brain*, 131(Pt 1), 39–49. doi: 10.1093/brain/awm270.

Shaw, P., Greenstein, D., Lerch, J., Clasen, L., Lenroot, R., Gogtay, N., & Giedd, J. (2006). Intellectual ability and cortical development in children and adolescents. *Nature*, 440, 676–679.

Simner, J. (2012). Defining synaesthesia. *British Journal of Psychology*, 103, 1–15.

Simner, J., Mayo, N., & Spiller, M. J. (2009). A foundation for savantism? Visuo-spatial synaesthetes present with cognitive benefits. *Cortex*, 45, 1246–1260.

Simner, J., Mulvenna, C., Sagiv, N., Tsakanikos, E., Witherby, S. A., Fraser, C., et al. (2006). Synaesthesia: The prevalence of atypical cross-modal experiences. *Perception, 35,* 1024–1033.

Snyder, A., Bahramali, H., Hawker, T., & Mitchell, D. J. (2006). Savant-like numerosity skills revealed in normal people by magnetic pulses. *Perception, 35,* 837–845.

Snyder, A. W. (2009). Explaining and inducing savant skills: Privileged access to lower level, less processed information. *Philosophical Transactions of the Royal Society of London Series B Biological Sciences, 364,* 1399–1405.

Söderqvist, S., Bergman Nutley, S., Peyrard-Janvid, M., Matsson, H., Humphreys, K., Kere, J., et al. (2012). Dopamine, working memory, and training induced plasticity: Implications for developmental research. *Developmental Psychology, 48,* 836–843.

Solari, S. V., & Stoner, R. (2011). Cognitive consilience: Primate non-primary neuroanatomical circuits underlying cognition. *Frontiers in Neuroscience, 5,* 65, [Epub]. doi:10.3389/fnana.2011.00065.

Squire, L. R., & Wixted, J. T. (2011). The cognitive neuroscience of human memory since H.M. *Annual Review of Neuroscience, 34,* 259–288.

Stix, G. (2011). Exceptional memory explained: How some people remember what they had for lunch 20 years ago. Observations, November 16, 2011. *Scientific American.* Retrieved December 20, 2011 from http://blogs.scientificamerican.com/observations/2011/11/16/group-with-exceptional-memory-remembers-what-was-for-lunch-20-years-ago/.

Sykes, C. S. (2012). *David Hockney: The biography.* New York, NY: Random House.

Takeuchi, H., Taki, Y., Hashizume, H., Sassa, Y., Nagase, T., Nouchi, R., et al. (2011). Cerebral blood flow during rest associates with general intelligence and creativity. *PLoS ONE, 6,* e25532.

Tammet, D. (2007). *Born on a blue day: Inside the extraordinary mind of an autistic savant.* New York, NY: Free Press.

Tavassoli, T., Latham, K., Bach, M., Dakin, S. C., & Baron-Cohen, S. (2011). Psychophysical measures of visual acuity in autism spectrum conditions. *Vision Research, 51,* 1778–1880.

Terhune, D. B., Tai, S., Cowey, A., Popescu, T., & Cohen Kadosh, R. (2011). Enhanced cortical excitability in grapheme-color synesthesia and its modulation. *Current Biology, 21,* 2006–2009.

Thioux, M., Stark, D. E., Klaiman, C., & Schultz, R. T. (2006). The day of the week when you were born in 700 ms: Calendar computation in an autistic savant. *Journal of Experimental Psychology Human Perception and Performance, 32,* 1155–1168.

This is Plymouth. (2008, August 22). *Bideford chess star on target to become International Chess Master. This is North Devon.* Retrieved January 20, 2012 from http://www.thisisplymouth.co.uk/Bideford-chess-star-target-International-Chess-Master/story-12160976-detail/story.html.

Treffert, D. A. (1989). *Extraordinary people.* New York, NY: Harper & Row.

Treffert, D. A. (2010). *Islands of genius.* London: Jessica Kingsley Publishers.

Turkeltaub, P. E., Flowers, D. L., Verbalis, A., Miranda, M., Gareau, L., & Eden, G. F. (2004). The neural basis of hyperlexic reading: An FMRI case study. *Neuron, 8,* 11–25.

Urdapilleta, I., Parr, W., Dacremont, C., & Green, J. (2011). Semantic and perceptive organisation of Sauvignon blanc wine characteristics: Influence of expertise. *Food Quality and Preference, 22,* 119–128.

van Bokhoven, H. (2011). Genetic and epigenetic networks in intellectual disabilities. *Annual Review of Genetics, 45,* 81–104.

Van Hulle, C. A., Schmidt, N. L., & Goldsmith, H. H. (2012). Is sensory over-responsivity distinguishable from childhood behavior problems? A phenotypic and genetic analysis. *Journal of Child Psychology and Psychiatry, 53,* 64–72.

Viskontas, I. V., Boxer, A. L., Fesenko, J., Matlin, A., Heuer, H. W., & Miller, B. L. (2011). Visual search patterns in semantic dementia show paradoxical facilitation of binding processes. *Neuropsychologia, 49,* 468–478.

Wakefield, A. J., Murch, S. H., Anthony, A., Linnell, J., Casson, D. M., Malik, M., et al. (1998). Ileal-lymphoid-nodular hyperplasia, non-specific colitis, and pervasive developmental disorder in children. *Lancet, 351*, 637–641.

Wall, D. P., Esteban, F. J., Deluca, T. F., Huyck, M., Monaghan, T., Velez de Mendizabal, N., et al. (2009). Comparative analysis of neurological disorders focuses genome-wide search for autism genes. *Genomics, 93*, 120–129.

Wallace, G. L., Happé, F., & Giedd, J. N. (2009). A case study of a multiply talented savant with an autism spectrum disorder: Neuropsychological functioning and brain morphometry. *Philosophical Transactions of the Royal Society of London Series B Biological Science, 364*, 1425–1432.

Ward, J. (2004). Emotionally mediated synaesthesia. *Cognitive Neuropsychology, 21*, 761–772.

Waterhouse, L. (1988). Extraordinary visual memory and pattern perception in an autistic boy. In L. K. Obler & D. B. Fein (Eds.), *The exceptional brain* (pp. 325–338). New York, NY: Guilford Press.

Wates, R. E. (2010). *Mozart: An introduction to the music, the man, and the myths*. Milwaukee, WI: Amadeus Press.

Weigelt, S., Koldewyn, K., & Kanwisher, N. (2012). Face identity recognition in autism spectrum disorders: A review of behavioral studies. *Neuroscience and Biobehavioral Reviews, 36*, 1060–1084.

Woollett, K., & Maguire, E. A. (2011). Acquiring "the Knowledge" of London's layout drives structural brain changes. *Current Biology, 21*, 2109–2114.

Yaro, C., & Ward, J. (2007). Searching for Shereshevskii: What is superior about the memory of synaesthetes? *Quarterly Journal of Experimental Psychology, 5*, 681–695.

Young, R. L., & Nettelbeck, T. (1995). The abilities of a musical savant and his family. *Journal of Autism and Developmental Disorders, 25*, 231–248.

Zarei, M., Mataix-Cols, D., Heyman, I., Hough, M., Doherty, J., Burge, L., et al. (2011). Changes in gray matter volume and white matter microstructure in adolescents with obsessive-compulsive disorder. *Biological Psychiatry, 70*, 1083–1090.

Zmigrod, S., de Sonneville, L. M., Colzato, L. S., Swaab, H., & Hommel, B. (2012). Cognitive control of feature bindings: evidence from children with autistic spectrum disorder. *Psychological Research*. [Epub December 6, 2011]. doi: 10.1007/s00426-011-0399-3.

CHAPTER 7

Increasing Prevalence and the Problem of Diagnosis

Contents

Rethinking Autism
http://dx.doi.org/10.1016/B978-0-12-415961-7.00007-1

Gillberg and Wing (1999) reviewed all available autism prevalence studies and concluded that autism was more prevalent than earlier estimates of approximately 2–5 in 10,000 children. They divided the total number of individuals diagnosed with autism by the total number of individuals screened in the studies they reviewed and concluded, "the most reasonable conservative estimate is about 1 in 1,000 children" (Gillberg & Wing, 1999, p. 404). A decade later, Fombonne (2009) reviewed 43 studies of prevalence of autism. He reported that 63.5 in 10,000 was the median prevalence rate for the 19 newer of the 43 studies. Fombonne (2009) declared that there was a striking convergence of prevalence rates at around 60–70 in 10,000, and he concluded, "one child in about 150 children can be confidently derived for the prevalence of autism spectrum disorders" (p. 157).

Thus in the 10 years between 1999 and 2009 there appeared to be a 650% increase in estimated general autism prevalence, from 10 in 10,000 (Gillberg & Wing, 1999) to 65 in 10,000 (Fombonne, 2009). In 2009, the United Stated Centers for Disease Control reported a 1 in 110 prevalence rate for a set of regions in the United States for the year 2006 (Autism and Developmental Disabilities Monitoring Network Surveillance Year 2006 Principal Investigators, CDC, 2009). In 2012, the Centers for Disease Control reported that in 2008 the prevalence rate monitored in the US had increased to 1 in 88 (Autism and Developmental Disabilities Monitoring Network Surveillance Year 2008 Principal Investigators, CDC, 2012).

Table 7.1 identifies autism prevalence rates reported for different countries for the years 2001 to 2010. The lowest prevalence rate of autism was 2 in 10,000 for children in China for 2005 reported by Li et al. (2011). Zaroff and Uhm (2012) reviewed prevalence rates around the world and concluded that the prevalence of autism was generally lower in countries outside of North America and Europe. However, Kim et al. (2011) published a prevalence rate for autism of 2.64% in Korea that was the highest rate ever reported anywhere in the world. Kim et al. (2011) defended this startlingly high prevalence rate, claiming, "validated, reliable, and commonly accepted screening procedures and diagnostic criteria in a total population may yield an ASD prevalence ... in the range of 2%–3%" (p. 7).

Zaroff and Uhm (2012) claimed, "Perhaps the only unifying feature of ASD prevalence data worldwide is the well-publicized increase in prevalence over time" (p. 397). Although increased prevalence was reported by many studies, it was unclear what increased prevalence rate should be accepted. For example, in Table 7.1 the median, or midpoint between the two most extreme prevalence rates of 2 in 10,000 (China 2005, Li et al., 2011) and 264 in 10,000 (Korea 2010, Kim et al., 2011) yielded a rate of 133 in 10,000, or 1 in 75. This ad hoc prevalence rate of 1 in 75 is double the 1 in 150 prevalence rate asserted by Fombonne (2009), but half the rate of 1 in 38 (Kim et al., 2011). Should the accepted prevalence rate be the largest, 1 in 38 as Kim et al. (2011) reported for Korea? Should the accepted prevalence rate be the midpoint of the lowest and highest recent prevalence rates, 1 in 75? Nazeer and Ghaziuddin (2012) reported that autism now occurred "in at least 1 out of every 100 children" (p. 21). This rate was an approximation of the average autism prevalence rate for 11 United States regions of 9.0 per 1000 children (Centers for Disease Control and Prevention, 2009).

Only an international study assessing whole population groups of the same age range, using the same diagnostic measures conducted within the same period would provide a sound basis for determining world prevalence. Of course, the wide differences reported for prevalence from country to country, and from region to region within a country, might represent real differences in incidence between countries and regions. If so, estimating a world prevalence rate for autism would not be of value.

The key unknown in the rising prevalence of autism was whether the increase was real. Leonard et al. (2010) lamented that, "Despite more than a decade of epidemiological investigation, it is still unclear whether the rising trend in prevalence reflects a true increase or changes in diagnostic trends and improvements in case ascertainment" (p. 548). Most researchers did not believe the actual incidence of autism was increasing (Brugha et al., 2011; Fombonne, 2009; Gernsbacher, Dawson, & Goldsmith, 2005; Leonard et al., 2010; Rosenberg, Daniels, Law, Law, & Kaufmann, 2009; Matson & Kozlowski, 2011). Fischbach (2011) stated, "Leo Kanner in 1943 gathered a group of children and said there is something common about these children ... but the definition has just kept expanding since then." Frances and Widiger (2012) cavalierly called the increasing prevalence of autism a fad, arguing

Table 7.1 Comparison of Prevalence Rates for Autism Spectrum Disorder for Countries Reporting Prevalence Rates from 2001 to 2010

Country	2001	2002	2003	2004	2005	2006	2007	2008	2009	2010
Number of Children or Adults Diagnosed with Autism Spectrum Disorder per 10,000, Rounded to the Nearest Whole Number										
Australia (Western), children (Parner et al., 2011)				51						
Australia, children (Williams, MacDermott, Ridley, Glasson, & Wray, 2008)				12–36						
Canada, (Montreal), children (Lazoff, Zhong, Piperni, & Fombonne, 2010)								79		
China (Hong Kong), children (Wong and Hui, 2008)					30					
China, children (Li, Chen, Song, Du, & Zheng, 2011)					2					
Denmark, children (Parner et al., 2011)				69						
England (London), children (Baird et al., 2006)					116					
England (Cambridgeshire), children (Baron–Cohen et al., 2009)									157	
England, adults (Brugha et al., 2011)							98			
Faroe Islands, children (Ellefsen, Kampmann, Billstedt, Gillberg, & Gillberg, 2007)		56								
Faroe Islands, children (Koovská et al., 2012)									94	
Iran (Shiraz), children (Ghanizadeh, 2008)							190			

Study	3–7	3–8	4–9	5–11	6–13	8–15	8–17			
Japan (Toyota), children (Kawamura, Takahashi, & Ishii, 2008)		181								
Korea (Southern), children (Kim et al., 2011)									264	
Scotland (Glasgow), children (Campbell, Reynolds, Cunningham, Minnis, & Gillberg, 2011)							111			
Sweden, children (Nygren et al., 2012)										80
Taiwan, children (Lin, Lin, & Wu, 2009)						29				
United Arab Emirates, children (Eapen, Mabrouk, Zoubeidi, & Yunis, 2007)										
USA (14 areas), children (Centers for Disease Control and Prevention, 2007)		66								
USA (14 areas), children (Centers for Disease Control and Prevention, 2009)				80		91				
USA (14 areas), children (Centers for Disease Control and Prevention, 2012)								114		
Venezuela (Maracaibo County), children (Montiel-Nava & Peña, 2008)						17				
Wales (Rhondda, Taff Ely), children (Latif & Williams, 2007)			61							
Averaged Prevalence per 10,000 Across Countries by Year where Two or More Rates are Identified	—	77	34	46	40	37	103	97	172	—

"fads in diagnosis come and go and have been with us as long as there has been psychiatry" (p. 7.7). Fombonne (2009) stated, "As it stands now, the recent upward trend in estimates of prevalence cannot be directly attributed to an increase in the incidence of the disorder" (p. 597).

Brugha et al. (2011) found autism prevalence in English adults to be 1 in 100, a rate "essentially the same as recently reported in systematic surveys of children up to age 15 years" (p. 464). The researchers argued that, because prevalence for adults was the same as for children, autism prevalence must be stable, not increasing. Brugha et al. (2011) proposed that the field should be "looking for causes of autism that have always been there, and not just for causes that have developed in recent years or decades" (Weintraub, 2011, p. 23). Ouellette-Kuntz et al. (2007) reported a significant trend for increased diagnosis of autism from 1997 to 2004 in British Columbia, Canada. However, unlike Brugha et al. (2011), Ouellette-Kuntz et al. (2007) argued that their findings did "not support the notion that rates of autism are stabilizing" (p. 1947), and proposed that because "of the uncertainty as to whether the real risk of ASDs is increasing, continued monitoring of the prevalence of this group of disorders is warranted" (p. 1947).

Broader Diagnostic Criteria Increased Autism Prevalence

Fombonne (2009) claimed that four factors caused increased autism prevalence, but that none of the four factors caused a true increase in incidence. Fombonne (2009) identified the first factor as broader diagnostic criteria for autism. Broader criteria increased prevalence by simply allowing more individuals to meet the diagnostic criteria for autism. Gillberg and Wing (1999) pointed out that criteria for autism prior to DSM-III (APA, 1980) were narrow and absolute, requiring a profound lack of social contact to age 5 and elaborate repetitive routines. Gillberg and Wing (1999) claimed that, over time, psychiatrists and researchers found this narrow diagnosis of autism failed to include many children with serious social impairment, and inclusion of more children led to the spectrum model of autism. From DSM-III onward, autism criteria were altered in each new version of DSM, from DSM-III-R (APA, 1987) to DSM-IV (APA, 1994) to DSM-IV-TR (APA, 2000), and to the proposed DSM-5 (APA DSM-5 Development, 2012a). Among these changes were alterations in autism subgroups, in type of symptoms, in number of symptoms, and in age of onset. Wazana, Bresnahan, and Kline (2007), in fact, suggested that the cumulative changes in autism diagnostic criteria up to DSM-IV-TR might have caused a 28-fold increase in autism prevalence over time.

Another associated problem was the use of DSM criteria by practitioners. Rosenberg et al. (2009) found that DSM-IV-TR criteria were not universally accepted by all diagnosticians. Rosenberg et al. (2009) noted, "Although psychiatrists and psychologists were most likely to adhere to DSM-IV-TR categories, many other evaluators may have found them insufficient or less useful" (p. 1107). Rosenberg et al. (2009) suggested that the process of diagnosis was at the mercy of diagnostician practice, and argued that diagnosticians might have misinterpreted the DSM-IV-TR guidelines perhaps because those engaged in diagnosis felt "dissatisfaction … with the current system" (p. 1105).

Lord et al. (2012) confirmed the concerns of Rosenberg et al. (2009) regarding diagnostic practice. Lord et al. (2012) reported that clinicians at university-based sites did not share the same diagnostic vision of the diagnoses within the DSM-IV group, that is, autistic disorder, Pervasive Developmental Disorder Not Otherwise Specified (PDD-NOS), and Asperger syndrome. Lord et al. (2012) reported that patterns of clinician diagnosis were idiosyncratic and complex. The researchers found that "statistically significant differences emerged across sites in the proportion of probands assigned to … autistic disorder, Asperger syndrome, and PDD-NOS" (Lord et al., 2012, p. 308). Clinicians could not replicate one another's diagnoses. This suggested that diagnostic categories were not adequately defined, or that clinician judgment was variable.

Diagnostic Substitution Increased Autism Prevalence

Fombonne (2009) identified a second factor contributing to the increased prevalence of autism as substitution of an autism diagnosis for another diagnosis. Fischbach (2011) stated, "As the diagnosis of autism is increasing the diagnosis of mental retardation is decreasing. And … more children who are just a little bit off … now are being described as perhaps Asperger's syndrome." Rosenberg et al. (2009) suggested that diagnosticians might have diagnosed children with autism spectrum disorder when their symptoms were not fully consonant with an autism diagnosis, and may have substituted the autism spectrum diagnosis for many who had intellectual disability without autism. Rosenberg et al. (2009) also claimed that the Asperger syndrome diagnosis had come to serve as a general diagnosis for high-functioning children who had behavioral problems. King and Bearman (2009) studied diagnostic change in the state of California, and estimated that one-fourth of increased autism prevalence was the result of diagnostic substitution. King and Berman (2009) proposed that the substitution of the diagnosis of autism for intellectual disability was "likely contributing to the lower functioning portion of the autism spectrum ... developmental language disorder or other learning disabilities, may be contributing to an increase in higher functioning cases" (p. 1232).

Government Policy Changes Increased Autism Prevalence

Fombonne (2009) claimed a third factor contributing to the increased prevalence of autism was government policy changes that had an impact on special education. Coo et al. (2008) found that in British Columbia, Canada, autism prevalence increased by an additional 31 in 10,000 children aged 4–9 years over a 9-year period from 1996 to 2004. Coo et al. (2008) reported that one change in government policy that might have contributed to the increase in prevalence during this period was "the provision of direct funding to families of children with an ASD, to allow them to purchase intensive early behavioural treatment and intervention" (p. 1044).

Autism was added to the United States Individuals with Disabilities Education Act in 1991. This Act requires all educational institutions receiving federal funds to provide free and appropriate public education to children with disabilities. However, the United States federal government has typically contributed only 18% of the states' yearly funding for special education. Moreover, because public education depends on local property taxes in most school districts, there has been uneven funding for special education across the United States (Caruso, 2010). Hertz-Picciotto and Delwiche (2009) concluded that funding changes in the provision of services from 1992 to 2006 could have increased the identification of autism. They noted that from the early 1990s to 2006, California increased support for services for developmental disabilities from $72 million to over $400 million, possibly contributing to the rise in prevalence in autism in California during this period.

Not all government policies, however, resulted in an increase in prevalence of autism. Fountain and Bearman (2011) reported that in California in the 1990s, autism was systematically under-diagnosed in Hispanic children. Fountain and Bearman (2011) argued that this selective under-diagnosis of autism in Hispanic children was the result of a ballot initiative Proposition 187 and other California anti-immigrant legislation. The researchers noted that although these policy changes were intended to prevent access to public services by undocumented immigrants, the effect of these policy changes "was to discourage some families of citizen children from seeking diagnosis of and services for their developmental disabilities" (Fountain & Berman, 2011, p. 3).

Increased Availability of Services Increased Autism Prevalence

Fombonne (2009) proposed that a fourth factor causing a rise in autism prevalence was the increasing availability of services for children with autism. Autism researcher Bookheimer (2011) noted, "the availability of some interventions and some treatments makes it much more likely that people will want to get a diagnosis because then you have a place to go" (Bookheimer, 2011). Fountain, King, and Bearman (2011) reported that, as autism prevalence increased significantly in California from 1992 to 2006, the age of first autism diagnosis grew earlier and earlier. Fountain et al. (2011) found that most of the drop in age at diagnosis occurred after 1996, and they reported that autism diagnoses occurred for younger children in wealthier communities. The researchers proposed that availability of services for the youngest children diagnosed with autism, combined with the knowledge that earlier treatment improved prognosis, led to the age of diagnosis becoming younger year by year in California. The researchers warned, "If early intervention is important, this disparity in the age of diagnosis has the potential to amplify socio-economic differences in outcomes later on" (Fountain et al., 2011, p. 6).

Increased Social Awareness of Autism Increased Autism Prevalence

In addition to the four factors Fombonne (2009) identified, Keyes et al. (2011) identified a fifth factor, heightened social awareness of autism, as driving the increase in autism prevalence without actually increasing the incidence of autism. Keyes et al. (2011) studied the diagnoses of autism for all children born in California from 1992 to 2003. They found that when compared with children born in 1992, every younger group for each birth year had "significantly higher odds of an autism diagnosis than the previous cohort" such that children born "in 2003 have 16.6 times the odds of an autism diagnosis compared with those born in 1992" (Keyes et al., 2011, p. 1). The researchers concluded that autism prevalence increased linearly year-to-year by birth cohorts, and the increase in prevalence was greater for high-functioning children. Keyes et al. (2011) concluded that the best explanation for their data was not that children were being diagnosed with autism at younger ages, but that changes in diagnostic practice and heightened social awareness of autism were likely to be driving the increased prevalence of autism in California.

Mazumdar, King, Liu, Zerubavel, and Bearman (2010) reported evidence for heightened social awareness arising from informal social networks of parents. The researchers found clusters of higher prevalence of autism in regions of California for every birth cohort for every year they studied from 1993 to 2001. They reported that children born in a primary prevalence cluster were nearly four times more likely to be diagnosed with autism than children living in any non-cluster region of California. Mazumdar et al. (2010) also found secondary clusters that supported the primary clusters. Primary diagnostic clusters that included only autism were centered on West Hollywood in Los Angeles. Children born in this set of clusters centered on West Hollywood were at four times greater risk of autism than children born any other place in California. The researchers argued that the California Department of Developmental Services was not providing different diagnoses within and outside primary clusters. Instead, Mazumdar et al. (2010) concluded that advocacy organizations might be directly or indirectly helping parents in primary clusters obtain diagnoses for their children. The researchers also suggested it was likely that parents spread information about autism to other parents through informal social networks within primary clusters. The researchers concluded, "If these dynamics are operating, even very small environmental risks could yield the amplification of autism risk we observe in the primary cluster areas" (Mazumdar et al., 2010, p. 8). Zaremba (2011) reported that Bearman concluded the influence of neighbors alone accounted for 16% of the increase in autism in California between 2000 and 2005.

A True Increase in the Incidence of Autism is Possible

Most researchers accepted the evidence that diagnostic criteria changes, diagnostic substitution, special education policy changes, increased availability of services, and heightened awareness of autism all had contributed to the increased prevalence of autism without increasing the true incidence of autism.

A number of researchers, however, remained concerned that there was a true increase in the incidence of autism. For example, Hertz-Picciotto and Delwiche (2009) suspected that some portion of the increased prevalence was a true increase in incidence. They reported autism rose 7–8-fold in California from the early 1990s to 2009, but that changes in diagnostic criteria, earlier diagnosis, and inclusion of milder cases together only accounted for a 5-fold increase. The researchers proposed that, "With no evidence of a leveling off, the possibility of a true increase in incidence deserves serious consideration" (Hertz-Picciotto & Delwiche, 2009, p. 89). Similarly, Schieve et al. (2011) found that although fertility treatment, low birth weight, preterm delivery, cesarean section, multiple births, and breech presentation were all associated with increased risk for autism, together the increase in these factors over time did not add up to enough additional risk coverage to account for the rise in autism prevalence.

Dr. Thomas Insel, Director of the National Institutes of Mental Health in the United States, and acting director of the National Center for Advancing Translational Sciences at the National Institutes of Health, stated that he believed the increase in the prevalence of autism might be a true increase in incidence. Insel wondered why "This whole idea of whether the prevalence is increasing is so contentious for autism, but not for asthma, type 1 diabetes, food allergies—lots of other areas where people kind of accept the fact that there are more kids affected" (Weintraub, 2011, p. 22).

The DSM Diagnostic System and Increased Autism Prevalence

A major point of contention for autism researchers was the causal role of the American Psychiatric Association (APA) Diagnostic and Statistical Manual (DSM) diagnostic criteria in increasing the prevalence of autism. Volkmar et al. (1997) argued that the DSM-III-R (APA, 1987) autism criteria broadened the concept of autism and thereby increased prevalence, but predicted that DSM-IV (APA, 1994) autism criteria were narrower and would reduce autism prevalence. However, Volkmar et al. (1997) were mistaken in their prediction. A decade later, Williams, Higgins, and Brayne (2006) reported that DSM-IV criteria had not reduced autism prevalence, but had increased autism prevalence 200% to 300% compared with DSM-III-R criteria.

In 2012, echoing the claim Volkmar et al. (1997) had made 15 years earlier, Volkmar asserted DSM-5 criteria would narrow the autism diagnosis so much that fewer than half of children diagnosed by DSM-IV criteria would meet criteria for a DSM-5 diagnosis (Carey, 2012). Volkmar used the proposed DSM-5 autism criteria to re-diagnose 372 children and adults originally diagnosed in 1993 and found that 25% of those diagnosed with "classic autism" in 1993 would not be diagnosed with autism spectrum disorder by DSM-5 criteria (Carey, 2012).

The Proposed DSM-5 Criteria were Predicted to Narrow the Diagnosis of Autism Spectrum Disorder

Box 7.1 lists the four proposed criteria for a DSM-5 autism spectrum disorder diagnosis. The first proposed criterion is the presence of social impairment symptoms. The second proposed criterion is the presence of a subset of restricted repetitive behaviors, interests, or activities or sensory abnormalities. The third criterion is that onset must occur in childhood. The fourth criterion identifies the degree of impairment in daily functioning on a scale of 1, needs some support, to 3, needs substantial support in daily living.

BOX 7.1 Summary of the Four Proposed Required Elements for the Provisional DSM-5 Autism Spectrum Disorder Criteria as of January 29, 2011 (APA DSM-5 Development, 2012a)

Proposed Required Element 1: Social Impairment

The individual expresses global impairment in social communication and social interaction that is not caused by developmental delay. The impairment must be demonstrated in three types of behaviors.

Impaired social-emotional reciprocity (abnormal social approach, failure of normal conversation, to total lack of initiation of social interaction)

Impaired nonverbal communicative behaviors used in social interaction (impaired eye contact, body-language, to total lack of facial expression or gestures)

Impaired development and sustaining of relationships with others than care-givers (impaired social flexibility, impaired imaginative play, failure to make friends, to apparent absence of interest in people)

Proposed Required Element 2: Restricted Repetitive Behaviors, Interests, or Activities or Sensory Abnormalities

The individual expresses a restricted, repetitive pattern of behavior, interests, or activities. This dysfunction must be demonstrated in two of four types of behaviors.

Stereotyped or repetitive speech, motor movements, or use of objects (motor stereotypies, echolalia, repetitive use of objects, or idiosyncratic phrases)

Excessive adherence to routines, ritualized patterns of verbal or nonverbal behavior, or excessive resistance to change (motor rituals, insistence on same route or food, repetitive questioning, or extreme distress at small changes)

Highly restricted, fixated interests, abnormal in their intensity or focus (strong attachment to or preoccupation with unusual objects, excessively narrow or perseverative interests)

Hyper- or hypo-reactivity to sensory input or unusual interest in sensory aspects of environment (apparent indifference to pain/heat/cold, adverse response to specific sounds or textures, excessive smelling or touching of objects, fascination with lights or spinning objects)

Proposed Required Element 3: Childhood Onset

Symptoms must be present in early childhood.

Proposed Required Element 4: Degree of Impairment

Symptoms must limit and impair daily functioning. The degree of impairment is coded as three levels: level 1 indicates the individual needs support; level 2 indicates the individual needs substantial support; level 3 indicates the individual needs very substantial support.

Chief concerns for many stakeholders were the exclusion of individuals with social impairment caused by developmental delay as defined in the first criterion, and the elimination of Asperger syndrome. The exclusion of individuals from a diagnosis of autism because they had serious neurodevelopmental social impairment with developmental delay was predicted to exclude many lower-functioning individuals from diagnosis. The elimination of Asperger syndrome was predicted to exclude higher-functioning individuals with serious neurodevelopmental social impairment from a diagnosis of autism spectrum disorder. These two changes, plus the elimination of a separate language impairment criterion, were predicted to significantly narrow the autism spectrum diagnosis.

Volkmar reported that he and his colleagues had found the proposed DSM-5 criteria would exclude 75% of individuals previously diagnosed with Asperger syndrome. Volkmar also reported that 85% of individuals previously diagnosed with PDD-NOS would not be diagnosed with autism spectrum disorder by the proposed DSM-5 criteria (Carey, 2012).

The report of Volkmar's preliminary findings triggered a firestorm of reaction in the community of researchers and parents. The chair of the American Psychiatric Association DSM-5 Task Force, Dr. David Kupfer, and the Vice-Chair, Dr. Darrel Regier, claimed the proposed DSM-5 criteria for autism were a significant scientific and clinical improvement over DSM-IV criteria (Kupfer & Regier, 2011). However, Volkmar's report did not appear to support their claim (Carey, 2012). A member of the American Psychiatric Association's DSM-5 Neurodevelopmental Disorders Work Group writing the autism DSM-5 criteria, Dr. Lord, discounted Volkmar's findings by saying that his "study numbers are probably exaggerated because the research team relied on old data, collected by doctors who were not aware of what kinds of behaviors the proposed definition requires" (Carey, 2012). A parent of children with autism thought it appeared, "Dr. Volkmar decided to take his issues with the DSM 5 autism criteria to the court of public opinion rather than to the scientific literature where they belong" (MJ, 2012).

Volkmar responded to critics by stating that he believed DSM-5 changes in autism criteria were a mistake because they would bar many affected individuals from receiving medication, medical services, and access to special schools (Wang, 2012). Dr. David Kupfer, chair of the DSM-5 task force, bluntly stated, "We have to make sure not everybody who is a little odd gets a diagnosis of autism or Asperger disorder. It involves a use of treatment resources. It becomes a cost issue" (Harmon, 2012). Volkmar wondered if the DSM-5 autism criteria revision was motivated by an effort to save money by limiting services for affected individuals (Wang, 2012). In support of Volkmar, Frances (2012a) reported that the Volkmar research team calculated that 2688 different combinations of DSM-IV criteria could confer an autism diagnosis, whereas only 6 different combinations of DSM-5 criteria would permit an autism diagnosis. Frances stated that these combinations suggested that DSM-IV allowed a broader and more heterogeneous group of individuals to be diagnosed with autism, but "The much narrower DSM 5 definition would (as claimed by APA) indeed be much more specific" (Frances, 2012a).

PRESSING PROBLEMS FOR THE DIAGNOSIS OF AUTISM

Research has not determined whether the increasing prevalence of autism has included a true increase in incidence. Therefore, Volkmar's claim that the proposed stringent DSM-5 autism criteria alone would stop the increasing prevalence of autism suggested arbitrary control of prevalence at a time when many researchers were trying to separate true incidence from prevalence. This disturbed researchers (Herbert, 2012; Mattila et al., 2011; Pinto-Martin, 2012; Wang, 2012; Weintraub, 2011). The claim that stringent DSM-5 autism criteria would halt the increasing prevalence also suggested that many individuals formerly diagnosed with an autism spectrum disorder would no longer meet diagnostic criteria, and thus would be excluded from medical and educational services. This disturbed researchers, parents, social workers, clinicians, teachers, and advocacy groups alike (Autism Speaks, 2012; Herbert, 2012; Knickerbocker & Waehler, 2012; Mattila et al., 2011; Ne'eman & Badesch, 2012).

The ensuing tempest revealed three problems for the diagnosis of autism. One problem was stakeholder conflict over the control of diagnostic criteria. Although only the American Psychiatric Association DSM-5 Neurodevelopmental Disorders Work Group was authorized to revise the DSM autism criteria, many researchers, concerned professionals, parents of affected children, and autism advocacy groups expressed ownership claims for the diagnosis of autism. In the public view, at a time of increasing prevalence of autism, the narrowed DSM-5 criteria might be tailored to insurance budget concerns and not public health concerns. Moreover, to many stakeholders, autism prevalence appeared to be willfully controlled by the American Psychiatric Association. One researcher stated, "The DSM giveth, and the DSM taketh away—this is the less-than-complimentary sentiment of many people within the autism community" (Whitehouse, 2012).

A second problem arose when Volkmar claimed that DSM-5 criteria would nip autism prevalence in the bud. In making this claim, Volkmar pulled back the curtain and revealed the troubled state of psychiatric classification (Carey, 2012). Most researchers knew that DSM criteria were the object of unrelenting criticism (Frances & Widiger, 2012; Nesse & Stein, 2012). Kelland (2012) reported that thousands of psychologists, psychiatrists, and mental health experts said the new DSM-5 classification was based on "tick-box diagnosis systems" that were "at best 'silly' and at worst 'worrying and dangerous'." Other criticisms of DSM classification included lack of attention to patient symptoms, poor boundaries between syndromes, and inadequate use of neuroscience findings to inform diagnostic categorization. Former director of The United States National Institutes of Mental Health (NIMH), Dr. Steven Hyman, wrote of DSM classification that he worried he had approved spending "large sums of taxpayers' money for clinical and translational projects that almost never questioned the existing diagnostic categories despite their lack of validation" (Hyman, 2010, p. 157).

One response to the need for a more valid system of diagnosis was the NIMH project to develop an alternate diagnostic system for mental disorders based on neuroscience findings, called the Research Domain Criteria (Cuthbert & Insel, 2010).

However, the public was largely unaware of shifting ground beneath the DSM criteria, and therefore, the revelation that diagnostic criteria might be, to any degree, arbitrary was unsettling. Moreover, because the DSM-5 label "autism spectrum disorder" defined only one disorder, this single diagnosis did not reflect autism heterogeneity, and did not make clear to non-researchers the difficulty inherent in classifying such a heterogeneous disorder. Walsh, Elsabbagh, Bolton, and Singh (2011) said of autism that, "The general public ... rarely appreciate this level of complexity and the broad spectrum of functioning that characterizes the condition" (p. 606). However, the general public could not be expected to appreciate the complex variation within autism when only one DSM-5 autism diagnostic category was proposed. Despite the word "spectrum" in its name, the proposal for only one DSM-5 autism category belied the heterogeneity of autism.

The third problem exposed in the conflict between Volkmar and the APA was the disparity between public expectation that, given sufficient money and time, researchers would find "a cure" for autism, and researchers' knowledge that autism heterogeneity precluded any single cure. A majority of researchers knew that, along with increasing prevalence, there was increasing variation in genetic risk factors, environmental risk factors, symptoms, and life outcomes for children diagnosed with autism. Coleman and Gillberg (2012) stated that autism was "a group of conditions with multiple etiologies" (p. 6). Amaral (2011) called autism "a large number of syndromes that manifest in behavioral alterations consistent with the diagnosis of autism" (p. 5). This meant finding "*a* cure" for autism was impossible. Nonetheless, public calls for a cure grew louder and louder. Dr. Gerald Fischbach, the Scientific Director of the Simons Foundation Autism Research Initiative, stated "The word 'cure' often gets in the way of autism research … I don't know of any neuropsychiatric disorder other than an infection that has been cured" (BigThink Editors, 2011). Researcher Dr. Susan Bookbinder stated, "I don't think we're going to find a cure for autism because I don't think autism is really a single disorder" (BigThink Editors, 2011).

However, not all researchers believed autism was heterogeneous, and a number of these researchers encouraged belief that a cure was forthcoming. For example, a parent blogger reported with optimism that she had been fortunate to speak with autism researcher Dr. Manuel Casanova. The parent reported Dr. Casanova told her that autism resulted from a defect in the minicolumns of the cortex that caused cortical hyperexcitability, and his research team was testing magnetic brain stimulation as the cure for defective brain minicolumns, wherein "by targeting one area of abnormality, and correcting it, the other areas will correct themselves" (Autismlearningfelt, 2011).

Despite the single-cause–single-cure autism claims proposed by some individual researchers, cumulative research evidence supported the view espoused by Amaral (2011), Bookheimer (BigThink, 2011), and Coleman and Gillberg (2012). There would be no single cure for autism because autism was not a single disorder. However, sudden public awareness that the proposed DSM-5 criteria for autism might control prevalence, coupled with existing public belief that autism was a single disorder for which a single cause might be found, led to frustration and helpless outrage in many. One autism blogger stated "Volkmar disagrees with Catherine Lord and the APA's proposals for changes to the DSM and he shows that the experts **STILL DON'T UNDERSTAND AUTISM** or know what in the world to do about it" (Dachel, 2012).

The following three sections of this chapter consider the conflicts in stakeholder ownership of the diagnosis of autism, the difficulties inherent in the DSM system of classification, and discussion of the problems in the proposed DSM-5 diagnosis of autism spectrum disorder.

CONFLICTS IN STAKEHOLDER OWNERSHIP OF THE DIAGNOSIS OF AUTISM

The public spat between autism researcher Volkmar and the American Psychiatric Association was a dispute between two stakeholders in the diagnosis of autism (Wang, 2012). The APA had an interest in maintaining that its work in constructing criteria for psychiatric diagnoses was scientific and clinically valid (Kupfer & Regier, 2011; Oldham, 2012). The APA also had a financial stake in the use of the diagnostic manual by professionals. Greenberg (2012) noted that the current edition of the diagnostic manual had earned the APA more than $100 million. As a clinician and researcher, Volkmar had a stake in finding the diagnostic criteria that best represented both his clinical experience of autism and his theory of autism. In the ensuing debate, stakeholders on both sides of the dispute voiced their concerns.

Stakeholders Expressed Concern that Narrowed DSM-5 Criteria would have Many Negative Effects

In support of the concerns expressed by Volkmar (Carey, 2012), another stakeholder, autism researcher Dr. Herbert, wrote a letter to *The New York Times* stating that a narrowed limit to diagnosis would impede early intervention:

> *Narrowing the definition of autism is a bad idea and narrows the opportunities to make significant inroads in helping children affected by this condition, their families and our nation. Autism still has many mysteries, but it is clear that early intervention makes a tremendous difference. A tighter definition means that parents, teachers and caregivers will wait longer to consider giving children specialized attention and care. It will mean less support for parents struggling to help their children communicate, adapt to social challenges and cope with a world that often feels overwhelming.*
>
> *Herbert (2012)*

Social workers also had a stake in the diagnostic criteria for autism. Two social workers concerned about the possible DSM-5 exclusion of high-functioning individuals with autism from diagnosis also wrote a letter to *The New York Times*. They argued,

> *To exclude these students from the services and supports they need throughout their education would be a great injustice and an attempt to save money now without considering the effect of their being unprepared to function fully as adults in our society. Changing the criteria to decrease the percentage seems dishonest and unethical.*
>
> *Knickerbocker and Waehler (2012)*

The most important stakeholders in the proposed DSM-5 criteria for autism spectrum disorder were the parents of children diagnosed with autism. One parent sarcastically identified the potential DSM-5 reduction in future autism diagnoses as a cure:

> To actually say that the overwhelming majority of persons diagnosed with some form of autism in the last two decades will no longer be considered autistic is Orwellian. How nice that the psychiatric community can somehow cure someone of autism overnight by changing the definition. Goodness if we parents of autistic children knew that was the way to do it, we would have asked for this definition change decades ago. We didn't need to go broke with therapists, doctors, neurologists and specialized programs.
>
> **Independent Patriot Westchester County (2012)**

Another parent was also shocked by changes in the proposed DSM-5 criteria. She could not believe that self-injurious behavior was not included in the proposed criteria:

> Has the American Psychiatric Association (APA) Lost Its Collective Mind? Have the "36,000 Physician Leaders in mental health" ignored history? After all, decades of autism research show self-injurious behavior is a hallmark trait of severe autism …. Yet, today, you see no mention of self-injurious behavior in DSM-5 autism diagnosis. Yes, the modern mental health leaders of the APA would have us believe autism with self-injurious behaviors doesn't exist.
>
> **Oakley (2012)**

In addition, a parent of three children with autism asserted that the proposed DSM-5 criteria would eliminate more than 40% of low-functioning individuals from diagnosis because DSM-5 criteria ignored language impairment and indirectly limited individuals with intellectual disability from a diagnosis of autism. The parent concluded, "DSM-5 is minimizing what is an extremely disabling aspect of some people's autism and has the potential to kick out a large segment because they also are intellectually disabled" (MJ, 2012).

One of the most vocal stakeholders was the psychiatrist who had directed the APA Task Force that developed the DSM-IV criteria, Dr. Alan Frances. In contrast to Volkmar, Frances was concerned that the proposed DSM-5 criteria for autism spectrum disorder would increase the prevalence of autism. Frances (2010) claimed, "the spectrum concept will likely further fuel the 'epidemic' of loosely defined autism that was already been triggered by the introduction of Asperger's in DSM4" (p. 4). Frances (2012b) also found much more to dislike in DSM-5. Frances scoffed that the low rates of agreement between clinicians assigning DSM-5 diagnostic categories were barely better than the "chance agreement two monkeys could achieve throwing darts at a diagnostic board" (Frances, 2012b). Frances judged that many DSM-5 changes were not supported by sufficient scientific evidence, and he denounced DSM-5 rationales for diagnoses as being "one sided, incomplete, and unsystematic; and sometimes giving undue weight to unpublished papers or papers authored by DSM 5 work-group members" (2012c). He predicted, "Because of its poor performance on DSM-5, the APA has probably forfeited its right to sole control of future revisions" (Frances, 2012b). When Volkmar's findings triggered a public reaction, he commented:

> people working on DSM 5 have difficulty getting their story straight. First they said they didn't care what impact DSM 5 would have on prevalence rates .... Last week, the New York Times ran a front-page story reporting that DSM 5 changes would dramatically reduce rates of autism. This produced an uproar in the autism community and instigated a petition against DSM 5 ... DSM 5 leadership was forced to change its tune.
>
> **Frances (2012a)**

The petition against DSM-5 identified by Frances was a statement made jointly by the presidents of two stakeholder advocacy groups, the Autism Society and Autistic Self Advocacy Network (Ne'eman & Badesch, 2012). They appealed to all stakeholders to sign their statement. Their petition demanded that DSM-5 criteria reflect all the diverse forms of autism because these diverse forms of autism had been discovered through scientific research. The statement's core claim was:

> One of the key principles of the medical profession has always been, "First, do no harm." As such, it is essential that the DSM-5's criteria are structured in such a way as to ensure that those who have or would have qualified for a diagnosis under the DSM-IV maintain access to an ASD diagnosis. Contrary to assertions that ASD is over diagnosed, evidence suggests that the opposite is the case – namely, that racial and ethnic minorities, women and girls, adults and individuals from rural and low-income communities face challenges in accessing diagnosis .... We encourage the DSM-5 Neurodevelopmental Disorders Working Group to interpret the definition of autism spectrum disorder broadly, so as to ensure that all of those who can benefit from an ASD diagnosis have the ability to do so.
>
> **Ne'eman and Badesch (2012)**

Other autism advocacy groups, also stakeholders in the diagnosis of autism, likewise responded to the possible limit to autism diagnosis. The charity founded by professional golfer Ernie Els posted a message on their website reporting they had received many concerned calls and emails about the proposed DSM-5 criteria from doctors, educators, therapists, parents and grandparents. The group encouraged all concerned stakeholders to lobby the APA:

As the DSM is the reference that healthcare providers must use to diagnose mental and behavioral conditions, it influences both the availability of treatments and insurance coverage. ... Advocacy is critical ....Voice your concerns to the American Psychiatric Association by email at apa@psych.org and your legislature.

Els for Autism (n.d.)

A group of 10 autism advocacy organizations, including SafeMinds, the National Autism Association, TACA–Talking about Curing Autism, The Autism File, The Canary Party, Exceptional Families Network, The Autism Society of Illinois, Elizabeth Birt Center for Autism Law and Advocacy, The Pilot House, and the Autism Action Network, issued a joint press release (Weisman et al., 2012). They claimed that the proposed DSM-5 criteria "will potentially disrupt appropriate and necessary services to hundreds of thousands of individuals in the US, hamper the ability to track the numbers of people with autism, and interfere with efforts to establish biological causes of autism" (Weisman et al., 2012).

The largest advocacy group, Autism Speaks, posted a statement on their website intended to reassure all stakeholders:

We have voiced our concerns and will continue to directly communicate with the DSM-5 committee to ensure that the proposed revision does not discriminate against anyone living with autism. While the committee has stated that its intent is to better capture all who meet current diagnostic criteria, we have concluded that the real-life impact of the revisions has, to date, been insufficiently evaluated. ... Autism Speaks will be working with leading experts in the field as well as community stakeholders to evaluate the potential impact of the DSM revision on our community and to ensure that all necessary adjustments be made to assure access to vital treatment and social support resources for all those who struggle with the symptoms of autism.

Autism Speaks (2012)

The APA Defense of the Proposed DSM-5 Criteria for Autism

The American Psychiatric Association reacted quickly to Volkmar's claim that the proposed DSM–5 criteria would exclude nearly 60% of individuals with serious social impairment from a diagnosis of autism spectrum disorder. The APA issued a press release that defended DSM-5 committee members as "the nation's top scientific and research minds," and that asserted anyone previously diagnosed with autism would receive an equivalent diagnosis with DSM-5 criteria (Brauser, 2012). Kupfer and Regier responded to concerned petitioners by claiming that individuals excluded from a diagnosis would still get services:

We understand the devastating impact that discontinuation of services can have on patients and families. We also recognize that services are determined not just by a diagnosis but also by the severity of symptoms and needs in areas such as education, social skills, activities of daily living, and maintaining personal safety.

Aspieside (2012)

In addition, Kupfer and Regier asserted that the DSM-5 criteria were scientific because they were "based on years of accumulated clinical, epidemiological, and neuroscience research which was thoroughly examined by the members of the DSM-5 work group on Neurodevelopmental Disorders" (Aspieside, 2012).

The President of the APA, Dr. John Oldham, rebuffed the request by Dr. David Elkins, President of the Society for Humanistic Psychology for an outside review of the proposed DSM-5 criteria. President Oldham claimed each revision of DSM was the best possible set of current criteria, and that an outside review would serve no purpose because there was "no gold standard for defining mental disorders" (Oldham, 2012).

Dr. Susan Swedo, chair of the DSM-5 Neurodevelopmental Disorders Work Group, defended the work of her group as having achieved a sound middle ground:

I suspect our recommended changes have struck the right balance between "lumping and splitting" .... We get an equal number of clinicians concerned that the new ASD category is too broad and those who think it is too narrow. It's a reminder that DSM is a manual of behavioral disorders that are diagnosed by observation, and those observations will always be influenced by a clinician's training and previous experience.

Moran (2012)

Similarly, another member of the DSM-5 Neurodevelopmental Disorders Work Group, Dr. Bryan King, argued that there was no validity to public concern that DSM-5 criteria would exclude affected individuals (Brauser, 2012). He claimed that the Neurodevelopmental Disorders Work Group never had an agenda to restrict or limit the number of children or adults who could be diagnosed. King implied that people had first worried the autism criteria were too wide, and now worried the criteria were too narrow (Brauser, 2012). However, King's assertion mistakenly conflated two different groups. The earlier criticisms that the autism criteria were too wide were professional speculation, but the concerns that DSM-5 criteria were too narrow were triggered by evidence reported in 2012, and the concerns came largely from parents and advocacy groups. Dr. King defended the group's work saying that he had received many calls from concerned parents and health workers and that he understood that if criteria are changed "it's reasonable to ask whether someone will still make it in that has been previously diagnosed;" however, he asserted, "We've only wanted to get the criteria right" (Brauser, 2012).

An apparent supporter of the APA DSM-5 changes in autism criteria, autism researcher Pinto-Martin (2012) suggested that the public should not engage in any debate over "whether the change is warranted or wise," but should instead focus on the effects of the new criteria. She affirmed that the new criteria were more restrictive, and therefore a child would have to have more pronounced autism symptoms to be diagnosed. She also affirmed that it might be more difficult for mildly affected children to qualify for insurance for special educational services and therapy. Surprisingly, Pinto-Martin (2012) claimed that, even with changes in eligibility, there would be no reduction in support for children who functioned at the higher end of the autism spectrum. Pinto-Martin (2012) claimed that the likely exclusion of higher- and lower-functioning individuals might be good, because this would necessarily require the development of services that were better targeted to these groups.

Pinto-Martin (2012) did see one major problem in the proposed DSM criteria: tracking long-term prevalence changes would be impossible. She argued that:

> monitoring changes in the prevalence of autism over time – an important, ongoing research initiative – will be hampered .... By changing the way in which children are labeled, we will face a decrease in prevalence. Finding out the real change in risk from an artificial increase or decrease can be difficult.
>
> **Pinto-Martin (2012)**

Another supporter of the DSM-5 changes, psychiatrist Paul Steinberg, suggested in *The New York Times* (Steinberg, 2012) that the elimination of Asperger syndrome was a good idea. He argued that a 1992 United States Department of Education directive requiring enhanced services for children with autism sent the diagnosis of Asperger syndrome skyrocketing, and that the Asperger diagnosis caused children to suffer poor self-esteem and poor social development. He also claimed that a serious negative effect of over-diagnosing Asperger syndrome was that the diagnosis left a blot on the medical records of children with social disabilities, hampering their ability to get jobs. Steinberg noted that the late Christopher Hitchens had speculated that George Orwell had Asperger syndrome. Steinberg (2012) claimed, "George Orwell might never have been able to write his brilliant essay about the shooting of an elephant if Asperger syndrome had been part of his permanent medical record."

Summary: Concerns of Stakeholders in the Diagnosis of Autism

Parents hoped that psychiatry would deliver a diagnostic system that addressed their children's needs. Researchers and clinicians hoped the DSM-5 diagnostic system would define autism according to research findings while maintaining the same level of diagnostic coverage. Kupfer and Regier (2011) and Regier, Kuhl, Narrow, and Kupfer (2012) posited that the goal of DSM-5 was to include basic research and epidemiological findings, but they stressed that all criteria had to "err on the side of clinical utility" (Regier et al., 2012, p. 4). However, for many parents, clinicians, and researchers, the proposed DSM-5 criteria for autism appeared to have less clinical utility than previous criteria. Consequently, stakeholders in the diagnosis of autism remained concerned.

THE DIFFICULTIES INHERENT IN THE DSM SYSTEM OF CLASSIFICATION

Three problems with DSM classification caused serious concerns. First, even though every mental disorder proposed in DSM was in fact a theory of a mental disorder, many people had come to believe that DSM categories were true diseases (Hyman, 2010). Second, neuroscience and genetics research had generated clear evidence that the behavior groups defined by DSM categories were unlikely to be valid (Craddock & Owen, 2010; Hyman, 2010). Third, the existing DSM diagnoses were plagued by heterogeneity and comorbidity (Frances & Widiger, 2012). Researchers were aware that the Research Domain Criteria were being developed as a neuroscience-based partner to the that DSM system but would take a number of years to be ready to use (Sanislow et al., 2010).

DSM Categories were Reified Theories

Reification means that an abstract concept comes to be seen as something concrete. Kupfer and Regier (2011) were frank in stating that reification of diagnostic categories had been a serious problem for DSM-III-R and DSM-IV. Despite the fuzzy boundaries of DSM diagnostic categories, and despite the fact that DSM diagnoses had not been validated by unique brain dysfunctions or other biomarkers (Nesse & Stein, 2012), many researchers mistakenly believed that DSM diagnostic criteria did represent valid mental disorders (Hyman, 2010). Hyman worried that this mistaken belief "was palpably impeding scientific progress" (2010, p. 157).

Many researchers were cognizant that reification led the field to sustain unproven diagnoses. For example, Kendell and Jablensky (2003) argued that Down and Huntington syndromes still existed, but formerly reified diagnoses of dropsy, chlorosis, and Banti's syndrome no longer existed because behavioral criteria for these diagnoses did not define clearly bounded groups. The researchers claimed, "typology will be abandoned and replaced by a dimensional classification" (Kendell & Jablensky, 2003, p. 8). Hyman (2010) hoped that researchers would construct alternatives to the DSM criteria that would help scientists "move beyond currently reified diagnoses in order to provide the information that will lead, ultimately, to a valid classification" (p. 171).

Neuroscience and Genetics Research Suggested that Behavior Classification by DSM Categories was Inaccurate

The emerging evidence that genetic and environmental risk factors linked many mental disorder diagnoses to one another strongly argued against the DSM classification of mental disorders by observable symptoms (Craddock & Owen, 2010; Arguello & Gogos, 2012). Consequently, the DSM system of organizing mental disorders by observed behaviors came under attack. Keshavan, Nasrallah, and Tandon (2011) asserted that defining "complex psychiatric disorders based on overt externally observable phenotypes (such as behaviors) is not optimal for determining etiology of these entities" (p. 8). Sweeney (2011) argued that psychiatry "may come to accept that major mental illnesses comprise a continuum of pathology with only modestly distinct clinical syndromes that have highly overlapping and heterogeneous clinical features and etiology" (p. 19). Kendler (2005) stated that the function of causal genes could not be understood in relation to psychiatric diagnoses, but could only be understood at the more basic level of "biological processes (e.g., neuronal cell migrations during development) and/or mental functions (e.g., processing of threat stimuli)" (p. 1250).

Akil et al. (2010) claimed that because many different neural circuit disruptions might converge on a common clinical manifestation, starting from a diagnosis and "searching broadly for genetic causes that are commonly shared across all affected individuals is not likely to succeed, because a great deal of biological heterogeneity lies at the basis of circuit dysfunction" (p. 1580). Akil et al. (2010) stated that schizophrenia, autism, and mood disorders shared genetic variant risk factors, and these disorders were each the result of very complex neural circuit dysfunctions. The researchers argued that because the neural circuits were very complex, there were many ways to disrupt them. Akil et al. (2010) noted that because the thousands of genes

regulating neural circuits worked in an interactive ensemble, even disturbance in a few genes could result in a complex neuropsychiatric phenotype.
The researchers recommended that personal genomics and neural circuit
analysis would do more to reveal the basis of neuropsychiatric disorders
than the use of DSM diagnostic groups in research.

DSM Diagnoses were Plagued by Heterogeneity and Comorbidity

Every edition of the Diagnostic and Statistical Manual of Mental Disorders
made clear that mental disorders were likely to include comorbidity because
most individuals diagnosed with one mental disorder could also be diagnosed with one or more additional disorders. In addition, significant heterogeneity was repeatedly demonstrated within diagnostic groups (Nesse &
Stein, 2012). Arguello and Gogos (2012) proposed that the main reason for
comorbidity and heterogeneity was the substantial etiological and pathophysiological variation within and across psychiatric disorders.

The Research Domain Criteria and the DSM

Although researchers knew the DSM classification was fraught with problems, researchers recognized that neuroscience and genetics findings were
generating a complex picture of gene, chromosome, epigenetic, and gene–
environment interactions influencing the development of the neural circuits of the brain. This emerging complex reality meant that there could be
no easy or quick solution to improving the classification of mental disorders. The Research Domain Criteria project or RDoC was organized to
address many of the concerns with DSM classification. The NIMH RDoC
project planned to construct a neural circuit pathophysiology-based classification (http://www.nimh.nih.gov/research-funding/rdoc.shtml) of mental disorders (Cuthbert & Insel, 2010; Sanislow et al., 2010). The goal of the
RDoC was to group mental disorders by similarities in underlying neural
circuit disruptions rather than solely on observed behaviors. Sanislow et al.
(2010) stated that the RDoC would build a "classification that incorporates
neuroscience and behavior, [something] necessary to free research from
constraint by current diagnostic entities" (p. 637). Sanislow et al. (2010)
predicted that what is now called a diagnosis "may turn out simply to be
indicative of a range of possible pathologies. ... for example, depression
might be viewed akin to the way that a fever is viewed today" (p. 637), that
is, as a sign that something is wrong, triggering the clinical search for possible neural processes that might underlie the depression.

The RDoC aggregated research findings for neural circuits that when disrupted either constituted or contributed to the pathophysiology of a mental disorder. Sanislow et al. (2010) stated that work began by collecting evidence for neural circuits in five domains: negative affect, positive affect, cognition, social processes, and arousal/regulatory systems. Neural circuits for the negative states of fear, distress, and aggression were one RDoC focus. These included: the basolateral amygdala connections with ventral medial areas of the prefrontal cortex, the amygdala and bed nucleus of the stria terminalis in fear and anxiety; shifts in the hypothalamic–pituitary–adrenal axis in stress; and the role of the amygdala, ventral tegmental area, nucleus accumbens, and mesolimbic dopamine pathway in regulating aggression. Neural circuits for positive affect were another focus of the RDoC. These included the mesolimbic dopamine system, the orbital frontal cortex, and the ventral and dorsal striatum. Circuits for cognitive processes were also central to the RDoC. These included: parietal areas governing attention; thalamic and occipital areas governing perception; dorsolateral prefrontal cortex regulating working memory, including executive functioning; hippocampus and distributed areas of the prefrontal cortex determining long-term memory; and the anterior cingulate contributing to cognitive control.

The RDoC project also studied neural circuits and neurohormones for social processes, with a focus on vasopressin and oxytocin, as well as circuits found for separation fear, facial expression recognition, behavioral inhibition, emotion regulation, and other social interaction functions. A fifth domain of the RDoC was the exploration of neural circuits for arousal/regulatory functions and the systems underlying them, including basic glutamatergic and cholinergic reticular systems regulating sleep and wakefulness, complex arousal circuits, the ventral tegmental area, locus coeruleus, and raphe nuclei.

The RDoC project began in 2010. The development was assumed to be a lengthy process but it was not clear when a formal RDoC classification would be published. Nonetheless, it was predicted that researchers would at some point shift from using DSM to using RDoC. Kupfer and Regier (2011) asserted that the RDoC neural circuit classification of mental disorders did not conflict with the DSM classification. They argued that the development of the RDoC intensified their "commitment to examining evidence from neurobiology" for DSM-5 categories (p. 673). Nonetheless, it was not clear how the two classification systems, the DSM for clinical practice, and the RDoC for research, would function in the future

(Cuthbert & Insel, 2010; Ghaemi, 2011; Sanislow et al., 2010). For example, grant applicants submitting proposals to NIH have used DSM criteria (Hyman, 2010). However, if the NIH viewed the RDoC as the scientific categorization of mental disorders, would grant applicants choose DSM criteria for research? (Ghaemi, 2011). In an article titled "Godzilla meets Tyrannosaurus Rex? DSM-5, RDoC and child bipolar disorder," Kaplan asserted, "Disagreement between the two systems about research classification is easy to imagine. Carrying the apparent mantle of better science, RDoC may be the winner in any such disagreement" (Kaplan, 2011).

Because the project to create the RDoC effectively defined the DSM criteria as the product of practical clinical considerations (Ghaemi, 2011), stakeholders might feel that their practical knowledge of autism entitled them to some ownership in the DSM-5, as well as in future DSM criteria. However, if the APA were to permit stakeholders who were not serving on the formal DSM Work Groups to shape or limit specific criteria for any DSM disorder, the APA claim to have developed scientific diagnostic criteria would be untenable.

PROBLEMS WITH DSM-5 AUTISM SPECTRUM DIAGNOSTIC CRITERIA

In a brief three-page outline of the goals for the overall DSM-5 classification, Kupfer and Regier (2011) singled out the proposed DSM-5 criteria for autism spectrum disorder for praise. They stated that:

> Beyond keeping pace with the science of psychiatry, many of DSM-5's proposed changes represent an opportunity to improve the field from clinical and public health perspectives. The proposal for a single "autism spectrum disorder" category that would include the current DSM-IV diagnoses of autistic disorder (autism), Asperger's disorder, childhood disintegrative disorder, and pervasive developmental disorder not otherwise specified was born from data suggesting that these disorders share a pathophysiological substrate. Changes in the wording of the criteria, however, help clarify symptom manifestation and provide diagnosticians with a more accurate example of how these children actually appear in clinics.
> **Kupfer and Regier (2011, p. 673)**

Kupfer and Regier (2011) also argued that the DSM-5 inclusion of dimensions in diagnostic criteria would reduce heterogeneity and comorbidities in all diagnoses, something especially valuable for autism.

The following sections evaluate three claims made by Kupfer and Regier (2011). One claim was that the proposed DSM-5 autism spectrum disorder criteria identified individuals who shared a pathophysiological substrate, i.e., shared the same autism-causing brain dysfunction. Another claim was that the proposed DSM-5 criteria provided an improved clinical picture of autism spectrum disorder. The third claim was that the use of dimensions in the DSM-5 criteria would reduce heterogeneity and comorbidities.

No Shared Pathophysiological Substrate has been Found for Autism

Kupfer and Regier (2011) asserted that the proposed DSM-5 elimination of Asperger syndrome, Childhood Disintegrative Disorder, and Pervasive Developmental Disorder Not Otherwise Specified diagnoses along with the creation of a single autism diagnosis was a scientific improvement over DSM-IV because evidence suggested individuals in the autism spectrum "share a pathophysiological substrate" (p. 673). This was a surprising claim. By contrast, Rutter (2011) theorized that, if a single diagnosis of autism were established, it would be characterized by "pathophysiological heterogeneity" (p. 649). Silver and Rapin (2012) reviewed brain deficits in autism and reported great heterogeneity, wherein autism was variably found with dysfunction in prefrontal cortex, inferior frontal region, primary and supplementary motor areas, orbital frontal cortex, temporal lobes, superior temporal gyrus, fusiform gyrus, hippocampus, parietal lobes, postcentral gyrus, posterior parietal lobe, occipital lobes, insula, cingulate gyrus, amygdala, septum, hypothalamus, cerebellum, and cerebellar vermis.

However, one recent study did provide partial support for the claim of a shared pathophysiology in autism. Via, Radua, Cardoner, Happé, and Mataix-Cols (2011) reported that although their meta-analysis of gray matter imaging found no global gray matter differences between affected individuals and typical controls, they also found no significant gray matter differences between Asperger syndrome and autism spectrum disorder. Moreover, Via et al. (2011) reported evidence for a possible common pathophysiology for autism and Asperger syndrome in reductions of gray matter volume in the amygdala–hippocampus complex and medial parietal regions, and a small increase in gray matter volume in the left, middle, and inferior frontal gyri in both Asperger syndrome and autism.

Via et al. (2011) thus provided evidence suggesting that two of four DSM-IV subgroups, autism and Asperger syndrome, might share a common pattern of brain dysfunction. However, Kendler et al. (2009) directed that DSM-5 "major changes should rarely if ever be based solely on reports from a single researcher or research team" and "we would not generally expect to support substantial and especially major changes if a significant proportion of the literature contained evidence that contradicted the change" (p. 5). There are three lines of evidence contradicting the idea that autism spectrum disorder has a shared causal brain dysfunction, i.e., pathophysiology. First, evidence has been reported for a smaller amygdala–hippocampal complex volume in other disorders such as depression (Masi & Brovedani, 2011), post-traumatic stress disorder (PTSD), and childhood maltreatment (Dannlowski et al., 2012). Second, contrary to the findings of Via et al. (2011), Nordahl et al. (2012) reported that scans of 85 boys with autism spectrum disorder 1 year apart revealed that the amygdala was significantly larger in boys with autism than in typical controls at both time points. Moreover, the researchers found the amygdala was relatively larger at time two, indicating the amygdala was growing faster in children with autism spectrum disorder. These findings are not consonant with the findings of Via et al. (2011) for a significantly smaller amygdala–hippocampal complex in autism spectrum disorder.

Finally, and most importantly, the vast set of brain studies in autism has not converged on any shared causal brain dysfunction. Walsh et al. (2011) stated, "despite huge advances in the basic scientific understanding of autism, comparatively little has been achieved to date with regard to translating the resulting evidence into clinically useful biomarkers" (pp. 609–610). Vissers, Cohen, and Geurts (2012) reported that current research findings contradicted one theory of common pathophysiology in autism: impaired long-range connectivity and enhanced local connectivity in the brain. They reported that there was no clear evidence for enhanced local over-connectivity in the brain in autism. Vissers et al. (2012) also reported that patterns of neural long-range under-connectivity were not consistent, and that EEG and MEG research did not provide converging evidence to support the notion of neural long-range under-connectivity in autism. In addition, under-connectivity could not be a unique pathophysiology for autism, because under-connectivity has been reported for many disorders, including dyslexia (Richards & Berninger, 2008), ADHD (Mills et al., 2012), schizophrenia (Cole et al., 2011), and depression (Cullen et al., 2010).

Pina-Camacho et al. (2012) reported that social communication impairments in other disorders were tied to brain connectivity problems similar to those found in autism. The researchers noted that there were abnormalities in neural connectivity in many groups with social impairment, including patients with psychosis and social cognitive deficits, patients with cerebellar malformations or cerebellar vermis damage, very low birth weight children, and individuals with the fragile X premutation or the fragile X syndrome. Pina-Camacho et al. (2012) effectively claimed that serious social impairment was likely to result from a range of brain connectivity abnormalities, regardless of an individual's diagnosis. If shown to be true, this is of importance for understanding the brain basis of social impairment as a symptom. However, this conclusion stands against the claim made by Kupfer and Regier (2011) that autism spectrum disorder was scientifically valid as a single diagnostic category because individuals diagnosed with autism share a pathophysiology.

Philip et al. (2012) conducted a meta-analysis of imaging studies of autism and reported they "could not draw firm conclusions from the research to date" because autism "does not represent a single disorder but is likely to be the result of multiple underlying causes leading to similar clinical features" (p. 938). Some individuals with autism have no identifiable pathophysiology (Silver & Rapin, 2012). Individuals with autism may or may not have gray matter abnormalities, white matter abnormalities, larger heads, or smaller heads (Philip et al., 2012; Stigler et al., 2011). They may or may not have deficits in serotonin, dopamine, glutamate, or GABA (Gupta & State, 2007; Lam et al., 2008). They may or may not express abnormalities in the neurohormones oxytocin and vasopressin (Andari et al., 2010; Insel, 2010). They may or may not have deficits in central-executive network, default mode network, or salience network (Gomot & Wicker, 2011; Taylor et al., 2012; Uddin et al., 2011).

Summary: There is no Compelling Evidence for a Common Pathophysiological Substrate for Autism Spectrum Disorder

Evidence has not established a shared pathophysiology for autism. Moreover, it is unlikely that a common pathophysiological substrate for autism spectrum disorder will be discovered. One reason is that the plethora of evidence for varied genetic and varied environmental risk factors has suggested that autism is many different disorders under one name. The many and varied causal risk factors for the autism phenotype have been found in association with many different patterns of brain deficit. Another reason why a common pathophysiological substrate is unlikely is that the two proposed criteria for autism spectrum disorder—serious social impairment and restricted or repetitive behaviors—have each separately been found in association with varied brain deficits, thus increasing the probability of individual variation in brain circuit dysfunction patterns in autism spectrum disorder.

Research Findings Supported some DSM-5 Criteria Changes for Autism Spectrum Disorder; However, Many Affected Individuals would be Excluded from Diagnosis

Kupfer and Regier (2011) claimed that DSM-5 criteria were clinically more informative than DSM-IV criteria because they clarified autism symptoms, giving clinicians "a more accurate example of how these children actually appear in clinics" (p. 673). However, research support for this claimed benefit of the proposed DSM-5 criteria was mixed.

There was research support for folding Asperger syndrome into autism spectrum disorder. Happé (2011) reported that there was insufficient evidence for the diagnostic distinction between high-functioning autism and Asperger syndrome. Children with autism who had typical early language development had the same outcome as those delayed in early language, consequently this diagnostic feature of Asperger syndrome did not differentiate Asperger syndrome from autism. Moreover, Happé (2011) reported that there was no evidence for a unique cause for Asperger syndrome, nor was there a differential response to treatment discovered for individuals diagnosed with Asperger syndrome.

Two published studies comparing DSM-IV and DSM-5 criteria found support for replacing the three DSM-IV criteria for autism with the two proposed DSM-5 criteria. Frazier et al. (2012) found that a mixed dimensional and categorical model of autism matched the two proposed DSM-5 autism symptom groups, social impairment and restricted, repetitive behavior. Mandy, Charman, and Skuse (2012) also found support for the two DSM-5 symptom groups, and noted that sensory abnormalities appeared as part of restricted and repetitive behavior. The researchers offered only one caveat: the associations they reported only applied to high-functioning individuals with autism.

Leventhal (2012) affirmed the two DSM-5 criteria for autism spectrum disorders, stating, "the parsimonious model that lumped all known ASD signs and symptoms into two factors was statistically significant, with a more than satisfactory level of specificity" (p. 6). But other research exploring autism criteria in typical samples found little or no correlation between the two criterial symptom domains. Robinson et al. (2012) reported that data from 5944 typical twin pairs revealed that "While genetic effects were substantial within each [autism symptom] domain, there was limited genetic overlap between domains" (p. 7). Identical and fraternal twins had nonsignificant cross-twin correlations ranging from .02 to .19 between the two DSM-5 autism symptoms of social impairment and restricted and repetitive behaviors and interests.

Szatmari (2011) noted another problem for the proposed two symptom domains. He pointed out, "social communication and repetitive behaviours may not be the most useful for categorising children with autistic spectrum disorder … because variation in these dimensions seems to be only weakly associated with variation in outcome and response to treatment, which are more closely related to cognitive and language abilities" (p. 2).

In addition, Mandy, Charman, Gilmour, and Skuse (2011) reported that within a group of individuals previously diagnosed with Pervasive Developmental Disorder Not Otherwise Specified, the two DSM-5 criteria—social communication impairment and restricted and repetitive behaviors—did not cohere. The researchers stated that "Despite their severe and impairing difficulties with reciprocal social interaction and communication," most of the children classified as having Pervasive Developmental Disorder "would not meet proposed DSM-V ASD criteria, due to a lack of unusual sensory interests and the absence of stereotyped, routinized patterns of behavior" (Mandy et al., 2011, p. 129). The researchers noted that 25% of their clinical sample expressed only the diagnostic social communication impairment. This meant that many individuals would be excluded from a DSM-5 diagnosis of autism spectrum disorder who, nonetheless, expressed significant social impairment that met the DSM-5 criteria for social communication deficits. Like Volkmar (Wang, 2012), Mandy et al. (2011) worried that excluding these individuals from a diagnosis of autism spectrum disorder would limit many individuals with severe social-communication difficulties from "receiving the benefits associated with diagnosis, such as funding for clinical and educational support" (p. 129).

Robinson et al. (2011) and Happé et al. (2006) found limited overlap in the etiology of the three DSM-IV autism trait domains of social impairment, communication impairment, and restricted and repetitive behaviors. The researchers reported that it was most likely that these three different components of the autism spectrum phenotype were associated with different genetic and environmental causality in individuals diagnosed with autism. Given this evidence, the subgroup identified by Mandy et al. (2011) of individuals who expressed social communication impairment alone might not have the separate etiological causal factor that yielded restricted and repetitive behaviors. Viewing the findings of Mandy et al. (2011) through the evidence reported by Robinson et al. (2011) and Happé et al. (2006) would suggest that this subgroup of individuals should not be excluded from a diagnosis of autism.

Similar to the findings reported by Volkmar comparing DSM-IV and DSM-5 criteria, Mattila et al. (2011) reported that their comparison of DSM-IV-TR and DSM-5 autism criteria found that all those diagnosed with Asperger syndrome and some high-functioning subjects with autism according to DSM-IV-TR failed to meet criteria for DSM-5 autism spectrum disorder. Mattila et al. (2011) were concerned that the individuals who had clinically significant social impairment would lose access to services. The researchers proposed that DSM-5 criteria be changed to include Asperger syndrome, PDD-NOS, and those high-functioning individuals with autism who might not meet DSM-5 criteria for autism spectrum disorder. Mattila et al. (2011) outlined the possibility of "combining them together and identifying them as one diagnosis" (p. 591), therefore creating an additional diagnostic category alongside DSM-5 autism spectrum disorder.

Summary: Evidence Supported Folding Asperger Syndrome into Autism Spectrum Disorder; However, the Proposed DSM-5 Criteria Appeared Likely to Eliminate Affected Individuals from Diagnosis

Hyman (2010) called for change in diagnostic classification for mental disorders. He argued that "the problems that have emerged within the DSM 'paradigm' … cannot be fixed by tinkering with existing criteria sets or by adding or subtracting diagnoses at the margins" (p. 171). However, the proposed DSM-5 criteria for autism spectrum disorder have done exactly that. Although some of the tinkering may prove to be sound, many individuals with serious social impairment will be excluded from diagnosis by "tinkering with existing criteria" and by subtracting three "diagnoses at the margin"—Childhood Disintegration Disorder, Asperger syndrome, and Pervasive Developmental Disorder Not Otherwise Specified.

Dimensionality in the Proposed DSM-5 Autism Spectrum Criteria Ignored Most Heterogeneity and Comorbidity in Autism

Regier et al. (2012) claimed that the addition of dimensions to the diagnostic criteria in DSM-5 would clarify heterogeneity and reduce excessive comorbidities. Box 7.1 lists the four requirements proposed for a DSM-5 autism diagnosis. The criterion for social impairment includes dimensions, and the fourth requirement states three levels or dimensions of functioning. Dimensionality was built into the proposed social impairment criterion by the provision of a dimensional range of somewhat impaired to severely impaired in social reciprocity, social communication, and developing and sustaining relationships. Dimensionality was also built into the proposed fourth requirement that autism symptoms impair daily life by grading support levels required for daily living: level 1 is "requires support"; level 2 is "requires substantial support; and level 3 is "requires very substantial support (APA DSM-5 Development, 2012a).

However, the proposed levels of daily living support, and dimensional range of social impairments in the provisional DSM-5 autism spectrum criteria did not address the major problems of heterogeneity and comorbidity in autism. The symptoms of comorbid disorders are the core component of autism heterogeneity. Autism heterogeneity "spans the entire range of IQ and language function and a wide array of communicative, social, and behavioral disabilities" (Jones & Klin, 2009, p. 471), and every biological feature measured in autism has demonstrated "enormous heterogeneity—far greater than in the general population" (Amaral, 2011, p. 6).

Box 7.2 lists the six major provisional disorder groups in the Neurodevelopmental Disorders Group in DSM-5 (APA DSM-5 Development, 2012b). Autism spectrum disorder is one of the six groups. The others are Intellectual Development Disorder, Communication Disorders, Attention Deficit/Hyperactivity Disorders, Learning Disorders, and Motor Disorders.

The major source of heterogeneity in autism is the co-occurrence of symptoms of the five other neurodevelopmental disorders. Before studies revealed that risk factors for autism generated a wide range of symptoms along with autism symptoms, these five, along with other neurodevelopmental disorders, were considered to occur as separate comorbid disorders along with autism. Intellectual Development Disorder has been reported for 55–70% of individuals diagnosed with autism by prior criteria (Chakrabarti & Fombonne, 2005; Charman et al., 2011). Because language impairment was a prior diagnostic criterion, all children previously diagnosed with autism expressed a variant of Communication Disorder. Stefanatos and Baron (2011) outlined the heterogeneity in language development in autism. They reported that children with autism may fail to orient toward speech, fail to respond to their name, fail to acquire words and word combinations, may have persisting receptive language problems, and may have impaired verbal imitation. Attention Deficit/Hyperactivity Disorder has been identified in nearly 30% of individuals diagnosed with autism (Ronald & Hoekstra, 2011). A majority of children with autism would qualify for some form of Learning Disorder. Moreover, more than 70% of individuals with autism have been reported to have some form of Motor Disorder (Levy et al., 2009; Downey & Rapport, 2012).

BOX 7.2 DSM-5 Proposed Neurodevelopmental Disorders Classifications (APA, DSM-5 Development, 2012b)

Intellectual Developmental Disorders
- Intellectual Developmental Disorder
- Intellectual or Global Developmental Delay Not Elsewhere Classified

Communication Disorders
- Language Impairment
- Late Language Emergence
- Specific Language Impairment
- Social Communication Disorder
- Speech Sound Disorder
- Childhood Onset Fluency Disorder
- Voice Disorder

Autism Spectrum Disorder
- Autism Spectrum Disorder

Attention Deficit/Hyperactivity Disorder
- Attention Deficit/Hyperactivity Disorder
- Other Specified Attention Deficit/Hyperactivity Disorder

Learning Disorders
- Learning Disorder
- Dyslexia
- Dyscalculia
- Disorder of Written Expression

Motor Disorders
- Developmental Coordination Disorder
- Stereotypic Movement Disorder
- Tourette's Disorder
- Chronic Motor or Vocal Tic Disorder
- Provisional Tic Disorder
- Substance-Induced (indicate substance) Tic Disorder
- Unspecified Tic Disorder
- Tic Disorder Due to a General Medical Condition

The dimensionality proposed for the first and fourth DSM-5 autism spectrum criteria did not address any of the symptoms of the other Neurodevelopmental Disorders known to co-occur with autism. The proposed DSM-5 rationale asserted that symptoms outside autism spectrum disorder diagnostic criteria were associated features, including genetic disorders, epilepsy, intellectual disability, and others (APA DSM-5 Development, 2012a). Moreover, the proposed DSM-5 rationale asserted that the criteria for autism reliably and validly differentiated autism spectrum disorder from non-spectrum disorders (APA DSM-5 Development, 2012a).

However, intellectual disability, attention deficit/hyperactivity disorder, language impairment, motor development problems, learning problems, and epilepsy are not "associated features" or comorbid "nonspectrum disorders." They are heterogeneous symptoms that co-occur with social communication and interactive impairment and restricted repetitive behaviors, interests, or activities, and sensory abnormalities. These heterogeneous symptoms co-occur in autism because they are all component deficits of complex phenotypes that result from various risk factors. Nazeer and Ghaziuddin (2012) reviewed findings for autism and noted that most individuals with autism suffer from intellectual disability that can vary from mild to profound, and that individuals with autism and intellectual disability are more likely to express ritualistic behaviors and abnormal movements.

Lord and Jones (2012) argued that the value of the proposed DSM-5 criteria "will not lie in links to etiology or even pathophysiology; it must be rooted in the provision of information that advises selection of services that will increase independence and quality of life" (p. 502). However, the proposed DSM-5 criteria do not provide the most comprehensive "information that advises selection of services" because they relegate the heterogeneity found in the full range of an individual's phenotypic symptoms to other disorders, even though genetic and environmental risk factors have been demonstrated to cause autism symptoms together with many co-occurring additional symptoms. Lord and Jones (2012) stated that "Having an ASD does not protect a child or family from having other disorders, and in fact, increases the risk of a number of co-occurring behaviors and difficulties" (p. 497). Lord and Jones (2012) concluded that the discussion of co-occurring other disorders was beyond the scope of their paper, but noted "what is important in measuring and describing core features" (p. 497) of autism.

Contra Lord and Jones (2012), symptoms linked to core autism features are important to measure. For example, Close, Lee, Kaufmann, and Zimmerman (2012) compared children with a current autism spectrum diagnosis with children who had previously been given an ASD diagnosis but no longer were classified with any ASD diagnosis. Close et al. (2012) found higher rates of moderate and severe learning disability and moderate and severe developmental delays in children currently diagnosed with an autism diagnosis. Close et al. (2012) also reported that the children currently diagnosed with autism had higher rates of reports of language problems and anxiety, and that adolescents with a current autism diagnosis had higher rates of moderate and severe speech problems and mild seizures and epilepsy.

Similarly, the findings from risk factor studies of autism have demonstrated that social impairment is one symptom group of many symptoms that result from risk factors for autism. Both genetic and environmental risk factor studies of autism, discussed in Chapters 4 and 5, have reported complex multi-symptom phenotypes for autism. Goh and Peterson (2012) asserted that individual risk factors for autism disturbed many varied neural circuits, thereby causing social, communicative, motor, and intellectual impairment in affected individuals. For example, Marshall and Scherer (2012) reported 22 chromosome number variants (CNVs) that linked autism to schizophrenia, attention deficit/hyperactivity disorder, and intellectual disability. They noted, "The fact that many of these pathogenic variants are pleiotropic has broad implications for diagnostics" (Marshall & Scherer, 2012, p. 125). A specific CNV may result in the phenotype of autism with intellectual disability and attention deficit/hyperactivity disorder symptoms, or even autism and schizophrenia symptoms. A meta-analysis of 85 studies of prenatal, perinatal, and neonatal risk factors for autism reported that environmental risk factors for autism also resulted in intellectual disability, language impairment, learning disorders, motor development problems, and general developmental delay (Guinchat et al., 2012b). Thus, environmental risk factors for autism may result in a complex multi-symptom phenotype of autism with intellectual disability and motor development problems. Genetic variants, chromosomal number variants, and environmental insults presumed to cause autism, therefore, cause co-occurring multiple symptoms which together comprise complex phenotypes of an etiology linked to autism symptoms.

In sum, the proposed DSM-5 criteria for autism have avoided the complexity of autism heterogeneity. However, defining co-occurring symptoms as outside diagnosis does not mean the many heterogeneous symptoms will no longer co-occur. Nearly all clinical presentations of autism social impairment and restricted, repetitive behaviors, interests, or activities, or sensory abnormalities are accompanied by additional heterogeneous symptoms. Importantly, risk factor findings have demonstrated that this heterogeneity in autism represents complex phenotypes that are etiologically valid. As noted in Chapter 1, Happé et al. (2006) called heterogeneity in autism "perhaps the biggest single obstacle to research at all levels" (p. 1220). Therefore, defining heterogeneity as outside the autism spectrum disorder by excluding heterogeneous symptoms as associated disorders or non-syndrome disorders is unhelpful to clinicians and researchers.

The exclusion of co-occurring symptoms reflects simplification in service of a theory. The data from Gregor Mendel's pea plant experiments were analyzed by Fisher (Stigler, 2008). Fisher concluded that Mendel had unintentionally eliminated the results of pea plant crosses that had not "bred true" to Mendel's expectations. A recent re-examination of Fisher's analysis of Mendel's pea experiments supported Fisher's assertions that Mendel's findings were a little too tidy (Stigler, 2008). Similarly, the proposed DSM-5 diagnostic criteria for autism spectrum disorder have framed a too tidy autism spectrum disorder. Like Mendel, the researchers developing the DSM-5 criteria are careful and dedicated scientists. It appears as if they have avoided including untidy heterogeneous symptoms that are part of the clinical reality of autism in the belief that a pure form of autism exists.

Specificity Problems in the Proposed DSM-5 Criteria for Autism Spectrum Disorder

A sound diagnostic classification should have good sensitivity and specificity. Sensitivity is the ability of diagnostic criteria to correctly identify and include individuals who have a disorder, and specificity is the ability of the diagnostic criteria to identify and correctly exclude from diagnosis those individuals who do not have the disorder. The proposed diagnostic criteria for autism spectrum disorder included two forms of specificity that would exclude many individuals with serious neurodevelopmental social impairment from a diagnosis of autism. Both points of specificity in the proposed DSM-5 criteria for autism spectrum disorder appear to be based on mistaken assumptions.

Specificity Problem One: Developmental Delay cannot Account for an Individual's Social Impairment

In the proposed DSM-5 criteria for autism spectrum disorder, one key point of diagnostic specificity was the exclusion of individuals with social impairment caused by developmental delay. Harmon (2012) reported that Dr. Lord, a member of the APA DSM-5 Neurodevelopmental Disorders Work Group, stated that the work group's goal "was to ensure that autism was not used as a 'fallback diagnosis' for children whose primary trait might be, for instance, an intellectual disability." The proposed DSM-5 description of social impairment stated that in order to diagnose autism spectrum disorder, the individual's social impairment "should not be accounted for by general developmental delays" (APA DSM-5 Development, 2012a). Developmental delay was not elaborated, but may be presumed to mean intellectual disability, or in DSM-5, Intellectual Development Disorder.

This point of diagnostic specificity effectively asserted social impairment caused by developmental delay was not really autism. This claim mistakenly assumed that when social impairment occurs along with developmental delay or intellectual disability, the developmental delay was *causing* the social impairment. In fact, this point of diagnostic specificity appeared to ignore the evidence of autism phenomenology, the evidence for autism etiology, and the evidence for brain circuitry for social and cognitive behaviors.

First, the proposed DSM-5 separation of social impairment from intellectual disability or general developmental delay ignored the phenomenological evidence that 55–70% of individuals diagnosed with autism by prior criteria experienced the developmental delay of intellectual disability (Chakrabarti & Fombonne, 2005; Charman et al., 2011). Second, all available current evidence for autism etiology suggested the reason why 55–70% of individuals diagnosed with autism have been found to have intellectual disability or developmental delay is that the genetic, chromosomal, and epigenetic factors, and environmental insults that cause serious neurodevelopmental social impairment also cause co-occurring multiple symptoms which together comprise complex phenotypes of that etiology. Goh and Peterson (2012) noted, "Genetic and molecular studies suggest that the pathophysiological mechanisms involved in ASD are likely to … [cause] disturbances in functioning across multiple neural systems, and consequently potential impairment in the acquisition of a wide range of skills, including social, communicative, motor, and intellectual skills" (p. 6). For example, van Bokhoven (2011) noted that single gene variants for *IL1RAPL1, SHANK2, SHANK3, NLGN3, NLGN4, GRIN2B, TCF4, AUTS2, CNTN4, CNTNAP2,* and *NRXN1* have been expressed in individuals as intellectual disability without autism, autism without intellectual disability, and autism with intellectual disability. The cumulative evidence linking autism to intellectual disability has indicated that social impairment and intellectual disability or developmental delay are co-occurring outcomes of many chromosomal and genetic variants. In addition, the Hallmayer et al. (2011) twin study suggested that environmental factors might account for more than half the variance in autism, and one demonstrated environmental cause for autism was extreme prematurity (Pinto-Martin et al., 2011). However, extreme prematurity may result in cerebral palsy, motor deficit, attention deficit/hyperactivity disorder, developmental delay, intellectual disability, and autism (Lubsen et al., 2011). Thus, the insult of prematurity may cause dysfunction in the neural circuits, transmitters, neurohormones, and synapses that mediate social behavior, but may also cause dysfunction in neural circuits that determine cognitive functions, and a range of motor functions.

Third, the theory that social impairment is not a feature of autism if it is "accounted for by general developmental delays" (APA DSM-5 Development, 2012a) is not consonant with existing neuroscience evidence for brain circuits. Neuroscience findings indicate that the neural basis for developmental delay cannot *account for* the neural basis for social impairment. When social impairment occurs along with developmental delays or intellectual disability, the developmental delay does not cause the social impairment. Research on the brain basis of social behavior (see Chapter 3) strongly suggests that human social communication and interaction behavior is governed by many diverse dedicated neural circuits, neurotransmitters, and neurohormones (Bos et al., 2011; Frith & Frith, 2012; Gallese & Sinigaglia, 2011; Gordon et al., 2011; Insel, 2010; Mar, 2011; Northoff & Hayes, 2011; Vickery et al., 2011). Consequently, when neurodevelopmental social impairment occurs in an individual, the neural cause is dysfunction in one or more circuits, neurotransmitters, or neurohormones regulating social behaviors. For example, from his meta-analysis of studies of Theory of Mind, the understanding that other people have different mental contents from our own, Mar (2011) concluded that the brain basis for Theory of Mind depends on a complex circuitry. Mar (2011) stated that this circuitry includes the right temporal-parietal juncture, prefrontal cortex, left and right posterior superior temporal sulcus, left and right angular gyri, left and right anterior temporal regions, posterior cingulate cortex, precuneus, and perhaps also the left inferior gyrus. Neurodevelopmental failure to develop a Theory of Mind, therefore, is likely to involve a failure of the function of elements of this complex circuit.

By contrast, general cognitive developmental delay or intellectual disability may be the result of dysfunction in any of the circuits for cognitive processes, such as: parietal areas governing attention; thalamic and occipital areas governing perception; dorsolateral prefrontal cortex regulating working memory, including executive functioning; hippocampal complex and prefrontal cortex determining long-term memory; and the anterior cingulate contributing to cognitive control.

Of course, neural circuits for social behaviors and cognition overlap and interact. However, where circuits mediating social behavior intersect and overlap circuits mediating other behaviors, the dysfunction in circuits causing intellectual disability does not cause the deficits in the neural circuitry that governs social behavior. Gu, Liu, Van Dam, Hof, and Fan (2012) noted that it remains unclear whether cognitive and social-affective processes work in parallel or in an integrated fashion. They proposed that their imaging study findings indicated that the bilateral anterior insula mediates the integration of cognitive and emotional processes. Similarly, Schilbach et al. (2012) reported evidence for a distinct circuit that integrated emotional processing, social cognition, and other cognition. The researchers identified this circuit as a connection between the precuneus and anterior medial prefrontal cortex, which they theorized determined the process of introspection. They speculated that social cognition, emotional processing, and resting state cognition might recruit different brain circuits for specific social and non-social functions (Schilbach et al., 2012). In fact, there are so many defined dedicated circuits for components of human social behavior that dysfunction in an integrative hub could not be interpreted as developmental delay causing social impairment (Bos et al., 2011; Frith & Frith, 2012; Gallese & Sinigaglia, 2011; Gordon et al., 2011; Insel, 2010; Mar, 2011; Northoff & Hayes, 2011; Vickery et al., 2011).

Specificity Problem Two: Individuals with Social Impairment but without Restricted Repetitive Behaviors, Interests, or Activities would be Excluded from Diagnosis

In the proposed DSM-5 criteria for autism spectrum disorder, a second key point of specificity was that an individual would be excluded from a diagnosis of autism spectrum disorder if he or she expressed social communication and interaction impairment but did not exhibit restricted repetitive behaviors, interests, or activities. However, Mandy et al. (2011) found that of 66 individuals with DSM-IV Pervasive Developmental Disorder Not Otherwise Specified, 64 met the social impairment and social communication criteria that would allow a DSM-5 diagnosis of autism spectrum disorder, but none of the 64 individuals met the requirement for restricted repetitive behaviors, interests, or activities. Interestingly, Mandy et al. (2011) noted that the majority of the 64 had no intellectual disability.

Therefore, the proposed DSM-5 criteria would exclude individuals without developmental delay who met diagnostic criteria for social impairment, because they did not have restricted repetitive behaviors, interests, or activities. Leekam et al. (2011) reviewed restricted repetitive behaviors, interests, or activities in autism and reported that this pattern of behaviors occurs in many other disorders including Tourette syndrome, fragile X, Rett syndrome, obsessive-compulsive disorder, Down syndrome, deafness, blindness, schizophrenia, and intellectual disability. Dysfunction in basal ganglia circuits may induce abnormal repetitive behavior, and dopamine abnormalities contribute to insistence on sameness. Leekam et al. (2011) argued that more research was needed to understand the development of basal ganglia, striatal and forebrain structures, and possible feedback dysfunction in corticostriatal circuits.

While restricted repetitive behaviors, interests, or activities have historically been a component of the autism diagnosis, as noted above, Robinson et al. (2011) and Happé et al. (2006) reported very little etiological overlap for social impairment, communication impairment, and restricted and repetitive behaviors in typical populations, and they argued that the three autism components were associated with different genetic and environmental causes. As demonstrated by the findings of Mandy et al. (2011), the elimination of the PDD-NOS diagnostic category in the proposed DSM-5 criteria for autism spectrum disorder would exclude a group of individuals that would meet the social impairment criterion of DSM-5 but not the restricted and repetitive behavior criterion. In previous DSM criteria, the diagnostic category PDD-NOS allowed a diagnosis for those individuals who met the social impairment criterion but not the restricted and repetitive behavior criterion.

Rutter (2011) argued that when clinicians and researchers interviewed a patient with autism symptoms, they selected the PDD-NOS category when they did "not recognize any meaning in the subcategories" (p. 649). That may be true in some instances. However, the PDD-NOS group studied by Mandy et al. (2011), who would be excluded from diagnosis by the proposed DSM-5 criteria, were not given a PDD-NOS diagnosis because clinicians failed to recognize subcategory meaning. Nor were these individuals diagnosed with PDD-NOS as a result of cleaving "meatloaf at the joints" (APA DSM-5 Development, 2012a). The data presented by Mandy et al. (2011), Mattila et al. (2011), and Volkmar (Carey, 2012) demonstrated that a significant group of individuals diagnosed with PDD-NOS expressed diagnostic neurodevelopmental social impairment. These patients will be excluded from diagnosis by the DSM-5 criteria.

The expression of social communication and interaction impairment co-occurring with restricted repetitive behaviors, interests, or activities has not been validated by a unique shared pathophysiological substrate, or by a unitary genetic cause, or by a unitary environmental cause. To the contrary, there is evidence for many different brain dysfunctions, many genetic risk factors, and many environmental risk factors for this combination of symptoms. Therefore, excluding a group affected by social communication and interaction impairment represents a new definition of the autism spectrum without a clear empirical justification.

Summary: Dimensionality in Proposed DSM-5 Criteria Failed to Address the Significant Heterogeneity of Symptoms that Co-occur with Autism, and Narrow Specificity will Exclude Affected Individuals

The dimensionality included in the first and fourth required elements of the proposed DSM-5 autism spectrum criteria avoided the significant heterogeneity caused by the clinical co-occurrence of symptoms such as intellectual disability and attention deficit/hyperactivity disorder with the criterial symptoms proposed for autism spectrum disorder. Because the known risk factors for autism disrupt multiple brain networks, thus producing complex phenotypes in affected individuals (Goh & Peterson, 2012), the failure to address heterogeneity will limit the ability of the proposed DSM-5 criteria for autism spectrum disorder to advance translational research.

The theory that serious neurodevelopmental social communication and interaction impairment is not a symptom of autism if it is "accounted for by general developmental delays" (APA DSM-5 Development, 2012a) ignores the clinical presentation of autism, the risk factor evidence for autism, and the evidence for neural circuitry for social behavior. Developmental delay that accompanies serious neurodevelopmental social communication and interaction impairment does not cause the social impairment, but co-occurs with social impairment as the phenotypic expression of etiological factors. The attempt to exclude social impairment if caused by developmental delay is not cutting nature at its joints, it is the judgment of Solomon.

In the proposed DSM-5 criteria for autism spectrum disorder, a second problematic specificity is the exclusion of individuals who express social communication and interactive impairment but not restricted repetitive behaviors, interests, or activities. The two diagnostic symptoms have not been validated by a neural substrate, genetic cause, or environmental cause. Moreover, there is a significant clinical population of individuals who express serious neurodevelopmental social impairment but who do not express restricted repetitive behaviors, interests, or activities (Carey, 2012; Mandy et al., 2011; Mattila et al., 2011). Therefore, the DSM-5 exclusion of known clinical populations of individuals expressing only social communication and interaction impairment appears an arbitrary decision not supported by evidence or a scientific rationale.

The proposed DSM-5 criteria for autism spectrum disorder (APA DSM-5 Development, 2012a) eliminate all prior subgroups. The proposed criteria reflect the choice to ignore etiologically validated heterogeneity in autism, the choice to exclude individuals with neurodevelopmental social communication and interaction impairment that co-occurs with developmental delay, and the choice to exclude individuals with serious neurodevelopmental social impairment who do not also express restricted repetitive behaviors, interests, or activities. As Pinto-Martin (2012) pointed out, the revised DSM-5 criteria for autism spectrum disorder will cause an immediate drop in prevalence. Affected children will be excluded from diagnosis, researchers will have to reformulate research designs, and monitoring the change in the prevalence of autism over time will have to start over using the DSM-5 theory of autism.

CONCLUSION: AN ORIGINALIST VIEW OF AUTISM AVOIDS THE COMPLEXITY OF EVIDENCE

It is unfortunate for researchers and parents of affected children that the proposed DSM-5 criteria include a stringent specificity that appears to reflect the originalist theory of autism. Originalism is a theory of text interpretation most often used to describe judicial explication of the United States Constitution. An originalist view of autism returns to Kanner's 1943 definition of autism as the original and correct basis for diagnosis. Originalist Kanner autism, also called classic autism, is theorized to occur without intellectual disability, and without heterogeneity. Folstein (2006) provided the clearest expression of the originalist position. Folstein stated that Kanner's first criterion for autism was: "Children with autism have an innate difficulty in understanding the nature of human interaction, what use it has, and how to go about it" (2006, p. 114). Folstein reported, "Kanner's second criterion was that autistic children cannot tolerate change of any type, either in their physical environment or in the sequence of activities during the day" (2006, p. 115). Folstein (2006) noted that Kanner required that children with autism look intelligent and alert, and that Kanner excluded children from diagnosis who had dysmorphic features or very low IQ. Folstein (2006) argued that a major cause for the increase in autism prevalence was the inclusion of children with mental retardation.

Because originalist theory assumed that Kanner's 1943 observations correctly defined autism as independent of developmental delay or heterogeneity, originalist theory drove the belief that diagnosis should provide stringent enough specificity to exclude development delay and heterogeneity from a diagnosis of autism. The proposed DSM-5 criteria for autism spectrum disorder are firmly in the originalist tradition. The proposed criteria carefully keep known heterogeneity as "associated disorders" outside autism. The proposed criteria would exclude a child from diagnosis if that child's social impairment were caused by developmental delay (argued above to be a neurological impossibility). In addition, the proposed DSM-5 criteria require a symptom from a category that is not identical to, but reflects Kanner's second criterion, insistence on sameness.

There has been a strong influence of originalist thinking on the design and goals of much research in autism. It has driven the fruitless quest for *the* single pathophysiological substrate of classic autism and the equally unproductive quest for *the* unifying symptom set for classic autism. Overall, autism research has been significantly hampered by the originalist vision of a unitary classic autism that existed in isolation, that is, without intellectual disability, epilepsy, identifiable genetic causes, or heterogeneous symptoms. Nonetheless, researchers discovered autism to be a causally complex, dauntingly heterogeneous phenotype linked to hundreds of genetic and environmental risk factors, a multitude of diverse brain deficits, and varied life courses. This evidence has demonstrated that autism is not the disorder Kanner construed in 1943.

Kanner could not have imagined the varied neural circuits governing human social behavior, or the ability to image the brain and explore its patterns of connection. Kanner defined autism before Watson and Crick determined the helical structure of DNA. The richness of discovery in genetics and neuroscience revealed new worlds of causal complexity.

Hyman (2011) claimed that the current DSM-IV criteria were ossified, and the many problems with DSM meant that DSM-5 revisions "must take more significant steps toward a new framework" (p. 661). While the proposed DSM-5 criteria heeded Rutter's (2011) wish to eliminate all subcategories of autism, the resulting single category as defined, unfortunately, is unlikely to advance translational research. Hyman (2011) argued that even though "psychiatry is not yet in a position to embrace a new paradigm" (p. 661), it would be a challenge for DSM-5 criteria not to get "ahead of the scientific evidence" (p. 661). Counter to Hyman's (2011) concern that the DSM-5 criteria not get ahead of the evidence, the DSM-5 autism spectrum disorder criteria have moved back in time to the period before genetic and neuroscience evidence for autism existed. Stringent originalist criteria step back in time to define autism without developmental delay or heterogeneity.

Overall, autism research has been significantly hampered by the originalist vision of a unitary classic autism that existed in isolation, that is, without intellectual disability, epilepsy, identifiable genetic causes, or other heterogeneous symptoms. The category "autism spectrum disorder" is a protem classification that will necessarily be changed as research provides a better understanding of the many complex phenotypes that include neuro-developmental social impairment. However, neither the premise that the proposed DSM-5 criteria are temporary, nor the evidence that the proposed criteria eliminate one unproven diagnosis, Asperger syndrome, justifies the imposition of diagnostic criteria for autism that take a giant and obstructive step back from the wealth of existing evidence.

REFERENCES

Akil, H., Brenner, S., Kandel, E., Kendler, K. S., King, M. C., Scolnick, E., et al. (2010). The future of psychiatric research: Genomes and neural circuits. *Science, 327,* 1580–1581.

Amaral, D. G. (2011). The promise and the pitfalls of autism research: An introductory note for new autism researchers. *Brain Research, 1380,* 3–9.

Andari, E., Duhamel, J. R., Zalla, T., Herbrecht, E., Leboyer, M., & Sirigu, A. (2010). Promoting social behavior with oxytocin in high-functioning autism spectrum disorders. *Proceedings of the National Academy of Sciences of the United States of America, 107,* 4389–4394.

APA. (1980). *Diagnostic and statistical manual of mental disorders* (3rd ed.). Washington, DC: American Psychiatric Association.

APA. (1987). *Diagnostic and statistical manual of mental disorders* (3rd ed., rev.). Washington, DC: American Psychiatric Association.

APA. (1994). *Diagnostic and statistical manual of mental disorders* (4th ed.). Washington, DC: American Psychiatric Association.

APA. (2000). *Diagnostic and statistical manual of mental disorders—text revised* (4th ed., rev.). Washington, DC: American Psychiatric Association.

APA. (2011). *DSM-5 development: A 09 Autism spectrum disorder.* Available at: http://www.dsm5.org/ProposedRevisions/Pages/proposedrevision.aspx?rid=94.

APA (American Psychiatric Association) DSM-5 Development. (2012a). *A 09 Autism Spectrum Disorders.* Retrieved February 8, 2012 from http://www.dsm5.org/ProposedRevision/Pages/proposedrevision.aspx?rid=94.

APA (American Psychiatric Association) DSM-5 Development. (2012b). *Neurodevelopmental disorders.* Retrieved February 8, 2012 from http://www.dsm5.org/proposedrevision/Pages/NeurodevelopmentalDisorders.aspx.

Arguello, P. A., & Gogos, J. A. (2012). Genetic and cognitive windows into circuit mechanisms of psychiatric disease. *Trends in Neurosciences, 35,* 3–13.

Aspieside. (2012, February 8). *APA responds regarding DSM5.* [Web log post]. Retrieved February 9, 2012 from http://aspieside.com/2012/02/08/apa-responds-regarding-dsm5/.

Autism and Developmental Disabilities Monitoring Network Surveillance Year 2006 Principal Investigators, Centers for Disease Control and Prevention. (2009). Prevalence of autism spectrum disorders—Autism and developmental disabilities monitoring network, United States, 2006. *Morbidity and Mortality Weekly Report Surveillance Summaries, 58*(SS10), 1–20.

Autism and Developmental Disabilities Monitoring Network Surveillance Year 2008 Principal Investigators, Centers for Disease Control and Prevention. (2012). Prevalence of autism spectrum disorders—Autism and developmental disabilities monitoring network, United States, 2008. *Morbidity and Mortality Weekly Report Surveillance Summaries*, *61*(SS03), 1–19.

Autism Speaks. (2012, February 2). *Autism Speaks statement on revisions to the DSM definition of Autism Spectrum Disorder.* Autismspeaks.org. Retrieved February 2, 2012 from http://www.autismspeaks.org/science/policy-statements/statement-revisions-dsm-definition-autism-spectrum-disorder.

Autismlearningfelt. (2011, April 15). *New autism research may lead to an autism cure.* [Web log comment], Autisable.com. Retrieved February 1, 2012 from http://www.autisable.com /745714448/new-autism-research-may-lead-to-autism-cure/.

Baird, G., Simonoff, E., Pickles, A., Chandler, S., Loucas, T., Meldrum, D., et al. (2006). Prevalence of disorders of the autism spectrum in a population cohort of children in South Thames: The Special Needs and Autism Project (SNAP). *The Lancet, 368,* 210–225.

Baron-Cohen, S., Scott, F. J., Allison, C., Williams, J., Bolton, P., Matthews, F. E., et al. (2009). Prevalence of autism-spectrum conditions: UK school-based population study. *British Journal of Psychiatry, 194,* 500–509.

BigThink (Ed.). (2011, February 9). *Why there may never be a cure for autism.* bigthink.com. Retrieved February 1, 2012 fromhttp://bigthink.com/ideas/26851.

Bookheimer, S. (2011, January 18). *BigThink panel discussion on autism. Is autism an epidemic? [Panel transcript].* bigthink.com. Retrieved January 8, 2012 from http://bigthink.com/ users/susanbookheimer.

Bos, P. A., Panksepp, J., Bluth, R. M., & van Honk, J. (2012). Acute effects of steroid hormones and neuropeptides on human social–emotional behavior: A review of single administration studies. *Frontiers in Neuroendocrinology, 33,* 17–35.

Brauser, D. (2012, January 25). *Concern over changes to autism criteria unfounded, says APA.* Medscape.com. Retrieved February 2, 2012 from http://www.medscape.com/viewarti cle/757515.

Brugha, T. S., McManus, S., Bankart, J., Scott, F., Purdon, S., Smith, J., et al. (2011). Epidemiology of autism spectrum disorders in adults in the community in England. *Archives of General Psychiatry, 68,* 459–465.

Campbell, M., Reynolds, L., Cunningham, J., Minnis, H., & Gillberg, C. G. (2011). Autism in Glasgow: Cumulative incidence and the effects of referral age, deprivation and geographical location. *Child Care Health Development.* [Epub November 1, 2011]. doi: 10.1111/j.1365-2214.2011.01340.x.

Carey, B. (2012, January 19). New autism definition will exclude many, study suggests. *The New York Times.* Retrieved January 20, 2012 from http://www.nytimes.com/2012/01/-20/health/research/new-autism-definition-would-exclude-many-study-suggests.html?_r=1&pagewanted=all.

Caruso, D. (2010). Autism in the U.S.: Social movement and legal change. *American Journal of Law & Medicine, 36,* 483–539.

Centers for Disease Control and Prevention, ADDM Network Surveillance Year 2002 Principal Investigators. (2007, February 9). Prevalence of autism spectrum disorders—Autism and developmental disabilities monitoring network, 14 sites, United States, 2002. *MMWR Surveillance Summaries, 56,* 2–28.

Centers for Disease Control and Prevention. (2009, December 18). Prevalence of autism spectrum disorders—Autism and developmental disabilities monitoring network, United States, 2006. *MMWR Surveillance Summaries, 58,* 1–20.

Chakrabarti, S., & Fombonne, E. (2005). Pervasive developmental disorders in preschool children: Confirmation of high prevalence. *American Journal of Psychiatry, 162,* 1133–1141.

Charman, T., Pickles, A., Simono, E., Chandler, S. E., Loucas, T., & Baird, G. (2011). IQ in children with autism spectrum disorders: Data from the Special Needs and Autism Project (SNAP). *Psychological Medicine, 41,* 619–627.

Close, H. A., Lee, L. C., Kaufmann, C. N., & Zimmerman, A. W. (2012). Co-occurring conditions and change in diagnosis in autism spectrum disorders. *Pediatrics, 129*, e305–e316.

Cole, M. W., Anticevic, A., Repovs, G., & Barch, D. (2011). Variable global dysconnectivity and individual differences in schizophrenia. *Biological Psychiatry, 70*, 43–50.

Coleman, N., & Gillberg, C. (2012). *The autisms.* New York, NY: Oxford University Press.

Coo, H., Ouellette-Kuntz, H., Lloyd, J. E., Kasmara, L., Holden, J. J., & Lewis, M. E. (2008). Trends in autism prevalence: Diagnostic substitution revisited. *Journal of Autism and Developmental Disorders, 38*, 1036–1046.

Craddock, N., & Owen, M. J. (2010). The Kraepelinian dichotomy—Going, going … but still not gone. *British Journal of Psychiatry, 196*, 92–95.

Cullen, K. R., Klimes-Dougan, B., Muetzel, R., Mueller, B. A., Camchong, J., Houri, A., et al. (2010). Altered white matter microstructure in adolescents with major depression: A preliminary study. *Journal of the American Academy of Child and Adolescent Psychiatry, 49*, 173–183.

Cuthbert, B. N., & Insel, T. R. (2010). Toward new approaches to psychotic disorders: The NIMH Research Domain Criteria project. *Schizophrenia Bulletin, 36*, 1061–1062.

Dachel, A. (2012, February 3). *Why do autism "experts" know so little? The DSM-5 debacle.* Ageofautism.com. Retrieved February 3, 2012 from http://www.ageofautism.com/2012/02/why-do-autism-experts-know-so-little-the-dsm-5-debacle.html#more.

Dannlowski, U., Stuhrmann, A., Beutelmann, V., Zwanzger, P., Lenzen, T., Grotegerd, D., et al. (2012). Limbic scars: Long-term consequences of childhood maltreatment revealed by functional and structural magnetic resonance imaging. *Biological Psychiatry, 71*, 286–293.

Downey, R., & Rapport, M. J. (2012). Motor activity in children with autism: A review of current literature. *Pediatric Physical Therapy, 24*, 2–20.

Eapen, V., Mabrouk, A. A., Zoubeidi, T., & Yunis, F. (2007). Prevalence of pervasive developmental disorders in preschool children in the UAE. *Journal of Tropical Pediatrics, 53*, 202–205.

Ellefsen, A., Kampmann, H., Billstedt, E. I., Carina Gillberg, C. I., & Gillberg, C. (2007). Autism in the Faroe Islands. An epidemiological study. *Journal of Autism and Developmental Disorders, 37*, 437–444.

Els for Autism. (n.d.). *Autism community voices concerns over reclassification.* Ernieels.com. Retrieved February 2, 2012 from http://www.ernieels.com/els_for_autism/Autism_Reclassification_Statement.html.

Fischbach, G. (2011, January 18). *Big Think panel discussion on autism: Is autism an epidemic? [Panel transcript].* bigthink.com. Retrieved January 8, 2012 from http://bigthink.com/users/geraldfischbach.

Folstein, S. (2006). The clinical spectrum of autism. *Clinical Neuroscience Research, 6*, 113–117.

Fombonne, E. (2009). Epidemiology of pervasive developmental disorders. *Pediatric Research, 65*, 591–598.

Fountain, C., & Bearman, P. (2011). Risk as social context: Immigration policy and autism in California. *Social Forum, 26*, 215–240.

Fountain, C., King, M. D., & Bearman, P. S. (2011). Age of diagnosis for autism: Individual and community factors across 10 birth cohorts. *Journal of Epidemiology and Community Health, 65*, 503–510.

Frances, A. (2010, February 10). Opening Pandora's box: The 19 worst suggestions for DSM5. *UBM Psychiatric Times*, 1–10. Retrieved March 19, 2011 from http://www.psychiatrictimes.com/display/article/10168/1522341.

Frances, A. (2012a, January 30). *DSM 5 will lower autism rates.* The Huffington Post.com. Retrieved January 30, 2012 from http://www.huffingtonpost.com/allen-frances/dsm-5-will-lower-autism-r_b_1240016.html.

Frances, A. (2012b, January 31). *APA should delay publication of DSM-5.* UBM Medica Psychiatric Times. Retrieved February 3, 2012 from http://www.psychiatrictimes.com/blog/frances/content/article/10168/2024394.

Frances, A. (2012c, February 9). *The DSM 5 follies, as told in its own words.* TheHuffington Post.com. Retrieved February 10, 2012 from http://www.huffingtonpost.com/allen-frances/dsm-5_b_1251448.html.

Frances, A. L., & Widiger, T. (2012). Psychiatric diagnosis: Lessons from the DSM-IV past and cautions for the DSM-5 future. *Annual Review of Clinical Psychology, 8,* 7.1–7.22.

Frazier, T. W., Youngstrom, E. A., Speer, L., Embacher, R., Law, P., Constantino, J., et al. (2012). Validation of proposed DSM-5 criteria for Autism Spectrum Disorder. *Journal of the American Academy of Child and Adolescent Psychiatry, 51,* 28–40.

Frith, C. D., & Frith, U. (2012). Mechanisms of social cognition. *Annual Review of Psychology, 63,* 8.1–8.27.

Gallese, V., & Sinigaglia, C. (2011). What is so special about embodied simulation? *Trends in Cognitive Neuroscience, 15,* 512–519.

Gernsbacher, M. A., Dawson, G., & Goldsmith, H. H. (2005). Three reasons not to believe in an autism epidemic. *Current Directions in Psychological Science, 14,* 55–58.

Ghaemi, N. (2011). Psychiatric diagnosis: Where's the science? *Medscape Psychiatry.* Retrieved February 1, 2012 from http://www.medscape.com/viewarticle/742619.

Ghanizadeh, A. (2008). A preliminary study on screening prevalence of pervasive developmental disorder in schoolchildren in Iran. *Journal of Autism and Developmental Disorders, 38,* 759–763.

Gillberg, C., & Wing, L. (1999). Autism: Not an extremely rare disorder. *Acta Psychiatrica Scandanavica, 99,* 399–406.

Goh, S., & Peterson, B. S. (2012). Imaging evidence for disturbances in multiple learning and memory systems in persons with autism spectrum disorders. *Developmental Medicine and Child Neurology, 54,* 208–213.

Gomot, M., & Wicker, B. (2012). A challenging, unpredictable world for people with Autism Spectrum Disorder. *International Journal of Psychophysiology, 83,* 240–247.

Gordon, I., Martin, C., Feldman, R., & Leckman, J. F. (2011). Oxytocin and social motivation. *Developmental Cognitive Neuroscience, 1,* 471–493.

Greenberg, G. (2012, January 29). Not diseases, but categories of suffering. *The New York Times.* Retrieved January 29, 2012 from http://www.nytimes.com/2012/01/30/opinion/the-dsms-troubled-revision.html?_r=1&emc=tnt&tntemail0=y.

Gu, X., Liu, X., Van Dam, N. T., Hof, P. R., & Fan, J. (2012). Cognition-emotion integration in the anterior insular cortex. *Cerebral Cortex.* [Epub January 23, 2012]. doi: 10.1093/cercor/bhr367.

Guinchat, V., Thorsen, P., Laurent, C., Cans, C., Bodeau, N., & Cohen, D. (2012b). Pre-, peri-, and neonatal risk factors for autism. *Acta Obstetrica Gynecologica Scandanavia, 91,* 287–300.

Gupta, A. R., & State, M. W. (2007). Recent advances in the genetics of autism. *Biological Psychiatry, 61,* 429–437.

Hallmayer, J., Cleveland, S., Torres, A., Phillips, J., Cohen, B., Torigoe, T., et al. (2011). Genetic heritability and shared environmental factors among twin pairs with autism. *Archives of General Psychiatry, 68,* 1095–1102.

Happé, F. (2011, March 29). *Why fold Asperger syndrome into autism spectrum disorder in the DSM-5?* Sfari.org. Retrieved February 6, 2012 from https://sfari.org/news-and-opinion/viewpoint/2011/why-fold-asperger-syndrome-into-autism-spectrum-disorder-in-the-dsm-5.

Happé, F., Ronald, A., & Plomin, R. (2006). Time to give up on a single explanation for autism. *Nature Neuroscience, 9,* 1218–1220.

Harmon, A. (2012, January 20). A specialists' debate on autism has many worried observers. *The New York Times.* Retrieved January 31, 2012 from http://www.nytimes.com/2012/

01/21/us/as-specialists-debate-autism-some-parents-watch-closely.html?_r=1&pagewan ted=all.

Herbert, M. (2012, January 27). *Narrowing the definition of autism.* [Letter to the editor]. *The New York Times.* Retrieved January 28, 2012 from http://www.nytimes.com/2012/ 01/28/opinion/narrowing-the-definition-of-autism.html2012, January 27.

Hertz-Picciotto, I., & Delwiche, L. (2009). The rise in autism and the role of age at diagnosis. *Epidemiology, 20,* 84–90.

Hyman, S. E. (2010). The diagnosis of mental disorders: The problem of reification. *Annual Review of Clinical Psychology, 6,* 155–179. doi: 10.1146/annurev.clinpsy.3.022806.091532.

Hyman, S. E. (2011). Commentary: Repairing a plane while it is flying—Reflections on Rutter (2011). *Journal of Child Psychology and Psychiatry, 52,* 661–662, discussion 673–675.

Independent Patriot Westchester County. (2012, January 19). Re: New autism definition will exclude many, study suggests. *The New York Times.* [Web log post]. Retrieved January 20, 2012 from http://www.nytimes.com/2012/01/20/health/research/new-autism-definition-would-exclude-many-study-suggests.html?_r=1&pagewanted=all.

Insel, T. (2010). The challenge of translation in social neuroscience: a review of oxytocin, vasopressin, and affiliative behavior. *Neuron, 65,* 768–779.

Jones, W., & Klin, A. (2009). Heterogeneity and homogeneity across the autism spectrum: The role of development. *Journal of the Academy of Child and Adolescent Psychiatry, 48,* 471–473.

Kaplan, S. L. (2011, July 4). Godzilla meets Tyrannosaurus Rex? DSM-5, RDoC and child bipolar disorder. *Psychology Today.* Retrieved January 31, 2012 from http://www.psycho logytoday.com/blog/your-child-does-not-have-bipolar-disorder/201107/godzilla-meets-tyrannosaurus-rex-dsm-5-rdoc-an.

Kawamura, Y., Takahashi, O., & Ishii, T. (2008). Reevaluating the incidence of pervasive developmental disorders: Impact of elevated rates of detection through implementation of an integrated system of screening in Toyota, Japan. *Psychiatry and Clinical Neurosciences, 62,* 152–159.

Kelland, K. (2012, February 9). *Grieving relatives could be classed as ill.* Reuters.com. Retrieved February 9, 2012 from http://www.reuters.com/article/2012/02/09/mental-illness-diagnosis-idUSL5E8D98MX20120209.

Kendell, R., & Jablensky, A. (2003). Distinguishing between the validity and utility of psychiatric diagnoses. *American Journal of Psychiatry, 160,* 4–12.

Kendler, K., Kupfer, D., Narrow, W., Phillips, K., & Fawcett, J. (2009, October 21). *Guidelines for making changes to DSM-V.* dsm5.org. Retrieved February 5, 2012 from http://www. dsm5.org/ProgressReports/Pages/Default.aspx.

Keshavan, M. S., Nasrallah, H. A., & Tandon, R. (2011). Schizophrenia, "Just the Facts" 6. Moving ahead with the schizophrenia concept: From the elephant to the mouse. *Schizophrenia Research, 127,* 3–13.

Keyes, K. M., Susser, E., Cheslack-Postava, K., Fountain, C., Liu, K., & Bearman, P. S. (2011). Cohort effects explain the increase in autism diagnosis among children born from 1992 to 2003 in California. *International Journal of Epidemiology, 41,* 495–503.

Kim, Y. S., Leventhal, B. L., Koh, Y.-J., Fombonne, E., Laska, E., Lim, E.-C., et al. (2011). Prevalence of autism spectrum disorders in a total population sample. *American Journal of Psychiatry, 168,* 904–912.

King, M., & Berman, P. (2009). Diagnostic change and the increased prevalence of autism. *International Journal of Epidemiology, 38,* 1224–1234.

Knickerbocker, H., & Waehler, K. (2012, January 27). *Narrowing the definition of autism.* [Letter to the editor]. *The New York Times.* Retrieved January 28, 2012 from http://-www.nytimes.com/2012/01/28/opinion/narrowing-the-definition-of-autism.html.

Koovská, E., Biskupstø, R., Carina Gillberg, I., Ellefsen, A., Kampmann, H., Stórá, T., et al. (2012). The rising prevalence of autism: A prospective longitudinal study in the Faroe

Islands. *Journal of Autism and Developmental Disorders*. [Epub January 25, 2012]. doi: 10.1007/s10803-012-1444-9.

Kupfer, D. J., & Regier, D. A. (2011). Neuroscience, clinical evidence, and the future of psychiatric classification in DSM-5. *American Journal of Psychiatry, 168*, 672–674.

Lam, Y. G., & Yeung, S. S. (2012). Cognitive deficits and symbolic play in preschoolers with autism. *Research in Autism Spectrum Disorders, 6*, 560–564.

Latif, A. H. A., & Williams, W. R. (2007). Diagnostic trends in autistic spectrum disorders in the South Wales valleys. *Autism, 11*, 479–487.

Lazoff, T., Zhong, L., Piperni, T., & Fombonne, E. (2010). Prevalence of pervasive developmental disorders among children at the English Montreal School Board. *Canadian Journal of Psychiatry, 55*, 715–720.

Leekam, S. R., Prior, M. R., & Uljarevic, M. (2011). Restricted and repetitive behaviors in autism spectrum disorders: A review of research in the last decade. *Psychological Bulletin, 137*, 562–593.

Leonard, H., Dixon, G., Whitehouse, A. J. O., Bourke, J., Aiberti, K., Nassar, N., et al. (2010). Unpacking the complex nature of the autism epidemic. *Research in Autism Spectrum Disorders, 4*, 548–554.

Leventhal, B. L. (2012). Lumpers and splitters: Who knows? Who cares? *Journal of the American Academy of Child and Adolescent Psychiatry, 51*, 6–7.

Levy, S. E., Mandel, D. S., & Schultz, R. T. (2009). Autism. *The Lancet, 374*, 1627–1638.

Li, N., Chen, G., Song, X., Du, W., & Zheng, X. (2011). Prevalence of autism-caused disability among Chinese children: A national population-based survey. *Epilepsy and Behavior, 22*, 786–789.

Lin, J.-D., Lin, L.-P., & Wu, J.-L. (2009). Administrative prevalence of autism spectrum disorders based on national disability registers in Taiwan. *Research in Autism Spectrum Disorders, 3*, 269–274.

Lord, C., & Jones, R. M. (2012). Annual Research Review: Re-thinking the classification of autism spectrum disorders. *Journal of Child Psychology and Psychiatry, 53*, 490–509.

Lord, C., Petkova, E., Hus, V., Gan, W., Lu, F., Martin, D. M., & Risi, S. (2012). A multisite study of the clinical diagnosis of different autism spectrum disorders. *Archives of General Psychiatry, 131*, 565–579.

Lubsen, J., Vohr, B., Myers, E., Hampson, M., Lacadie, C., Schneider, K. C., et al. (2011). Microstructural and functional connectivity in the developing preterm brain. *Seminars in Perinatology, 35*, 34–43.

Mandy, W. P. L., Charman, T., Gilmour, J., & Skuse, D. (2011). Toward specifying Pervasive Developmental Disorder—Not Otherwise Specified. *Autism Research, 4*, 121–131.

Mandy, W. P. L., Charman, T., & Skuse, D. (2012). Testing the construct validity of proposed DSM-5 criteria for autism spectrum disorder. Journal of the American Academy of Child and *Adolescent Psychiatry, 51*, 41–50.

Mar, R. A. (2011). The neural bases of social cognition and story comprehension. *Annual Review of Psychology, 62*, 103–134.

Marshall, C. R., & Scherer, S. W. (2012). Detection and characterization of copy number variation in autism spectrum disorder. In L. Feuk (Ed.), *Genomic structural variants: Methods and protocols, methods in molecular biology* (pp. 115–135). Totowa, NJ: Humana Press.

Masi, G., & Brovedani, P. (2011). The hippocampus, neurotrophic factors and depression: Possible implications for the pharmacotherapy of depression. *CNS Drugs, 25*, 913–931.

Matson, J. L., & Kozlowski, A. M. (2011). The increasing prevalence of autism spectrum disorders. *Research in Autism Spectrum Disorders, 5*, 418–425.

Mattila, M. L., Kielinen, M., Linna, S. L., Jussila, K., Ebeling, H., Bloigu, R., et al. (2011). Autism spectrum disorders according to DSM-IV-TR and comparison with DSM-5 draft criteria: An epidemiological study. *Journal of the American Academy of Child and Adolescent Psychiatry, 50*, 583–592, e11.

Mazumdar, S., King, M., Liu, K.Y., Zerubavel, N., & Bearman, P. (2010). The spatial structure of autism in California, 1993–2001. *Health and Place, 16,* 539–546.

Mills, K. L., Bathula, D., Dias, T. G., Iyer, S. P., Fenesy, M. C., Musser, E. D., et al. (2012). Altered cortico-striatal-thalamic connectivity in relation to spatial working memory capacity in children with ADHD. *Frontiers in Psychiatry, 3,* 1–17.

MJ. (2012 January 23). *The New York Times' DSM 5 autism coverage.* [Web log post]. Autismjabberwocky.blogspot.com. Retrieved February 3, 2012 from http://autismjabberwocky.blogspot.com/2012/01/new-york-times-dsm-5-autism-coverage.html.

Montiel-Nava, C., & Peña, J.A. (2008). Epidemiological findings of pervasive developmental disorders in aVenezuelan study. *Autism, 12,* 191–202. doi: 10.1177/1362361307086663.

Moran, M. (2012, February 3). DSM-5 may see major changes to autism, learning disorders. *Psychiatric News, 47,* 17a–32. Retrieved February 3, 2012 from http://psychnews.psychiatryonline.org/newsArticle.aspx?articleid=48120.

Nazeer, A., & Ghaziuddin, M. M. (2012). Autism spectrum disorders: Clinical features and diagnosis. *Pediatric Clinics of North America, 59,* 19–25.

Ne'eman, A., & Badesch, S. (2012, January 31). *The joint statement of the Autism Society and Autistic Self Advocacy Network on the DSM-5 and autism.* Autism-society.org. Retrieved January 31, 2012 from http://www.autism-society.org/news/in-the-news/the-joint-statement-of-the.html.

Nesse, R. M., & Stein, D. J. (2012). Towards a genuinely medical model for psychiatric nosology. *BMC Medicine, 10,* 1–5.

Nordahl, C. W., Scholz, R., Yang, X., Buonocore, M. H., Simon, T., Rogers, S., et al. (2012). Increased rate of amygdala growth in children aged 2 to 4 years with autism spectrum disorders: A longitudinal study. *Archives of General Psychiatry, 69,* 53–61.

Northoff, G., & Hayes, D. J. (2011). Is our self nothing but reward? *Biological Psychiatry, 69,* 1019–1025.

Nygren, G., Cederlund, M., Sandberg, E., Gillstedt, F., Arvidsson, T., Carina Gillberg, I., et al. (2012). The prevalence of autism spectrum disorders in toddlers: A population study of 2-year-old Swedish children. *Journal of Autism and Developmental Disorders, 42,* 1491–1497.

Oakley, K. (2012, January 31). *DSM-5 autistic spectrum disorder disaster.* [Web log post]. Autismseizureselfinjuriousbehavior.com. Retrieved February 1, 2012 from http://www.autismseizureselfinjuriousbehavior.com/.

Oldham, J. M. (2012, January 27). *Letter to David N. Elkins, Ph.D., President, Society for Humanistic Psychology. Coalition for DSM-5 Reform.* Retrieved February 9, 2012 from http://dsm5-reform.com/.

Ouellette-Kuntz, H., Coo, H., Lloyd, J. E., Kasmara, L., Holden, J. J., & Lewis, M. E. (2007). Trends in special education code assignment for autism: Implications for prevalence estimates. *Journal of Autism and Developmental Disorders, 37,* 1941–1948.

Parner, E. T., Thorsen, P., Dixon, G., de Klerk, N., Leonard, H., Nassar, N., et al. (2011). A comparison of autism prevalence trends in Denmark and Western Australia. *Journal of Autism and Developmental Disorders, 41,* 1601–1608.

Philip, R. C., Dauvermann, M. R., Whalley, H. C., Baynham, K., Lawrie, S. M., & Stanfield, A. C. (2012). A systematic review and meta-analysis of the fMRI investigation of autism spectrum disorders. *Neuroscience and Biobehavioral Reviews, 36,* 901–942.

Pina-Camacho, L., Villero, S., Fraguas, D., Boada, L., Janssen, J., Navas-Sánchez, F. J., et al. (2012). Autism spectrum disorder: Does neuroimaging support the DSM-5 proposal for a symptom dyad? A systematic review of functional magnetic resonance imaging and diffusion tensor imaging studies. *Journal of Autism and Developmental Disorders, 42,* 1326–1341.

Pinto-Martin, J. A. (2012, January 24). *It makes sense to redefine autism.* CNN.com. Retrieved January 24, 2012 from http://www.cnn.com/2012/01/24/opinion/martin-autism-definition/index.html.

Pinto-Martin, J. A., Levy, S. E., Feldman, J. F., Lorenz, J. M., Paneth, N., & Whitaker, A. H. (2011). Prevalence of autism spectrum disorder in adolescents born weighing <2000 grams. *Pediatrics*, 128, 883–891.

Regier, D. A., Kuhl, E. A., Narrow, W. E., & Kupfer, D. J. (2012). Research planning for the future of psychiatric diagnosis. *European Psychiatry*. [Epub June 13, 2011]. doi: 10.1016/j. eurpsy.2009.11.013.

Richards, T. L., & Berninger, V. W. (2008). Abnormal fMRI connectivity in children with dyslexia during a phoneme task: Before but not after treatment. *Journal of Neurolinguistics*, 21, 294–304.

Robinson, E. B., Koenen, K. C., McCormick, M. C., Munir, K., Hallett, V., Happé, F., et al. (2012). A multivariate twin study of autistic traits in 12-year-olds: Testing the fractionable autism triad hypothesis. *Behavior Genetics*, 42, 245–255.

Ronald, A., & Hoekstra, R. A. (2011). Autism spectrum disorders and autistic traits: A decade of new twin studies. *American Journal of Medical Genetics Part B*, 156, 255–274.

Rosenberg, R. E., Daniels, A. M., Law, J. K., Law, P. A., & Kaufmann, W. E. (2009). Trends in autism spectrum disorder diagnoses: 1994–2007. *Journal of Autism and Developmental Disorders*, 39, 1099–1111.

Rutter, M. (2011). Research review: Child psychiatric diagnosis and classification: Concepts, findings, challenges and potential. *Journal of Child Psychology and Psychiatry*, 52, 647–660.

Sanislow, C. A., Pine, D. S., Quinn, K. J., Kozak, M. J., Garvey, M. A., Heinssen, R. K., et al. (2010). Developing constructs for psychopathology research: Research domain criteria. *Journal of Abnormal Psychology*, 119, 631–639.

Schieve, L. A., Rice, C., Devine, O., Maenner, M. J., Lee, L. C., Fitzgerald, R., et al. (2011). Have secular changes in perinatal risk factors contributed to the recent autism prevalence increase? Development and application of a mathematical assessment model. *Annals of Epidemiology*, 21, 930–945.

Schilbach, L., Bzdok, D., Timmermans, B., Fox, P. T., Laird, A. R., Vogeley, K., et al. (2012). Introspective minds: Using ALE meta-analyses to study commonalities in the neural correlates of emotional processing, social & unconstrained cognition. *PLoS ONE*, 7, e30920.

Silver, W. G., & Rapin, I. (2012). Neurobiological basis of autism. *Pediatric Clinics of North America*, 59, 45–61.

Stefanatos, G. A., & Baron, I. S. (2011). The ontogenesis of language impairment in autism: A neuropsychological perspective. *Neuropsychological Review*, 21, 252–270.

Steinberg, P. (2012, January 31). Asperger's history of overdiagnosis. *The New York Times*. Retrieved February 2, 2012 from http://www.nytimes.com/2012/02/01/opinion/aspergers-history-of-over-diagnosis.html?_r=2.

Stigler, K. A., McDonald, B. C., Anand, A., Saykin, A. J., & McDougle, C. J. (2011). Structural and functional magnetic resonance imaging of autism spectrum disorders. *Brain Research*, 1380, 146–161.

Stigler, S. M. (2008). CSI: Mendel. [Review of the book Ending the Mendel-Fisher controversy by A. Franklin, A. Edwards, D. J. Fairbanks, D. L. Hartl & T. Seidenfeld]. *The American Scientist*, 96, 425.

Sweeney, J. A. (2011). Viewing the elephant from 200 feet: Reconstructing the schizophrenia syndrome. *Schizophrenia Research*, 127, 18–19.

Szatmari, P. (2011). New recommendations on autism spectrum disorder: Shifting the focus from subtypes to dimensions carries potential costs and benefits. *British Medical Journal*, 342, d2456.

Taylor, M. J., Donner, E. J., & Pang, E. W. (2012). fMRI and MEG in the study of typical and atypical cognitive development. *Neuropsychology Clinics*, 42, 19–25.

Uddin, L. Q., Menon, V., Young, C. B., Ryali, S., Chen, T., Khouzam, A., et al. (2011). Multivariate searchlight classification of structural magnetic resonance imaging in children and adolescents with autism. *Biological Psychiatry*, 70, 833–841.

van Bokhoven, H. (2011). Genetic and epigenetic networks in intellectual disabilities. Annual *Review of Genetics*, *45*, 81–104.

Via, E., Radua, J., Cardoner, N., Happé, F., & Mataix-Cols, D. (2011). Meta-analysis of gray matter abnormalities in autism spectrum disorder: Should Asperger disorder be subsumed under a broader umbrella of autistic spectrum disorder? *Archives of General Psychiatry*, *68*, 409–418.

Vickery, T. J., Chun, M. M., & Lee, D. (2011). Ubiquity and specificity of reinforcement signals throughout the human brain. *Neuron*, *72*, 166–177.

Vissers, M. E., Cohen, M. X., & Geurts, H. M. (2012). Brain connectivity and high functioning autism: A promising path of research that needs refined models, methodological convergence, and stronger behavioral links. *Neuroscience and Biobehavioral Reviews*, *36*, 604–625.

Volkmar, F. R., Klin, A., & Cohen, D. J. (1997). Diagnosis and classification of autism and related conditions: Consensus and issues. In D. J. Cohen & F. R. Volkmar (Eds.), *Handbook of autism and pervasive developmental disorders* (2nd ed., pp. 5–40). New York, NY: John Wiley and Sons.

Walsh, P., Elsabbagh, M., Bolton, P., & Singh, I. (2011). In search of biomarkers for autism: Scientific, social and ethical challenges. *Nature Reviews Neuroscience*, *12*, 603–612.

Wang, C. (2012, February 2). Redefinition of autism sparks concerns. *Yale Daily News*. Retrieved February 2, 2012 from http://www.yaledailynews.com/news/2012/feb/02/autism-redefinition-sparks-concerns/.

Wazana, A., Bresnahan, M., & Kline, J. (2007). The autism epidemic: Fact or artifact? *Journal of the American Academy of Child and Adolescent Psychiatry*, *46*, 721–730.

Weintraub, K. (2011). Autism counts. *Nature*, *479*, 22–24.

Weisman, K., Fournier, W., Ackerman, L., Shreffler, R., Taylor, G., Fish, A., et al. (2012, January 26). *Changes in DSM-5 autism definition could negatively impact millions*. Safeminds.org. Retrieved February 4, 2012 from http://www.safeminds.org.

Whitehouse, A. (2012, February 6). *DSM-V and the changing fortunes of autism and related disorders*. Theconversation.edu.au. Retrieved February 6, 2012 from http://theconversation.edu.au/dsm-v-and-the-changing-fortunes-of-autism-and-related-disorders-5071.

Williams, J. G., Higgins, J. P. T., & Brayne, C. E. G. (2006). Systematic review of prevalence studies of autism spectrum disorders. *Archives of the Diseases of Childhood*, *91*, 9–15.

Williams, K., MacDermott, S., Ridley, G., Glasson, E. J., & Wray, J. A. (2008). The prevalence of autism in Australia. Can it be established from existing data? *Journal of Paediatric Child Health*, *44*, 504–510.

Wong, V. C. N., & Hui, S. L. H. (2008). Epidemiological study of autism spectrum disorder in China. *Journal of Child Neurology*, *23*, 67–72.

Zaremba, A. (2011, December 12). Discovering autism: Unraveling an epidemic. *The Los Angeles Times*. Retrieved January 2, 2012 from http://www.latimes.com/news/local/autism/la-me-autism-day-one-html. 0, 1218038.htmlstory.

Zaroff, C. M., & Uhm, S. Y. (2012). Prevalence of autism spectrum disorders and influence of country of measurement and ethnicity. *Social Psychiatry and Psychiatric Epidemiology*, *47*, 395–398.

CHAPTER 8

Autism Symptoms Exist but the Disorder Remains Elusive

Contents

Rethinking Autism
http://dx.doi.org/10.1016/B978-0-12-415961-7.00008-3

> More than $1 billion has been spent over the past decade researching autism. In
> some ways, the search for its causes looks like a long-running fishing expedition,
> with a focus on everything from genetics to the age of the father, the weight of the
> mother, and how close a child lives to a freeway.
>
> **Stobbe (2012)**

The symptoms of autism exist. However, the billion dollars spent on autism research in the past decade has generated evidence for significant heterogeneity in autism. Chapters 1 to 6 documented heterogeneity in autism diagnostic behaviors, associated non-diagnostic behaviors, brain deficits, onset symptoms, and genetic and environmental risk factors. This evidence has found no shared pathogenesis, pathophysiology, or validated symptom set. The increasing evidence for heterogeneity makes autism a harder and harder problem to solve, while the increasing prevalence puts more and more pressure on autism researchers to solve the problem.

Shockingly, Frances and Widiger (2012) claimed that much of autism was a fad. Frances and Widiger (2012) stated, "fads meet a deeply felt need to explain, or at least to label, what would otherwise be unexplainable human suffering and deviance" (p. 115). From this definition, it would seem that psychiatry, with its deeply felt need to explain and label human suffering and deviance, must be a fad. The charge made against autism by Frances and Widiger (2012) is wrong. As outlined in Chapter 7, the increase in autism has been shown to stem from diagnostic criteria changes, diagnostic substitution, special education policy changes, increased availability of services, and heightened awareness of autism, and, also perhaps a true increase in incidence. Some portrayals of autism in novels, movies, or on television may be faddish, but autism symptoms are not a fad.

The majority of autism researchers currently hold one of two competing theories. One theory is that autism is a single multi-etiology heterogeneous disorder. The other theory is that autism is a spectrum of many closely related disorders. However, these two views shade together when researchers define autism. For example, Sato et al. (2012) stated, "Autism is the prototypic form of a group of conditions, also known as 'autism spectrum disorders'" (p. 1). Walsh et al. (2011) opened their paper by stating, "Autism spectrum disorder is the term used for a diverse group of developmental conditions that affect a person's ability to relate to and communicate with others" (p. 603). Three pages later Walsh et al. (2012) argued that researchers needed to develop "understanding of autism as a complex condition that is probably determined by multiple, yet to be understood pathways that lead to heterogeneous outcomes" (p. 606). Even reports of a unitary feature for autism open with a tip of the hat to the theory of many autisms. For example, Wolff et al. (2012) began their paper, "Autism spectrum disorders (ASDs) are *complex disorders of neurodevelopment* defined by impaired social communication and restricted, repetitive behaviors" (p. 1). The researchers, however, concluded, "aberrant development of white matter pathways may … [cause] this neurodevelopmental *disorder*" (p. 1). Elsabbagh et al. (2012) expressed both theories in the first five words of their first sentence: "*Autism spectrum disorders (henceforth autism)* are diagnosed in around 1% of the population" (p. 1).

Unfortunately, a clear understanding of the nature of autism has not been generated by the billion dollars in research funding. Worse still is the cost in missing translational findings for treatment and prevention. If autism is many distinct disorders with many varied causes, there is no translational value in searching for one unifying brain dysfunction for autism. Conversely, if autism is a single complex disorder, there will be no ultimate translational results from efforts to distinguish subgroups. Walsh et al. (2011) stated, "despite huge advances in the basic scientific understanding of autism, comparatively little has been achieved to date with regard to translating the resulting evidence into clinically useful biomarkers" (pp. 609–610). Unfortunately, most of the "huge advances in the basic scientific understanding" of autism are findings for massive heterogeneity in genetic variants, chromosomal number variants, and environmental risk factors, and these "huge advances" have not solved the core question of what entity "clinically useful biomarkers" would be identifying.

This chapter has five sections. The first section argues that the higher prevalence of males than females diagnosed with autism is likely to be a composite ratio, based on the male to female ratios for many different environmental and genetic risk factors. The second section demonstrates that, despite accumulated evidence to the contrary, most autism research has continued to search for unifying features and single predictors for autism. The third section summarizes three critical inferential problems that would be eliminated by abandoning the effort to unify autism as a disorder. The fourth section presents the argument for autism as symptoms. The fifth and concluding section proposes a way of seeing and documenting autism symptoms without defining autism as a disorder.

THE AUTISM MALE TO FEMALE RATIO IS LIKELY TO BE A COMPOSITE

No accepted model has explained the reason for the greater number of males than females diagnosed with autism. Recent estimates of the autism male to female ratio have remained at between 2.5 and 4 males diagnosed for every female diagnosed. However, Zwaigenbaum et al. (2012) studied 319 young siblings of children with autism and reported a significantly lower gender difference ratio of only 1.65 male siblings diagnosed with autism for every female sibling diagnosed. The researchers diagnosed autism in 57 boys among the 176 at-risk male siblings, and diagnosed autism in 28 girls of the 143 at-risk female siblings. Most surprising was that boy/girl ratios for cognition and symptoms in the autism sibling group did not differ from the boy/girl ratios for the same measures in a comparison group of typical children.

Sato et al. (2012) proposed there were three theories explaining the higher number of males than females diagnosed with autism: the extreme male brain, X chromosome gene variants, and a prenatal protective factor functioning in females.

The Extreme Male Brain Theory of the Autism Male/Female Ratio

Baron-Cohen et al. (2011) theorized that autism symptoms were caused by dysregulated fetal testosterone that resulted in autism symptoms being an exaggeration of typical male traits. This theory of autism argued that females are more empathetic than males, males are more analytic than females, and males have a greater drive to construct rule systems than females. Autism, in this view, is an extreme version of typical male systematizing. Challenges to this view include findings like those of Bejerot et al. (2012), who reported that women with autism displayed fewer feminine character-istics than did women without autism, and men with autism displayed fewer masculine characteristics than did men without autism. Bejerot et al. (2012) further noted that autism behaviors and traits correlated with effeminate body features in men with autism, and with less feminine facial features in women. Conversely, James (2012) concluded that the reports of more male siblings born to mothers of boys diagnosed with autism and mothers of boys with developmental language disorders supported the extreme male brain theory because they suggested that the maternal production of high androgen levels was persistent. James (2012) noted that there were two controlling factors for typical sex ratios at birth—hormone regulation at conception, and sex-specific effects of stressors during pregnancy—and dysfunction in either factor might contribute to developmental disorders.

The X Chromosome Theory of the Autism Male/Female Ratio

Noor et al. (2010) proposed that the male to female ratio in autism was due to effects of genes of the sex chromosomes. Zwaigenbaum et al. (2012) reported that more gene variants on the X chromosome have been discovered in association with autism symptoms, each of which might confer a higher number of males with autism: neuroligins 3 and 4; *PTCHD1*; *TMLHE*; *MECP2*; some cases of fragile X syndrome; and, possibly, epigenetic effects from paternally imprinted X-linked genes. Baron-Cohen et al. (2011), however, argued that X-linked mutations are insufficiently prevalent in autism to account for the autism sex ratio.

The Female Protective Factor Theory of the Autism Male/Female Ratio

Szatmari et al. (2012) proposed that females possessed some trait that protected brain development, such that more genetic risk factors were needed to trigger the expression of autism symptoms in females. Sato et al. (2012) reported a rare autosomal *SHANK1* deletion only in males with autism. Mutations in *SHANK2* and *SHANK3* have been found in association with autism symptoms; however, Sato et al. (2012) found autism symptoms only in the males in a family carrying *SHANK1* deletions, and noted that their finding was the first report of an autosomal sex-limited risk factor for autism. Because the researchers also found a male with autism who carried a de novo deletion of *SHANK1*, they concluded that the *SHANK1* deletion in the family studied was the primary cause of autism in affected male family members. Sato et al. (2012) reasoned that carrier females in this family did not express autism symptoms because they had some neural feature that protected them from the effects of the *SHANK1* deletion.

Many Risk Factors are Likely to Contribute Many Different Sex Ratios to Autism

Given multiple risk factors, it is likely that the male to female sex ratio in autism is a composite of hundreds of separate male to female sex ratios, each of which is determined by a specific causal risk etiology and the ensuing mediation of brain development.

As outlined in Chapters 4 and 5, many varied genetic, chromosomal, epigenetic, and environmental risk factors have been linked to autism symptoms. Autism symptoms may also result from prenatal interaction of maternal and child genes and the gestational environment, and may result from the effects of fetal immune system genes in the environment of the developing fetal brain. If the autism male/female ratio is a composite of many varied ratios, then gene variants on the X chromosome, epigenetic effects from paternally imprinted X-linked genes, the rare autosomal *SHANK1* deletion found only in males with autism, and intrauterine testosterone might all contribute to the ratio of more males than females in autism.

Genetic and environmental risk factors have tied autism symptoms to schizophrenia, anxiety, attention deficit/hyperactivity disorder, Tourette syndrome, intellectual disability, and language development disorders. Copeland, Shanahan, Costello, and Angold (2011) conducted a prospective population study of psychiatric disorder prevalence in 1400 children aged 9–16 years. They found a 1.6 to 1 ratio of males to females for any psychiatric diagnosis. The neurocognitive disorders whose symptoms have been linked to autism through shared risk factors have demonstrated a higher prevalence of diagnosed males than females. Attention deficit/hyperactivity disorder has a 10 to 1 male to female ratio, language development disorders have a variable ratio of 2 to 4 males for 1 female, Tourette syndrome has a 6 to 1 male to female ratio, and intellectual disability has an approximately 1.8 to 1 ratio of males to females. Therefore, when autism shares risk factors with these disorders, it is likely those risk factors may contribute to the male/female diagnosis ratio found for autism.

Notably, the twin study of Hallmayer et al. (2011) suggested that environmental factors might account for more than half the variance in autism, and the researchers argued that disruptive events in the prenatal environment were likely to be an important cause for autism. Although replication of the Hallmayer et al. (2011) twin study is needed, findings for environmental risk factors outlined in Chapter 5 suggest that sex ratios for these environmental risk factors would be likely to contribute to the composite male/female ratio for autism.

Initial Structural and Hormonal Differences Between Male and Female Brains

Hines (2011) summarized initial differences between male and female human brains. In general, the brain is larger in males. The amygdala is also larger in males, but the hippocampus is larger in females. Female brains have greater cortical thickness in many regions than do male brains. Human female brains show greater gyrification in parts of frontal and parietal cortex, and female brains appear to use white matter with greater efficiency than do male brains. It may be that differential features such as cortical thickness and greater white matter efficiency confer protection for the female brain.

Differences in gonadal hormones and the social neuropeptides arginine vasopressin and oxytocin between males and females may contribute to the higher male to female ratio in autism. Gonadal hormones differentiate males and females. Insel (2010) and Gordon et al. (2011) proposed models of social motivation and social behaviors that began from gonadal hormones and the social neuropeptides, arginine vasopressin and oxytocin. Insel (2010) noted that the process of mammalian pair bonding differentially involves arginine vasopressin (AVP) in males, and oxytocin (OT) in females. Ebstein, Knafo, Mankuta, Chew, and Lai (2012) argued that the OT–AVP neural pathways regulate social behavior under the influence of six crucial genes: *AVP-neurophysin II*, *OXT neurophysin I*, and their receptors, *AVPR1a*, *AVPR1b*, *LNPEP*, and *CD38*. Ebstein et al. (2012) reviewed evidence for abnormalities in AVP and OT in autism, and presented evidence for the association of autism with variants of these genes. Ebstein et al. (2012) argued, "these genes not only account for individual differences in behavior in socially intact individuals but also contribute the vulnerability to disorders of social cognition especially autism" (p. 374).

Initial sex differences in brain structure and circulating hormones, when disrupted may contribute to autism symptoms. Initial sex differences in brain structure and circulating hormones may also leave male brains more vulnerable to a range of disruptive processes, and may confer protection from disruptive processes for female brains.

Male Brain Vulnerability During the Prenatal Period

As noted above, Hallmayer et al. (2011) proposed that environmental factors causing autism were likely to have their effect during the prenatal period, and Chapter 5 reviewed evidence for prenatal risk factors for autism symptoms. The high male to female sex ratio found for autism may, in part, reflect that male brains, in general, are more vulnerable to insult during prenatal life (Howerton & Bale, 2012; James, 2012; Kent, Wright, Abdel-Latif, & New South Wales and Australian Capital Territory Neonatal Intensive Care Units Audit Group, 2012; Murphy et al., 2012; Peacock, Marston, Marlow, Calvert, & Greenough, 2012).

For example, Murphy et al. (2012) reported that maternal cigarette smoking significantly affected the epigenetic process of DNA methylation only in male newborns. The researchers reported that only male infants born to current smokers showed significantly elevated methylation relative to those born to mothers who quit smoking during pregnancy, and those born to mothers who never smoked. In addition, Peacock et al. (2012) reported that among 787 very preterm infants, a significantly higher percentage of the 428 male infants died, required oxygen, had a pulmonary hemorrhage, or had a major cranial ultrasound abnormality than did very preterm female infants in the their sample. These findings were significant even after adjusting for differences in male and female birth weights and gestation duration. In addition, a follow-up of these children found significantly more motor disability and cognitive delay among boys than girls.

Initial Male–Female Brain Function Differences may be Increased During Brain Development

Given the initial differences in male and female brain structure, gonadal hormones, and social neuropeptides, and given the risk factor disruptions mediating autism symptoms, it is possible that interaction of the initial brain differences with the disruption may confer some additional harm for male brains or stimulate protection for female brains during the processes involved in brain development. These processes include programmed brain alterations, very early learning, and even developmental brain changes occurring during sleep (Karmiloff-Smith, 2012; Reeb-Sutherland, Levitt, & Fox, 2012). Wolff et al. (2012) stated, "Both highly experience-dependent and less environmentally mediated processes contribute to the functional and structural organization of the brain, and the dynamic interplay of these processes over time yields specialized cortical circuits designed to optimally process complex information" (p. 8). Brain development produces alterations in many varied aspects of the brain. For example, the anterior insula and the anterior cingulate cortex together contribute to social responsiveness in behavior. Uddin, Supekar, Ryali, and Menon (2011) reported significant developmental changes in brain interconnectedness for right fronto-insular cortex, tissue that contributes to switching attention between outside the self and inside the self. Consequently, the anterior insula, a contributor to social responsiveness, if disrupted earlier in development may suffer additional disruption during this programmed change as the brain develops (Uddin et al., 2011). Sex differences in the disrupted brain in autism may differentially influence programmed developmental processes such as this.

Reeb–Sutherland et al. (2012) reported that individual differences in associative learning measured at 1 month of age were associated with later measures of social behavior. The researchers found a significant link between 1-month associative learning and brain activity pattern in response to familiar and unfamiliar faces. Reeb–Sutherland et al. (2012) proposed that their findings were not the result of individual differences in general cognition, and argued that infant "associative learning may serve as a major building block for the development of social behavior" (p. 2). Karmiloff–Smith (2012) noted that impaired sleep processes characterized most neurodevelopmental disorders. She pointed out that the brain changes during sleep, consolidating and reorganizing information. Because consolidation of information during sleep depends on gene expression, brain biochemistry, and psychological processes in response to environmental stimuli, abnormal sleep processes may contribute to aberration in brain function.

Sex differences in brain structure, function, gonadal hormones, and social neuropeptides, as well as other initial sex differences, may contribute to sex differences in programmed developmental changes in the brain, in associative learning, or in sleep processes subsequent to the initial effects of brain disruptions for autism.

Summary: The Male to Female Diagnosis Ratio in Autism is Likely to be a Composite Ratio

There is evidence that male brains are more vulnerable to insults and disruptions. Male and female differences in brain structure, function, gonadal hormones, and social neuropeptides, as well as other initial sex differences, may variably contribute to male prenatal brain vulnerability to insult and disruption, and may variably confer some protection against prenatal insult or disruption for female brains.

The existing evidence for multiple varied risk factors for autism makes it likely that the male to female ratio in autism is not generated by any single cause, but rather reflects the collocation of hundreds of separate male to female prevalence ratios. It is likely that different causal risk factors for autism generate distinct male to female ratios each of which is determined by a specific causal risk etiology and consequent mediation of brain development.

MUCH RESEARCH IS STILL FOCUSED ON TRYING TO UNIFY AUTISM AS A SINGLE DISORDER

Even though many researchers would define autism as a spectrum of related disorders, most researchers have continued the quest to find unifying features for autism as if autism were a single disorder. Why this research continues is unclear. Tatsioni et al. (2007) concluded that "it can be difficult to discern whether perpetuated beliefs are based on careful consideration of all evidence and differential interpretation, inappropriate entrenchment of old information, [or] lack of dissemination of newer data" (p. 2525).

The Quest to Find a Unifying Feature for Autism Persists

There are hundreds of alternate unifying feature claims for autism. Claims for unifying features in autism have often not been replicated, or have been found to be true only of a small subset of individuals with autism. Moreover, unifying feature claims for autism have often sidestepped evidence that the unifying feature was not specific to autism.

Even in genetic research, where multiple genetic variants have been explored as causes for the autism spectrum, many researchers have worked to create unified accounts of the genetic etiology for autism. Unifying models of related gene variants and/or chromosomal number variants for autism have rarely been replicated, and there has been a rapid replacement of one genetic model with another subsequent to the discovery of new data (Abrahams & Geschwind, 2010; Bill & Geschwind, 2009; Girirajan et al., 2010; Holt & Monaco, 2011; Voineagu et al., 2011; Zhao et al., 2007).

Following are brief discussions of four selected unifying feature claims. One reports that autism includes a superior mental process of touch-to-vision memory (Nakano, Kato, & Kitazawa, 2012). A second reports that autism includes a superior visual speed discrimination skill (Chen et al., 2012). A third asserts that atypical response to eye gaze in infants predicts later autism diagnosis (Elsabbagh et al., 2012). A fourth asserts that an early atypical pattern of the brain's white matter development predicts later autism diagnosis (Wolff et al., 2012). Following the discussions of these four unifying feature claims are brief discussions of two multi-gene models.

Two Empirical Unifying Earliest Feature Claims for Autism
Event-Related Potential Pattern to Eye Gaze Before 12 Months Predicts Autism

Elsabbagh et al. (2012) reported that 40 infants at risk for autism, when compared with 45 healthy controls, showed less P400 brain activity at 6–10 months while viewing faces with eye gaze directed toward versus away from the infant. Thus, a particular brain activity pattern known to be specifically responsive to human faces (P400) was found to be atypically relatively less active in individuals at risk for autism in infancy. The researchers proposed that their findings were consonant with evidence that brain function measures can distinguish infants at risk for autism from typical children, and consonant with evidence for various other early predictors of risk, including a visual processing marker, an attention-switching marker, a face response marker, and a marker based on sensitivity to eye direction gaze. Elsabbagh et al. (2012) argued that atypical brain function related to eye gaze reaction precedes the onset of autism behavior.

Limitations for the Claim that Event-Related Potential Pattern to Eye Gaze Before 12 Months Predicts Autism

The researchers found that neither static gaze nor face-versus-noise contrasts reliably distinguished the ASD group from the two other groups. Thus, there was only a single significant data point (P400 on dynamic gaze shift), demonstrating lower responsivity, differentiating children at risk who later were diagnosed with autism. Moreover, Elsabbagh et al. (2012) did not discuss the implications of delayed cognitive development found for children at risk for autism.

Infant White Matter Development Pattern Predicts Autism

Wolff et al. (2012) reported that imaging of white matter tracts revealed that development of a majority of tracts differed significantly between 17 infants at risk and later diagnosed with autism, and 33 at-risk infants not diagnosed with autism. The 17 infants who later were diagnosed with autism showed evidence of larger white matter tracts at 6 months. However, these 17 infants then were found to have slower development of white matter tracts compared with infants not diagnosed with autism, and at 2 years the brains of the 17 diagnosed children showed evidence for less white matter in fiber tracts compared with children without autism. Wolff et al. (2012) concluded, "Most fiber tracts for the ASD-positive infants were characterized by higher fractional anisotropy at 6 months followed by blunted developmental trajectories such that fractional anisotropy was lower by 24 months" (p. 6).

Limitations for the Claim that Infant White Matter Development Pattern Predicts Autism

The 17 children who were later diagnosed with autism differed not only in diagnostic features. The children later diagnosed with autism had significantly lower scores on a measure of cognitive development at age 6 months, 12 months, and 24 months. Atypical white matter development is likely to be the cause of both developmental delay and abnormal social behavior. However, the Wolff et al. (2012) research report did not discuss developmental delay. Also possible is that the pattern of white matter development in the 17 was a collection of different patterns of white matter development. The report offered no analysis or discussion of individual variation within the group of 17 children diagnosed with autism.

Wolff et al. (2012) cited the study of Barnea-Goraly, Lotspeich, and Reiss (2010) with the comment, "Studies of ASDs using diffusion tensor imaging have identified evidence of widespread abnormalities in white matter fiber tract integrity" (p. 2). However, Barnea-Goraly et al. (2010) reported that the brains of children with autism and their unaffected siblings both had reduced prefrontal white matter, and reduced white matter in the corpus callosum, cingulate gyrus, thalamus, left and right superior temporal gyrus approaching the hippocampus and the amygdala, and left and right temporoparietal junctions. Barnea-Goraly et al. (2010) found white matter structure in the children with autism and their unaffected siblings differed significantly from that of typical children, and they concluded that atypical white matter was likely to be a family trait "not directly related to the actual psychopathology" of autism (Barnea-Goraly et al., 2010, p. 1058). Wolff et al. (2012) included no discussion of these relevant Barnea-Goraly et al. (2010) data and conclusions in the interpretation of their own white matter findings.

Two Empirical Unifying Superior Skills in Autism
Superior Perceptual Integration in Autism
Nakano et al. (2012) reported that 14 adults with autism demonstrated superior performance on a test of touch-to-vision delayed matching of shape compared with 20 healthy controls. The study participants touched a shape without seeing it, and then had to identify it visually after a delay. The researchers argued that success on this task required integration of sensorimotor percepts of the felt shape into an object representation that could be mentally visualized. Nakano et al. (2012) argued that the integration of sensorimotor percepts of a shape that was later correctly identified visually contradicted the weak central coherence theory of autism. Happé and Frith (2006) had proposed the weak central coherence theory of autism, which claimed that cognitive processing in autism relied on abnormally superior processing of sensory details in the absence of ability to integrate sensory information. Nakano et al. (2012) noted that the superiority of adults with autism on the touch-to-vision task did not reflect a superiority of local or detail-focused processing because the adults with autism were no better than typical adults in their ability to discern object orientation or length. Nakano et al. (2012) proposed that future studies were necessary to explore whether superior haptic-to-visual shape perception skill was linked to savant skills found "in 10–30% of persons with ASD" (p. 7).

Superior Discrimination of Visual Movement Speed in Autism

Chen et al. (2012) reported that 19 adolescents with autism had better speed visual discrimination performance scores than 17 healthy controls when visual comparisons were made after a delay. In the study, all adolescents had to determine which of two displays of 200 random dots on a computer screen was moving faster. The regular interval between dot displays to be compared was a half second, and the prolonged comparison delay was six times as long, 3 seconds. The researchers argued that superior discrimination for the individuals with autism could not be the result of enhanced working memory because previous studies had reported impaired working memory in autism.

Chen et al. (2012) theorized that superior visual discrimination skill in autism was a function of an atypically longer process of visual encoding in autism. The researchers proposed that the visual system in autism had shifted visual speed processing to a slow speed range, such that brain activity in the visual system had longer latencies with smaller receptive fields. Chen et al. (2012) argued that the 3 second delay allowed for extended coding that "would afford additional processing of speed signals and allow for a perceptual advantage in this visual motion domain" (p. 737).

Limitations for the Findings of Nakano et al. (2012) and Chen et al. (2012)

Shared limitations of the studies of Nakano et al. (2012) and Chen et al. (2012) are small sample size and isolation of the specific finding. Sample sizes of 14 and 19 individuals cannot provide compelling evidence. Second, both findings exist in isolation from other findings in the field, and represent one data point of superiority within testing that otherwise found no differences between the sample with autism and the control sample. As noted in Chapter 2, Ioannidis (2005) stated, "There is increasing concern that in modern research, false findings may be the majority or even the vast majority of published research claims …. However, this should not be surprising. It can be proven that most claimed research findings are false" (p. 696). Ioannidis argued that small samples, selective measures, a bias for significance, and highly creative measures operating in a "hot" field all contribute to invalid significance measures. All the factors identified by Ioannidis apply to these two studies.

Two Empirical Multiple Gene Models of Autism

The Multiple Hit Model of Autism

LeBlond et al. (2012) studied 260 individuals with autism and found a deletion within the *SHANK2* gene in one individual with autism and moderate intellectual disability. Because the affected individual's parents did not carry this deletion, the deletion was a de novo event, new in the affected individual. LeBlond et al. (2012) reported, "In patients, the only feature associated with carriers of *SHANK2* mutations compared with other patients was a trend for low IQ" (p. 11). The researchers also noted that 5% of the Finnish population was heterozygous for a *SHANK2* variant without negative effects, and that "deleterious *SHANK2* variants were detected in a heterozygous state in parents and in the general population without causing severe phenotypic consequences" (LeBlond et al., 2012, p. 11). The researchers concluded that the co-occurrence of de novo mutations, together with inherited variations, might be the genetic source of autism. In a larger sample, the researchers identified three patients with de novo *SHANK2* deletions who also carried inherited CNVs at 15q11–q13, a region associated with neuropsychiatric disorders. The researchers concluded that these three cases supported the theory of autism as resulting from multiple genetic mutations.

Limitations for the Multiple Hit Genetic Causal Model for Autism
It is likely that cases of autism do result from "the co-occurrence of de novo mutations, together with inherited variations" (LeBlond et al., 2012, p. 12). However, the multiple hit theory cannot apply to all cases of autism. The evidence for various forms of syndromic autism, discussed in Chapter 4, has demonstrated that autism symptoms can appear as the result of single gene effects. In addition, there is evidence suggesting different forms of "myriad hits" wherein many gene variants contribute to autism symptoms.

Tumor Necrosis Factor and Beta-Estradiol Regulators as Priorities for Genetic Research in Autism
Lee, Raygada, and Rennert (2012) proposed that autism was linked to gene clusters related to *PTEN/TSC1/FMR1* and *mTOR/PI3K* gene regulation. Lee et al. (2012) created a theoretical network of possible genes by examining 35 genes that had been linked to impaired social interaction, 8 genes linked to repetitive behavior, 74 genes linked to obsessive behavior, 146 genes linked to impaired communication, and 98 genes tied to intellectual disability. The researchers analyzed relationships between the aggregated genes and found complex regulatory networks. Two key factors in the regulatory network they constructed were tumor necrosis factor (TNF) and beta-estradiol.

The researchers proposed that TNF would be expected to operate in a systemic molecular network in autism because TNF decreases serotonin transporter function. However, Lee et al. (2012) were surprised to find beta-estradiol-related effects in the constructed network. They noted that beta-estradiol was involved in neuroprotective and neurotropic functions mediated by estrogen receptor signaling cascades.

The researchers tried to replicate the constructed networks using evidence of actual genes found in association with autism. However, the researchers stated that, because so few genes had been identified for autism in genome-wide association studies, they could not construct a network based on genes actually found in autism. In a third analysis, the researchers reported finding a cluster for increased expression of the *PTEN*, *TSC1*, and *FMR1* genes, and a cluster including genes with deletions and reduced expression linked to the mTOR/PI3K signaling pathways. The researchers concluded that a large number of non-overlapping gene networks might be the basis for autism heterogeneity.

Limitations of the Network Model

Although the researchers stated that the goal of their study was to "prioritize molecular interactions" (Lee et al., 2012, p. 9), it was not clear from the report of their study how genetic research priorities had been advanced by their efforts, nor did they propose specifically how their constructed network information might be used in future research.

Summary: All Six Studies Sought to Find a Unifying Feature or Pattern in Autism

This brief review reported four claims for behavioral unity in autism: infant diminished P400 wave to dynamic gaze shift predicting autism (Elsabbagh et al., 2012); abnormal trajectory of infant white matter development pattern predicting autism (Wolff et al., 2012); adult superior touch-to-vision delayed matching (Nakano et al., 2012); and adult superior dot movement delayed discrimination (Chen et al., 2012). Elsabbagh et al. (2012) found one pattern of brain activity, and Wolff et al. (2012) found one pattern of brain development. Each finding was proposed as a predictive early signal of autism. However, because neither research team conducted an exploratory data analysis to look for individual variation, possible evidence for variation in these proposed early predictors was not explored. Although all disorders under the autism umbrella would benefit from early intervention, autism variation might be crucially important for intervention strategies, and the patterns of individual variation cannot be adequately explored in small samples.

This section also sketched a report supporting the multiple-gene-hit model (LeBlond et al., 2012), and a gene network model (Lee et al., 2012). The translational value for these models is, as yet, unclear.

ABANDONING AUTISM AS A SINGLE DISORDER WOULD ELIMINATE THREE INFERENTIAL PROBLEMS IN AUTISM RESEARCH

Diagnostic Criteria that have Never been Validated would no Longer be Needed

As noted in Chapter 7, Hyman had worried that, as director of NIMH, he had funded hundreds of studies predicated on DSM criteria "that almost never questioned the existing diagnostic categories despite their lack of validation" (2010, p. 157).

Links Between Autism Diagnostic Symptoms have not been Validated or Explained

As noted in earlier chapters, Happé et al. (2006) provided evidence from twin studies of typical individuals that the three DSM-IV autism diagnostic symptoms of social impairment, communication difficulties, and rigid and repetitive behaviors were genetically unrelated, and resulted from three separate sets of non-overlapping genes. They concluded that the symptoms were independent of one another. Happé et al. (2006) stated, "Clearly a question remains of why these three features co-occur at above-chance rates" (p. 1219) in autism.

Similarly, Robinson et al. (2012) tested 5944 typical twin pairs and found almost no genetic causal overlap for the proposed DSM-5 two symptom groups: social impairment, and restricted and repetitive behaviors and interests or sensory abnormalities. The researchers noted that identical and fraternal twins had non-significant cross-twin correlations ranging from .02 to .19 between the two DSM-5 autism symptoms.

Boucher (2011) noted that autism symptoms were not correlated, and expressed concern that there was no explanation for how the varied etiologies, brain deficits, and diagnostic symptoms did manage to converge on a single autism brain abnormality. She hypothesized that heterogeneous brain deficits, heterogeneous etiologies and diagnostic symptom behaviors must "fan in" to converge onto a single brain abnormality. Boucher (2011) proposed that the autism diagnosis be redefined as a spectrum of many separate symptoms and physical disorders that happened to occur together in autism more than would be expected by chance. Similarly, Lord and Jones (2012) defined autism as an "as-yet-not-understood combination of social-communication deficits and repetitive/restricted behaviors and interests that interact together to form a pattern that appears to be more than the sum of its parts" (p. 504). As Boucher (2011) noted, research has not discovered how the symptoms "interact together to form a pattern that appears to be more than the sum of its parts."

Autism Diagnostic Symptom Set has not been Validated

Kanner (1943) defined infantile autism as a single disorder with two key symptoms: the profound failure to understand social interaction, with an insistence on sameness. Kanner has rightfully been honored for his identification of severe social impairment in children. However, neither neuroscience nor genetics research has validated Kanner's autism. Researchers have not found any brain circuit or region that when disrupted will cause his two symptoms, insistence on sameness and the inability to understand social interaction, and only these two symptoms (Campbell et al., 2011; Ebisch et al., 2010; Leekam et al., 2011; Lewis & Kim, 2009; Lombardo et al., 2011; Schulte-Rüther et al., 2011). Similarly, researchers have not found a genetic or environmental cause that generates all and only all the three DSM symptoms of social interaction failure, communication impairment, and restricted and repetitive behaviors or activities (Addington & Rapoport, 2012; Geschwind, 2011; State & Levitt, 2011; Yrigollen et al., 2008).

Moreover, no animal models have been found that produce animal homologues of the three DSM symptoms. For example, Peñagarikano et al. (2011) reported that mice lacking the *Cntnap2* gene associated with autism exhibited abnormal vocal communication, repetitive and restricted behaviors, and abnormal social interactions. However, Peñagarikano et al. (2011) reported that the mice were also hyperactive and suffered epileptic seizures. Malkova, Yu, Hsiao, Moore, and Patterson (2012) created a mouse model of environmental risk of autism by stimulating the immune system of female mice. Male offspring of the immune-activated mothers had truncated vocalization, decreased sociability, and high levels of repetitive behaviors. However, Malkova et al. (2012) noted that offspring of immune-activated mouse mothers "also display features of schizophrenia. These include enlarged ventricles, enhanced responses to amphetamine and hallucinogens, alterations in dopamine and serotonergic pathways, as well as … enhanced anxiety and eye blink conditioning" (p. 8).

Abandoning the quest for autism as a single disorder would eliminate the need to validate autism diagnostic criteria that have never been validated.

Viewing Behavioral Symptom Heterogeneity as Comorbidity would be Unnecessary

Coghill and Sonuga-Barke (2012) argued that heterogeneity and comorbidity made classification of diagnostic groups difficult. The researchers pointed out that comorbidity is common in childhood mental disorders. When comorbidity is reduced by eliminating some diagnostic categories, then the remaining diagnostic categories necessarily will have increased heterogeneity. In the case of autism, as argued in Chapters 4 and 7, comorbidity has often been the assignment of selected symptoms of one general brain disruption to separate disorders. Pushing out selected symptoms of complex autism phenotypes into other disorders has been an error similar to Mendel's setting aside and discarding pea phenotypes that seemed errantly and extraneously heterogeneous thus interfering with the orderly clarity of Mendel's inheritance model.

In fact, the extensive variation in symptoms found for individuals with autism is rarely the result of the comorbidity of a truly independent additional disorder (Addington & Rapoport, 2012; Fernandez et al., 2012; Rommelse et al., 2011; Tabet et al., 2012). Despite claims of errant clinical practice (Lord, 2011), problems in diagnosis often reflect the difficulty in assigning simplified labels to complex phenotypes. Diagnostic social impairment and diagnostic motor and sensory behaviors occur with intellectual disability or developmental delay, epilepsy, motor delay, language impairment, attention deficit/hyperactivity disorder, and other symptoms because the brain is complex, brain development is complex, and brain disruptions are so varied.

Equally important, the exclusion of non-diagnostic associated symptoms from autism phenotypes leads to problematic inferences. For example, Guinchat et al. (2012a) reported that parents' early concerns about their children at risk for autism did not include autism symptoms:

> We found that the earliest warning signs were frequently not specific to autism …. Motor peculiarities, sensory reactivity, atypical regulation of emotions, a lack of attention, an abnormal level of activity, or sleeping problems were some of the common features … and it is noteworthy that most of the concerns related to a diagnosis of autism were clearly not the earliest concerns evoked by parents.
>
> **Guinchat et al. (2012a, p. 598)**

Although Guinchat et al. (2012a) declared that motor peculiarities, sensory reactivity, atypical regulation of emotions, a lack of attention, an abnormal level of activity, or sleeping problems were features not specific to autism or a diagnosis of autism, these features have all been found in complete autism phenotypes. If Guinchat et al. (2012a) were to view the children's phenotypes as including all expressed symptoms, the researchers would then find that parents had been reporting symptoms relevant to their children's neurodevelopmental disorder.

As discussed in Chapter 7, Close et al. (2012) provided another example of an inferential problem that occurs when symptoms are assigned to a disorder thought to be comorbid with autism. The researchers compared symptoms of children who "lost" the diagnosis of autism with symptoms of children who did not lose the diagnosis of autism. The researchers looked at data from 1366 children where 453 of the children's parents reported a past but not current diagnosis of autism spectrum disorder. The remaining parents reported a current diagnosis of ASD for their child. Close et al. (2012) found that children aged 2–5 years with a current diagnosis of autism were 9.20 times more likely to have developmental delay and 4.76 times more likely to have two current comorbid conditions than children who had a former diagnosis of ASD. Children aged 6–11 years with a current diagnosis of autism had a 3.85 times greater odds of having a past speech problem, 3.51 greater odds of having current anxiety, and were 3.19 times more likely to have two current comorbid conditions.

Do the symptoms Close et al. (2012) described as comorbid "belong to" the autism phenotype or do they belong to another comorbid disorder? A British newspaper, *The Daily Mail*, reported the Close et al. (2012) study findings in an article headlined "Can some children simply grow out of autism?" (Naish, 2012). England's National Health Service (NHS) responded to the *Daily Mail* article by arguing that children do not grow out of autism (NHS Choice, 2012). The NHS asserted that "diagnosing ASD is challenging, especially since the condition is often accompanied by other neurodevelopmental disorders with overlapping symptoms" (NHS Choice, 2012).

The NHS claim effectively proposed that a symptom such as speech delay would be an "overlapping symptom" in a child with autism and a comorbid language disorder, because speech delay could result from the child's autism or result from the child's comorbid language disorder. However, the brain disruption causing the speech delay does not recognize or respect diagnostic assignment. More importantly, risk factors for autism symptoms may cause social impairment, behavioral rigidity, sensory abnormalities, and attention deficit/hyperactivity disorder, developmental delay, language development problems, and motor problems in the same individual. Therefore, when speech delay and social impairment both occur in one child, it is unlikely that the speech delay is an overlapping symptom of a separate comorbid language disorder.

Although Close et al. (2012) argued that future autism research should "focus on the factors that discriminate the co-occurring conditions whose symptoms overlap with ASD" (p. e315), this discrimination would be likely to be scientifically counterproductive. Autism genetic and environmental risk factors produce non-diagnostic and diagnostic symptoms in an individual because risk factors cause brain-wide disruptions (Gilman et al., 2011; Wei et al., 2011). Therefore, co-occurring symptoms are most likely to be component impairments of the complete autism phenotype and are unlikely to be evidence of separate comorbid disorders.

Abandoning the diagnosis of autism as a disorder would free researchers to recognize and study the complete phenotype of children expressing neurodevelopmental social impairment.

The Problem of the Failure to Reconcile Data and Synthesize Theories in Order to Establish the Features of Autism would Disappear

Autism research has spent little effort to reconcile competing theories and conflicting findings (Waterhouse, 2008, 2009). Theories of autism as a single disorder are replaced repeatedly without efforts to reconcile findings or synthesize theories. Because no unifying brain dysfunction has been established, many of us conducting autism research have generated a series of varied theories of autism brain dysfunction.

As outlined in Chapter 1, the Duhem–Quine principle proposed that no scientific theory will fully account for all the existing variation in available evidence. Consequently, scientific understanding moves forward from one not-fully-explanatory theory to the next not-fully-explanatory theory. However, there are limits to the scientific acceptability of not-fully-explanatory theories. The extreme heterogeneity of autism has meant that far too little of the variation in autism has been explained by theories claiming autism is a single disorder.

Meehl (1990) argued that when theories explain too little variation, they are so weak that they can easily be replaced in a process that Meehl called "ad hockery." The weak support for an existing theory allows for the creation of a new ad hoc theory whenever new empirical evidence is discovered. Viewed from a Meehl (1990) perspective, the repeated replacement of one theory of autism after another has been "ad hockery." Rejected ad hoc theories eventually require synthesis, not replacement. Although normal science does involve a "point–counterpoint" competition between data claims, reconciliation of contradictory findings and competing theories is necessary to drive productive research.

Meehl (1990) argued that eventually, "As more and more 'ad hockery' piles up" (p. 112), researchers begin to doubt that they have correctly conceptualized the problem. Researchers begin to conclude, as Szatmari (2011) did, that the research field should start over in conceptualizing autism.

Lack of Subgroup Synthesis

The proposed DSM-5 autism criteria have collapsed all former DSM-IV-TR diagnostic subgroups into one group, autism spectrum disorder. Unfortunately, the rationale proposed for collapsing the individual subgroups was that they shared a common pathophysiology (Kupfer & Regier, 2011), a rationale that has not been supported by empirical evidence (see Chapter 7).

Veenstra-VanderWeele and Blakely (2012) argued that because autism spectrum disorder was a heterogeneous condition, researchers should create subgroups "based on biomarkers, such as macrocephaly or indicators of mitochondrial dysfunction, or genetic findings, such as the neurexin–neuroligin system …. [or] abnormal mTOR and 5-HT signaling" (p. 206). Eapen (2011) proposed three genetic subgroups of autism. She defined syndromic ASD caused by rare, single-gene disorders as having a more complex phenotype. She defined de novo mutation ASD as a severe and specific phenotype. Eapen (2011) defined a third genetic type as broad autism caused by genetic variations in single or multiple common genes distributed across the general population.

Many indirect biomarker subgroups have also been proposed for autism. Aldridge et al. (2011) conducted a facial feature analysis of boys with autism. Aldridge et al. (2011) determined that all the boys with autism had a distinct facial phenotype characterized by an increased breadth of the mouth, orbits, and upper face, combined with a flattened nasal bridge and reduced height of the space between the nose and mouth. Aldridge et al. (2011) noted that this facial phenotype signals disruption of the embryological frontonasal process that contributes to forming the face. The researchers also found two distinctive face types within the autism group. One face pattern subgroup of 12 boys had increased autism severity scores and lower cognitive scores. A second face pattern subgroup of 5 boys had less severe autism symptoms and larger heads.

Fountain, Winter, and Bearman (2012) proposed six subgroups of autism based on the course of development: high, bloomers, medium-high, medium, low-medium, low. The low-medium and low subgroups showed little improvement in behavior from age 3 to 14. The high and medium-high groups demonstrated continuous improvement in behaviors during this same period. The one surprising group called "bloomers" showed the steepest upward development trajectory from low functioning to high functioning within the time period.

It is not clear how evidence for the six developmental trajectory sub-groups proposed by Fountain et al. (2012) and the two face structure sub-types proposed by Aldridge et al. (2011) might be synthesized with the three proposed genetic subgroups—syndromic autism, de novo mutation autism, and broad autism—proposed by Eapen (2011). Similarly, it is not clear how the evidence for many hundreds of subgroups based on a wide array of different features might be reconciled.

The Hundreds of Theories Proposing a Unifying Feature for Autism would not Require Synthesis if Autism were no Longer Viewed as a Single Disorder

Data reconciliation and theory synthesis have been rare in autism research. Many researchers believe the variation in autism will be resolved by the next, better, new unifying brain dysfunction. For example, Kana, Libero, and Moore (2011) argued, "Given the complexity, heterogeneity, and the developmental nature of ASD, a global explanation or a set of explanations seems optimal … disrupted cortical connectivity may be one such explanatory model" (p. 428). Thus for Kana et al. (2011) the best response to complexity and variation was to provide a broad but unifying explanatory theory.

However, the disrupted cortical connectivity theory espoused by Kana et al. (2011) to explain all autism has been countered by other findings. Barnea-Goraly et al. (2010) reported that individuals with autism and their unaffected siblings had the same pattern of atypical white matter. Vissers et al. (2012) carefully reviewed evidence for the underconnectivity theory of autism. Vissers et al. (2012) found insufficient evidence for frontal cortex local overconnectivity. More importantly, they reported that varied patterns of abnormal functional connectivity fell outside the bounds of the theory, and thus were not explained by the theory. Wass (2011) also reviewed the underconnectivity theory of autism. Wass argued that increased short-range connectivity and decreased long-range connectivity reflected immaturity of the cortex, and are found in many other disorders, including depression, schizophrenia, Tourette's, Williams syndrome, and developmental language disorder. Wass (2011) stated, "The overlap between how connectivity is disrupted in ASD and in other disorders remains poorly understood" (p. 25).

If autism continues to be conceptualized as a single disorder, these contradictory findings for connectivity need to be reconciled, and the theories of underconnectivity need be synthesized.

Kaiser and Pelphrey (2012) argued that although previous autism research had not found any "consistent neurochemical, neurophysiological, or neuroanatomical abnormality" (p. 29) for autism, the researchers none-theless argued that "disruptions in the visual perception of biological motion were a hallmark of ASD which may serve as a channel to the pathogno-monic deficits of the disorder" (p. 33).

However, Koldewyn, Whitney, and Rivera (2010) stated, "current results do not support either a general dorsal stream deficit or a bias towards local perception as explanations for visual perception differences in those with autism" (p. 608). Koldewyn et al. (2010) and Rutherford and Troje (2012) found that the detection of biological motion in individuals with autism was correlated with intelligence level. More significantly, Rutherford and Troje (2012) found no group differences in the detection of biological motion between individuals with autism and controls, and reported that the pattern of decline across levels of masking was similar between groups.

Can the contradictory findings for impaired detection of biological motion be reconciled with the contradictory findings for the theory that autism is caused by underconnectivity? Again, normal science does involve a "point–counterpoint" theory competition, but reconciliation of contradictory find-ings and theory synthesis are required in order to drive productive research.

Theory Predictions from Autism Data Sets Require Reconciliation
Noted and productive autism researcher Eric Courchesne has proposed more than a dozen separate theories of autism. Only four of them are described here (Akshoomoff, Pierce, & Courchesne, 2002; Chow et al., 2012; Kennedy & Courchesne, 2008; Schumann, Barnes, Lord, & Courchesne, 2009). In 2002, Akshoomoff et al. theorized that autism resulted from aberrant timing of neu-ron growth leading to a larger than normal cerebrum and reduced cell num-bers in the cerebellum and limbic regions. In 2008, Kennedy and Courchesne reported evidence that the attention network regulating attention to external events was intact in autism, but the default mode network regulating self-internal attention was disrupted in autism. Kennedy and Courchesne (2008) theorized that the spared dorsal external attention network supported spared and enhanced skills in autism, while the impaired self-internal attention net-work resulted in attention being shifted away from "social and emotional pro-cessing, but toward a particular non-social and non-emotional cognitive processing style" (p. 1882). In 2009, Schumann et al. reported finding larger amygdalae in toddlers with autism and that amygdala size in males was associ-ated with severity of autism symptoms. Schumann et al. (2009) theorized that the larger amygdala was hyper-aroused in people with autism in response to socially relevant stimuli, thus impairing social interaction functioning.

In 2012, Courchesne and his research team (Chow et al., 2012) compared gene expression levels in postmortem frontal lobe samples from 9 males with autism and 7 males without autism who died when they were between 2 and 14 years old. The researchers also compared gene expression levels in postmortem frontal lobe samples from 6 males with autism and 11 males without autism who died when they were between 15 and 56 years old. This total sample of 33 was selected from a larger initial sample of 57 individuals. Chow et al. (2012) found that 2017 genes had significantly different expression levels in the 15 autism brain samples compared to the 18 non-autism brain samples, and they reported that 736 genes were differentially expressed in the two age groups within the total autism sample. Chow et al. (2012) theorized that the gene expression differences they found for the younger autism sample reflected abnormal brain activity regulating cell number, proliferation, cell cycle, cortical patterning and differentiation, DNA damage response and apoptosis and survival. The researchers argued that this dysregulation was the possible cause of the 67% excess of neurons they found in the prefrontal cortex of children with autism (Courchesne et al., 2011).

All four theories proposed by Courchesne and colleagues were well developed and supported by empirical evidence. However, these four theories effectively replaced one another in the ad hoc fashion described by Meehl (1990) because Courchesne and colleagues did not attempt to reconcile conflicting claims of their own research team's four papers, or to reconcile their findings with conflicting findings of others.

The four theories make contradictory predictions and report contradictory findings. Akshoomoff et al. (2002) theorized that abnormal growth patterns led to a smaller cerebellum and smaller limbic regions in autism. The core elements of the limbic region that would be smaller would be the hypothalamus, hippocampus, and the amygdala. Conversely, Schumann et al. (2009) found evidence for larger amygdalae in children with autism, and theorized that autism social impairment reflected hyper-activation of the amygdala. For Akshoomoff et al. (2002), the amygdala, as part of a smaller limbic system, should be smaller, not larger. Similarly, Chow et al. (2012) theorized that a set of aberrantly expressed genes explained their own team's finding for excess neurons and aberrant organization of those neurons in autism frontal lobe tissue. If there is more tissue in the cerebrum in autism, according to Akshoomoff et al. (2002), the cerebellum and the amygdala should be smaller, but Schumann et al. (2009) found evidence for larger amygdalae in children with autism. In addition, Ecker et al. (2011) reported finding reduced amygdala size associated with autism symptoms in adults with autism. Ecker et al. (2011) also noted that studies have reported larger amygdalae, smaller amygdalae, and normal sized amygdalae in autism.

If the cerebrum were larger in autism as proposed by Akshoomoff et al. (2002), it would be expected that head size would be likely to reflect the larger cerebrum. However, Barnard-Brak et al. (2011) reported in the Early Childhood Longitudinal Study Birth Cohort, a nationally representative, community-based sample of approximately 9000 children, that the 100 young children with autism did not show significant head circumference difference at age 9 months, 24 months, and 36 months compared with the head circumference of the 8900 children without autism.

Kennedy and Courchesne (2008) reported evidence that the external attention network was not disrupted in autism. However, Chow et al. (2012) reported that many brain development genes have aberrant expression in the frontal lobe in autism and theorized that aberrantly expressed genes accounted for their findings of more neurons in frontal lobe tissue in autism (Courchsne et al., 2011). Given the importance of frontal lobe function to external attention (Posner, 2011), it is surprising that an aberrantly developed frontal lobe (Chow et al., 2012) in autism would cause no disruption of the external attention network (Kennedy & Courchesne, 2008). In addition, external attention deficits have been widely reported for autism (Rommelse, 2011). These discrepant findings require reconciliation.

Chow et al. (2012) did note that their gene expression results differed to those of a similar study by Voineagu et al. (2011), and suggested that genetic heterogeneity in autism and sample characteristics might explain the differences. However, Chow et al. (2011) offered no synthesis of their findings with those of Voineagu et al. (2011).

As exciting and interesting as the four theories have been (Akshoomoff et al., 2002; Chow et al., 2012; Kennedy & Courchesne, 2008; Schumann et al., 2009), this brief exercise suggests that the effort to reconcile findings and theories, if undertaken, might have been problematic.

THE EXISTING QUANDARY AND THE ARGUMENT FOR AUTISM AS SYMPTOMS

The Existing Quandary: Should the Current Paradigm of Autism be Abandoned?

Kendler and First asked the question:

> *At what point does it make sense to abandon one paradigm in favour of another? Ideally, the shift should be organic, occurring at a point at which the advantages of*

the new paradigm become so overwhelming that to continue with the existing paradigm would make no sense. However, what happens if a shift is driven by a new paradigm whose advantages over the existing paradigm are tentative, more theoretical than practical, appealing but not "road tested"?

Kendler and First (2010, p. 264)

What paradigm of autism should researchers follow?

Should researchers keep searching for *the* unifying pathophysiology of autism in samples defined by DSM criteria and DSM diagnostic instruments? Elsabbagh et al. (2012), Chow et al. (2012), Kaiser and Pelphrey (2012), Kana et al. (2011), Wolff et al. (2012) and many other researchers have argued for this course. Lord and Jones (2012) noted that finding the neural basis for autism symptoms was "particularly important if the focus is on earlier or better diagnosis … we do want to link the neurobiology to the behaviors that we are trying to explain in ASD" (p. 492).

However, the search for the neurobiological basis for autism has a long history of failure. As noted throughout this book, no validated pathophysiology has been discovered for autism, and even the core autism symptom of social interaction impairment has not been linked to any single neurobiological cause. The existing evidence for heterogeneity of behaviors, brain deficits, and etiologies for autism argues against the possibility of finding autism-specific "valid patterns of brain function that are associated with reliably measured behavioral dimensions of ASD" (Lord & Jones, 2012, p. 492).

Should researchers attempt to exclude what they interpret as non-diagnostic symptoms from autism symptom sets in the belief that there is a unitary autism disorder or meaningful spectrum of closely related autism disorders? Close et al. (2012), Guinchat et al. (2012a), Lord and Jones (2012), and the APA DSM-5 Neurodevelopmental Disorders Work Group have argued for this view.

Lord and Jones (2012) stated that, in comparison with neurobiological research in autism, the research on social impairment was "notable in its consistency and replicability across studies" (p. 494). However, this consistency cannot include the measurement of individual variation. As noted in Chapter 1, Jones and Klin (2009) concluded, "Individuals with autism show a vast clinical variability in the expression and severity of their symptoms. This heterogeneity spans the entire range of IQ and language function and a wide array of communicative, social, and behavioral disabilities" (p. 471). Schultz noted, "If you've seen one child with autism, you've seen one child with autism. Autism's like a snowflake" (Scott, 2011). Even Lord (2011) observed that anyone who has met more than one person with autism is struck by the variation between diagnosed individuals.

Lord and Jones (2012) proposed that "Finer-grained descriptions of behaviors associated with ASD are still needed in order to better define dimensions of social-communication deficits and restricted/repetitive behaviors on an individual level for both clinical and neurobiological purposes" (p. 504). Although finer-grain descriptions of autism symptoms would certainly yield increasing detail that would better inform differentiable clinical descriptions of individual variation within autism, finer-grain behavioral descriptions are unlikely to add information that would help to link behavior to neurobiology. To date, no validated causal specificity for autism symptoms has been determined from the wealth of heterogeneous neurobiological findings. Because finer-grain symptom descriptions will not explicate how varied neurobiological causes converge on one clinical symptom, and will not explicate how divergent clinical symptoms are generated by a single neurobiololgical cause, finer-grain descriptions of autism symptoms are unlikely to be useful for determining the complexities of autism neurobiology.

Should researchers view autism as a spectrum of related disorders that can be successfully divided into subgroups? Aldridge et al. (2011), Eapen (2011), Veenstra-VanderWeele and Blakely (2012), and many other researchers have held this view, but this view has yet to provide improved clarity in diagnosis and has yet to establish standard subgroups within autism. The proposed DSM-5 criteria for autism have eliminated all diagnostic subgroups for lack of distinguishing evidence to differentiate the diagnostic subgroups, and because a shared pathophysiology for autism was claimed to exist.

Kendler and First (2010) argued that psychiatric disorders could not be divided into etiological subgroups because the genetic bases for disorders have proven to be so complex that finding single etiology subgroups would be unlikely. However, genetic single etiology subgroups already exist in autism. Called syndromic autism, the diagnosis of autism has been made in individuals with fragile X syndrome, Rett syndrome, tuberous sclerosis, Joubert syndrome, Timothy syndrome, Down syndrome, Klinefelter syndrome, and Angelman syndrome, as well as in many other defined genetic syndromes.

In fact, syndromic autism demonstrates that autism symptoms may appear in association with many different forms of neurobiological brain disruption caused by many different genetic etiologies. The findings for syndromic autism also suggest that the Lord and Jones (2012) goal of linking "neurobiology to the behaviors that we are trying to explain in ASD" (p. 492) may be fraught with complex overlapping links.

Should researchers view autism as many hundreds of different autisms resulting from multiple genetic causes and multiple environmental causes?

Coleman and Gillberg (2012) have argued for this view, but the prospect is daunting. Dame Stephanie Shirley, founder of Autism Speaks in Britain, had hoped that "the causes of the various autisms should be understood by 2012" (Feinstein, 2010, p. 297). This has not happened, and for good reason: the causes are many and complex.

Most importantly, nature has blocked any easy path to inference for the discovery of multiple autisms. As noted frequently in this book, autism symptoms appear with other symptoms in association with a shared risk factor, and many different patterns of brain disruption may produce the same autism symptom. Together these two lines of evidence mean that clear causal mapping of risk factor to brain disruption to symptom will be unlikely, and suggest that etiological agents and developmental brain disruptions have *not* created hundreds of clearly distinguishable autism syndromes.

An additional inferential problem for forming multiple subgroups is the difficulty in identifying discrete brain deficits. The widespread brain disruptions found to date in association with autism, and the complexity of brain networks both stand against the identification of discrete brain deficits for autism subgroups. An example of the potential underlying complexity is the proposal that Schilbach et al. (2012) made for three overlapping brain networks. The researchers conducted a meta-analytic study and concluded that there was a social cognition network reflected in brain activation in the left dorsomedial prefrontal cortex, the left precuneus, the temporoparietal junction, the anterior temporal cortex, and the left superior frontal gyrus. They defined a network for emotion processing that included bilateral activation in the amygdala, the ventral and dorsal striatum, the anterior cingulate cortex and dorsomedial prefrontal cortex, the posterior cingulate cortex, precuneus, dorsal visual area V5, and insular cortex (Schilbach et al., 2012). Finally, they defined a network for introspection, the default mode network active when a person is not focused on a task, including posterior cingulate cortex, precuneus, anterior cingulate cortex, ventromedial and dorsomedial prefrontal cortex, bilateral supramarginal gyrus, bilateral temporoparietal junction, left superior and right middle temporal gyrus, left middle occipital gyrus, and left middle frontal gyrus. Schilbach et al. (2012) found two points of overlap for all three systems—the precuneus and anterior medial prefrontal cortex—which the researchers viewed as hubs that connected the three systems.

Given the existing evidence for widespread brain disruption caused by many risk factors for autism, linking disrupted components of complex systems as described by Schilbach et al. (2012) to discrete variations in autism symptoms is likely to prove impossible.

Rethinking Autism

Insel and Wang called on researchers to rethink the nature of psychiatric disorders:

> With no validated biomarkers and too little in the way of novel medical treatments since 1980, families need science to provide more than hope. Genetics and neuroscience finally have the tools to transform the diagnosis and treatment of mental illness. But first, it is time to rethink mental disorders, recognizing that these are disorders of brain circuits likely caused by developmental processes shaped by a complex interplay of genetics and experience.
>
> **Insel and Wang (2010, p. 1971)**

This book has taken Insel and Wang's call seriously. The research findings for autism have been reconsidered here in an effort to understand why none of us conducting research in autism has been able to find a valid shared brain deficit in autism, or a standard diagnostic symptom pattern, or replicable and meaningful clinical or neurological subgroups.

Like Insel and Wang (2010), Kendler (2012) called for empirical pluralism in psychiatry. Kendler (2012) argued that psychiatric disorders "are stunningly complex" (p. 385), and he, too, claimed that "having overly simplified views of them, often ideologically driven, has only hampered our field" (p. 385).

If autism is not a single disorder, if autism is not hundreds of distinct subtypes of autism, what is the entity being studied?

The Argument that Autism is Symptoms and not a Single Disorder or a Spectrum of Related Disorders

Given the totality of the existing research evidence, I believe the least speculative scientific position is that autism symptoms are just that, symptoms. The following series of claims together lead to the conclusion that autism symptoms are symptoms and not a single disorder or multiple disorders.

Claim One: Autism has not Been Validated as a Symptom Set, and Heterogeneity in Symptoms, Brain Deficits, and Etiologies Argues that Autism is not a Single Disorder

Kanner (1943) defined autism with two diagnostic symptoms: the profound failure to understand social interaction, and an insistence on sameness in the environment. There has been no validation of this pairing of symptoms. DSM criteria before DSM-5 defined autism with three symptoms: social impairment, communication impairment, and restricted and repetitive behaviors. There has been no validation of this triad of symptoms. The proposed DSM-5 criteria for autism spectrum disorder have defined autism with two diagnostic symptoms: social interaction impairment; and restricted or repetitive behaviors, interests, or activities, or sensory abnormalities. Given previous findings, this pairing is unlikely to be validated.

In addition to the lack of validation for the connection between autism diagnostic symptoms, the heterogeneity of diagnostic and associated symptoms, the wide variation in brain deficits, and the immense range of etiologies make it implausible that autism could be one disorder. No unitary pathogenesis exists for autism. No unitary pathophysiology exists for autism. No consistent unitary phenotype exists for autism.

Claim Two: Environmental and Genetic Risk Factors for Autism Cause Brain Disruptions that are not Causally Specific to Autism Symptoms

Genetic and environmental risk factors yield autism symptoms along with other symptoms and disorders. As Lord and Jones (2012) posited, "the most significant scientific challenge to the concept of autism as one 'disease' or even 'diseases' is the heterogeneity of the genetic findings" (p. 491). Fragile X syndrome (Bray et al., 2011), Rett syndrome (Goffin et al., 2012), and other genetic risk factors for autism symptoms have been associated with varied brain disruptions and a range of phenotypes. Variant phenotypes have included complete autism phenotypes, partial autism phenotypes, and phenotypes comprised of non-autism symptoms along with or independent of autism symptoms (Hoeft et al., 2011; Wulffaert, Van Berckelaer-Onnes, & Scholte, 2009). For example, Fernandez et al. (2012) reported evidence for three large de novo (new and unique to the set of individuals studied) chromosomal copy number variants that caused both autism symptoms and tic disorders. Fernandez et al. (2012) argued that their findings supported the idea of shared genetic bases for different clinical diagnoses. As Addington and Rapoport (2012) noted, the study of mental disorders has "little reason to expect phenotypic specificity from a particular genetic variant" (p. 2).

Talkowski et al. (2012) explored balanced chromosomal abnormalities that index single gene disruptions in a large sample of individuals diagnosed with autism and individuals diagnosed with other neurodevelopmental disorders. The researchers found possible causal gene variants previously linked to neurodevelopmental disorders, single gene contributors to microdeletion syndromes, new gene variants, and genes associated with schizophrenia and bipolar disorder. Talkowski et al. (2012) proposed a polygenic basis for autism, in which differing mutations in the same sets of genes contributed in an overlapping fashion to autism, schizophrenia, psychosis, bipolar disorder, and intellectual disability.

State and Levitt (2011) made the essential point about the widespread nature of brain disruptions caused by genetic variants. They stated, "Complex functions … mediated by hierarchically organized circuitries that include sensory and motor, autonomic regulatory, social-emotional, and cognitive domains" (State & Levitt, 2011, p. 1) are altered in autism by varied disruptions in the "neurodevelopmental processes that are guided by thousands of genes" (State & Levitt, 2011, p. 1). In fact, alterations or combinations of alterations in organizing factors, including gene variants, chromosomal number variants, altered epigenetic processes, and untoward gene–environment interactions may impair brain circuits for many behaviors: social, perceptual, motor, cognitive, and others (Goh & Peterson, 2012; Sivakumaran et al., 2011).

Similarly, environmental risk factors for autism symptoms have yielded many varied outcomes including individuals with all diagnostic autism symptoms, with some autism symptoms, and with many other symptom patterns, along with or independent of autism symptoms. These outcomes include intellectual disability, cerebral palsy, motor disorders, and other neurocognitive impairments (Guinchat et al., 2012b). A wide range of environmental insults are possible, and evidence for environmental risk factors suggests that environmental risk factors are unlikely to disrupt only brain circuits that generate social impairment and aberrant motor and sensory behaviors. Mwaniki, Atieno, Lawn, and Newton (2012) reviewed outcomes of intrauterine and neonatal insults. They reported that epilepsy, vision problems, hearing problems, cognitive impairment, motor impairment, and social impairment were all possible outcomes of insults before or during delivery. Rees et al. (2011) stated that an adverse intrauterine environment, including fetal neuroinflammation from any cause, could confer death of gray matter in the cerebellum, hippocampus, and cortex, and cerebral white matter damage causing long-term deficits in neural connectivity. Lubsen et al. (2011) argued that glial and neuronal cell death in various brain regions occurred for children delivered prematurely. The researchers also found evidence suggesting that there was damage to neurobiological processes directing axonal growth and synaptogenesis.

An additional problem is that interconnected networks increase the vulnerability of individual circuits to developmental disruption. The many brain circuits mediating social behavior are woven through the brain's interconnections (Akil et al., 2010; Berntson et al., 2012; Koch, 2012; Molenberghs, Cunnington, & Mattingley, 2012; Solari & Stoner, 2011; Van Essen & Ugurbil, 2012). For example, consider the central autism symptom of social interaction impairment. As outlined in Chapter 3, social neuroscience research has demonstrated that social interaction depends on many different neurochemicals and many brain circuits, including those mediating social motivation, social cognition, behavioral flexibility, perceptual processing, and many others. Evidence suggests there are multi-purpose processing centers, such as the amygdala, that mediate both social and non-social behaviors. Even presumptively dedicated social brain processing centers such as the fusiform face area may serve more general processing functions, such as discrimination and categorizing of objects. A meta-analysis of 125 studies of human mirror neuron system function conducted by Molenberghs et al. (2012) suggested that, depending on the tasks involved, the mirror system provides comprehension of action or comprehension of the emotions of others. Berntson, Norman, Hawkley, and Cacioppo (2012) argued, "complexities associated with navigating social systems in primates ... led to the evolutionary development of some of the most complex networks of the brain ... the complexity of these networks has thus far precluded a clear mapping between social and neurological processes" (p. 65).

In sum, there are many circuits mediating social behavior, many of these circuits are multi-purpose, and circuits mediating social behavior are interwoven with the totality of cortical and subcortical circuits, systems, and networks. Therefore, in order for genetic and environmental risk factors to impair social interaction, risk factors must necessarily cause brain disruptions that impair not only social-behavior-mediating brain circuits, but also brain circuits mediating other behaviors. A brain disruption yielding social impairment would therefore be likely to cause varied additional symptoms such as developmental delay, atypical motor behaviors, and language impairment or delay. As noted earlier, neuroscience findings for regional circuits, systems, and networks within the larger connectome do not suggest that there could be an easy mapping of these interwoven, overlapping, and shared circuits to specific symptoms.

For example, Wei et al. (2011) hypothesized that three major brain development processes were disrupted in autism: neuron migration; the balance of excitatory and inhibitory synapses; and synaptogenesis. All three are global brain development disruptions. Consequently, the brain disruption model outlined by Wei et al. (2011) effectively predicts that intellectual disability, motor delay, language impairment, attention deficit/hyperactivity disorder symptoms, and other non-diagnostic symptoms would be likely to co-occur with autism symptoms.

Of course, there may be rare cases, like the famous HM of memory research, wherein an individual has severe neurodevelopmental social impairment because of a specific lesion. However, there are myriad brain circuits and neurochemicals that determine the many skills needed for typical social interaction behavior. As outlined in Chapter 3, our many social brain circuits reflect the behavioral evidence that human means for social communication are overbuilt. We have many alternate ways of communicating with one another, such as eye gaze, facial expressions, gestures, body movement, voice tone and pattern, and language. Consequently, a specific focal lesion is less likely to be able to cause severe developmental social interaction impairment.

In sum, the totality of evidence demonstrates that developmental brain disruptions caused by genetic and environmental risk factors for autism will not map one-to-one with autism symptoms. Thus, because these brain disruptions will not be causally specific for autism, efforts to validate autism as a single disorder will continue to fail. Moreover, the presence of associated symptoms with autism symptoms suggests that the autism spectrum of symptoms and the broad autism phenotype will also continue to fail to be validated.

Claim Three: Because Risk Factors Tie Autism Symptoms to Non-Autism Symptoms, Behavioral Subgroups cannot be Uniquely Autism Subgroups

Finally, because most individuals diagnosed with autism express one or more additional non-diagnostic symptoms generated by the causal risk factors for autism, associated non-autism symptoms cannot be excluded from any subgroup formation. Consequently, subgroups formed would include various combinations of symptoms, and thus would not be uniquely autism subgroups.

Taken together, these three claims and associated lines of evidence argue against the existence of autism as a single disorder, spectrum, or set of autism subgroups. If autism symptoms are not one disorder, and are not many disorders, what are they? The most parsimonious and least speculative view is that autism symptoms must be symptoms.

Summary: Autism Symptoms as Symptoms

Sanislow et al. (2010) proposed,

> *a diagnosis may turn out simply to be indicative of a range of possible pathologies .... for example, depression might be viewed akin to the way that a fever is viewed today, suggesting specific tests for a panel of potentially active diagnostic markers that will steer the clinician to the appropriate treatment among any number of possible disordered processes that might underlie the depression.*
>
> **Sanislow et al. (2010, pp. 637–638)**

Are autism symptoms similar to the way in which fever is a symptom? Fever is characterized by a rise in core body temperature, and the activation of immune systems. Fever is generally temporary; autism is not. However, fever, like autism symptoms, is a sign of many different diseases, and fever, like autism symptoms, results from complex mechanisms. Gensini and Conti (2004) noted that Galen believed that fever was a disease in itself, and many theories of fever as a disease existed for several thousand years.

Fever is now understood as a physiologic response to disease mediated by immune system agents called pyrogenic cytokines (Mackowiak, 1998). Yang, Zhuang, and Servaes (2012) noted, however, that there is still much fever of unknown origin (FUO).

The discovery of pathogens was necessary in order for fever to be understood as a symptom of a pathogen's effect on the body. The pathogen is the etiology, the pathogen's disruption of body function is the disease, and a fever is one observable symptom of the immune system's reaction to the pathogen, and its disruption of body functions.

Similarly, the discovery of many different brain deficits associated with autism, and the discovery of many different genetic and environmental risk factors as causes for those various brain deficits were a necessary precondition in order that autism symptoms could be seen as symptoms and not a disorder. Autism symptoms are the observable behaviors that reflect the existence of developmental brain disruptions *and* the causal chains leading to those brain disruptions that begin with an etiology or multiple etiologies.

CONCLUSION: AUTISM SYMPTOMS WITHOUT A DISORDER

Talkowski et al. (2012) reported that a "profound collective contribution of the disrupted genes on neurodevelopment" (p. 534) crossed many diagnostic boundaries, and Leckman and Pine (2012) asked what the best nosological approach should be given that genetic risk variants are shared by many different disorders.

Lord and Jones (2012) argued that the finding that autism shares causal risk variants with other disorders "is an important addition to, but in no way a replacement for a behavioral diagnosis" (p. 491). In fact, however, the findings for the many shared risk factors for autism and other disorders, the resultant broad and variable brain disruptions, and the mixed symptom phenotypes do argue that the behavioral diagnosis of autism as a disorder is likely to be wrong. Moreover, because the evidence, as reported in this book, has demonstrated that no form of the behavioral diagnosis of autism has been validated, and the evidence for many shared risk factors, broad brain disruptions and multi-symptom phenotypes suggests that the behavioral diagnosis of autism is unlikely ever to be validated, scientific progress will continue to be stalled if the DSM-5 diagnosis remains in use. The most simple and minimal solution would be to replace the DSM-5 diagnosis with an open set of symptoms that makes no claims to be a disorder.

Many changes in diagnostic criteria, clinical practice, and research practice would result from the acceptance of the view that autism symptoms are symptoms. For example, while autism is understood as a disorder, the co-occurrence of the two symptoms of social impairment and intellectual disability defy a diagnostic boundary. But if social impairment and intellectual disability are seen as two observable symptoms of brain disruption, then just as a physician would never say that a person who had a rash could not be diagnosed with a fever, a clinician would no longer say that a child who had developmental delay could not be identified as having social impairment.

Box 8.1 uses the proposed DSM-5 first criterion for autism spectrum disorder as an illustration of a possible starting point for describing two neurodevelopmental social impairment symptom sets. The proposed use of DSM-5 criteria listed in Box 8.1 includes both the description of a simple neurodevelopmental social impairment symptom set and the description of a complex symptom set. The first symptom set is defined by neurodevelopmental social impairment only. The rationale for this symptom set of social impairment without other symptoms is that this phenotype has been reported in clinical populations (Mandy et al., 2011; Mattila et al., 2011). If there is a group with social impairment and no other neurodevelopmental or psychiatric disorders, this group would be of importance for research.

The second symptom set documents autism social impairment with all additional co-occurring neurodevelopmental symptoms. The rationale for this complex symptom set is that heterogeneous symptoms have been found with genetic and environmental risk factors for autism and require explanation as complex symptom sets.

The British Psychology Society recommended that any classification system should begin from symptoms. They claimed that because "two people with a diagnosis of 'schizophrenia' or 'personality disorder' may possess no two symptoms in common, it is difficult to see what communicative benefit is served by using these diagnoses" (Alan, 2011, p. 3). The British Psychological Society stated, "We believe that a description of a person's real problems would suffice" (Alan, 2011, p. 3), and they argued that a symptom list would be preferable to DSM-5.

Adequate description of social impairment and other symptoms requires that many symptoms must be included. The range of symptoms, such as that

BOX 8.1 Two Possible Neurodevelopmental Social Impairment Phenotypes for a Transitional Symptom Nosology

Neurodevelopmental Social Impairment Only Phenotype

A. *Persistent deficits in social communication and social interaction across contexts for all three types of social impairment appearing in childhood:*

Deficits in social-emotional reciprocity; ranging from abnormal social approach and failure of normal back and forth conversation, through reduced sharing of interests, emotions, and affect and response, to total lack of initiation of social interaction.

Deficits in nonverbal communicative behaviors used for social interaction; ranging from poorly integrated verbal and nonverbal communication, through abnormalities in eye contact and body language, or deficits in understanding and use of nonverbal communication, to total lack of facial expression or gestures.

Deficits in developing and maintaining relationships, appropriate to developmental level (beyond those with caregivers); ranging from difficulties adjusting behavior to suit different social contexts, through difficulties in sharing imaginative play and in making friends, to an apparent absence of interest in people.

B. *Does not express any other neurodevelopmental symptoms including*

Atypical sensory behaviors:

Hyper- or hypo-reactivity to sensory input or unusual interest in sensory aspects of environment (such as apparent indifference to pain/heat/cold, adverse response to specific sounds or textures, excessive smelling or touching of objects, fascination with lights or spinning objects).

Atypical motor behaviors:

Hypotonia, motor stereotypies, self-injurious behavior …

Atypical rigidity in behaviors and interests:

Excessive adherence to routines, ritualized patterns of verbal or nonverbal behavior, or excessive resistance to change (such as motoric rituals, insistence on same route or food, repetitive questioning, or extreme distress at small changes).

Highly restricted, fixated interests that are abnormal in intensity or focus (such as strong attachment to or preoccupation with unusual objects, excessively circumscribed or perseverative interests).

Atypical language development:

Absence of language

Delayed onset of speech

Stereotyped or repetitive speech, echolalia, idiosyncratic phrases

Attention deficit/hyperactivity disorder symptoms

Intellectual disability or developmental delay

Seizures

BOX 8.1 Two Possible Neurodevelopmental Social Impairment Phenotypes for a Transitional Symptom Nosology—*cont'd*

Neurodevelopmental Social Impairment Multi-symptom Phenotype

A. *Persistent deficits in social communication and social interaction across contexts appearing in childhood:*

Deficits in social-emotional reciprocity; ranging from abnormal social approach and failure of normal back and forth conversation, through reduced sharing of interests, emotions, and affect and response, to total lack of initiation of social interaction.

Deficits in nonverbal communicative behaviors used for social interaction; ranging from poorly integrated verbal and nonverbal communication, through abnormalities in eye contact and body language, or deficits in understanding and use of nonverbal communication, to total lack of facial expression or gestures.

Deficits in developing and maintaining relationships, appropriate to developmental level (beyond those with caregivers); ranging from difficulties adjusting behavior to suit different social contexts, through difficulties in sharing imaginative play and in making friends, to an apparent absence of interest in people.

B. *Neurodevelopmental deficits manifested in any to all subdomains:*

Atypical sensory behaviors:

Hyper- or hypo-reactivity to sensory input or unusual interest in sensory aspects of environment (such as apparent indifference to pain/heat/cold, adverse response to specific sounds or textures, excessive smelling or touching of objects, fascination with lights or spinning objects).

Atypical motor behaviors:

Hypotonia, motor stereotypies, self-injurious behavior …

Atypical rigidity in behaviors and interests:

Excessive adherence to routines, ritualized patterns of verbal or nonverbal behavior, or excessive resistance to change (such as motoric rituals, insistence on same route or food, repetitive questioning, or extreme distress at small changes).

Highly restricted, fixated interests that are abnormal in intensity or focus (such as strong attachment to or preoccupation with unusual objects, excessively circumscribed or perseverative interests).

Atypical language development:

Absence of language

Delayed onset of speech

Stereotyped or repetitive speech, echolalia, idiosyncratic phrases

Attention deficit/hyperactivity disorder symptoms

Intellectual disability or developmental delay

Seizures

suggested in Box 8.1, could be listed and identified. The underlying brain disruptions would be known or unknown. Current unknown risk factors would continue to be identified as new findings for causal environmental insults developed over time, and as knowledge of causal gene, chromosomal, epigenetic, and gene–environment disruptions of brain development accumulated.

Rutter (2005) warned, "There is no disgrace in being wrong, but there is a disgrace in persisting with a theory when empirical findings have made it apparent that the hypothesis or claim was mistaken" (p. 255). This book has argued that empirical findings have made it apparent that the theory of autism as a single disorder or spectrum was mistaken. However, the continued quest to unify autism is not a disgrace, but a desperate search for a single clarifying solution where none is likely to exist.

Prassad, Cifu, and Ioannidis (2012) pragmatically concluded that often, "established standards must be abandoned not because a better replacement has been identified but simply because what was thought to be beneficial was not" (p. 37). This book has argued that the established theory and standard diagnosis of autism should be abandoned not because a better replacement has been identified but because the totality of empirical research has failed to validate autism as a disorder, and the evidence for heterogeneous symptoms for risk factors requires a more inclusive explanation. Translational research requires a neurobiological mechanism. Because autism symptoms are symptoms of a multitude of neurobiological mechanisms, the abandonment of belief that autism will eventually be found to have a single neurobiological mechanism should be beneficial for research.

The vision suggested here is simple. Neurodevelopmental social impairment is a symptom, sensory abnormalities are a symptom, intellectual disability is a symptom, restricted and repetitive interests and behaviors are symptoms, and other neurodevelopmental associated disorders are symptoms, all of which result from varied complex developmental brain disruptions.

Although the descriptive shift may be simple, and although shifting to a symptom view has the power to end fruitless efforts to prove that a set of symptoms is a unique disorder, the resulting research problem is immensely more difficult than searching for a singular unity. Etiologies, brain disruptions, the process of brain development, and the structure and function of the brain are each complex worlds. Finding lines of causality through and across these worlds will be a lengthy and extremely demanding challenge.

REFERENCES

Abrahams, B. S., & Geschwind, D. H. (2010). Connecting genes to brain in the autism spectrum disorders. *Archives of Neurology, 67*, 395–399.

Addington, A. M., & Rapoport, J. L. (2012). Annual Research Review: Impact of advances in genetics in understanding developmental psychopathology. *Journal of Child Psychology and Psychiatry, 53*, 510–518.

Akil, H., Brenner, S., Kandel, E., Kendler, K. S., King, M. C., Scolnick, E., et al. (2010). The future of psychiatric research: Genomes and neural circuits. *Science, 327*, 1580–1581.

Akshoomoff, N., Pierce, K., & Courchesne, E. (2002). The neurobiological basis of autism from a developmental perspective. *Development and Psychopathology, 14*, 613–634.

Alan, C. A. (2011, June). *The British Psychology Society Response to the American Psychiatric Association: DSM-5 Development, 1–26.* Bps.uk.org. Retrieved January 23, 2012 from http://www.bps.org.uk/news/societys-critical-response-dsm-5.

Aldridge, K., George, I. D., Cole, K. K., Austin, J. R., Takahashi, T. N., Duan, Y., et al. (2011). Facial phenotypes in subgroups of pre-pubertal boys with autism spectrum disorders are correlated with clinical phenotypes. *Molecular Autism, 2*(15), 1–12.

Barnard-Brak, L., Sulak, T., & Ivey Hatz, J. K. (2011). Macrocephaly in children with autism spectrum disorders. *Pediatric Neurology, 44*, 97–100.

Barnea-Goraly, N., Lotspeich, L. J., & Reiss, A. L. (2010). Similar white matter aberrations in children with autism and their unaffected siblings: A diffusion tensor imaging study using tract-based spatial statistics. *Archives of General Psychiatry, 67*, 1052–1060.

Baron-Cohen, S., Lombardo, M. V., Auyeung, B., Ashwin, E., Chakrabarti, B., & Knickmeyer, R. (2011). Why are autism spectrum conditions more prevalent in males? *PLoS Biology, 9*, e1001081.

Bejerot, S., Eriksson, J. M., Bonde, S., Carlström, K., Humble, M. B., & Eriksson, E. (2012). The extreme male brain revisited: Gender coherence in adults with autism spectrum disorder. *British Journal of Psychiatry.* [Epub April 12, 2012]. doi: 10.1192/bjp.bp.111.097899.

Berntson, G. G., Norman, G. J., Hawkley, L. C., & Cacioppo, J. T. (2012). Evolution of neuroarchitecture, multi-level analyses and calibrative reductionism. *Interface Focus, 2*, 65–73.

Bill, B. R., & Geschwind, D. H. (2009). Genetic advances in autism: Heterogeneity and convergence on shared pathways. *Current Opinion in Genetic Development, 19*, 271–278.

Boucher, J. (2011). Redefining the concept of autism as a unitary disorder: Multiple causal deficits of a single kind? In D. Fein (Ed.), *The neuropsychology of autism* (pp. 469–482). New York, NY: Oxford University Press.

Bray, S., Hirt, M., Jo, B., Hall, S. S., Lightbody, A. A., Walter, E., et al. (2011). Aberrant frontal lobe maturation in adolescents with fragile X syndrome is related to delayed cognitive maturation. *Biological Psychiatry, 70*, 852–858.

Campbell, D. B., Datta, D., Jones, S. T., Lee, E. B., Sutcliffe, J. S., Hammock, E. A.D., et al. (2011). Association of oxytocin receptor (OXTR) gene variants with multiple phenotype domains of autism spectrum disorder. *Journal of Neurodevelopmental Disorders, 3*, 101–112.

Chen, Y., Norton, D. J., McBain, R., Gold, J., Frazier, J. A., & Coyle, J. T. (2012). Enhanced local processing of dynamic visual information in autism: Evidence from speed discrimination. *Neuropsychologia, 50*, 733–739.

Chow, M. L., Pramparo, T., Winn, M. E., Barnes, C. C., Li, H. R., Weiss, L., et al. (2012). Age-dependent brain gene expression and copy number anomalies in autism suggest distinct pathological processes at young versus mature ages. *PLoS Genetics, 8*, e1002592. [Epub March 22, 2012].

Close, H. A., Lee, L. C., Kaufmann, C. N., & Zimmerman, A. W. (2012). Co-occurring conditions and change in diagnosis in autism spectrum disorders. *Pediatrics*, *129*, e305–316.

Coghill, D., & Sonuga-Barke, E. J. S. (2012). Annual Research Review: Categories versus dimensions in the classification and conceptualisation of child and adolescent mental disorders: Implications of recent empirical study. *Journal of Child Psychology and Psychiatry*, *53*, 469–489.

Copeland, W., Shanahan, L., Costello, E. J., & Angold, A. (2011). Cumulative prevalence of psychiatric disorders by young adulthood: A prospective cohort analysis from the Great Smoky Mountains Study. *Journal of the Academy of Child and Adolescent Psychiatry*, *3*, 252–261.

Courchesne, E., Mouton, P. R., Calhoun, M. E., Semendeferi, K., Ahrens-Barbeau, C., Hallet, M. J., et al. (2011). Neuron number and size in prefrontal cortex of children with autism. *Journal of the American Medical Association*, *306*, 2001–2010.

De Jaegher, H., Di Paolo, E., & Gallagher, S. (2010). Can social interaction constitute social cognition? *Trends in Cognitive Sciences*, *14*, 441–447.

Eapen, V. (2011). Genetic basis of autism: Is there a way forward? *Current Opinion in Psychiatry*, *24*, 226–236.

Ebisch, S. J., Gallese, V., Willem, R. M., Mantini, D., Groen, W. B., Romani, G. L., & Bekkering, H. (2010). Altered intrinsic functional connectivity of anterior and posterior insula regions in high-functioning participants with autism spectrum disorder. *Human Brain Mapping*, *32*, 1013–1028.

Ebstein, R. P., Knafo, A., Mankuta, D., Chew, S. H., & Lai, P. S. (2012). The contributions of oxytocin and vasopressin pathway genes to human behavior. *Hormones and Behavior*, *61*, 359–379.

Ecker, C., Suckling, J., Deoni, S. C., Lombardo, M. V., Bullmore, E. T., Baron-Cohen, S., et al. (2012). Brain anatomy and its relationship to behavior in adults with autism spectrum disorder: A multicenter magnetic resonance imaging study. *Archives of General Psychiatry*, *69*, 195–209.

Elsabbagh, M., Mercure, E., Hudry, K., Chandler, S., Pasco, G., Charman, T., et al. (2012). Infant neural sensitivity to dynamic eye gaze is associated with later emerging autism. *Current Biology*, *22*, 1–5.

Feinstein, A. (2010). *A history of autism: Conversations with the pioneers.* New York, NY: Wiley Blackwell.

Fernandez, T. V., Sanders, S. J., Yurkiewicz, I. R., Ercan-Sencicek, A. G., Kim, Y. S., Fishman, D. O., et al. (2012). Rare copy number variants in Tourette syndrome disrupt genes in histaminergic pathways and overlap with autism. *Biological Psychiatry*, *71*, 392–402.

Foss-Feig, J. H., Heacock, J. L., & Cascio, C. J. (2012). Tactile responsiveness patterns and their association with core features in autism spectrum disorders. *Research in Autism Spectrum Disorders*, *6*, 337–344.

Fountain, C., Winter, A. S., & Bearman, P. S. (2012). Six developmental trajectories characterize children with autism. *Pediatrics*. [Epub April 2, 2012].

Frances, A. (2012, February 21). *DSM 5 freezes out its stakeholders.* Huffingtonpost.com. Retrieved February 21, 2012 from http://www.huffingtonpost.com/allen-frances/dsm-5-freezes-out-its-sta_b_1269838.html.

Frances, A. J., & Widiger, T. (2012). Psychiatric diagnosis: Lessons from the DSM-IV past and cautions for the DSM-5 future. *Annual Review of Clinical Psychology*, *27*, 109–130.

Gensini, G. F., & Conti, A. A. (2004). The evolution of the concept of "fever" in the history of medicine: From pathological picture per se to clinical epiphenomenon (and vice versa). *Journal of Infection*, *49*, 85–87.

Geschwind, D. H. (2011). Genetics of autism spectrum disorders. *Trends in Cognitive Sciences*, *15*, 409–416.

Gilman, S. R., Iossifov, I., Levy, D., Ronemus, M., Wigler, M., & Vitkup, D. (2011). Rare de novo variants associated with autism implicate a large functional network of genes. *Neuron*, *70*, 898–907.

Girirajan, S., Rosenfeld, J. A., Cooper, G. M., Antonacci, F., Siswara, P., Itsara, A., & Eichler., E. E. (2010). A recurrent 16p12.1 microdeletion supports a two-hit model for severe developmental delay. *Nature Genetics*, *42*, 203–209.

Goffin, D., Allen, M., Zhang, L., Amorim, M., Wang, I. T., Reyes, A. R., et al. (2012). Rett syndrome mutation MeCP2 T158A disrupts DNA binding, protein stability and ERP responses. *Nature Neuroscience*, *15*, 274–283.

Goh, S., & Peterson, B. S. (2012). Imaging evidence for disturbances in multiple learning and memory systems in persons with autism spectrum disorders. *Developmental Medicine and Child Neurology*, *54*, 208–213.

Gordon, I., Martin, C., Feldman, R., & Leckman, J. F. (2011). Oxytocin and social motivation. *Developmental Cognitive Neuroscience*, *1*, 471–493.

Guinchat, V., Chamak, B., Bonniau, B., Bodeau, N., Perisse, D., Cohen, D., et al. (2012a). Very early signs of autism reported by parents include many concerns not specific to autism criteria. *Research in Autism Spectrum Disorders*, *6*, 589–601.

Guinchat, V., Thorsen, P., Laurent, C., Cans, C., Bodeau, N., & Cohen, D. (2012b). Pre-, peri-, and neonatal risk factors for autism. *Acta Obstetrica Gynecologica Scandanavia*, *91*, 287–300.

Hallmayer, J., Cleveland, S., Torres, A., Phillips, J., Cohen, B., Torigoe, T., et al. (2011). Genetic heritability and shared environmental factors among twin pairs with autism. *Archives of General Psychiatry*, *68*, 1095–1102.

Happé, F., & Frith, U. (2006). The weak coherence account: Detail-focused cognitive style in autism spectrum disorders. *Journal of Autism and Developmental Disorders*, *36*, 5–25.

Hoeft, F., Walter, E., Lightbody, A. A., Hazlett, H. C., Chang, C., Piven, J., et al. (2011). Neuroanatomical differences in toddler boys with fragile X syndrome and idiopathic autism. *Archives of General Psychiatry*, *68*, 295–395.

Holt, R., & Monaco, A. P. (2011). Links between genetics and pathophysiology in the autism spectrum disorders. *EMBO Molecular Medicine*, *3*, 438–450.

Howerton, C. L., & Bale, T. L. (2012). Prenatal programing: At the intersection of maternal stress and immune activation. *Hormones and Behavior*. [Epub March 23, 2012].

Hyman, S. E. (2010). The diagnosis of mental disorders: The problem of reification. *Annual Review of Clinical Psychology*, *6*, 155–179.

Insel, T. R. (2010). The challenge of translation in social neuroscience: A review of oxytocin, vasopressin, and affiliative behavior. *Neuron*, *65*, 768–779.

Insel, T. R., & Wang, P. S. (2010). Rethinking mental illness. *Journal of the American Medical Association*, *303*, 1970–1971.

Ioannidis, J. P. A. (2005). Why most published research findings are false. *PLoS Medicine*, *2*. e124.

James, W. H. (2012). The relevance of the epidemiology of human sex ratios at birth to some medical problems. *Paediatric Perinatology and Epidemiology*, *26*, 181–189.

Jones, W., & Klin, A. (2009). Heterogeneity and homogeneity across the autism spectrum: The role of development. *Journal of the American Academy of Child and Adolescent Psychiatry*, *48*, 471–473.

Kaiser, M. A., & Pelphrey, K. A. (2012). Disrupted action perception in autism: Behavioral evidence, neuroendophenotypes, and diagnostic utility. *Developmental Cognitive Neuroscience*, *2*, 25–35.

Kana, R. K., Libero, L. E., & Moore, M. S. (2011). Disrupted cortical connectivity theory as an explanatory model for autism spectrum disorders. *Physics of Life Reviews*, *8*, 410–437.

Kanner, L. (1943). Autistic disturbances of affective contact. *The Nervous Child*, *2*, 217–250.

Karmiloff-Smith, A. (2012). Perspectives on the dynamic development of cognitive capacities: insights from Williams syndrome. *Current Opinion in Neurology*, *25*, 106–111.

Kendler, K. (2012). The dappled nature of causes of psychiatric illness: Replacing the organic–functional/hardware–software dichotomy with empirically based pluralism. *Molecular Psychiatry*, *17*, 377–388.

Kendler, K. S., & First, M. B. (2010). Alternative futures for the DSM revision process: Iteration v. paradigm shift. *British Journal of Psychiatry, 197*, 263–265.

Kennedy, D. P., & Courchesne, E. (2008). The intrinsic functional organization of the brain is altered in autism. *NeuroImage, 39*, 1877–1885.

Kent, A. L., Wright, I. M., Abdel-Latif, M. E., New South Wales and Australian Capital Territory Neonatal Intensive Care Units Audit Group (2012). Mortality and adverse neurologic outcomes are greater in preterm male infants. *Pediatrics, 129*, 124–131.

Koch, C. (2012). Neuroscience: The connected self. [Review of the book Connectome: How the brain's wiring makes us who we are, by S. Seung], *Nature, 482*, 31.

Koldewyn, K., Whitney, D., & Rivera, S. M. (2010). The psychophysics of visual motion and global form processing in autism. *Brain, 133*, 599–610.

Kupfer, D. J., & Regier, D. A. (2011). Neuroscience, clinical evidence, and the future of psychiatric classification in DSM-5. *American Journal of Psychiatry, 168*, 672–674.

Lane, A. E., Young, R. L., Baker, A. E. Z., & Angley, M. (2010). Sensory processing subtypes in autism: Association with adaptive behavior. *Journal of Autism and Developmental Disorders, 40*, 112–122.

LeBlond, C. S., Heinrich, J., Delorme, R., Proepper, C., Betancur, C., Huguet, G., et al. (2012). Genetic and functional analyses of *SHANK2* mutations suggest a multiple hit model of autism spectrum disorders. *PLoS Genetics, 8*, e1002521.

Leckman, J. F., & Pine, D. S. (2012). Editorial commentary: Challenges and potential of DSM-5 and ICD-11 revisions. *Journal of Child Psychology and Psychiatry, 53*, 449–453.

Lee, T. L., Raygada, M. J., & Rennert, O. M. (2012). Integrative gene network analysis provides novel regulatory relationships, genetic contributions and susceptible targets in autism spectrum disorders. *Gene, 496*, 88–96.

Leekam, S. R., Nieto, C., Libby, S. J., Wing, L., & Gould, J. (2007). Describing the sensory abnormalities of children and adults with autism. *Journal of Autism and Developmental Disorders, 37*, 894–910.

Lewis, M., & Kim, S. J. (2009). The pathophysiology of restricted repetitive behavior. *Journal of Neurodevelopmental Disorders, 1*, 114–132.

Lombardo, M. V., Chakrabarti, B., Bullmore, E. T., MRC AIMS Consortium, & Baron-Cohen, S. (2011). Specialization of right temporo-parietal junction for mentalizing and its relation to social impairments in autism. *NeuroImage, 56*, 1832–1838.

Lord, C. (2011). Unweaving the autism spectrum. *Cell, 147*, 24–25.

Lord, C., & Jones, R. M. (2012). Annual Research Review: Re-thinking the classification of autism spectrum disorders. *Journal of Child Psychology and Psychiatry, 53*, 490–509.

Linden, D. E. J. (2012). The challenges and promise of neuroimaging in psychiatry. *Neuron, 73*, 8–22.

Lubsen, J., Vohr, B., Myers, E., Hampson, M., Lacadie, C., Schneider, K. C., et al. (2011). Microstructural and functional connectivity in the developing preterm brain. *Seminars in Perinatology, 35*, 34–43.

Mackowiak, P. A. (1998). Concepts of fever. *Archives of Internal Medicine, 158*, 1870–1881.

Malkova, N. V., Yu, C. Z., Hsiao, E. Y., Moore, M. J., & Patterson, P. H. (2012). Maternal immune activation yields offspring displaying mouse versions of the three core symptoms of autism. *Brain, Behavior, and Immunity, 26*, 607–611.

Mandy, W. P. L., Charman, T., Gilmour, J., & Skuse, D. (2011). Toward specifying Pervasive Developmental Disorder—Not Otherwise Specified. *Autism Research, 4*, 121–131.

Mattila, M. L., Kielinen, M., Linna, S. L., Jussila, K., Ebeling, H., Bloigu, R., et al. (2011). Autism spectrum disorders according to DSM-IV-TR and comparison with DSM-5 draft criteria: An epidemiological study. *Journal of the American Academy of Child and Adolescent Psychiatry, 50*, 583–592.

Meehl, P. E. (1990). Appraising and amending theories: The strategy of Lakatosian defense and two principles that warrant it. *Psychological Inquiry, 1*, 1–141.

Molenberghs, P., Cunnington, R., & Mattingley, J. B. (2012). Brain regions with mirror properties: A meta-analysis of 125 human fMRI studies. *Neuroscience and Biobehavioral Reviews, 36,* 341–349.

Murphy, S. K., Adigun, A., Huang, Z., Overcash, F., Wang, F., Jirtle, R. L., et al. (2012). Gender-specific methylation differences in relation to prenatal exposure to cigarette smoke. *Gene, 494,* 36–43.

Mwaniki, M. K., Atieno, M., Lawn, J. E., & Newton, C. R. (2012). Long-term neurodevelopmental outcomes after intrauterine and neonatal insults: A systematic review. *The Lancet, 379,* 445–452.

Naish, J. (2012, February 21). *Can some children simply "grow out" of autism? One mother tells how her son's life has been transformed.* dailymail.co.uk. Retrieved February 22, 2012 from http://www.dailymail.co.uk/health/article-2103940/Autism-Can-children-simply-grow-One-mother-tells-sons-life-transformed.html.

Nakano, T., Kato, N., & Kitazawa, S. (2012). Superior haptic-to-visual shape matching in autism spectrum disorders. *Neuropsychologia, 50,* 696–703.

NHS Choices. (2012, February 22). "Kids grow out of autism" claim unfounded. *NHS.uk.* Retrieved February 22, 2012 from www.nhs.uk/news/2012/02February/Pages/children-grow-out-of-autism-claim.aspx.

Noor, A., Whibley, A., Marshall, C. R., Gianakopoulos, P. J., Piton, A., Carson, A. R., et al. (2010). Disruption at the PTCHD1 locus on Xp22.11 in autism spectrum disorder and intellectual disability. *Science Translational Medicine, 2.* 49ra68.

Norris, M., Lecavalier, L., & Edwards, M. C. (2011). The structure of autism symptoms as measured by the Autism Diagnostic Observation Schedule. *Journal of Autism and Developmental Disorders, 42,* 1075–1086.

Peacock, J. L., Marston, L., Marlow, N., Calvert, S. A., & Greenough, A. (2012). Neonatal and infant outcome in boys and girls born very prematurely. *Pediatric Research, 71,* 305–310.

Peñagarikano, O., Abrahams, B. S., Herman, E. I., Winden, K. D., Gdalyahu, A., Dong, H., et al. (2011). Absence of CNTNAP2 leads to epilepsy, neuronal migration abnormalities, and core autism-related deficits. *Cell, 147,* 235–246.

Pies, R. W. (2012, February 8). *Beyond DSM-5, psychiatry needs a "third way."* Thepsychiatrictimes.com. Retrieved February 8, 2012 from http://www.psychiatrictimes.com/blog/pies/content/article/101682029546.

Prasad, V., Cifu, A., & Ioannidis, J. P. (2012). Reversals of established medical practices: Evidence to abandon ship. *Journal of the American Medical Association, 307,* 37–38.

Reeb-Sutherland, B. C., Levitt, P., & Fox, N. A. (2012). The predictive nature of individual difference in early associative learning and emerging social behavior. *PLoS ONE, 7,* e30511, 1–7.

Rees, S., Harding, R., & Walker, D. (2011). The biological basis of injury and neuroprotection in the fetal and neonatal brain. *International Journal of Developmental Neuroscience, 29,* 551–563.

Robinson, E. B., Koenen, K. C., McCormick, M. C., Munir, K., Hallett, V., Happé, F., et al. (2012). A multivariate twin study of autistic traits in 12-year-olds: Testing the fractionable autism triad hypothesis. *Behavior Genetics, 42,* 245–255.

Rommelse, N. N. J., Franke, B., Geurts, H. M., Buitelaar, J. K., & Hartman, C. A. (2011). A review on cognitive and brain endophenotypes that may be common in autism spectrum disorder and attention-deficit/hyperactivity disorder and facilitate the search for pleiotropic genes. *Neuroscience & Biobehavioral Reviews, 35,* 1363–1396.

Rutherford, M. D., & Troje, N. F. (2012). IQ predicts biological motion perception in autism spectrum disorders. *Journal of Autism and Developmental, 42,* 557–565.

Rutter, M. (2005). Autism research: Lessons from the past and prospects for the future. *Journal of Autism and Developmental Disorders, 35,* 241–257.

Sanislow, C. A., Pine, D. S., Quinn, K. J., Kozak, M. J., Garvey, M. A., Heinssen, R. K., et al. (2010). Developing constructs for psychopathology research: Research domain criteria. *Journal of Abnormal Psychology, 119,* 631–639.

Sato, D., Lionel, A. C., Leblond, C. S., Prasad, A., Pinto, D., Walker, S., et al. (2012). SHANK1 deletions in males with autism spectrum disorder. *American Journal of Human Genetics, 90,* 879–887.

Schilbach, L., Bzdok, D., Timmermans, B., Fox, P. T., Laird, A. R., Vogeley, K., et al. (2012). Introspective minds: Using ALE meta-analyses to study commonalities in the neural correlates of emotional processing, social & unconstrained cognition. *PLoS ONE, 7,* e30920.

Schulte-Rüther, M., Greimel, E., Markowitsch, H. J., Kamp-Becker, I., Remschmidt, H., Fink, G. R., et al. (2011). Dysfunctions in brain networks supporting empathy: An fMRI study in adults with autism. *Social Neuroscience, 6,* 1–21.

Schumann, C. M., Barnes, C. C., Lord, C., & Courchesne, E. (2009). Amygdala enlargement in toddlers with autism related to severity of social and communication impairments. *Biological Psychiatry, 66,* 942–949.

Singer, T. (2012). The past, present and future of social neuroscience: A European perspective. *Neuroimage, 61,* 437–449.

Sivakumaran, S., Agakov, F., Theodoratou, E., Prendergast, J. G., Zgaga, L., Manolio, T., et al. (2011). Abundant pleiotropy in human complex diseases and traits. *American Journal of Human Genetics, 89,* 607–618.

Solari, S. V., & Stoner, R. (2011). Cognitive consilience: Primate non-primary neuroanatomical circuits underlying cognition. *Frontiers in Neuroscience, 5,* 65. [Epub]. doi: 10.3389/fnana.2011.00065.

Spiker, M. A., Lin, C. E., Van Dyke, M., & Wood, J. J. (2012). Restricted interests and anxiety in children with autism. *Autism, 16,* 306–320.

State, M., & Levitt, P. (2011). The conundrums of understanding genetic risks for autism spectrum disorders. *Nature Neuroscience, 14,* 1–8.

Stobbe, M. (2012, April 9). *Autism research may be about to bear fruit.* Associatedpress.com. Retrieved April 20, 2012 from http://www.google.com/hostednews/ap/article/ALe qM5gXNsF87xp3fq4T2MKsWVZ3D5IwPA?docId=a87f8d58fe4a4875a5e3cc2539 2f038c.

Szatmari, P. (2011). New recommendations on autism spectrum disorder: Shifting the focus from subtypes to dimensions carries potential costs and benefits. *British Medical Journal, 342,* d2456.

Szatmari, P., Liu, X. Q., Goldberg, J., Zwaigenbaum, L., Paterson, A. D., Woodbury-Smith, M., et al. (2012). Sex differences in repetitive stereotyped behaviors in autism: Implications for genetic liability. *American Journal of Medical Genetics B, Neuropsychiatric Genetics, 159B,* 5–12.

Tabet, A. C., Pilorge, M., Delorme, R., Amsellem, F., Pinard, J. M., Leboyer, M., et al. (2012). Autism multiplex family with 16p11.2p12.2 microduplication syndrome in monozygotic twins and distal 16p11.2 deletion in their brother. *European Journal of Human Genetics, 20,* 540–546.

Talkowski, M. E., Rosenfeld, J., Blumenthal, I., Pillalamarri, V., Chiang, C., Heilbut, A., et al. (2012). Sequencing chromosomal abnormalities reveals neurodevelopmental loci that confer risk across diagnostic boundaries. *Cell, 149,* 525–537.

Tanguay, P. E. (2011). Autism in DSM-5. *American Journal of Psychiatry, 168,* 1142–1144.

Tatsioni, A., Bonitsis, N. G., & Ioannidis, J. P. N. (2007). Persistence of contradicted claims in the literature. *Journal of the American Medical Association, 298,* 2517–2526.

Uddin, L. Q., Supekar, K. S., Ryali, S., & Menon, V. (2011). Dynamic reconfiguration of structural and functional connectivity across core neurocognitive brain networks with development. *Journal of Neuroscience, 31,* 18578–18589.

Van Essen, D. C., & Ugurbil, K. (2012). The future of the human connectome. *NeuroImage*. [Epub January 10, 2012]. doi: 10.1016/j.neuroimage.2012.01.032.

Veenstra-VanderWeele, J., & Blakely, R. D. (2012). Networking in autism: Leveraging genetic, biomarker and model system findings in the search for new treatments. *Neuropsychopharmacology, 37*, 196–212.

Vissers, M. E., Cohen, M. X., & Geurts, H. M. (2012). Brain connectivity and high functioning autism: A promising path of research that needs refined models, methodological convergence, and stronger behavioral links. *Neuroscience and Biobehavioral Reviews, 36*, 604–625.

Voineagu, I., Wang, X., Johnston, P., Lowe, J. K., Tian, Y., Horvath, S., et al. (2011). Transcriptomic analysis of autistic brain reveals convergent molecular pathology. *Nature, 474*, 380–384.

Walsh, P., Elsabbagh, M., Bolton, P., & Singh, I. (2011). In search of biomarkers for autism: Scientific, social and ethical challenges. *Nature Reviews Neuroscience, 12*, 603–612.

Wass, S. (2011). Distortions and disconnections: Disrupted brain connectivity in autism. *Brain and Cognition, 75*, 18–28.

Waterhouse, L. (2008). Autism overflows: Increasing prevalence and proliferating theories. *Neuropsychology Review, 18*, 273–286.

Waterhouse, L. (2009). Autism is a portmanteau syndrome. *Neuropsychology Review, 19*, 275–276.

Wei, H., Malik, M., Sheikh, A. M., Merz, G., Brown, W. T., & Li, X. (2011). Abnormal cell properties and down-regulated FAK-Src complex signaling in B lymphoblasts of autistic subjects. *American Journal of Pathology, 179*, 1–9.

Wolff, J. J., Gu, H., Gerig, G., Elison, J. T., Styner, M., Gouttard, S., et al. (2012). Differences in white matter fiber tracts development present from 6 to 24 month in infants with autism. *American Journal of Psychiatry, 169*, 589–600.

Wulffaert, J., Van Berckelaer-Onnes, I. A., & Scholte, E. M. (2009). Autistic disorder symptoms in Rett syndrome. *Autism, 13*, 567–581.

Yang, J., Zhuang, H., & Servaes, S. (2012). Fever of unknown origin: The roles of FDG PET or PET/CT. *PET Clinics, 7*, 181–189.

Yrigollen, C. M., Han, S. S., Kochetkova, A., Babitz, T., Chang, J. T., Volkmar, F. R., et al. (2008). Genes controlling affiliative behavior as candidate genes for autism. *Biological Psychiatry, 63*, 911–916.

Zhao, X., Leotta, A., Kustanovich, V., Lajonchere, C., Geschwind, D. H., Law, K., et al. (2007). A unified genetic theory for sporadic and inherited autism. *Proceedings of the National Academy of Sciences of the United States of America, 104*, 12831–12836.

Zwaigenbaum, L., Bryson, S. E., Szatmari, P., Brian, J., Smith, I. M., Roberts, W., et al. (2012). Sex differences in children with autism spectrum disorder identified within a high-risk infant cohort. *Journal of Autism and Developmental Disorders*. [Epub March 28, 2012].

Page numbers followed by "f" indicate figures, and "t" indicate tables, and "b" indicate boxes.

Supervisory control of lower level
processes, 132
Supplementary motor area, 103t–113t
Supramarginal gyrus, 103t–113t
Symptom convergence, 75
Symptom divergence, 75–76
Syndromic autism, 9, 13, 56, 159, 173,
210–211, 253–254. *See also* Comorbid disorders; Idiopathic autism
causes, 176
genetic risk factors, 175–176
individuals with, 173
as symptom set, 211
Synesthesia, 284t–291t, 300–301
emotional, 301
as evidence for brain bases, 326–328
forms, 300–301
ordinal linguistic personification, 301
Systemic lupus erythematosus (SLE),
237–238

T

TACA. *See* Talking about Curing Autism
(TACA)
Tactile sensitivity, 301–302
Talking about Curing Autism (TACA), 364
Taste memory, 284t–291t
Temporal lobe, 103t–113t
Testosterone, 98–99, 103t–113t
and oxytocin, 129–130
Thalidomide, 245
adverse outcome of, 246
Theory of Mind, 16, 103t–113t
Threat detection, 128
Tic disorder due to general medical
condition, 379b
Tick-box diagnosis systems, 359
Timothy syndrome, 160t–164t
TNF. *See* Tumor necrosis factor (TNF)
TORCH infections. *See* Toxoplasmosis,
Other, Rubella, Cytomegalovirus,
Herpes (TORCH) infections
Tourette syndrome (TS), 55, 142–143,
385–386, 404
Tourette's disorder, 379b
Toxoplasmosis, Other, Rubella, Cytomega-
lovirus, Herpes (TORCH)
infections, 10

Tracking the intentions of others, 132
TS. *See* Tourette syndrome (TS)
TSC. *See* Tuberous sclerosis complex (TSC)
Tuberin, 160t–164t
Tuberous sclerosis, 13
Tuberous sclerosis complex (TSC), 55
with autism, 55
with autism symptom in identical twin
brothers, 55
Tuberous sclerosis type I, 160t–164t
Tuberous sclerosis type II, 160t–164t
Tumor necrosis factor (TNF), 412
Tumor necrosis factor alpha (TNFα),
259–260
Turner syndrome, 167
22q11.2 deletion, 194
Two genetic mechanisms, 172
idiopathic autism, 173–174
causes, 176
genetic basis for, 174
genetic risk factors, 175–176
syndromic autism, 173
causes, 176
genetic risk factors, 175–176
individuals with, 173
Two-hit genetic mechanisms, 176
chromosomal deletion or duplication,
177
mutations in genes, 177
two-cause model, 177
Type 1 diabetes (T1D), 237–238

U

Ubiquitination ligase, 160t–164t
Underconnectivity theory, 195–196,
201–202
genetic contribution model, 196
multigene model, challenges for,
196–197
Understanding the other, 132–134
Unloving mother theory, 226–229
Unspecified tic disorder, 379b

V

Valproate, and autism, 254
Valproic acid, 245. *See also* Valproate, and
autism
adverse outcome of, 246